W9-CHD-552

SONIC COOL
THE LIFE & DEATH of ROCK 'N' ROLL

JOE S. HARRINGTON

HAL•LEONARD®

Cover and interior illustrations by Jon Langford.

Copyright © 2002 by Joe S. Harrington

All rights reserved. No part of this book may be reproduced or utilized in any form or by any means, electronic or mechanical, including photocopying, recording, or any other information storage retrieval system, without permission in writing from the Publisher, except by a reviewer, who may quote brief passages for review.

Published by Hal Leonard Corporation
7777 West Bluemound Road
P.O. Box 13819
Milwaukee, WI 53213, USA

Trade Book Division Editorial Offices:
151 West 46th Street, 8th Floor
New York, NY 10036

Visit Hal Leonard online at www.halleonard.com

Library of Congress Cataloging-in-Publication Data

Harrington, Joe S.
  Sonic cool : the life and death of rock 'n' roll / Joe Harrington.--
1st ed.
    p. cm.
Includes bibliographical references (p.   ) and index.
  ISBN 0-634-02861-8 (alk. paper)
  1. Rock music--History and criticism. 2. Music--Philosophy and
aesthetics. I. Title.
  ML3534 .H395 2002
  781.66'09--dc21

                              2002014827

Printed in the United States of America
First Edition

10 9 8 7 6 5 4 3 2 1

CONTENTS

PREFACE

THIS SHOULD BE THE LAST BOOK ABOUT ROCK. Surely, here at the onset of the new millennium, that which passes itself off as popular music bears only a faint relationship with the Rock of the past and is a product of a completely different evolutionary process, and a nonorganic one. Surely this new process forms an interesting thesis of its own, as evidenced by a wave of books on the subject—i.e., the cheapening corporatization of popular music—that will no doubt continue to appear for many years to come. It's probably about time that the word *Rock* be retired and come to signify music from the past. Which is the whole point about this being the "last" book about Rock—not so much that other books shouldn't be written (once again, they undoubtedly will), but that this is the first book that approaches the whole topic of Rock (and the phenomenon thereof) as having *finality* (crushing conclusion).

When I first conceived this book some twenty-odd years ago, it was because I did not believe an adequate history of Rock existed. Although other books may have loosely traced Rock's chronological history, they seldom explained its essential meaning. There were, of course, books filled with great essays about the topic, from Marcus's *Mystery Train* to Guralnick's *Feel Like Goin' Home*, as well as a host of great biographies (Nick Tosches' Jerry Lee Lewis epic *Hellfire* immediately comes to mind) and oral histories (*Please Kill Me*). But what I was seeking was something that explained the phenomenon of Rock—why it became so monstrously popular, and also why it was destined to fail. I guess I conceived it as an epic that would tie in all the cultural manifestations that Rock has come to represent, along with its musical legacy.

As a phenomenon, the kind of *belief* that Rock 'n' Roll inspired in its listeners was, in a very real way, closer to religion than mere entertainment. The Rock 'n' Roll lifestyle has lasted, too—as one can witness in any major city, judging by the hordes of kids walking around in the latest fashion statement of the moment (not to mention the self-destructive practices they routinely engage in). In fact, it could be argued that, within the popular culture itself, Rock has been the single most important disseminator of freethinking (as well as free love). In the annals of twentieth-century art forms, Rock 'n' Roll was pretty goddamn important, not only as music but as a *way of life*—one that, in fact, offered a viable alternative to the accepted hegemony. But the fact that Rock, in its soul-selling inevitability, in turn became perhaps the ultimate bastion of conformity actually means that its capitulation to the corporate god was a dire kind of self-fulfilling prophecy of biblical proportions.

If one sees the history of Rock 'n' Roll as analogous to the Bible—and I do believe there's a moral to this book—let this be Rock's apocalypse, with the chapter entitled "Punk" as the dividing line between Old Testament and New Testament. This book is an attempt to reconcile the Rock of the Baby Boomers and the post-Punk Rock of all subsequent generations. The culture of the '80s was a symptom of the world ultimately growing larger—and leaving a thousand disparate diversions in its wake. In the '90s, we'd see this more emphatically in the form of fringe religious, political, and sexual preoccupations of all varieties. Rock 'n' Roll itself would fragment into so many subcategories that there was no longer any consensus even as to what "Rock 'n' Roll" actually was.

The thing that made Rock 'n' Roll unique and the thing that has made it the subject of so many exhaustive—but ultimately inaccurate—surveys is that it was the first form of music that was intrinsically related to the culture overall. For this reason, Rock 'n' Roll is perhaps the greatest oral history of the twentieth century. This is something I think those other books have perhaps missed. Rock 'n' Roll is folklore more than it is history. That's why I like to think of this book as more the story of Rock than the history of Rock.

It's also why some may argue that this book cannot serve as a truly proper history of Rock because so many groups or artists are ultimately excluded—not only individual artists, but also whole genres (for example, the whole worldwide satanic metal subculture is hardly even mentioned, nor is Techno music). Michael Jackson is barely in this book at all. But like all hot topics of postmodern research—"Cultural Studies," if you will—this book deserves to be written. This is one author's view of a subject I've made myself almost fatally familiar with for nearly three decades.

As far as history goes, it gets harder to pinpoint any kind of mass consensus after the dissipation that occurred after Punk; starting then, the history of Rock becomes utterly subjective. That's why the final chapter is entitled "Post Everything"—at a certain point it simply doesn't matter anymore; leaving Limp Bizkit out of the text does very little to alter its theoretical conclusions. Perhaps it's best to see *Sonic Cool* as not so much a straight history but a book closer in spirit to Richard Meltzer's *The Aesthetics of Rock*, Joe Carducci's *Rock and the Pop Narcotic*, and LeRoi Jones's *Black Music*: more of a theoretical/philosophical entity as opposed to an all-inclusive "study."

It's called *Sonic Cool* because those are the two sides of Rock's soul. "Sonic" is the sound of the music, which—despite the cultural trappings—was, once upon a time, the main thing. "Cool"—the posture of Rock and the Rock culture—is the more facile side of the music's success, perhaps the seductive element that was ultimately responsible for Rock becoming a fixture of what I call the Entertainment Industrial Complex. The point of the book: Never again shall the twain meet. And although I eulogize this fact, I by no means lament it—it is only Rock 'n' Roll. There was no guarantee it was going to last forever. In this sense, *Sonic Cool* is satire as well (Tom Wolfe was another inspiration).

Call it a cultural history of Rock. Or call it the history of the Cultural Revolution. Either way, it's over. The future will bring something else. Who knows what they'll call it? But if they continue to call it Rock, they're clutching onto something that no longer exists. If you think somehow I've missed my mark, or left something out, or failed to explain some essential element of the true meaning of Rock, its history or its sociopolitical connotations, by all means feel free to write your own goddamn book.

Joe S. Harrington
Portland, Maine
April 18, 2002

Acknowledgements

SO IT'S FINALLY COME DOWN TO THIS, HUH? First off, thanks are in order for what I call the holy trinity—the three people who were chiefly responsible for turning a dream into not only a reality but what eventually got to feel like a conspiracy. As far as credits go, this triumvirate is in a class of their own, which I call the "Beyond the Call of Duty" category. First among them is John Strausbaugh: When I first told him about my concept for *Sonic Cool* sometime in early 1999, he was already eminently familiar with my style, and in a way, he'd been partly responsible for helping nurture it, as he'd already published more than fifty reviews of mine in the *New York Press*, the paper he edited. It should be noted here for posterity's stake that he's the best editor I've ever had the pleasure of working with, for the simple reason that he eschews the usual schoolmarm-ish precision bullshit, easy-reading tactics, and putting-words-in-writers'-mouths practices of most editors, who are so afraid of their own shadows and so unsure of their own literary oats that they apparently get a quick-fix kick out of emasculating their legions of underpaid writers. It was Strausbaugh who recommended an agent for me, Jim Fitzgerald, who turned into the second conspirator of the trinity. Luckily for me, who had very little experience treading in these waters, Jim was the possessor of a genuine Rock 'n' Roll sensibility that is rare in most literary folks. From the beginning, he believed in the project and never once flagged in his support.

It was this kind of dedication that eventually landed the manuscript in the lap of Ben Schafer, at that time the editor at Hal Leonard. Ben was another godsend: not succumbing to the pressures of the politically correct and thus robbing the book of its satirical implications just for the sake of appeasing the thought police, he's the one most responsible for this book finally coming out the way it was intended to. As we embarked on this project, Ben proved from the very beginning that he was truly "in on the joke," and I feel very fortunately to have crossed paths with him at this point in time. I'm very confident when I say that perhaps no other editor would've given a first-time author such a wide wingspan as well as unflailing support.

I'd also like to thank John Cerullo at Hal Leonard for recognizing a winner when he sees it, as well as everyone else at Hal Leonard for their support during the two years it took to complete the project.

And thanks also to the great Jon Langford, for coming up with an appropriate cover illustration that matches the irreverent spirit of the book itself.

Thanks are also in order to the following people who contributed in no insignificant way to the final outcome, be it by loaning a record or two; providing advice, guidance, or moral support; as well as any ideas, thoughts, punch lines, or even a sentence or two that I might have appropriated wholesale: "Metal" Mike Saunders, Eva Neuberg, Jon Decker, Dave Daley, Jon Reisbaum, Jim DeRogatis, Ted Drozdowski, Joan Foley, Tony Mayberry, Steve Perry, Robert Brooker, Ben Goldberg, Lisa Kearns, MC Kostek, Mike Doughty, Gilbert Doughty, Brendan Bourke, Spencer Gates, Steve Aylett, Tris McCall, Anna Price, John O'Hara, Barbara Manning, George Tsetsilas, Peter Lebares, Keith Wasmund, Robert Morris, Jeff Morris, Randy Haecker, Chris Jacobs, Steve Manning, Ron Schneiderman, Bob Dubrow, Kris Thompson, Connie Adams, Angus Merry, Rick Oulette, Ben Lowengard, Spencer Ackerman, Erin Franzman, Terri Hinte, Todd Cronin, Andria Lisle, Warren Lemond, Rick Grazul, Jacob Hoye, Jeff Niesel, Jeff Dice, Patrick Corrigan, Cassie Gagne, Lael Morgan, David Tyler, Chris Busby, Laurie Blackwood, Pam Nashel, Nina Ippolito, Brian Coleman.

Extra special thanks to: Delerium Archives, David Simpkins, Lauri Bortz, Mark Dagley, Marianne Nowottny, Allison Tanenhaus, Erin Hosier, Tom Warren, John Fahnley, Julie Underwood, Kris Gillespie, Tim Shea, Chris Irving, Scott Irving, Jim Pinfold, Steve Prygoda, Sue Minichiello, Carl and Susan and Max and Miles Treicel, Noel Ventresco, Craig Ventresco, Lisa LeeKing, Lisa Carver, Dave Goolkasian, Sean Dillman, Penny Day, Julie and

Jere Nickerson, Daniel and Cecelia Nickerson, William Hobbs, Andrew and Pam Smith, Andy and John and Carol Bogner, Eric and Rachel Youngling, Raymond Ross, Michael Galinksy, Matt Martinez, Adam Stern, David Treemarcki, Tom Mafrici, Liz August, Tim Smart, Bernard Stollman, Johnny and Mellow Lomba, Phuong Baum, Anne Streng, Patrick Sabatini, Mum, Dad, Doris Storer, and anyone else I forgot.

To Jon Fox, who started it all and always kept it real

CHAPTER 1

THE FIFTIES

In the '50s, a decade of expanding goodwill, few people doubted their government. America, after all, had won the war. Young men who'd spent a couple of years fighting overseas were anxious to buy homes and raise families in the new plenteous utopia of postwar America. Around them raved a new culture—particularly television—that promoted a new kind of affluence. This was the bounty of the World War II daddies whose right it was to inherit the world because they'd saved it ("and don't you forget it, kid" went the refrain). They'd fought abroad to defend the American way of life, and now they were reaping its rewards. But there were millions of people whose lives went on, devoid of the American Dream.

For those who were left behind, the '50s was an extremely grueling time when conformity was rewarded and individuality was judged with suspicion. The specter of the witch-trial-like McCarthy hearings put a lot of fear in anyone thinking of dissent. It was definitely an era of hiding in the closet—for gays, political dissidents, druggies. But these "dissenters" existed, beneath the exterior of neatly mowed lawns and *Leave it to Beaver* benevolence.

In the recent past, Franklin Roosevelt had been such a popular president that he almost put the Republicans out of business. People still blamed them for the Depression, and FDR's emergence as a world leader during the war years helped him achieve a prolonged presidency that enabled him to complete the social and economic agenda that was the New Deal. His inevitable successor, Harry Truman, solidly embraced a small-town, Midwestern working class ethic and was given to plain language. But Dean Acheson, Truman's Secretary of State, came to embody the Eastern establishment: Educated at Groton and Harvard, a product of Wall Street, he was young, rich, and, in terms of foreign affairs, chiefly Eurocentric. Even after China fell to Communist rule, he tended to concentrate more on European affairs.

In his first year as Secretary of State, Acheson was dogged by an incident that would prove to be a historic turning point in the Cold War: A man named Whittaker Chambers, his own background quite dubious, charged that someone named Alger Hiss was at one time a member of the Communist Party. At the time, Hiss was the head of the Carnegie Endowment, an organization long vilified by the Republicans as a liberal organ. Although Hiss eventually got out of the whole thing on a charge of perjury, the main target amongst Red-haters was Acheson, who continued to support Hiss long after the trial was over.

The event that really jump-started the Cold War was the Soviet Union's testing of the nuclear bomb on August 29, 1949. Soon the bomb became part of modern folklore, this almighty force that, in an instant, in the hands of those dirty Reds, could extinguish all the things Americans had fought so hard for. It wasn't that long ago that Soviets and Americans had fought side by side in World War II, but by becoming our nuclear equals, the Soviet Union had now emerged as the new enemy.

On other fronts, the contours of society were changing: Harry Truman would be the last president not to go to college. The country was entering a whole new era in which the overriding goal of most Americans would be *to succeed*. It was no longer going to be a world where one could hang a man from a tree if one didn't like the color of his skin. Harry Truman came from the Old School, the last of the unbuffed political heroes (like James Curley and Huey Long) just as Eisenhower, his successor, would be the last of the real brave war heroes who could display his bloodlust in public.

With the escalating nuclear arms race and the Cold War, spying and espionage became huge issues of national security. These were the years when Americans were literally looking in every garbage can for "commies." It was also the golden age of the FBI, led by J. Edgar Hoover (who, as history has proven, had some secrets of his own).

It was an era of fear and entrapment, as proven by Joe McCarthy, a demagogic senator from Wisconsin, who at one time let it slip that he had a list of

"205 *proven commies*" in the State Department. This was in many ways the first of the modern-day press scandals, as the hearings were among the first big nationally televised media events, and everyone from politicians to actors to coffee-getters was accused.

McCarthy hurt Truman. He also hurt the Democrats in the long-term, because he made them look soft on Communism. The final blow came during the Korean War, when Truman replaced the ever-popular General MacArthur with Matt Ridgeway. This caused MacArthur to accuse the president of "not wanting to get the job done." To most Americans, MacArthur was a national hero admired for his outspoken bravado. Now that he was no longer taking direct orders from the president, he was even less checked in his criticism.

In those days, people's speech wasn't policed by politically correct do-gooders, nor was their conduct checked by international bodyguards. This was still the day and age when people—not just working class zealots, but national policy leaders—openly admitted that they wanted to totally maim their enemies. With both the Soviet Union and the United States having access to the bomb, the stakes got a lot higher, and the public relations rhetoric intensified. Most people now realized that this rhetoric could have fatal consequences. A lot of hip thinkers—artists as well as academics—began questioning the country's overt nationalism, but for the most part Americans in the '50s continued to have blind faith in their leaders (and deftly built bomb shelters).

The '50s saw the invention of "leisure time," which would have seemed inconceivable during the war years when men and women worked day and night to keep the war effort running effectively. With the rise of new technology—the birth of electronics and the conversion of coal-fueled energy to crude oil—industry itself was becoming more efficient. This meant the average worker was able to work fewer hours for more money. Americans became *consumers*. They began to spend money on home furnishings, clothes, cuisine, and automobiles in order to gain status among their peers.

Cars, for instance, had once been thought of only as a means of transport. But with the mass production of autos that accompanied the postwar economy, automakers like General Motors began to design cars for the different strata of society. So while a Pontiac was a sporty model perfect for, say, a horse breeder or truant officer, the Cadillac was aimed at corporation heads, movie stars, and the owners of baseball teams. As the desire to succeed was being bred in all

Americans, the Cadillac became the ultimate status symbol. That's why when Elvis finally made it, the first thing he did was to buy a Cadillac. Back then, the automobile still had a *mystique* to it, and mechanics were looked upon as skilled professionals. The increasing need for gasoline meant that soon the giant chains like Gulf and Esso were going to be popping up on every highway. This meant that soon the American road would look exactly the same from New York to Florida, even as Jack Kerouac was putting the finishing touches on *On the Road*, his epic saga of life on the American highway.

Although in the first half of the century there were towns in rural outposts that hadn't actually changed much in 100 years, after the '50s there was little chance of such isolation. The thriving America of Wall Street and Madison Avenue wouldn't allow it, because they knew that if they could reach all those folks there were several more millions to be made. American enterprise was, in a sense, *reaching out* to rural Americans, encouraging them to buy into what would become known as "mainstream" culture. Which, in many cases, was the lowest common denominator.

Despite its prominence as a military and industrial stronghold, the United States was routinely mocked by Europeans for its lack of true culture. The '50s changed all of this. With the rise of pop culture, this country would extend its cultural influence beyond even the Iron Curtain (although it was strictly hush-hush).

Housing had changed dramatically in the postwar years: With the birth of independent contracting, it had become more affordable for the American of modest income to buy a house. The automobile had eliminated the need to live right in the urban center for employment purposes. The cities were, in fact, stretching out, with the more affluent occupants moving to the outlying regions. This was the beginning of suburbia, which opened up even more avenues of leisurely pursuit—which ultimately led to Americans standing around the water cooler at work talking about their new air conditioners.

The chain stores began opening up: Korvette's, Woolworth's, and all the other retailers. Eugene Ferkauf, the founder of Korvette's, once noted that what made the new consumers different from their parents was that they did not fear debt. And *their* children, the dreaded Baby Boomers, would be the first ones born into a world where disposable income was a given.

Postwar Americans were more adventurous than their parents in that they were willing to explore new boundaries in order to fulfill their ambitions. They were willing to marry outside of their own religious or ethnic backgrounds, or relocate to new areas if the promise of a new job or career demanded it. The automobile and jet also made this possible, but it was more than that—these Americans believed in the endless possibilities of the future.

Americans were becoming more mobile and thus living farther from the workplace. The new reality of commuting produced a need for faster services—not only gas stations, but fast food as well. This was the beginning of the "rat race"—the hustle and bustle and all that came with it. It was also the beginning of the stand-up hamburger stand: McDonald's and the like. The down-home diner was on its way out, as people were increasingly willing to forsake things like personal service and a familiar atmosphere in order to eat more quickly. There were also all kinds of new instant foods, like the "TV dinner," for instance, which went along with the rise of television and a more sedate lifestyle in general for Americans who'd earned the right to leisure.

The combination of increased leisure time and the proliferation of the automobile helped expand the tourism industry in the '50s. The new motel chains proliferated: first the Sheraton, then Holiday Inn and the Ramada Inn. These were family motels that encouraged you to bring the kids. Thus, the Baby Boomers were privileged in yet another way their parents and grandparents weren't. Kids were getting more sophisticated—and thus jaded—earlier in life.

What *really* helped jade those kids even faster was the fact that, with the economy being so good, many of them could afford to have their own cars by working as the proverbial "soda jerk" after school. The car would become part of the '50s mythology, and for good reason: it enabled teenagers to get away from their parents' houses and mingle with their peers. The car helped bring about the sexual revolution as well by revamping the whole notion of courtship: Sexual initiation was naturally a lot easier in a car than it had been in, say, a barn. And the new drive-in theaters gave the kids a destination (or an alibi).

Television was another big factor in the increasingly early sophistication of the Baby Boom generation. Television wasn't only changing the face of entertainment and advertising, but politics as well. Although comedy and variety shows dominated the world of early television, network owners were finding out that televised events like the McCarthy hearings and the famous Costello mob trial pulled the highest ratings. There were even newspaper articles about how some husbands returned home after a hard day's work and found their wives glued to the TV, housework undone, supper unmade (a cardinal sin in those days).

People were growing accustomed to seeing events actually unfurl instead of reading about them after the fact. This would be a pivotal factor in the opposition to the Vietnam War in the next decade. The line between what people saw on television and what was happening in real life began to fade. Many young couples were now living far away from their families in brand-new housing developments where they hardly knew their neighbors. They began to feel closer to the characters in a show like *I Love Lucy* than they did to the people around them.

TV was so important that, in 1952, the Republicans hired a huge advertising firm to teach Ike how to groove to the new medium. This permanently changed the face of politics in America. Prior to that, political campaigns had been unrehearsed. By contrast, Ike's spots were concise and well edited so that he was always cast as the returning War Hero—and cut off before he said anything stupid (which he was more than capable of). This was a technique that both Richard Nixon and Ronald Reagan, the next two Republicans elected president in the twentieth century, would incorporate.

If Eisenhower was just learning how to master the medium of television, his vice presidential candidate, Richard Nixon, was soon to pull off a major coup with his Checkers speech. To answer questions about the acceptance of supposedly illegal funds, Nixon called a major press conference, televised in prime time by the three major networks, during which he played on the sympathies of his audience by installing his wife as a prop and making reference to the family dog. This helped teach politicians a new tactic—mainly to remember that the print media was irrelevant to "real Americans." TV was the new medium with which to reach the mainstream.

In those years, it was still Eisenhower and his generation who were running the country, and the America they remembered was the one from their turn-of-the-century childhood. As a whole new generation of young minds was uprooting the fields of art, entertainment, technology, science, medicine, and education, the governing class was still very much based in a much simpler day and age. Many of the tensions of the time arose from this rather obvious paradox.

The Kinsey Report, *Sexual Behavior in the Human Male* by Alfred Kinsey, was published in 1948. Kinsey tried to dispel many of the common myths about sex in those days, such as the belief that masturbation led to brain damage or that homosexuality was a form of mental illness. He also concluded that healthy sex led to healthier marriages and that premarital sex tended to produce better marriages. Although these opinions seem like common knowledge nowadays, they were very controversial in the '50s.

The Sexual Revolution was still a few years away, but medical science was already working on the birth control pill, and when it finally arrived, it wasn't long before all the old taboos went out the window. In the '50s, however, such thinking was still almost inconceivable except to a small minority of liberals. The Catholic Church still held that the Pill and prophylactic devices interfered with the natural progress of God. But young families, even religious ones, had found God's progress to be too much of a burden, even in the Promised Land. With the advent of birth control, young families figured there was no reason they should have to have six, seven kids. The American Dream came to encompass "family planning," which essentially meant that newlyweds could regulate the course of nature itself. All of American life—even such previously sacred realms as childbirth—was becoming programmable. Life was becoming less of a mystery. People felt less indebted to the things they had previously relied on to make life explainable—like religion, for instance.

The courts were also changing. The new Chief Justice of the Supreme Court, Earl Warren, was a former Republican governor of California with very moderate tendencies who sought to declare racial segregation illegal. Ever since the Jim Crow laws were passed in the late nineteenth century, a "together but not equal" dictum had existed in the United States, particularly in the South. This discrepancy was in complete defiance of the Fourteenth Amendment, which said that state governments couldn't deny Blacks the right of equal protection—which, argued Warren, was exactly what the Southern states were doing by segregating public schools.

In 1951, in *Brown vs. the Board of Education*, a Black welder named Oliver Brown had filed suit with the court in Topeka, Kansas against the local school board, claiming that his eight-year-old daughter had to travel twenty-one blocks by bus to attend an all-Black school. Eventually the case worked its way to the Warren court and, in a historic decision, they unanimously declared segregation illegal. The hard part, though, was ahead for the courts and law enforcement officials who had to make the law stick. It was one thing to put it on the books, but to enforce it was a different thing entirely. People didn't know it at the time, but we were about to enter a violent period in which the U.S. would come dangerously close to a second Revolution. What they also didn't know was that a whole generation was going to get high on it.

Southern Black leaders were surprised to find out how sympathetic the mostly white press corps was to their cause. The racial stigma would also start to be broken down by the presence of Blacks in sports and Rock 'n' Roll. In 1955 both Chuck Berry and Little Richard would place records in the Top Ten, and Elvis Presley, a white Southern performer said to be haunted by the Black vibe, was bubbling under.

In the nation at large, the event that seemed to galvanize the racial struggle was the murder of Emmitt Till that summer (1955). Till was a fourteen-year-old Black proto-gangbanger from Chicago; his mother had sent him south to visit an uncle, Moses Wright, who lived in the thick of the Mississippi Delta cotton country. During his visit, Till apparently whistled at a white woman, within earshot of her redneck husband. Later that day, the man and his cracker cronies bashed Till's skull in and threw him into the Mississippi River, weighed down by the fan from a cotton gin. It took authorities three days to find the body, and when they did, it was badly decomposed. They sent the corpse back to Chicago, at which time the boy's mother decided to hold an open-casket funeral, exposing the brutality of the crime to anyone with the guts to look. The national media had a field day. The fact that Till's murderers got off the hook only further emphasized the racial divide.

The Black population was growing. Particularly in the northern cities like Chicago and Detroit, Blacks already made up a sizable part of the workforce. Ever since the '40s, a large portion of Southern Blacks had been migrating north, mostly for work-related reasons, but also to escape the rampant racism of the South. In cities like Toledo and Cleveland, Blacks found that they were able to get decent jobs with decent wages in the factories and thus become consumers themselves. But the idyllic picture of the American Dream, as manifested by TV shows like *Leave it to Beaver* and *Ozzie and Harriet*, was something that Blacks would never feel a part of.

In these TV programs, the formula was the same: two kids (usually brothers, as in the case of both the Cleaver and Nelson families), the omniscient, all-powerful father (who worked somewhere during the day, although the series never made clear where), and the dutiful housewife-mother. They were inevitably white, as were their neighbors and virtually all their social contacts. Obviously, someone was being left out of the American Dream. In *Ozzie* as well as *Beaver*, it was always the younger son who was seen as being most vulnerable to the rebellious factors that were just beginning to manifest themselves in the culture at large. There was always the threat that the Beaver might "go bad."

While television was portraying its cleansed version of America, Hollywood was presenting a more unsettling vision of American life. James Dean, the new star of American cinema, had emerged in 1954 on the heels of Marlon Brando (who'd already created a stir with his sexually charged performance in *A Streetcar Named Desire*—Elvis was watching). Younger, prettier, and even more confused, Dean was an immediate sensation following his debut in *East of Eden*. One thing about Dean was that he method-acted, which was a new trend. That is, he became the role he was playing. His next role, in the eponymous *Rebel without a Cause*, suited him perfectly: mainly, that of the confused loner who flirted with danger and blamed his parents for the way he'd turned out.

Young Americans no longer felt tied to the sexual mores of their parents. The advent of the bomb—and the great Fear that was prevalent during the Cold War—helped foster the philosophy of "why wait 'til tomorrow?" Not just in terms of premarital sex, but in terms of everything—like buying a house, for instance. The whole notion of buying on credit came about in the '50s. People were much more likely to eschew caution when they truly believed that tomorrow might never come.

In 1954, Joe DiMaggio, perhaps the greatest baseball player of his era, married Marilyn Monroe. The actress had made a name for herself that year by being filmed in *The Seven Year Itch* with the wind blowing up her skirt. At the same time, a young Methodist named Hugh Hefner had dug up some smutty pictures of Monroe dating back to when the actress was young and struggling in Hollywood. Hefner used these to launch a new magazine called *Playboy*. The whole idea of "scoring" as a lifestyle came about, and it didn't take long for a plethora of "alternative lifestyles" to crop up. The very notion of "lifestyle" was a new concept because, previously, people had never had the leisure to afford such dalliance. *Playboy*, on the other hand, was devoted to the pursuit of lifestyle as a form of identity (in this case, the swinging bachelor).

Playboy was and is essentially a soft-core sex magazine. Their bunnies were (and are) airbrushed kewpie dolls, almost always white, fresh-faced bimbos who, in the personality profiles that accompany their photo spreads, confessed that they longed to be homemakers and man-pleasers. There had always been much harder-core pornography around, even in the '50s, but *Playboy* appealed to a certain mentality more than to actual prurience. There were articles about hi-fis and liquor, and seduction tips from Hef himself. *Playboy* was essentially treating sex as a reward for success and affluence. In other words, it was still very much tied into '50s ideals, no matter how much Hefner loathed his straight-laced upbringing.

In 1956 the surprise best-seller of the year was *Peyton Place*, written by a hard-drinking woman named Grace Matalious about the backdoor indiscretions of a small town in New Hampshire. Like the Kinsey Report, *Playboy*, Rock 'n' Roll, and the films of Marlon Brando, James Dean, and Marilyn Monroe, *Peyton Place* showed the seething sexual underbelly of American society. Topics like adultery, abortion, and incest were, in those days, seldom talked about...*except* in small towns like the one Metalious wrote about. It proved that sex sells and Americans were anxious to read about other people's indiscretions, even if they weren't willing to admit their own. The book revolutionized the oncoming paperback book industry by proving that a book was infinitely resalable even after it had peaked on the best-seller lists. Year after year, *Peyton Place* sold more copies, and even inspired a television show by the same name (which more or less brought about the soap opera craze).

The heroines of *Peyton Place* were not only sexually liberated, but also frank and up-front about their desires and disgruntled about the myth of the American Male as breadwinner and provider. No one knew it at the time, but along with the advent of the Pill, this was an important step in the birth of Feminism. Indeed, the author, Grace Metalious, was an independent woman who'd been married a few times and was a well-known nonconformist in the small town she called home.

In the '50s, women's independence was actually *discouraged* by magazines like *Redbook*, *McCall's*, and *Ladies' Home Journal*. These magazines argued that the few women who did go to college and try to pursue a career must have had something wrong with them. They were vilified for wanting to be single and have a career instead of raising a family. But a few women began to ask the question: "Whose American Dream is it anyway?" Even if a woman did graduate college with the idea of embarking on a professional career, the outside world gave her little to be optimistic about. Women were being taught that the most valuable thing they could do with their lives was to fulfill their preordained roles of wife and mother. The culture at that time took no account of women who might possibly desire to be neither.

During the '50s it seemed like everyone was at war with someone else: Black against white, young against old, communist against capitalist, the CIA against everybody. Nowhere did the frictions of the era come together more dramatically than in the upstart musical form that was soon to be labeled "Rock 'n' Roll." However, the musical—as well as cultural—factors that had helped create Rock 'n' Roll had been going on for half a century.

CHAPTER 2

WHERE THE MUSIC CAME FROM

POPULAR MUSIC IN THE TWENTIETH CENTURY CAME FROM A VARIETY OF SOURCES: Country, Folk, and down-home music. Its roots go deeper than that: much twentieth-century American song derived from British and Celtic balladry, brought to these shores by nineteenth-century immigrants. The other major influx came from Africa. As Blacks came to this country because of slavery, and as slavery started in the South, perhaps we should start there.

Slaves in the field had every opportunity to invent new work songs. The only salvation for them at that time was the church itself, and that was the other side of the slave's musical experience: spirituals. These spirituals were structurally very similar to the Anglo/Celtic folk ballads. It was inevitable that these two sources would merge, particularly after emancipation, when Black performers were allowed to play music in front of white audiences for the first time.

As the twentieth century dawned, Blacks and whites were drawn together by the demands of industries such as mining, railroads, and manufacturing. However, in the rural South, change was slow to come. In this region, music was the only thing uniting Blacks and whites. There were very few telephones, paved roads, or homes with plumbing. Blacks and whites lived in total squalor. The poor Southern redneck (the "prole" or "plebe" of European descent) was in reality much like the "nigger" he so despised.

There was something about the isolation—Black or white—that bred a need for song. With little else to live for besides God, it was in many ways the only uplifting part of the day when the folk gathered for singsong. A song can travel in the air with very little guidance, and, after a while, some of the Black (spiritual) and white (ballad) work songs became intermingled. Hence, the sources of Blues, Folk, and Country were very similar. This is because they described hardships like poverty and sickness, plights known by both Blacks and whites at the time. This was the preoccupation of the rural farmer, share-cropper, and mountaineer, and this was the source for almost all twentieth-century song forms.

In the days before mass communication, many of the songs were popularized and distributed by the traveling tent-shows, medicine shows, and circuses, all of which featured live music along with the vast array of "freak" acts also on display. This is how vaudeville spread, and minstrelsy also, as many white performers appeared in blackface, which was another way for the Southern white to denigrate the Negro.

The emergence of the railroads helped break down the isolation of the rural South, helping bring people—particularly Blacks—to the bigger cities. Slowly, the South grew into a more industrialized region, as people by the thousands flocked to urbanized centers like Nashville, Memphis, New Orleans, St. Louis, Atlanta, and Houston. The railroad also helped replace agriculture as the chief source of southern industry. Most of all, it changed people's whole perspective on the hopelessness of their own situation—here was a world now where rapid motion (and thus "transcendence") was possible. This notion was best expressed through music (think of all the train songs), and, more than any other cultural preoccupation of the century, music has come closest to replacing religion in people's lives.

Music created a culture of its own that came from the devil and competed against the Lord. This less-than-holy ethos derived chiefly from the blue light districts popping up in the larger Southern cities. The two chief American musical forms that began the century, Ragtime and Blues, were both Black-derived. This contributed to the "evil" connotations of the music because, to most whites, those "jigaboos" were speaking in tongues.

The publication of Scott Joplin's "Maple Leaf Rag" sparked a nationwide Ragtime craze. It couldn't have been only Blacks that bought the sheet music, as the arrangement was intended as much for pianos as it was banjo, and most

Blacks didn't own pianos at the time—these instruments were still chiefly display items for rich plantation owners. The only time Blacks saw a piano was when they saw the one in the lobby of the pubs and taverns and whorehouses in the bigger cities, where a "house" pianist would often perform until dawn. This was where the first wave of Black Rag composers originated from, including Joplin, who'd named his famous rag after a popular club in Sedalia, Missouri. Later Ragtime pianists like Eubie Blake and Jelly Roll Morton played endless variations of the same bar chords, creating many of the "licks" that came to characterize twentieth-century music. Most of these were disseminated to northern regions through the sale of sheet music.

The first exposure many Southerners got to nonindigenous forms of music was through the invention of the radio. Not only was it a cheap and abundant source of entertainment, it narrowed the gap between urban and rural cultures. Southerners heard the latest wares from Tin Pan Alley, and Northerners smelled the turd of nationally syndicated programs like *National Barn Dance* and *The Grand Ol' Opry*. Southern white Country music had been developing at precisely the same time as Black Blues and Ragtime, and these radio shows were the first to expose this kind of rural stomp to the nation at large.

An important part of Country music's development was the introduction of stringed instruments like the fiddle, banjo, mandolin, and guitar. These were the primary musical tools of Southern Folk expression, but, for the first half of the twentieth century, this was a world ignored by the music industry (save for the field recordings of John Lomax, which he began making in 1933 under the sponsorship of the American Council for Learned Studies). It was the same story as always: Northern music biz moguls feared that the raw technique of the Southern rural musician, Black or white, would repel the sophisticated urban consumer. Until they realized that the rural market represented a whole new untapped source of revenue (sell the Southern trash back to the Southerners, in other words).

The rise of the recording industry occurred in the early twentieth century when the 78 RPM phonograph record supplanted the cylindrical disc as the chief source of home entertainment. Among the early record labels were Vocalion, Victor, Paramount, Columbia, and Okeh. The record industry was stunned by the invention of the radio, because it meant a decline in sales. People could now, with the initial purchase of a radio, hear an unlimited source of music for free. The industry was left having to mine less radio-friendly segments to develop a whole new audience—and that turned out to be Southern Negroes and rednecks.

In the spring of 1920, the Okeh record label recorded a young Black vaudeville singer named Mamie Smith singing "Crazy Blues." This recording set off the Blues boom and made Okeh into a ranking record label. A market for Black music was found to exist among Blacks. Okeh's Ralph Peer dubbed the new category "Race Music." By the mid-'20s, all the major labels had introduced a "race" line, and RCA even started its own "race" subsidiary, Bluebird, in 1933.

Although most of the Black records came not from rural but from urban sources, it was discovered that Southern Blacks were buying the recordings as fervently as Northern ones. This sent enterprising men like Peer into the Deep South seeking more "authentic" exponents of "race music." While they were down there, they discovered a whole new source of white "hillbilly" music as well.

Many of these hillbilly records were made up of fiddle players performing what Columbia tagged "old familiar tunes," or Okeh called "old-time music." The Brunswick label, meanwhile, called their early Country sides "songs from Dixie." In any case, the rural flavor was preserved throughout. By being the first to record these sounds, these performers succeeded in turning what was once rural "folk" music into a new form of American popular music (to rival Tin Pan Alley, no less).

By far, the most important practitioners of this popularized folk art were the Carter Family, the first of the Southern "American musical families" to hail from a traditional background and achieve commercial success. Their renditions of songs like "Engine 143," "Wabash Cannonball," "Worried Man Blues," and "Will the Circle Be Unbroken" were the ones that taught these songs to most Americans. Although Carter Family recordings weren't big sellers, they proved to have incredible resilience in the years to follow, helping to shape the whole mythology of the American South coming out of the Depression. The Carters also helped shape the sound of Country, which in turn helped shape the sound of Rock 'n' Roll. Mother Maybelle Carter's finger-picking lead-guitar style popularized the Gibson hollow-body guitar, making it the predominant instrument in Country & Western music. The Carters were also one of the first Country acts to become known primarily through recording, as they seldom ventured north of Virginia.

The other major country recording artist to emerge out of the Depression era was Jimmie Rodgers, the so-called yodelin' cowboy. In sharp contrast to the Carters' image of down-home stability, Rodgers represented the more restless side of Country music's identity—that of the hard-luck loser and singing brakeman. Rodgers was in many ways considered the first white Blues singer, a fate later bestowed upon Hank Williams and others (on some occasions, Rodgers actually sounded like a weird precursor to the "talking" style of Bob Dylan). The fact that he died young, from TB, only enhanced his legacy.

At the same time as artists like the Carter Family and Jimmie Rodgers emerged, record labels were starting to document the many Black Blues singers coming from the rural South who, like Rodgers, told tales of hard times and woe. During the Depression, many pioneering Country–Blues singers and guitarists made their recording debuts, helping to popularize traditional material that would form the root of modern, electrified Blues. Sleepy John Estes recorded the first "Milk Cow Blues" for Victor in 1930; Bukka White, meanwhile, popularized the "Fixin' to Die Blues" (later redone by Bob Dylan, among others). But, by far, the most influential Blues pioneer to record during these years was the mysterious Robert Johnson.

Johnson was originally a disciple of the skilled guitarist Charley Patton, often credited as being the Father of Delta blues. Patton's use of the twelve-bar (or, in his case, the thirteen-and-a-half-bar) structure and the rhythmic density with which he utilized it on such classics as "Pony Blues," "Revenue Man Blues," and "Rattlesnake Blues"—not to mention his gravelly voice—was the source behind the subsequent Delta style of such practitioners as Johnson, Howlin' Wolf, Muddy Waters, Elmore James, and John Lee Hooker.

Johnson was the first of Patton's descendents to achieve notoriety, but, like Jimmy Rodgers, he died at an early age. In Johnson's case, his death seemed to be the devil's work, and part of his mystique was that, during his brief recording career, he was almost always conjuring the evil spirit through evocations like "Hellhound on My Trail," "Me and the Devil Blues," and "Devil Got My Woman." There were even rumors that he'd sold his soul to the devil in exchange for his virtuoso guitar style. His strange vocal style truly sounded like a man possessed.

Johnson's legendary recordings for Columbia in the mid-'30s set the stage for many subsequent Blues and Rock experiments, introducing a lot of the hard-luck clichés, sexual innuendoes, and basic rhythm patterns that would characterize both genres. Nearly all his songs became "standards" in one form or another, particularly "Terraplane Blues," "Love in Vain," "Stop Breaking Down," "Dust My Blues," and, especially, "Standing at the Crossroads," which introduced the whole mythology of Johnson's ill-fated deal with the devil, as the crossroads off of Highway 61 in Clarksdale, Mississippi was where he'd supposedly sold his soul.

Johnson died as a result of poisoning in August 1938 after flirting with the wife of a man who'd hired him to play a house party that night. It was a Rock 'n' Roll murder. Johnson had a reputation for being a heavy drinker, a woman-izer, and a hell-raiser. Along with his supernatural obsessions and early death, this made him the first burnout legend, setting the pace for Charlie Parker, Hank Williams, Johnny Ace, James Dean, Elvis Presley, Eddie Cochran, Jim Morrison, Sid Vicious, Lester Bangs, John Belushi, Johnny Thunders, and all the rest. So the cast was set already. In 1938.

Many innovators of Rock 'n' Roll were already perfecting their technique in the '30s: Howlin' Wolf, Muddy Waters, Bukka White, Elmore James, John Lee Hooker, and Sonny Boy Williamson. They were all more or less peers, but it took their eventual migration to the big cities to draw attention to what they were doing (the root of which all went back to the Delta). In most cases, this meant Chicago, although Hooker actually ended up in Detroit. But that wasn't for another twenty years.

In the 1930s the "urban blues" of performers like Big Bill Broonzy and Tampa Red were among the most popular. Both of these artists can be credited with expanding the basic line-up of the typical Blues band, from what was often just a singer/guitarist, string bass, and piano to perhaps two guitars and a couple of horns plus the normal rhythm section. This was a natural result of urbanization: Broonzy, for example, was originally from Mississippi but moved to Chicago in the '30s. Larger venues meant larger and louder bands. Most of them emulated the large Swing bands of Duke Ellington or Benny Goodman. Although white, Goodman was accepted by Blacks for allowing the revolution-ary Black guitarist, Charlie Christian, to record for the first time.

The Swing boom was the inevitable by-product of the economy finally get-ting better and people having more money to spend to go to dance halls and the like. When World War II came along, Swing was another way for people to get closer to one another and to forget about their troubles and about their loved ones being overseas. Swing was purely an American phenomenon: because it seemed so patriotic, Swing endured as the primary "pop" music of the day. The Dorsey Brothers, Benny Goodman, and even Duke Ellington provided the soundtrack for the generation coming of age in the '40s—the same generation who would spawn the Baby Boomers the next decade.

Jazz was not a popular phenomenon upon its inception in the '20s. Its origins were in the whorehouses of New Orleans's legendary Storyville district. New Orleans was always one of America's bawdiest cities, considering the multiracial melting pot that made up its population. As a port of entry in the Gulf of Mexico, New Orleans proved to be an inviting horn of plenty to sailors from all over. The population consisted of French, Negro, English, Creole, Spanish, and Native American folks. The culture it produced was Jazz—the sound of which was shaped by this diversity. The early Dixieland brass bands were based on the English model, and instruments like the cornet and clarinet seem to have been introduced by the Creoles.

The Creoles were not found in the more landlocked regions like Chicago. Essentially Black natives of the West Indies, they spoke an especially sweet brand of French that influenced the intonations of Jazz itself. American music in the twentieth century belonged to everyone from Native Americans banging on their drums, to the "coon songs" of Southern Blacks, to the wailing of mountain hillbillies, to conservatory-trained neocool classicists, to Tin Pan tricky-men. It is this kind of diversity that has made this country's musical legacy perhaps its most valuable and lasting gift to the world.

In the late '20s and early '30s, Jazz was economically tied to Prohibition, which outlawed many of the places jazzmen had previously played. For many years, the whole format of the jazz "band" was scaled back—the most the speakeasys could hold were three- or four-man bands. With the repeal of Prohibition, a new phenomenon began taking place in the form of the Big Bands, who'd learned a thing or two from New Orleans pioneers like Louis Armstrong and his Hot Seven. With this group, Armstrong, the pioneer of modern trumpet playing, proved that a soloist could have an individual voice, even with a fairly large band behind him. The bands only got bigger when it once again became legal to drink.

Even though Big Band ultimately became more a form of Pop than Jazz, some legitimate innovators did come out of it. Edward "Duke" Ellington, the

Washington, D.C.-born pianist, emerged as the reigning leader among fully orchestrated composers. He was also the only Black to achieve the same respectability as Goodman or the others. Ellington wrote "scores" not only for ensemble, but individual sections for each player, which made many of his works, especially the later ones, almost neo-Classical pieces.

During the Big Band era, a similar phenomenon was sweeping the southwest region of the United States. Labeled "Western Swing," the music of bands like Bob Wills & His Texas Playboys was a combination of traditional down-home Country sources and the more elaborate Big Band format. The Western Swing bands employed brass, reeds, and woodwinds like the Jazz bands, but also featured fiddles and maintained the distinctly Southern personality of the region.

Wills was by far Western Swing's most important practitioner. Born in East Texas in 1905, he was subject to a variety of influences most purely Southern parties weren't—not only Anglo, but also Chicano, Black, German, Cajun, Native American, and Mexican. According to Country music historian Bill Malone: "A passion for dancing was common among all these groups, and in this heterogeneous society musical styles flowed freely from one or another, modifying the old Southern rural style." [1]

The whole "western" of Country & Western came from this element. Until then, all hick expression had been called "Hillbilly," much like all Black manifestations were lumped under the heading of "Race." Starting with the huge ballroom bands of Texas and Oklahoma, the whole Western motif and the mythology of the cowboy began to be absorbed into music. Everyone knows how important cowboy hats have become to Country music (if not Rock 'n' Roll). In those days, some of the participants actually were cowboys, and the mythology of the Old West has been prevalent in the culture ever since. As far back as 1910, John Lomax published his popular songbook *Cowboy Songs and Other Frontier Ballads*. Gene Autry, the "singing cowboy," made millions. Dime store novels about the Old West proliferated, and of course we all know what Hollywood did with the image. It was only natural that the cowboy element of "kick the stirrup and ride the dusty trail" would become a popular motif in popular music, to the point where, by the late '30s, you had Tin Pan Alley hacks affecting the ways of the Old West and Bing Crosby singing "San Antonio Rose."

In 1934, Wills—a fiddler by trade—moved his Texas Playboys to Oklahoma, where, throughout the '30s, they held residence at one of Tulsa's largest ballrooms, Cain's Academy. Although the Playboys were definitely stressing a true down-home flavor, they were as adept at straight Jazz as they were with so-called Country. The clarinet playing in Wills's "The Girl I Left Behind Me" (1941) was very close to New Orleans Jazz. The steel guitar work of Leon McAuliffe went on to inspire the whole form of Country music, lending the "crying" sound that would become such an integral feature of the classic Country made by people like Hank Williams a decade or so later. Like Ellington's band, when the Playboys rocked, they rocked—their version of "Four or Five Times" sounds rhythmically very much like the New Orleans Rock 'n' Roll standard "Don't You Just Know It."

But that's just the way American music was progressing in the early- to mid–twentieth century. What's really amazing is that it was all happening at once. Regions and cultures were still sealed off enough from one another to allow each one's own individual characteristics to flourish. However, all these disparate styles were starting to merge through the various migrations that were occurring. The sounds of Black, white, urban, and rural expression was beginning to sound more alike. Radio abetted this homogenization. Because of the Depression, the record labels had consolidated into three majors: Decca, Victor, and Columbia. Two of these, Victor and Columbia, had their own subsidiaries, Bluebird and Okeh, respectively, to handle the more rawboned acts. Decca, under the leadership of Dave Kapp, sought to expand their roster as well. This was an important part of Country music's eventual evolution into a "popular" category, which would in turn influence Rock 'n' Roll. The labels were finding out, particularly after the Depression, that whatever sold was worth hanging onto, even if it sounded like nonsense—which much Western Swing no doubt did to Northern executives and talent scouts, just as Rock would years later.

With bands not only swelling to larger ranks themselves, but also playing to larger and larger audiences, there was a need to increase volume. This was most commonly achieved through the use of amplification. This was another historic turning point because, thereafter, the electric guitar became the most popular and sought-after instrument in American popular music. Blues artists were experimenting with the instrument at the same time, but certainly with none of the national exposure that being in one of the Big Bands or Western Swing ensembles offered.

Electrification made its debut in 1934 with Bob Dunn's work with the original Musical Brownies, one of the first "country jazz" outfits. Dunn accomplished this by jimmy-rigging a keg amp. However, by 1936, Gibson was already introducing their own electric models with built-in pick-ups and volume controls. In September '36, Leon McAuliffe had a huge hit with "Steel Guitar Rag," which helped popularize the sound of the electric guitar to the whole nation. Within a couple of years, the Black guitarists Charlie Christian and Aaron "T-Bone" Walker defined how the instrument would be played for generations: Christian with a fluid style that more or less introduced the instrument as the lead voice, and Walker with a less polished but more emotional style of "picking."

After Prohibition ended, jukeboxes became increasingly popular. Beer halls and taverns that were now allowed to operate needed some sort of musical entertainment to keep the drinkers happy. Not all of them could afford live talent, and the jukebox presented the perfect alternative: a coin-operated phonograph containing a vast number of records. In 1933 the Wurlitzer Company became the first to market the invention—by 1940 more than 300,000 jukeboxes had been sold.

In the ensuing years, the jukebox would play a pivotal role in the emergence of the whole "kiddie kulture," with its steadfast presence in the malt shop and other teen haunts. In the prewar years, however, there were no teen clubs, and the primary function of the new invention was to provide entertainment for the patrons of drinking establishments which, in the wild Southwest, were called juke joints or, more likely, honky-tonks.

According to Bill Malone: "When country music entered the honky-tonk, it had to change…the older pastoral or down-home emphasis…could not survive in such an atmosphere. Songs about 'poor old mother at home' and 'the Old Country Church' seemed somewhat out of place…Instead, songs reflecting the problems and changing social status of the ex-rural dweller became paramount."[2]

In other words, the songs became topical, and nine times out of ten the topic was drinking. This is the kind of environment Rock 'n' Roll grew out of— Rock *music*, that is. The *culture* of Rock 'n' Roll was eventually taken over by the kids who at this time were virtually nonexistent. The average honky-tonk musician worked some obscure hard-labor day job and then played music all night. Even Bob Wills was a factory dock worker throughout much of his early career. This is an element clearly missing from modern music.

The honky-tonk also represented the move back toward the small-band for-mat. They were, after all, merely drinking bars and not large dance halls that could accommodate the huge ballroom crowds. By the early '40s the tonks were pulling sizable crowds of servicemen, civil defense workers, and other outsiders who often clashed with the local folk. There was a lot of violence, and the whole mythology of the fist fight became interwoven in Country music's legacy.

Much of the violence was over women, and as a result, cheatin' songs became as rampant as drinkin' ones. Floozies were prevalent at the honky-tonks, but, like the bordellos of New Orleans, this bawdy environment was an ample breeding ground for a whole new musical style. As the popular honky-tonk pianist Moon Mullican recalled: "The only place a piano playing kid like me could get work in those days wasn't exactly high class. The ladies of the evening, who worked there, would come and set on the piano bench and fan me while I played." [3]

Wasn't exactly high class: there was still that Christian guilt about it! What bluesmen and subsequent rockers added was a gleeful sense of sin. This hadn't happened yet, but the factors marking honky-tonk's proliferation were leading to something more closely resembling the American Rock band. Musicians were still using fiddle and stand-up bass, but the electric guitar had been added as a full-time effect among most bands, and for the first time drummers actually began accom-panying Western-style bands also. This was undoubtedly a big influence on such important pre-Rock units as Hank Williams & His Drifting Cowboys.

Another dynamic that influenced the proliferation of the small bands was World War II. With so many men being drafted, it was hard to keep up per-sonnel in the mammoth Big Band or Western Swing orchestras. The small band made it easy to train new members and replace departed ones. The whole country was in a state of mobilization anyway, and it was not unusual for some-one to suddenly move to another region entirely because of service or the promise of war-related employment. This panic-stricken sense of flux would permanently change the tempo of American life—and intensify the shape of its culture. As for the small-band concept, it would change the whole manner in which music was composed. It would also put more emphasis on the individual musician, not to mention the singer. American "popular" music soon became almost exclusively a vocal art.

The war effort affected the recording industry in other ways. The war-related demand for shellac instigated a freeze on supply. The record industry was at the bottom of the need list, even though shellac was a vital ingredient in the manufacture of phonograph records. As a result of the war, studios were unable to operate at full capacity because personnel were scarce and new machinery was unobtainable.

In the midst of all this, there were other circumstances that would permanently alter the face of American popular music. On Dec. 31, 1940, a contract between the National Association of Broadcasters (NAB) and the American Society of Composers, Authors, and Publishers (ASCAP) expired. In subsequent negotiations, ASCAP apparently made demands that exceeded the wishes of NAB, so NAB set up their own licensing association, called Broadcast Music, Inc. (BMI). Going against a giant like ASCAP, which owned most of the music published in this country since 1884, BMI naturally started head butt first. One thing they had going for them was that they were owned by the radio stations, which meant that their stuff was guaranteed to get airplay. On January 1, 1941, the broadcasters banned all ASCAP material from the airwaves, which gave rise to a number of independent publishers like Acuff-Rose and helped break Tin Pan Alley's monopoly on composing.

When the two sides settled their differences in October 1941, BMI had secured its rank in the entertainment world. This encouraged the great flow of material coming from nontraditional sources to proliferate: Blues, Be Bop, hillbilly music, and, eventually, Rock 'n' Roll. Adding to the confusion was the musicians' strike that occurred months after the ASCAP/BMI controversy was settled. James C. Petrillo of the American Federation of Musicians claimed that the jukebox industry and the radio stations were putting musicians out of work and insisted on establishing funds, payable by the record industry, to unemployed musicians. When his demands weren't met, the American Federation of Musicians went on strike in 1942. That meant no licensed recording. The big labels like Decca and Columbia were left only with their backlists. This was actually a boon to the many smaller independent labels, which popped up to fill the void and which endured long after the strike was settled due to the quality of the music they produced.

One such independent label was Capitol. Founded in Hollywood by the famous Tin Pan Alley tunesmith Johnny Mercer, the company was able to pilfer the film industry for talent while taking advantage of the large number of Southern and Southwestern musical performers who'd flocked to California during the war. In the ensuing years, Capitol would introduce many of the leading figures in Country & Western: Tex Ritter, Buck Owens, Tennessee Ernie Ford, Merle Haggard, and the Louvin Brothers. They also proved quite formidable in the Pop field, from Frank Sinatra to, eventually, the Beatles. By the '60s, they weren't even considered an independent anymore, but one of the four major labels.

The great thing about the indie label boom of the '40s was that it was most beneficial to musicians who were playing musical forms that may have otherwise been ignored, such as Hillbilly, Bebop, or R&B. Labels like Blue Note and Savoy were responsible for epochal recordings by jazz pioneers like Miles Davis and J.J. Johnson, but they also dabbled in the newborn "jump" Blues idiom, which, through a myriad of twists and turns, led to Rock 'n' Roll. Because they were left with the dregs of the recording industry that no one else wanted—the rednecks and Blacks—the independent labels were a big step towards integration. By being together on the same record labels, Blacks and whites came to know and ultimately share each other's idioms.

A perfect example was the legendary King label, founded by Syd Nathan in Cincinnati, Ohio in 1944. Nathan was as important a pioneer of early rock as Sam Phillips and was one of the many Jews who took a liking to the new R&B format, which, as a musical form, was an important melting pot of styles and cultural elements. King originally began as a hillbilly-based label with releases by Grandpa Jones, Moon Mullican, and the Delmore Brothers, whose raunchy "Hillbilly Boogie" in 1945 was a worthy predecessor to Rock 'n' Roll. By the '50s, King had branched off into a sister label called Federal, which specialized in the new "jump"/R&B vocal groups like the Midnighters and Five Royales. Nathan encouraged both his white and Black artists to cover each other's material, which meant more royalties for the label. This not only helped integrate the two distinctive styles of white Country "boogie" and urban Black "jump" Blues, but paved the way for important crossovers, like Elvis Presley covering Arthur Crudup. King finally got lucky and beat Chess Records to the punch by signing a young singer/composer from Macon, Georgia named James Brown, who would go on to influence the direction of American music for the next twenty years.

In the postwar years, the country was undergoing immense prosperity. The end of the war freed Americans from material restraints. Having "won the war," there was a great urge on the part of the populace to live it up. Recorded music flourished. The World War II daddies had just come home and were having parlor parties with lots of drinking and a few discs always on the phonograph. The record industry had made significant advances that furthered the accessibility of recorded music. By the '50s, the heavy, disc-like 78 RPM record was being phased out in favor of the lighter 45 RPM and the 33 RPM LP, which really didn't take off 'til the mid-'50s but eventually came to dominate the industry.

Before the grim specter of the Cold War set in, the postwar years were a period of great jubilation, and everyone wanted to let go a little. The names of the various genres of music that arose during those years said it all: Juke, Jump, Honky-Tonk, Boogie Woogie, Bebop, Rock 'n' Roll—all joyous-sounding expressions signifying wild times. Some of the craziest stuff that ever rocked the Earth came about in the years 1945–1950.

During those years, a large number of Country musicians recorded Boogie material, starting with the Delmore Brothers and running through such important pre-Rock artists as Hardrock Gunter and Roy Hall. The origins of Boogie Woogie" date back to Birmingham, Alabama, where, in 1928, Pinetop Smith recorded "Pinetop's Boogie Woogie" for Brunswick. A mining town, Birmingham had its share of brothels and redneck bars, and these were the origins of the new, repetitious style perfected by pianists like Smith who were faced with having to keep the action going all night. In this ribald environment, the sound, the feel, was more important than the individual song (or player) per se.

In the pre-Rock years, Boogie Woogie was another catch-all term that basically meant…Rock. The old fogeys would say, "Waaah, those kids and their Boogie Woogie!" The form reached the height of absurdity when the Andrews Sisters performed "Boogie Woogie Bugle Boy" in 1948. But it was never a "form" anyway; it was a meaningless term that meant "noise parents didn't understand." Which is, of course, exactly what Rock became.

It had some help getting there from Louis Jordan, the only Black artist other than Nat "King" Cole to cross over to the Pop charts in the pre-Rock era. When he cut his classic sides for Decca in the mid-'40s, Jordan and His Tympani Five were the essence of the commercially successful Boogie band, as evidenced by songs with titles like "Choo Choo Ch'Boogie," "Boogie Woogie Blue Plate," and "Blue Light Boogie." The important thing about them was, despite the fact Jordan was the obvious frontman, the rhythm section actually swung, providing many of the rhythms that would later constitute Rock 'n' Roll.

The term "jump blues" originally meant bands like Jordan's, but, by the '50s, there was a recognizable new genre emerging that not only included the good-time jive of honkers and shouters like Jordan, but the harder-edged guitar-oriented urban Blues coming out of places like Chicago. For want of a better term, it became Rhythm & Blues, but it still basically meant Black music, much like the old "Race" category had, since Nat "King" Cole and the Ink Spots charted alongside the more raucous new sounds. Although the term has endured, it's even more meaningless today, as most of what constitutes "R&B" no longer possesses either rhythm *or* Blues.

Interestingly enough, the term *rock 'n' roll* was already in use. Between 1947–1952, several songs made use of the verb *to rock*: Wild Bill Moore's "We're Gonna Rock," "Rockin' Boogie" by Joe Lutcher, "Rockin' the House" by Memphis Slim, Hattie Noel's "Rockin' Jenny Jones," "Rockin' at Midnight" and "Good Rockin' Tonight" by Roy Brown, "Rock the House" by Tiny Grimes, and "All She Wants to Do Is Rock" by Wynonie Harris. Most of these came from the smaller Black- or hillbilly-oriented record labels. Although there was no common thread between any of these artists, all of these songs, and others using the term *rock* or *rock 'n' roll* during this period, embraced a feel-good/fuck-all ethos, with an emphasis on tempo and volume. *Billboard* even hissed over a Johnny Otis release in 1949: "Mmmmnn! One of the loudest records ever made," as if to suggest this was a *bad* thing.

Real "country music" was coming to an end due to the appearance of the quixotic Hank Williams, who, in many ways, was the last of the real rural country stars. Williams embraced the contradiction between down-home and uptown. On the one hand, his roots couldn't have been more rural. On the other, the fact he had a performance-ready band behind him and that he wore tailor-made cowboy suits made him one of the first true recording "stars" of the '50s. Through his success emerged the subsequent Nashville override: "Country music" after Hank became as self-conscious and commercially oriented as any other form of Pop.

The son of a farmer, Hank Williams was born in the small community of Mt. Olive, Alabama in 1923. Illness having forced Papa into a veteran's hospital, the boy was raised by his mother, Lilly, who exerted an overbearing influence on her son for the rest of his life. But like with many a mama's boy—Duke Ellington, Elvis, Jack Kerouac, Andy Warhol—this smothering maternal influence helped shape the psyche that would create great works of art.

As early as age fourteen, Williams demonstrated a prodigious talent for music-related endeavors. Like most country artists, Williams wasn't only influenced by the popular Honky-Tonk and hillbilly performers of the day such as Ernest Tubb and Roy Acuff, but also by the many Black Blues artists he no doubt heard growing up in the South. His big break came in late 1946, when he signed on as a staff songwriter with Acuff-Rose. Fred Rose had apparently been bowled over by Williams's first recordings for the Sterling Company in New York (which *Billboard* had dismissed as "way back in the woods"). A few months later, Rose helped Williams secure a recording contract with a budding new company named MGM, which probably could be called the House That Hank Built, as Williams was their first successful artist (you can thank him for Connie Francis, in other words).

Like most hillbilly artists, Hank's career was marked by alcoholism. In his case, it was probably in part due to feelings of guilt stemming from his complicated relationship with his mother. But it also had to do with the fact that performers like him were emerging straight out of the backyard shithouse to take over the world. For instance, a decade before, Bob Wills and Tommy Duncan in the Texas Playboys would wear heavy cowboy suits and hats, despite the fact that there was no air conditioning, because they really believed that, as entertainers, they should dress "proper"—unlike later t-shirt-and-jeans-wearing cretins (the Ramones, AntiSeen, Nirvana). They were literally sweating their asses off in the name of art, and all there was to do was...drink!

The folks at the *Grand Ole Opry* had been warned about Hank's drinking, but they saved him a place because they realized genuine backwoods talent when they saw and heard it. They made the kid a star, just like they'd later attempt—unsuccessfully—to do with Elvis. But even at the height of his fame, Hank was in great pain for several reasons, including his mom's overbearing nature and his wife Audrey's infidelity, and also a congenital birth defect that made him walk in a slightly stooped manner and necessitated the use of many prescription drugs. Add to the stage heat—which he combated with beer—the myriad of mind- and body-numbing pills and you have the makings of one truly twisted individual. This set a pattern that would continue in Rock 'n' Roll for the next fifty years.

Williams also held the unique distinction of being the first white "hillbilly" artist to cross over to the Rhythm & Blues charts—that was because songs like "Move It on Over" and "Rootie Tootie" owed as much to the rhythms of Black music as they did to Honky-Tonk. Nevertheless, I'm sure ol' Hank still called 'em "niggers." At least he had the self-deprecating sense of humor to sing: "I've had a lotta luck and it's all been bad."

Bad luck befell Hank with crushing finality on New Year's Day in 1953, when he died unexpectedly of a heart attack at age 29 (he had to die cryptically on a holiday). By then he'd already been fired by the *Opry* and had remarried. He was a national hero, but a flame burned inside of him that made him an oddity among the people of his time, which is ultimately what killed him but also what still enshrines him today with the post-everything crowd. Is it postmodernism only when the so-called artist is self-conscious of the time he/she lives in, or when he/she is unselfconscious about the time but is misunderstood by it? That's the question posed by someone like Hank Williams, as well as the thousands who followed in his wake.

Before Hank sputtered out, he'd returned to the place where he'd begun: the *Louisiana Hayride*, the *Opry's* only regional competition and one even more open to raucous brands of hick hoedown. As the *Opry* became more famous and Nashville-oriented, it became more generic and less rustic, like a hick version of Lawrence Welk and a grim foreboding of *Hee Haw*. Hank was drunk off his feet, holding a guitar with horseshit under his fingernails and high on whatever prescriptions he could get his hands on. Hell, he could've ended up becoming Neil Young. And don't think for a moment that Neil Young doesn't know it.

The *Louisiana Hayride* originated in Shreveport, Louisiana, on KWKH, a powerful station with a 50,000-watt signal and central proximity in a tri-state area (Louisiana, Texas, Arkansas) that was experiencing an economic revival due to the area's expanding gas and oil industry. The show was broadcast live from the Shreveport Auditorium every Saturday night, which was traditionally the wildest night of the week for the working stiffs. They came out to drink and naturally could appreciate a Hank Williams, who joined the show shortly after its debut and split from the Opry a year later, a trend repeated by countless Country greats and fellow badasses: Webb Pierce, Faron Young, Johnny Cash, and George Jones.

By far, the most famous alumnus of the *Hayride* was Elvis Presley. Before he joined, Elvis was just another country bumpkin with aspirations of Williams-like success. Growing up in Memphis, Elvis heard the *Hayride* almost as a rule, and the version of "Old Shep" that he later appropriated for his own actually belonged to *Hayride* regular Red Foley. Like Williams, Elvis was naïve and passionate enough to dig the Black music of the region without the stigma some others attached to it.

When Elvis arrived, he was abetted by several factors: (a) many more people "arriving" with him, like D.J. Fontana, his drummer, whom he picked up from the *Hayride*; (b) people to help him along, like Sam Phillips; and (c) a whole new segment of the population to target, "the kids." Hank Williams sang about broken marriage and the like, but what Elvis and others of his ilk were expressing was pure adolescent frustration—it was in his nervous movements, and in his quavering, hiccuping voice. Amongst prairie regulars, there was a lot of scorn and condemnation for him. But soon Elvis and his ilk would transcend into a world where they never even had to worry about what such hayseeds thought.

Which would become the whole point of Rock 'n' Roll.

CHAPTER 3

ELVIS GOTTA GUN

THERE WERE OTHER WEIRD POCKETS OF ALTERNATIVE CULTURE GROWING IN POSTWAR AMERICA: biker clubs, for instance. The original Hell's Angels were actually a grudge-harboring collective of shell-shocked war veterans. These were the days before the bastions of political correctness had established any kind of "therapy" for such displaced souls. So-called crazies were more or less on their own (lest they wanted to end up in one of the notorious "snake pits" with pants-pooping droopy-haired Grumpus lookalikes). Bikers were veterans who couldn't adapt to the "morality" that had seized American culture in the '50s. They also couldn't fit in with the table manners of June Cleaver. They were animals, and they remained animals even as they rode hippie winds in the '60s. That's what the hippies never figured out: these guys were *war veterans* as opposed to anti-establishment creeps. They were harboring such repressed anger and resentment that it would inevitably erupt into violence. They needed the wide-open spaces that riding their hogs provided. And soon they'd have women, too—the fallen daughters of every bedroom community, who were seeking their own liberation from '50s-style training-bra too-goodness.

The biker and the redneck mentality often merged. As everyone from Charlie Rich to AntiSeen would eventually prove, rednecks were the original longhairs.

In the South, where poverty was more real, Country music served as a form of Blues. Hank Williams, the most popular Country artist of his time, was essentially doing a Blues as pure as Robert Johnson's. Williams would one day explain his Blues this way: "You got to have smelt a lot of mule manure before you can sing like a hillbilly." [1]

To today's superhip it might seem inconceivable, but once upon a time, in the South, before the automobile, before movies, before paved roads even, the barn dance was the big event on Saturday night. The idea was simple: lots of chicken-eating and bottle-passing, with some local yokels providing the musical accompaniment. This uproarious form of hokum was so popular that when radio began the barn dance would serve as the blueprint for some of its most popular programs: like *The Grand Ole Opry*, for instance.

Broadcast over 50,000-watt WSM, the *Opry* was the first heavily syndicated radio program, setting the stage for Symphony Sid and all the rest. Coming from Tennessee, this was pure hick shtick with Minnie Pearl's improvised hayseed skits as well as an enormous variety of corn-fed talent: Roy Acuff, Bill Monroe, Eddy Arnold, Bob Wills, Hank Williams, and eventually Elvis Presley. Based in Nashville, the show helped establish that city as an important Country music Mecca.

The *Opry* was broadcast for four and one-half hours per night, so the performers had to be good to sustain the length of the performance. We hadn't reached the point yet where it all became bullshit—as it would, starting with MTV or even before that. But in 1947, many people didn't have anything better to do on a Saturday night than sit glued to their radios for four and one-half hours. It's a pretty safe bet that they were passing the corn-liquored bottle the whole time without one single concern about what MADD mothers thought. It was a different world then. And it was the South.

By the '50s, Hillbilly music had become so popular that more than 600 radio stations broadcast *Opry*-like shows. Most of the performers were amateurs who plied the muse only because they loved it. As Bill Monroe noted, they could not "give up their day jobs." This put them more in line with today's "indie" rockers as opposed to major label glory seekers. In fifty years, we really have come full circle. But the difference was, a day job for a Southern hillbilly meant something like dock loading, not copy shop slacking. These randy hillbillies would've put a fist through the face of today's super-ironic hordes.

Billboard, the leading music-trade publication in the nation, didn't know what to make of Hillbilly music's rising popularity. Before 1942, the magazine lumped Hillbilly with "foreign" numbers, meaning that, ironically enough, the most genuine of American white song forms was being listed beside recordings that came from abroad. But to the metropolitan editors of *Billboard*, the sounds coming from the Deep South at that time sounded as alien as whatever Europe had to offer.

By 1942, things weren't much better. The new "Western & Race" category did what civil servants and pandering half-mad politicians had been trying to do all along, and ever since: lump "white trash" and Negroes together. It wasn't until the early '50s that *Billboard* finally inaugurated its "Country & Western" category, forever changing the definition of American popular music. Now such disparate elements as Western Swing, rural white Southern Blues, and Appalachian Bluegrass were united in the public consciousness.

Country & Western music was reaching its golden period in the early '50s via not only Hank Williams, who was basically the last of the honky-tonk stylists, but also Nashville's emergence as the epicenter of the Country music-making business. Nashville represented the commercialization of the form. The rough-hewn honky-tonk style was absorbed by the new rockabillies who tended to make their home in Memphis. Nashville, meanwhile, became kind of the Tin Pan Alley of the hick world.

"We made this town," said Frank Rose, one-half of the famous Acuff-Rose publishing partnership that acted as the phoenix for Nashville's rise to prominence. As the firm gained credibility, they began to attract a stream of aspiring songwriters who soon learned to pen the classic country song: "*Waaah*, mah baby dun left me" or, later on, "*Waaaah*, the plant dun closed down again/I been laid off n' drinkin' all day." The addition of the pedal steel guitar (heard most prominently on the recordings of Webb Pierce, as played by Bud Isaacs) reshaped the sound of Nashville. Initially pioneered by West Coast musicians, the sobbing tone lent Country music the "crying" sound that became its trademark.

Another important innovation was the invention of the electric bass guitar, which Fender introduced in the '50s. Held like a guitar, the new instrument freed both Blues and Country artists from the heavy burden of the stand-up bass. As Country music historian Bill Malone noted: "When bands no longer roamed across the country with the 'bass fiddle' tied to the top of the touring car, an era in American music had truly come to an end." [2]

Fender had already introduced its electric guitar a couple of years earlier, and it had met with phenomenal success. The "cool" twang of the instrument came to dominate the sound of Country & Western for years to come. Other important guitar manufacturers like Rickenbacker had sprung up on the West Coast during the postwar years. With more and more musicians getting a hold of the instrument, they were bound to produce a sound that resembled Rock 'n' Roll, even if they didn't have any idea what they were doing.

In 1947, Arthur Smith, a country-poke from Charlotte, North Carolina who'd later relocate to the West, had a huge hit with "Guitar Boogie," a song that helped popularize the sound of the electric guitar nationwide. At approximately the same time, Les Paul was making his historic recordings with wife Mary Ford that not only used electric guitar but such revolutionary new recording techniques as multitracking as well. Paul would go on to design his own line of guitars for Gibson, which became Fender's biggest competition.

The guitar was, for the most part, portable, which was another reason the instrument proved so popular among vagabond musicians. Because of its immense popularity, the guitar became the catalyst for virtually all of the subsequent major musical developments of the next twenty years. Because of the accessibility and low cost of the equipment, performing musicians were able to literally revolutionize their sound overnight. It wouldn't be long before what they were playing would evolve into something resembling Rock 'n' Roll.

The volume of the new electric bands, usually featuring both amplified guitar and bass, created the necessity for drummers. This was another step towards Rock 'n' Roll, because the success of most good Rock 'n' Roll rests firmly on the backbeat. Or as Chuck Berry would soon say: "It's got a backbeat you can't lose it."

In many historical movements, the pivotal events occur chiefly by accident, and Rock's early years are riddled with examples of such fortuitous happenstance. Take the case of Ray Butts, for example—here was the man who was actually the architect of the Rockabilly sound, and no one's ever heard of him. Butts lived in Memphis during the era when Rock 'n' Roll was exploding. According to legend, he hand-built four amplifiers with echo built in. Although such devices were soon to become commonplace, Butts's amps were originals. Who were the four people who ended up with the amps? Only the founders of the next generation of Southern guitar-speak: Chet Atkins, Scotty Moore, Roy

Orbison, and Carl Perkins. According to Perkins: "I was a fool and sold that amp…I wish I hadn't. That amp did something those echoplexes can't do. It was a sound of its own. It was the Sun sound in person." [3]

Despite Ray Butts's innovations, not to mention those of his messengers, the "Sun sound" was not born overnight. The South may have been an incredibly fertile musical region in the early '50s, but other than the increasingly slick music-biz Mecca of Nashville, the mainstream record industry avoided the region. Even the majority of new "indie" labels that were handling the new pre-Rock sounds were geographically too far out of bounds for most Southern musicians. King was in Cincinnati, Chess was in Chicago, Specialty and Modern were in Los Angeles, and Atlantic and Savoy were in New York. Labels like King had already taken a big step towards Rock by blending white and Black artists within their rosters. This was an idea that no doubt caught the ear of Sun Records founder Sam Phillips. Such musical miscegenation was already indigenous to the Memphis region, which is why in all his early interviews Elvis Presley claimed to be equally influenced by B.B. King and Hank Williams.

As has often been stated, Elvis was the artist Phillips had been seeking ever since he became a talent seeker—doing Artists and Repertoire (A&R) work—for the aforementioned indie labels in the late '40s. But it didn't start out that way: Phillips hadn't initially set out to find "a white man who could sing the blues." He'd set out to find a *Black* man who could sing the blues. Born on a farm near Florence, Alabama in 1923, Sam Phillips had worked the cotton fields as a child alongside Blacks. According to Phillips, hearing them sing their work songs and spirituals while they baled cotton sparked his interest in Black musical expression. Something about the emotional force of the idiom captivated him, and it was this primal experience, similar to the one experienced by Alan Lomax, that indirectly led to the foundation of Sun Records (and subsequently the birth of Rock 'n' Roll).

A career in radio helped land Phillips in Memphis in 1945. At that time the city was an incredibly diverse spawning ground for a number of important musical developments, many of them aided by the presence of an excellent radio station, WDIA, which pioneered the first all-Black format in the country. One of the DJs on the radio station, B. B. King, was a Blues performer in his own right. It was hearing King that eventually led Phillips to set up his first recording studio, at 706 Union Street, in 1949. Having begun his career as an engineer,

Phillips was able to make demos of all the local Black musicians in the area, including B. B. King and Howlin' Wolf. To supplement his income, Phillips also recorded speeches, weddings, funerals, and graduations for a fee and continued to work at WREC radio in Memphis. Phillips was no fool—he knew that a market for Rhythm & Blues had sprung up, particularly in the Northern cities and on the West Coast, and he was successful in persuading faraway labels like Chess in Chicago and Modern in L.A. to lease his wares.

Modern was the province of Joe, Jules, and Saul Bihari, and their first release was Hadda Brooks's "Swingin' the Boogie." Brooks was another important transitional figure in the history of Rock, a pianist who boogied the boogie ad infinitum, even going so far as to boogalarize Grieg in "Concerto Boogie." That was *definitely* the first time a classical reference was made in the name of Rock 'n' Roll.

The Biharis would make frequent trips to the Deep South in search of potential talent. During one such trip to Memphis they discovered B. B. King, who made his first recordings under the aegis of Sam Phillips. The pianist on the sessions was a young jazz musician named Phineas Newborn, whose style didn't suit the Biharis (they were looking for a more down-home quality). Shortly thereafter, they fired Newborn and replaced him with a cocky kid from Clarksdale, Mississippi, named Ike Turner. Clarksdale was the site of the legendary crossroads where Highway 49 met Highway 61, which was where Robert Johnson supposedly sold his soul to the devil. It would only go to follow that Turner, who'd sprung literally from the same Delta mud, was one of the gutsiest musicians of the era.

Like Sam Phillips and B. B. King, Turner had an earlier career in radio. In the late '40s, he'd been a DJ on WROX—"We rocks!"—where he'd played the latest in jump Blues by people like Louis Jordan, Amos Milburn, and Charles Brown. It was during this stint that he first met King, which is probably how he ended up playing on the session. Turner was not only ambitious but also versatile: Although he played fairly straight for B. B. King, he also led a more raucous combo of his own, the Kings of Rhythm. It was only a matter of time before Sam Phillips was holding the microphone in front of them as well.

Bands like Turner's were important, because they were the first Black musicians to hail from the South who didn't rely on the oral tradition passed down by Blues musicians from Charley Patton on up. That is, they drew as much inspiration from radio and recordings as they did from what they heard in the clubs and honky-tonks. This opened up many possibilities: more exotic marriages of musical styles as well as forms of instrumentation, and more sophisticated lyrical insights. What they were in the process of was modernizing the Blues. Someone like Son House, for instance, had no chance of appealing to a larger audience, but a band like the Kings of Rhythm did.

On March 3, 1951, Turner and crew assembled at Sam Phillips's Union Avenue studio to cut four songs. One of them, "Rocket 88," was to have a profound impact in several different areas. For one, it helped establish Sam Phillips as a major A&R man. For another, it helped establish Chess Records in Chicago as one of the early Rock 'n' Roll labels. Not surprisingly, "Rocket 88" has often been referred to as "the first Rock 'n' Roll record" (and Sam Phillips would sure like to have you believe it). However, by 1951 there were already several records in the same raucous vein, but perhaps none as gloriously irresponsible as "Rocket 88." After all, the saxophone was slightly off-key, and the lyrics proclaimed, "Everybody in my car's gonna take a little pill." Beyond that, it was credited to the *wrong person*—mainly Jackie Brenston, who was merely the bass player in Turner's band, although he did compose the song. The recording was actually by Ike Turner's Kings of Rhythm, but on the label it said "Jackie Brenston." This must've angered Turner at first, considering that the band was more or less his baby, but it couldn't have angered him long when "Rocket 88" became the best-selling R&B record of 1951 (in the process putting both Chess and Sam Phillips on the map). Not surprisingly, when Chuck Berry would have his first hit several years later—also on Chess—it would be with "Maybellene," a rollicking car song in the "Rocket 88" tradition.

Like a lot of the indie labels that were springing up in the postwar years specializing in Black Rhythm & Blues, Chess was a family-owned business, in this case by two brothers, Phil and Leonard Chess. Like the good Jewish businessmen they were, they'd sensed a market growing for the new Black Rhythm & Blues ever since the Delta bluesmen began flocking to Chicago in alarming numbers during the years before World War II. The Chess brothers, in fact, operated a succession of after-hours clubs where Black and white musicians hung out together and jammed until sunrise. Like Sam Phillips, Leonard Chess reasoned that if he could somehow capture the sounds he heard in these clubs, he could tap into a revolution. So he set up a makeshift studio, in this case in the garage, and persuaded local singers and musicians to record. It didn't end there, however: while Leonard dealt with operations back home, Phil scouted the country looking for talent. This led him to Sam Phillips.

At that time Phillips was leasing most of his material to the Bihari Brothers in Los Angeles, and Ike Turner was acting as his go-between. But when Chess somehow secured Howlin' Wolf to a contract while he was supposedly under license to Modern, the Biharis accused Phillips of double-dealing and severed the relationship. Phillips had no choice but to rush readily into the arms of Chess, the Biharis' main competition. The Chess brothers were naturally more than willing to employ Phillips's estimable talents in this area. Thus they began a fruitful partnership that continued until Phillips launched his own label, Sun, a couple of years later. When he did, he was clearly influenced by Leonard Chess's recording methods—like rigging a microphone and a loud speaker at both ends of a sewer pipe to produce echo. According to Leonard's son, Marshall, who later went on to work for the Rolling Stones, the big thing was percussion: "My father wanted drum, drum, and more drum. I think he was responsible for doing that to blues, to bring out a heavy beat." [4]

Chess Records was fortunate that a lot of the greatest Delta bluesmen like Muddy Waters and Howlin' Wolf had moved to Chicago in the '40s. These artists helped build Chess as a serious label with their new, more urbane Blues styles. An artist like Muddy Waters, who was born in the heart of the Delta, now found himself in the heart of the American Dream. His reaction: "I'm drinkin' TNT/I'm smokin' dynamite/I hope some screwball/Start a fight." The machismo displayed by someone like Waters was truly threatening to the white-bread world of the '50s. In this way, it was kind of a strange premonition to Rap (Muddy even sang in "I Can't Be Satisfied": "I feel like snappin'/My goddamn pistol in your face.")

Songs like "I Just Want to Make Love to You" and "Hoochie Coochie Man" became readymade classics for the first line of Black and white Blues revivalists a decade later. There's a reason this music caught on with white kids like Keith Richards, Eric Clapton, and Mike Bloomfield: Blues represented a kind of underground. It was only later, in the hands of the prissy folk-revivalists of the Kennedy years, that Blues would become a sacred institution. Then Muddy Waters would finally be given his just due. However, in the '50s, when Chess was putting out all these great records, artists like Muddy were considered the scum of the Earth by the recording industry. But they were having their impact nonetheless.

Another important thing about Muddy (and another important precursor to Rock): he was one of the first to employ a full band containing six players, unprecedented in the field of Blues at that time. It's clear that Waters (real name: McKinley Morganfield) was making a self-conscious decision to expand the parameters of his chosen art.

Which probably could not be said about Howlin' Wolf, Muddy's Chess counterpart, who epitomized "raw talent" in the form of an unwitting mystic who was so down-home he actually frightened people. That was probably due to the fact that Wolf (a.k.a. Chester Burnett) was a surly, foul-mouthed, 300-pound behemoth, born and bred in the Delta, black as night, who never appealed to the same supper-club set as B. B. King and eventually Muddy. That's because Wolf's whole delivery was a primal yowl tinged with anger and sadness, perhaps a little *too* close to the spirit of the Blues to ever cross into the mainstream like so many of his peers. The little bit of acclaim he received mostly came at the hands of the Brit brigade a decade later.

Wolf was actually one of the artists Chess discovered through Sam Phillips. In November 1952, Phillips launched his own label, Sun, to compete with the flood of indies who were already having some chart success (some of them with *his* recordings). In August 1951 the Dominoes' "Sixty Minute Man," released on the independent Federal label, surprised everyone, particularly label owner Syd Nathan, by jumping onto the pop charts. This was especially surprising because "Sixty Minute Man" was a bluesy tune with a rattling guitar riff and somewhat bawdy lyrics ("20 minutes of huffin'/And 20 minutes of puffin'/And 20 minutes of blowin' my top"). Within the next couple of years, several more Black vocal groups would cross over onto the Pop charts: the Orioles, Cadillacs, Charms, Penguins, Spaniels, Chords, El Dorados, Teenagers, and a plethora of others who literally came right off the street. This was not lost on Sam Phillips, who'd been recording Black talent for years. He also must have been aware when, the year after he founded Sun, a white performer from Ohio named Bill Haley had a huge hit covering Blues shouter Joe Turner's "Shake, Rattle & Roll." Here was a novel idea: a white guy bastardizing what was essentially an authentic piece of Blues. It was an idea that Phillips had been thinking about a long time.

The early releases on Sun Records were mostly authentic Blues by people like Dr. Ross the Harmonica Boss or Little Walter. Good records, but they weren't selling. Phillips kept thinking: "If I could only find a white boy who could sing the blues I could make a million dollars." He didn't quite make his million—somebody else did. But he did find the artist to put Sun on the map in the form of a young truck driver who'd been bugging "Mistah Phillips" for weeks to record him. Phillips remembered the boy because of his flamboyant style of dress. As Phillips's secretary, Marion Keisker, recalls: "He wore the most outlandish clothes, he really did. I had to call back my dog once."

Here was this typical hick working class nobody with stars in his eyes. Probably hadn't even been laid yet. And like Hank Williams, the boy suffered from the too-close-to-his-mommy syndrome. It was his mom, Gladys, who'd bought him his first guitar in 1946, when he was eleven years old, and he carried it everywhere—not because he knew how to actually *play* the thing but because, like a big security blanket, it reminded him of his mommy. Already Elvis Presley was establishing the little-lost-rebel-boy persona that would carry him for the rest of his years.

Phillips had a service whereby, for two dollars a pop, anyone could make a record—but you only got one copy as a kind of keepsake. When Elvis decided to cut a record, it was a gift to his mother. He'd always been interested in singing, practicing for hours to sound like the crooners he listened to on the radio or the Blues artists he heard around Memphis. The record he cut that day was actually kind of conventional: a pair of Ink Spots songs, "My Happiness" and "That's Where Your Heartaches Begin." But for some reason, Phillips didn't forget about the boy in the pink suit.

The idea of trying to find a white kid to sing the Blues kept plaguing him. Then it dawned on him one day that the solution was right there before his eyes in the form of Elvis. As the legend goes, when Phillips finally called the young boy, he ran six blocks to the audition. At first it was Phillips' idea to have him record straight Blues, but in a cosmic twist of fate, Elvis and his band decided to cover a Blues song on one side, and a Country & Western one on the other. In both cases, Elvis improved on the original versions. In the case of Arthur Crudup's "That's All Right," the Blues number, many people mistakenly believed Presley was Black. But Elvis wasn't consciously emulating anyone— he was just letting his emotions go overboard with unabashed youthful exuberance. In "Blue Moon of Kentucky," the Bill Monroe number that had been a big regional hit, he changed the whole tune around so that it literally *jumped* instead of swung. It is significant that Elvis would choose to record two different styles of music on his debut record and make them sound strangely akin. The common denominator between both Blues and Country was the funky down-home quality that enabled one to let go of his/her emotions and not feel self-conscious about it. Elvis realized this, and it was through his realization that the synthesis of these two musical forms could finally take place (hence "Rock 'n' Roll").

The band Sam Phillips assembled behind Elvis provided the perfect backdrop for Elvis's unique musical vision. More than likely, it was they who spurred him on. Scotty Moore's guitar playing, for one thing, was as influential to the whole school of Rock guitar players as Chuck Berry's; Bill Black's stand-up bass playing was the prototype for the whole subsequent Rockabilly style of slap-bass playing; and D.J. Fontana's drumming had the steady rhythm that distinguished this music once and for all from that of straight Country cats. Together these four men would virtually invent the Rockabilly craze, a Southern white invasion of would-be Country pluckers infected by the Rock 'n' Roll bug.

As for Presley's vocal quality, he may have been a hick with no worldly experience to speak of, but he infected each tune with enough gusto to compete with more sophisticated Blues and Hillbilly singers. His manipulation of Black idioms while still maintaining his choirboy persona was the perfect juxtaposition of wide-eyed wonder and lascivious intent, a confusing but engaging paradox that suited the increasingly confused mood of the times as well.

There's an insurgency to the sides Elvis and his cronies cut for Sam Phillips during the years '54–'55 that gives the impression that no one involved felt that what they were doing was in any way "ordinary." Like Charlie Parker's Savoy sides, or Robert Johnson's Columbia recordings, Elvis's Sun sessions are among the few instances when we actually get to hear a specific style of music being born. Elvis was one of the first recording artists who wanted *creative* freedom. This sometimes chagrined Phillips, who can be heard admonishing the young Elvis on a demo of "When It Rains, It Pours": "Don't git too *complicated*, bah!" But Elvis was a genuine stylist who imparted his unique trademark on everything he did. That's why even though Elvis seldom wrote his own material, he soon came to own the versions he cut of other people's songs—case in point being "Hound Dog," originally a hit for Willie Mae "Big Mama" Thornton.

The minute "That's All Right" was waxed, a dub of the song was delivered to Sam Phillips' friend Dewey Phillips, who hosted the popular *Red, Hot and Blue* radio program in Memphis. Although the two Phillipses weren't related, there was something thicker than blood between them—mainly payola (a form of bribe for airplay, a common practice among disc jockeys at the time, a factor that would soon come back to haunt them when the Feds caught wind of it). That's undoubtedly why Phillips played the song thirty times one night. It paid off: although the song went nowhere nationally, it made number one in Memphis, and a (local) star was born.

Elvis didn't "invent" Rock 'n' Roll, but his subsequent recording, "Good Rockin' Tonight," showed he was making a self-conscious attempt to introduce the masses to what had already made a believer out of him (in this case in the form of Roy Brown's 1946 original on King). The way Elvis introduced the song, with a mighty reverberating hiccup that elongated the word "well" to salacious proportions, was like a premonition of all that was to come. Keeping to the spirit of the first single, the B-side, "I Don't Care if the Sun Don't Shine," was a more Pop-oriented number, originally done by Patti Page in 1950, but Elvis's version shed the gentility of her version, to say the least. When he sang the line "we're gonna kiss n' a-kiss n' a-kiss n'a-gunna kiss sum more" he got downright excited and almost started panting in an open display of lust that must've dismayed City Fathers in Anytown U.S.A. circa 1955. Hence the controversy—hence the King!

In 1955, Elvis was verging on territory that was virtually nonexistent until that time. Although his sound was a mixture of both Black and white resources, because he was white he got lumped in with the Hillbilly singers. The Country audience was none too enamored with the young kid, not to mention the Country music establishment. A good example was when Elvis finally went on the *Grand Ole Opry*. The figureheads of that organization told him in no uncertain terms: "go back to driving a truck, boy." Elvis cried all the way home.

Elvis borrowed a lot of his image from Hollywood, so it's no surprise he eventually ended up there. But Rock 'n' Roll was different from the movies in that it represented movement—not pictures of movement, but a living, breathing performance art. Not surprisingly, Elvis gained a lot of recognition from his frenetic stage act. Until then, very few musical performers did more than just stand there and play (although contemporaneous sax blowers like Illinois Jacquet and Flip Phillips were literally rolling on the floor during the Jazz at the Philharmonic Shows). Elvis also had mighty appeal as a sex symbol even though he was actually all thumbs: "Aw shucks, ma'am!" But in his naïveté lay his charm.

Rockabilly essentially came out of the combination of Hillbilly and Rock. And even though it probably wasn't called that at the time, it was a pretty apt description of a kind of music whose essential elements were the echo chamber and the concept of "getting real gone." Sam Phillips once described the "magic" of the early Sun studios this way: "I didn't want to get those people in some stupid-ass studio and lead them astray from what they had been doing. To put it another way, I didn't try to take them uptown and dress them up. If they had broken-down equipment or their instruments were ragged, I didn't want them to feel ashamed. I wanted them to go ahead and play the way they were used to playing. Because the *expression* was the thing." [5]

What better definition of Rock 'n' Roll has there ever been?

By 1955, Rock 'n' Roll, in most senses, was already a reality. Several more songs had "crossed over": the Eldorados had declared "Crazy Little Mama (Come Knockin' on My Front Door)" which was the same thing as saying, "Let's get real gone." Later that year, the Cadillacs (*black* Cadillacs, that is!) proclaimed: "My name is Speedo." What the hell was a Speedo? The kids were obviously communicating in a whole new language that sounded like freakish nonsense to the uninformed (i.e., the *squares*).

Rock 'n' Roll was given a mighty boost in 1955 by the unprecedented success of Bill Haley's "Rock around the Clock." Here was the first incidence of a modern tradition—mainly that the song became popular after it was featured in a movie. In this case, the movie was Richard Brooks's teen-delinquent drama, *The Blackboard Jungle*, which caused teens all over the country to rip up the seats of their local theaters. Even though it wasn't really that much of a song— a clattering opus with adenoidal vocals—it turned out to be a bigger sensation than the movie itself, another unprecedented move.

The song had actually been recorded a year earlier, and Haley was no overnight sensation. He'd been playing music since he was thirteen, mostly Hillbilly with some Western Swing thrown in. At twenty-one, he took a job as a DJ at WSNJ in Bridgeport, New Jersey and then transferred to WPWA in

Chester, Pennsylvania, where he became program director. Like a lot of DJs at the time, Haley mixed in his share of Black Rhythm & Blues. And like a lot of other famous performing DJs—B. B. King, Howlin' Wolf, Rufus Thomas—Haley was also in a band. They were called the 4 Aces of Western Swing, which gives you some idea what they sounded like.

In 1949 the Aces became the Saddlemen, once again sticking to the Western theme. They signed with Atlantic, Ahmet Ertegun's upstart label that would soon come to dominate the field of R&B but that, at that time, still released their share of Hillbilly. The Saddlemen only released two records on Atlantic, both flops. In 1951 Haley signed with Decca, took off his cowboy hat, fashioned a "spitcurl" on his forehead like Alfalfa, and put on a trashy dinner jacket. And…Rock 'n' Roll was born?

Well, something closely approximating it, anyway. Although not as overtly Black-sounding as the Sun artists, Haley was nevertheless working on a similar Country/R&B fusion. Finally changing the band's name to Bill Haley & the Comets, he was the undisputed leader, and he preferred a clean but rollicking upbeat "dance" music. He also helped popularize the term *Rock 'n' Roll* with a string of recordings using the phrase, such as "Rock the Joint" and "Rock Rock Rock." The Comets weren't a manufactured "product" either, but a legitimate touring/performance unit. As a friend's dad, who saw them perform in the '50s in Old Orchard Beach, Maine, once told me: "Waaaah, they had that whole pier *a-rockin'*!"

In 1955, Chess also had its first share of crossover success, first with the Moonglows, whose "Sincerely" was basic Ink Spots crooning with some orgasmic groans thrown in, and then with the launching of two of Rock's most important pioneers: Bo Diddley and Chuck Berry. What these two did once and for all was assert the importance of the riff in Rock 'n' Roll, which meant a short rhythmic phrase repeated constantly. It was this development that finally made Rock distinguishable from the forms of music that it had originated from—mainly, Country & Western and Rhythm & Blues.

Diddley (real name is in dispute but may have been Ellas McDaniel) was another Mississippi product transplanted to Chicago. He learned to play guitar at age ten and was one of the first musicians to really appreciate the new technological aspects of the instrument. This accounted for his weird use of vibrato as well as the fact that he played a custom-designed square-shaped guitar.

Diddley himself was no square, however—songs like "Hey Man" and "Cops and Robbers" were streetwise screeds that foreshadowed Rap: the former a play on the whole school of "your girl's so ugly" dissing; the latter a pretty graphic narrative of street crime with Bo playing narrator. As for the basic Bo Diddley guitar riff—a thumping two-chord pattern that doubled back on the beat—it's probably one of the two or three most-copied Rock riffs of all time (as epitomized by Buddy Holly's "Not Fade Away," Johnny Otis's "Willy & the Hand Jive," the Strangeloves' "I Want Candy," Humble Pie's "The Light," David Bowie's "Up the Hill Backwards," X's "The Hungry Wolf," the Smiths' "How Soon Is Now," U2's "Desire," and many other examples).

Bo, never one to feign modesty, summed up his importance in the annals of twentieth century Jive this way in a *Premiere* magazine interview in 1991: "I made the first record to be called Rock 'n' Roll by Alan Freed. I even started that hipshake thing that Elvis copied. The same for rap—we called it *signifyin'*, and it came out of the ghetto. And in 1955 I was one of the first Blacks on Ed Sullivan's *Toast of the Town*. They paid Elvis $5000 but only gave me $750...I was only 26 years old and just figured maybe that was the way things went."

Chuck Berry proved more capable of conforming to the public's expectations without necessarily "selling out." Sure, he was another Chicago (by way of St. Louis) bluesman (and full-time hairdresser) who was urged, at the behest of the Chess Brothers, to try more "upbeat" (read: Rock 'n' Roll) material. But he wrote the stuff himself and it was no more compromising, sound-wise, than that of the early Chess Records masters. It was downright *raw*, as a matter of fact, and with early material like "Thirty Days" and "Maybellene," he achieved the ultimate, electrified hybrid of chord-based Blues and Country clatter (his runs were almost Bluegrassy).

Berry was extremely versatile: "Havana Moon" was an almost Jamaican takeoff years before "bluebeat" had its day (proving that, when it did, it was partly Berry-based). As a lyricist, Berry wrote the book in terms of teen exploit—with a somewhat cynical twist. After all, he was already thirty when he wrote most of his golden gassers. Given his degenerate history as far as underaged women go, perhaps the only lyric he ever wrote that he truly believed in was "Sweet Little 16." His love for having honeys shit on his face gives new meaning to songs like "Wee Wee Hours" as well as "No Particular Place to Go," about not being able to find a public restroom.

Despite his perversions, however, Chuck has been one of the most copied Rock guitar stylists, inspiring everyone from Lonnie Mack to Keith Richards to Johnny Thunders. He's also been one of the most venerable composers: "Johnny B. Goode," Berry's autobiographical take on his own mythical ascendance, is an American standard that has been translated into just about every "popular" category of music, from Country to Reggae to Disco. With this kind of sideways mobility, Rock was not to remain an isolated phenomenon for long. The book was already being written.

"How did we know it was changing?" recalled Phil Chess. "From what our kids were listening to. You could feel it. You could tell it was crossing over. We just didn't know how big it was gonna be." [6]

The Chess brothers were among the first to market Rock 'n' Roll as a distinct category of its own, as evidenced by the '50s albums of artists like Chuck Berry, where there was a minimum of Tin Pan Alley-derived filler. The fiction that all Rock LPs before the Beatles were utter crap does a grave disservice to some brave, groundbreaking work.

In this regard, the Vee Jay label of Chicago seemed to be Chess's closest rivals. Like Chess, they specialized in relocated Delta transplants such as John Lee Hooker and Jimmy Reed. Hooker was actually based out of Detroit, and his early work for Vee Jay, as well as the sides he cut before that for Modern, were some of the recordings that helped define the electric guitar to the next generation. Hooker was one of the first to appreciate the varying degrees of control that a musician could exercise over noise itself. He understood the amplifier-as-instrument concept and the fact that the resulting power struggle between guitar and amp could be intensely gratifying in an almost sexual way. This was the part of his whole routine that influenced such latter-day destructos as Jimi Hendrix and Bernie Worrell of P-Funk, who were basically doing an update of his Blues a decade later.

Jimmy Reed, on the other hand, built the foundation upon which a further groove could be laid. Like Bo Diddley and Chuck Berry in regards to their own distinctive riffs, Reed repeated his classic shuffle ad infinitum. It wasn't as if these guitarists were limited in capacity; it was that they were stylists who didn't feel the need for any extraneous bullshit. Most likely, they plundered their very singular idioms to death because they knew this would be the trademark that would get them noticed. Like the makers of all folk art—the man who spun the pottery vase or whatnot—it wasn't so much *what* they did, but their undying perseverance to the task at hand. It was so repetitious it was memorable, in other words. True to the primitive ethos of early Rock 'n' Roll, Jimmy Reed's recordings were often crudely made and sparsely orchestrated. That meant utilizing such makeshift techniques as banging two blocks together to replicate actual drums ("Big Boss Man"). This definitely influenced future skeleton-crackers like the Velvet Underground, but this wasn't intentional primitivism—it was more a case of make do with what you have, go for the feeling first. Many of the early Rock records were made cheaply because the major labels weren't willing to spend much time or money on Rock 'n' Roll, and the indie labels like Vee Jay simply didn't *have* any money.

Sonny Boy Williamson was the perfect example of an authentic Blues artist drawn into the Pop cultural landscape by accident. Williamson perfected the idea of harmonica-as-lead-instrument, and his arrangements were still based almost entirely on the twelve-bar form, but he wasn't opposed to taking the Blues uptown either, as such material as "Help Me" demonstrates. Chess had a harder time grooming him than some of their other artists, and Sonny Boy was never able to fully cross over, even though most of his sessions were recorded with the same musicians who backed all of Chess's major artists: Otis Spann, Willie Dixon, etc. In the end, he helped develop the language of the harp as a distinct *voice*, influencing such players as Paul Butterfield, Tony Glover, and Bob Dylan, among others.

Elmore James was another transplanted Southerner who left his stylistic groove on the future of uptown music making. Literally the son of a whore from the heart of the Mississippi Delta, James stood 6'2" and was drunk most of the time. By the time he got to Chicago, he'd already been playing for years, having been one of the actual protégés of Robert Johnson. His voice was a curdling high-pitched blare, which was only matched by his guitar, a distorted staccato burst of notes that ripped with passion and abandon. If one needed an argument for why the Blues had to be electrified, Elmore James would be a prime example. His simple songs came alive through the wonders of amplification, even if many of his "classics" sounded surprisingly similar: "Dust My Broom," "Shake Your Money Maker," "Standing at the Crossroads," et al. Along with Jimmy Reed, Elmo was the absolute king of repetition. For this reason, he was similarly enshrined among the next generation of musicians, particularly those from England like Brian Jones of the Rolling Stones and Peter Green of Fleetwood Mac. In his own time, however, his reckless lifestyle—which helped build his myth to future generations—damaged his career. Bouncing from label to label (Chess, Modern, Trumpet, Philo, etc.), his recorded legacy was spotty, to say the least. He died in 1964, right before the Blues revival really took off.

Although the Blues had become an unexpected urban phenomenon, for its purveyors it was not an easy life. The exposure, the fame, the biracial audiences all brought new problems that bluesmen from an earlier time, like Robert Johnson for instance, never had to face. For many prominent Blues musicians in the '50s, it was a world rife with contradictions. A perfect example of the down-home-goes-uptown paradox was Lightnin' Hopkins. The legendary Texas guitarist began in the '40s with a rural-sounding arpeggio-filled style. However, by the mid-'60s, he was sporting a neon electric suit and playing Rock 'n' Roll, as evidenced by the classic *Electric Show and Dance* featuring the bona fide staple, "I Want to Play with Your Poodle."

Blues had always been a ribald form, and bluesmen had always been outspoken. Not just in the case of sexually explicit material, but also with politically laced broadsides as well, like J. B. Lenoir's "Eisenhower Blues" as well as the many anti-Prohibition and pro-marijuana Blues from the 1930s, or the antisegregation material from the '40s. But as Blues became more intertwined with the Pop market, the lyrics became increasingly teenage-oriented.

The New Orleans pianist Fats Domino helped filter this transition. Influenced by Boogie Woogie pianists like Albert Ammons and raised in the same whorehouse environs, Domino was comfortable with blues ("Please Don't Leave Me") or standards (the infamous "Blueberry Hill") but tailored many of his songs to the Pop or novelty market. This made it easy for Ricky Nelson to bleach "I'm Walkin'" in the same way that Pat Boone would destroy Little Richard's "Tutti Frutti." Domino hit his stride in the mid-'50s with a kind of rolling boogaloo personified by such songs as "My Girl Josephine," "Ain't That a Shame," "Boll Weevil," and the classic "Blue Monday." A big, lovable teddy bear persona helped establish Domino as a definite crowd pleaser, and in the '50s he sold more records than any other Black artist save Nat "King" Cole.

New Orleans was coming into its own as a regional entity as far as Black music went. The precedent for the New Orleans sound was established by Dave

Bartholemew, the popular bandleader of the '40s who more or less tutored all the musicians who helped define the city's musical tradition: Fats Domino, drummer Earl Palmer, saxophonists Lee Allen and Alvin Tyler. The influence of Louis Armstrong & His Hot Seven still cast a mighty shadow over the city's musical heritage, and one thing that made New Orleans music distinct from that of other regions was the emphasis on swinging Jazz-like rhythms and instrumentation. As far as recording goes, the harbinger for the "New Orleans sound" was Cosimo Matassa's J&M Studios, where they employed a similar lack of embellishment to Sam Phillips at Sun: no overdubbing and not many rehearsals. This made for a "live" sound that jumped right out of the radio once the finished product had been waxed.

No one tested this approach more readily than Little Richard, a young singer from Macon, Georgia who perhaps best came to epitomize the instantly polarizing effect Rock 'n' Roll had on the older generation. There was the typical World War II Daddy in the living room—a sanctum he'd fought hard for—reading his evening paper, and there was sonny boy—a dumbsquat who hadn't done shit yet—in his room blasting a Little Richard platter. Obviously this was going to cause some friction, especially because, to Daddy-o, Little Richard undoubtedly sounded like total noise. He'd *never* heard anything like that before and didn't even possess the frame of reference to understand it, but his children could understand it perfectly because they'd grown up in a world without limitations. Think of how most older Americans view Rap nowadays and you'll have a pretty good idea the kind of reaction that greeted Rock 'n' Roll—only a thousand times worse because when Rock 'n' Roll arrived, there simply was no precedent. And no one was more responsible for this total assault on the senses (and sensibilities) of the American public than Little Richard.

Born Richard Penniman on December 5, 1935 in Southern Georgia, he is—along with Elvis, Chuck Berry, Jerry Lee Lewis, and Buddy Holly—one of the true mythic heroes of early Rock 'n' Roll. He was born the same year as Elvis, about a day's travel away by car. The similarities ended there: although both were products of poverty, Elvis at least had the love of a nurturing family. Richard, on the other hand, grew up the son of a bootlegger who was *not* tolerant of his son's slightly effeminate characteristics. Enraged by his son's flamboyance, he tossed Richard out at an early age. Richard joined a traveling show, which, considering the circumstances, was probably akin to saying, in the words of the Geto Boys: "Nigger you wuz onna goddamn punk tank." Probably some of the crusty old clowns and vaudeville sleazers manhandled the young boy, but you can't rape the willing, as they say, and Little Richard, almost from birth, seemed predisposed to sybaritic excess.

The turning point came when a white club owner and his wife adopted Richard. Before long, the boy began to perform at the Tick Tock Club, a Macon hot spot owned by the couple, Johnny and Ann Johnson. Richard still credits the Johnsons with being the only true "family" he ever had and claims he wrote "Miss Ann" about Ann Johnson. After reading his autobiography it's easy to see why—he apparently lusted after her big country bosoms!

In 1951, at age sixteen, Richard won a local talent contest at WGST in Atlanta and landed a contract with RCA. There he made a series of recordings that have since been underestimated in the annals of pre-Rock. Given what was going on at the time, Richard's early stuff was as axiomatic as that of Ike Turner's Kings of Rhythm. It's just that his later work would so totally blow away *everything* else that these early sides would come to seem irrelevant. However, one can already hear the roots of what would soon follow. The voice, for one thing—a combination of raw bluster and Gospel testimony—was already powerful. Like a lot of performers, Richard just needed a little nurturing.

Little Richard ended up on Specialty Records, a successful Los Angeles indie that had had a crossover hit of sorts with Guitar Slim's "The Things I Used to Do." At the time, Specialty president Art Rupe was recording a lot of his sessions at J&M, so it was perhaps inevitable that Little Richard, a regional product, would record there. But Little Richard turned out to be not just another homegrown singer plying the same Cajun/Creole mix—he was a screaming wild man who made the whole *country* uptight! Newspapers wrote about him as early as 1955, before Elvis even, trying to discredit him, but how can you discredit someone who's *purposely* crass? Unlike, say, Fats Domino, Little Richard had no shame (which, along with the fact that he put parents in a state of total fear, was another vital symbol of Rock being born).

Little Richard's first big hit was "Tutti Frutti," a song that made a whole generation of Uptights—parents, broadcasters, college professors—proclaim that Rock 'n' Roll was just a bunch of screaming nonsense. And all because of the line "wop bop a lu bop a wop bam boom!" (If they'd only heard Dorothy LaBostrie's non–Hit Parade–intended original, which was apparently so profane that even the normally uninhibited Little Richard was ashamed to sing it!) What Little Richard brought to it was, as Richard Meltzer once noted, "The spirit of wrestling." Capes, gowns…a persona! From Elvis to Jerry Lee, all the original rockers were virtual cartoon characters!

That's what's missing from today's Rock: true style. For instance, Little Richard wore a cape and makeup with an eight-inch pompadour. Elvis and other rocka-hillbillies piled their hair atop their heads like crazed roosters. Jerry Lee played the piano with his feet. Screamin' Jay Hawkins crawled out of a coffin. Bo Diddley wore glasses and played a rectangular guitar. They were a colorful bunch, outrageous and, by nature, vital, simply because no one had ever seen anything like them—except in the circus.

The kids got the message, right down to nonsensical expressions like "Be Bop a Lula" and "Wop Bop a Lu Bop." Factors such as this have subverted the language ever since (eventually leading to Rap as well as Ebonics). As non-English speaking immigrants continued to pour into the country over the next few decades, the language became even more diluted. Rock 'n' Roll served as a linguistic filter as well as a musical one, as it is, by its very essence, a microcosm of the larger "melting pot" (see Richie Valens's "La Bamba," for instance). It was also, as people were finding out, chiefly a vocal art despite the finest attempts of instrumentalists like Bill Doggett, Ace Cannon, Link Wray, etc. As opposed to the vocal music of the earlier twentieth century—show tunes and the like—the lyrics weren't so much compositional as they were slang. This outraged the denizens of Tin Pan Alley as much as it did English teachers. Time and again in the following years, Rock lyrics helped introduce slang expressions into the mainstream vocabulary.

The same year Little Richard broke with "Tutti Frutti," Chuck Berry was experiencing his initial burst of fame with "Maybellene," a classic rock song about the automobile. Once again, it was a new suburban culture that the IRT subway–taking Tin Panners couldn't understand. In the past, lyricists had stuck to ballads, which meant songs with a neat morality play enclosed, or songs about love. But with artists like Chuck Berry, lyrics for the first time took on an almost journalistic sense of describing actual events, which is why Rock became so topical in future years. Folk music, which is usually given the credit for this, was actually mired in tradition until the advent of Bob Dylan in the '60s—an artist who was primarily influenced in his formative years by Rock 'n' Roll.

To the '50s generation, nothing was more symbolic of their self-made kid-culture than the automobile. Time and again, rockers celebrated their wheels, from "Rocket 88" to "Maybellene" to the Flamingos' *insane* "Buick 59," which featured coughing, upchucking noises and auto-destruct sound effects. It was only matched in tastelessness by the Treniers' "Get Out of the Car," a song that, in another stunning premonition to Rap/Hip Hop, tells the tale of a chick who gets the boot and has to walk home from Lovers' Lane because she wouldn't put out.

At about the same time Chuck and Little Richard were making their grand entrance onto the national scene, RCA was busy trying to sway Elvis out of Sam Phillips's grasp. By now, the singing hillbilly had garnered considerable recognition. Even the *Grand Ole Opry* had relented and let the boy perform. So it was inevitable that, before long, he'd be swept up in a massive swirl of hype and media attention. The turning point came in November 1955 when RCA finally persuaded Phillips to relinquish Elvis's contract for what now seems like the paltry sum of $40,000. Considering Presley's shelf life during the ensuing years, I'm sure Sam Phillips kicked himself many times.

Elvis's new manager was a former tent-show barker and carney hawker named Colonel Tom Parker. Given that Parker's experience included giving the world a ten-foot dancing bear, it's no wonder Elvis became such a crass spectacle once he'd succumbed to the Colonel's grasp. By the time Elvis signed with RCA, the cast was set: Rock 'n' Roll had become carnival, spectacle, wrestling, show biz! And no form of music ever made itself so readily available to spiritual and aesthetic corruption so early in the game as Rock 'n' Roll.

Part of the reason was Elvis. He set the precedent or, more accurately, Colonel Tom did. Parker had already successfully managed Hank Snow, at that time RCA's best-selling Country artist, and Elvis was certainly ripe for being molded into a national superstar. Actors like Marlon Brando and James Dean had already captivated the nation with their sullen demeanors and amoral preoccupations, and Elvis was much bigger because he didn't belong to the internal pecking order of Hollywood. At least at that time, Elvis's success was still primarily a musical phenomenon that occurred outside of the framework of the music "industry." But Elvis's signing with RCA represented the commercialization of Rock, period. So there you have it— Rock 'n' Roll lasted all of about two years as an uncorrupted force. Despite the fact that some of Elvis's later stuff proved that he was an adequate "stylist," it can't be construed as Rock 'n' Roll. Elvis lost that when Colonel Tom swept him out of the cornfields and pointed him towards...Babylon. Then the kiddies had to find new hot rods to help get their rocks off.

Gene Vincent would do just fine in this capacity. Launched by Capitol a few months after RCA acquired Elvis, the Norfolk, Virginia native would have a big hit with "Be Bop a Lula," and his Blue Caps were an able-bodied Rockabilly outfit in their own right. Vincent, who'd been in the Navy and had a bum leg, went much further than the King did with sex-crazed yelping and heavy breathing. In later years, whole cults would form around Vincent, particularly in England, where he served as the role model for the original "Teds"—from John Lennon to Sid Vicious.

As Elvis was exploding all over the nation and imitators started springing up everywhere, what of Sam Phillips? Well, Sam didn't quit the Rock 'n' Roll game just because he lost the Big Cheese. Rock 'n' Roll was so new at that time that Sam didn't realize that not *all* potential rockers were going to be as big as Elvis. For all Phillips knew, Carl Perkins could be the country's next major recording star. Sam had a whole stable, and, of course, most of them did go on to some degree of fame, if not fortune.

Well, maybe not Malcolm Yelvington, but he was every bit as eponymous as Elvis (albeit less polished). One of the great characteristics of early Rock 'n' Roll was that anyone could play it. Beyond that, anyone could outdo the acknowledged masters of the game because Rock 'n' Roll in the '50s was, above all, a *moment*. And no breed of musicians better epitomized this than the pioneers of Rockabilly, that most insane of musical forms. From their hiccupping vocal reverberations to their bizarre style of dress (high collars, pink suits, classic leather James Dean garb), these mad cats were "real gone" all right. Since most of 'em were hicks raised on the *Grand Ole Opry*, it was purely their own doing that they ended up playing this music in the first place. It was only the humbleness of their surroundings that provided them with the kind of isolation necessary to come up with something so pure and untainted. Elvis might have provided the blueprint, but musically it had very little to do with Elvis, at least after he left Sun—and much more to do with Malcolm Yelvington.

The sound of Rockabilly came from echo. This was a perfect example of how technology was now playing a major role in the music business, sometimes a bigger role than the "artists." Time and again over the next few decades, we'd see major musical trends—Disco, Synth-Pop, Rap, even to some extent Heavy Metal—that owed their very existence to technological advancements. The electric guitar was a prime example—in order for something to "rock," it seemed there had to be electric guitars. Instrumentalists like Scotty Moore, Carl Perkins, and James Burlison (of the Rock 'n' Roll Trio, another pioneering Rockabilly outfit) were the catalysts, popularizing a wealth of amplification techniques that would resonate around the world. Consequently, many white, would-be Country artists were turning to Rock.

Of Sam Phillips' original Sun roster, none were really Country artists save Johnny Cash. The drum-based density of something like Carl Perkins's "Blue Suede Shoes" was (and still is) Rock 'n' Roll by definition even if, as an instrumentalist, Perkins obviously took his cue from the Western pickers on the *Opry*. Unlike the well-rehearsed Country music of Nashville, Rockabilly was punctuated by the sense of raw discovery—amplification, after all, couldn't always be controlled, and sometimes when the original rockabillies hit upon something new it was as much a surprise to them as it was to their audience. These guys may have been hicks more than hipsters, but they were blatantly degrading the whole God-fearing mentality of the South with their deliberate vulgarity. And when they finally got the chance to flee the region, they did. Carl Perkins, for instance, went to England. And when he got there, what did he find? The Beatles!

Of all the acts in Sam Phillips' stable, the most outrageous one—and the one most likely to rival Elvis's sacred stature in the Sun roster—was Jerry Lee Lewis, whose inflammatory stage act and persona could rival Little Richard's. Lewis was a white country bumpkin pianist from Louisiana whose primary influences were honky-tonk artists like Moon Mullican and Merrill Moore. These artists were on the verge of Rock anyway, and Lewis was readily adaptable to the form due to his deliberate outrageousness. His cousin Jimmy Swaggart claims that Jerry was "hossing" around as early as age nine. According to Lewis: "Oh sure…I had an act then, of course it was not quite as polished…it was just more naturally good."[7]

Many of Lewis's early performances were in the church, but as he grew older he drifted toward the houses of ill repute like so many other musicians, probably because, at that time, that's where the money was. It was in such an environment that he picked up his ribald technique, which involved kicking the piano bench over and other theatrical maneuvers. He also heard Hillbilly pianist Roy Hall performing the original "Whole Lotta Shakin' Goin' On." Hall was another interesting pre-Rock character, and he befriended both Elvis and Jerry Lee, schooling them in the early days before either became famous.

By the time Sam Phillips found Lewis, he was the most raucous performer this side of Little Richard. The advent of Rock 'n' Roll no doubt helped this flashy hillbilly perfect his brand of arrogance. Part of Rock 'n' Roll being born was the birth of a kind of "superstar" that had never existed before—flashy and outrageous. As Peter Guralnick noted: "Jerry Lee…perfected the art not only of deliberate outrageousness but of creating a distance between himself and the outrageousness which permits him to be extravagant and to make commentary on the proceedings all at the same time." [8]

Making commentary on the proceedings: This was a kind of mythic, nearly godlike understanding of the world that previous entertainers never had. That's why the masses gobbled it up with the kind of fervent devotion usually reserved for holy rollers.

The early Rock may have been deliberately crass, but it was nevertheless commercial. And when tested, even some of the true pioneers grayed, or got scared. Elvis and Little Richard chose the Army and God, respectively, as means of redemption from their formerly rocking selves. Those who didn't back down were quickly tamed in other ways: both Chuck Berry and Jerry Lee, for instance, got hung out to dry for little-girl lust. In Jerry Lee's case it was his own cousin, news that spread like buckshot through the media and brought a little of the Southern bedroom/backwoods tradition to the eyes of the nation. Although the kids couldn't have cared less, the moral watchdogs of the 1950s— of which there were many—weren't about to let Lewis off the hook, especially when he showed no remorse for his brazen act. Sam Phillips had lost another money-making teen idol as Lewis slid into a period of blacklisted notoriety before being redeemed as a successful Country artist in the next decade.

At the time, Phillips's trough of potential Elvises was still knee-deep. Texan Roy Orbison came up with "Ooby Dooby," an all-time Rockabilly classic later covered note-for-note by Creedence Clearwater Revival. But Orbison never really caught on until he'd changed his style completely, becoming the consummate crooner he was in the '60s. By that time he'd left Sun, and Sam Phillips was slowly seceding from the record industry. The Sun Studios would remain an active base of recording for years to follow, but Sun's days as an innovative label were numbered. The industry had caught up with the echo-laden sound created in Memphis. Even Sam's old rivals at Chess cut a Rockabilly record, "Suzy Q" by Dale Hawkins.

Soon a performer would come along to shake up the whole Pop/Rockabilly paradigm. In 1956 in Clovis, New Mexico, a producer named Norman Petty led a would-be superstar named Buddy Holly through a series of recordings that could loosely be termed Rockabilly. Holly's own songwriting was based more on Western and even Pop sensibilities, but his band the Crickets were a worthy precursor to the modern Rock 'n' Roll line-up. The fact that bassist Jerry Allison used a Fender electric bass as opposed to the stand-up bass, which was still the standard at the time, was a big influence on future performing units (like the Beatles, for instance). Petty's embellishments weren't always for the better, however, particularly after 1958 when Holly began being groomed as a potential "teen idol." The maudlin string arrangements on songs like "Reminiscing" and "Lonesome Tears" were dangerously close to Connie Francis. Like a lot of great Rock artists, from Elvis to Alice Cooper, Buddy Holly started to go downhill when he lost his original band. Without the Crickets, he cut "It Doesn't Matter Anymore," which proved that he was no less prone to schlock than Elvis. But this wasn't a self-conscious "sellout" of the type pulled by today's goats—Holly was a twenty-one-year-old kid in a whole new business. The fact that he died in a plane crash soon after that means no one really knows what his true musical aspirations were. One thing's for sure— his influence was immense, particularly on the next generation.

The most successful Country crossover act was the Everly Brothers, largely due to the fact that they were a Nashville product. The Everlys were in fact the first successful recording artists from that city to attempt to reach a more youthful audience, and it paid off for years to come. They began developing their unique harmonizing talents as children in a family group led by their father, Earl Everly. The Everly Brothers were heirs to the whole brother-duet tradition in Country music that included the Blue Sky Boys and Louvin Brothers. They may have worn tight pants and swung their guitars around, but their harmonies were perfectly angelic. Songs like "All I Have to Do Is Dream" and "Devoted to You" were hypnotically close to dream music, way ahead of the Memphis pack harmonically. No less a personage than John Cale has claimed that certain tonal qualities perfected by the Everlys were the inspiration for some of the primal noise pioneered by the early Velvet Underground.

In Hollywood, the proximity of the film and TV industries imposed even stricter standards on would-be "rockers." Take, for example, Ricky Nelson. Like the Everlys, he was part of a show-biz family—in his case, the popular real-life family of TV's *Ozzie and Harriet*. Using the show as a springboard, Ricky launched a career that, while certainly manufactured, was not entirely devoid of passion. Backed by an excellent band featuring the exceptional guitarist James Burton, Ricky was an above-average singer, putting honest emotion into songs like "Believe What You Say" and "Hello Mary Lou." Nelson proved his sincerity by choosing to pursue a more purist singer/songwriter path in the '60s as opposed to the crooner style epitomized by many of his '50s peers (including Elvis). And to prove he wasn't stuck in that era, he rebuked "retro" before it had really begun, in 1972, with the hit "Garden Party."

The other white Rock 'n' Roll artist from L.A. who proved to have enduring talent was Eddie Cochran. He wasn't a Hollywood brat but a legitimate Rockabilly artist with an even more sophisticated knowledge of sound than his Southern counterparts, thanks to his proximity to the legendary Gold Star studios. Far from being a pawn to some producer, Cochran produced his own sessions, wrote his own songs, and was responsible for such innovations as using a cardboard box for a drum in "Summertime Blues," once again proving that the actual sonic sphere of Rock 'n' Roll is very close to avant-garde. Cochran was saying "why not?" in the same way John Cage or Cecil Taylor were saying it in their respective fields. And "why not" is often the root of true genius.

Cochran's musical influence spread all the way across two musical generations. His innovative technique of aligning the bass and guitar to the same harmonic frequency created a "heavy" sound that would subsequently influence the Ramones: compare their "Suzy Is a Headbanger" to his "C'mon Everybody," for instance. The Sex Pistols went so far as to cover the latter, as well as "Somethin' Else," Cochran's 1959 juvenile delinquent anthem. To Rockabilly purists, Eddie Cochran became a venerated institution second only to Gene Vincent, with whom he moved to England before his—Cochran's—untimely death in 1960 in a car accident, as the curse of Buddy Holly continued.

Right about that time, Elvis was getting out of the army, but he didn't go back to Rock 'n' Roll. He—and mostly Colonel Tom—had a much shrewder agenda in mind, mainly to become a long-term commodity in the entertainment business, even if it meant staying in Hollywood for ten years making lousy movies. People didn't realize at the time, but this was to have a grim effect on the whole Rock 'n' Roll process. We were already seeing the pattern developing: Rock 'n' Roll had in a few short years already doomed itself to mass merchandising and crass commercialism. It would soon become the most popular music the world has ever known, but in its assimilation to the wills of the corporate devil, Rock would invent a system of control and dissemination that would ultimately rob it of its intrinsic value: the ability to *rock*, free of pretense or ambition.

CHAPTER 4

KILL THE BUSINESS

WE MAY BE FORGETTING SOMEONE HERE: Thomas Edison. Because if there hadn't have been any reproduction of sound, there wouldn't have been any Jazz, Rock 'n' Roll, record business, *nothing*. Despite the popularity of hoedowns and jamborees in the early half of the twentieth century, recordings have proven to be the most effective means of bringing music to the masses.

Edison's blueprint for recorded sound came from the telephone—he figured that any instrument that could carry the human voice could also retain it. In a weird predecessor to today's answering machine, Edison's first sound-recording device was designed to deliver messages from people with a phone to people without one: a talking telegraph, in other words.

When completed, the phonograph was cylindrical in shape and capable of both recording and playback. Edison tested the machine by reciting "Mary Had a Little Lamb." He had to give it a good old-fashioned crank to get it to play back, but when he did, he was amazed by what he heard. The machine was patented on February 19, 1878, and initially marketed as a novelty. The Edison Speaking Phonograph Company was formed shortly thereafter, thus beginning the recording industry.

Flash ahead ten years. A young, self-taught scientist and German immigrant named Emile Berliner discovers that a lateral-moving stylus is a more efficient means of recording than Edison's model. Berliner's first upgrade is the disc itself—from cylinders to flat sheets, which are more easily transcribable.

Eventually, Berliner discovers that a coating of zinc with an acid solution makes reproduction possible, and there you have it: the first records.

While all this was taking place, Edison's cylindrical disc player was at the height of its popularity. It wasn't until the beginning of World War I that the cylinder became entirely extinct. Through newer and finer recordings, disc manufacturers were able to produce more enduring works, such as whole operas, on disc. Columbia and other early producers of cylinders mocked this with ads that accused the makers of records of only reproducing "cut and dried subjects," which is, of course, what the whole history of recorded music was going to come down to eventually.

Shortly before cylinders went all the way into the clunker, the Victor Company emerged to court America's nascent record-buying public. The switch to platters had spurred a flurry of recording activity. The "music business" had officially begun. This created the need for composers of the popular songs that would come to dominate the Hit Parade. Anybody could now make a record, but not anyone could compose a tune that millions of people would want to hear again and again. Record companies found that in order to satisfy the appetite of the mass populace, they had to feed them shovels full of swill.

Swill is always mass-produced. It is never a frontier explosion, soul purge, or spontaneous eruption like Hillbilly, Bluegrass, Country & Western, Jazz, Folk music, Blues, Soul, Gospel, Rhythm & Blues, or Rock 'n' Roll. These categories are so named because they describe a certain style of music. But all Pop does is go pop. The only thing that qualifies music as "pop" is the fact that it's popular.

America's foremost music composing factories were all located in the same lower midtown neighborhood of New York, named Tin Pan Alley. Through years of bar mitzvahs, piano lessons, and synagogue singalongs, these boys had learned a nice way with a tune. Put into a factory setting, where they would literally bang away until they came out with a song, men like George Gershwin and Irving Berlin were soon to become the best-known composers in the world. The musical legacy of the first half of the century was dominated by the hacksmiths who rolled out of Tin Pan Alley: Berlin, Gershwin, Cole Porter, Johnny Mercer, Rodgers and Hart, Rodgers and Hammerstein, Hoagy Carmichael, and others. From their repertoires came the Book of American Standards—so much so that forty years later, John Coltrane would still be playing them, and Bob Dylan was heard to remark: "Eeeeh, none of us claimed to be as good as Johnny Mercer."

Pre-1910, the only way a composer could profit from his/her compositions was through the sale of sheet music. However, once recording came about, there arose whole new questions about rights of ownership, such as: should a composer be compensated for every rendition of his/her work? This brought up the issue of royalties. But the issue didn't really accelerate until the advent of radio, which meant that anybody could just pluck any song off the air and steal it. That is, if it wasn't protected.

This caused the formation of the ASCAP, or American Society of Composers, Authors, and Publishers. However, "American Society" once again didn't include Blacks or rural whites. ASCAP was the publishing domain of Tin Pan Alley, and for years they had a contractual monopoly over what broadcasters were allowed to play on the air. But ASCAP never properly came to terms with radio, which is why in 1940 the National Association of Broadcasters felt the need to establish BMI—Broadcast Music, Inc. The name says it all: "broadcast music." Whereas ASCAP had been the domain of song-and-dance men who'd more or less received their musical training in vaudeville, BMI basically belonged to anyone who could be considered a "recording artist"—which meant all they had to do was put out a record. This opened up the door to a wealth of musical resources, including ones ASCAP would've never bothered licensing—like Blues and Country & Western. The difference between ASCAP and BMI was that ASCAP was copyrighting the *song*, whereas BMI was copyrighting the *performance* itself. This was advantageous to BMI because, by that time, the "hit parade" was almost totally reliant on radio.

In the years preceding the ASCAP/BMI controversy, some important inroads had already been made in American popular music. In 1938, the Vocalion recording of Big Joe Turner and Pete Johnson doing "Roll 'em Pete" became the biggest-selling Blues record since Mamie Smith's "Crazy Blues" in 1920. This reawakened the industry to the expanding growth of the Black record market. Within a few years, thousands of independent labels had opened up to accommodate such Black-oriented fields as Bebop, Blues, and Gospel. Many times, the labels recorded white Hillbilly artists as well (King Records in Cincinnati, for instance).

"Roll 'em Pete" showcased a whole new idiom in American popular music—the "blues shouter." Coming from Kansas City, at one time America's lewdest locale, Turner was a veteran of the red light districts that also produced the Count Basie Orchestra, whose version of Swing was a great deal more soulful than that of their Northern counterparts. Along with fellow shouter Jimmy Rushing, Turner helped introduce a more robust style of vocalizing to the popular idiom that contrasted with the polished slickness of Cab Calloway. A good example of Turner's impact was the success of Frankie Lane, the first white singer to employ the "shouting" technique as opposed to the crooning style of Perry Como and Frank Sinatra.

Another important development was the advent of the boogie woogie piano style, as epitomized by barrelhouse pianists like Albert Ammons, Meade Lux Lewis, Jimmy Yancey, Clarence "Pinetop" Smith, and Cow Cow Davenport. Ammons, Lewis, and Pete Johnson formed the Boogie Woogie Trio and played a successful series of concerts at Carnegie Hall in 1938 and '39 that did much to alert the public to the arrival of this new idiom. The result was a series of rip-offs culminating in Tommy Dorsey's "Boogie Woogie." The Will Bradley Orchestra made a whole series of popular recordings with Boogie Woogie themes.

If the "Spirituals to Swing" concerts in 1938 featuring Ammons, Lewis, Johnson, and Count Basie can be seen as the "official" start of the Boogie Woogie craze, it can also be seen as a year when many significant changes occurred in the relationship between Black and white musicians. That year, the Famous Door, a nightclub in New York, opened its doors to Black patrons for a series of engagements by Count Basie. Far from an altruistic act, it's more likely the club owners sensed it was commercial suicide to continue their whites-only policy, considering that 90 percent of Basie's audience was Black. That same year, the Black Blues singer Billie Holiday joined the Artie Shaw Band. At around the same time, the Benny Goodman Orchestra hired a series of Black musicians, including vibraphonist Lionel Hampton, pianist Teddy Wilson, and electric guitarist Charlie Christian.

Under FDR, Blacks were allowed union membership for the first time. This went for musicians as well. This created a whole new element of Black nightlife, where Black musicians found themselves infinitely employable. In cities like Detroit and Chicago, where America's increasing industrialization had resulted in better opportunities for Blacks, some of them were able to open their own nightclubs where they could employ Black musicians almost exclusively. Although it appeared on the surface that Blacks were finally experiencing what it was like to be part of American society, the country was still segregated, and Blacks still faced discrimination wherever they went. But in the music industry, Blacks were about to exert a newfound importance on the buying trends of the public.

Although there were as many Black Big Bands as white ones, the popular Swing bands who dominated the Hit Parade in the '30s and '40s were chiefly white. But overly slick pros didn't appeal to a significant number of Blacks that now had buying power of their own. To cater to their tastes, a more emotionally compelling style of music emerged. Perhaps the pinnacle in this genre was "Flying High" by Lionel Hampton, the vibraharpist who'd played with Benny Goodman. Based on a repetitive riff, not unlike later Rock riffs, with a honking saxophone solo by the Texas-bred tenor Illinois Jacquet, "Flying High" introduced a new style called "jump Blues."

Louis Jordan & His Tympani Five, who recorded for Decca in the '40s, utilized typical Swing rhythms but in a more downscaled format (hence "Tympani Five"). Jordan, who'd played and sung in the Big Band of Chick Webb, told Arnold Shaw: "I didn't think I could handle a big band. But with my little band, I did everything they did." [1]

There were many factors that caused the Big Bands to shrink in the 1940s (chiefly the draft). By the time Be Bop and Rhythm & Blues had taken hold, it was a conscious decision on the part of the musicians to scale down the proceedings and concentrate on a smaller unit. Whereas the music of the Swing bands had been chiefly designed for dancing, the new music was more lyrical and in many ways cerebral. In the case of a performer like Louis Jordan, he was able to incorporate both Black and white resources in order to achieve this metamorphosis. This ensured his popularity with white audiences as well as Black. As a result, Jordan & his Tympani Five racked up a string of hits that crossed over during the '40s, many of them with a "novelty" base: "School Days," "Caledonia," "Ain't Nobody Here but Us Chickens," "Five Guys Named Moe." But these weren't mere novelty sides, because the musicianship was tight and because Jordan was a brilliant arranger who incorporated everything from typical jump Blues to Caribbean rhythms in songs like "Run Joe" (a big influence on Chuck Berry). Jordan added a lot of comic voices and other laugh-getters to ensure his popularity with mixed audiences. This trait would be picked up readily by nascent Rock 'n' Rollers (like Bo Diddley for instance). In many ways, the Tympani Five were the blueprint for the R&B jump bands that would in turn spawn the Rock revolution. Bill Haley & the Comets, a white act who also recorded for Decca, copied Jordan's whole sound and, in 1945, the popular white bandleader Woody Herman covered Jordan's "Caledonia." And Jordan was years ahead of his time in terms of promotion, creating what amounted to the first "videos," in the form of cinematic shorts featuring the band performing that could be shown in movie theaters between features.

Another thing Louis Jordan accomplished was to bring Black popular slang into the mainstream. Whereas, for years, white bandleaders had been trying to parrot Black hipster jive and had been making fools of themselves, Jordan's use of the vernacular was "authentic." Jordan's records were the first time many whites encountered the nuances of hip urban blackspeak. In this sense, the Tympani Five were not only a premonition of Rock, but Rap as well.

In the years following Jordan's ascendance, Blacks began to see the first signs of mass acceptance in the recording field. Part of this was the war ending: the recording industry was booming, as were all industries. There was no short-age of shellac now. Record companies had a little more freedom to experiment with new talent. There was a proliferation of small, independent labels, many catering to Black recording artists. The postwar economy had convinced many people that starting a small, independent record label was a worthy entrepre-neurial venture.

Even Capitol, by no means a Black label, made their first million with a Black artist: Nat "King" Cole. Cole's early recordings were made with a trio consisting of bass/guitar/piano before he branched off to make a series of recordings in the crooner style. One of these, "Mona Lisa," crossed over into the Pop charts and eventually sold half a million copies. There were other Black ersatz crooners, like the "Singing Private," Cecil Gant—so named because at the time he made his first record, "I Wonder," he was still enlisted in the U.S. Army. The song never crossed over on a Nat "King" Cole scale, but at one point the label that issued it, Gilt Edge, reported that they were selling 100,000 records per month. Surely that kind of success inspired the rush of small, independent labels that were popping up all over the West Coast in the late 1940s.

Further developments were occurring in the field of commercial Black music. Not only were the hits of the Ink Spots and Nat "King" Cole adorned with the kind of lush arrangements usually afforded white crooners like Como or Sinatra, but in L.A., the revolutionary electric blues guitarist, T-Bone Walker, cut his first sides for Capitol. "Mean Old World" and "I Got a Break Baby" were Rock prototypes, considering that they utilized the classic Rock lineup about ten years before the fact: bass, guitar, piano, drums, and no horns. Walker would go on to greater fame in the '50s, when electrified Blues really caught on.

The proliferation of independent labels caused whole new strains of Black music to reach a mass audience. With no A&R budgets to speak of, most of the indies relied on local talent or on demos people sent them in the mail. For this reason, most of the early independents showcased an eclectic mix of talent. The whole range of Black music was changing so rapidly that terms like "boogie woogie" or "jump Blues" suddenly became antiquated because they weren't inclusive enough. *Billboard*, which until that time had been dumping all "race" records into a catch-all chart called the "Harlem Hit Parade," came up with the perfect appellation for the wide variety of new sounds emerging: "Rhythm & Blues." On June 25, 1945, they instituted the new category. Before they ever had any records place in the actual "hit parade," labels like Exclusive, Savoy, National, Apollo, Jubilee, DeLuxe, and King had number-one R&B hits. These were the records being played in Black bars and nightclubs, and at dances and hops in Black high schools.

With the advent of BMI—which catered to the independent labels—the airwaves opened up to foreign sounds. In order to fill air time, the notion of playing records on the air, with royalties paid to musicians and songwriters licensed to BMI, came into being. In order to accommodate this process, a whole new industry emerged—mainly that of the radio station "jock," who spun records and shilled for sponsors in between. Eventually the "DJs," as they were almost instantaneously branded, became personalities in their own right. This was all adding up to the kind of environment in which Rock could flourish.

As the '50s dawned, there was a new generation forming, one who'd never known a nonnuclear, nonelectric world. Teenagers became downright possessive about their music, but in order for that to happen the older, wiser, somewhat more jaded DJs had to come along to introduce the transistorized generation to the almighty Beat. Hand it to the DJs for realizing one thing (and thus revealing it to the rest of the world): the hillbilly Boogie Woogie, the sanctified Gospel shout, and the lowdown grit of R&B weren't that far apart. And it was all these factors that would eventually come together under the banner of Rock 'n' Roll. So in a sense, it was actually the DJs that invented Rock 'n' Roll, at least as a phenomenon (as a music, the ingredients were already there as early as '46–'47).

In Los Angeles, where a lot of the impetus for postwar Rhythm & Blues occurred, it was no surprise that as early as 1948, a white DJ named Hunter Hancock was showcasing R&B on his show. At first he was playing Jazz on KFVD in L.A., until someone told him that if he really wanted to reach the Negro audience, Jazz wasn't cutting it anymore. He soon switched to R&B, which at that time meant Cecil Gant, Nat "King" Cole, Louis Jordan. For the next couple of years, L.A. was the hotbed for R&B development. The wartime economy had brought more than 2 million people to California, many of them Blacks. This led to the expansion of the Watts section of Los Angeles, one of the largest concentrations of Blacks in the country. It was in this environment that a lot of the independent labels formed. One of them, Specialty, was literally founded in a shoebox: owner Art Rupe paid some guy two bucks a month to keep a shoebox on his desk to file all of Specialty's correspondence, phone messages, and unpaid bills. The label eventually became one of the most important of the early Rock 'n' Roll merchants, featuring the recordings of Little Richard, among others.

However good their intentions, independent record label owners, whether Black or white, met with resistance from the industry at large. There was no way the major labels were going to let these upstarts encroach upon what was basically a monopoly. So they made it difficult for the indie owners to gain access to pressing plants, limiting the quantity they could press and making them press the records in the middle of the night. However, when the sales of R&B records began to accelerate, the pressing plants—many of them co-opted in some way by the major labels—had no choice but to relent, if only for commercial purposes.

Meanwhile, DJs across the country were getting hip to the R&B buzz. In the South, white disc jockeys like John R. Richbourg, Gene Nobles, Hoss Allen, and Zena Sears were making believers out of people. Because these jocks played mostly Black music, their programs were relegated to the late-night hours. As far as parents were concerned, the DJs were messengers of a bad vibe.

The DJs, on the other hand, understood this kind of notoriety perfectly, and the best ones played it up.

No one applied this principle more effectively than Alan Freed, whose notoriety served as a gateway into Rock 'n' Roll. Born in Johnstown, Pennsylvania in 1921, son of a traveling salesman, Freed moved to Ohio shortly after he was born. In high school, he played trombone, eventually leading his own combo called the Sultans of Swing. When the Big Bands hit, he became a big fan of Benny Goodman, among others. Later on, when Freed was presenting his spectacular concerts at places like the Brooklyn Paramount, he claimed he sympathized with the kids who waited in line for hours to get tickets because he'd done the same thing with Goodman. That was Freed's whole aesthetic in a nutshell: he sympathized with the kids.

Freed's whole approach to broadcasting was indeed proselytizing. After a stint as a classical DJ at WKST in New Castle, Pennsylvania, Freed settled in Akron, where he landed a job as the host of a local TV show. Unfortunately, Freed wasn't the most photogenic individual, and he didn't have TV appeal. However, he'd soon find his real niche in the world of radio.

Like most disc jockeys, Freed bounced around the dial a lot. By June 1951 he was working for WJW in Cleveland. This stint proved to be the turning point in Freed's career—and, curiously enough, in the history of Western popular music. During that time, a business called the Record Rendezvous Shop, run by someone named Leo Mintz, became one of Freed's sponsors. One day Mintz told Freed that he'd recently had a lot of requests from white kids for Black R&B records like Lloyd Price's "Lawdy Miss Clawdy." This came as no surprise to Freed, as he'd been following such developments through industry tip sheets at the time and was about to go to an all-R&B format.

Calling his late-night show the *Moondog House Party*, Freed confined his playlist almost entirely to Rhythm & Blues and punctuated his presentation with hipster jive. He opened his show every night with a record on King called "Blues for a Moondog" by Todd Rhodes, a Black record featuring the kind of honking saxophone solo that had by now become the mainstay of R&B. Because his vocal chords had been damaged due to an earlier operation in which he'd had some polyps cauterized, Freed's voice was low and gravely. For this reason, a lot of people assumed he was Black, and he made no attempt to rectify this misconception.

Freed became hugely popular in Cleveland during the early '50s. This enabled him to organize a series of concerts that were profitable not only to him but to WJW as well. One particular package show, held at the Cleveland Arena on March 21, 1952, helped bring national attention to the rising phenomenon of Black Rhythm & Blues. Called "the Moondog Coronation Ball," it pulled an estimated 25,000 to the arena to see such acts as Billy Ward & His Dominoes, the Orioles, the Moonglows, Charles Brown, and others. The write-ups in the local paper were superb, and editorials focused on the growing potential of radio as an effective advertising method. In other words, the whole industry was a winner from Freed's efforts.

Freed was one of the few DJs who could break the color barrier—that is, Blacks liked him too. This was partly due to the fact that he played—and promoted—mostly Black music. But there were also a number of Black DJs spinning R&B on their respective shows. Oftentimes, though, their delivery was even more frenzied than Freed's, taking on the pitch of a gospel preacher (which isn't surprising, considering that so much Black music came straight out of the church). In Philadelphia there was Jocko Henderson, whose show on WDAS, with its strong signal, could be heard all the way up and down the East Coast. In some markets where the population was overwhelmingly Black, many stations found that it was in their best interest to switch over to R&B. Stations that would've never touched Negro music a few years earlier were now faithfully following the lead of men like Freed.

This set the whole record industry into a tailspin, because radio was quickly becoming the most effective medium for promoting a record. Played extensively in one geographical location, a song could become a regional hit. However, if the record "broke out" and got picked up by, say, twenty-five more stations, the label might have a national hit. So the whole relationship between the disc jockeys and record companies got a lot friendlier, so to speak. This spawned the first flowerings of payola, or the practice of steady palm-greasing, which would almost bring Rock 'n' Roll to its knees in the late '50s. In a McCarthyesque campaign that befit its era, a Senate subcommittee would later purge the industry of all such illegal practices, but not before a lot of loose cash had already changed hands. In the interim—perhaps as a result of all the palm-greasing—Rock 'n' Roll would explode as a popular phenomenon.

It was easy to see why it was in the record companies' best interests to keep the DJs happy. For a couple grand, or even a couple hundred, most DJs could be bribed to play *any* record. If this was a hastily made recording by some local performer on an indie label—which most of the early Rock 'n' Roll records were—the potential profits were immense. On the local level, DJs could be bought cheap—maybe a wad of bills, or some marijuana or a whore. These expenditures got worked right into the budget of small labels as a necessary evil inherent in the big, bad record business—which was becoming bigger and badder by the day. Because radio was chiefly responsible for making Rock 'n' Roll a popular phenomenon, the coercion to make such expenditures was immense. Alan Freed bought four houses before anyone caught up with him. But by the time they did, he had bigger problems.

Because Freed was the most famous of the Rock 'n' Roll DJs, when the Payola Scandal happened in 1959, he was one of the hardest hit. But his problems actually began as far back as 1954, when he first came to prominence. For one thing, a famous New York street musician named Moondog successfully sued Freed for infringing on his right to the name. Then Freed was in a life-threatening auto accident that left his internal organs permanently damaged, including his liver. For a heavy drinker like Freed, this meant, basically, that his days were numbered. But the final blow for Freed came when the IRS essentially froze his assets, and he was subsequently blacklisted by the radio industry. By 1960, no radio station would touch him.

Long before then, payola had become rampant: whenever a small label lacking in resources felt they had to help a record "break out," they'd send a representative to any given town to grease the palms of local DJs. These were the days before there was such a thing as program lists—the time slot occupied by a DJ was essentially his or her own. It was not unusual to hear the same song two times, or over and over again if the DJ liked it enough—or had a vested interest in the record. But as Rock 'n' Roll would continue to increase in popularity, it would become more of a business. This would put an end to these corrupt and haphazard practices. In the meantime, certain cities became key "breakout" areas in the early days of Rock 'n' Roll: Philadelphia, for one; or Cincinnati, where it was reported by *Variety* that without payola a record stood little chance of getting airplay.

Mob influence was another prevalent factor in the early days of Rock 'n' Roll. Take, for instance, the case of Morris Levy, founder of Roulette

Records, original owner of Birdland, and a pivotal figure in the birth of Rock 'n' Roll. Like a lot of the early moguls, Levy was literally born on the streets of New York. His father died when he was two, and his mother, saddled with many ailments, raised him and his brother Irving alone. Irving ended up joining the Navy, but Morris found himself expelled from school and in reform school for assaulting a seventy-five-year-old woman—namely his teacher, over whose head he poured a quart of black ink. From that point on, he turned his back on education. At age fourteen, he became a hat check boy at the Greenwich Village Inn. By doing so, he caught the favor of Tommy Eboli, future head of the Genovese crime family. Eboli took the boy under his wing. End result was, when it came time to purchase Birdland, for some reason the juvenile delinquent and first-time business owner Morris Levy had no trouble securing the loan.

When Rock 'n' Roll hit, Levy wanted a piece of the action. In 1956 he started Roulette Records. The label's first hit was "Party Doll" by a Texas rockabilly performer named Buddy Knox. It was a big hit, but Levy's success as a label owner can more or less be attributed to one thing: he was the first to realize the enormous assets to be gained from publishing. He understood that a hit record was infinitely redeemable—that is, if he owned the copyright. So early on, he literally pilfered copyrights from composers, in essence selling them their own contracts in exchange for exclusive rights to their own songs. To the struggling Black R&B artists from the ghetto who'd never even imagined fame, it seemed like a good deal. Once Levy had gained the publishing rights to their songs, he would in turn resell them again and again. Not surprisingly, Roulette became a leader in the repackaged oldies field.

The way Levy accomplished this was to devour other record labels through shady business dealings. One of his primary victims was George Goldner, who set the precedent for the New York indies with his Rama and Gee labels, but who'd sold the back catalogs of both labels to Roulette by the end of the '50s. Goldner got lucky in 1956 when he discovered Frankie Lyman & the Teenagers, a Black New York vocal group who, despite their instant popularity, worked cheap. When Goldner met Frankie Lyman he was singing "I'm Not a Juvenile Delinquent"; by the late '60s he'd died a penniless junkie in a New York ghetto. But Goldner and Levy were essential to the birth of Rock 'n' Roll because, like Alan Freed, they saw the dollar signs.

After Freed had conquered the Midwestern radio market, it was inevitable that he would end up in New York, at WINS. When he did, it was in collusion with Morris Levy. Because Levy had such enormous influence in the New York nightclub scene due to his success with Birdland as well as his mob connections, Freed asked Levy to become his manager. Now Levy also had an interest in the most successful radio personality in America. But Freed was no dummy either— part of the arrangement was that Freed would own twenty-five percent of Roulette Records. Although history has tended to paint Alan Freed as an inno- cent victim who was terrorized by the sharks of New York, Freed was not above reproach himself when it came to business dealings. By the late '50s, he owned a lavish estate in Connecticut as well as an apartment on Fifty-Eighth Street in New York, and additional property in Palm Springs, California and Miami, Florida. He also owned his share of numerous record labels and had even appro- priated a songwriting credit or two, most notably Chuck Berry's "Maybellene" (which he in turn received a royalty for every time he played it on his show).

As Rock 'n' Roll gained momentum—fueled by such factors as the arrival of Presley—it had plenty of detractors, not only within the mainstream music industry but also morally offended legislators, city councilors, radio program- mers, politicians, and civic-minded do-gooders of every stripe. Everyone's seen the famous '50s footage in which the bullnecked Southerner breaks the record and proclaims: "Waaah, Rock 'n' Roll has got to go!" That kind of reaction probably would've greeted any institution that resulted in the intermingling of Blacks and whites, but Rock 'n' Roll was particularly vulnerable because of the shaky business practices that governed it.

At the center of the controversy once again was Alan Freed. In Connecticut, the police, fearing riots, tried to revoke a theater in Hartford's license after Freed hosted a three-day rockfest there. Freed went on the coun- terattack: having no small vested interest in the Rock 'n' Roll business, he was rather outspoken in his support for the burgeoning industry. This did not endear him to anti-Rock forces in the government or elsewhere. But there were a few young moguls who were able to profit from the rising Rock trend and still endear themselves to the establishment. One of them was Dick Clark, who rose to prominence as the popular host of TV's *American Bandstand*.

Clark was born in Mount Vernon, New York and, like Alan Freed, had begun his career in local radio, doing station breaks and occasional live commercials for a small station in Syracuse before moving to Philadelphia in 1952. The station Clark worked for, WFIL, also had a television affiliate who hosted a local music program called "Bandstand." The original host, Bob Horn, was fired for public drunkenness, and Clark was his replacement. The station's management liked Clark's all-American preppy looks and personable demeanor.

However, when one looks at either Freed's or Clark's outside business interests, they don't look that different. Like Freed, Clark was a small-time DJ who stumbled onto national fame. Clark's break came when *American Bandstand*—as the show was now called—got picked up by ABC. Clark would stand there and shill hair tonic between lip-synched performances by current pop sensations. It was a formula that proved popular with the ever-expanding teen market: in its first year alone, *American Bandstand* reached an estimated 20 million teenagers per day. Clark's power in the industry grew even more when it was discovered that exposure on *Bandstand* more or less guaranteed a record's success in the national charts. Not surprisingly, a lot of record execs began trying to strike the kind of deals with Clark that they had with Freed a few years earlier. But Clark proved to be a lot shrewder and was better at covering his tracks. As a result, when the payola scandal hit, Clark came out unscathed.

That didn't mean that Clark wasn't as deep into the soup as Freed was: he owned three music publishing companies, was a partner in number of record labels, and managed Duane Eddy, a popular instrumental performer of the late '50s (who, not coincidentally, appeared frequently on *American Bandstand*). The difference was, when the Payola Hearings struck, Clark divested himself of all questionable holdings and took a loss just to clear his name, knowing full well he could easily recoup the profits from *Bandstand* alone.

Among the record labels co-owned by Clark were three based in Philadelphia: Cameo, Parkway, and Swan. These labels helped spawn the teen idols, prefabricated singing sensations whose sole purpose was to bleach the Black influence out of Rock 'n' Roll: Fabian, Frankie Avalon, Bobby Rydell, Paul Anka, Annette Funicello, Connie Francis, Freddy Cannon, Bobby Curtola, Johnny Crawford, Shelly Fabares, etc. Not ironically, *American Bandstand* was where most of these acts got their first national exposure. Clark was more than happy to play the host for these adenoidal crooners and give them a mainline right into the mainstream because he adhered to a strictly capitalist philosophy. As he would later tell Lester Bangs, "One must learn to screw the system from within." [2]

The kind of homogeny personified by *American Bandstand* soon spread to radio. The concept of top forty helped dilute the radio stations further, from bastions of ribaldry to a structured format that relied solely on the music industry to feed it new product. Top forty created a structure whereby the same forty records were played over and over again all day, making airtime much more valuable—and the national record charts like *Billboard* much more important. Radio became a lot less regionalized. Now, it was the same records being played in every town. Top forty also took a lot of influence away from the DJs: whereas spontaneity had been their original province, now they found themselves having to curtail their own unique personalities for the sake of generic complacency.

Thanks to all this concentration on teenybopper tastes, the purveyors of Rock 'n' Roll in the '50s, perhaps due to forces beyond their control, had screwed themselves out of a vital new market—mainly that of the 33-RPM Long Playing Record Album. Although the twelve-inch long player had made its debut right around the time that Rock 'n' Roll was first invading the industry, very few Rock 'n' Roll artists made the transition to the full-length format. Other than Elvis, almost no Rock 'n' Roll performers charted albums in the '50s. This was partially due to the attitude of the record labels: they knew albums cost more to press, and most of them honestly didn't feel, at that time, that Rock 'n' Roll was worth making the investment in. As opposed to "long-term talent," most labels at that time preferred to score a big hit with a no-name group, then dump them before paying them their royalties and repeat the formula with another faceless group. Labels like Roulette and Gee lived by such practices. Some labels like Atlantic, King, Imperial, and Chess exercised a little more foresight as far as nurturing long-term talent went, but in the case of most of the indies it was: "What have you done for me lately?"

The anti-Rock forces in the '50s asserted that the music was just a passing fad, mindless garbage for an immature audience (a charge Alan Freed would always deny). Nobody knew what kind of mileage to expect out of the form, and if you'd told the founders of Rock that their work would still be getting reissued—as well as *analyzed*—fifty years later they would have laughed at you. It was a whole different world then—everything was new and unchallenged. It wasn't like nowadays, when someone takes something stillborn and sells it off right away. Things were allowed to develop a bit more organically.

The early album market was dominated by schmaltzmeisters like Lawrence Welk, Percy Faith, Jackie Gleason, Morton Gould, Ray Conniff, Mantovani, and Nelson Riddle. Occasionally a more eccentric bandleader would come along, like Juan Esquivel or Les Baxter or Martin Denny, who'd do something slightly off-the-wall in the same light Jazz vein. But for the most part it was this type of genteel cocktail music that dominated most Americans' record collections between the years 1956–1964, at which time the Beatles came along and blew the album market wide open.

As for the cocktail craze, it's easy to see where America's collective heads were by just looking at the album covers. Typical of the kind of repressed sexuality that dominated the age, much of the artwork showed buxom babes in suggestive poses with come-hither looks and accompanied by come-on titles: *Music for Lovers, I'm in the Mood, Romantic Moods, Music to Put Her in the Mood*, or any variation thereof. Another reason for the facelessness of the album market at the time was that the medium itself had become the message. With the invention of stereophonic sound, the whole notion of hi-fi came into being, and it wasn't so important what you *played* on your new stereo as much as the fact that you *owned* one, to go along with your TV, lawnmower, and other consumer items. The new two-speaker technology literally dwarfed the little phonographs that had previously been the norm, and the new albums were specifically tailored to audiophiles' expectations. Here was a format that could support the indulgence of serious musical appreciation, so the Classical fan could sit down in his easy chair and listen to an entire symphony without having to get up and change the record. The average LP could support up to twenty minutes of music per side, and not surprisingly a lot of the early "Living Stereo" albums manufactured by RCA were Classical releases. It was evident that the record industry was aiming the new album market at a more "mature" audience (hence the suggestive nature of the album covers). The implication was that Rock 'n' Roll was not a serious form of music and it didn't warrant the new long-play format.

Part of Rock's self-imposed anonymity in the era between Elvis and the Beatles was brought about by the rise of instrumental Rock. As all Rock lyrics were presumed to be garbage anyway, groups like the Ventures and Johnny & the Hurricanes figured, why not eschew vocals altogether and concentrate on the musicianship? In other cases, the choice to eschew the vocals was probably by accident—a lot of the early instrumental hits like Bill Doggett's "Honky Tonk" and Link Wray's "Rumble" were nothing but jams anyway, probably last-minute takes never aimed at a radio audience. Then there were performers like drummer Sandy Nelson, who milked a singular musical idea—in his case the incessant drum pattern of "Teen Beat," his 1959 hit—into a whole career. Along with drums and twangy guitar, the other big instrumental trend during that era was the organ craze. The electric organ had been invented in the '50s, and there was a rash of artists who parlayed the instrument's popularity into fairly fruitful careers: Dave "Baby" Cortez, Jesse Crawford, Jimmy Smith, Jack McDuff, Shirley Scott, Big John Patton, and others. Also notable were the organ experiments of Ray Charles and James Brown, who dabbled with the instrument in their spare time.

Aside from the diluting process that was occurring in the form of the Teen Idols and the constriction of Top Forty radio, other problems were about to beset the nascent musical form of Rock 'n' Roll. One of the biggest stories in the press in 1959 was the rigging of a television quiz show called *The $64,000 Question*. The news media, more or less responsible for making celebrities out of DJs like Alan Freed and Dick Clark, found an inevitable link between the game show scandal and the world of radio. In its sixtieth anniversary edition, *Billboard* ran an article about the expanding influence of DJs like Freed. In another article, *Billboard* revealed that many of the famous disc jockeys had holdings in record store chains, songwriting, publishing, jukebox routes, and managerial duties. They also received money for public appearances. In short, stardom as a radio jock was a quick route to more lucrative ventures. It might be safe to say that, at the time, the most successful AM disc jockeys were probably a lot better off than the artists whose records they played on their shows.

At the same time *Billboard* divulged this information, ASCAP was launching an investigation of its own. Since Rock 'n' Roll had come along, the corporation had been losing its stronghold on the publishing industry. This was because most Rock and R&B songs were published by BMI, ASCAP's competitor. ASCAP's backlog of records and sheet music couldn't match the exposure BMI publishers were getting from all the radio play.

What really blew the lid off the radio industry was a notorious disc jockey convention in Miami in May 1959. All through the '50s, the record business had been currying the favor of DJs with cash or other forms of material persuasion. Record promo men initially took DJs out to lunch or dinner, or gave them a bottle of whiskey, in an attempt to get them to play certain records. But as competition increased, the stakes grew higher. By the late '50s, it was not unusual for a record company to buy a certain target disc jockey a new car or, on some occasions, a new house. There were other methods that could be employed as well. In the *Billboard* article, one record agent spoke of taking several "New York models" on the road with him to "promote a tune." One Texas record honcho was known to toss $100 bills into a DJ's wastepaper basket. Another producer revealed that his monthly payola budget alone came to $2,000.

The smarter, more ambitious broadcasters like Dick Clark and Alan Freed set up their own companies so they could legitimately tap into the market. Although this was de facto legal, there were still a lot of loopholes that needed explaining. In the world of promotion, it was impossible to keep track of all the expenditures because "promotion" was such a vague term. Nowhere was this more apparent than at the Miami DJs Convention. Far from trying to keep their extravagant practices a secret, the DJs seemed to be flaunting it. The week they arrived, the mayor had declared it "Disc Jockey Week," claiming their presence would help boost the local economy. If the number of hookers hanging around the Miami airport were any indication, he was right.

The record companies intended to make good use of all the sitting ducks they had assembled in one place. It was a wise investment for the record companies, who hoped to make 1959 their greatest year ever, with sales exceeding the previous year's $450 million. It was estimated that $90 million of that was based solely on the sale of 45s, at that time still the primary medium for Rock 'n' Roll (which, at the time, still only represented 20 percent of the overall market). Although their influence had been somewhat eroded due to newly formulated programming restrictions, DJs were still the primary link between the record companies and their target audience. And for that audience, companies were willing to pay dearly.

At the Miami convention, they did just that. Cadillac convertibles were waiting for the DJs the moment they stepped off their planes, and things got progressively better for them after that. Several DJs were invited to a side excursion to Cuba where the new dictator, Fidel Castro, had yet to shut down the nightclubs and gaming facilities. The more low-rent DJs were hoarded onto a private yacht carrying a special cargo of booze and an all-female crew.

Fifteen miles from the mainland, everyone stripped naked. The more elite DJs were flown to Cuba in a plane chartered by a record company and taken to the most exclusive sex clubs in Havana. Meanwhile, back at the convention, the booze literally flowed like water: one record label had outfitted a suite with faucets whose spigots poured Martinis and Manhattans. Needless to say, this room was much frequented by the DJs.

Unfortunately for them, all this conspicuous consumption was not going to go unnoticed for long in an America still spooked by the memory of the McCarthy Hearings, entrenched in the Cold War, getting uptight about civil rights, and just coming off a major scandal concerning game show fraud. The headline in the *Miami Herald* on the Sunday following the convention told the story: "Booze, Broads and Bribes." To the DJs who attended the convention, it signaled the end of their glory days. From that point on they would become mere pawns in the industry as opposed to the kind of major power brokers they had become in the '50s.

A *Miami News* article disparagingly referred to the DJs as "little tin gods" and reported that an unnamed PR man had claimed he'd doled out $1 million per year in payola to radio jocks. Concurrent articles in *Time* and *Newsweek* mocked the event, the former renaming the convention "The Big Payola" and the latter describing it as "the flipside of success." Wrote *Time*: "One of the most pampered trades in the U.S.—the disc jockeys—had come to town and Big Daddy, in the shape of U.S. record companies, were there to take care of them."

In the next few weeks, further disclosures of misconduct haunted the disc jockeys. Amidst the testimonial, one name seemed to come up the most: Alan Freed. Although at the Miami Convention he was partying as loosely as ever, at one point even throwing his wife into a swimming pool, Freed was worried. During the convention, Freed had indignantly told members of the press that payola in the radio business was no different than what was known as "lobbying" in Washington. Freed was right: in most businesses, similar gratuities were looked upon as "perks." But the DJs were especially vulnerable because of what they represented to the public. One of the big charges against them was that they inspired race mixing. An easy way to nail them was to unearth their financial inequities and expose the corrupt practices of their trade.

During 1959, the Federal Trade Commission filed complaints against a number of record labels on charges of unfair competition. In New York, the district attorney called a grand jury to investigate whether bribery charges should be brought against the DJs and record execs. But what really brought the house down was the investigation into payola brought about by the U.S. House Subcommittee on Legislative Oversight, led by Representative Oren Harris of Arkansas, specifically citing the Miami Convention as evidence.

Payola had long been looked upon as a shaky practice, but there was nothing illegal about it because the laws had yet to be written. That is unless, of course, an enterprising recipient of slush-money "forgot" to note it on his taxes. This is where Alan Freed went wrong. This is also what caused a lot of prominent DJs under investigation to sing like canaries. But, in the end, if the laws enacted to stamp out payola are any indication, the government didn't really consider it a very serious crime. Although as a result of the hearings Congress passed a statute making payola a crime punishable by a maximum fine of $10,000 and one year in prison, no one has ever served time on payola charges. The whole scandal was, in many ways, a witch-hunt.

Even the commercial bribery laws that came about because of the scandal were not very stringent. Although a lot of local DJs folded under pressure, an equal number of them defiantly mocked the proceedings. Unless it could be directly proven that DJs took money to play specific records, there was nothing illegal about it. So the DJs didn't dispute receiving cash and gifts but, rather, why they received them in the first place. As the more imaginative DJs explained, the cash they received was not a "bribe" to play a certain record, but a "thank you" for services already rendered. And there was no law against that.

When the investigators finally called Dick Clark to the stand, he proved to be more articulate than his older, more roguish counterparts. He'd also done his homework. The panel was impressed that Clark had brought his own statistician, who had to draw an actual diagram to explain the intricate web of Clark's financial holdings. In the end, Clark would forsake all his holdings in outside firms to walk away scot-free, and the committee would pronounce him "a fine young man." There was a lesson in there somewhere: screwing the system from within.

Alan Freed, on the other hand, didn't make out as well. The panel prolonged his actual trial until December 1962. Because of his notoriety, he was more or less unemployable during this time. Broke and in ailing health, Freed pleaded guilty to two counts of commercial bribery and was given a light sentence. It should have ended there, but a little more than a year later, on March 16, 1964, he was indicted by another grand jury, this time for tax evasion. The IRS wanted him to cough up about $38,000, but he never had to pay one penny, mainly because he died a broken man shortly thereafter.

As for Dick Clark, it didn't take him long to rebound from his losses. In 1960 he took a Black chicken-plucker named Ernest Evans, rechristened him Chubby Checker, and had him record a version of "The Twist"—originally a failed would-be hit by R&B artist Hank Ballard—for Clark's own Cameo label. The record managed the amazing feat of getting to number one on the charts on *two separate occasions*, a feat that, thus far, has never been duplicated. The success of "The Twist" also spawned a major dance craze that helped propel Rock 'n' Roll out of the malt shop as well as the cow pasture and into the realm of sophisticated urban nightlife. Jackie Kennedy was seen doing the twist at the Peppermint Lounge, which meant Rock 'n' Roll had become the toast of discotheque society. As Tom Wolfe wrote: "The prole vitality of rock and roll…has made it the darling holy beast of intellectuals in the United States, England and France. Intellectuals, generally, no longer take jazz seriously. But rock and roll! Poor old arteriosclerotic lawyers with pocky layers of fat over their ribs are out there right now twisting with obscene clumsiness to rock and roll." [3]

In the early '60s, Rock 'n' Roll was an up-and-coming "racket" (in more ways than one). But this wasn't necessarily a bad thing—it meant that some of the brightest young talents on the musical horizon were turning to Rock 'n' Roll as opposed to Jazz, Classical, or other more formalized techniques. Similarly, the main source of the music was shifting from the rural outposts to a more sophisticated domain. One didn't have to have "smelt a lot of manure" (as Hank Williams once said) in order to produce "authentic" Rock 'n' Roll any longer. Rock 'n' Roll was on its way to becoming an art form. It was also becoming mass-produced.

One of the first people to approach the making of Rock 'n' Roll records as an artistic venture was Phil Spector, perhaps the first superstar record producer. He took groups off the street who had no particular finesse and put them in the studio with the best musicians he could find, almost as if they were merely another component. Working them through exhaustive sessions, he'd sometimes demand to do a take thirty, fifty, one hundred times until he'd achieved the desired level of perfection. When this pissed off the record companies who'd hired him, he formed his own label with Lester Sill called Philles (an amalgam of "Phil" and "Les"). He was the first of the temperamental spoiled brats of Rock 'n' Roll who approached the business on his own terms, as if he were a mini-Mozart, and *won*—at least temporarily. This was a great boost for artistic freedom in the name of Rock 'n' Roll.

Originally from the Bronx, Spector moved West to Los Angeles with his mother after his father committed suicide when Phil was eight. Phil would later take the words from his father's grave for the title of his first production: "To Know Him Is to Love Him." With his mousy demeanor and New York City complexion, the young Spector was out of place among the sun-worshipping Californians. A withdrawn kid, he took to music as his refuge. In L.A. he took guitar lessons from the acclaimed Jazz guitarist Howard Roberts and started hanging around Gold Star studios in Hollywood, hoping he'd meet someone who'd let him record his songs. It was at Gold Star in the '50s that Spector first came in contact with the massive echo chambers that would eventually become his trademark. The studio had not one but two echo chambers, probably due to its size—Gold Star was relatively small compared to many of the other studios in L.A., and to compensate, they'd built an extra echo chamber in the bathroom. Although it sounds weird, this innovation would be much copied in the '60s.

In the meantime, Spector was conducting recording experiments of his own. With a pair of high school friends, one male, one female, he cut a demo of "To Know Him Is to Love Him," a typical saccharine ballad based on the kind of "group harmony" that was popular at the time. Calling the group the Teddy Bears, he somehow managed to sell the homemade recording to a local label, Dore, and in a fluke, it went all the way to number one on the national charts. Spector's legend as a "boy genius" was born. What the whole experience taught him was that he could easily orchestrate people as well as instruments to mimic the sounds that were in his head. Seeking artists who had some innate talent but perhaps couldn't project themselves, he would write the songs and then surround them with the embellishments of the modern recording studio, creating intricate pop melodramas.

After the Teddy Bears folded, Spector worked as a court stenographer during the day and heard his share of court cases dealing with finance in the movie industry and other entertainment fields. This wised him up to the economic factors of the business, a learning experience that would help him become a millionaire by the time he was twenty-one. He knew the deck he was playing with from the start, and this helped him get ahead in the budding Rock 'n' Roll industry. However, by the early 60's Spector was tired of the L.A. treadmill, which centered on teen idols and other pubescent fantasies. Through his association with Lester Sill, he was introduced to one of the most successful songwriting teams in Rock 'n' Roll, Jerry Leiber and Mike Stoller. Not only had the duo written some of the biggest hits of the Rock 'n' Roll era like "Hound Dog" and "Ruby Baby" (both covered by Elvis, which meant big bucks), they were well ensconced in the Brill Building. This was the creative hub of the New York Rock 'n' Roll industry where Phil Spector longed to be.

At the time, Leiber and Stoller were extraordinarily successful as the producers of the Drifters, the most popular Black vocal group in the country. The Drifters recorded for Atlantic Records, which is how Spector first came in contact with the label. Moving to New York, Spector got a job as an "assistant" at Atlantic, which meant serving in whatever capacity was needed at the time, writing or producing. This helped him further hone his chops.

Atlantic Records was one of the original independent labels that had sprung up in the postwar years to record Boogie Woogie and Rhythm & Blues. It was formed in 1947 by Ahmet Ertegun, the son of the Turkish ambassador to the U.N.; his original explanation for starting the label was: "I didn't want to go in the army, and I didn't want to work." A philosophy student and a collector of Jazz and Blues 78s, Ertegun met Herb Abramson sometime in the late '40s during the Be Bop craze. Ertegun's older brother, Nesuhi, was also a Jazz devotee. The three of them conceived the idea of the label originally to record Jazz, which Abramson already had some experience in. Borrowing $10,000 from a dentist friend, Ertegun moved in with Abramson in Greenwich Village while Nesuhi headed west. Because of Abramson's Jazz background, the first artists they signed were Pete Johnson and Joe Turner, veterans of the raucous Kansas City Swing scene of the late '30s and '40s.

Atlantic was one of the first companies not to shuck their songwriters by giving mysterious credit to Alan Freed or whatnot. At the time, the common practice for most record labels was to steal the copyright away from the original songwriter, paying him a small retainer's fee, and then pocket all the royalties. As Syd Nathan, the owner of King Records, once said: "We are not here to soothe the feelings of starry-eyed amateur songwriters."

At the time, the major record labels had a standard formula: they'd take a "name" act into the studio, hand him an arrangement of a staff-written song, and hire an orchestra to accompany him. This resulted in the bland state of the Hit Parade in the years prior to Rock 'n' Roll. Like many of the smaller labels, Atlantic discovered that there was a veritable ocean of uncharted territory in the small nightclubs where mostly Black musicians plied their trade. Most of these combos were playing something approximating Rhythm & Blues, and Atlantic's first hit was a juke-joint number by Sticks McGhee called "Drinkin' Wine Spo Dee O Dee," which was cut in the Louis Jordan vein.

The small labels discovered that although the major labels weren't willing to go out and discover Rhythm & Blues talent on their own, they were willing to whip out a prefab "cover" version of a potential R&B hit just in time to cancel out the "authentic" version. The whole recording environment in those years was not favorable to musicians, Black ones in particular. For instance, no one got paid advances. Most of the musicians received a standard session fee and that was it (a lot of Jazz musicians augmented their income through this method). Promotion was nonexistent, other than radio, which is why payola was so prevalent in those days. And songwriters had their material bought forthright—that is, once they sold it, they no longer "owned" it.

Until the early '50s, Atlantic concentrated most of its A&R resources in and around New York. However, they soon discovered that a lot of their competitors like King in Cincinnati, Chess in Chicago, and Specialty in L.A. were making frequent pilgrimages to the South to mine the incredibly fertile musical resources that region had to offer. L.A.'s Imperial Records was particularly lucky: a foray to New Orleans in 1949 led them to discover the artist who would build their label into a commercial entity, Fats Domino. But Atlantic didn't really gain much from their inaugural trip down South, other than acquiring the legendary New Orleans pianist Professor Longhair in an attempt to compete with Fats Domino. Unfortunately, despite some fine records, Longhair never equaled Domino's success.

If the trip proved anything, it was how far the label was willing to go to enlist outside help to improve the quality of their records. This distinguished them from other, lesser fly-by-night labels. Hiring outside arrangers, songwriters, musicians, and producers—like Tom Dowd, for instance—the company crafted a more sophisticated product than that of its peers. They were also willing to let musical forms run together in a more organic manner, such as Frank Culley's sax solo on the Clovers' "Don't You Know I Love You" which, at that time, seemed incongruously jazzy for an R&B record. However, Atlantic was an innovator: in a few years, the honking saxophone solo would become one of the signatures of R&B.

When Herb Abramson got drafted in 1952, a young journalist who'd recently been brought into the publishing wing of Atlantic, Jerry Wexler, became Ahmet Ertegun's new right-hand man. His work habits proved much more businesslike than Ertegun's, and soon he was running the day-to-day operations of the label. In the future, Wexler would prove to be the company's true visionary, producing almost all of the acts who, over the years, would make the company famous: Ray Charles, the Coasters, the Drifters, and Aretha Franklin. One of the first records he produced was "Sh-Boom" by the Chords in 1954. Although more "pop" than anything Atlantic had done yet, the song still contained a fairly tough sax solo by Sam Taylor. Although the Crewcuts' subsequent whitewashed version outsold the Chords' original, "Sh-Boom" was Atlantic's first crossover hit. Later that year, Joe Turner's "Shake, Rattle & Roll" also landed on the Pop charts and was subsequently scooped by Bill Haley & the Comets. By the time Abramson returned from the army, he found an upstart record label on the verge of success. But the chemistry at the label had changed—Wexler was the New Kid in Town and Abramson found himself slowly being squeezed out.

At the same time Atlantic was becoming a leader in the field of R&B, Nesuhi Ertegun was heading up the label's Jazz division and taking equally big chances with such idiosyncratic talents as the Modern Jazz Quartet, Charles Mingus, Ornette Coleman, and John Coltrane. By doing so, the company was building its reputation as an alternative to the "one take out-of-key" approach that characterized most of the indies at that time. Such considerations could only pay off in the long run.

Atlantic was also smart in other ways. For example, putting Lieber/Stoller under contract as staff writers/producers gave the label a tie-in with Elvis's lucrative publishing company, Hill & Range (to whom the songwriting duo were also contractually obligated). Through the Leiber/Stoller connection, Atlantic also gained access to other songwriters in the Brill Building, the song-writing factory located at 1619 Broadway that served the same function as Tin

Pan Alley had to an earlier generation. At this time, very few Rock 'n' Roll artists wrote their own material, thus creating a need for mass-produced fodder. Music publisher Don Kirshner got rich in those years, building his publishing company, Aldon, into one of the most successful of its era. At one time he had under contract the songwriting teams of Neil Sedaka & Howard Greenfield, Gerry Goffin & Carole King, and Barry Mann & Cynthia Weil. Among them, these three songwriting pairs wrote more than two hundred hits that charted during the years 1958–1963.

Leiber and Stoller never really fit into the Kirshner clique at the Brill Building. They were older, more grizzled veterans than the young kids who worked there, and they were under contract to an independent publisher, Hill & Range. They did, however, introduce Phil Spector to the other songwriters in the building, just as they'd brought him to Atlantic. Writers like Jeff Barry and Ellie Greenwich became Spector's partners in composing arch-teen dramas like "(Today I Met) the Boy I'm Going to Marry," "Da Doo Ron Ron," "Then He Kissed Me" and "Be My Baby."

The marriage of these composers' acute narratives combined with Spector's massive orchestration helped create the "girl group" genre in the early '60s. By that time, the basic street-corner harmony style of vocalizing had been overshadowed by new studio innovations, like the introduction of strings on the Drifters' "There Goes My Baby" or the thundering echo chamber employed by Spector. But it wasn't always that way; many an enterprising record producer built his dreams on "doo wop," the music of the mostly-ethnic vocal groups. George Goldner comes readily to mind—combing the streets of Harlem and the ghettos of Brooklyn for amateur Black and Puerto Rican harmonizers, he discovered some of the most successful vocal groups of the era: Frankie Lyman & the Teenagers, Little Anthony & the Imperials, the Crows, and the Flamingos. More importantly, Goldner launched the Chantels, who in many ways were the prototype for the girl groups like the Ronettes and Crystals.

Consisting of five Black women from the Bronx, led by the powerful voice of Arlene Smith, the Chantels epitomized the life-and-death struggle of teenage romance in the '50s. "Maybe," their first hit, had all the breadth of a hymn and took on apocalyptic overtones in its lament for unrequited love. The automobile had changed the concept of courtship, and the World War II

Daddies were gravely concerned over the fact their daughters seemed to be rushing into romance, "going steady" instead of dating casually. Nowhere was this passion more apparent than in the sound of Rock 'n' Roll during the years 1956–1962.

Goldner wasn't the only record producer to influence Spector. Another innovator was Morty Craft, originally an arranger with Glenn Miller, who went on to produce Bill Haley & the Comets. After Haley helped build Essex into a respectable label, Craft branched out and started labels like Melba and Lance. On the latter he recorded the Shepherd Sisters, who, despite their sororal connection, weren't really a girl group but a vocal group more in the style of the McGuire or Andrews Sisters. On their recording of "Alone," Craft used glockenspiel, a chimelike instrument played with two hammers. This was to have an enormous impact on Spector, who was just developing his penchant for weird studio embellishments.

By 1962, Spector was busy consummating his teen empire with groups like the Crystals, whose number one hit "He's a Rebel" heralded the coming age with its vindication of nonconformity: "Just because he doesn't do what everybody else does" went the refrain, and that seemed to sum up Spector. He'd made a name for himself in the industry by acting obnoxious, and now he was making ultra-obnoxious records as well (one of them was called "He Hit Me and it Felt Like a Kiss"). Soon Spector was to find the group who would become his ultimate sculpted jewel—the Ronettes. Originally a recording act for Colpix, another one of Dick Clark's labels, the group of two sisters and a cousin were snatched up by Spector and turned into every male teenager's fantasy—three chicks packed into tight dresses singing "Be My Baby." But Spector's interest in the group wasn't strictly commercial or artistic—he'd become taken with the lead singer, Ronnie Bennett, and eventually they were married.

The marriage didn't last and neither did the Ronettes, despite the lavish productions that Spector had erected around them. By that time other labels, producers, and songwriters were testing the same waters. Labels like Dimension, Cameo, Swan, Scepter, and Laurie became specialists in the kind of heartbroken drama that characterized the releases on Spector's own Philles label. Once again utilizing the resources of the Brill Building, most of the prototype girl groups—the Chiffons, Shirelles, Angels, Shangri Las—resided on the East Coast. There were exceptions, like the Mermaids, who epitomized the

West Coast strain with the dreamy "Popsicles and Icicles" (which painted a portrait of the Perfect Boy with its exotica-like weeping guitars). A lot of this stuff was just teenage fantasy fodder, but what made it great was the intense relationship between the artist, the songwriter, and the producer. It was a package deal, and if the chemistry was right, it resulted in nothing short of a masterpiece. This was to have a profound effect on all subsequent commercial assembly line music. Not surprisingly, many of Motown's earliest successes were girl groups like the Marvelettes, Martha & the Vandellas, and the Supremes (or solo female artists working in that vein, like Brenda Holloway or Mary Wells).

The Baby Boomers were really the first generation to experience adolescence as a state of mind. Unlike the World War II Daddies who were literally thrust into adulthood by the war, the generation of the '50s and '60s were able to experience adolescence as a period of protracted development. That meant they had more time to dwell on the problems of youth. And this is what the girl groups did—magnified all the aches and pains of adolescence into high drama. No group was better at this than the Shangri Las, four tough chicks from the Bronx who painted dramas so intense that the only solution to their eternal plight seemed to be suicide. Not to be outdone, a group called Whyte Boots released the apogee of the girl group sound in the form of "Nightmare," the story of a catfight gone too far in which the protagonist ends up killing her adversary—all for the love of a boy.

The girl groups proved that American popular music was still very much a vocal group medium. The Instrumental Rock trend came and went, its only enduring legacy being the Ventures. But ever since Elvis had arisen in the mid-'50s in the midst of talented instrumental stylists like Chuck Berry and Jerry Lee Lewis, he had helped sway the focus back to singers. The Beatles—and a lot of technology—would come along soon and reintroduce instrumental prowess to Rock 'n' Roll. But at least up until that time, Rock 'n' Roll musicians treaded in obscurity while singers ruled the record charts. Not surprisingly, during the early '60s, group harmonizing was still the primary medium. Particularly in cities like New York and Philadelphia, the street-corner sound was prevalent. Groups like the Rays, Danny & the Juniors, the Crests, Dion & the Belmonts, Jay & the Americans, and the Four Seasons epitomized the East Coast style. New York and Philadelphia were also the centers of the Twist craze. In New York, a kind of discotheque sound emerged in the form of the organ-laden dance bands like Joey Dee & the Starlighters, whose hit singles like "Mashed Potatoes and Hot Pastrami" were also borderline Instrumental Rock (unless one considered moronic shouts of "mashed potatoes yeah" to be actual singing).

The New York vocal groups were mostly of Italian-American descent. This included the majority of solo singers as well, many of whom were more derivative of the "crooner" tradition set forth by Frank Sinatra and Dean Martin a decade earlier. Bobby Darin, one of the most popular young vocalists of the '50s, had already made his decision to adopt the supper club style that would eventually land him in Vegas where he belonged. Dion DiMucci, on the other hand, pursued a more bluesy approach, first with his group the Belmonts and then on his own. In the form of songs like "A Teenager in Love," it was a whiney Blues but it was Blues nevertheless. Dion had clearly followed the advice of his friend Paul Anka: "Write songs that make the girls feel sorry for you."

What separated Dion from other teen idols was that his street credibility was a little more real: he was a heroin addict. Like Frankie Lyman, he got hooked at an early age just as fame was coming upon him. That means while he was doing all those stupid shows—*Ed Sullivan* and whatnot—he was whacked out on smack. Nevertheless, he achieved tremendous success in the early '60s with "Runaround Sue" and "The Wanderer," songs that revealed his slightly streetwise persona. This resulted in a huge contract with Columbia in 1962, after which he moved into more "mature" terrain despite obvious schlock like "Donna the Prima Donna," which, even then, had a slightly cynical edge that exposed Dion's darker side. With his covers of Drifters songs like "Ruby Baby" and "Drip Drop," he was also a top-notch purveyor of white soul. These songs sold, too, which pleased Columbia. Dion was sort of the label's first experiment with Rock (Dylan was still a folk singer at that time). Even after the heroin began to take its toll, Dion proved uncompromising in his desire to explore a more bluesy directive with covers of Howlin' Wolf's "Spoonful" and Sonny Boy Williamson's "Don't Start Me Talkin'." When Tom Wilson came to Columbia in 1965 to produce Bob Dylan, Dion attempted to cash in on Dylan's success with songs like "Two Ton Feather." Of course, he was hardly the only one doing this in 1965. The Dylan act did little to revive Dion's sagging career.

Eventually he cleaned up his act and sold his story to Warner Brothers with the admirably nonpreachy drug-rehab song "Your Own Back Yard."

In New York, the sounds on the street stayed the same, but the echo had changed—this time it came back in the voice of a girl! Mainly, from Frankie Valli, lead singer of the Four Seasons, whose shrieking falsetto was the most popular voice in America for a brief season. Originally hailing from New Jersey, the group was able to ride the novelty of Frankie's voice into a pretty durable career. Their best work of the early period was probably "Walk Like a Man," in which the kid's father tells him to walk away from the bitch. The Four Seasons shared Dion's machismo. In songs like "Dawn," Frankie tells the girl to get lost. Although obviously R&B-influenced, there might have been some other *influence* as well considering the group's Italian-American roots. For years, men like Morris Levy of Roulette records had maintained inextricable ties to organized crime. Frankie Valli & the Four Seasons were probably not immune to this influence either.

Not to suggest that the Four Seasons' bountiful success was entirely due to graft. Some of their performances in the mid-'60s were like the last word on the whole Doo Wop/street-corner style, like "Working My Way Back to You," a production so soulful that it was later covered note-for-note by a Black group, the Spinners. And, once again, it was macho: "I used to love to make you cry/it made me feel like a man inside," Frankie sang. Their songs spoke to all the struggling working class Joes coming home with lipstick on their collar to the young wife holding the screaming baby: "Joey, *you promised!*" You know, sometimes he might just have to take a swing. *Rocky*-type stuff, but at that time it worked. So much so that the Four Seasons enjoyed hit after hit, not officially disbanding until 1970. By then even they wore hippie clothes.

What the success of the Four Seasons and others of their ilk proved was, the '60s weren't actually as hip as everyone says they were. Despite the media distortion of the '60s as a decade-long protest/drugfest, there was a whole forgotten half of young people who grew up in the '60s and pursued business as usual, totally oblivious to the "counterculture." Perhaps this was the first Bill Gates generation—astute middle class kids who were enjoying the academic wealth that the postwar environment had provided without the radicalization. These were the first yuppies—successful college-educated urban professionals striving for the American Dream in droves. Considering such subsequent bummers as Altamont as well as two Nixon presidential victories, the so-called unity of the more radical factions turned out to be a hoax. While a certain, highly visible number of Baby Boomers were out in the streets calling attention to the "movement," many of their peers off campus were reaping the capitalistic rewards of living in the most prosperous time ever, and loving every minute of it. (Hey, they thought that was the revolution!)

If the "popular music" of any given time is an accurate barometer of what was really going on in the culture, this more traditional faction of '60s youth has been underreported. Take, for example, Jay & the Americans, who actually did a patriotic song called "Only in America." Or Nancy Sinatra, Frank's daughter, who may have fooled around with leather but was known to leave parties where pot smoking was going on. The Vogues' "Five o' Clock World" is a perfect example of '60s yuppie Rock: to the heaving hammer of the beat, a young yup "workin' on money I ain't made yet" struggles to get through the work day in order to enjoy some of that longed-for leisure time. Neil Diamond expressed some of the same frustration with the daily grind in "Thank the Lord for the Nighttime" only in hipper terms: "9 to 5 ain't takin' me where I'm bound." But at least he *knew*—he hadn't officially "dropped out" like the hippies. Speaking of Neil Diamond, his first major hit, "Solitary Man," was perhaps the epitome of square '60s Rock, vowing monogamy and celibacy at a time when "free love" was just beginning.

Artists like these missed the boat on the '60s "revolution" but continued to have hits all the same. Others of this ilk included Bobby Vinton, Billy Joe Royal, B. J. Thomas, Lou Christie, Bob Lind, Roy Orbison, Dusty Springfield, the Association, Herman's Hermits, Johnny Rivers, the Cyrkle, Gary Puckett & the Union Gap, the Happenings, the Classics IV—not to mention decidedly non-Rock artists like Tom Jones, Dionne Warwick, Engelbert Humperdinck, and the Walker Brothers. The success of these groups, however limited, proves that, to a certain extent, the '60s "revolution" might've been a hoax.

With the arrival of the Beatles, Dylan, and the ensuing counterculture, Rock would increasingly become a forum for self-expression and a million different ideologies. Suddenly, groups who were merely feckless mouthpieces for some producer seemed passé. It was the misfortune of a good-time group like Tommy James & the Shondells to happen at the same time as Rock's maturity. James himself has gushed, "I loved making records! You could always hear it...and I think that's why there's so many good feelings surrounding our music.

We were really having fun, and you can hear that in the grooves." Golly! But in a way he was right—the Shondells reeled off hit after captivating hit in the '60s, hits that have, by the way, lived a longer, more luminous life than a lot of the failed experiments of their more adventurous peers. "I Think We're Alone Now" was in many ways a primal influence on the Ramones. "Mony Mony," meanwhile, seemed to influence the Stooges' "Down on the Street"—not all that surprising, considering that the album it was on, *Funhouse*, was produced by Don Galucci, who was originally in the Kingsmen and whose "Louie Louie" was the prototype for all garage groups like the Shondells. The group wasn't entirely devoid of artistic pretensions, either: "Crimson & Clover" from 1968 was an opulent cornucopia of psychedelic embellishments and pseudopoetic fancy, proving that, once again, Tommy shouldn't be overlooked entirely. He wrote most of his own material, which means he didn't fall short of the promise brought about by the Beatles and Dylan—it's just that his experience was not as troublesome. There was a lesson in there somewhere for future purveyors of mirth in the name of Rock 'n' Roll.

No group took the fall for Rock's sudden "maturity" harder than the Beach Boys. More than any other of their era, the group epitomized not only the sunny utopia of the West Coast, but the promise of Rock 'n' Roll itself as a way for educated, affluent, perhaps slightly alienated young whites to make millions of dollars and achieve "respectability." The Beach Boys were the first American Rock 'n' Roll band to have *any* artistic control whatsoever: there's very little question that Brian Wilson was by far the most innovative producer–composer of his day, eclipsing even Phil Spector. But alas, the *aura* that surrounded him—that of the talented hometown ham that everybody knew was always destined for greatness—ultimately ensured that he'd sit on the sidelines during the subsequent age of anarchy. Because Brian and the Beach Boys were so ultimately a product of '50s values that they could never truly break free in a day and age when "freedom" was everything. Right up until the time Brian checked himself into his first loony bin, his father, Murray—a World War II Daddy if there ever was one—managed the group's career and was often at odds with his eccentric son. Phil Spector's father had died. Lennon's left home. Guys like Bob Dylan, Keith Richards, and Brian Jones broke free of the old man. Brian couldn't do that, because all of the things he held dear—hot rods racing around a track, burgers cooking on the open grill, the prom queen and the ideal of love and marriage—were totally born out of his father's world: mainly, the white suburban middle class. These were just the ideals that, in the '60s, were being questioned, and Brian, not the happiest guy in the world, began to question *himself*. Exacerbated by the copious amount of acid he took during the psychedelic era, these feelings of insecurity eventually drove him crazy.

In short, you couldn't be a "hippie" and still be bossed around by Dad. But Brian couldn't betray his family roots because, after all, the Beach Boys were a family affair: Wilson, his two younger brothers, Dennis and Carl, a cousin, Mike Love, and a neighbor, David Marks (soon to be replaced by Al Jardine, another high school friend). At the time, Instrumental Rock was the big trend on the West Coast—Dick Dale & the Deltones were the perfect example of a "surf" instrumental combo. What the Beach Boys introduced to the surf culture was the bleached-white collegiate matching-sweater vocal harmony, borrowed from groups like the Four Freshmen. In other words, they yuppified what was essentially a "punk" genre to begin with.

Hawthorne, the section of Los Angeles where the Wilson brothers grew up, was a fairly well-to-do suburb. It was a great community for a youth to grow up in during the postwar years, with its endless strip just right for cruising and its close proximity to Manhattan, Hermosa, and Redondo Beach. Because of his background, Brian Wilson really saw life from the myopic view of the American Dream in progress: burgers, girls, and the endless pursuit of mindless leisure. It was only later that he'd become aware of the irony, and by then it was too late— the joke was on him. But, in the early '60s, the Beach Boys epitomized the American West Coast teenage experience.

With Murray taking the managerial hand, the band inked a one-off deal with a local indie called Candix and released "Surfin'," their first single. The song was a typical Rock 'n' Roll romp for its day—the only thing distinctive about it was the weird use of falsetto, possibly influenced by another California act from around the same time, Jan & Dean (soon the paths of the two groups would cross). Murray Wilson actually had a brief career as a songwriter in the '50s; however, a small business importing drills and lathes from England was what kept the Wilson household afloat. It was inevitable he would project some of his musical frustrations onto his very talented oldest son, Brian. By all reports, he was a grinding taskmaster and he delighted in humiliating Brian— in fact, friends who knew the family claim that Brian's partial hearing loss was caused by a smack Murray gave him to the head when he—Brian—was only six years old. Nevertheless, Murray would remain the Beach Boys' official manager for years to come.

Despite Murray's faults, he was as relentless in his promotion of the boys as he was in his brutal browbeating of Brian. His persistence paid off—Murray got the group a deal with Capitol, who'd just hired a hot young producer named Nick Venet to help them penetrate the "youth market." Only twenty-one, Venet had already produced the Lettermen, another white vocal group, and the Beach Boys seemed to fit into his musical frame of reference. Sticking with the surfing theme, the group had recorded a follow-up to "Surfin'" called "Surfin' Safari," and it became their first national hit. According to Venet, the first time he heard it, the thought occurred to him: "this song is going to change West Coast music."

All up and down the West Coast, the surfing fad was giving credence to a whole new teenage way of life that in many ways predated a lot of the other subcultures that would sprout up later in the decade. In surf culture, for a few moments anyway, all the rules and restrictions of the "straight" world were eliminated, and life came down to a beautiful unity of man and nature—riding the waves. There were no rules. Like other later countercultural manifestations, surfers created their own language, dress code, and way of life. Which, in their case, was the ultimate California sun-worshipping reality: surfing all day and then having enormous beach parties deep into the night before drunkenly grabbing the boards once more and hitting the midnight surf. True surfers slept on the beach, ate on the beach, danced on the beach, fucked on the beach. As the Beach Boys, the penultimate surf group, proclaimed: "We're on safari to stay."

As a result of the Beach Boys' success on Capitol, Brian earned himself considerable clout in the West Coast music scene. Despite Murray's interference, it was evident who the real brains of the Beach Boys was. The fact that Brian soon took control of production duties only enhanced his stature—at a time when most Rock production was handled by an in-house staff producer, it was truly unusual for a group member to assume the task, especially when he was a twenty-one-year-old novice. But, from the beginning, the level of "artistic control" that the Beach Boys—and Brian specifically—maintained was truly unique. Brian's production methods, while in many ways primitive, were still innovative: for instance, his use of double-tracking and multiple overdubs was matched only by Phil Spector.

Like Spector, perhaps the first West Coast-bred super producer, Wilson surrounded himself with an array of talented collaborators. Chief among them was Gary Usher, another Hawthorne neighbor, who was soon to become an important producer in his own right. It was Usher who collaborated on the Beach Boys' first hot rod song, "409," thus anticipating another trend. In fact, thanks to the Beach Boys, Capitol was able to fully exploit both the surf and hot rod trends. The actual personnel on most of these records were, many times, the same—mainly the hip coterie that had begun to revolve around Brian Wilson in the L.A. music scene of the '60s.

Another Wilson collaborator was Roger Christian, a former DJ who set a fire under Murray Wilson's ass when he dumped on the lyrics to "409" on the air. Apparently with a "you think you could do better?" tone in his voice, Murray Wilson called the radio station and within minutes had coerced Christian into a meeting with his famous son. The whole gist of Christian's put-down had been that the 409 itself was not the hot rod the Beach Boys had claimed it was, and with that in mind he and Brian proceeded to write another hot rod tune that was an even bigger hit, called "Shutdown." They followed that with "Little Deuce Coupe." By then the hot rod trend was firmly estab-lished—after all, the automobile was even more of a mainstay of teenage cul-ture than the surfboard.

Before long there were a host of makeshift "hot rod" groups just as there'd been a plethora of "surf" groups—and most of these were just Brian and his friends. Gary Usher, in particular, was the catalyst for a wealth of surf- and hot rod-related schlock. For Capitol alone he masterminded the Knights, the Ghouls, the Super Stocks, and, for Mercury, the Weird-Ohs, Silly Surfers, Hondells, and others. Monster and "weirdo" records were in vogue for a season, and at one point the strange fusion of monster and hot rod records actually exist-ed in the form of Mr. Gasser & the Weirdos—who were actually Gary Usher and a bunch of studio musicians.

And where was Brian during all this? Only writing and producing some of the most enduring American Pop classics ever: "Surfin' USA," "Don't Worry Baby," "Fun, Fun, Fun," "Dance, Dance, Dance," "I Get Around," "Help Me Rhonda"—all million-sellers that inspired an almost devout following amongst the denizens of the L.A. musical establishment. Among Brian's biggest disciples were Jan & Dean— the aforementioned "surf" duo who were doing it as early as the Beach Boys, only with lesser success until Brian came along to write their greatest triumph, "Surf City." With its utopian vision of "two girls for every boy" it was a message even the landlocked masses of the Midwest or the cynical denizens of the East Coast could understand. The result was Brian's first number one hit before even the Beach Boys themselves had topped the charts, a fact that so enraged Murray Wilson that he labeled Jan & Dean "pirates." When Jan Barry heard this, he showed up at a Beach Boys recording session wearing an eye patch. This type of wise-ass humor was typical of the duo that left piss-takes in the can, like their version of a new song Brian had written called "New Girl in School," in which they made creative use of the word *woody*—a term theretofore used to describe a favorite surfer ride.

The success of the Beach Boys revolutionized West Coast Rock. Many groups that were primarily instrumental revamped their sound to include more echo and their image to include surfboards (whether they rode the waves or not was irrelevant—of the Beach Boys, only Dennis was a surfer). Despite the prevalence of Beach Boys knockoffs—whether Wilson-related or not—surf music remained for the most part an instrumental sound. Dick Dale & the Deltones are the obvious prototype, as Dale was performing something akin to later Fender-heavy hits like "Let's Go Trippin'" and "Mr. Eliminator" as early as '59. During the early '60s, bands with names like the Chantays, Surfaris, Marketts, Pyramids, and Rumblers helped reinvigorate American Rock 'n' Roll at a time when crooners and vocal groups ruled the hit parade.

The Pacific Northwest was one of the first regions to help popularize the notion of the "garage band." The area already had its own local legends in the Ventures, five bricklayers from Seattle who "horsed around" with instruments in the evening after work. They happened to make it big with a fluke instrumental hit called "Walk-Don't Run"—and turned it into a decade-spanning career. Along with Dick Dale, the Ventures helped make the Fender guitar the brand of choice among American Rock bands at the time. In Washington, as well as the whole Northwest, the Ventures' influence was dominant, even as a more raucous variation of the same idiom was being worked on at roughly the same time.

In nearby Tacoma, a group called the Wailers had begun around 1958, performing a hybrid of saxophone-driven R&B and good old Chuck Berry Rock 'n' Roll. As group member Buck Ormsby explained: "There were no precedent 'bands' to work from, there were none. But we wanted to play music, create it, form a band and perform. We started practicing in bedrooms, garages, living rooms, or wherever there was space." This was the original "punk"/underground scene, evidenced by the fact that, like latter-day indie rockers, the Wailers started their own label, Etiquette. Soon an equally feisty Seattle outfit made their debut on Etiquette as well—the Sonics. With wailing saxophone and singer Gerry Roslie's pre-Iggy vocals, they challenged the very notion of the Beach Boys' existence.

The "punk" credence of the Northwest can be further attested to by the fact that the region was where "Louie Louie," perhaps the prototype Punk anthem, originated. The song had originally been an R&B hit for Richard Berry, whose 1956 original was slower and had more of a Latin feel. It was only when the Wailers recorded it as a backing band for singer Rockin' Roberts that it took on the characteristics of its trademark 1-2-3, 1-2, 1-2-3 riff. When it was covered a few months later by a Portland band called the Kingsmen, it was downscaled even further. The Kingsmen were an even more rudimentary group than the Wailers or Sonics, and they could only afford to book time in a local studio—one that had little going for it as far as technical features went. The end result was a garbled, distorted demo that was barely audible. Miraculously, the record was picked up by radio stations in Boston, of all places, and became a *Billboard* breakout hit. The reason for its sudden ascendance seemed to be that it had somehow mistakenly been declared "obscene." Typical of the leftover witch-hunt mentality of the payola years, the fact that the lyrics couldn't be fully understood led investigators to believe they were "dirty." A full-bore investigation by the FCC and FBI in which both Richard Berry as well as the singer of the Kingsmen, Jack Ely, were dragged in to testify, came up short. In the end, the FCC concluded: "We found the record unintelligible at any speed." In a way, this statement summed up the record's whole ragged appeal—as well as its "punk" aesthetic.

The garage-band scene that surf music had helped spawn didn't end on the West Coast either. There were even several landlocked "surf" bands, like the Astronauts from Denver, who released a succession of LPs for RCA with "surf" themes even though they'd probably never seen the ocean before they toured California. Perhaps the most notorious of the ersatz surf bands were the

Trashmen from Minneapolis, whose "Surfin' Bird" sounded like the Rivingtons' "Papa Oom Mow Mow" minced through a trash compactor. A Punk classic, it has been covered by everyone from the Ramones to the Cramps to AntiSeen.

Back in California, there was an obvious Latino element to bands like the Premieres, Cannibal & the Headhunters, and The Midnighters. To these bands, Ritchie Valens was the obvious influence—dead at nineteen, killed in the same plane crash as Buddy Holly, he remained a martyr figure to Latino musicians. Whatever nuances bands like this were adding to the overall figuration of Rock in the early '60s was soon obscured by the arrival of the British, who may have shared their devotion to Valens but were oblivious to the more organic connotations of the music. We'll never really know what direction West Coast Rock would've taken had the Beatles and their ilk never invaded. (The East Coast is easier to figure out because of its denizens' affinity for Folk music, a more intellectual reckoning that probably would have allowed for such deviations as Bob Dylan, the Fugs, and the Velvet Underground—albeit in slightly muted form.)

Whatever the case may be, there was evidence that Rock 'n' Roll as a purely musical form had weathered the late '50s/early '60s drought signified by the payola probe and other factors and was about to undergo a massive renaissance. Nobody could have predicted at that time how massive. Even without the arrival of the Beatles, Rock 'n' Roll would have survived—but it might have remained a very small speck on the whole landscape of popular music. As it was, the arrival of the Beatles created just the opposite—namely, a guarantee that songs as relatively insignificant as "Louie, Louie" and "Surfin' Bird" would live forever.

CHAPTER 5

THE BEATLES

THE GREATEST MUSICAL SUCCESS STORY OF THE TWENTIETH CENTURY BEGAN ON OCTOBER 9, 1940. While the Battle of Britain raged and Hitler's bombs made dust out of some of England's more formidable structures, a baby was born to a mother in Liverpool. Daddy wasn't present because he was away at sea. Soon he would be away altogether, abandoning the boy, whose name was John Winston Lennon (after Churchill).

The baby's mother, Julia, found the burden of raising the boy alone to be too much and sent the child to live with her sister Mimi. Julia still visited on occasion, but the relationship she established with her son was more that of an older "friend." In fact, together they made fun of Mimi's stricter ways.

When John Lennon reached adolescence in the mid-'50s, he presented an ever-growing problem for his aunt. Although he showed bursts of creativity and even brilliance, his energies were channeled into mischief and aggressive behavior. Lennon established early on that he was a leader, and it was he who initiated the small-time thievery and pranks among the other boys at Liverpool's Quarry Bank High School. This did little to endear him to his educators, who predicted that he'd come to a rotten end.

Somewhere along the line, Lennon discovered Rock 'n' Roll. There wasn't much of a pre-Rock music scene in England—just the spinal remains of the Big Band era. The most original sound to emerge during those years was skiffle, a shuffling brand of weak-kneed vaudeville shtick best personified by Lonnie

Donegan's "Rock Island Line." Skiffle was played on a washboard, string bass, and *tea chest*, with a guitar providing the primary rhythm. Lennon chose to become a guitar player.

His first band, the Quarrymen, was a typical skiffle organization, performing giddy "traditional" tunes and goofy novelties and playing school and social functions. It was at one such outing that John Lennon met the man who, with him, would forge the music partnership of the century: Paul McCartney. It was McCartney who encouraged Lennon to begin writing songs.

McCartney, born on June 18, 1942, was a musical prodigy: his father Jim had been a Jazz bandleader in the years following World War I, and Paul had begun playing guitar when he was fourteen. At that time, the first strains of the Rock boom were coming over from America, and McCartney was at the perfect age to be usurped by it. He didn't really apply himself to music, however, until his mother Mary died prematurely of cancer in 1954. From that point on, he never stopped. By the time he met Lennon in 1956, he was already composing his own material.

As McCartney recalls: "I used to know all the words to '20 Flight Rock' and a few others. John didn't know the words to many songs, so I was valuable. I wrote a few words and showed him how to play '20 Flight Rock' and another one. He played all this stuff and I remember thinking he smelled a bit drunk. Quite a nice chap, but he was still a bit drunk. Anyway, that was my first introduction, and I sang a couple of old things." [1]

When McCartney speaks here of singing "a couple of old things," he's not kidding—Paul's sensibilities, even at that time, ranged from the toodle-doo Jazz of his father's generation to the "Pennies from Heaven" style of Fred Astaire. He always had conventional Pop tastes, and he brought them to the Quarrymen. Who knows what direction Lennon, who was more Rock-oriented, would've taken had he never met McCartney? But it was McCartney who gave Lennon the conviction to pursue his own musical ideas in the first place. It would become a unique and eventually strained partnership, but there's no underestimating its significance. Neither of them could have made it in precisely the same way without the other. On the other hand, the combination of their talents was a force to be reckoned with.

Soon a tragic event would occur that would further cement their relationship: on July 15, 1958, John's mother stopped by Mimi's for her usual visit, and on her way out, she was struck fatally by a car. This tragedy would have much bearing on Lennon's psyche. Initially he reacted with bitterness, becoming even more withdrawn, abusive, and mean-spirited. But it brought him closer to McCartney, whose own mother had also prematurely passed away four years earlier. Now they really were "brothers," psychically linked through circumstance and misfortune.

From that point on, they attacked their music with a vengeance. Although the Quarrymen quickly rose to some degree of prominence on the Liverpool music scene, the scene itself didn't really offer much of a future for the two musical aspirants. Nevertheless, they had a very professional attitude about their music. No doubt when Lennon later said "nothing affected me 'til Elvis," what he meant was that Presley's *celebrity* affected him, and he would use it as a blueprint for his own.

Both Lennon and McCartney were devoted to honing their musical chops as well. One way to do this was to add another guitarist to the Quarrymen's ranks. Paul's friend, George Harrison, was three years Lennon's junior, which put him in the unenviable position of being Lennon's proverbial "whipping boy." Even Lennon had to admit that the youngster was a much more accomplished guitarist than either himself or McCartney. Harrison had been playing since he was six and possessed a mastery of the basic Rock licks as well as many twangy Country & Western influences. The prevailing influence of Carl Perkins on the Beatles' early recordings no doubt stemmed from Harrison's entrance into the group.

In 1958, the disillusioned Lennon began attending the Liverpool College of Art. A lot of wayward British youths in the late '50s found themselves enrolled in art school, probably because the curriculum was easy and they could just slide. This included Lennon, Pete Townshend, Keith Richards, Eric Clapton, and the various Kinks. Considering the arty pretense of a great deal of subsequent British Rock, it's not hard to see how the art school "occupation" has left its mark. In Lennon's case, the most significant thing to happen to him while at art school was that he came to admire another student, Stuart Sutcliffe, who became the next big influence on his life after McCartney. Although Sutcliffe apparently had some musical ability, it was his *style* that Lennon liked. One of the first of the real "teddy boys," Sutcliffe flirted with the kind of rebellious imagery that Lennon found instantly beguiling. So when the Quarrymen needed an electric bass player in their effort to become more of a Rock 'n' Roll band and less of a skiffle one, Lennon nominated Sutcliffe. As has been the case with many a Rock legend ever since—most particularly Sid Vicious—it didn't matter whether he actually knew how to play his instrument yet. He'd learn. For now it was more important that he *looked* the part.

The next task at hand was to find a drummer. Johnny Hutchinson, a well-known local stand-in, provided the support needed for the band to embark on their first tour. At the urging of Liverpool impresario Larry Parnes, they accompanied a hackoid singer named Johnny Gentle on a two-week tour of Scotland. This gave them their first taste of the road. It was an experience they'd become infinitely familiar with in the years to follow.

Shortly thereafter they hired their first permanent drummer, Thomas Moore. But he didn't work out, and soon they were looking for a replacement. Pete Best would prove to be perfect—at least for a while. Although he was plain and dumpy, he did own a full drum kit, a big consideration at that time. More importantly, his mom owned the Casbah Club, the most well-known club in Liverpool. It was inevitable that the Quarrymen became the "house band"—except by then they weren't calling themselves the Quarrymen anymore: they'd become the Silver Beatles and then simply the Beatles, apparently in honor of Buddy Holly's Crickets (although there are just as many historians who would claim the name was a reference to "the Beats"—which is doubtful, considering that the Beatles in their original form were more rockers than readers).

At this point the band gained their first manager, Allan Williams. Not only did he own two clubs in Liverpool—the Blue Angel and the Jacaranda—but he also had connections in Hamburg, Germany, where a nighttime sleaze scene had thrived since the '30s. In the early '60s, the strip in Hamburg was just beginning to feature live Rock bands as part of the debauchery. As the Beatles were, at that time, playing at least a close approximation of standard American Rock 'n' Roll, they were hired.

As Lennon remembered: "We hated the club owners so much that we jumped around until we broke through the stage. We'd all end jumpin' 'round on the floor. Paul would be doing 'What I Say' for an hour and a half. All these gangsters would come in…They'd just send a crate of champagne onstage and we'd have to drink it even though it killed us. They'd say 'Drink it and then do "What I Say".' So we'd have to do this show for them, whatever time of night.

If they came in at five in the morning, and we'd been playing for seven hours, they gave us a crate of champagne and we were supposed to carry on." [2]

This nightmarish experience helped them hone their chops, and they soon returned to Liverpool with renewed self-confidence. The British Rock scene was just getting underway, with Cliff Richard ("Move It," "Living Doll"), Vince Taylor & the Playboys ("Brand New Cadillac"), Johnny Kidd & the Pirates ("Shakin' All Over," "Restless"), Tony Dangerfield ("She's Too Way Out"), and the Tornadoes ("Telstar"). Although these and many other fine examples represented an attempt on the part of the British to establish a Rock scene of their own, the majority of British Rock 'n' Roll attempts until that time had constituted wimpy regurgitations of already-outdated American styles. The Beatles realized immediately how superior they were to the competition. They returned from Hamburg as conquering heroes.

The nexus for the Liverpool explosion was a former Jazz venue known as the Cavern Club, which became the stomping ground for the new wave of Liverpool "beat" groups: Kingsize Taylor & the Dominoes, Rory Storm & the Hurricanes (featuring soon-to-be-crowned Beatle drummer Ringo Starr), and, of course, the Beatles themselves. According to Peter McCabe and Robert Sconfeld: "The attraction to 'beat' soon brought a wide cross-section of Liverpool's children flocking to the new clubs. They ranged from young school kids to art students and poets...Slowly they acquired a group consciousness that went beyond the fact that they appreciated the same music. The musicians were close to each other, but more important, the audience and the musicians were friends. Much of the inevitable hero worship was contained because many of the band members were old school friends of the onlookers...for the most part, the audiences were...impressed that their friends had matched, and in some cases even surpassed, their American heroes, Presley and Little Richard." [3]

By description this scene sounds very much like the Punk or indie scenes of subsequent years—a sophisticated and supportive pack of peers jammed into a basement club to witness the pinnacles and pratfalls of their peers. As Richard Meltzer has observed, the Beatles and their ilk were: "a pack of basic limey post-teens with no illusions of takin' over the world...yet there's already *somethin'* to indicate that ENGLAND IS SOMEHOW FINALLY ABOUT TO ENTER THE 20TH CENTURY AND EMERGE FROM THE DUST OF SHAKE-

SPEARE/CHURCHILL/QUEEN VICTORIA/LESLEY HOWARD. And where's this emergence takin' place: the CBGBs of its time." [4]

Mick Jagger of the Rolling Stones described the uniqueness of the "Liverpool Sound" this way: "I can remember the first time the Stones ever went to Liverpool the drummers played completely different. I can't remember what it was, but I do know that they played four to the bar on the bass drum as opposed to what drummers in the south played—a more choppy pattern. They did have a different sound, and the other thing was all those harmonies." [5]

While the bands in London who coalesced around Alexis Korner & His All Stars were preoccupied with American Rhythm & Blues, the Beatles and their Mersey-side ilk were mining a myriad of Colonial resources. Along with the Blues, they turned to American "girl groups," white-bread harmonizers like the Everly Brothers and Four Freshman, and countrified rockabillies like Carl Perkins and Chet Atkins for their inspiration. The bottom line was, the Beatles *had* to be versatile, having to maintain nine-hour sets and all. There simply wasn't that much Blues to go around, and the Beatles were never a "purist" outfit to begin with—they were perfectly willing to supplant such tendencies in favor of pure Pop if it paid off.

At that time, the connotations of "pop" weren't that ominous. Although some musicians strove for Blues purity, hardly anyone at that time strove for Rock purity. It was expected of every musician playing the form to eventually join the Hit Parade. This was the precedent set by Elvis Presley, and that was the world the Beatles were coming into. The Beatles did something no other group had done, however—they *elevated* the form at the same time. Some would argue that they killed "Rock" in the process by foisting upon it a bunch of high-minded ideals, but if they hadn't, who knows what would have happened? Rock 'n' Roll could've been relegated to the same terminally retro status as lounge music. As it was, the Beatles forever solidified Rock's status as the ultimate "popular music"—even if they emasculated it in the process (which is debatable anyway).

The Beatles were also catching long stares for their hairstyles—a shaggy type of mane that resembled the pudding-bowl clips of mentally retarded kids locked up in the notorious "snake pits" before the days of enlightenment. Sutcliffe had introduced the haircut to the group, influenced by Astrid Kirchherr, a beautiful blonde pre-Nico German artist/bohemian who'd become acquainted with Sutcliffe a few months before he joined the Beatles. It's hard to say what other influences Sutcliffe would've brought to the group had he not quit and decided to stay in Hamburg with Kirchherr. Shortly thereafter, Sutcliffe died of a brain hemorrhage on April 10, 1962.

By this time, the Hamburg scene had become a thriving circuit for not only British Rock musicians, but the American originals as well. After all, bad boys like Gene Vincent, Carl Perkins, Eddie Cochran, and even instrumental acts like Johnny & the Hurricanes weren't exactly welcome anymore in the Pop-oriented music scene back home. Many of them moved to Europe in the early '60s, where they found themselves the objects of widespread cult adulation. Cochran loomed particularly large on the British music scene, having moved to England before dying in a car crash in 1960.

European musicians everywhere began aping these expatriates' juvenile delinquent mannerisms and style of dress. In Hamburg, a young vocalist named Tony Sheridan was cultivating a leatherboy image close to that of Vincent and Cochran. It was during one of their many trips to the legendary Star Club that the Beatles first met the singer. Sheridan was getting ready to make a record and asked the group to accompany him. By this time McCartney had switched to bass, replacing Sutcliffe. Lennon, Harrison, and Sheridan played guitar on the session, and Best added the beat. The song was called "My Bonnie," and the B-side, "Ain't She Sweet," marked the first recorded appearance of a Lennon vocal.

"My Bonnie" led to a strange request for a record store owner in Liverpool. It seems while the Beatles had been away in Hamburg they'd built up a cult following back home. In a few months, the group would top all categories in the *Mersey Beat* year-end poll. *Mersey Beat* was the brainstorm of one Bill Harry, who started the magazine in reaction to the *Liverpool Echo*'s failure to recognize the "beat" scene. This was early fanzine pioneering at its best. "Mersey" referred to the famous river, which reached a vortex in Liverpool. From its banks came the sound that would rock the world.

During the 1960s, British culture became highly exportable, particularly in America, where Anglophilia was at an all-time high. As Meltzer noted, the Brits were finally shaking off the cobwebs of Elizabethan formality. In 1963 the Profumo Scandal, in which top-ranking government officials were leading girls around on leashes, rocked Britain. Soon after, Swingin' London would implode. Thanks to the English, fashion and Rock would become inextricably linked.

However, the day that young Raymond Jones strolled into the Nems Record Store requesting "My Bonnie," the Beatles and their ilk had yet to achieve anything beyond local notoriety, and British working class fashion was still more in the league of docker boots and Navy trousers. The store's proprietor, Brian Epstein, had never even heard of the group, despite the fact that they were from Liverpool. Intrigued by the notion of a local scene, Epstein jammed into the Cavern one night to hear the Beatles play. It was likely that, even at that time, Epstein was thinking in entrepreneurial terms. His interest in Rock music was limited, but as a manger of a successful music outlet, he was at least curious about the sudden popularity of these upstarts. Upon his first visit to the Cavern, Epstein's impression was: "It was black as a deep grave, dark and damp and smelly, and I regretted my decision to come." [6]

Epstein introduced himself to the band, and while they—and chiefly Lennon—were skeptical, they agreed to meet him at Nems the following day. It was at this time that he offered to take over managerial duties. The Beatles had never really had a responsible manager. Allen Williams was able to help them establish themselves in Liverpool and Hamburg but had no eye on the future as long as his pockets were being filled. Epstein realized the group's potential in a much larger sense.

Brian was not a likely party to get involved with a Rock group: Jewish, homosexual, and almost thirty, he'd been working in the family business for most of his adult life. Although the store was prospering, having become the most successful record store in Liverpool, Brian's relationship with his father was still testy. That probably stemmed from an incident that happened when Brian was a teenager. As he recalled: "I wrote home and asked to be taken away from school so that I could become a dress designer." [7]

Brian and his ilk were emblematic of the whole "Swingin' London" phase of the '60s: young, elegant, and slightly pouffy, these nonconformists were rebelling against the stifling repression of the '50s by flouncing the fashion. Soon they would become millionaires.

Despite his lack of experience in the field of Rock, Brian obviously knew a winner when he saw and heard one. Having the group record a demo, he began shopping it around to the various record labels in England whom he knew from his connections in the retail business. At that time, the "beat" explosion was still mostly a provincial phenomenon, and the London-based British record industry wasn't entirely interested. Finally, on the first day of 1962, he got them an audition with Decca, at that time Britain's most successful record label (who'd later sign the Rolling Stones). But the label rejected the Beatles, and Decca A&R man Dick Rowe's immortal comment on the occasion still stands among the greatest blunders of history: "Groups of guitars are on their way out, Mr. Epstein."

Groups of guitars *weren't* on their way out, however. Thanks to the Beatles and their ilk, the guitar-based four- or five-man performing unit was about to become the wave of the future.

After subsequent rejections by several other major labels, the Beatles went back to toiling at the Star Club in Hamburg. It was not an encouraging prospect, and the group began to have second thoughts about Epstein. He, on the other hand, never lost faith in his charges and was always confident that the Beatles were going to take the British music industry by storm. In the summer of 1962, Epstein decided to have the Beatles' demo pressed onto a one-sided plastic record. As luck would have it, the person he enlisted to do this, Syd Coleman—an old record biz contact—happened to also be doing similar work for EMI. Coleman was blown away by the Beatles and arranged an audition with a friend who at that time was a staff producer for Parlophone, an EMI subsidiary.

George Martin was the right person at the right place at the right time to hear the Beatles. Parlophone was kind of EMI's "offbeat" branch that, up until then, had specialized in comedy records, which meant Martin had a taste for the absurd. For this reason, he wasn't quite as opposed to Rock 'n' Roll as some of his peers. The Beatles didn't lay a heavy Rock trip on him from the start anyway, auditioning with lightweight fare like "Til There Was You." Martin was impressed enough to grant them a recording session. Almost immediately, the band began rehearsing new material.

There was one stipulation: Pete Best would have to go. This didn't entirely displease the Beatles, as he'd never really fit in anyway. By that time they already had their eye on another Liverpool drummer, Ringo Starr, who'd become friendly with the group when his own band, Rory Storm & the Hurricanes, had backed them up in Hamburg. Starr was told he could join the group on the eve of their EMI debut if he shaved his beard. "No beards in the Beatles," said Brian. Not yet anyway.

For their first recording, the Beatles chose a song John and Paul had written back in the '50s, "Love Me Do." Although not a complex construction by any means, it was unique because it was self-penned, an anomaly in those days when Tin Pan Alley still dominated the charts. On the basis of this, Martin had a hard time convincing his uppers that he hadn't lost his mind. EMI needn't have worried—although the record was only a modest hit on the British charts, from this point on the Beatles would repay all dividends.

By the time of the Beatles' second release, however, the company was still not entirely convinced. As a result, they tried to convince the young upstarts to record a cover song, but the ambitious Lennon and McCartney were having none of it, insisting on recording another new self-composed tune called "Please Please Me." This was the turning point of the group's career.

The Beatles' forthrightness in this area was unique and trendsetting—most artists would've succumbed and gone for the gold. For instance, look at all the crap that Presley cut. The Beatles, however, had total faith in their capabilities and knew they were destined to turn the record industry inside out. That's why every subsequent Beatles hit would be an original and they'd restrict cover material to their album filler—and even then they'd discontinue that after 1965.

Part of this had to do with a deal Brian cut with publisher Dick James. Until then a not-very-successful entrepreneur, James was looking for a passport out of Tin Pan Alley. He was convinced that, within five years, Lennon/McCartney would be the most successful composing team in England. In cahoots with Epstein, he created Northern Songs to exclusively publish Beatles songs. James realized that Rock music *publishing* was another whole field ripe for the taking—a fact already proven by Hill & Range, Elvis's publishers. After the Beatles, it was considered very passé for bands to do nothing but covers. The Beatles were the first to stress that Rock was an art form, not merely a way to entertain sock hop morons or lovelorn teenagers.

"Please Please Me" was indicative of the band's high musical and lyrical standards. The first thing one noticed about a Beatles song was that there was a hell of a lot going on, as opposed to most records of the day (save for those produced by Phil Spector or Brian Wilson). "Please Please Me," for instance, moved rapidly through several vexing variations. The "c'mon c'mon" call-and-response buildup set the tone for the next several years of record making, in which the songs themselves would build to explosive climaxes (almost a lost art now).

The Beatles were all about excitement, no question. Sure, they threw in schmaltzy stuff for a quick sellout. But they weren't becoming famous for "This Boy" and "Til There Was You"—they were becoming famous for their string of walloping hit singles like "Please Please Me," "From Me to You," and "She Loves You." George Martin's excellent production helped render everything else anachronistic, primitive, and, worse yet, square. Bye-bye, Four Seasons.

The excitement was infectious. Crowds started to scream. Girls started to faint. And a few music biz people began to draw comparisons to names like "Sinatra" and "Presley."

Under their breath, that is, because at that time the Beatles were still considered very freaky. One way the Beatles would change all this was to weigh in heavily on the album market, which is where all the royalty money was. Save for Presley—who fell more into the "entertainer" category anyway—no one in Rock had been able to make a dent in this area. Like a heavyweight boxer who had to come up the hard way, the Beatles had to fight for respect every inch of the way, and it's to their credit that they succeeded, KO'ing the competition on almost every front until at least 1966 or so.

The Beatles' first album, *Please Please Me*, was recorded during a sixteen-hour all-night session in early 1963. The Beatles were used to doing such marathons, thanks to their experience in Hamburg. EMI was determined to not go over budget on such a dubious venture and urged the boys to work quickly. The result was as "live"-sounding a recording as could be hoped for, considering the circumstances.

That didn't help it sell in America, where Vee Jay records, the Four Seasons' label, had leased it. Vee Jay didn't seem to know how to promote the group, and the record languished in obscurity. A few weirdos heard it, but otherwise it went unnoticed. Americans would have to wait eight more months to discover the Fab Four (as they were becoming known back home).

Meanwhile in England, as Epstein had predicted, things were happening fast. During the spring of '63, the Beatles headlined a national tour for the first time with American pop legend Roy Orbison in tow. This helped propel *Please Please Me* to the top of the *Melody Maker* charts, where it stayed for an unprecedented thirty weeks! When it was finally knocked off the top slot, it was by the Beatles' second album. That kind of popularity was simply unheard of, even for Presley.

Nothing signaled the Beatles' arrival more than the "Sunday Night at the London Palladium" broadcast on October 13, 1963. By now the Beatles had long since surpassed the Cavern and were playing national—and soon to be international—venues. The Palladium was the biggest, and their performance drew so many fans that they blocked the streets. The next day the papers carried pictures of girls fainting and bobbies carrying them away. It was definitely a sign of things to come.

The Beatles kept recording at a frenetic pace. Their second album, *With the Beatles*, showed a marked technical improvement over their first. EMI was by now prepared to spend the big bucks to both promote and record the "lads" (as they affectionately became known). The cover, with its four ear-cropped moptops shrouded in the shadows, was one of the most mimicked album cover concepts of the '60s. As for the music contained in the grooves, at least half of the new compositions—"It Won't Be Long," "Not a Second Time," "All I've Got to Do" and George Harrison's "Don't Bother Me"—were shimmering in their brilliance.

At this point EMI knew they had a winner on their hands and was willing to take another aim at the American market—unfortunately, that was right about the time Lee Harvey Oswald was taking his aim at President Kennedy, and suddenly the country was beset by tragedy. For the next month, the assassination hung over the nation like a black cloud. As some sociologists have surmised, perhaps it was the void caused by the death of a president who had seemed to possess such youthful vigor that enabled the Beatles to so totally capture the imagination of America's youth.

EMI was relentless in its hype—the Beatles were scheduled to arrive in the United States on February 7, 1964. As early as December '63, Capitol Records, EMI's North American wing, was pressing copies of the "I Want to Hold Your Hand" single and *Meet the Beatles* album (an amalgamation of their first two British albums). They also distributed stickers, press releases, and other hype, including one million Beatles wigs, which became a popular novelty before the countercultural hordes got brash and grew their own.

Even all the hype couldn't have prepared the public, or the Beatles themselves, for what happened next. When the Beatles finally arrived at Kennedy

Airport—so named after the slain president—literally thousands of screaming youths were there to greet them, and the media were there to cover it. One airport official told the press: "We've never seen anything like this before. Not even for presidents and kings."

But the times they were a-changin'. Two days after their arrival, the Beatles made their successful debut on *The Ed Sullivan Show*, which was the American equivalent of the televised Palladium show back home. This was brilliant strategy on Epstein's part: Sullivan's show was, at that time, the most watched in America, and he was one of the most powerful moguls in the industry. Although he'd later have run-ins with other groups (the Rolling Stones, the Doors), he'd continue to host the Beatles whenever they appeared on these shores—and pay Epstein a sizable portion for the right.

Despite the Beatles' phenomenal success, acceptance from the "straight" world was slow in coming. Take, for instance, the opening paragraph of the *Newsweek* cover story dated February 24, 1964: "Visually they are a nightmare: tight dandified Edwardian beatnik suits and great pudding-bowls of hair. Musically they are a near-disaster: guitars and drums slamming out a merciless beat that does away with secondary rhythms, harmony and melody. Their lyrics (punctuated by nutty shouts of yeah, yeah, yeah!) are a catastrophe, a preposterous farrago of valentine-card romantic sentiments."

In light of this kind of condescension, the Beatles had their own ideas about America. As Lennon said: "When we arrived we knew how to handle the press. The British press are the toughest in the world; we could handle anything…And when we got here you were all walking around in fuckin' bermuda shorts with Boston crewcuts and stuff on your teeth…The chicks looked like 1940s. There was no conception of dress or any of that jazz. We just thought what an ugly race…and we thought how hip we were." [8]

McCartney concurred: "There they were in America, all getting house-trained for adulthood with their indisputable principle of life: short hair equals men, long hair equals women. Well we got rid of that small convention for them. And a few others too." [9]

All this talk about hair would have been irrelevant if it wasn't for the fact that the Beatles kept outdistancing the competition where it really counted—mainly, on the record charts. On April 4, 1964, they held the top five slots on the *Billboard* Top 100, with seven in the top ten as well as a smattering of hits in the lower depths. Even Elvis had never achieved this feat. When the Beatles weren't at number one that year, there was a good chance that a John-and-Paul-penned number for another group or artist—like Peter & Gordon's "A World Without Love"—was dominating the top slot.

The Beatles' arrival signaled the start of the British Invasion, so named because it meant that other British groups could start descending upon the American hit parade in alarming quantities. In 1964 alone, such significant British musical acts as the Rolling Stones, Manfred Mann, the Searchers, the Animals, the Kinks, and the Zombies would all place records in the top ten. As all these groups relied on heavily amplified guitars or organs, electricity became the navigating force of Rock 'n' Roll.

The Beatles were at the forefront of all this joyful noise. They were nothing if not clever, and the level of enthusiasm with which they approached their work—and that they subsequently injected into it—was palpable. Nowhere was this more apparent than in their first film, *A Hard Day's Night*, and its accompanying soundtrack. Lennon and McCartney were composing at a new level of sophistication with songs like "I'll Be Back," "When I Get Home," "I'll Cry Instead," and "Things We Said Today." The harmonies were getting stronger, and there was a complexity to the work that bespoke maturity—until then a foreign concept in Rock 'n' Roll. Part of the reason for this sudden maturity was the frantic pace that fame demanded, which would make anyone age overnight. As a result of their increasing sophistication, their work in the next few months would become simply airborne: songs like "Eight Days a Week" were downright ecstatic—the notes and harmonies literally hung in the air.

The film, meanwhile, showed that the Beatles, unlike Presley, had depth as "personalities" as well. It was in *A Hard Day's Night* that their four distinct personas came to the fore: John was "the smart one," Paul, "the cute one," George, "the quiet one," and Ringo, the normal average Joe with a heart of gold. At this point, the Beatles began to be taken seriously by cultural spokespeople like Dr. Joyce Brothers, Norman Mailer, and Arthur Schlesinger, Jr. The Beatles had now completed their assault on the public consciousness via two mediums: music and "celebrity."

Musically, the band continued to evolve. Albums like *Something New* and *Beatles '65* were pivotal in that they confirmed the fact that Country & Western was as much a part of their sound as Pop or Rhythm & Blues. This would be an important influx on the American music scene, helping young musicians discover redneck roots that might've otherwise evaded them. One need only mention the Byrds, the International Submarine Band, Lovin' Spoonful, Buffalo Springfield, etc.: country bumpkinism, and the English did it first! Coincidentally, the Beatles' American record label, Capitol, was a leader in the Country field, with down-home music makers like Merle Haggard and Roy Clark being their main money-pullers until the Fabs.

Another thing these albums established was Paul's role as the chief balladeer in the group. Songs like "And I Love Her" and "I'll Follow the Sun" became readily adaptable "standards" easily covered by non-Rock artists, which could work in the positive (Herbie Mann) or negative (New Christy Minstrels). In any case, it worked in favor of the Beatles' pocketbooks as far as publishing went. Because of this romantic manifestation in the Beatles' music, rockers were inspired to display their more "sensitive" leanings, which is why the Rolling Stones added sop to their repertoire like "As Tears Go By." This would in turn influence the wistful romanticism of the singer/songwriters in the next decade (Neil Young, Jackson Browne, James Taylor, Elton John, and other guys who wore their hearts on their sleeves).

The Beatles' innovations sparked a creative revolution in the world of Rock 'n' Roll. For instance, the mere *spurt* of feedback at the beginning of "I Feel Fine" foreshadowed the electrified eruptions of the Yardbirds and Who. The chiming twelve-string guitar played by George Harrison in *A Hard Day's Night* provided the impetus for the Byrds and a thousand other "folk-rockers." Even Bob Dylan, the only one besides perhaps the Rolling Stones to actually challenge the Beatles' mantle in the '60s, had gone electric.

Dylan became a colossal phenomenon in 1965 and, all of a sudden, critics were paying enormous attention to lyrics. Dylan had come from a folkie background, and his "protest" songs were rife with peculiar allegorical imagery. This put him in a decisive advantage over either Lennon or McCartney in the lyric writing category because, up until that time, most of their songs had been of the contrived boy/girl quality.

John Lennon was the first Beatle to explore more topical lyrical terrain. "I'm a Loser" on *Beatles '65* (*Beatles for Sale* in England) hinted that the smiley-face Beatle façade might not be entirely on the level. Lennon would pursue this vein of self-doubt even more on the next album with songs like "Help!" and "You've Got to Hide Your Love Away."

One of the things that might have inspired the Beatles to delve further "into their heads" was the fact that they'd began smoking marijuana. According to legend, it was Dylan who introduced them to pot during their first American tour in 1964. The Beatles, however, were no strangers to drugs: all during the Hamburg/Cavern years they used uppers to maintain their vigorous performance level. In the '60s, psychedelic drugs like marijuana and LSD became the preference of the young, rich, hip, and famous. Soon it would trickle down to the sandlot leagues. That's when the *real* revolution would begin (e.g., the Stooges).

The "artists" of the '60s viewed chemical consumption as an integral part of the creative process. The Beatles were no exception. According to Lennon in an interview much later, the whole time the band was making their second film, *Help!*, they were baked.

Although the Beatles' personal interests drifted towards the bohemian fringe, their public image was squeaky clean. Not only did they gleefully frolic through the uninspired *Help!*, but in May 1965 it was announced that they'd been awarded the royal MBE (Medal of the Order of the British Empire). This was Mother England repaying them for all the money they'd helped pump into the British economy. They were, at that time, Britain's most exportable item.

On a performance level, the Beatles were by now going through the motions. Such was the volume of the screaming fans that they couldn't even hear themselves play (sound systems in those days were much less efficient). This would soon convince them to give up touring altogether. In 1965, however, they couldn't just jump off the whirlwind they'd created. For one thing, Brian Epstein had sealed up engagements for the rest of the year. There's no doubt that the Beatles were at their absolute *zenith* when Sid Bernstein booked them for the legendary Shea Stadium concert on August 15 before 55,000 screaming fans. This event, more than any other, helped awaken promoters to the lucrative potential of live Rock. Within a few years, "stadium" concerts would be the norm.

The Beatles' dissatisfaction over performance conditions led them to become more ensconced in the womb-like security of the recording studio. The result was *Rubber Soul*, released in December 1965. By this time, the group's ambitions were clear—not only did they compose every song on the album (gone were the Rock 'n' Roll oldies) but also, almost as if to stress the album's cohesive singularity, no singles were released from it. So confident were the Fabs by now in the ability of their images alone to sell an album that nowhere on the front cover did the name "Beatles" appear. The cover was innovative in another way: the strange, distorted image of the Beatles' stretched faces—rendered with typical '60s "fisheye" photo technique—would inspire further visual trickery in the album packaging field. Rock album artwork was soon to become an industry in itself, in which the groups would demand to have their favorite artists design their record sleeves, such as the Stones with Michael Cooper, the Grateful Dead with Stanley Mouse and Big Brother & the Holding Company with R. Crumb. This all had to do with the rise of drugs.

Rubber Soul was the first Beatles album in which drug use was readily apparent—not just on the cover, but in the hypnotic lilts in the songs that could only have been conceived in the seclusion of the studio (and dreamed of in an altered state). Lyrically, the songs proved no less perplexing. *Rubber Soul* was also the first album on which George Harrison came into his own as a songwriter: "Think For Yourself" was full of weird harmonic shifts on a par with anything John or Paul had written.

Harrison was soon to exert an even bigger influence on the group due to his interest in Eastern music and philosophy. Already a big buzz among poets and intellectuals, Eastern religion was another by-product of the drug culture and consciousness-raising in general. Fortunately, Harrison's mystical inclinations were at this time still mostly musical. "Norwegian Wood" marked perhaps the first appearance of the Indian sitar on a Rock 'n' Roll record. By this time, however, there was a question as to whether what the Beatles were recording was even Rock 'n' Roll anymore. In any case, they were definitely pushing the boundaries of the form. Many times this meant outright non-Rock moves like the semi-Classical piano solo George Martin played on "In My Life," which once again confirmed their reputation with highbrows. The Beatles were having it both ways—inducing the hippie hordes on the one hand but charming the knickers off the bowtie and cufflink set on the other. All those comparisons to Schubert were starting to add up. In December 1965 it was reported that there had already been more than three hundred versions of "Yesterday." The song had only been out for three months.

The thing about the Beatles in those days was that they were always moving. Changing styles, instrumentation, even their appearance with every album, they were able to create a momentum that has seldom been matched. Lennon later admitted that, during those years, he saw himself "sending messages." For instance, in "The Word," Lennon states: "the word is love." Sure enough, within the next few years "love" *would* be the word among the hippies. Similarly, in "It's Only Love," he uses the phrase "I get high" in typical Tin Pan Alley fashion to describe the elation of love, but the fact was, he knew the double meaning and that's precisely the way he meant it.

Ah, yes: double entendres, hidden meanings, and the like. It could only have made sense under LSD. The implosion of acid in 1966 was to have a profound effect on the whole mindset of Rock 'n' Roll. The Rock scene in San Francisco, haven of the hippies, was based entirely around the experience of tripping. The whole record industry went mad for a while with psychedelic imagery, so much so that Petula Clark had multicolored florals exploding on her album covers. The shape, sound, and visual image of pop culture were becoming lysergically distorted.

LSD was originally conceived as an agent to help people overcome psychosis. This naturally resulted in a lot of deep inner reflection and emotional overhaul. Sometimes a person would relive his or her whole life in the course of one "trip." The whole soul-searching notion of "self-help" that became so popular in the next decade began with the acid. The first time the Beatles tried acid it was thanks to a dentist friend of George's, and they went mad driving their limos like submarines, etc. In other words, their shenanigans on the drug were akin to their winky-blink dope-smoking antics: pure fun. In Lennon's case, the drugs would eventually produce full-blown paranoia (as reflected by his later work).

To produce the accompanying psychedelic sounds, the Beatles became increasingly reliant on the properties of the modern recording studio (in large part assisted by George Martin). Like the Beach Boys at around the same time, who were also embarking on their own psychedelic voyage, the Beatles were becoming less of a performance unit and more of a studio tool—albeit a multifaceted one. To the band, touring had become all but irrelevant. The Beatles were seeking isolation so they could continue their "experiments" unfettered. This included drugs as well as music. By now the acid had magnified their musical vision to an almost Utopian sense of mission. Such were the trappings of guru-dom.

This was the age when acid freaks sat next to roto-styluses trying to decipher the "message" of each Beatles record. In 1966 they got plenty of 'em: "Nowhere Man" seemed another autobiographical step in John Lennon's road toward total alienation. "Rain," the flip side of the "Paperback Writer" single, was a reverberating piece of proto-psych that foretold doomsday woe and had Lennon chanting backwards through an oscillator. This was a technique George Martin would help him perfect on the next two albums.

Lennon was quickly becoming the most adventurous Beatle, not just in terms of his drug taking but also in the tunes he was composing at that time. "I'm Only Sleeping" was a creative collage of tape loops and interzoidal head sounds. Lennon, as dopefied jester, sneers and literally *coos* about how much he cherishes his precious sleep, a theme he'd repeat again in the near future. It was a very regal attitude, and it reflected a lot of the arrogant trappings that Rock was about to take on.

Lennon was also becoming the most publicly outspoken Beatle on other issues. In 1966 the group found themselves in the midst of controversy over a comment he'd made earlier that year to a reporter from the *London Evening Standard*: "Christianity will go. It will vanish and shrink. We're more popular than Jesus now." When these comments were taken out of context in August 1966, essentially being interpreted in the media as "Beatles Proclaim They're Bigger Than Christ," the group found themselves in the midst of an awkward and unwanted controversy just as they were about to embark on what was to be their final American tour (although no one knew it at the time). Brian Epstein made Lennon hold a press conference to apologize, mostly for PR reasons: some of the venues in the upcoming tour, particularly in the southern Bible Belt, had threatened to pull out at the last minute if Lennon didn't retract his "blasphemous" statements.

When the Beatles quit touring, Brian Epstein's role became minimal. For three years he had vigorously sold his boys to the world—at a higher price each time. He took care of their tours, film deals, and public image—but he had little influence on their music. It was during this period, however, that they were entering their most musically fruitful period. Epstein's days of dressing them up were over, in other words. And although this gave him more time to pursue the nightlife of London's "underground," it left him increasingly despondent. It was only when he died unexpectedly of a sleeping pill overdose the following year that it became apparent how important he'd actually been to the group.

In 1967 Rock had reached its apex as a cultural phenomenon. One of the great factors of '60s Rock was that such incredible refinement took place in such a short period of time. The Beatles always seemed to be at the forefront of it all. Still, as the Rock scene grew larger, reliance on superficial "leaders" like the Beatles, Elvis, or Bob Dylan (who'd warned against them anyway) became irrelevant. The "movement" itself had become more important than any single entity.

Before the Beatles ceased to be relevant they had one last fling, and it was the most momentous event of their career—and of the counterculture. Conscious of their musical development—and of their highly inflated but not totally unfounded myth—the Beatles set out in late '66 to create an album that would put the seal on the whole movement, an actual *event* that would rival the collective achievements of Western civilization itself. It's hard to believe a Rock n' Roll album could create such a stir, but in the primitive frenzy of the Rock Boom, that's what happened. Right place, right time…happens all throughout history.

There was more to it than that, though: the Beatles, at that time, *had* to come up with an ambitious offering because so many of their peers were challenging the parameters they'd established. The Beach Boys had just released "Good Vibrations," a construction so intricate that it took one hundred takes to perfect. Pink Floyd was out-hallucinating the Beatles with their light shows and with material like "Arnold Layne." Frank Zappa was cutting two-record sets with songs that all ran together. The Velvet Underground was playing screeching songs about whips. And Captain Beefheart & His Magic Band were distorting the Delta Blues through a weirdo-dadaist dope-soaked filter.

The Beatles were conscious of all these developments, which is exactly how *Sgt. Pepper's Lonely Hearts Club Band* came about. On a purely technical level, I suppose *Sgt. Pepper* was purty big cheez. But like *The Doors*, it hasn't aged well. The sound is technically proficient, playful, even fascinating, but it's not timeless. The Beatles marching through the purple haze in their bright band uniforms pledging to save the world "with our love" (this last courtesy of the acid-soaked Harri). They really had reached their stride, perfected their craft. You really could see how a whole generation of dopeheads could be gobbled up by its euphoric good vibes. But the big hoopla surrounding the album was hype— all it ultimately wrought was circus carousel sounds (the Hollies' "Carrie Ann,"

Spanky & Our Gang's "Sunday Will Never Be the Same," and a host of others) and psychedelic poesy lemon-drop lyrics—next thing you know someone invented the Strawberry Alarm Clock (Did I hear Lemon Pipers?).

"Getting Better" was a slap on the back from McCartney to the hippie hordes…we're winning, *we're winning*! But there was a darker side to it all: "Silly people stand there and disagree/And wonder why they don't get past my door." The paranoia had begun, in other words. (Or "I Choose the Sycophants I Want"—Paul.)

"She's Leaving Home" incorporated strings, which raised highbrows even higher. It was quintessential mid-'60s generation-gap fare dealing with a teenage runaway who leaves the nest because "fun is the one thing that money can't buy." Runaways were another whole aspect of the culture that grimly blossomed in the '60s (along with VD and serial killers). There was a grim malevolence that was beginning to pervade every aspect of the "underground." In many ways, *Sgt. Pepper* was like the last blast of uncorrupted '60s "fun." Soon such exuberant idealism would be replaced by cynicism, and the Beatles would pipe in on that one too, but in 1967 they had other priorities—like drugs, gurus, money, and women, in that order.

After all the accolades afforded *Sgt. Pepper* by everyone from Leonard Bernstein to the *Opera Times*, there seemed to be some distance between the Fab Four and the average kid on the streets. The myth is that all Rock at that time was undergoing similar highbrow pretensions, but that simply wasn't true. There was potent Rock being made everywhere, from the Pretty Things and Them in England to the MC5 and Shadows of Knight in the United States. But in 1967 it was all overshadowed by McCartney's music-hall sensibilities—inherited from his *father* for chrissakes—on pap like "When I'm 64." This must have helped turn a few hip rockers into Beatle-haters at that time. And the world has been full of Beatle-haters ever since (generally, anyone wishing to downplay the wuss quotient in Rock 'n' Roll). The Fabs' whole dalliance with cutesy-pie techniques—which sounded great to them because they were stoned—turned them into lightweights in the minds of rockers (and Rock historians) everywhere.

So while the Beatles "refined" the sounds/sensibilities of Rock 'n' Roll, supposedly for art's sake, they turned it into Pop as well. One thing people nowadays have a hard time understanding is that they weren't always one and the same. Little Richard was not Pop, nor was Chuck Berry or Gene Vincent.

They were Rock artists who had crossover success. They never compromised their basic sound/premise to achieve success. Starting with the advent of Elvis and then Buddy Holly and Phil Spector, Rock began to aspire to "hit parade" standards. But Rock, as a purely brutalizing musical form, went on nevertheless. Occasionally in the '60s Rock and Pop were on the same par (e.g., the Rolling Stones hits like "Get off My Cloud" and "19th Nervous Breakdown," which were enormously popular while still being uncompromising Rock 'n' Roll). But this was purely by accident. If the record companies had their way, they'd never have to deal with anything that creates friction, and when the Beatles made their move toward housewife muzak, they made it that much easier for companies to ignore the more eccentric—nay, *genuine*—artists and pad their rosters with people-pleasing tunesmiths. The Beatles were aware of this, which is why the remainder of their hits were astoundingly lightweight.

The Beatles ultimately left psychedelia behind, but it left a lasting impression on their psyches, particularly Lennon's. Always the group's most complex personality, Lennon came to feel stifled by what the Beatles had become. His reawakening came when he met Yoko Ono, a Japanese conceptual and performance artist who became his Earth Momma. Yoko had been staging "happenings" on the Lower East Side of New York for years, to little acclaim. When London gallery owner John Dunbar introduced Lennon to her in 1968, John apparently became smitten. Lennon's infatuation led to an open affair with the "artist," which brought about the demise of his marriage (since '63) to Cynthia Powell. It also helped bring about the demise of the Beatles.

The Beatles' partnership had been forged in blood back in the day, a brotherhood so righteous that women were not permitted to come between them. The wives waited at home while the band toiled endless hard day's nights in the studio or on tour. But as the partnership began to splinter in the late '60s, the various members of the group found themselves more interested in their own personal endeavors than those of the group—very often, this included their girlfriends. In Lennon's case it was the panorama of radical notions that Yoko exposed him to, which was just the excuse he was looking for to free himself from the "pop" confines of the Beatles.

In perfect hippie fashion, Lennon *refused* to be apart from Yoko—even while he was in the recording studio with the other chaps. This has proven time and again to be a detrimental factor to any band's existence. In Lennon's case, the other boys had to indulge him because he was, after all, the leader. He didn't just bring Yoko into the studio, however—he also brought her influence into the group: "Revolution #9," for instance, was a weird avant-garde melange that sounded more like John Cage than the Beatles.

Almost as if to stress the dissolution of the group's collective identity, the next album was simply entitled *The Beatles* and came in a plain white sleeve. There were four separate giveaway photos of the Beatles, but none of them together. As Lennon would later claim, they were, at this point, "acting as each other's session men." This would, of course, become the domain of Crosby, Stills, Nash, & Young as well as the patent for much of the sterile El Lay studio Rock of the '70s (Fleetwood Mac even did their own "white album"). The "white album" was in many ways the Beatles' last stand—even by today's standard, it's a pretty hip sonic barrage. It also showed that, for the most part, the Beatles had left the psychedelic circus-sounds of *Sgt. Pepper* behind and were getting ready to rock again.

Besides the slow disintegration of the group itself, there were other problems on the Beatles' horizon. In March 1969, both Lennon and McCartney were married: John to Yoko, Paul to American Rock photographer/groupie Linda Eastman. Linda's family were well-to-do New Yorkers, and Paul soon found himself assimilating to their middle class values. He also decided he wanted his brother-in-law, Lee Eastman, to represent his fortunes. Meanwhile, Lennon, Harrison, and Starr had chosen New York strong-arm lawyer Allen Klein to run their affairs. To further complicate matters, Dick James had sold his shares of Northern Songs, the Beatles' publishing company, to Sir Lew Grade, and there were many problems to sort out.

A year before, the Beatles had started their own record label, Apple, not only to represent them but to nurture new and "unusual" talent as well. *Unusual* was the key word here—Lennon in particular was in the midst of a radical rebirth (partly due to Yoko). As a result, the Beatles found themselves playing sugar daddies to any crazies who walked in off the streets. Unfortunately, most of the duds they sponsored never made it off the starting ramp (Magic Alex indeed!). *After* the Beatles paid them large sums of money, of course.

The Beatles' lack of business acumen was probably their undoing—which goes back to the death of Brian Epstein. The Beatles were basically unprepared to represent themselves. In retrospect, it probably wasn't a good idea for them to launch their own label. The jet set whirlwind they'd grown accustomed to—not to mention the drug indulgence—didn't leave much time for running a business. As a result, hippie hangers-on ripped them off left and right.

That was the problem with the Beatles: when they had ceased to be the number one most noteworthy group, their *moment* died. It had lasted a long time, but by 1970, when they officially split, they were merely spectators in the revolution they'd created. No one was looking to the Beatles for "the word" anymore. The only thing people in Rock 'n' Roll were looking for was a way to make money. Ultimately the Beatles failed in this regard, as they ended up giving away the store (Apple failed miserably). In this sense they had joined the realm of people like Elvis, Judy Garland, and Erroll Flynn: fossilized myths whose identities would always be preserved within the times they lived in. As far as Rock 'n' Roll went, it was the groups who'd followed in the Beatles' footsteps who'd ultimately go on to shape the future while the Beatles remained forever encapsulated in wax—and the minds of television documentary makers—forever.

CHAPTER 6

THE ROLLING STONES

THE ROLLING STONES HAVE OFTEN BEEN DUBBED "THE WORLD'S GREATEST ROCK 'N' ROLL BAND" but, in many ways, they represent the last decrepit bastion of genuine '60s hedonism. The fact that, as fifty-something billionaires, they're still out there prancing around makes matters even worse. They grew up to become what they always most abhorred. Then again, the game has changed a lot since then, and they had a lot to do with that too.

At their best, the Stones accomplished a polished hybrid of Black and white sources. In doing so, they breathed new life into each—no easy feat. Of all white Rock artists, the Stones have, time and again, proven themselves the most capable of interpreting Black material. At least in the beginning, the Stones existed solely from this "white blues" perspective—they sought to assimilate Black culture as well as music (Mick's rubbery-lipped moves weren't by accident, after all). It's partly through the filter of the Stones that people like Chuck Berry, Bo Diddley, and Muddy Waters became cultural touchstones.

One has to also understand how incredibly popular the Rolling Stones were in the '60s. It's a pretty safe bet that if a person listened to Rock in the '60s, he or she probably listened to the Stones. There isn't anyone that one can say that about now. Things have become more diversified. Once upon a time there were probably only a couple dozen "significant" Rock 'n' Roll bands in the known world. In the '60s, the Stones consumed a large enough slice of the pie to be second only to the Beatles.

The Stones' purist tendencies may have become corrupted as the years went by, particularly after the departure—and subsequent death—of founding member Brian Jones in 1969. However, they never stopped copping Black trends, from Reggae to Disco. In many cases, this won them the respect of the Black artists they were emulating. In the '60s, when all the British cats were copping Black sounds, only the Stones could claim that one of the most sacred of all Soul performers, Otis Redding, actually returned the favor ("Satisfaction" on his *Otis Blue* album from 1965). For purists this was the ultimate fait accompli.

It was no surprise that the Stones produced such a winning vibe, considering their musical backgrounds: drummer Charlie Watts and bassist Bill Wyman hailed from the Jazz milieu, and Brian Jones had played a myriad of instruments including clarinet, alto, and guitar before forming the Stones in 1962. The band's roots, however, did not lie in Jazz.

To the north of London, the Beatles and the Liverpool scene were beginning to make a stir. By contrast, in London at that time, a major Blues revival was underway. Chief among these purist aggregations were the musicians of Alexis Korner's Blues Incorporated, who deserve special credit for providing a virtual spawning ground for the first wave of British blues musicians. Korner's group was among the first to stress things like *chops*—they were a professional organization that took themselves seriously as musicians. Once the Beatles broke the doors wide open for English acts in general, Korner was too much of a geezer to cash in, but many of the bands that subsequently made it in America contained graduates of his musical finishing school.

Eventually Korner's group came to hold a residency at the Ealing Blues Club in London. Flyers for the band billed them as "the most exciting blues band in England," but what they were playing was probably closer to washed-out versions of American R&B. There simply wasn't much Blues impetus in London during that time. As the records all came from the United States, a musician's mastery of the idiom all relied on what he or she had or hadn't heard. Even musicians like Korner who were well versed in Black American music were dealing from a twice-removed perspective: once removed because they were English, and twice because they were white. It was difficult to be a purist in a country that hadn't produced any significant role models in one's chosen mode of expression.

The denizens of the early British Blues scene were like a small extended family: fellow travelers who swapped ideas and influences and sat in with each other's bands. In the early '60s, the clubs in London hadn't totally opened their doors to Blues yet, and there wasn't much work to go around. For this reason it was common for a committed Blues purist to be in several bands at once.

When the first wave of British Blues musicians came around, they weren't doing it to become famous. They looked at what they were doing as an act of fanatical, almost religious devotion. Once again, they were purists. They had no idea where it was all leading. As with any visionary quest, the process alone was stimulating enough.

One such Blues disciple was Brian Jones. From a well-to-do family in Cheltenham, the young Jones fit the description of a musical prodigy, but a rebellious streak soon put him at odds with his engineer father, who gave the boy the boot. That was after the young Brian had fathered two children out of wedlock before he was even eighteen years old. Adrift in London, the young punk eventually gravitated towards the Blues scene (which represented a certain subcultural element in itself). With Pat Andrews, the mother of his second child, in tow, Brian began his transformation into the life of a musician—which included staying out all night at clubs and sleeping all day. Needless to say, he was soon sans woman and child.

Jones apparently impressed Korner enough that Korner invited him to join Blues Incorporated. During that time, Korner's harmonica player, Cyril Davies—himself no spring chicken—taught Jones to play the instrument, adding to an impressive repertoire that already included clarinet, cornet, piano, saxophone, and guitar. Not surprisingly, later on, when the Stones started fooling around with more "eclectic" instrumentation in the studio, it was usually at Brian's behest.

Despite his prodigious talents, Brian's instrument of choice soon became the guitar, especially after he'd discovered the work of the American R&B great, Elmore James. Brian was entranced by the legend of the 6'2" Mississippian who made it a practice to play so drunk that he often fell off the stage. James's standard chord progression was a typical twelve-bar shuffle based on Robert Johnson, which he repeated ad infinitum. The guitarist left his mark on the entire first wave of Brit blues players, from the Stones to Eric Clapton, but he died before being able to reap the fruits of his enormous influence.

Jones soon formed a group of his own, using Korner alumnus Ian Stewart on piano. Playing informally without a name, they eventually merged with another group that was gigging around the same time: Little Boy Blue and the Blues Boys. Little Boy Blue was one Michael Philip Jagger and, like Jones, he was a Blues fanatic. The difference was, where Jones had chosen the musician's lifestyle unconditionally, Jagger was merely slumming—playing in a Blues combo while he waited around to get his degree from the London School of Economics.

Despite the security of this fallback position, Michael (or "Mick," as he was called) pursued his love of American R&B with vigor, even going so far as to send away to Chess Records in Chicago for albums. One day during a train ride home from the university he bumped into Keith Richards, the son of an electrician from the poorer side of the tracks, who'd attended grammar school with Jagger years earlier and had recently begun playing the guitar. Jagger happened to be carrying a Chuck Berry album that day and, coincidentally, Berry happened to be Richards's hero. This instantly rekindled their friendship. Jagger told Richards he was singing with a band, and Keith followed by saying he'd been jamming with someone named Dick Taylor at Sidcup Art School. The art schools at that time served as a refuge for wayward youths who were killing time until something more interesting came along; in many cases, this turned out to be music.

As Taylor remembered, Richards was a rebel from the start: "He was a real Ted, just a hooligan, and I used to really like him for that. I remember once the art school took us on a trip to Heal's, the furniture shop, because we were studying graphic design, and they wanted us to see well-dressed furniture. And Keith was sitting in this really nice sofa worth hundreds of pounds and quite casually dropping his cigarette on it and burning a hole in it and not giving a monkey's ass about it." [1]

This kind of behavior did little to endear him to even the liberal educators at Sidcup, and Keith—unlike Jagger—soon gave up all hopes of formal education with not so much as a twinge of regret (later on he'd recollect that what he liked best about Sidcup was "the bog"). From that point on, it was almost destiny that Richards would cross paths with the similarly rebellious Brian Jones. Shortly thereafter, the first incarnation of the Rolling Stones was born even though, at that time, they were still using the Blues Boys moniker.

As several members of Alexis Korner's band—Jones, Ian Stewart, drummer Charlie Watts—were now moonlighting as Blues Boys, it was inevitable that Jagger and Richards would be introduced to the influential bandleader as well.

Blues Incorporated was still the proving ground for virtually all the young British blues musicians emerging in those days. Korner had been a member of Chris Barber's pioneering "trad" Jazz unit in the '50s. As he remembered: "Chris…started bringing over electric blues players from the States—Otis Spann, John Lee Hooker, Muddy, people like that. And he was cutting his own throat and killing the trad jazz scene by having this R&B unit within the band. He knew exactly what he was doing, fostering the thing that was going to come next in music." [2]

At a time when Blues-worshipping Brits looked upon Black American musicians as almost supernatural beings, seeing their idols right there onstage helped lend additional validity to their purist intentions. If their idols were willing to come over and jam with them, the Brits figured they were doing something right. This helped them maintain their integrity.

In 1962 Jagger et al. were still weathering their internships within the patriarchy of Blues Incorporated. Jagger had already begun to express his distaste for some of the more trad-based arrangements. Korner, meanwhile, had begun to notice that the increasingly younger audience was paying more attention to Jagger's flamboyant antics than to the band itself. For an outfit that had always prided itself on its chops, this was somewhat illuminating. Inevitably, before the end of the year, Mick, Keith, Brian, and Ian Stewart decided to branch off from Blues Incorporated. Watts would remain for at least a few more months, while Dick Taylor drifted back to art school only to re-emerge with the seminal Pretty Things a couple of years later.

After adding drummer Tony Chapman, the band changed their name to the Rolling Stones after Muddy Waters's "Rollin' Stone." This kind of indebtedness to Black R&B pioneers on the part of the British musicians ultimately benefited the Blues artists themselves. Whereas before, in a record store, a Muddy Waters album would be filed under Folk or some other hoary category, after the Rock explosion of the '60s, these guys became Rock stars in their own right. It was this kind of foresight on the part of the Stones and other groups that helped establish the mutual admiration society that would soon exist between the Britons and the Blacks. This resulted in situations like Sonny Boy Williamson having the Yardbirds record an album with him upon his first trip to England in 1964 (which also served as the band's recording debut).

The Stones' arrogant, aggressive nature caused riots and violent episodes wherever they played. According to legend, Brian was the primary catalyst. As

Anthony Scadutto observed: "His insecurity made it necessary for him to prove something. He would pick an argument with a customer in a club, knowing he was certain to get beat up…jumping on the edge of the stage and snapping a tambourine in their faces, leering at them, daring them to attack. His performances made his friends worry about Brian's balance." [3]

Sounds kind of like G. G. Allin, doesn't it? With Mick perfecting his flimsy rubberman persona and Brian and Keith acting the part of the prototypical bad boys, the Stones were already honing the image of the modern Rock band. The only part of the musical equation lacking at this point was a bassist, a gap soon filled by Bill Wyman, an ex-RAF (Royal Air Force) man who possessed the necessary amplification to make him a shoe-in for the role. Wyman was also married, which pleased Jagger, who was already getting possessive about the limelight. The fact that Wyman was content to remain in the background made him an instantly tractable factor.

Convincing Charlie Watts to join the group full-time proved to be more difficult. Although the Stones had a full-time drummer in Tony Chapman, nobody had gelled with the group as effectively as Watts. Like Wyman, Watts was married and perfectly willing to remain in the background and keep the beat. Finally, in February 1963, he consented, and the Rolling Stones' lineup was complete. The band also found a manager of sorts in filmmaker Giorgio Gomelsky. The Russian immigrant also owned the Crawdaddy Club in London, and the Stones were able to parlay a Sunday night residency of sorts. George Harrison came down and checked 'em out, and the press began to take notice (England at that time enjoyed a much more sophisticated music press than the United States).

Because Gomelsky had never signed the band to a proper contract, he had no real safeguard against other sly entrepreneurs coming along trying to usurp his managerial duties—an inevitability in the case of property as hot as the Stones. But the manager who hustled the Stones away from Gomelsky was no seasoned hustler. In fact, he was even younger than the Stones themselves and, as a result, shared their flair for outrageousness.

Andrew Loog Oldham had worked his way his way up into the thick of Swingin' London via apprenticeships with two of the most prominent British pop culture sensations: designer Mary Quant and the Beatles, for whom he served as publicist during the *Please Please Me* era. However, when the Fabs ultimately settled on Tony Barrow to perform that function, Oldham was out of a job. By then he had his eye on the Stones, an act whose flamboyance seemed to match his own (Oldham was one of the first men to openly wear mascara).

Encouraging the Stones to play up their more "camp" tendencies, Oldham was the first manager to play off the negative contrast between his charges and the Beatles, who had a very "cuddly" image as opposed to the Stones' darker, uglier image. In other words, by positioning themselves as the opposite of the Beatles, the Stones gained a lot of notoriety. Enough anyway to get them signed to Decca, whose A&R man Dick Rowe was undoubtedly looking for a way to save face after having turned down the Beatles. Part of the deal was that each Stones record would bear the imprint of something called "Impact Sound," the name of Oldham's production company. This guaranteed him an extra percentage of every record sold, even though he'd confessed that he didn't know a "bloody thing" about record production. It was also a clever disguise for a ripoff perpetrated by Oldham, Jagger, and Richards (unbeknownst to Brian Jones, who apparently was left out of the proceedings).

Although soon, at the urging of Oldham, Jagger and Richards would begin writing their own material, at this point the Stones were still basically a glorified cover band. Not surprisingly, their first recording for Decca, released in June 1963, was a rendition of an obscure Chuck Berry tune called "Come On," which the Stones wimped out considerably. Whereas in Berry's version he'd spewed invective against the idiot who kept bugging him with incessant phone calls, labeling him "some stupid jerk," Jagger gentrified it into "some stupid guy." The band wasn't much to brag about either. This was probably due to the fact that they felt rushed making the record, as Decca had afforded them only three measly hours of studio time. Obviously, at that time the label didn't consider the Stones to be of much consequence. Jagger was already starting to mouth off, which angered Decca engineer Roger Savage but delighted Oldham.

Although Ian Stewart played on these and almost all subsequent Stones releases, it was decided around this time to trim the group down to a five-piece, probably for monetary reasons as much as image. The thirty-year old "Stu" didn't fit the group's juvenile delinquent persona anyway, so he became their official "road manager" and session pianist, a demotion that didn't seem to bother him in the least, considering his continued loyalty to the group (the money probably didn't hurt).

For the Stones' next record, Oldham wisely looked to his former employ-
ers, the Beatles, for a helping hand. Lennon/McCartney-penned compositions
had already proven a successful formula in the hands of Cilla Black, the
Fourmost, Gerry & the Pacemakers, and others. Why not the Stones? John
and Paul gave them a song they'd written in about ten minutes called "I Wanna
Be Your Man." The Stones went ahead and totally *shredded* the Beatles' version.
The rivalry was on, and it would not cease for the next six years.

While Epstein dressed the Beatles up, Oldham dressed the Stones down.
That is, he encouraged them to deliberately wear ratty, mismatched threads,
which only enhanced the band's nihilistic persona. Apparently the band members were more than happy to live up to the image: Jagger's girlfriend at the
time, model Chrissie Shrimpton, told tales of how he pushed her around; Brian
Jones, meanwhile, was a well-known purveyor of domestic violence. It was
almost as if they were trying to become the living embodiment of Anthony
Burgess's novel, *A Clockwork Orange*, which had just come out. There was even
talk of a film version, with the Stones portraying the droogies. Girls may have
screamed and fainted when Elvis or the Beatles played, but when the Stones
played, people *rioted*. Many times this was due to the band's direct provocation,
like the time in Scotland when Keith Richards lowered the Cuban heel of his
Chelsea boot into the face of one of his detractors and the three hundred or so
onlookers went apeshit and tore up the place.

It wasn't long before word about these provocateurs spread to the United
States. The Beatles had already landed on February 9, 1964. This opened the
floodgates for an onslaught of limey bands to invade the American market.
Perceived as being the only British group, at least at this point, with a style distinctly different from the Beatles, the Stones were able to establish their niche
immediately. Their first album, *England's Newest Hitmakers*, sold fairly well for
what was essentially a hardcore R&B record. The album cover was classic—they
looked at you with a leer…cold, unforgiving—and in unmatched suits! Unlike the
Beatles, the Stones never smiled in pictures. This whole punk aura would become
the prototype for a million bands, from the Pretty Things to the Stooges.

On the Stones' first album, musical role models included Chuck Berry
("Carol," "Route 66"), Jimmy Reed ("Honest I Do," "Little By Little"), Muddy
Waters ("I Just Want to Make Love to You"), and Phil Spector ("Tell Me"). In
the case of the latter, this was primarily Oldham's influence as, according to

Jagger: "Andrew was so influenced by Phil Spector it was disgraceful." Spector happened to be in England while the Stones were recording the album and ended up playing piano on "Now I Got a Witness." The album may not have been recorded in the highest fidelity—thanks to Oldham—but in almost every other regard the Stones sounded ready to take on the United States.

When they finally arrived in the U.S. for their first tour in the summer of 1964, far from starting riots, the bands had a hard time filling even the most modest-sized auditoriums. Still, they received a lot of publicity, if only for their ungainly appearance. Their close friend, David Bailey, who was the most successful fashion photographer in England, was quick to expose the Stones' zit-laden faces in all the glossy magazines. Once the Stones hit New York they flocked right to Andy Warhol's Factory for a "screen test" and Baby Jane Holzer, one of Warhol's "superstars," gushed about how sexy they were compared to the "fat" Beatles (which apparently anguished the increasingly paranoid John Lennon).

A pair of excellent albums, *12 x 5* and *Now*, helped solidify the Stones' status among hardcore fans and fellow musicians. The liner notes on *Now*, written by Oldham, were a classic attempt to shore up the group's bad boy image in almost *Clockwork*-ian terms: "Thrust deep into your pocket for loot to buy this disc of grooves and fancy words. If you don't have the bread, see that blind man, knock him in the head, steal his wallet and behold, you have the loot. Another one sold."

From the moment Mick and Keith saw how quickly the Beatles had knocked off "I Wanna Be Your Man," they began thinking about composing their own material. Brian Jones's big mistake was that he believed the group should stick with the more traditional material that had made them famous. This would be a conflict for many musicians coming out of the incestuous London Blues scene, most notably Eric Clapton, who quit the Yardbirds on similar grounds. In Jones' case, he was merely outvoted, which may have been his downfall in the group. It was possible he was jealous of Jagger and Richards—after all, it was said that, although Jones was capable of coming up with a riff or two, he was incapable of ever finishing anything. In that case, who knows how many "Jagger/Richards" tunes contain sections Mick and Keith nicked from Jones? Although one thing that's clear in retrospect is that, even at this point, Jones's role as a productive member of the group was diminishing.

Once Mick and Keith started writing, they forged a brotherhood that was impossible for Brian to infiltrate.

Early hits like "Heart of Stone," "The Last Time," "Play with Fire," and "Satisfaction" demonstrated the first flowering of the Stones' more chauvinistic traits. This was the element they would bring to Rock—a worldly kind of machismo that resigned women to the role of faithful lapdogs. The Stones were merciless in their assumed superiority. This would have a profound impact on future generations of rockers, mainly because it was such an easy role to assume once the ephemera of fame had attached itself. The result was an almost Roman mentality concerning sybaritic excess.

Because of their sexual sophistication, the Stones would aid the Rock maturation process considerably. "The Spider and the Fly" told the tale of the rocker on the road looking for the quick sex fix, which, in this case, took the form of an aged floozy. "She was *common*," scoffs Mick, once again betraying his elitist tendencies. If there were any doubt about Mick's casual attitude concerning sex, one only had to listen to "The Singer Not the Song" from *December's Children* (1965) in which Mick compares his current lover to the string of groupies who "do it without thrilling me." He seemed to be saying that women were expendable.

The group's sexism took an even more vicious turn after months on the road had taken its toll. "19th Nervous Breakdown" took deadly aim at a spoiled rich bitch to a Punk-Rock juggernaut of breakneck guitars and clattering drums. On *Aftermath*, the first album on which they composed all their own songs (copying the Beatles, who'd done the same thing six months earlier with *Rubber Soul*), the subject matter was usually women, and it was not often flattering. "Under My Thumb" was the classic macho putdown in which the girl takes on the role of sexual servant. Mick came from a fairly affluent background and was conscious of class as well. "Your manners are never quite right," he sang on "Back Street Girl," relegating the girl to private, Lewinsky-like suck-buddy status.

The Stones' contempt wasn't reserved for women, however. They were not only among the first to express the travails of Rock star life ("Flight 505"), but they even lampooned the music industry itself. In "The Under Assistant West Coast Promotion Man" they sent up the record company flak that accompanied them on their first American tour. This showed total disrespect for the protocols of "show business," which the Stones and their ilk were about to transform into the youth-based industry it is nowadays. At least the Stones admitted that hack George Sherlock was "the necessary talent behind every Rock 'n' Roll band" (particularly, one supposes, the *Stones*, nudge-nudge, wink-wink).

Despite such playful barbs, there was an even darker side to the Stones that was beginning to manifest itself in songs like "Paint It Black." What else would a person say about a song that proclaimed "my heart is Black"? The song itself moved along in violent jerks, punctuated by manic drum rolls courtesy of Charlie Watts, punk-strum from the guitarists, and Jones doubling on the then-trendy sitar (which once again outraged John Lennon, who claimed the Stones had ripped off the Beatles again).

The Stones were also the first group to be publicly busted, which stirred up a lot of controversy in the Summer of Love in 1967. There they were, in all their glory, relaxing at Keith's home in Redlands enjoying a few joints or whatever, when there was a knock on the door. They'd all taken acid earlier in the day—as British or American Rock stars were wont to do at the time—and it seemed like a big joke when they opened the door only to see all these Keystone-like constables lined up behind the one bearing the search warrant. At that time in England, busting a famous Rock star was a badge of pride among law enforcement officials, and the Stones were a prized catch.

In the Stones' case it only helped solidify their rep as the princes of debauchery, especially when it was revealed that British chanteuse Marianne Faithfull—Mick's girlfriend at the time—was wrapped naked in a fur rug. To make examples of them, the British authorities threw Jagger and Richards in prison. But the Stones chose to reflect the experience with humor. "We Love You" from the summer of '67 featured slamming guitar "jail" doors and the sardonic refrain "we love you/of *course* we do!" Humor was always one of the Stones' fortés, as in "Miss Amanda Jones" on the underrated *Between the Buttons* album in which they hint that the girl in question might actually be a *man*. The Chuck Berry rhythms were a little too fast, almost as a sarcastic reminder of how far the Stones had come from their humble origins already.

Although Andrew Oldham had been partially responsible for encouraging the Stones to play up their darker side, by 1967 the group was beginning to have reservations about his PR tactics, not to mention his business acumen. After a bitter argument with Mick during the recording of *Their Satanic*

Majesties' Request, Oldham stormed out, never to return. By then he'd already started his own label, Immediate, whose artists inevitably relied on songs written by Mick and Keith, such as "Sittin' on a Fence" by Twice as Much, or "Out of Time" by Chris Farlowe (who was Mick Jagger's brother).

Brian Jones, at this point, was on his way to being slowly edged out of the group as well. The real friction began when his girlfriend, Anita Pallenberg, began going out with Keith instead of Brian. Jones had beaten her regularly, and after he started taking acid, he was a perpetrator of bad scenes in general, from emotional breakdowns to violent episodes. Whereas good ol' Keith was utterly passive: give the guy a fifth of whiskey and some heroin, and put on a Hound Dog Taylor album, and he'll have a perpetual shit-eating grin on his face. Henceforth, Anita, who aspired to be an actress, found Keith to be a much more suitable boyfriend. It was important that she bagged a *Stone*, after all, but which one didn't really matter. (Her subsequent movie career proved that heroin and bad teeth are never criteria for on-screen glory.)

There was more to Brian Jones's demise than the defection of his girlfriend to the arms of another Stone. Between his constant drug hassles and ego problems, there was also the fact that Brian openly hated the new psychedelic direction the Stones were taking. Always a purist, Brian wished to return them to the Blues firmament that they'd built their reputation on. In this case, he was right: *Their Satanic Majesties' Request*, released at the tail end of 1967, was a lame attempt to mimic *Sgt. Pepper*, and the critics savaged it.

The year 1968 was one of decisions for the Rolling Stones. It posed new questions about not only management and Brian, but also what direction their music should take. The decision came in the form of "Jumpin' Jack Flash," a slab of three-chord mayhem that helped the Stones once and for all solidify their position as the dark princes of Rock 'n' Roll. No lutes or harpsichords on this one—it was all rhythm, caused by distortion, caused by power chords, caused by guitars—probably caused by drugs. The band had finally worked out its Chuck Berry fixations, finding a way to combine their basic Blues compulsions with the sinister underpinnings of their new liege-like status. The promo clip (read: Rock video) that accompanied the track foreshadowed the New York Dolls and other glam rockers by about four years.

In November 1968, the Stones released one of their best albums, *Beggar's Banquet*. In sharp contrast to *Satanic Majesties*, the album was rustic and unadorned, harking back to the band's Blues roots with songs like "Parachute Woman" and "Prodigal Son" (a cover of an obscure Fred McDowell song). The track that caught the most attention was the opener, "Sympathy for the Devil," in which the Stones parodied the aura of "evil" that was increasingly being attributed to them. "Street Fighting Man" was an incendiary track celebrating the anarchy that was occurring all over the world in the form of youth riots, first in France that May, and then later in Chicago. "Stray Cat Blues," on the other hand, was an ode to jailbait that utilized the Velvet Underground's "falling spikes" guitar sound to evoke malice.

It was a great comeback for the Stones, but by this time, Brian Jones was barely part of the picture. In fact, judging by the "documentary" that filmmaker Jean-Luc Godard made about the group around this time (called *Sympathy for the Devil*), they weren't even miking him in the studio anymore (unbeknownst to him, of course). Jones had become too temperamental and erratic to maintain even a secondary role in the band, and in early 1969 it was announced that the guitarist had parted ways with his old cronies over "musical differences." It went a lot deeper than that, but that was at least part of it— Jones in many ways viewed his separation from the band as a chance to re-emerge as a bandleader of some sort. There were even rumors that he might start a band with John Lennon, who was feeling similarly disenchanted about the Beatles' musical direction (nothing ever came of it, although the pair did produce the unusual track "You Know My Name," which later appeared on the B-side of a Beatles single).

The Stones replaced Jones with a young blond guitarist named Mick Taylor, who'd replaced Peter Green (who'd replaced Eric Clapton) in John Mayall's Bluesbreakers. Taylor's style was more fluid than Brian's, and it would play a large part in shaping the Stones' sound in the '70s. Three weeks after Taylor joined the band, Brian was found drowned in his swimming pool, on July 3, 1969. It was well known that he'd been suffering in a severe depression ever since he was edged out of the Stones, the band he'd created, and many suspected that his death was a suicide. The Stones immediately threw a free concert in London's Hyde Park to eulogize him and also took the opportunity to preview Taylor to the masses (as well as Mick's new white dress, which he wore for the occasion).

One of the problems that Jones had saddled the Stones with was the fact that his frequent drug busts had prevented him from leaving the country. This was of serious consequence to a band whose most lucrative success came from abroad. Almost from the beginning, the Stones had staked their reputation on being one of the premiere live attractions in Rock 'n' Roll. The fact that they were unable to take the show on the road irked Jagger and Richards in particular. Brian's departure from the group—and subsequently all earthly existence—enabled the group to tour the United States for the first time in three years. Commencing on November 7, 1969, the tour proved that timing was everything. Although hugely successful for the most part, it would culminate in an event that would solidify the Stones' reputation as Evil Incarnate. It would also drive a stake into the heart of the utopian '60s myth.

In 1969, Woodstock had just happened, and everyone was thinking in terms of community. The time seemed ripe for the Stones to cash in on the good vibes by offering a free concert of their own. This wasn't a totally altruistic gesture on their part: they planned to film the event and beat the founders of Woodstock at their own game. As usual for the Stones, the whole thing was one massive publicity stunt.

One has to remember, this was the beginning of the era when Rock stars were buying castles in France, and the Stones would be among England's first expatriate tax exiles. Other than Elvis Presley, no one in Rock 'n' Roll had ever made the kind of money that bands like the Stones were garnering at that time. These young millionaires were undoubtedly on a heavy narcissism trip, and all their whims seemed obtainable. As a result, the record companies were bending over backwards to accommodate them. It's no wonder that Jagger, perhaps the preeminent pampered Rock star, envisioned an event so magnum that it would cap off not only the tour, but the '60s as well.

Woodstock had been relatively free of casualties. The Rolling Stones' freebie, on the other hand, was doomed from the start. Under sneaky politics, the concert site was changed at the last minute, from the Sears Point Raceway outside of San Francisco to the Altamont Speedway in Livermore, twenty miles east. Melvin Belli, the famous trial lawyer, stepped in to help the Stones and, at this point, as Anthony Scaduto observed: "The free concert—love and peace and good vibrations for the kids—was starting to be seen for what it was: corporate strategy, big business, and all the sleazy elements of Western society that the underground and the 'Woodstock Nation' said it despised, and for which the Stones had once seemed to offer a revolutionary antidote."[4]

To make matters worse, the Stones had decided, apparently on the suggestion of the Grateful Dead, to hire the San Francisco chapter of the Hell's Angels to "police" the event. This was a common practice within the hippie culture at that time, but anyone who's ever read Hunter Thompson's *Hell's Angels* knows that bikers are no hippies. Their gestalt is based on brute force, not radical ideology. During the acid age, however, there became a common bond between the nascent youth culture and the bike gangs—mainly, drugs. Although the Stones reputedly settled their tab with the Angels by giving them fifty cases of beer, it wouldn't be unreasonable to assume that some kind of narcotics payoff may have also taken place. Given the circumstances— mainly, the preference for drugs by both parties involved—it would, in fact, seem most likely.

The concert went on as planned, on December 6, 1969: by all reports, a good time was had by no one. This included the Stones, who were finally overwhelmed by their own grandiose hellfire fantasies. There was Mick prancing around onstage in a red velvet cape trying to look like a little devil, all the while being flanked by a bunch of psychopaths. The Angels had already knocked out Marty Balin of the Jefferson Airplane, and the hippies were finding out that the bikers weren't the type of people you can reason with. The Stones now found themselves held hostage to their own bizarre ego trip.

It was a frigid December night, and the mood of the event had taken on a dark hue from the start. The irony was, there was Mick onstage singing "Sympathy for the Devil." When it was over, a Black teen had been beaten and stabbed to death by the Angels. It probably didn't help that he had a white girlfriend. The Angels weren't known for being racially tolerant either. As for the Stones, they got their movie out of it anyway (despite being sued by the victim's mother).

To coincide with the American tour, the Stones released a new album, cryptically entitled *Let it Bleed*. Although it was the band's first album with Mick Taylor, the texture was still largely the same as the previous album, *Beggar's Banquet*. There were a lot of rustic Blues and Country elements combined with several decadent rockers, not the least of which was "Gimme Shelter," a cathartic performance that seemed to serve as the swan song of the '60s with its foreboding vision of imminent apocalypse. Other songs like "Midnight Rambler" and "Monkey Man" were equally steely-eyed. But the Stones were still hard to take seriously, because the whole time they were creating this frightening music, Mick was onstage grasping his fanny.

Mick was soon to venture even further into narcissism with a starring role in the film *Performance*. In the movie he played an aging Rock star cooped up in a country estate with two groupies (one played by Anita Pallenberg). A gangster on the lam, James Fox, appears and the two slowly swap identities until Mick ends up getting snuffed by underworld figures and Fox fucks the chicks. The theme song, "Memo From Turner," was probably the most depraved Stones opus yet, with a plethora of dark images running through it, from gangland-style violence to sadomasochism. It demonstrated that, far from learning their lesson from Altamont, the Stones were plunging into the new decade with the same decadent abandon as always.

Changes were brewing for the Stones in the '70s. For the past seven years the band had been signed to Decca in England. Although the deal was lucrative enough for its time, the market had expanded threefold since then and the Stones, perhaps the top grossing concert act in the world, wanted a bigger slice of the pie. They were also displeased with Decca over other issues, such as distribution and the fact the label had refused to issue the original album cover art for *Beggar's Banquet* (which featured a toilet).

In 1971, they left Decca for Atlantic, a label the band very much admired due to its pioneering efforts in the field of R&B. Part of the deal was that the Stones would launch their own subsidiary, called Rolling Stones Records, which would bear the logo of the eponymous red lips and tongue. Long rid of the unscrupulous Allen Klein, whom the Stones had pawned off on the Beatles, they were now totally in charge of their internal affairs.

The Stones' first album on their own label, *Sticky Fingers*, gave a good idea where the band was headed in the '70s: a lot of long jams and sloppy material like "Sway" that showed they'd become consummate drunks as opposed to acidheads like a lot of their '60s brethren. The music was earthy, grounded in the same elements they'd always utilized, from Chuck Berry ("Brown Sugar") to Memphis Soul ("I Got the Blues") to Country ("Dead Flowers"). It was laid back music, and the Stones, to their credit, were among the first to realize that the apocalyptic vision of Altamont and "the revolution" was soon to fade into the mere hedonistic excess—and boredom—of the '70s. The album also established Mick Taylor as a genuine factor and served as the prototype for the band's sound for the next several years.

Besides Mick's media-event marriage to Bianca, the big news in the Stones camp during 1971 was that they were moving to the South of France to become England's first Rock 'n' Roll tax exiles. This was due to England's harsh tax laws, whereby performers and entertainers were only allowed to keep ten percent of their earnings. When the Stones arrived, they made themselves right at home as usual, staying awake on three-day drug and alcohol binges in Keith's basement studio, recording all the new songs Mick and Keith had written with whatever musicians happened to be passing through. By the time the band finished recording, they had enough material for two LPs, which they decided to release as their first-ever double album, *Exile on Main Street*. The band took a lot of heat from the critics when the LP was first released in 1972, but by the end of the year most of them had reversed their opinion. The music had a certain thickness, partly thanks to Jimmy Miller's production, which rendered most of the lyrics indecipherable. Nevertheless, all the band members played to the fullest extent of their talents, and, as a result, *Exile* was probably the peak of the Rolling Stones' career.

To correspond with the album's release, the Stones once again embarked on a cross-country American tour, which turned out to be their biggest one ever, at least until the days of *Steel Wheelchairs* et al. Barnstorming across the country in what was an election year, the Stones garnered almost as much media coverage as the presidential race. Mick was on the cover of *Life*, and the whole spectacle was featured on the CBS-TV news magazine *60 Minutes*. Filmmaker Robert Frank was there as well, but the resulting documentary, *Cocksucker Blues*, proved even too scandalous for the Stones, who forbid its release because it depicted them indulging in a host of scurrilous—as well as illegal—activities.

The irony of being thirtysomething and still living the Rock 'n' Roll lifestyle was not lost on the Stones, and the next two albums, *Goat's Head Soup* (1973) and *It's Only Rock' n' Roll* (1974) were attempts to come to terms with that. The musicianship certainly couldn't be faulted even if at times the energy level sank to armchair proportions. Being the youngest member of the band, Mick Taylor was always pushing to discover his own voice, and his sinuous leads during those years did a lot to help jell the rhythm section. But as the veteran Stones settled into their Old Fart personas, Taylor grew bored and quit the group shortly after *It's Only Rock 'n' Roll*. With his departure, they lost something they were never able to regain—mainly the opportunity to have two excellent guitarists with two distinctly different styles. His replacement, Ron Wood, was fine, but he played in basically the same style as Keith Richards— in fact, his earlier band, the Faces, were almost a carbon copy of the Stones. After Wood joined, the Stones' music grew increasingly uniform, almost to the point of self-parody (which, admittedly, they were already verging on as early as "Jumpin' Jack Flash").

The first thing the new lineup did was to embark on another major U.S. tour in 1975. Although, unlike in '72, they had no new product at stake this time (save for a couple of lame "greatest hits" albums), the fans came out in droves anyway. This was important because it proved to the record companies that the Rock audience was chiefly indiscriminate and would pay for the "name" alone. The Stones' own lack of productivity during this period as far as recording goes can be attributed to Keith Richards's ongoing struggles with the law over his various heroin offenses. It took the group more than a year to record their next album, and then when it came out it was no great shakes. The most important thing about *Black & Blue* was that it demonstrated the Stones' new preoccupation with Reggae, but in the year of the Ramones, it sounded tired.

Some Girls in 1978 was hailed as a big breakthrough and "comeback," but it actually rocked no harder than *It's Only Rock 'n' Roll*. The Stones could still come up with inventive rhythms when they tried ("When the Whip Comes Down"), but most of the time it was down to rote. Credit the stalwart rhythm section, particularly drummer Charlie Watts, with rescuing otherwise mundane material. There was little distinguishing one song from another, but despite this fact all the aging Rock critics, from Jann Wenner to Robert Christgau, vindicated the album for "coming to terms" with the Punks. What they—the critics—were actually doing was grabbing a hold of the last fleeting vestige of youth, which they saw receding as quickly as Charlie's hairline or Keith's bridgework.

The Stones did some serious jamming one last time, on side two of the *Tattoo You* album in 1981, but that was absolutely the *last* time they were "relevant" in any way. The best they could do after that was to make use of their celebrity and to survive. They couldn't really break up, because it was unthinkable that any member other than possibly Mick or Keith could ever have a solo career. It was in all of their vested interests to just keep going. Their collective identity as the "bad boys of Rock 'n' Roll" sealed their fate. It also made them an anachronism in light of Punk, Rap, Grunge, and other musical and cultural developments that would come along in the '70s, '80s, and '90s.

That didn't stop the aging grannies—in the form of the Baby Boomers this time—from coming out in droves, just like they had for Elvis. The dinosaur/oldies status befitted a group who'd stopped exploring in an artistic sense ever since Taylor had left the group (Charlie Watts's stand-up Jazz tributes or Keith's L.A. thrashing doesn't count—not to mention Jagger's pathetic "acting" career). The Stones didn't give a hoot about their "legacy"—staging tour after tour, each one more grandiose, they milked the legend for all it was worth. By doing so, they'd effectively negated their own value in the annals of the music that they were so instrumental in helping define two generations ago.

"When I'm 33, I quit. That's the time a man has to do something else. I can't say what it will definitely be. It's still in the back of my head— but it won't be in show business. I don't want to be a rock n' roll singer all my life. I couldn't bear to end up as an Elvis Presley and sing in Las Vegas with all the housewives and old ladies coming in with their handbags. It's really sick. Elvis probably digs it." [5]   —Mick Jagger

CHAPTER 7

BOB DYLAN

THE '40S WERE A TIME OF GREAT PROGRESS IN AMERICAN MUSIC, but few people knew it because most of the developments were taking place in either the Black or redneck fields. All through the Southern states, the Appalachians, the West Coast, and Texas, pioneering sounds were being wrought, but most people only heard the Swing bands of Gene Krupa and the Dorsey Brothers. By the end of the '40s, however, many of the nascent musical forms that had been gurgling beneath the surface would begin to impact the popular culture, from Country & Western to the first inchoate rumblings of Rock 'n' Roll.

You didn't hear any of it in Hibbing, Minnesota, however, which is why, almost from the time he was born, Robert Zimmerman wanted to escape. Born on May 24, 1941, son of an appliance store owner, the young Zimmy showed a natural predisposition toward music. As a teenager, he was withdrawn. He wasn't the type to toss a football around with the other neighborhood boys. He could usually be found playing guitar—or listening to the huge record collection he'd already begun amassing (Little Richard was an early favorite). Zimmerman would later pursue a Folk direction, but at that time, like any other white American teen, he was enamoured with Rock 'n' Roll.

He was not disrespectful to his parents, nor was he a textbook "hood"/J.D. type, but he did manifest his rebellion in subtle ways, like buying a motorcycle and forming a band called the Golden Chords. His father was naturally not happy about these developments and decided to put the boy to work in the store. One of Bob's duties was repossessing appliances from negligent customers, and friends say this experience deeply grieved the young Dylan, so much so that he would always have a lifelong affinity with the underprivileged and downtrodden.

The '50s may have seemed like a grimly restrictive time, but underneath the surface the first flowerings of mass bohemia were brewing. Jewish Americans were at the forefront of it all, from the poison-penned satire of *Mad* magazine to Allen Ginsberg's perverse poetry to Lenny Bruce's freeform monologues. No coincidence that, in the next decade, Bob Dylan, another Jew, would synthesize all of these influences and introduce them to Rock 'n' Roll.

Bob was adamant to his friends that he wanted out of Hibbing. During his teenage years, he began spending more time in Minneapolis, more than two hundred miles south. Even before he'd enrolled as a student at the University of Minnesota, Zimmerman began hanging around the off-campus hobo quarter, Dinkytown. It was here that he was first exposed to folk music. The coffeehouse scene was just beginning, where some frazzled hobo would strum an out-of-tune acoustic guitar and sing the same songs everyone else was singing in front of a dozen people.

By the time Zimmerman graduated high school in 1959, Rock 'n' Roll was his main obsession. Acquaintances remember that he was already talking about being a star. When he agreed, for his parents' sake, to attend the University of Minnesota, he had no intention of graduating. It was a means to an end, to put him closer to Dinkytown. Along the way, Zimmerman would reinvent his past and re-emerge as Bob Dylan. But even before that, he was making up stories that he had no parents at all and that he was an "orphan" from Oklahoma. A lot of this came from the yarn-spinning methods of the bluesmen he listened to, like John Lee Hooker and Lightnin' Hopkins, whose own backgrounds were clouded in myth. Besides building a mystique, such ravings would help Dylan perfect his narrative style of songwriting.

Mystique was all-important to Dylan. Unlike the Beatles, there was nothing about Dylan's musical style that was that unusual or appealing: he was an average guitar player, a poor harmonica player, and an even worse singer. Many a youngster had dreams about escaping his dull surroundings by becoming a star. Dylan seemed to be just another starry-eyed kid, but he had an uncanny knack for making it all seem believable. He was obsessive in his quest for fame, as evidenced by his high school graduation photo, which bore the legend: "To join Little Richard."

Contrary to belief, Dylan didn't "go Rock" from a primarily Folk base; it was the other way around. When Dylan arrived at college, he was already familiar with Dinkytown. It was inevitable that he would end up spending most of his time there, as his interest in academic studies was negligible. In the late '50s, Folk music was sweeping the college campuses because the students saw it as an honest form of self-expression uncorrupted by capitalist hands. Young Folk singers of all descriptions were beginning to fill the coffeehouses of bohemian enclaves like Dinkytown. Dylan's style at the time was still primarily "hillbilly," but that didn't stop him from taking the stage at the Ten O'Clock Scholar, the local Folk hangout. According to Dylan biographer Anthony Scaduto, the youngster's "adenoidal" singing often caused patrons to flee in disgust.

As for the name, he told Scaduto: "I needed a name in a hurry and I picked that one. Wasn't Dylan Thomas at all...I knew about Dylan Thomas but I didn't deliberately pick his name."[1] Inventing a new name was just the beginning—soon Dylan was fabricating tall tales about how he played piano behind Little Richard and ran away with the circus. He even told people *he was Bobby Vee*, the American teen idol who'd just had a big hit with "Take Good Care of My Baby." His coffeehouse routine may have been bombing, but "Bob Dylan" was already a celebrity at the on- and off-campus parties he attended that fall.

Dylan only lasted about six months in college before dropping out and drifting further into the Minneapolis Folk scene. The folkies were at their peak then: artists like the Kingston Trio and Pete Seeger were selling a lot of albums. Woody Guthrie, an Okie born and bred, was considered the catalyst for the movement. Born in 1912, Guthrie lived a nomadic life and wrote songs about the various injustices he'd encountered during his travels. Almost instantly, he became Dylan's idol. Dylan became Guthrie reincarnate, and suddenly it became important to him to write his own material "like Woody." This put him apart from the other young Folk singers that were tied to "traditional" material and seldom wrote their own stuff. It was inevitable that, at the rate Dylan was moving, he would soon become bored with the quaint little Minneapolis milieu.

This boredom gradually led him to New York's Greenwich Village, the hotbed of the Folk movement. There were many would-be Woodys in this environment, but none like Dylan—he wheezed and cackled, stomped his foot, stopped mid-song and made comedic Charlie Chaplin-esque gestures and then started over again. Audiences were agog over this little hillbilly from Hibbing, Minnesota. Of course he didn't *tell* them that he was from Hibbing—he told them he was from Sioux City! "*Eeeeh!* Raised by *Indians!*"

The "eeeh" was a trait he'd perfected. Said with a sneer through a cloud of cigarette smoke, it was the final cutting phrase to stop a conversation dead in its tracks. Soon Dylan would begin taking amphetamines, and his delivery would take on the staccato jab of Lenny Bruce. He'd also cultivate a physical image to go along with all this negative energy. Since he'd been slightly chubby as a youth, he'd become obsessed with thinness (hence the speed). At times he sank to sallow skin and bone, but in the early days in the Village he used this emaciated look to enhance his hobo/boho image, claiming: "Eeeeh! I can't *afford* to eat!"

Dylan would accent some words, hang on to syllables, yodel—anything to make his delivery more distinct. Another thing that put Dylan ahead of the pack was his seemingly endless repertoire. He seemed to know a thousand songs and had even written a few by then. But when anyone tried to press him on his musical origins, he came back with a standard put-on: "Eeeeh! I learned 'em in the *carnival!* I was a *roustabout*. A lot of songs people are singin' today, I learned these songs in the carnival. That's why I know all these songs!"

One of the first songs Bob Dylan wrote was "Song for Woody." He'd met his mentor, who lay dying of Huntington's Disease at Greystone Hospital in central Jersey, a few days after he moved to New York. Arriving at the hospital, he announced "I'm Bob Dylan," almost expecting the legend Guthrie to have heard of him. Then sitting at the Master's feet, he played a few songs. Because of his health, Guthrie was mostly despondent, but he appreciated the boy's devotion. To a few close friends Guthrie confided: "The boy's gonna be a big star someday."

At that time, Guthrie was *the* sacred figure in American Folk music, and his embrace of Dylan added yet another feather in the young man's cap. But Guthrie's blessing didn't win over Dylan's harshest critics. As Scaduto explained: "There were two distinct groups of folk singers at the time: 'Low folk' and 'high folk' they called it, and the highs considered Dylan to be the lowest of the low." [2]

The purists thought that folk music was an antique art and that the songs should be sung the same way they'd always been. Whereas Dylan and his ilk were more concerned with music than with intellectual arguments about a song's "purity." Dylan even committed the cardinal sin of incorporating humor into his act, a no-no amongst the ultraserious purists. Dylan refused to toe the line on any of the accepted conventions, from the way he dressed to his inter-pretation of any of the so-called classics. A good example of his brashness at this stage in the game was his refusal to play the same harmonica solo again and again on a Harry Belafonte session that he'd accepted to supplement his income. Dylan quit after one song, claiming he was bored by the repetition.

Word about Dylan spread through the Village and caught the ears of John Hammond, the legendary Columbia Records impresario who'd discovered Bessie Smith, Benny Goodman, Billie Holiday, and more recently, a young gospel singer from Detroit named Aretha Franklin. Folk singer Carolyn Hester introduced Dylan to Hammond after Dylan had played harp on her debut album (another session gig that Dylan apparently *didn't* walk out on this time). Hammond liked Dylan immediately. "What a wonderful character," he thought. "Playing guitar and blowing mouth harp, he's gotta be an original. I gotta talk contract right away."

As is the case with a lot of "originals," Dylan didn't do anything technical-ly that fascinating, but he dared to do things other people didn't—and that got him noticed. Columbia at that time was trying to hippen its image after Mitch Miller's stewardship in the '50s had left the company with a stodgy veneer. Although the label was best known for Johnny Mathis, it was slowly building up its repertoire of artists designed to appeal to a younger audience: Miles Davis, Pete Seeger, Johnny Cash, Barbra Streisand, and, finally, Dylan. By the mid-'60s, with all of the aforementioned exceeding in their respective cate-gories—Jazz, Folk, Country, Pop, and Rock 'n' Roll—Columbia had become the top-grossing record label in America.

Dylan recorded his first album for a cost of just over four hundred dollars. Produced by Hammond, the album was released in October 1962. The num-ber one song in the nation at that time was "Sherry" by the Four Seasons.

Given a high-class packaging job by Columbia, the album still failed to make the top two hundred. That didn't stop a few intuitive critics from taking notice of the strange young man. The album featured a reprint of Robert Shelton's gushing review in the *New York Times* from the previous year: "Mr. Dylan's voice is anything but pretty. He is consciously trying to recapture the rude beauty of a southern field hand musing in melody on his porch."

The rural fixation played a big part in the album's sound, particularly the opener, a version of Jesse Fuller's "You're No Good," which had Dylan whooping like a straw-sucking cracker. Shelton was right: the voice wasn't pretty, but it helped Dylan propagate his hillbilly image (even if it was partly false). This also carried over to the liner notes, where Dylan continued his string of Huck Finn-ish folk tales: "Eeeeh, my first professional job was at a stripjoint in Colorado City."

The original material on Dylan's first album was largely autobiographical. "Talkin' New York" was a hilarious account of his first year in the city. It reiterated the experiences of the past twelve months, including the indignation he faced from the Folk community as well as the failed Belafonte session. Dylan made it a point to note that, at the time he'd arrived, the *New York Times* had said it was the coldest winter in seventeen years. To which Dylan responded: "Eeeh! Didn't feel so *cold* then!" He was already trashing the institutions. "Song for Woody" was a premonition of Dylan's later protest period, with its vision of a world that "looks like it's dying." These were words as good as any of Guthrie's, and Dylan had done it with the same rapid speed as his mentor.

After his first album, Dylan's songs became more topical and political. His radicalization happened quickly because he was hanging out with self-proclaimed Marxists like Pete Seeger. According to a friend at that time, Dylan considered playing a radical social function for twenty dollars, but she intervened, warning him that he was too young to hurt his career by supporting a "cause" like Seeger had. Dylan's girlfriend at the time was a beatnik chick named Suze Rotolo who encouraged him to follow the radical path. He later wrote some of his most pointed love songs about her.

Rotolo appeared clutching Dylan's arm on the cover of his second album, *The Freewheelin' Bob Dylan*. Both the album's title and the cover were indicative of how Columbia was marketing Dylan: a restless hobo beatnik vagabond free spirit. Mass Bohemia was just about to flourish, and Dylan was at the forefront of a whole new breed of angry young men. In 1963, Dylan still had to prove himself, but to whom? That was the question. The Rock audience at that time was still a bunch of zit-faced juvenile delinquents—nobody took them seriously. Dylan, meanwhile, had been reviewed in the *New York Times* and had played Newport. This was pre-Rock now. This was Folk. Rock at this time was still Rock 'n' Roll, and Dylan at this point was anything *but* Rock 'n' Roll—although interestingly enough, right about the same time he was cutting his first album, he recorded a Rock n' Roll single with a six-piece band entitled "Mixed Up Confusion." When it went nowhere, he temporarily hung up his Rock 'n' Roll shoes, but he was always experimenting with the idea, so his so-called conversion to Rock a couple of years later wasn't really all that surprising.

It's no wonder Dylan was already starting to appeal to the radical/protest set, seeing that songs like "Masters of War" were vituperative rants destined to endear him to flag-burners. There was a gentler side to Bob Dylan also: "Blowin' in the Wind," an ode to human endurance, was his most widely hailed composition yet. Within months there were hundreds of cover versions, which more or less *made* Dylan as a songwriter on a Seeger or Guthrie level. The most successful version was by a shiny white trio named Peter, Paul, & Mary. Their manager was the ruthless, arrogant, and irascible Albert Grossman, and in 1963 he became Dylan's manger too.

JFK was shot in November '63, and suddenly the beaming optimism that had characterized the Folk movement was replaced by anger, grief, and disillusionment. As a result, Dylan's next album, *The Times They Are a-Changin'* was even more wrathful than its predecessor. His compositional skills were coming to the fore with a kind of intensity that many people mistook for arrogance, but he couldn't be faulted for lack of integrity, at least not at this stage of the game. He played all the Civil Rights marches, which brought him face to face with Blacks while performing ironic material about racism like "Only a Pawn in Their Game." This was great experience for any performer.

In early '64 Dylan was still firmly entrenched in the Folk scene. On *Freewheelin'*, he even made fun of Rock 'n' Roll with a parody of a Rock 'n' Roll nobody called Rockaday Johnny ("I Shall Be Free"). Soon that would change. Like Lennon and McCartney, Dylan, from the beginning, had set his sights on the top of the mountain. So when the Beatles became a sensation in early '64, some of the folkies may have smirked but Dylan listened intently.

In January 1964 Dylan embarked on a cross-country trip à la Kerouac, taking along English journalist Peter Karman, singer Paul Clayton, and his new road manager, Victor Maimudes. For the trip, Dylan purchased a brand new Ford station wagon. During the third week of the trip, as Dylan and his cronies were cruising through Colorado, the Beatles broke in America. Dylan was impressed by the enormity of their sound, commenting: "They were doing things nobody was doing. Their chords were outrageous, just outrageous, and their harmonies made it all valid. You could only do that with other musicians. Even if you're playing your own chords you had to have other people playing with you. That was obvious. And it started me thinking about other people." [3]

Dylan's next LP, *Another Side of Bob Dylan*, was marked by more personal and less political material. Recorded in one session on several bottles of Beaujolais, the album was taken by many in the Folk community as one big Fuck You. Critic Irwin Silber simpered in *Sing Out*: "*Mmmmmnnn!* Your new songs seemed to be all inner-directed, inner-probing, self-conscious...even a little cruel on occasion."[4] An English fan in the film *Don't Look Back* told him: "It sounds like you're just trying to have a good *laugh*." To which Dylan replied, in his inimitable way: "Eeeeeeeh! Don't I deserve to have a good *laff* once n' a while?"

By now Dylan's mantle was enormous, and he was a recognized star everywhere he went. The Youth Movement was just beginning to implode, and Dylan was its most visible commodity. He began to surround himself with a vast array of goons and glory-seekers, and the amphetamine he was taking guaranteed that many paranoid scenes would get played out. He was working at a frenetic pace and—as the documentary *Don't Look Back*, made around this time, amply demonstrates—barely missing a punch. On *Another Side* Dylan had mused about "shadow boxing with Cassius Clay" and indeed, in several scenes in the movie—with a *Time* reporter, a snooty hotel clerk, a pretentious student—his verbal acumen was nothing short of gladiatorial. No one seemed to escape his vitriol, and his exaggerated "punk" mannerisms became the role model for many an aspiring singer/songwriter/radical.

Don't Look Back was filmed during a tour of England in the spring of 1965 when Dylan was right at the crossroads between Folk and Rock star. The American folksinger Joan Baez accompanied Dylan on the tour, but her professional, as well as personal, relationship with Dylan was nearing an end. After

Dylan had broken up with Suze Rotolo, he began having a relationship with Baez, the woman most people considered "the queen of the folkies." For a brief moment they stood united as King and Queen, but Dylan's relationship with that audience was about to reach its tumultuous conclusion at Newport in 1965, and Baez was part of the baggage that he had to let go. Dylan's new friends were Village hipsters like Bob Neuwirth as well as the members of the new Rock bands like the Beatles, the Rolling Stones, and the Byrds.

The transformation to Rock icon was almost complete by the time Dylan released his fifth album, *Bringing It All Back Home*, in March 1965. Peering through a fisheye lens of the type that was soon to become commonplace, Dylan stared blankly and fondled a pussycat while a swank-looking woman in a red dress sat in the background smoking a cigarette (this was actually Grossman's wife Sally). Although Dylan still performed acoustically throughout the British tour, at least one side of *Bringing It All Back Home* was recorded with a full electric band.

By 1965, influenced by the Beatles, sales of electric guitars and basses had doubled. The pioneers of the American "Folk-Rock" sound were the Byrds, who scored a number one hit with a version of Dylan's "Mr. Tambourine Man." Dylan released his own Rock 'n' Roll single, "Subterranean Homesick Blues," around the same time, and it was similarly infused with drug imagery. Here for the first time was a chance for Rock to achieve some sort of lyrical maturity. Even if the lyrics were, for the most part, indecipherable abstractions, Dylan's rhapsodic delivery—fueled by the speed—seemed to suggest that his unique knack for wordplay was limitless. It was if the language and poetry of the beatniks had been boiled down into a three-minute burst of lyrical and musical adrenaline.

Things moved faster then. The Rock industry was still new, and the artists, instead of making calculated moves, were following their instincts and learning as they went along. That's why there was such a sense of urgency to the Rock of the '60s. It wasn't like the "product" of today that sits stale in the can until accountants peg the perfect time it should be released. The artists wanted to get the stuff out as quickly as possible, not only because they were eager to reveal their artistic selves to the world, but also because they wanted to beat their competitors to the punch. Such competition is healthy, and this had a nurturing effect on the entire body of Rock music at that time.

Dylan was at the epicenter of the renaissance, and he was beginning to surround himself with a fine array of talented accompanists to help him make his transition to electric troubadour. This included the Hawks, a Canadian band that had moved to New York in 1964 and would soon be rechristened the Band; Mike Bloomfield, the Jewish guitarist from the Butterfield Blues Band who'd been playing electric Blues since he was a teenager; and Al Kooper, the organist from the Blues Project, one of the first electric Rock bands in the Village. In May 1965 Dylan used many of these musicians, and others like drummer Bobby Gregg, to lay down the track that many consider his greatest achievement, "Like a Rolling Stone." Designed as a hit single, it defied conventional wisdom, running six minutes in length. Mounting with tension in each verse, until the dam finally burst with a fury so cathartic it seemed like Dylan was evoking all the doubts and desires of his generation, the song became an anthem, and Dylan achieved the mythic stature he'd always aspired to.

Not everyone was happy with Dylan's transformation to Rock deity. To many in the Folk movement, Dylan had long seemed to abandon the "cause." He was still technically the most visible "Folk singer" in the world, however, so when the Newport Folk Festival rolled around in 1965, Dylan was asked to play, just as he had been every year since 1963. There was a difference this time, though—Dylan invited his Rock buddies to join him onstage. For his backing band he'd chosen the Butterfield collective, a tough bunch of blue-collar kids from Chicago who'd been playing Rhythm & Blues on the bar circuit for years. They weren't Folk purists by any means. For Dylan to bring them onstage at Newport was seen as sacrilege. The folkies booed him offstage—ironically enough, this event occurred just as "Like a Rolling Stone" was beginning its chart ascendance. In truth, from their standpoint, the folkies had a right to complain—Dylan's conversion to Rock was what finally brought the Folk movement to its knees.

Coinciding with the rise of both dope and radical beliefs, this was also the age when people started reading into Dylan's lyrics for hidden meaning. This raised the stakes of Rock composition even higher, because now someone was actually analyzing the contents. In a few years the Rock press would emerge, and whole reams of analytical discourse would be written in the name of Rock 'n' Roll. Dylan was in many ways the catalyst.

In October 1965 Dylan released what was arguably his best album, *Highway 61 Revisited*. At this point he was working at such a rapid pace that the album was recorded in a matter of weeks, and it seemed to sum up his creative energies all at once. As a hi-fi expert, Bob Johnston did a production job that was far advanced over the competition (excepting Gary Usher's work with the Byrds and George Martin with the Beatles). The richly textured, organ-laden sound would provide the inspiration for many bands over the next few years, from Procol Harum to Traffic to Mott the Hoople.

Dylan's put-downs reached their apotheosis on *Highway 61*. In songs like "Tombstone Blues," he trashed American institutions left and right. This included the sacred halls of higher learning, which Dylan still had bitter memories of since his own brief college experience in the early '60s. This inspired his immortal comment: "The only difference between an old folks' home and a college is that more minds die in college."

In November 1965 Dylan secretly married Sarah Lowndes, but it did little to quell his fervor. Shortly after the wedding, Dylan embarked on an extensive tour abroad, including Canada, Australia, and England. Accompanied by the Hawks, Dylan was at the peak of his prowess as a live performer (as the many bootlegs recorded during the tour attest). He'd also reached his commercial zenith, selling millions of records all over the world. Still, many say Dylan secretly resented Grossman for putting him through such a grueling regimen so soon after his marriage.

As the stakes got higher, the music got better. *Blonde on Blonde*, released in 1966, was a bold move for any performer: a double album, it was a testament to Dylan's ego at the time that he would even attempt such a grandiose gesture—and a testament to his genius that he would pull it off so effortlessly. *Blonde on Blonde* was even more influential than the previous album. The fact that Dylan recorded it in Nashville set a precedent for the Country Rock that would emerge later in the decade. Many of the cuts were purposely sloppy and down-home, like "Rainy Day Women," for instance. Dylan was stewed the whole time he made the album, and undoubtedly the fans that thought he was having a "laugh" ever since the days of *Another Side* and *Bringing It All Back Home* had long since abandoned him.

Lyrically speaking, Dylan was often merely trilling hallucinatory gibberish, but like hipsterspeak earlier and Rap music later, it was the *rhythmic* orientation of the words that made it work. One of the reasons Dylan was able to move so fast was that he recorded semi-improvisationally. This was the period when a speed-fueled Dylan would fill notebook after notebook with lyrics (he even wrote a book, *Tarantula*, which would be published later) and bring 'em into the studio while the band cooked up a riff or, more likely, a groove. Consequently a song could end up being eleven minutes long ("Desolation Row") or even take up a whole side of an album (as "Sad Eyed Lady of the Lowlands" did on side four of *Blonde on Blonde*). Self-conscious experiments in longevity were very much a part of the Rock-becoming-aware process as well.

Dylan had been one of the first composers to deal with the new realities of love and sexuality in the modern age by writing intelligent songs expressing self-doubt and introspection that could serve either side of the relationship. This was a seminal influence on the crop of ultrapersonal singer/songwriters who'd emerge in his wake. What Dylan was doing, albeit inadvertently, was creating "adult Rock," that genre that no longer dealt with the adrenaline burst of teenybop Rock but instead with romantic situations and the "emotions" they entailed. What this meant was that, in Rock terms, Dylan was already dead by 1966. And for him to be able to shift gears so effortlessly proves all along that his much-vaunted "Rock" period of '65–'66 was merely dabbling of the most detached kind.

If what happened next had *not* happened, who knows what direction Dylan would have taken? It's one of those famous "what ifs" that are ultimately meaningless. Just as *Blonde on Blonde* was making its ascent up the charts, Dylan suffered a near-fatal motorcycle accident that laid him up for nearly two years. As quickly as he'd risen, Dylan vanished from national prominence just as Rock was about to make its most baron-like influx into mass culture. If Dylan had died, he would have become immortal. As it was, he healed and reappeared in very mortal form. Such is the crux of "legend."

Dylan's rehabilitation was gradual. For several months he holed up in his new home in Woodstock, New York with the members of the Band, producing what would later be known as the *Basement Tapes*, which wasn't officially released until 1975 (although many bootlegs had surfaced before that). The whole mysterioso aura was alive and well the whole time he was in exile, and the myth grew even stronger.

When Dylan reappeared in 1968 with *John Wesley Harding*, it wasn't exactly what people expected, especially in light of the "progressive" experiments being wrought at the same time by his peers (the Beatles, Byrds, et al.) In 1966, Dylan had apparently found it important to "compete" with the Beatles and their ilk. But *John Wesley Harding* was hardly the album to "top" *Sgt. Pepper.* That was Dylan's choice, and at this point he was more or less abdicating his Rock star mantle. The problem was, the purveyors of the movement weren't willing to let him slide away so easy. Because of this, Dylan would forever be measured against these mythical terms. Considering the path he's taken in the past three decades—which, one must presume, is exactly the direction he wanted to take—he probably would've been better off if he'd never left the Folk scene in the first place.

Dylan's work in the '70s was, to be kind, unfocused and, to be unkind, downright careless, almost as if to trash the legend by its own hands. In a perverse way, this is probably just what Dylan intended. He's asserted time and time again that he doesn't really care what the critics *or* public expect of him, thus rendering all further analysis irrelevant.

When Dylan *was* "relevant," he achieved three things: he parlayed a few verbal tricks into the annals of American songform; he was Rock's first mythical cult superstar and the first one to be taken seriously as an "artist"; and he brought certain hip elements and radical notions into the public consciousness once and for all.

CHAPTER 8

THE REVOLUTION

THE '60S WERE THE BIRTH OF THE MODERN AGE, when all of the things that seemed so amazing in the '50s became predictable and run-of-the-mill like they are now. The reason for this was the great acceleration of life itself, the mag-malike mixture of everything coming together at once: technology, education, the economy, and the media. After fifteen years of postwar prosperity, America was reaping the benefits of its own excess. At the beginning of the decade there was still a faith that the American Frontier would fulfill its own bountiful promise. The significance of the '60s was that, by the end of the decade, the faith had fallen out.

In the '60s it was easy to believe that a "revolution" was going on, just by the immense changes that were occurring in almost every facet of American life. The technological revolution had allowed for Rock music to get louder and the basic Folk structure to become electrified. A growing youth population was suddenly realizing that they had a culture of their own apart from John Wayne and Lawrence Welk. But as subsequent electoral contests proved, that was about the extent of it. Other than sex, drugs, and Rock 'n' Roll, what other trappings of "the movement" have endured?

The '60s also marked the birth of the Sexual Revolution: in the horrific afterglow of the bomb, who was gonna wait for tomorrow? Some may have still been asking "Will you still love me...?" but most were willing to suspend disbelief for a few minutes. What the aging prudes of yesteryear failed to understand as they decried the "new permissiveness" was that the kids of the modern age saw no convincing argument for abstinence. With Rock 'n' Roll having already taken the place of God in the Baby Boomers' lives, and the furious sense of the here and now eclipsing any sense of moral tradition, they seemed gloriously born into a time when there was no longer anything or anyone to answer to. Most of them were continuing farther in education than their parents had—didn't that entitle them to make their own decisions? In the '60s, sex was no longer something people were secretive about—it became a recreational rite of passage. And like Rock 'n' Roll, that was something that the moral standard bearers simply could not prevent.

The Sexual Revolution was enabled by other factors besides the Baby Boomers' insatiable thirst for endless gratification. The invention of the birth control pill made saying yes a lot easier, as did the arrival of such publications as *Cosmopolitan*, which was the flip side of the whole *Playboy* thing—mainly, a magazine for women that dealt frankly with sex. Its founder, Helen Gurley Brown, had actually predated the philosophy of *Cosmo* with her book, *Sex and the Single Girl*, in 1962, which said basically: "Go ahead, *do it*! What are you waiting for?" Even before then, the great glut of pulp literature had made sex more accessible. Now at the end of every supermarket checkout lay: *The Velvet Underground*!

A lot of the new sexual awareness coincided with the rise of psychology, psychiatry, and psychoanalysis that became popular in the '50s, most of it based on the teachings of Sigmund Freud, who surmised that everything was latently sexual. This was another privilege of the postwar brats: a shrink to peck their minds and delve into their psyches to find out what caused their "problems." The predisposition towards emotional problems was another thing that set the Baby Boomers apart from their parents' generation. Whereas previously on the American Frontier the John Wayne model of parent would've smacked Junior in the face and said: "get over it, boy—stop acting like a *weirdo*," now they shipped him off to a shrink. It only exacerbated the problem when the shrink told the parents that they were actually to blame. This tied in with the "child psychology" of people like Dr. Benjamin Spock, whose *Baby Book* became the Bible of child rearing in the '60s with its urging of parents to try "reasoning" with their children instead of bossing them around.

Psychoanalysis had been around for years, served up in offices all over the Upper West Side of New York, with long couches and Freudian doctors nodding their heads saying: "yes, tell me more." It was the generation of the '50s who'd really come to embrace the necessity for mind-plumbing, not only because they were the most self-obsessed generation ever, but because they were the most sex-obsessed—and hence *confused*. Psychoanalysis was the first step toward the inward preoccupations that would totally usurp the culture in the next decade. Whereas, say, being a member of the Communist Party in the '30s might have been a badge of distinction for a young free thinker, now a person was more proud of being a mind-fucked head case because it was another excuse to say: "See where our parents went wrong! It's *their* fault!" In other words, the parents were "the enemy" merely because of their age, not because of any fundamental philosophical disagreement. This syndrome would help create the Generation Gap.

Beyond that, psychoanalysis was a kind of status symbol because it showed that one could afford to have his/her problems analyzed while the plebeians had to learn to cope for themselves. Not surprisingly, a lot of the proto-yuppies were first introduced to psychoanalysis while in college (that bastion of self-serving redundancy).

The college campus in the '60s was the hotbed for the social upheaval. It was the first time many youths had ever been away from home. It was the place where the culture of Butte, Montana met the culture of Long Island, New York. It was the place where most kids first got drunk and got laid. It was *freedom*, and it was a place where young minds could foment new ideas and ideals. It also provided a draft deferment for many men who were just beginning to question the logic of having to give two years of their increasingly luxurious life to Uncle Sam. Part of the Baby Boomers' birthright was that they were "entitled" to continuing education, and as Vietnam drummed on and on, many of them *did* continue, right into their thirties (the "Mike Stivic" syndrome). As the counterculture grew, the children of the '60s would even come to question these institutions. But in the early '60s, college campuses were bastions of youthful idealism. It had been mostly academics who had been imperiled by the McCarthy Hearings, and in the '60s they began getting their revenge. Higher education in America has been entwined with the politics of the Left ever since.

Kennedy's youthful vigor made politics a lot more endearing to college-age youths who might not have otherwise become politically active. There was a ray of hope that shone amid the youthful idealism of the '60s—Kennedy had created programs like the Peace Corps, and the olive branch was genuinely being extended to underdeveloped nations in an effort to keep the "free world" safe from Communism. The biggest shock to the fortitude of the United States was the astronomical rise of Castro in Cuba, which placed a Communist dictatorship right in its own hemisphere. In those days, the New Left hadn't really begun attacking the military yet. After all, wasn't it JFK himself who said: "Ask not what your country can do for you but what you can do for your country"?

The issue most at stake on campuses at that time, free speech, turned out to be the catalyst for the whole movement. Berkeley, California had been one of the first cities in the nation where a radical community had manifested itself. Its close proximity to San Francisco, long a leftist foothold, made it part of a Bay Area axis of liberalism. In 1960, students from UCal Berkeley protested capital punishment at San Quentin; a year later they joined the Civil Rights Movement. In 1963, there were more than seven hundred students arrested during a rally against racist hiring practices at a San Francisco hotel. This set the stage for the Free Speech Movement, which began as protest over whether students could raise money for social causes on campus. Despite pressure from school officials and threats of expulsion, the students maintained their demonstrations for four grueling months. The college radicals, like the leaders of the Civil Rights Movement before them, had learned how to use the television medium to publicize their cause. As the '60s slogan went, "the whole world is watching," and from that point on there was no turning back. Small skirmishes would begin popping up on campuses all over until the protest rally became as much a part of college life in the '60s as the pep rally had been in the '50s.

Student radicals didn't listen to Rock 'n' Roll; they listened to Folk. At this point, Folk music was the place where, lyrically, anti-establishment sentiment was being registered. Folk had always been "protest music," ever since the Depression, when ramblers and raconteurs like Woody Guthrie and Jimmie Rodgers crossed the country singing songs about social injustice. Guthrie, in particular, was brazenly outspoken in such songs as "Deportee," which dealt with discrimination against migrant workers (Guthrie was the main influence on Bob Dylan, among others). The Folk form—vocal "ballads" with sparse accompaniment (usually one guitar)—had a big revival in the '50s. That's because the idea of such a proletariat art form was appealing to the ranks of the New Left. The folkies showed their support for such causes as the Civil Rights and Free Speech movements by playing at all the fundraisers. At that time, Folk music was the domain of the college campuses, and Rock 'n' Roll was still the province of the high schools.

Despite its purest (or purist) intentions, Folk music was actually *selling* in the late '50s and early '60s. The Weavers, the Kingston Trio, the Rooftop Singers, Odetta, Joan Baez, and Peter, Paul, & Mary actually experienced chart success. There was a growing enthusiasm on college campuses for nonelectric music, perhaps as a backlash against Rock 'n' Roll, which was viewed by members of the New Left as crass commercialism. Labels like Vanguard and Elektra emerged to mine the more adventurous Folk practitioners, and there was also a folkie press: *Sing Out* and *Broadside*, which anticipated the Rock press a lot more than the teen mags like *16* and *Hit Parader*.

For all the pinkos squatting stoned on dormitory floors listening to Bob Dylan sing "The Times They Are a-Changin'," the checks from home kept coming. Which is why the concept of a white, middle class "protest" music was loaded from the start. Besides, the plebeians once again weren't listening. In that case, the market in 1964 was open to just about anyone: Rock 'n' Roll was still selling but had to compete with Bobby Vinton. Other than Dylan, the album market in particular was dominated by crud (soundtracks, mood music, and lame comedy). No one could have guessed that within a few months a Rock 'n' Roll band from England, of all places, would transform the industry so dramatically that everything that had come before would suddenly sound outdated, and record companies and musicians alike would have to begin thinking on whole new terms.

There are many reasons a unifying force like the Beatles had to come from abroad. Elvis, the only similar phenomenon, came from a background that was similarly alien to most Americans—the rural south. With the advent of the highway system and mass communication, such isolation within the country itself was diminishing. It now took a truly foreign element to shake things up. Coming from England, the Beatles held the same potent combination of awe and mystery that Elvis had—for what most people in America knew about England at the time, it was if they came out of nowhere. As far as music goes, it meant an entire rebirth for Rock 'n' Roll—which unilaterally put the folkies out of business.

England in the '50s was coming into its own postwar identity much the same as the United States, but English youth didn't have a unifying factor like

Rock 'n' Roll to signify their rebellion. For a time, the English had a dalliance with their own timid brand of "folk music" called skiffle. There was also the "trad jazz" movement, but this tended to consist of watered-down recreations of already-stale American musical forms like Dixieland and Ragtime. Nevertheless, some of the finer players in the first wave of English Rock groups would hail from this background (Charlie Watts of the Rolling Stones, for instance, or the various members of the Animals).

In the seaport towns like Liverpool, music fans and budding musicians were perhaps more fortunate than the folks in the Midlands in that they had access to exportable goods, including records, coming from the American trade vessels that were pulling into port. As the legend goes, the sailors sold American R&B records fresh off the boat to the British kids for five shillings a shot. Since this was a pretty lofty tab, the records took on an almost sacred aura. This explains the reverence with which this stuff was treated—most Brits didn't realize the American scene held a virtually endless cornucopia of such down-home resources.

In Liverpool, the scene revolved around the Cavern Club, where the Beatles were the house band. Not only did scores of would-be Beatles pop up but other clubs, viewing the success of the Cavern, soon opened their doors to Rock 'n' Roll. This was not a genteel, overly professional scene—it was a rude, raucous uproar. This put it in stark contrast with the first wave of English Rock 'n' Roll stars: Cliff Richard, Tommy Steele, Lonnie Donegan, the Shadows, the Tornadoes, Tony Dangerfield, Adam Faith, Johnny Kidd, Tommy Quickly. Although some of these were modeled on the Elvis/Gene Vincent J.D. role model (particularly Kidd), a great deal of these artists were merely manufactured "teen idols" on the level of Fabian and Frankie Avalon in the United States. The Beatles and their ilk were the "alternative" scene, the *Punk Rock*, per se. Which means that they were slow to be embraced by the national music scene. This meant that bands like the Beatles found themselves having to commute to places like Hamburg, Germany in order to get engagements. But the grueling regimen of playing sixteen hours per night with a minimum of breaks on a brutal strip club circuit helped them hone their chops. Because of their rigorous musical training in clubland, the Brits sounded a thousand times more sophisticated than their American counterparts by the time they hit these shores.

Liverpool became the bastion of the "Mersey sound"—tight arrangements, clanging guitars, two- and three-part vocal harmonies, and kick-start drumming. This is the sound that would infest towns all up and down the Mersey River as well as nearby cities like Manchester, and the sound utilized by the first wave of British bands to make it big in the United States. London, by contrast, seemed to be a Blues-dominated scene, centering on formalized purist institutions like Cyril Davies' All Stars and Alexis Korner's Blues Incorporated. These organizations acted as a finishing school for the next wave of British musicians: the Rolling Stones, the Yardbirds, the Pretty Things, the Animals, and Cream. There was an incredibly fertile crossbreeding of musical minds at work, and this was by far the first time in Rock history that "virtuosity" was taken into account (save perhaps with somebody like Scotty Moore).

In the United States, no such scene was ensuing. The Instrumental and Surf bands existed on a competitive level among one another so their chops were adequate, but save for Dick Dale, none of them thought about what they were doing in *formal* terms. The Northwest Frat-Rock scene—the Kingsmen, the Sonics, the Wailers, Don & the Goodtimes, Paul Revere & the Raiders, the Frantics—was going strong, but it didn't really become marketable until after the arrival of the British. By then bands like the Raiders were being sold as if they were the latest Brit invaders off the boat.

The first Beatles records to make any dent on the American market were released in January 1964. By that time, the group had been recording for a year and a half. EMI's American counterpart, Capitol, had initially passed on the group. When they finally relented, it was with a massive media campaign unrivaled in music history. They used sound bites to exploit the Beatles' accents and paid off the Powers That Be to get their pictures in the papers. This made the Beatles an instant "novelty," but anyone who thought they were merely a passing fad like so many other "freak" acts had seriously underestimated not only their musical quality but their ambitions as well.

The Beatles raised, not lowered, the standard of "pop." Their most notable innovation was the fact that they composed their own material. Discounting the odd Chuck Berry cover, their albums were devoid of the usual "filler" that polluted most "pop" albums of the day. It's to the Beatles' credit that, by the time of their fourth British album, *Beatles for Sale*, the Rock 'n' Roll oldies sounded tired compared to the innovative new material the group was composing.

Needless to say, the industry was thrown for a loop. Largely unprepared for the "Rock revolution," the major labels like Capitol were, at that time, run by old men who had no ear for Rock 'n' Roll. The Beatles, as well as the other Brit groups, left them scrambling around in a desperate effort to discover the Next Big Thing. As a result, even the most inept bands were signed (providing they had long hair). It's funny nowadays to read the backs of albums by utterly worthless groups like the Royal Guardsmen and see the hype that accompanied them: "Their music is stamped with excellence and precision which clearly indicates that these boys will be around a long time."

Even the British bands who *didn't* write their own material were either excellent interpreters, like the Rolling Stones or Yardbirds prior to their own innovations starting in about 1965 or so, or were given the finest Brill Building material to work with (Animals, Manfred Mann). Forced to hone their chops for years in the sweaty club scene, these bands were much more sophisticated than their American counterparts. A band like the Animals, for instance, were such original stylists that it hardly mattered whether they composed their own material. Although most of their best-known material—"It's My Life," "Don't Bring Me Down," "We Gotta Get Out of This Place"—wasn't written by them, the performances were so distinct that they came to own these songs in the minds of their generation.

It took a while for such innovators to penetrate the American marketplace, however. In England, Brian Epstein had a whole empire of second-echelon groups who existed in the Fabs' shadow, and they were the first-runs over here (the Fourmost, Gerry & the Pacemakers, Peter & Gordon, Billy J. Kramer & the Dakotas). Even groups not affiliated with Epstein *sounded* like the Beatles: the Dave Clark Five ("Because"), the Hollies ("I'm Alive"), Freddie & the Dreamers ("I Like It"), the Merseybeats ("See Me Back"), Herman's Hermits ("A Must to Avoid"), the Searchers ("Don't Throw Your Love Away"), etc. When the Beatles themselves shifted gears, as they did successfully so many times, these groups—with the exception of the Hollies— were unable to keep pace.

At the same time, the more sophisticated British groups—the Rolling Stones, the Kinks, the Who, the Yardbirds, the Animals, the Pretty Things, Them, the Bluesbreakers, Spencer Davis Group—found themselves having to deal with the American Pop marketplace. It must have been disillusioning for some of them to find that the more idiosyncratic their music became, the less popular it was in the United States. Just think of the Yardbirds, the Animals, the Kinks, and the Zombies, all of whom started out having "hits" only to see their popularity wane as their music grew more innovative. And the Who, who started out innovative, never really had "hits" at all, at least not until later. Some of the more extreme British groups—the Downliners Sect, the Birds, the Exiles, the Primitives, Creation—despite being stars in England, never made the translation over here.

Even somewhat known entities like the Kinks, the Pretty Things, Them, and the Who were far from popular in the mid-'60s. To those who followed such things, however, they were incredibly influential, not only in their arrangements but in the overdramatic way they wailed on their instruments. Their primal pound was always sexual, whereas bands like Herman's Hermits were flirtatious and light-hearted. The Rolling Stones, at that time considered perhaps the darkest of the bad boys, aped American Blues and Country (dig Keith's *twang*) and stole their aggresso-posture from the Black bluesmen they emulated.

The Yardbirds were in many ways even more "authentic" than the Stones. Not only did they mine the Blues more aggressively than most—even backing American Blues legend Sonny Boy Williamson on an album—but their experiments with techniques like feedback and distortion predated two important genres of the late '60s: Heavy Metal and Progressive Rock. Apparently that wasn't "authentic" enough for original lead guitarist Eric Clapton, who was so much of a purist that he split as soon as the group agreed to record a "pop" single (undoubtedly to get a better shot at the American market). The group then entered their most fruitful period with replacement Jeff Beck, whose raga-esque forays on songs like "I'm a Man" and "Mr. You're a Better Man Than I" influenced a whole generation of Rock guitarists.

The Bluesbreakers, the organization Clapton joined after leaving the Yardbirds, were so "authentic" they never got around to having hits. This despite serving as a finishing school in the Alexis Korner model for a whole new fleet of musical prodigies: Clapton, Mick Taylor (Rolling Stones), Peter Green (Fleetwood Mac), Keef Hartley (Keef Hartley Band). The same can be said of the Graham Bond Organization, another pioneering Blues outfit whose use of organ (hence "Organ-ization") was as unique as Mayall's use of saxophone. As a bandleader, Bond turned out as many future superstars as Mayall, including Jack Bruce, who'd soon join Clapton and fellow Organization dropout Ginger Baker to form the ultimate "purist" supergroup, Cream. The Blues as motif was so popular during this era that even somewhat pedestrian outfits like Manfred Mann ("Got My Mojo Working," "Smokestack Lightnin'") and the Nashville Teens ("Tobacco Road") made a pretense of Blues purism.

Them, from Ireland, were less contrived in their pursuit of the Blues. Even when they tried to approach "pop" styles, their more rough-hewn impulses bled through. Consequently they had little success finding a niche in the United States, despite a wealth of fine material and a vocalist of ample capability in Van Morrison. However, they lasted further into the next quarter than many other groups of this period (long after Morrison had flown the coop, in fact). There was a small order of groups who simultaneously evoked both the aggressive posture of the purists and the pop impulses of the more mainstream groups. These were mostly the "mod" groups like the Small Faces, the Who and, to some extent, the Kinks. The Mods were an interesting youth subcult that happened in England but not the United States: partial to motor scooters, which they decorated with lights and other ornaments, they were dedicated to fashion and pill-popping as a lifestyle. They clashed with their rivals, the Rockers, in legendary street and beach battles throughout the '60s. The Rockers apparently favored the old greaser style of pre-Beatles Rock over the new dance hall edition.

Which hardly mattered to a group like the Who—but it gave them an *identity* to bring the kids in. Like the Beatles, they did their share of American R&B and girl group covers, and their original compositions were more Pop-oriented than someone like the Yardbirds, but they performed them at aerodynamic velocity with a multitude of guitar effects. Their experiments with feedback and distortion were legendary, and it wasn't that far of a leap from "The Ox" to the Velvet Underground's "European Son" or the primal guitar exorcisms of Jimi Hendrix (Pete Townshend was reputedly in awe of Hendrix). A lot of this was just frustration—angst literally ripples through the twelve tracks on the group's first album. When the Clash debuted a dozen years later, they were basically doing a complete rewrite of the Who (not fundamentally but "theoretically"). Plus, the Who invented the stage show (smashing the instruments and the like).

The Kinks shared with the Who the producer Shel Talmy, an American who must have been partly responsible for the splurge of sledgehammer sounds on their early sides. "You Really Got Me," "All Day and All of the Night" and "I Need You" were predecessors of the whole three-chord genre—the Ramones' 1978 "I Don't Want You," for instance, was pure Kinks-by-proxy. In other words, the Kinks did a lot to help turn Rock 'n' Roll (Jerry Lee Lewis) into Rock (Led Zeppelin, Black Sabbath, the Stooges). Leader Ray Davies's original inspiration was probably the Beatles ("If You Still Want Me"), but he soon became an able balladeer in his own right, adding a jagged twist to songs like "A Well Respected Man" and "A Dedicated Follower of Fashion" that even the Beatles couldn't match in terms of social commentary. Among the more iconoclastic groups of the day, the Kinks were actually banned from performing in the United States during the years 1965–1969. Years when, by chance, they were doing their greatest work: "See My Friends," "I'm Not Like Everybody Else," "She's Got Everything," "Sitting on My Sofa," "David Watt," "Days," and "Waterloo Sunset"—brilliant singles released during this period that went unnoticed in the United States.

The Small Faces were even less successful than the Kinks in making a dent on the American market. Only in their case, it happened in the reverse order, as it was their early "mod" singles that failed to make a dent and their later psychedelic work that was moderately successful. Like the Who, another "mod" band, they experimented with both drugs and feedback (John Cale once claimed the feedback solo in "Whatcha Gonna Do About It" almost convinced the Velvet Underground to move to England). As far as Hard-Rock dynamics go, the Small Faces shouldn't be discounted: songs like "Come on Children" and "Tin Soldier" were musically sophisticated while still maintaining their essential rawness. They were blessed to have a fairly good R&B growler in the form of vocalist Steve Marriott, who later fronted the proto-Boogie band Humble Pie (who also had their moments). Dig the Fleshtones sometime and then listen to something like the Small Faces' "Own Up" for proof that they were "punk" progenitors. Even the Sex Pistols liked 'em.

The Spencer Davis Group was a more polished unit, also blessed with a capable young R&B-influenced singer, Stevie Winwood. Bandleader Davis was a Birmingham keyboard player who shied away from the limelight, transferring the focus to Winwood. A child star in England, Winwood was apparently the man to beat for a season in the U.S. too (that is, if Bob Seger's "Heavy

Music"—in which he sings "Stevie Winwood got nothin' on me"—is to be
believed). For a youngster, Winwood played it tough on songs like "Watch
Your Step," possibly because, like the Beatles of the Hamburg days, he was
being schooled in a rough environment. As drummer Ritchie Yorke remembered: "I don't know what was supposed to happen to people of 16 in a pub, but
Steve was well able to take care of himself." [1]

Too bad the same couldn't be said about Winwood's forays with heroin.

The Troggs were named after another short-lived British youth tribe named
the Troglodytes who predated hippies in moving back to the mountainside. The
group actually had nothing to do with the back-to-nature fad, but the cave-
dweller thing fit them perfectly, as they were thuggishly primitive in their musical approach. They were also unabashedly outspoken about their primal desires,
all voiced lasciviously by vocalist Reg Presley. Their cover of an obscure song by
a group called the Wild Ones, "Wild Thing," was a number one hit in the
United States in 1966. But despite a killer first album in which they etched the
prototypes for both bubblegum Rock ("A Girl Like You") and Heavy Metal
("From Home," "I Want You"), their stardom in the United States was momentary. Like the Kinks, the Who, and other angloids, they released plenty of excellent singles that failed to chart stateside, partly due to the subject matter:
"Cousin Jane" was the most incestuous Rock 'n' Roll song between Elvis's
"Kissin' Cousins" and AntiSeen's "Little Sister"; "66-54321" was a distant
cousin to the Velvet Underground with the same kind of scraping, droning riff,
but the lyrics about "going too far" guaranteed it wouldn't get on the radio. And
what can one say about a song called "I Can't Control Myself" in 1966?
Meanwhile, musically speaking, the Troggs were the unlikely prototype for the
riff structure of such important bands as the Stooges and Black Sabbath.

Those are just a few of the more musically significant English bands that
sprang up during the heyday of the British Invasion. For all their hardships,
they were much luckier than the groups in other foreign countries who stood
even less of a chance of ever cracking the monster American market.
Nevertheless, the "beat group" explosion was a worldwide phenomenon:
France had Les Lutins and the Downbeats, Spain had Los Bravos, Italy had the
Shakers, Germany had the Rattles, and Japan had the Mops and the Beavers.
These are only the tip of the iceberg, of course—who knows how many thou-
sands of bands rocked the continents? The legacy of the bands in the English-

speaking countries has been more effectively documented. Among cultists, the '60s scenes of countries like Canada, Australia, and New Zealand are the stuff of legend. Canada had its share of proto-punk rockers like the Ugly Ducklings and the Haunted, who proved that, once folkies like Joni Mitchell and Neil Young had expatriated themselves to warmer climates, it wasn't a bad place to be in the '60s (especially for American draft dodgers). Australia had a full-blown scene led by the Easybeats, who even had their own Lennon/McCartney in Vanda/Young, a team that would continue to shape Aussie rock right up until AC/DC. Judging by the evidence, New Zealand had a well-defined scene as well with bands like the Craig, the Blue Stars, and the Pleazers (whose "Don't Give Me No Lip Child" was later covered by the Sex Pistols).

Because the United States is a consumer-driven society that devours every-thing in its path and then regurgitates it in more grandiose terms and numbers, the influence of the British groups was felt most emphatically here. Virtually overnight, the British re-awoke the Rock instincts of American youth. As Ron Schaumburg wrote: "The Beatles had revolutionized America's musical orien-tation: In 1960 a Manhattan music store sold two guitars a week; two years later it was selling sixty a day. Everyone was forming his own band—the Basement Beatles in every neighborhood were emerging into light." [2]

The frat-Rock scene, which had been going on all along, was rejuvenated by the arrival of the British. Northwest bands like the Sonics and Wailers who'd had their own styles were suddenly adapting to the ways of the Brits: the Beatles in the case of the Wailers ("You Better Believe It") or the Yardbirds in the case of the Sonics ("You've Got Your Head on Backwards"). The most successful band from this scene, Paul Revere & the Raiders, even moved to Hollywood and got their own TV show. That's after they adopted Colonial uniforms in a routine utterly similar to the Beatles. Nevertheless, their best work—"Just Like Me," "Steppin' Out," "Hungry," "Ups & Downs"—had a legitimate punk edge to it.

In a town like Chicago where the legacy of the Blues was real, not roman-ticized like it was with the Brits, a legitimate white-Blues scene had existed since the '50s. Guitarist Mike Bloomfield had been jamming with actual Blues musicians since he was sixteen; Paul Butterfield was a notorious freak act as a white kid blowing Blues harp. With Blues as an indigenous form, these musi-cians probably didn't need the Brits to lead the way. There would have been some kind of white electric Blues upsurge in America without the Brits. But until the British arrived, the audience for Blues was still restricted by the same "purist" hangups as the folkies—mainly, that it had to be of the reverential variety of a Dave Van Ronk or John Hammond, Jr. (or Dion). The British added some much-needed inauthenticity.

The first wave of American bands to absorb the British influence was highly derivative of the Beatles (Byrds, Beau Brummels, Vejtables, Golliwogs, Rockin' Ramrods, Knaves, Gants, Remains, Knickerbockers, Choir, Clefs of Lavender Hill); Rolling Stones (Lyrics, Chocolate Watch Band, Electric Prunes, Harbinger Complex, Leaves); or Yardbirds (the Litter, the Del Vetts, Count 5, Other Half, the Shadows of Knight.). This was the original era of the widely hailed '60s Garage Rock genre, which has continually been accredited as the origin of Punk Rock. But unlike the bands who acted as the self-conscious antecedents of Punk—the Velvet Underground, the MC5, the Stooges, the New York Dolls—the '60s garage-rockers were most likely unwitting prophets. The thing that distinguished them from the more polished acts of the day was their raw, uninhibited, and often inept "street" ethos. Most of them were barely out of their teens and caught up in the excitement of the moment. But the grim reality was that they were teen fuck-ups, not international Rock stars like their British idols (although many of them charted hits). Given this frustrating irony, it's no wonder some of the performances of mid-American garage bands like the Swamp Rats, the Spades, the Shadows of Knight, Lollipop Shoppe, the Seeds, Music Machine, MC5, the Banshees, Third Bardo, and others represent the birth of real ANGER in Rock 'n' Roll. These groups might not have been formalized punk theorists like the Velvet Underground or even Rolling Stones, but they were attitude punks (originals).

The proliferation of bands bred intense local competition in every major city. "Battle of the Bands" was a mainstay of the era. This was the day and age when the first wave of "Rock classics" emerged: "Louie Louie," "Hey Joe," "Gloria." These were the songs that every '60s Rock musician had to learn. This helped define what constituted "Rock" in the first place—that is, away from Tin Pan Alley standards. The new medium was almost totally guitar-driven, and the groups made their presence known on TV shows like *Shindig*, *Hullabaloo*, and *Upbeat*. Suddenly hairy boys and girls were everywhere, frugging in go-go boots while musical incompetents like the Seeds performed.

In May 1965 the mainstream media took notice of the Rock phenomenon in the form of *Time's* cover story: "Rock 'n' Roll: Everybody's Turned On." Although it was an interesting list of bands the magazine selected in the first paragraph to exemplify "Rock 'n' Roll," it's obvious that they merely picked the ones with the funniest names (e.g., Raparata & the Delrons). In other words, the editors of the piece knew little the difference between Pop and legitimate Rock 'n' Roll. Like the AM radio of the day, they merely lumped it all together under one category. But that was about to change.

We were about to enter the hyphen-Rock era. Now there would be different schools of Rock—subgenres! Folk-Rock, one of the first hybrids, was pretty much just that: Folk sensibilities (Dylan) and Rock instruments (Beatles). In many ways, it was the first attempt to bring a self-conscious element of "maturity" (read: sophistication) to Rock 'n' Roll. The Byrds' first two albums, both released in 1965, were the primers of Folk-Rock and the most mimicked sound in American Rock for about a year. The way their sound evolved wasn't all that different from Paul Revere & the Raiders, another mid-'60s product of the L.A. studio system, who also recorded for Columbia. In fact, many of the same studio musicians played on albums by both groups. They even shared the same producer in Gary Usher. But the Byrds aspired to more poetic frontiers, and in rhythm guitarist David Crosby they had at least one token New Left stereotype. They were one of the first groups to be taken "seriously," and through the prism of chiming twelve-string guitars, a million "heads" exploded.

Like a lot of the British groups, the Byrds found that the more complex their music became, the less interested the public—or more aptly, radio programmers—were. Singles like "Eight Miles High," a celebration of drugs, and "So You Want to Be a Rock 'n' Roll Star," a cynical look at the record industry, were over the heads of most of the audience at that time. Although they'd been fashioned as a Pop group, the Byrds were suddenly failing on those terms. If their music is any indication, this suited them fine, because they grew more adventurous as they went along, resulting in one of the most enduring musical legacies of their era. Songs like "I'll feel A Whole Lot Better" and "The World

Turns All Around Her" were, in terms of the harmonic lilt perfected by the Beatles, the next logical step and provided the fuel for the whole next wave.

Los Angeles as a recording center really came into prominence during the era of Surf-Rock, perhaps the first real hyphen category. The creators of the Surf sound were a small coterie of producers including Brian Wilson, Terry Melcher, Gary Usher, Dean Torrence, Roger Christian, P. F. Sloan, and Steve Barri. The descendants of Brian Wilson and his cronies (not to mention Phil Spector) were producers like Sonny Bono and Lou Adler who fashioned pristine Folk-Rock singles to compete on the charts against the Beatles. Bono was actually a Phil Spector protégé who'd been trying to have a hit for years, finally succeeding when he teamed up with wife Cher and they waxed such adenoidal fare as "I Got You Babe." "Why do they laugh at me?" Sonny lamented. Maybe it was because he was 5'6", had a Beatles haircut, and had bad taste in bell-bottoms? But since Sonny & Cher were a couple, they represented the first streak of domesticity in Rock, and the Mamas & the Papas weren't far behind: Once again, there was husband-wife interaction in the group, this time in the form of John and Michelle Phillips. Phillips sang in a kind of Dylan rasp, while the music was super-embellished studio-slick product (once again, the usual L.A. hacksmiths: Russ Kunkel, Hal Blaine, Leon Russell, et al.).

The impetus behind the Mamas & the Papas was Lou Adler, a mogul of sorts—a couple years later he'd help organize the Monterey Pop Festival. In the '70s he'd give us Cheech & Chong and Carole King, among other things. In the '60s his forte was Folk-Rock. Besides the Mamas & the Papas, he also launched Barry McGuire, a former member of the New Christy Minstrels who waxed Dylanesque on the "protest" classic, "Eve of Destruction." The apocalyptic vision of the lyric must have ultimately spooked McGuire, because he soon cashed in on the God-Rock craze of the late '60s and renounced his brief tenure as a Pop star (a premonition to "finding yourself" if there ever was one). The author of "Eve of Destruction" was P. F. Sloan, former partner of Steve Barri in the Fantastic Baggys, a Surf-Rock group. Once the surf had crashed—Hendrix's immortal eulogy, "You will never hear surf music again," was imminent—Sloan began writing "protest" material for groups like the Turtles, whose "Let Me Be" was Punk-Rock defiant with exuberant Beatles/Byrds dynamics.

The Byrds had introduced Dylan into the Rock lexicon, and in 1965–66 his extensive catalog of self-penned classics became the currency amongst many up-and-coming groups looking for some instant credibility. Manfred Mann, Them, the Chocolate Watch Band, Thirteenth Floor Elevators, Grass Roots, Rascals, and the Grateful Dead, among others, all waxed Dylan covers in '65–'66. Those not content to cover Dylan merely appropriated his technique. Some of the culprits included John Phillips, Donovon (dubbed "the Scottish Bob Dylan"), Tom Rapp, Lou Reed, Jerry Garcia, Country Joe McDonald, Bob Seger, the Hombres, Mouse, and Sonny Bono. Dylan's own Rock conversion had been partly the result of producer Tom Wilson. As staff producer at Columbia, Wilson was responsible for the orchestration of "Like a Rolling Stone" as well as the electric side of *Bringing It All Back Home*. Although he was soon to leave Columbia to fulfill a similar function at Verve/MGM (which became a prominent Folk-Rock label in its own right), his parting shot was to do a similar Folk-to-Rock conversion for a duo named Simon & Garfunkel. "Sound of Silence" got tricked up in the same fashion as "Like a Rolling Stone," with a lot of jangling guitars, pounding drums, and celestial organ. The result was a number one single, something even Dylan never had. In the end, Simon & Garfunkel sold more albums in the '60s than anyone other than the Beatles and Rolling Stones.

Dylan's successful transition from Folk to Rock, and the success of the Beatles and other electric groups, made a lot of Folk clubs begin hiring Rock bands. The coffeehouses in Greenwich Village—the Café Wha, Night Owl, the Bitter End, the Café Au Go Go, and the Bizarre—began featuring electric music on a regular basis. This spawned the first wave of New York Rock bands: the Rascals, Lovin' Spoonful, Blues Project, Magicians, Blues Magoos, Youngbloods, Velvet Underground, Lothar & the Hand People, Fugs, Vagrants, the Good Rats, and even Jimi Hendrix in his pre-acid phase. All of these bands had a unique approach to the new electric format that brought in elements of everything from Blues to Folk to ragas to avant-garde to cabaret to R&B. At the coffeehouses, all styles and substances melded. There was undoubtedly a lot of marijuana and acid floating around at the time—as evidenced by the increasingly trippy graphics of the city's biggest underground newspaper, the East Village Other. The drugs shaped the music as well.

It also tied in with the rise of mass bohemia, which was quickly encroaching on the culture at large thanks to a new awareness about the war in Vietnam. The war had been going on for ten years by the time it became unpopular in the mid-'60s. That's because it began to hit closer to home once America was fielding ground troops and watching the carnage on TV every night. America's involvement in Vietnam had been a gradual result of bad policy unraveling: after the 1954 Geneva summit that created the nation of South Vietnam, America had been holding on to it with a lame life-support system of "advisors." What President Eisenhower and his secretary of state, John Foster Dulles, didn't realize, however, was something the French had learned the hard way: Far from being incompetent savages, the Viet Minh were a skilled fighting force with nothing to lose and everything to gain. They were accustomed to jungle terrain and fought in an unconventional manner that baffled their adversaries. They'd been fighting the French for seven years, with the smell of imminent victory in their nostrils, and they weren't about to give up. But in the midst of Cold War hysteria, American intervention in Vietnam seemed like the right thing to do.

By the time Kennedy, and later Johnson, took office, they'd inherited the war and weren't about to be daunted by the dire projections of their advisors. By 1966, there were 385,300 U.S. servicemen committed to ground battle. Vietnam was a brutal, new breed of warfare—"search and destroy" missions and "free-fire" artillery that mowed down everything in its path. As Americans watched, they began to realize that this was all happening in another hemisphere in a jungle country most of them had never heard of. A 1967 Gallup poll revealed that half of Americans believed the war was a mistake. With this kind of consensus growing, it was only a matter of time before the more outspoken antiwar factions began fusing with some of the other factions of the New Left. Magnified by the drugs, it seemed easy to believe that a "revolution" was happening.

Chief among the radicals were the Fugs, who formed in the East Village in 1964 in the backroom of Ed Sanders's Peace Eye bookstore (a self-described "scrounge lounge," according to Sanders). Sanders, an ex-beatnik from Cleveland who moved to New York in the late '50s to "meet Allen Ginsberg and become a poet" and had sailed around the world in a Polaris submarine in 1962 to protest the proliferation of nuclear weapons, was also the publisher of *Fuck You: A Magazine of the Arts* (which just proved that *Forced Exposure* wasn't far behind). Sanders would make his presence known at all the important "happenings" of the '60s, so the Fugs—who were named after Norman Mailer's substitute for the f-word in *The Naked and the Dead*—were destined to appeal to a more "aware" audience than the average Rock 'n' Roll band. This despite the fact they weren't really a "band" at all but a ragtag assemblage of poets and radicals who played a weird mélange of Folk music, Blues, Eastern chants, and dirty poems. This was good enough to get them signed to ESP-Disk, a bizarre record label in New York founded by Bernard Stollman that specialized in avant-garde Jazz and pledged total artistic freedom (their slogan was "the artists alone decide what you hear on their ESP disk").

By the time of their second album, *The Fugs* (which actually made the top forty), the group had evolved into a kind of primitive clatter marked by lustful evocations and mantralike prepsychedelic trance-Rock. There was also room for the eleven-minute "Virgin Forest," perhaps the first Rock song to run eleven minutes or more. This was also when they began attracting attention, not only from the media, but the FBI as well (especially after they burned an American flag onstage). This was the classic '60s pop/radical paradox: being on Hoover's shit list and the cover of *Life* (which Sanders was on February 17, 1967).

Along with the Fugs, there were the unholy Godz, who also recorded for ESP and shared with their label-mates a penchant for primitive bashing, heavy breathing, and dirty words (these were still the days when it was a big deal to say "shit" on a record). They also shared a love of exotica (the *psaltry?*). Whereas the Fugs were poets, the Godz were more like ad executives—slightly older, more cynical guys with day jobs on Madison Avenue who looked at the invading British groups with skepticism (they mangled the Beatles' "You Won't See Me" on their second album, which predated the deconstructionist tendencies of Punk).

In many ways, the "drug culture" was the most far-reaching effect of the "revolution." People wanted things *instantly* in the '60s—that's why the kids rioted instead of going about it via conventional means like the student council meeting. As leisure time increased and television promoted instant gratification, the rise of recreational drug use was inevitable. Drugs like marijuana, LSD, and psylocibin gave people a chance to achieve instant euphoria without even leaving their chairs. Prescription drugs, not to mention alcohol, were so much a part of American culture anyway that no matter how much the kids were rebelling by using these newfangled "psychedelic" drugs, they were still being just like their parents.

In the '60s, the cure for everything was supposed to come from a pill, right down to the futuristic promise that someday we wouldn't have to eat—we'd simply pop a capsule. This all had to do with the race to the moon. It also had to do with the hedonism of the time, whereby drug taking could become a new national pastime. It was the rich Pop stars of the day who were instrumental in pushing this trend onto America's soft white underbelly. To the parents of the middle class, their children's embrace of the drug culture was a chasm from which many a parent/child relationship never recovered.

New York seemed to experience a proliferation of amphetamine in the '60s, perhaps because the pace of life there was accelerated anyway. Speed, a controlled substance that stimulated the nervous system, had been used for years to treat depression and assist in weight loss. In the '50s, housewives gulped "diet pills" that not only improved their waistlines, but made them whirling dervishes with the housework as well. This kind of instant artificial energy also aided truck drivers, traveling salesmen, and other people whose occupations relied on prolonged stamina. It was also not uncommon in the political arena: even JFK reportedly used amphetamines on occasion. As for sports, so-called pep pills had been common for years in basketball, and, in baseball, pitchers popped "greenies" in order to stay "up" for a game. Meanwhile, on and off Broadway, whole chorus lines were speed-eating chatterboxes.

In bohemian quarters, speed helped spur such enduring countercultural benchmarks as Jack Kerouac's *On the Road* and the rambling monologues of Lenny Bruce. In the early days of the Beatles, when they were toiling away in the dingy clubs of Hamburg and Liverpool, they often bought speed from the sailors who frequented clubs like the Ratskeller in order to maintain their rigorous performing schedule. But speed also caused hallucinations—as evidenced by the career of Bob Dylan at this juncture. Thanks to his use of amphetamines, he'd become the master of the put-down, a feisty chain-smoking fiend who sensed people's weaknesses and subsequently ran numbers on them. His lyrics had taken on a hallucinatory quality as well as they rambled on for eleven minutes at a time through elaborate dreamscapes and poetic free flights.

But flourishing in New York at the time was an even more decadent scene than the one that surrounded Dylan, a milieu so demure that even Dylan was considered unhip by its fractured denizens—mainly, the one coalescing around Andy Warhol's Factory (where Dylan was unceremoniously referred to as "the creep"). It was an environment conducive to heavy amphetamine usage, which in turn prompted massive paranoia (another symptom of the drug). By that time, Warhol, the ex-window dresser and shoe designer turned Pop artist and film-maker, was the central figure in the whole downtown art and film netherworld. His point-blank images of soup cans and car wrecks had struck a nerve with the public, and his vague, self-effacing nonimage had enhanced his mystique.

Like a lot of media figures in the mid-'60s, Warhol was impressed by the increasing scope of Rock music. He realized that conventional "art" was soon to become a graveyard of highbrow pretensions whereas Rock was a whole new field waiting to have a splotch of paint—or semen—tossed in its as-of-yet-unblemished face. Warhol's own "underground" movies delved into the hitherto unexplored: drugs, decadence, poor-little-rich-girl fantasies, suicide, homosexuality, transvestism, alienation. When he set out to "discover" a Rock band, he sought one that would mirror these themes with their music.

He didn't have to look far. In December 1965 his dancer–poet friend Gerard Malanga took him to see a group called the Velvet Underground, named after a sex paperback the lead singer found lying in the gutter one day in the spring of that year. The band had been slumming around the Village for months and were on the verge of being fired from the Café Bizarre for playing their "Black Angel's Death Song" one too many times. The various members, in their spare time, jammed with several self-professed "avant-garde" collectives around town and were bringing elements to the coffeehouse scene that clearly didn't "belong" there.

Warhol instantly liked their appearance (dressed in black) and was impressed by the fact that their strange songs seemed to deal with the same topics as his films (drugs, kinky sex). The Velvet Underground was also one of the first bands to feature a woman, in the person of drummer Maureen Tucker. However, with her short hair, black slacks, and shades, she looked like a boy. No wonder Warhol licked his lips.

The "Velvets," as they became known, gave "street" credibility a new name. Considering the musical backgrounds of the various members, it's no surprise their legacy has lasted longer than most. John Cale was a classically trained pianist brought to America from his native Wales on a Bernstein scholarship to Tanglewood Conservatory in 1963—his use of electric viola in the Velvets gave the band's music a disturbing undertow. Lou Reed had been playing piano since age five and, since switching to guitar, had been a member of one Rock 'n' Roll band or another since the '50s. Sterling Morrison had played trumpet in his youth but had switched to rhythm guitar after his discovery of Rhythm & Blues. He and Reed met when both were English Lit students at Syracuse University. This literary calling was not lost on their music—Reed's songs about detachment and decadence had a descriptive quality and personal uniqueness heretofore unknown to Rock. Reed was a genuine anomaly: a Long Island youth whose parents made him endure "shock therapy" to combat "homosexual feelings" (obviously, if his future incarnations were any indication, it didn't work).

John Cale recalls first meeting Reed: "He was a staff writer for some publishing company. He played me the songs he had written but they were nothing new or terribly exciting. But then he played me several which he claimed they wouldn't publish. He played 'Heroin' first and it totally knocked me out. The words and the music were so raunchy and devastating. What's more, his songs fit perfectly with my musical concept." [3]

Thus began the saga of the group that writer Diana Clapton called "the most powerfully innovative, enduringly influential and organically self-destructive...of its time." [4] Maybe so, but as the early demos, not released until 1995, reveal, the Velvet Underground could've just as easily ended up another weird avant-garde Folk-Rock act signed to ESP-Disk. As the original nucleus—Reed, Cale, and Morrison—rehearsed in their Ludlow Street apartment all through the summer of '65, songs like "Heroin" and "Venus in Furs" grew into more elaborate soundscapes, partly due to Cale's viola. The addition of Moe Tucker added a lot—a female drummer schooled on Olatunji and Bo Diddley records, she gave them a pulse that enabled them to more sharply focus their attack. In a song like "Lady Godiva's Operation," on their second album, the drums are everything. If Warhol had never come along and added Nico, the blonde chanteuse, and pricked Lou Reed's ego, who knows what direction their music would have taken? Most importantly, Warhol gave them a place to rehearse where they could play for hours at unlimited volume, and it's probably at the Factory that their more heavily amplified tendencies evolved. The songs were always there, but compare the demo version of "I'm Waiting for the Man" to the finished product: what had started as a kind of sleazy Blues had been transformed into a raging juggernaut of well-sculpted noise. And this was what would become their trademark (along with their fag/junkie image—despite the fact that they were neither).

The Velvets became the perfect freak act to augment Warhol's mixed-media show, the Exploding Plastic Inevitable, which toured the United States in 1966 and '67. The EPI was the total '60s event, a clashing multimedia "happening" combining light shows, films, dance, and Rock 'n' Roll. In many ways, it set the precedent for all subsequent "psychedelic" light shows: flashing strobes, florescent lights, and visual images projected off the musicians while they played. Marshall McLuhan more or less acknowledged the influence of the EPI with a photo in *The Medium is the Massage*.[5] However, at the time, reaction was almost always negative, as demonstrated by the famous quote in the *Chicago Tribune*: "The flowers of evil are in full bloom."

Few other mixed-media extravaganzas were as extreme as the EPI, but visual stimulus was to become a requirement of the "psychedelic" experience, a process by which, through the use of chemicals, one could alter his/her perception of "reality." The idea was, the more people understood the various levels of their own perception, the more they could "get it together." LSD was supposed to deliver humankind to the final stages of its psychic evolution.

As Jay Stevens, author of the ultimate LSD book *Storming Heaven*, explained: "This was a question the authorities were interested in…the way to 'live' scale. One dose of LSD stimulated enormous changes. Whereas the person [taking the test] might have said, 'It's important for me to get a corporate job' now they were saying 'I think maybe a contemplative lifestyle might be what I want.'"[6]

Think about it: a drug so powerful that just one dose could alter a person's whole philosophical outlook. Can you imagine the societal implications if this substance was unleashed on the throbbing masses? And what if it was all promoted in a massive media campaign—Turn On, Tune In, Drop Out! In the '60s, that's precisely what happened: as the foundation of society was being shaken by a controversial war, drugs—powerful drugs—came into the picture.

LSD, or lysergic acid diethylmide, was known throughout the research community as the "drug capable of shattering the ego." Invented in 1943 as a treatment for psychosis by the Swiss physicist Albert Hoffman, LSD was supposedly the key to unlocking the subconscious mind—that is, it changed the perception of what was "real," which is why it was used to treat such imagination-related disorders as schizophrenia. Outside of the medical community, there were people who were interested in the drug for consciousness-expansion purposes. This included the writer Aldous Huxley, whose *Doors of Perception* was an early psychedelic manifesto. Beatnik authors like Allen Ginsberg and William Burroughs were also interested in hallucinogens (Burroughs' South American search for the hallucinogenic *yage* plant was legendary), although their pal Jack Kerouac was just a good ol' drinker—upon being given psilocybin by Ginsburg, he remarked: "Walking on water wasn't built in a day."

By the early '60s, a young psychology professor was conducting grant-funded LSD experiments at Harvard, supposedly to study the drug's effects on human behavior. Timothy Leary was among the new breed of academics: affluent and liberal, he'd already raised eyebrows in Newton, Massachusetts (where he lived) for hosting pool parties featuring bikini-clad college girls and marijuana smoke. It wasn't long before his "research" sessions at Harvard took on a similarly libertine atmosphere.

The lucky few chosen for the "experiment" were sent through the revolving doors of consciousness. Reactions varied, because LSD affected everyone differently. For Dr. Leary, who'd already achieved wealth and success, twittering the knobs of consciousness provided a suitable playtime, a recreational extravagance. But to college students with still-fragile psyches, it could be cause for a full-blown psychotic reaction.

It was such issues that were dividing the entire medical community over LSD's merits. Such division led to Leary and his colleague Richard Alpert being dismissed from Harvard in 1963. Shortly thereafter, Peggy Hitchcock, an heir to the Mellon family fortune, informed Alpert that her brothers had just purchased a mansion in Millbrook, New York, as a tax shelter. In a move that could have only happened in the free-wheeling days of '60s philanthropy—when legitimate "patrons of the arts" were more plentiful—she handed the estate over to Leary and Alpert, who soon began dropping acid day and night and providing the impetus for similarly lost souls to do the same.

If Leary and his swanky mates introduced acid to the intelligentsia, then who unleashed it on the masses? For the answer, we must look toward the West. In the first half of the twentieth century, the region still held the promise of "wide open spaces"—particularly the Pacific Northwest region with its picturesque redwood-strewn mountainsides on the one hand, and the crashing blue surf of the Pacific on the other. Not surprisingly, between the years 1910–1935, some twenty thousand families migrated to the area. That kind of massive upheaval within the country itself may seem inconceivable nowadays, but, especially during the Depression, people literally packed up and moved two thousand miles, all for the promise of "better times ahead."

It was under such conditions that Ken Kesey was born. His family had migrated to Springfield, Oregon during the '30s, and Kesey, who was born in 1940, experienced a typical Baptist upbringing. Although he was gifted both academically and athletically, his strongest forté was his verbal skills, which led him to compose several scholarship-winning essays. Ending up at Stanford in 1958, Kesey was intrigued by the burgeoning "bohemian" scene that was taking place at that time in Northern California.

Kesey's closest friend in the early '60s was Vic Lovell, to whom he dedicated his first novel, *One Flew Over the Cuckoo's Nest*. It was Lovell who, in 1960, told Kesey about a volunteer program being held at the Menlo Park Veteran's Hospital. They were seeking human lab rats basically, to test the effects of certain "psychomimetic" (i.e., to mimic psychosis) substances. For the twenty dollars they offered, plus an ever-growing writer's curiosity about such things, Kesey was apparently game.

One of the drugs Kesey was given was LSD, and it impressed him so mightily that he soon took a job as an orderly at the hospital in order to procure more of the drug. Working the graveyard shift, his duties were minimal. This allowed him not only time to write, but to sample the drug supply as well (these were the days before such things were kept under close scrutiny). It was during this period that he wrote *One Flew Over the Cuckoo's Nest*. For a first novel, it won the twenty-two-year-old author an unprecedented amount of acclaim. Kesey credited his amazing success to LSD, and believed he had found "the answer."

After the phenomenal success of *Cuckoo's Nest*, Kesey penned what was essentially his *Ulysses*: entitled *Sometimes a Great Notion*, an epic about loggers in Oregon, the novel painstakingly described every tree branch in lysergic detail. Although the book was another enormous success, Kesey soon hung up his literary shoes to concentrate solely on…the party!

This marked the essential difference between Kesey and Leary: although Leary thought the acid should be treated as an official "sacrament," to only be used in a controlled environment, Kesey took a more evangelical point of view—one that would presage the subsequent West coast hippie movement. With the money he earned from his books, Kesey bought an old 1939 International Harvester bus and filled it with his zany friends (dubbed "the Merry Pranksters"). They were like an old-time medicine show, but the medicine they were dispensing was a very potent brew: LSD. Eventually the Pranksters perfected their "let's put it in the drinking water" brand of populism with a series of events called the Acid Tests, where the ex-football star Kesey would literally ladle out his magic potion to…those kids! But these kids weren't necessarily the privileged hordes who'd been subjected to Leary's experiments, just your average beer-drinking juvenile delinquents from all over California who'd hitchhiked up the coast to check out the scene. Unlike Leary's tour-guided extravaganzas, this atmosphere was anything but controlled. Anyone could come, and as a result Hell's Angels blended with teenyboppers: a perfect case of *Satan Meets the High School Cheerleaders*, in other words.

It wasn't long before this kind of debauchery caught the eyes of the Feds. LSD went unregulated until September 1966, when the state of California, under then-governor Ronald Reagan, officially made it illegal. By that time, however, the damage had already been done: not only had a definite "drug culture" already taken hold; but chemists-gone-awry like Owsley Stanley were making tubs full of the stuff that was as potent as the supply coming from the Sandoz lab in New Jersey.

Drugs have always played a large role in the lives of musicians. It's not hard to guess what acid did to the structure of Rock music. No longer were the players tied to the limitations of Top Forty. The whole notion of Rock improvising came about. In San Francisco, where psychedelia found its strongest foothold, the new dance halls gave the musicians a forum to expound on their more lysergically fueled musical notions, and the emergent hippie culture gave them an audience. After the groups started taking acid, there was no way the facile Pop process was going to make sense to them anymore. Acid revolutionized the whole basic sound of Rock 'n' Roll.

Chief among the early acid experimenters were the Grateful Dead, who were the band Kesey chose to accompany the Acid Tests. The kids nowadays may have vilified them as granola heads and lames, but the fact is, in the '60s they were miles ahead of most groups. Although guitarist Jerry Garcia had

Revenant

CHARLEY PATTON
It had all been done by 1929.

MILES DAVIS
Shee-it, Norman Podhoretz,
Norman Mailer . . . they all
named Norman.

Don Hunstein/Courtesy of
Columbia Records

FIFTIES ALBUM ART

Some early examples of rock 'n' roll album cover art.
(What, did they think the audience was a bunch of morons?)

Holdo

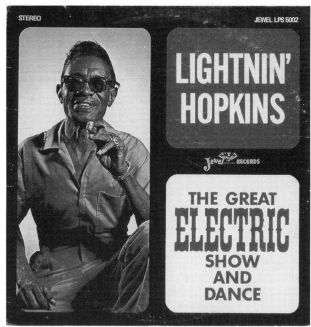

LIGHTNIN' HOPKINS
ALBUM
The blues in neon
(batteries optional).

Holdo

BO DIDDLEY
The guitar was
the only thing
that was square.

John Fahnley

RICKY NELSON
Dino was apparently not amused.

Capitol Records

BEACH BOYS
Where's Brian?

Holdo

THE ROLLING STONES   Clacking teeth.

John Fahnley

THE YARDBIRDS
Oy, wot say, mates. Isn't that the old lady from the cover of the Doors album?

PRETTY THINGS ALBUM
File under "Archaeology."

Holdo

VELVET UNDERGROUND
Free meth at the supermarket opening (right next to the Brillo boxes).

Holdo

THE FUGS
On Hoover's shitlist—and the cover of *Life*.

Raymond Ross

SUN RA
Ray Charles in the 88th dimension.

DAVID BOWIE
Chameleon in a clown suit.

Raymond Ross

John Fahnley

RETURN TO FOREVER
In favor of scarves.

Courtesy of Columbia Records

BOB MARLEY
Marijuana martyr.

John Fahnley

excellent chops (based in Bluegrass), it took the band a while to polish their act and transcend their meager jug-band beginnings. But the acid came along to help with that, and no one embraced the psychedelic ethos more readily than the Grateful Dead (on an early album, Garcia is referred to as "Captain Trips"). The band was capable of Blues, and on many occasions, they took "traditional" material—which was actually the folkie thing again—and transformed it into this new kind of jam-based "psychedelic" Rock with swirling organ (courtesy of Pigpen) and Garcia's crystalline guitar lines. They were also champions of amplification—they helped put the cheesy "public address" systems that had been the norm for Rock bands, right down to the Beatles, out of business.

The Dead had "high" ambitions in more ways than one: their second album, *Anthem of the Sun*, was a kind of sound collage, mixing live and studio performances, that sounded unlike anything else at the time. This was something the record labels didn't know how to handle yet (i.e., artistic control) but soon were going to have to learn. The days of the generic teen Rock band with giddy sock hop hopes were dying out. Rock was turning into two things overnight: Art and Big Money! The groups weren't dupes anymore. As they wrested "artistic control" from their labels, the sounds got wilder and wilder.

Groups like the Dead were pioneers of the ballroom scene that had sprung up in San Francisco in the wake of LSD. The Avalon, Matrix, Fillmore West, and all the others provided cavernous spaces where the loose jamming of the psychedelic bands could rebound off the walls and high ceilings. By holding the Acid Tests at Longshoreman's Wharf in San Francisco, Kesey had established the precedent for more expansive performance spaces. The ballrooms allowed the hippies not to "feel closed in, man" which would in turn have bred massive "paranoia." Plus the volume of bands like the Dead was simply too much for the small clubs to handle. The larger halls were the only places that could accompany the new heavily amplified Rock.

The Bay Area had never really enjoyed much of a Rock scene prior to the Dead and their ilk. San Francisco was always a hip town that had played host to a variety of anti-establishment manifestations, from hip to beat to gay. The music clubs tended to focus on Jazz, Blues, and Folk. There wasn't really a "teenybopper" scene, or a meaningful one anyway, until the arrival of the Beau Brummels in 1964. They were San Fran's essential Beatles copy band, and their second album, *Vol. 2*, was actually an overlooked classic occupying a strange niche between that era and the one coming in—like the missing link between *Rubber Soul* and *Surrealistic Pillow*. The Brummels recorded for Autumn Records, run by one Sylvester Stewart, also known as Sly Stone, whose own Funk powerhouse would start up soon. So, by the mid-'60s, there were signs of life.

The group that really changed everything was the Jefferson Airplane, formed by an ex-folkie named Marty Balin, who needed a band to play at his own club, the Matrix. Ralph J. Gleason, the influential jazz critic at the *San Francisco Chronicle*, came down to check out the scene and wrote a vastly influential article that drew national attention to "the San Francisco sound." The Airplane reaped the rewards by being one of the first San Fran groups to sign to a major label, RCA. The first album, *The Jefferson Airplane Takes Off*, brought the San Francisco sound to the world: an evangelical wail combining crisp, clean guitar lines with soaring male/female vocal harmonies. "My Best Friend" sounded like the Mamas & the Papas on acid.

After the original chick singer, Signe Toly, left to have a baby, the group went on to even greater heights with her replacement, Grace Slick. With Slick they recorded *Surrealistic Pillow*, the first entirely psychedelic Top Ten album, which made them the first hippie millionaires (of course, they lived communally in a big house on Fulton Street). "Somebody to Love" was a yowling classic: Grace tongue-lashes the "straight" in a manner not unlike Dylan's repudiation of "Mr. Jones" while guitars play mind-bending patterns. Guitarist Jorma Kaukonen was right behind Jerry Garcia in defining the mercurial guitar sound of vintage San Francisco (also credit Moby Grape's Jerry Miller and Quicksilver's John Cipollina).

Grace Slick's role in the artistic direction of the Jefferson Airplane shouldn't be underestimated: for a woman to have a defining role in a Rock 'n' Roll band of that magnitude was unprecedented. A former fashion model, Slick was a new model liberal, rebelling against the staunch morality of the '50s in every way possible. That meant giving up her career and her marriage (she was recently divorced) and joining a Rock 'n' Roll band (and fucking every one of them save Marty). She was the first independent female in Rock, the first one not specifically pandering to male ideals (although by fucking the whole group—and then bragging about it—she did kind of fall into the classic '60s "old lady" trap). In her lyrics, when she took aim she could be as acerbic as Dylan: a frequent target of scorn were the men of her father's generation (the World War II daddies). But as she pointed out in "Two Heads": "Eeeeh, you call that *men*, darling?" She also figures as a pre-indie Rock chick with stuff like "Lather," in which she utilized the "little girl voice" in a direct premonition of Barbara Manning, Rebecca Odes, Heather Lewis of Beat Happening, etc.

The other Big Mama of the Frisco scene—and not coincidentally Slick's only peer in the Female Rock pantheon of the '60s—was Janis Joplin, a Texas import who moved to the city in 1966. Growing up in Port Arthur, and staking out a path as a fairly dowdy Folk singer, she was the subject of much derision, culminating in some frat organization naming her "ugliest boy" in one yearbook category. This event more than anything convinced her, at the urging of her friend Chet Helm, to leave the small town behind once and for all. Joplin didn't exactly "see the bright lights" and pursue some ideal of fame—it was more a case of needing a more nurturing environment to practice her art, and San Francisco at that time seemed ideal. In the late '60s, the rules about what a "star" constituted—and how a person became one—were changing. In that sense, Janis Joplin was perfect—a true freak during a period when "freaks" of all dimensions were becoming prominent.

The band she joined when she got to Frisco, Big Brother & the Holding Company, were a sloppy garage-Blues band, but they suited her perfectly. There was chemistry within the group that allowed Joplin to go off on her Bessie Smith/Aretha Franklin Blues fits and frequently attain the emotional heights that had previously been reserved for Black performers. By the time Dylan's manager, Albert Grossman, had taken Joplin under his wing in 1968, he was urging her to dump Big Brother, which turned out to be her downfall. No matter how sloppy they were, Big Brother understood their star better than any slick cats ever could. When she made some more "professional" records in the late '60s, her music suffered from loss of character (i.e., blandness). But she had bigger problems by then—like heroin, for instance, which eventually killed her in 1970.

A lot of the early Frisco bands were folkies prior to the psychedelic revolution. The Quicksilver Messenger Service is a perfect example of a band that combined very basic Blues and Folk elements transformed by acid and electricity into something totally original. The word "mercurial" is always used to describe the heavy vibrato of guitarist John Cipollina—indeed there seems to be some kind of chemical compound coursing through it. Like most of the hippie bands, Quicksilver did good-time songs like the classic "Dino's Song" followed by hypnotic instrumentals like "Gold and Silver," which showcased the guitar duels between Cipollina and Gary Duncan in a direct premonition of Tom Verlaine and Richard Lloyd in Television. Verlaine, as well as the Patti Smith Group's Lenny Kaye, has cited Cipollina as a direct influence.

Country Joe & the Fish, like the Dead, had jug-band roots, but what Country Joe brought to the scene was his New Left politics. Raised a liberal by Marxist parents—in *Berkeley*, no less—he embraced the radical notions of the "movement" instantly and with reckless abandon. Flaunting his drug use, he pressed an EP on his own Rag Baby label, once again in a direct premonition of indie. The record contained the classic fogged-out San Francisco anthem "Bass Strings," with its immortal refrain: "Just one more trip/And I'll stay high all the time." Later Joe became a bigwig in the "protest" category, playing all the benefits, smoke-ins, love-ins, be-ins, etc. (including a classic appearance at Woodstock). Recording for a folkie label, Vanguard, the Fish were a Frisco institution that reveled in their "underground" status. It was a testament to the way San Francisco was changing the whole politics of the record industry that a group like this could actually thrive in the climate of the late '60s without having *any* mainstream "hit" potential whatsoever.

The same cannot be said of Moby Grape, a band that was signed to Columbia in the feeding frenzy following the Monterey Pop Festival. Unlike the other Frisco bands, the Grape weren't prone to long excursions, and their first album consisted of tightly constructed, heavily harmonized Rock of the Beatles/Byrds variety. But Columbia botched the job by releasing five singles at once from the album, an exercise in overkill that confused radio programmers and blew the band's chances of being the only other Frisco band that could follow the Jefferson Airplane into the Top Forty. The group seemed to react with total narcissism, making their next album a jam-based excursion that also included brass and other incongruous elements. It was becoming evident to the record companies that, despite the hype, the chances of getting these stoners to commit anything memorable to vinyl was like trying to get Allen Ginsberg to put his pants on. You had to be there, I guess.

The Steve Miller Band—actually a Chicago transplant—signed to Capitol for an unprecedented sum in 1967, but once again the experience didn't really translate to vinyl. Miller found himself jetting back and forth between Frisco and England, enlisting the aid of Brit session heavies like Glyn Johns, Nicky Hopkins, and Lee Michaels in order to get his sound right. When he did, such as on mammoth productions like "Baby's House," it sounded like the missing link between the Beatles and Elton John. It had nothing to do with the classic "San Francisco Sound," in other words, nor did such other late arrivals as Santana, who perfected a kind of Latin Jazz-Rock hybrid, or It's a Beautiful Day, who were just tired folkies in hippie drag.

The San Francisco groups brought national attention to the city. In the eyes of the world, San Francisco became the capital of the hippies. On the promise of Scott McKenzie's "San Francisco (Wear Some Flowers in Your Hair)," thousands of teen runaways flooded the streets of San Francisco during the summer of 1967 (the "Summer of Love"). The dupes fresh off the bus never thought about such considerations as money, food, or hygiene. Fortunately for them, there were altruistic forces like the Diggers and the Haight-Ashbury Free Clinic in place. That didn't stop VD from becoming the new childhood disease of the '60s. The neighborhood known as the Haight became the crossroads for a whole new kind of depravity.

What was a "hippie" anyway? According to California governor Ronald Reagan: "A hippie is someone who dresses like Tarzan, has hair like Jane, and smells like Cheetah." They were the Great Unwashed, no question! In fact, when Jefferson Airplane named their third album *After Bathing at Baxter's*, they probably felt the need to document the occasion because it was something that happened so infrequently. But hippies relished their reputation as dirtballs because it grossly offended Mom and Pop America (who'd always preached that cleanliness was next to you-know-what). "Hippie" came to connote a vast array of political and social implications, but as a generic term in the '60s, it meant a person had long hair, took drugs, scorned work (and "materialism" in general), and listened to Rock music.

The San Francisco groups—the Grateful Dead, the Great Society, the Jefferson Airplane, the Charlatans, Big Brother & the Holding Company, Moby Grape, 50 Foot Hose, the Loading Zone, Mother Earth, the Steve Miller Band, Quicksilver, Sopwith Camel, the Serpent Power, Country Joe & the Fish, Santana, Dan Hicks & His Hot Licks, Kak, Aum, Cold Blood, Mad

River, Sly & the Family Stone, the Harbinger Complex—helped introduce a lot of the tendencies that made Rock "mature." These included the Jazz-like notion of the extended jam, amplification, better equipment, higher production values, horn sections and other eclectic instrumentation, real long hair, communalism, light shows, acid, album-oriented Rock, big contracts, artistic independence, underground radio, and the underground press.

In a weird premonition of the ensuing hippie culture, the Beatles played their last live performance as a group in San Francisco on August 29, 1966. At this point, the touring had become drudgery, and the reclusive tendencies of the recording studio held the greatest allure. When the Beatles returned to England that fall, they found a whole new "psychedelic" scene emerging at clubs like the UFO and Speakeasy. They also found a new standard of musicianship to be reckoned with and an environment of elevated intent, primarily in the form of two upstart acts that also both happened to be trios: Cream and the Jimi Hendrix Experience. In the form of these "power trios" lay the prototype for "heavy metal."

Cream perfected the notion of Rock one-upmanship by their name alone (they considered themselves the "cream" of British musicians). Surely their lumbering versions of "Spoonful" and "Sittin' on Top of the World" exhibited a kind of arrogance bordering on contempt. This wasn't Herman's Hermits, in other words. Cream considered themselves accomplished enough musicians to subject their audience to their every artistic fancy. This resulted in bloated eighteen-minute versions of "Spoonful," but it also resulted in some of the most well-crafted Rock of the period: "Tales of Brave Ulysses," "I'm So Free," "Sweet Wine," "White Room," "Swlabr," "Badge," etc. In songs like "Cat's Squirrel" they were already putting Zeppelin-oid fluctuations to use. Cream's ambitions often overshadowed the resulting music, but they were self-consciously trying to elevate the art form of Rock (even if they were still under the mistaken impression that Rock was merely an extension of the Blues—guitarist Eric Clapton had earned his rep being "Blues or nothing," remember?). Ginger Baker's wild, cyclical drumming wouldn't have made sense in the conventional (Beatles/Stones) nonimprov format (i.e., Pop). With the high-art notions came a gentlemanly detachment: "Who needs the hurry, the worry of city life?" Cream presaged the whole wave of English Rock Aristocracy, buying castles and the like.

The Jimi Hendrix Experience came about no more organically than Cream, despite its leader's dues-paying as a backup musician to such R&B artists as Little Richard, Wilson Pickett, and the Isley Brothers on the chitlin circuit in his pre-psychedelic incarnation. His being a Black man from Seattle, Washington, Jimi Hendrix's arrival in England was the epitome of "freak" acts in a freak era. Hendrix had already fronted a band in New York called Jimmy James & the Blue Flames, and although it was still R&B-based, he was already experimenting with distortion and odd special effects. It was during this time that he caught the attention of Chas Chandler, the former bass player of the Animals, who was looking for a new kick—and managing Hendrix was more than he could have ever dreamed of. Taking him back to England, Chandler bedecked Hendrix in psychedelic garb and introduced him to a pair of Brit musicians: Mitch Mitchell (drums) and Noel Redding (bass). The appearance of these two white kids with the Big Black Stud completed the freak picture, but Hendrix lucked out—they could actually play. Hendrix, a man who wore his guitar around his neck seventeen hours per day, was carving out such a distinct path as an instrumentalist that it's likely he elevated his accompanists just by sheer force of will. Credit Mitchell and Redding for being able to make the cosmic jump. Along with Ginger Baker and Keith Moon, Mitchell was the best of the British drummers, a polyrhythmic powerhouse who made every rimshot a force to be reckoned with. Because Hendrix was a lead-based guitar player, Redding had to sometimes compensate rhythmically, and he was more than capable in this category.

As evidenced by the band's first album, *Are You Experienced?*, Hendrix never abandoned the Blues impulse. Songs like "Hey Joe," "Remember," "The Wind Cries Mary," "51st Anniversary," "May This Be Love," and "Highway Chile" were nothing less than the final word in the Blues, before the whole genre became a vaudeville act (a few modern-day purveyors like R. L. Burnside excepted). The drugs undoubtedly helped him propel the Blues into outer space, but no matter what vibe he was pursuing, be it Blues or psychedelic, his basic language was absolute. Like Charlie Parker, Miles Davis, John Coltrane, Ornette Coleman, Cecil Taylor, or any of the other Jazz pioneers, Hendrix invented his own musical language. As far as Rock goes, in the field of "heavy metal," he was essential with crunching riff-rockers like "Purple Haze," "Foxy Lady," "Manic Depression," "Voodoo Chile," and the rest. And when he mastered the recording studio with albums like *Axis: Bold as Love* and *Electric Ladyland,* he was inheriting the Beatles' baroque art-Rock mantle, albeit with a much heavier edge. There's no telling what he would have done had the drugs not snuffed him in 1970. Posthumous releases like *Nine to the Universe* hint at perhaps a jazzier direction (a merger with Miles, not to mention Funkadelic, might have been the inevitable result).

The Rock virtuoso era coincided with the pastoral bliss of psychedelia. British groups moved to the countryside in droves, not only to live like squires but also to escape the heat of narco agents, who were starting to hound the English superstars with alarming persistence.

Traffic came together under such conditions. As drummer Jim Capaldi remembers: "They had an amazing image...in America of us all wandering around the countryside. Woody (Chris Wood) used to wander around with an Ordnance Survey map looking for ancient burial grounds...People like Ginger Baker would come driving up in Jaguars and get stuck in the muddy tracks." [7]

Despite such indulgences, Traffic provided yet another unique variation on the basic Rock structure combining Soul, Jazz, and psychedelic elements. Formed by Steve and Muff Winwood, two brothers recently exiled from the Spencer Davis Group, with guitarist Dave Mason in tow, Traffic were in many ways the forerunners of Prog-Rock. Their licks were tasteful, and—in contrast to bands like Cream and the Jimi Hendrix Experience—not flashy at all, but always proficient. Because of Steve Winwood's R&B background with Spencer Davis, Traffic carried its weight as a somewhat Blues/Gospel-influenced band as well ("Medicated Goo" sounded like a great lost Stax/Volt single). Their best material—"Mr. Fantasy," "Feelin' Alright," "Empty Pages," "The Low Spark of High-Heeled Boys"—was still redolent of the Blues.

Procol Harum mixed Classical tastes and poetic images and combined organ/piano to create a somber demeanor that evoked the cathedral as much as Winwood's organ playing in Traffic evoked a revival meeting. Matthew Fisher's organ playing was still a basic update of the whole Zombies/Georgie Fame formula, but there was little Pop quotient at this point. Their riff-based numbers like "Whisky Train" helped introduce yet another Brit guitar god in the form of Robin Trower.

The effects of the acid on the British Rock scene at this time were profound. No group epitomized this more than Pink Floyd (formerly the Architectural Abdabs), who featured a psychedelic light show à la the Exploding Plastic

Inevitable. Original leader/guitarist Syd Barrett, who insisted on going onstage loaded, proved himself a songwriter of some competence with such acid-altered entities as "Arnold Layne," "See Emily Play," and "Bike," which epitomized the first wave of British psych as much as the Beatles' similar experiments ("Strawberry Fields Forever," et al.). However, in Barrett's case the dementia was real, not feigned—even before Floyd recorded their second album, *A Saucerful of Secrets*, he'd gone too far, as they say. Legend varies as to what actually happened (one report has it that he consumed a whole thimblefull of acid), but Barrett was Britain's first full-blown acid casualty. Later on, he made a couple of landmark psych-Folk albums, *The Barrett* and *Madcap Laughs*, that influenced David Bowie, among others.

Kaleidoscope combined Pop and music hall sensibilities with psychedelia to create a structurally sound dynamic that sustained them through three fine LPs. Despite this fact, they were never introduced to this continent, perhaps to avoid confusion with an American band of the same name. The Move were another British band that was more or less ignored in the United States despite charting several hits in England during the heyday of British psych, '67–'69. Combining the influence of the Beach Boys with vaudeville/music hall, the Move shared a propensity with the Who for their high-energy delivery and weird subject matter. Leader Roy Wood was a genuine eccentric capable of psychedelia like "Cherry Blossom Clinic Revisited," which told the tale of a full-blown freak-out in the best Brit "Rock opera" fashion.

Other British "freakbeat" bands went even more ignored in the U.S., despite some groundbreaking work. Perhaps the biggest tragedy of the era was that of the Pretty Things, who got ignored even while they were making powerful records like "Midnight to Six Man" and "LSD," a pair of songs combining sophisticated lyrics with active musical centers. The Pretty Things were punk-prototypes and, like the Floyd, they were another group who went overboard on the acid (*SF Sorrow*, supposedly their version of *Sgt. Pepper*, was overrated). But when they came right out and said it, as they did on "LSD," it was a ballsy move in light of all the "veiled" drug references that were making the rounds in Rock lyrics in those days. The fact that they backed it up with blistering R&B ensured that they would not be forgotten by history. Many of the Brit psych bands were also verging on Heavy Metal by this time (the Move, "Sunshine Help Me"). The increasing amplification required to enhance the

psychedelic experience, first introduced by the San Francisco groups, was leading to a wealth of musical possibilities. As groups wandered off musically in
their own directions to explore the limits of their musical imaginations, spontaneous combustion was an inevitable result.

The Yardbirds have often been credited with creating "heavy metal."
Their greatest period of experimentation came during the Jeff Beck era.
Despite the Pop arrangements of songs like "For Your Love" and "Heart Full
of Soul," by the time the Yardbirds got to stuff like "Lost Women" and "Over
Under Sideways Down," they were creating a whole new muse. It wasn't metal
just yet, but it was aggressive in nature and musically hewn of new shapes and
forms that the previous structural impositions of Rock, pre-acid, hadn't
allowed. This was an important step towards all subsequent improv-based
Rock (Metal, Prog, Fusion), but it should be clarified: for the most part the
Yardbirds conducted their improvs still firmly within the context of the three-
minute single à la the Beatles, Stones, Kinks, Who, etc. They were also still
having people write some of their songs for them (e.g., Graham Gouldman).
They were also throwing in the hackneyed Blues covers (albeit psychedelical-
ly transformed). Whatever jamming they did must have been concentrated
into these little doses—or perhaps onstage. By the time of their last album,
Little Games, Jimmy Page had replaced Beck as the lead guitarist and, by the
sounds of it, was already setting the dynamic for Led Zeppelin ("Tinker Tailor
Soldier Spy," "White Summer").

The entire first wave of British groups was transformed by the acid insurgence. Eric Burdon, the leader of the Animals, even went so far as to fire the
original band and reconstruct a whole new one—dubbed "Eric Burdon & the
Animals"—that centered around his psychedelic excesses. His "A Girl Named
Sandoz" was the trippiest evocation of the psychedelic experience this side of
the Blues Magoos' "Dante's Inferno." Scotsman Donovon Leitch began as a
Folk troubadour in the Dylan tradition but went overboard on the psychedel-
ic stuff, as the song titles demonstrate: "Mellow Yellow," "Epistle to Dippy,"
"Wear Your Love Like Heaven," "Jennifer Juniper," "Sunshine Superman."
Still, producer Mickey Most—who'd also worked with the Animals and
Yardbirds—framed Donovon's most naïve flights of fancy in fairly appealing
psych/Pop pastiches.

Like everything they did, the Beatles' psychedelic experiments were vastly influential, starting with the introduction of the sitar on *Rubber Soul*. George Harrison's forays into Eastern mysticism had led to a fascination with the musical attributes of the Far East. Because he was a hippie millionaire, he could afford to engage in dabbling of the highest order and did so by enlisting India's sitar maestro, Ravi Shankar, to give him lessons. The sitar is a very difficult instrument to play, and it takes years of discipline. It doesn't really correspond with the psychedelic lifestyle at all, so Harrison soon grew bored with the instrument. He'd used it on "Norwegian Wood" and then again on "Love You To," and he even went to India and made an album, *Wonderwall Music*, with native musicians playing traditional instruments. But George Harrison wasn't going to give up his career in the Beatles to be a sitar virtuoso, no matter how honorable it looked underneath the glowing eye of his swami. Ravi Shankar, on the other hand, was able to ride the Harrison association to some degree of crossover success, even performing at the Monterey Pop Festival.

Despite such attempts as Vincent Bell's *Pop Goes Electric Sitar* (1966), the sitar ended up being mostly a novelty. Songs like Donovon's "Sunshine Superman," Traffic's "Paper Sun," Eric Burden & the Animals' "Monterey," and the Rolling Stones' "Paint it Black" utilized the instrument as strictly an embellishment (the sitar did nothing to form the structure of the song itself, in other words). But the preponderance of such attempts shows that the artists themselves were desperately yearning for a kind of eclecticism that playing Rhythm & Blues apparently no longer offered. It's difficult to say whether they were trying to actually refine the rough-hewn textures of Rock 'n' Roll like later Art-Rock practitioners, or if they were just stoners on a lark. In any case, Rock was turning into a canvas for an infinite number of musical variations. Hyphen-Rock would know no bounds in the years to come.

The Beatles at that time were still the conduit through which all of these ideas were filtered. It was producer George Martin's idea to play a baroque harpsichord solo on "In My Life" (1965). The next thing you know, there was Baroque-Rock in the form of the Rolling Stones' "Lady Jane," the Left Banke's "Walk Away Renee," and, to some extent, Procol Harum's "A Whiter Shade of Pale." That was only outdone by Vaudeville-Rock: "Winchester Cathedral," "The Egg Plant That Ate Chicago," the Beatles' "Your Mother Should Know," the Monkees' "D. W. Washburn," the Sopwith Camel's "Hello, Hello," Donovon's "Mellow Yellow," and the immortal "Acapulco Gold" by the Rainy

Daze. It seemed like, by 1967, a great number of Rock musicians were simply engaging in a kind of eclecticism that really had little to do with Rock 'n' Roll and only served to cloud the picture for future generations.

Nowhere was this more apparent than on the Beatles' magnum opus, *Sgt. Pepper's Lonely Hearts Club Band,* released in June 1967. Here was an album made as an album—that is, as a contiguous entity as opposed to a mere collection of songs. The Beatles had given up touring to supposedly concentrate solely on their music, and the counterculture awaited the next installment of their musical saga with bated breath. The result was a Rock 'n' Roll album that bore little resemblance to Rock 'n' Roll. That's why it ultimately became known as Art-Rock (or Prog, as in "progressive," Rock): it was Rock 'n' Roll that carried with it the pretense of Fine Art. In reality it was just a purer form of Pop—a more pretentious version of the schmaltz that, despite the insurgence of the past three years, still dominated the hit parade.

The first evidence that the album was a departure from the norm was the whole presentation itself—*Sgt. Pepper* was an upgrade of album-making aesthetics. The sleeve, for example, was a gatefold, a type usually reserved for Jazz and soundtracks, as record execs at that time believed Rock was a shuck that didn't warrant such grandiose trappings. Ditto for a lyric sheet, as Rock was believed to be a bunch of blathering nonsense. The Beatles apparently disagreed—they obviously thought the new social commentary they were penning at the time in the form of "She's Leaving Home" and "A Day in the Life" warranted being read as *poetry*, hence a lyric sheet for the first time in a Rock album. This was also the day and age when Rock stars were having their designer friends do the art for their album jackets as well. The bands were telling the record companies what they wanted, and the companies were footing the bill. Bands were packaging themselves now—they were totally in control of how they wanted to be perceived by their "public."

The artistic reckoning, as well as the drug experience, stimulated the need for more visually elaborate album packaging. With Rock LPs becoming thematic entities, the covers had to be evocative of the music therein. As Dominy Hamilton explained: "The psychedelic poster and record sleeve were, literally, objects of contemplation. Listening to records in the late '60s was a matter of 'getting into it'; you put the record on the turntable, you got high, and probably looked at the record cover while listening." [8]

As Rock groups wrested more artistic control from their corporate sponsors, they were given to not only embellishing their albums with more intricate graphics but also embellishing their music with artier musical devices. Taking a hint from the Beatles, who used a string section on songs like "Eleanor Rigby" and "She's Leaving Home," the Moody Blues brought in literally a whole symphony orchestra to augment the maudlin ditties on *Days of Future Passed*. In the years to follow, the concept of the hippie Rock band "jamming" with the symphony orchestra became commonplace. Although it was reasonable enough that a classically trained prodigy like Frank Zappa might attempt such a feat, it became ridiculous when a group of English heavy-oids like Deep Purple attempted to sit in with the Royal Philharmonic (*Concerto for Rock Group and Orchestra*, 1970).

As for actual Classical musicians playing Rock, perhaps the most notable converts were the various Juilliard-trained members of the New York Rock & Roll Ensemble, who added such unlikely instruments as cello and oboe to the basic guitar/drums framework. They also attempted to adapt Bach to Rock in a move that predated the real Prog-Rock era—King Crimson, Yes, ELP, etc.—by a couple of years. As proof of how much the Art-Rock preoccupation had taken hold, Leonard Bernstein, the flamboyant leader of the New York Philharmonic, hosted a TV special in 1967 about Rock's increasing sophistication, concentrating on *Sgt. Pepper* and a young singer/songwriter named Janis Ian.

In Los Angeles, increased musical sophistication was a given considering the proximity of the industry at large as well as the abundance of studios and producers. As far as recording technique went, L.A. had already played host to some of the most sophisticated producers of the day: Brian Wilson, Terry Melcher, Lou Adler, and Gary Usher, among others. As the record industry became more industry and less hype for teen-hops, a much broader definition of Rock emerged encompassing everything from Blues to Folk to Ragas to Country influences, to symphony orchestras, along with avant-garde ideas from the visual arts, social satire, fashion.

The psychedelic era caught Brian Wilson by surprise. Then again, just about everything caught Brian Wilson by surprise. By 1967 he'd more or less succumbed to the sandbox. The Beach Boys had helped build L.A. into the capital of fun, sun, and surf, but by the mid to late '60s, protest was selling, and Brian's idyllic paradise was starting to look more like a concentration camp (especially to him). *Pet Sounds*, released in June 1966, was Brian's attempt to come to terms with the strange sounds he was hearing in his mind (under acid). Luckily, at that time he hadn't entirely abandoned his musical gifts, so the songs were still tuneful enough. The teenyboppers turned their backs on it, which hurt Brian even further, but several budding young Rock critics paid great allegiance (big deal).

Hooking up with a collaborator, Van Dyke Parks, Wilson set out to create a masterpiece that would rival *Sgt. Pepper* in the annals of album-making grandeur. The album was to be called *Smile*, and the centerpiece was "The Fire Suite." Brian went so far into the deep end during the recording sessions that he made the other musicians wear actual fire hats, supposedly to capture the right "vibes." When a factory across the street from the studio burned down, Brian panicked, and, in a fit of paranoia, erased the whole tape. It was around this time that he also installed the sandbox—a four-thousand-dollar monstrosity that sat in the middle of his living room, where he would sit and contemplate the "vibes." Needless to say, the Beach Boys had a hard time convincing the emergent "serious" Rock audience that they were indeed serious. Parks cashed in on his association with Brian and made a few albums of his own, but they were the most fey meanderings imaginable.

The Byrds were also early pioneers of immaculate studio proficiency and had taken the dive towards progressivism early with "Eight Miles High," a complex work of art before such things were the norm. They'd always been a slick outfit: the guitar solo in "I'll Feel a Whole Lot Better" was twelve-string heaven. Even when the Byrds aped the Beatles directly ("She Has a Way"), there was still a deliberate warping of Country & Western sensibilities that revealed a greater ambition. They were musical adventurers from the start, so the era of greater awareness suited them perfectly. As far as psychedelia goes, the Byrds had been hinting at evocations of flying all along, from their name to Roger McGuinn's "whooooosh concept" in the liner notes of *Turn Turn Turn*. As the band evolved, Chris Hillman's country fixation ("Time Between") and David Crosby's hippie-dippie tendencies ("Triad," "Mind Gardens") became more pronounced. But like Brian Wilson, McGuinn apparently saw the other members of the band as interlocking fixtures and "programmed" them as such (eventually resulting in their departure—Crosby in '67, Hillman in '68). *The Notorious Byrd Brothers* (1968) was McGuinn's attempt to match *Pet Sounds* and *Sgt. Pepper*, and it outdistanced both of them—a glistening pastiche of studio-made perfection.

After the Byrds had elevated their flight patterns far above the Sunset Strip, other bands carried on the Folk-Rock tradition. Love was a perfect example. Could you get more '60s than a band called *Love*? They packed 'em at Ciro's once the Byrds had finished their residency there, and they were the first Rock group signed to Jac Holzman's Folk label, Elektra, thus paving the way for the Doors, MC5, and the Stooges. Their first LP was chock-full of seemingly innocent Folk-protest Rock, but the sound was primitive, more in the tradition of the garage bands. They sounded like an overamplified, underskilled Byrds. This was still the day and age when groups who'd only been playing for six months were whisked into the studio to record their debut albums. But what Love lacked in technical proficiency they made up for in terms of ambition— by the time of their second album, *Da Capo*, they were incorporating string sections, Jazz elements, and a boring Blues tune that took up an entire side of the LP ("Revelation," clocking in at 18:45). Like the Fugs before them, who'd trilled "Virgin Forest" for eleven minutes, or the Stones, who'd pounded "Goin' Home" for a similar duration, Love were correct in assuming that Rock should have the license to be an improvisational forum. But it would take the Doors ("The End," "When the Music's Over") and Velvet Underground ("Sister Ray") to finally get it right: lengthy Rock excursions that actually added up to something.

Love was so big in L.A. at a certain point that there were even Love copy bands (Sons of Adam, Soul Benders). L.A. in the '60s seemed predisposed to cults. Original Love member "Snoopy" Pfister freaked out and joined the Manson Family. It hardly mattered to Love leader Arthur Lee—like McGuinn, he looked at his band members as interchangeable. This eventually led to the departure of Brian McLean, the only other composing member of Love, who played Brian Jones, haircut-wise, to Lee's Hendrix/Dylan (Lee was Black). McLean stuck around for one more album, which actually turned out to be Arthur Lee's magnum opus, *Forever Changes*. Released at the tail end of 1967, it was everything a psychedelic album should be. Here Lee's baroque concept came to full fruition: matched against arranger David Angel's lush string sections, songs like "Andmoreagain," "You Set the Scene," and "The Red Telephone" were among the most evocative summations of their era. But the era was coming to an end. Despite the fact that *Forever Changes* often ranks with *Sgt. Pepper* in the recollection of the old fossils who were actually there when it happened, at the time it didn't sell. Lee seemed to take the public's indifference, as well as the fall of psychedelia, with some degree of duress. As he remarked to *Creem* in 1981: "Who would have ever thought there'd be no more *hippies*?"

And where did that leave art?

Just ask Jim Morrison. He was a kid who always had a book by Lord Byron in his back pocket. He was also a massive fan of Love, and when he got his band going, they signed to Elektra as well. In fact, the Doors are what made the label a permanent Rock fixture once and for all. The whole thing began in typical '60s fashion: two UCLA School of Film students, Morrison and Ray Manzarek, flopping around the beaches and coffeehouses, discussing their concept of a band, influenced by the British groups in their musical, as well as theoretical, outlook. They were both unusual cases: Manzarek was a classically trained pianist who looked like a college professor—in a kind of pre-Lou Barlow mode, he predated nerd-Rock. Morrison, on the other hand, was a natural-born hell-raiser with a genuine loathing for law and order. The runaway son of a Naval admiral from Miami, Florida, Morrison copped out of the draft by telling them he was gay (he wasn't), then enrolled in film school and never looked homeward again. Enamored by the sun-drenched lifestyle that California had to offer, he eventually dropped out of school altogether. By that time, he'd found a more suitable outlet for his Apollonian vision: Rock 'n' Roll.

With Manzarek on organ and Morrison on vocals, the duo soon adopted a pair of aspiring Rock musicians, Robbie Krieger (guitar) and John Densmore (drums), and became the Doors, named after Aldous Huxley's LSD appreciation *The Doors of Perception*. This gives you a pretty good idea where they were coming from—the Doors were one of the first bands to be *specifically* related to the drug scene. From the start, they had no bass player, which gave them a unique sound (session men handled the duties on record). Through a series of club dates that bordered on performance art and psychodrama, the group—and especially Morrison—became notorious. "The End" was the centerpiece of their set: a long, unwinding piece peppered with apocalyptic images and Oedipal fantasies. Many people were shocked, but Elektra owner Jac Holzman understood the group's power and passion. He also knew that packaged chaos of any kind was selling.

The Doors (1967) was one of the classics of its era, with Manzarek's hypnotic organ, Morrison's poetic free flights, and the basic-Rock support of Densmore and Krieger (both excellent players). Borrowing a bit of Elvis Presley's baritone, with his own Southern roots in there as well, Morrison was capable of gritty down-home Blues shouting. It was his stage act, however, that was catching all the attention. Iggy Pop, who would represent the next step *beyond* Morrison, saw Morrison perform in Michigan at some local teen outlet in the '60s and recalled how he would bait the jocks in the audience by switching into an impromptu "pussy voice." It was just this kind of confrontational theater that Morrison specialized in.

The thing that made the Doors unique was that while they were pushing the envelope with radical notions, they were also having Top Forty hits. For a brief period they were probably the most popular band in America, but the more famous they became, the more desperate Morrison was to legitimize his poetry. This resulted in his most exhibitionist tendencies coming to the fore— which resulted in his numerous scrapes with the law. This helped fortify his outlaw mythos while holding the other members of the group hostage to his self-destructive hellride. The group was banned, dates were cancelled, narcs hounded them, and, ultimately, the music suffered.

If Jim Morrison was one of the first Rock performers to refer to himself as a "poet," Frank Zappa was one of the first performers to claim identity as a "composer." Whether such grandiose notions were valid, and whether they were a good influence on future generations of musicians and listeners, is a moot point at this late date. Fact is, in the mid-'60s, Rock was taking on a heightened sense of artistic merit. No one helped put the seal on the Rock-as-art transformation more than Frank Zappa. A classically trained child prodigy and Los Angeles native, Zappa had as his musical idol Edgar Varèse, the expatriate French composer whose compositions in the '20s and '30s were prototypes of electronic music. A natural eccentric, Zappa had already enjoyed a career as a teenage songwriter in the '50s selling his lyrics to Doo-Wop groups like the Penguins, who covered his "Memories of El Monte." With his barbed sense of humor, Zappa was one of the first exponents of *satire* (i.e., not stupidity) in the name of Rock. Unlike the other artists of the era, Zappa approached Rock 'n' Roll with distance (thus irony). This would become the calling card of all subsequent Rock that sought to explore more than a brain-to-booty response. Zappa's music played to the id. Even at its most Jazz- or R&B-influenced stages, it was none too funky. Zappa's own chops-laden guitar moved the music through a wide spectrum of polymorphous changes, with the support of an ever-changing array of eclectic musicians cloaked under the all-purpose Mothers of Invention moniker. This would greatly influence such Prog-Rock giants as King Crimson as well as the slick-but-cynical pop of Steely Dan.

Zappa formed the Mothers of Invention in 1965, after trying his hand at film and other avant-garde ventures. One of the first true Rock tapehounds, Zappa collected sounds and married them to live instruments in a move probably as influenced by Spike Jones as it was by Varese. Through the strength of good management (in the form of Herbie Cohen) and Zappa's own connections, the group became a main attraction on the L.A. circuit. They were one of the first bands to develop true "freak" appeal, through their theatrical stage antics that were tantamount in many ways to what the Fugs were doing in New York at the same time. Zappa was crafty—he reasoned that attracting contingents of freaks would generate publicity, so he encouraged misfits like hippie vagabond Vito and impresario-turned-pervert Kim Fowley to bring their respective entourages, thus turning Mothers gigs into "happenings" (or "freak-outs" as Zappa dubbed them). Although the freak scene at that time revolved around drugs, Zappa, in a stunning refutation of the hippie mentality, was an avowed teetotaler.

The Mothers' first album, *Freak Out*, was an enormous blow for creative freedom in Rock. Not only was it a double album—absolutely unprecedented for a new group—but also Zappa had total control right down to the liner notes, which basically lambasted the audience itself with barbed jibes. "This piece of trivial nonsense," Zappa wrote, "is included in this collection because in a nutshell kids, it is intellectually and emotionally ACCESSIBLE for you. Hah!"

Zappa and his tribe were the first Rock group to have absolutely zero teen appeal. They couldn't be featured on *Upbeat* because they were ugly and had beards, and because go-go girls couldn't gyrate to their odd, quirky music accentuated by bursts of ugly white noise and kazoo, marimbas, and Zappa's own foreboding voice. Lyrically, Zappa lambasted the teen culture by writing mock-bubblegum tunes like "Wowie Zowie." In many ways, Zappa represented the birth of true negativity in Rock—songs like "You're Probably Wondering Why I'm Here," "I'm Not Satisfied," "Ain't Got No Heart," and the six-minute "protest" song "Trouble Comin' Everyday" weren't exactly uplifting. Although the noise experiments ("Who Are the Brain Police," "Help I'm a Rock," "The Return of the Son of Monster Magnet") didn't really hold up as improvs, they were a big step toward progressive freedom in Rock. It was this direction—extended composition laced with barbed social commentary—that Zappa would explore further on his next two albums, *Absolutely Free* and *We're Only in it for the Money*. The former took aim at Mom and Pop America, including the crass commercialism of Madison Avenue in general and television in particular. The intricately woven tracks leapt from one stylistic variation to another while Zappa maintained his somewhat tenuous connection with the Rock audience through his relentless parodies of well-known Rock tunes ("Louie Louie" was a frequently picked-on target).

We're Only in it for the Money* (1968) was an even more scathing put-down of the so-called hip factions than *Absolutely Free* had been of their parents. Almost as if to drive this point home, the whole LP was posed as a parody of *Sgt. Pepper*, complete with a gatefold sleeve that mocked the Beatles' masterpiece. Zappa's montage concept had been perfected at this point: the songs all ran together, interspliced with everything from tape manipulations to foreign voices to cryptic whispering (the last courtesy of engineer Gary Kellgren). As the '60s progressed, Zappa's eclecticism got the best of him: experiments like the lost film soundtrack *Uncle Meat* as well his Doo-Wop tribute *Cruisin' with Ruben & the Jets* were ambitious but ultimately flawed projects. But *Hot Rats*, released in 1969, was one of the great early electric Jazz-fusion improv albums. By that time Zappa had become one of the longest-running contradictions in Rock: a "freak" who created "psychedelic" music but didn't take drugs.

Speaking of freaks, none were freakier than Zappa's boyhood buddy Don Van Vliet, a.k.a. Captain Beefheart. Van Vliet had hung out with Zappa and collaborated on some of the latter's early film experiments before forming his

own Magic Band and moving out to the desert of the San Fernando Valley.
The original group was one of the toughest white R&B acts of the period,
competing with Brits like the Pretty Things for the title of roughest-hewn
Blues combo. They found success early, being signed to A&M and recording
singles like "Diddy Wah Diddy" and the hypnotic "Moonchild." But
Beefheart proved too weird to be molded into any kind of Pop success, and
soon he and his band of merry men retired to their Valley digs in order to perfect Van Vliet's unique concept of "Earth music." The resulting album, *Safe as
Milk*, was one of the lost classics of the '60s, but it was also the last Beefheart
album bearing any semblance of conventional song structure. According to
legend, Beefheart taught his band to "un-play" their instruments at this point,
resulting in a series of weird, dada-esque albums like *Strictly Personal, Trout
Mask Replica* (produced by Zappa), and *Lick My Decals Off, Baby*, which detonated the limitations of standard Rock structure once and for all.
Unfortunately, their influence wouldn't become readily apparent until the rise
of Punk later in the next decade, when arty experimenters like Pere Ubu,
Devo, the Electric Eels, MX-80 Sound, the Residents, and many others would
borrow a page or two from the good Captain.

In the '60s, the canyons were creeping with craziness. A case in point was
Beefheart's communal living arrangement with his band of merry men.
According to another L.A. musician, Merrill Fankhauser, who knew Beefheart
at the time, things got pretty weird out there in the desert:

"So we go over there and Don has this strange look in his eye. Don
gets Jeff and I to go with him into this large bathroom they call the
Magic Bathroom. They lock all three of us in there and Don starts to
demoralize Jeff (Cotton, Beefheart's guitar player AKA Antenna
Jimmy Semens)...saying all this negative stuff about him. I felt like I
was dealing for Jeff's soul because all of a sudden Jeff turned to putty
and was agreeing with Don saying 'Yeah maybe I should go back with
Don.' It seemed like Don was trying to hypnotize us both. Jeff started
crying and fell into the bathtub slumped into a fetal position.

"Then Don brings out this little cage that had all these spiders in it,
including a black widow. Then he says, 'What would you think if I
could make one of these spiders smoke a cigarette?' He pulled his

beard and said 'Wouldn't that be heavy, ha ha ha.'" [9]

Another "freak" musician who also had a Zappa association was Tim Buckley, a waiflike singer/songwriter who'd actually migrated from New York and fallen in with the West Coast Folk scene. Buckley sounded like a tormented soul with his weird timbre and his wavering, disjointed compositions. Although most of his tunes were still based on Folk melodies, they had a weird and unique druggy undertow due to Buckley's use of unconventional instrumentation like vibes and marimbas, not to mention his own melancholic weirdness. In the works of Tim Buckley one finds some of the most individualistic musings of the '60s. Mind-expanding masterpieces like "I Never Asked to be Your Mountain" were heavily orchestrated affairs full of hyped-up marimbas and wildly-strumming guitars, which created the perfect launch pad for Buckley's wailing, unearthly voice. Music like this could only have come out of the increasingly freaky environment of L.A. in the late '60s. Sometimes it got a little drawn out, such as the ten-minute hippie opus, "Love Song from Room 109 at the Islander (on Pacific Coast Highway)," but it was always undeniably original. On songs like the classic "I Must Have Been Blind," Buckley created haunting melodies that hinted that he was a deeply troubled soul. Like so many troubled souls, he finally found an end to his torment through the drugs, dying of a heroin OD in 1976. He's since been enshrined by the indie-Rock hordes that are always looking for antiheroes and obscuros to venerate. He was survived by a son, Jeff, who was talented enough to map out a musical path of his own that, oddly enough, met with the same tragic fate (by drowning this time).

No tragedies befell Buffalo Springfield, however—they were the slickest of the L.A. hippie bands, and they reaped the rewards, being the first white Rock band signed to Atlantic records. Their sound was a mix of the Beatles' *Rubber Soul* with some odd Country influences, a prescient move considering the Country-Rock revival that they anticipated by about a year with rustic material like "Go Ahead and Say Goodbye." Other recordings like "Do I Have to Come Right Out and Say It" and "Nowadays Clancy Can't Even Sing" possessed a shimmering brilliance that evoked the whole *moment* coming alive. Why do you think so many people got caught up in that moment? It was because the music was so powerful. Even a relatively minor group like Buffalo Springfield had high-minded ideals about what they wanted to do with their music. They were no slouch at ornate Art-Rock constructions either: Neil Young's magnum opus, "Broken Arrow," was an intricate pastiche that took ninety-eight takes to perfect, replete with *Sgt. Pepper* orchestrations. In three short years, Rock 'n' Roll had moved out of the garage, and the garage bands who did still exist were soon to be left in the dust, or would turn into Heavy Metal. Buffalo Springfield was the other side of the coin: in their slick professionalism, they influenced the sound of L.A. Rock for the next decade (the Eagles and Fleetwood Mac, as well as the direct spinoff "supergroup" Crosby, Stills, Nash, & Young).

Not every group in L.A. was as prophetic. Considering its stature as the center of the entertainment industry, Los Angeles is naturally predisposed to schlock. Once the acid culture had infiltrated Hollywood, bubblegum psych flourished. Uni Records, the recording division of Universal Studios, produced some of the trashiest flower-power groups of all time: Strawberry Alarm Clock, the Rainy Daze, the Lollipop Shoppe, the Giant Crab, etc. These groups were the crossroads between prototypical '60s Garage-Rock (Seeds, Standells, Electric Prunes, Chocolate Watch Band) and Bubblegum Rock (Ohio Express, 1910 Fruitgum Company, Archies). The actual prototypes were the Monkees, Don Kirschner's TV version of the Beatles, who, in 1967, sold more records than any other American band despite the fact they were a bunch of actors merely *portraying* a Rock band. At least the Monkees were capable of occasional brilliance: "(I'm Not Your) Stepping Stone" became somewhat of a Punk classic, covered by the Sex Pistols, Minor Threat, Johnny Thunders, and others.

The Monkees were not alone in the annals of bogus freakdom. Girl-chasing lecher-men like Vito and Kim Fowley were staging the L.A. equivalent of New York's "happenings." Fowley made some of the most obnoxious psych-bubblegum albums of all time, and for a while led a fringe freak element called "the Canyon People" who were kind of the stateside equivalent of the Troglodytes (the English troupe who influenced the Troggs)—kids living off "nature" without any floor plan for tomorrow. But conditions were the same everywhere: once the going got rough, they returned to the womb of suburban comfort. Not before Fowley got his hands on the pretty ones, though.

All these disparate freak elements came together under one umbrella in June 1967. Based on the Folk and Jazz festivals, the Monterey Pop Festival was a joint venture of the Frisco (Bill Graham) and L.A. (Lou Adler, John

Phillips) communities with a few helping hands coming from abroad (Paul McCartney, Brian Epstein, Andrew Oldham). The whole hippie market had been growing for about a year—whereas, before, most Rock albums other than the Beatles/Stones/Dylan had been sleepers saleswise, all of a sudden groups like the Doors and Jefferson Airplane were placing albums in the Top Ten. In a way the festival was an opportunity for the hippies to announce themselves to the world, their "coming out" party, if you will. But the ones who really came out were the record magnates. As the saying goes: "The real action took place backstage."

One person who had his life changed by Monterey was Clive Davis, the newly appointed head of A&R at Columbia. The young lawyer had taken over operations of the label a couple of months before Monterey in a bid to make the label more competitive in the new Rock wars. As far as Rock went, Columbia was at a standstill with its two most significant acts, Bob Dylan and the Byrds: the former due to a debilitating motorcycle accident that kept him from recording, and the latter due to their increasingly esoteric music (which the public wasn't buying). Davis was looking for a shot in the ass for the label, and got it in the form of Moby Grape, Laura Nyro, Tom Rush and, most importantly, Big Brother & the Holding Company. When Janis Joplin became one of the most successful Rock performers of the late '60s, Columbia hit the jackpot. Joplin's performance at Monterey had been one of the event's most memorable and became a standout of D. A. Pennebaker's movie version, which started the whole era of "concert" films, another lucrative slice of the ever-sweetening Rock 'n' Roll pie. As for Clive, he would recall a few years later: "I was so impressed by what I saw at Monterey that I was convinced it was going to usher in a social revolution."[10]

It ushered in a revolution all right, but it wasn't the one the hippies were hoping for. Still, in the late '60s, as cosmic latitudes verged on the Age of Aquarius, it seemed like the whole world was on the cusp of some existential retuning. On Broadway, *Hair* opened and was a huge hit despite the fact that it featured nude hippies. On TV, *The Mod Squad* presented cops in hippie garb that preached a more "with it" style of law enforcement than Joe Friday's. The fact that they were interracial and included a woman in their ranks was a strange premonition of the Equal Rights Amendment and political correctness, among other things.

No medium exploited the hippie insurgence more than the music business. It was a great thing for the creative groups of the day to suddenly be given artistic freedom and financial security at once, and to their credit, most the '60s musicians—from the Byrds to Led Zeppelin—responded honorably. They didn't just serve up the ultimate dreck and take the paycheck; they consciously tried to push the envelope. But the companies didn't know that—they were just following the market ledgers as usual. So when anti-establishment sentiment was in vogue, the record companies suddenly began siding with the "revolutionaries." This resulted in embarrassing ad campaigns like Columbia's "The Man Can't Bust Our Music." It was embarrassing because ten years earlier the company had been the domain of Mitch Miller—who could be more "the man" than him?

The biggest gaffe came from MGM Records, which launched one of the most fiendish cash-ins ever in 1968. Dubbed "the Bosstown Sound," it consisted of a bunch of post-frat bands gone psychedelic with outlandish names like Ultimate Spinach, Phluph, the Beacon Street Union, Orpheus, and the Chamaeleon Church. Some of the music was OK—the Spinach had their moments, particularly their third album, which featured future Doobie Brother Jeff "Skunk" Baxter; and the Beacon Street Union proffered the immortal "Speed Kills." But the unprecedented glut of hype gave psychedelia a bad name within the industry—it also proved to be MGM's last stand as a respectable Rock label. After that, the label cut its losses and launched the Osmonds.

Before such crass commercialism doomed the hippie age to the realm of nostalgia, there remained one crowning moment: Woodstock. After the precedent set by the Monterey Pop Festival, the huge festivals briefly became mainstays of the era. In the whirl of egalitarian spirit that surrounded the Movement, a lot of the more practical implications got swept under the rug. Promoters drooling for a big payoff routinely oversold shows and failed to provide standard water, food, and toilet facilities. The masses of hippies let loose in the cow pasture sensed Eden and let nature take its course—it was a public health official's nightmare, in other words. It only got worse as the drugs got harder: from pot and acid in the '60s to barbiturates and cocaine in the '70s.

All things considered, the countercultural factions who gathered at Woodstock for three days in August 1969 put on a good show for the masses—so much so that they earned the name "Woodstock Nation." Organizer John Roberts, a millionaire investor who had no prior experience in the music business, made such a killing off the event that he never attempted to repeat history. Although he whined when the barricades eventually crumbled down, allowing ten thousand gate crashers to get in free, he refused to sell his rights to the festival to Albert Grossman for a million dollars cash on the spot—a wise decision considering that Woodstock ended up being an infinitely recyclable investment. The direct result was the film of the same name—which played on the midnight movie circuit for years—as well as two separate soundtrack albums.

Woodstock was the high point of the hippie culture, but it presented some obvious contradictions. Not only the financial finagling that went on in the name of Peace, Love, & Flowers, but also the fact that the gas-guzzling iron machines manufactured by General Motors backed up the highways for eight miles blowing smog into the air. The field became a giant mud pie when it rained during the second night of festivities. Not only had the hippies never sussed that they might want to actually *bathe* over the course of three days, but they also didn't think about the fact that they might get hungry. Fortunately the women's group from the local Jewish Community Center in Bethel, N.Y.— where the festival was held—sent a giant care package of thirty thousand peanut butter sandwiches to keep the hippie hordes from starving to death. There was never any shortage of drugs, however.

In a real "revolution," the voices leading the insurrection would never have accepted spoon-fed handouts from the opposing forces. But such contradictions were becoming rampant within the Movement. Among the splintering factions, one of the big questions was violence—whether or not to employ it. Militant groups like the Weathermen and Black Panthers said yes, which scared away a lot of would-be politicos. When four demonstrators were shot dead by National Guardsmen during an antiwar demonstration at Kent State University in Ohio on May 4, 1970, a lot of students probably decided to join the Young Democrats—or stay home—instead.

There were also health considerations: the drugs had gotten harder and more prevalent, and the age of introduction had decreased so that now even preteens were turning on. As the '70s dawned, the glassy stupor of downers had replaced the mystical powers of grass and LSD. The massive freak-outs that had plagued festivals like Woodstock had reached epidemic proportions in neighborhoods like San Francisco's Haight-Ashbury. Dr. David Smith had opened the Haight-Ashbury Free Clinic in 1967, but by the end of the '60s, it had become impossible to meet the health care demands of all the hippie casualties. At one point they were averaging five hundred cases of the clap each week.

The kids who bought the antimaterialist "live for today" party line had never given any consideration to what they would do when tomorrow came. In San Francisco, for instance, it got cold at night, and once the dance halls had closed, there was nothing to do but wander the streets, tripping aimlessly. Sleeping in Golden Gate Park was risky—there were winos and other predators. Young women who were arriving off the bus every day to the hippie capital were par-ticularly vulnerable. With the streets littered with what amounted to runaways, a whole new element of sharks—criminals, hucksters, pushers, whoremongers, and mystical shamans—moved in. Ed Sanders made the perfect analogy in his excel-lent Manson book, *The Family*: "From the standpoint of vulnerability the flower movement was like a valley of thousands of plump white rabbits surrounded by wounded coyotes." [11]

Into this soft white underbelly came the most notable killjoy of the hippie culture: Charles Manson. The ex-con son of a prostitute had spent more than half of his life in institutions, so when he was finally dumped onto the streets in 1967, he found a whole new world waiting. Gravitating to San Francisco, Manson found the New World much to his liking—Rock bands, drugs, crash pads, dance halls, free love, and girls in miniskirts. Manson immediately drift-ed toward the more devious elements of the hippie culture—not only biker gangs but weird witchcraft cults. He also attracted his own sort of odd groupies: masochistic runaways looking for a father figure (a bill Manson fit, being thir-ty-three at the time).

The sad thing was, it wasn't just these wayward bimbos that Manson horn-swaggled, it was also some of the more reputable figures in the "under-ground"—like producer Terry Melcher, who thought Manson was talented enough as a singer to warrant a screen test. Or Beach Boy Dennis Wilson, who allowed Manson to commandeer his house as a hippie crash pad with his harem of devoted worshippers. What did Murray Wilson think?

The mood turned ugly in 1969. Suddenly, perhaps scared off by a violent episode or two, Melcher weaseled out of his agreement to make a documen-tary/album with Manson. One supposes he was on some good acid when he signed him. When he finally came down, he realized Charlie was bonkers and sought to avoid him, even moving out of his house so Charlie wouldn't pull one of his unannounced drop-bys with his typical entourage of twenty filthy hippies. The next tenants of the deluxe mansion in the Hollywood Hills were film director Roman Polanski and his wife Sharon Tate. Unfortunately, Tate and a few of her friends became the celebrity victims of Charlie's knife-wielding zombies. There's speculation as to why Manson chose them—it might have been the Melcher association, but it also might have been something more insidious, like a dope-burn for instance. In any case, just the fact that Manson was hobnobbing with celebrities in the Hollywood Hills tells you something about the times. The kinky *nouveau riche* of the '60s liked to keep street trash like Manson around as a kind of anti-establishment totem/bogeyman. This explains the appeal of biker groups with the same crowd. You can hear them now: "Oh, he's been in *prison*! If that isn't street credibility, then what is?"

In any event, after Manson conducted his celebrity slaughter, the decadent millionaires were a little more careful whom they let into their parties. When Manson finally got caught, the headlines screamed "hippie cult murders." For Mom and Pop America, that pretty much put the stamp on the hippie culture once and for all. Hippies were something to be feared, and law enforcement organizations began to take a longer look at them. The days of hippies living "free" in the park were ending. A whole new climate was dawning…a climate of fear.

Fear was the primarily catalyst at Altamont, the Stones' botched concert spectacle, which occurred appropriately enough in December 1969 and, at least symbolically, shut down the decade for good. Like the Hollywood elite trying to pal around with hardened criminals, the Stones displayed the same dilettante mentality by thinking they could enlist a bunch of Hell's Angels as bodyguards and "security" forces. When the Angels wreaked havoc—once again in the form of murder—the Stones turned tail and ran (courtesy of their private helicopter). Besides seriously damaging their unholy rep as badasses, it made the Stones and others requestion the validity of the "movement"—or at least made them have their doubts about how close they wanted to get to the action. In the case of the Stones, they abandoned universal consciousness for sheer hedonism (so much for "it's just a shot away").

Another disillusioning factor about Altamont, at least to the hippies, was that this time the insurrection happened from within. The Angels had been perceived as "sympathetic cousins"—it was one thing when cops or National Guardsmen beat up on hippies, but when it came from within the ranks of the revolutionary hordes themselves, then maybe they had miscalculated the universality of their "cause" to begin with. To many people, this revealed not only the frailty of the Movement, but the hypocrisy of it as well. Occurring within a few days of Manson's arrest, this revelation was devastating to the counterculture. No wonder so many of them went out to pasture—or joined the "system."

In the '60s, the difference between "us" and "them" had been clearly defined. As events like the Manson massacre and Altamont—not to mention Kent State and the Weathermen Days of Rage, four days of violent protest when cars were overturned and windows smashed in Chicago—proved, we were about to enter a new era in which the lines wouldn't be as clear. And the targets of violence might not be the most philosophically justified ones, but whatever or whoever happened to be standing in the way.

CHAPTER 9

THE BACK TO
THE ROOTS REVIVAL

BOB DYLAN'S STATURE WAS SUCH THAT, BY 1968, the counterculture waited with
collective bated breath for his return after a lengthy hiatus resulting from a
motorcycle accident. Dylan had sat out the psychedelic era and, recuperating
from the crash, had a lot of time to reconsider his beliefs and redirect his energies toward something perhaps more redemptive. As he began the healing
process, he began writing songs with a somewhat different message than the
speed-fueled hallucinations on *Highway 61 Revisited* and *Blonde on Blonde*. Rife
with biblical imagery, many of the songs dealt with themes of moral conflict
and spiritual redemption: "I Shall Be Released," "The Ballad of Frankie Lee &
Judas Priest," "All Along the Watchtower," "I Dreamed I Saw Saint
Augustine," "This Wheel's on Fire."

The radical difference between the Dylan of '65/'66 and the postcrackup
period was that of a man who'd had a near-death experience. The harrowing
accident had apparently provided Dylan with his own shock of recognition.

When Dylan finally did come around again, it was in his secluded country
hideaway in upstate New York with the help of a few select friends. His days of
holding court amongst the New York Superhip were over. After being magnified to the level of a prophet by many within the movement, Dylan wanted out
of the celebrity trip. He also realized that, after such a lengthy hiatus, high
expectations would await his return. It was a long journey back to center stage
(a forum he never truly recaptured).

When Dylan finally reappeared in January 1968, it was with an album that made apparent his new down-home sensibilities. Entitled *John Wesley Harding*, the album was as oblique as the cover photo of Dylan with a passel of Woodstock yokels. Gone was the sardonic *Eeeeh*, replaced by a more contemplative demeanor. Dylan had even changed his style of singing, from the arch wheeze of the mid-'60s period to a more mellow kind of drawl. The music was understated—it rocked, but softly (Dylan used many of Nashville's top session men—Kenny Buttrey, Charlie McCoy, Pete Drake—as he had on the previous album, *Blonde on Blonde*).

During his seclusion Dylan surrounded himself with the same musicians who'd backed him on his legendary world tour in '65–'66, a bearded collective known as the Band (formerly the Hawks). Originally from Canada, the group eventually relocated to upstate New York and became Dylan's constant companions during the recovery period that ran through the entirety of 1967. It was easy to ignore the psychedelic era in Woodstock, and that's pretty much what Dylan and the Band did. The sessions they cut at that time, although widely bootlegged, would officially remain in the vaults for almost a decade. But many of the songs from the period would wind up on the Band's first album, *Music from Big Pink*.

When the album came out in 1968, it bespoke the same kind of rustic simplicity as *John Wesley Harding*. The group's down-home combination of organ, piano, and at least four capable vocalists—Levon Helm, Garth Hudson, Richard Danko, and Richard Manuel—gave the songs an almost sanctified quality. This was reinforced by weirdly evocative pieces like "The Weight," which spoke in weird parables as the music built to emotive crescendos. Their plain-folk mentality was in many ways at odds with the self-aggrandizement that was increasingly coming to typify the Movement. They stood outside of the hippie culture, even as they were embraced by it.

Dylan's other old cronies, the Byrds, were also tempering the psych-out with *Sweetheart of the Rodeo* (1968). The previous album, *The Notorious Byrd Brothers*, had been one of the most intense Acid masterpieces of its day, with songs about dope and outer space in a tightly compressed production style—courtesy of Gary Usher—that heralded the oncoming face of Progressive Rock. By this point, the individual Byrds had become snap-in components of leader Jim McGuinn's increasingly complex—and eccentric—musical vision, and members were flying the coop left and right. Rhythm guitarist David Crosby found his exodus following *Notorious* and was replaced by Gram Parsons, whose Country leanings rubbed off on McGuinn. Fans who'd flight-trained to "Eight Miles High" must have been surprised when they heard "traditional" material like "The Christian Life" on *Sweetheart*. The album didn't sell that well, but it heralded another new trend: Country-Rock.

Shortly after *Sweetheart* was released, Parsons and original Byrds bassist Chris Hillman left to form the Flying Burrito Brothers, who were basically a low-flying version of the Byrds. They were important because they were the first group to devote themselves solely to the Country revival. The cover of their first album, *The Gilded Palace of Sin*, told the story: the Burritos as brown-dirt hippies flanked by their honky-tonk women (whom they presumably fucked in teepees). The Burritos gained hip credibility by being asked to perform at Altamont. Undaunted, McGuinn replaced Parsons with guitarist Clarence White and continued in the Country-Rock vein, making albums like *The Ballad of Easy Rider* and *Untitled* with a group who were the Byrds in name only.

Besides Byrds alumni, there were other participants in the burgeoning L.A. Country-Rock scene: Poco, founded by two ex-members of Buffalo Springfield, Richie Furay and Jim Messina, and featuring the pedal steel guitar of Rusty Young, were an even more lightweight version of the countrified ethos. Monkee Mike Nesmith, who'd been the only member of the group to play his own instrument, proved himself an adequate purveyor of countrified twang in the form of "Papa Gene's Blues," "You Just May Be the One," "What Am I Doin' Hangin' 'Round," "Circle Sky," and "The Door Into Summer." When the hoax that was the Monkees finally dissolved, Nesmith made several Country-esque albums with his own First National Band (interestingly enough, Pacific Arts, the record label he founded in 1971, was one of the first to explore the field of video).

Although they were from Berkeley, Creedence Clearwater Revival never really fit in with the dopey hippie-mania. Like the Hawks up in Canada, Creedence had been playing in one form or another since the late '50s. As far as Rock 'n' Roll went, they'd already honed their chops long before they heard the Beatles. Creedence were "old school" before there was such a thing—they believed in the tradition of Elvis and the Beatles, which is to be "of the people" and serve the masses (i.e., by having hit singles). This was actually a much more populist ideal than the Marxist-inclined hippies, and Fogerty more than anyone sensed the reality that hippie was just a passing phase and in a few years all those trippy-cosmic vibes would sound hideously outdated, whereas a good Rock 'n' Roll record lasts forever. He was right—there's no doubting Creedence's legacy as far as the popular culture goes (i.e., equal to Elvis or the Beatles). Within the parameters of their basic sound was a complete rewrite of the Sun Records formula, along with some '60s-influenced density. The result was a sound that crackled off the radio in hit after hit, all of them a rich kind of Americana: "Proud Mary," "Lodi," "Green River," "Bad Moon Rising," "Down on the Corner," etc. No other band embraced such working class sensibilities without shame in the era when elitist academics and radicals were otherwise leading the way. It was a conflict, and when leader John Fogerty confronted it, as he did on "Fortunate Son," one could hear his anger. Above all, CCR were the real Rock deal: the rhythm section of Doug Clifford (drums) and Stu Cook (bass) provided a sturdy backbone for the Fogerty brothers, whose guitars carved in and out of one another with a chunky consistency. Their fusion of Blues and Country made a lot of people wake up to the richness of down-home resources. They were messengers of simplicity and purity during an increasingly complex and impure era.

Although Creedence's musical roots were firmly planted in the American South, the other Berkeley-Frisco bands seemed to be preoccupied with the mythology of the Old West. Consider the Grateful Dead (*Workingman's Dead*), Quicksilver (*Happy Trails*), Steve Miller ("Space Cowboy"), the Charlatans (they wore cowboy hats), and Dan Hicks & His Hot Licks (who played a hippie version of Western Swing). This would in turn lead to Love's "Singin' Cowboy," McGuinness-Flint, and Indian-Rock, a short-lived trend that exploited the hippies' commingling with Native Americans in the late '60s. This took the form of Cher ("Halfbreed"), the Cowsills ("Indian Lake"), Don Fardon ("The Lament of the Cherokee Reservation"), the Raiders ("Indian Reservation"), Keef Hartley (*Halfbreed*, different from Cher's), and the 1910 Fruitgum Company ("Indian Giver"). It also influenced such cinematic ventures as *Butch Cassidy and the Sundance Kid* and Dennis Hopper's *Chincero*.

Real Country & Western also had a revival at the end of the decade. Contrary to popular myth, it hadn't just shriveled up and gone away during the

Rock era. What do you think the hordes in redneck bars listening to Merle Haggard thought about the Beatles? It's not hard to guess their reaction: "*Waaaah*, they look like a bunch of girls." This was the Silent Majority Nixon would call on to help him win the election in 1968. They proved to be a more powerful demographic than anyone imagined, and Country & Western was more popular than ever. Artists like Johnny Cash, Tammy Wynette, George Jones, Merle Haggard, Roy Clark, and Dolly Parton became superstars (although their humble origins seldom allowed them to accept the mantle). Even Bob Dylan Cash'd in on his association with Johnny, featuring him on his own Country album, *Nashville Skyline* (1969). There was also a whole new generation of singer–songwriters like Joe South, Kris Kristofferson, Tony Joe White, Jerry Reed, Ray Stevens, B. J. Thomas, and others who personified the new breed of urban cowboy: hip, but still with a trace of sorghum on their boots.

Country artists weren't the only ones getting their just due in the late '60s. Just as the Country-style formulations of groups like the Byrds and Creedence influenced the Country & Western revival, the move back towards traditional Rock by many groups spawned a renewed interest in the original Granddaddies of Rock 'n' Roll, and the old rockers returned in force. In the late '60s, Elvis, Muddy Waters, Howlin' Wolf, Little Richard, Chuck Berry, Bill Haley, B. B. King, and Fats Domino all staged successful comebacks. Rock 'n' Roll, although officially only a little over a decade old, was beginning to achieve its own sense of tradition. This was partly due to the fact that many members of Rock's second generation were acknowledging their musical debt to their elders, but also it was due to a general dissatisfaction among Rock fans over the increasingly complex nature of the music. Many fans felt that not only the musicians but also the *audience* were losing touch with the basic tenets of Rock 'n' Roll. As a result, some members of the Rock audience began developing a sense of nostalgia over the greaser ethos of the '50s.

Nowhere was this more apparent than in England, where the first wave of teddy boys had originated. First the Brits had feasted on Blues and now they were hell-bent on consuming every last morsel of authentic Memphis twang. Brit collectors routinely made expeditions to the South to buy up all the remaining Sun 45s—in fact, this was the origin of the dreaded "record collector" mentality that would plague subsequent generations of Rock hipsters.

The Rock 'n' Roll revival was on and revival bands were popping up everywhere: Sha Na Na, Cat Mother & the All Night Newsboys, Daddy Cool, Brownsville Station, and the Persuasions all paid homage to the '50s (albeit in varying degrees of "authenticity"). Once in a while, a group like the Flamin' Groovies—who, like Creedence, hailed from the Bay Area but also, like Creedence, didn't fit the hippie mold—would deliver a salient rethink of '50s ethos mixed with a more modern aggressive style (hence Punk in a few years' time). Rock 'n' Roll oldies became a prominent component of many bands' set lists, particularly in England, where Heavy groups like Mott the Hoople and Uriah Heep regularly respun '50s hits in a more bombastic updated vein.

Even luminaries like the Beatles, the Rolling Stones, and the Who were not immune to this repurification process. In 1968, the Beatles and Stones both reverted to Rock after bouts with psychedelia—the Beatles in the form of "Lady Madonna" and the *White Album*, the Stones in the form of "Jumpin' Jack Flash" and *Beggar's Banquet*. This sudden fit of purity would sustain both groups throughout 1969 as well. The Beatles toyed with the idea of playing live again but settled for the semi-loose mock-live atmosphere of *Let it Be* while John Lennon moonlighted in the Plastic Ono Band (whose *Live Peace in Toronto* album featured a whole side of Rock 'n' Roll oldies). The Stones went on tour in America and res-urrected such chestnuts as "Little Queenie" and "Carol" (both written by Chuck Berry). As for the Who, they left the pastoral pursuits of Rock operas and the like behind, at least long enough to revive Eddie Cochran's "Summertime Blues" and muscle up one of the most brain-demolishing live albums of all time, *Live at Leeds*. In Detroit, the MC5—who were definitely influenced by the Who—revived "Tutti Frutti" and "Back in the USA" in the spirit of the Revolution. Frank Zappa paid tribute to his lifetime love of Doo Wop with *Cruising with Ruben & the Jets*. And "story of Rock" songs—from Cat Mother's "Good ol' Rock 'n' Roll" to the Turtles' "The Story of Rock & Roll"—proliferated.

The most significant development to come from Rock's new sense of self-awareness was the birth of the Rock press. By the late '60s, two important jour-nals had emerged: *Rolling Stone* in San Francisco and *Crawdaddy* in Boston. They were important because they were the first to treat Rock 'n' Roll as a seri-ous art form and social force as opposed to mags like *Sixteen* and *Hit Parader*, which treated it like teenage fodder. Although writers like Paul Williams,

Langdon Winner, Barry Hanson, Lenny Kaye, and Greg Shaw, among others, were only in their early twenties, they'd already developed a scholarly sense about Rock history. Not surprisingly, the major labels were soon enlisting their aid in compiling the endless string of oldies compilations that began appearing at the tail end of the '60s. From Shaw's handling of United Artists' "legendary masters" series to Kaye's programming of such important archival documents as *I Dig A Cappella* and the original *Nuggets*, these young critics had obviously done their homework. Because they were the first generation to write about Rock, their words in many ways became irrefutable truths in terms of aesthetic consensus (at least until the post-Punk era, when some of their opinions would begin to be reversed).

In the meantime, a group of about twenty-five people were shaping Rock's aesthetic heritage. In a revelatory article entitled "Rock Critics: Why They're Morons," published in *Creem* in 1987 just before the magazine went down for good, writer Hercules "Archie" Bovis makes a good point: "All of today's under-35s absorbed these opinions in their formative years—and they trusted them completely. So completely, in fact, that this 'new' breed of Rock writers never learned to go back and listen to that era's critically lauded music *without* always being conscious of its alleged greatness."[1]

As the Rock audience's awareness of its own roots became more defined, the whole context became more formalized. There was "good" and there was "bad" now. There were "standards." Most of all—at least according to a Jon Landau or Robert Christgau—there was a "right" and "wrong" way to play Rock 'n' Roll. According to the critics, the Jimi Hendrix Experience was "right" and Blue Cheer was "wrong." And for years, the twain would never meet. Somewhere a kind of *Emperor's New Clothes* mentality developed whereby critics ascribed an incredible amount of significance to favored artists like Van Morrison, the Band, Rod Stewart, the Who, and others, and a whole generation of Rock listeners and magazine readers were held hostage to these pronouncements. Later on, whole tomes would be written to debunk the formalized history of Rock, such as Joe Carducci's stinging indictment against the mainstream Rock press, *Rock and the Pop Narcotic*.

In the late '60s, however, the whole idea of taking Rock seriously was novel in itself. In England, the erosion between the Pop audience and the more formalized entities was inching further apart. The British Blues scene, since its inception in the early '60s, had split sometime about mid decade into two camps—the ones who went psychedelic and the ones who didn't. The psychedelic purveyors were primarily those like the Rolling Stones, the Animals, the Yardbirds, and Pretty Things who weren't even necessarily "purists." The purist scene, meanwhile, seemed to derive philosophically from Eric Clapton's crucial decision to quit the Yardbirds in protest of their more Pop-oriented tendencies. The unit Clapton joined after quitting the Yardbirds, John Mayall's Blues Breakers, could in many ways be seen as the prototype for the new traditionalists: Fleetwood Mac, Chicken Shack, and the Keef Hartley Band among them. Meanwhile, Clapton's post–Blues Breakers outfit, Cream, seem to have influenced the more flashy purveyors: 10 Years After, Savoy Brown, Free, Jethro Tull, the Jeff Beck Group, Humble Pie, and the Aynsley Dunbar Retaliation. Meanwhile, latent psychedelic tendencies were still present in such late '60s Brit arrivals as the Groundhogs, Man, Blodwyn Pig, Family, Argent, Love Sculpture, Spooky Tooth, and Tomorrow.

Folk music also had a revival in England via Fairport Convention, the Incredible String Band, Pentangle, Bert Jansch, Steeleye Span, Strawbs, Nick Drake, Lindisfarne, Trees, Amazing Blondel, and Hedgehog Pie. Many of these artists, like the Fairports, Trees, and the Incredible String Band, combined the hallucinogenic male/female vocal harmonies of the American West Coast psych-groups like the Jefferson Airplane with traditional material and, as a result, were responsible for the first truly revolutionary twist on folk music since Bob Dylan. Other British bands like Led Zeppelin and Jethro Tull combined elements of both Folk and Blues but weren't "traditional" in any sense of the word.

Another important influx into the British music scene in the late '60s was Jamaican Blue Beat, Ska, and Reggae. The first wave of Jamaicans in England arrived after World War II, when the citizens of the various British colonies were encouraged to emigrate in order to assist the restoration effort. The Jamaicans brought their own unique brand of culture, including Ska, a form of music popularized in England by such imported talents as Laurel Aitken, Prince Buster, and Millie Small, among others. In 1969, a Jamaican named Desmond Dekker had a number one hit with "The Israelites" for the Trojan label, which would prove to be an important early exponent of authentic Reggae sounds (including the first recordings by Bob Marley & the Wailers). There was also Chris Blackwell's

Island label: son of a wealthy Jamaican planting family, Blackwell, who was white, parlayed his love of traditional Jamaican music into the most successful British indie label of the '60s. Island broke ground not only with its Reggae imports but also by introducing such significant Brit groups as Traffic, Fairport Convention, Free, Mott the Hoople, and Roxy Music.

The Black population in England definitely had some impact on the subsequent Soul revival, as evidenced by the appearance of such interracial groups as the Foundations and Equals. The soul boys would have their say in the '70s of course, as everyone from David Bowie to Rod Stewart would cop blatant R&B stylings. England's original youth tribe, the Mods, had been soul fanciers all along, and when Reggae appeared they were quick to embrace that as well: the dance hall implications apparently suited their always-intense love of movement, and they dug the fashion statement—porkpie hats and the like—as well. England was about to burst into an era when a diverse array of youth subcults would take to the streets, from Mod to ted to skinhead to glam. Out of the fragments of all of these, British Punk would emerge in the mid-'70s.

Meanwhile in America, hippie steadfastly remained the only recognizable subculture. Because the U.S. is such a large country, regional differences were a primary factor in determining the musical styles of bands that were all basically purveying the same organic experience—mainly, the late '60s Blues-Rock dig-out. Of the American Blues revivalists, the Allman Brothers Band best personified the Southern hippie boogie band. Formed around the nucleus of brothers Duane and Greg, the Allmans had existed in one form or another since 1964, recording as the Allman Joys and the Hourglass before ever stepping foot out of Georgia. Duane was one of the region's most sought-after studio musicians, having logged numerous sessions at Muscle Shoals with the likes of Aretha Franklin and Wilson Pickett. The endless guitar duels of Duane and Dicky Betts that would stretch a song like "Whipping Post" out to thirty-five minutes became their signature. Not surprisingly, in an era when downers were coming in, the Allmans became one of the top concert attractions of the era. When Duane died in a motorcycle accident just as the band was reaching its zenith, and then bassist Berry Oakley died in *exactly the same manner in almost the exact same place* thirteen months to the day after Duane's death, it only increased their mystique as Southern voodoo blueshounds. With Betts and Greg Allman now ruling the roost, their music grew more mundane.

Guitarist Johnny Winter had a similarly long-standing rep in his home state of Texas, having logged the same kind of credentials as the Allmans as far as homegrown recordings go. In 1968 he figured into Clive Davis's new regime at Columbia, and the label handed him a hefty contract, accompanied by a barrel full of hype, based mostly around the fact he was an albino. His growling vocal style and frenetic guitar playing in many ways set the standard for all subsequent white Blues legends, from Roy Buchanan to Stevie Ray Vaughn. But Winter failed to live up to his potential, because somewhere between the honky-tonks in Texas and the cover of the *Rolling Stone*, he'd become a junkie. He survived, and eventually was able to turn his career around and become a somewhat venerable "Blues legend" of his own making. In the '60s, he also qualified as a "Rock revivalist" with his inspired covers of Chuck Berry, Little Richard, the Rolling Stones, and Bob Dylan.

The Northern exemplars of the American Blues scene tended more towards R&B and less towards druggy indulgence. A perfect example was the J. Geils Band, who came from Boston but took their cue from the social end products of the larger Midwestern R&B centers like Detroit and Chicago (Junior Wells was a big favorite). They were one of the first white bands to feature a permanent harmonica player and were as tight and concise as the Stones and felt just as comfortable with Motown covers and the like. A consummate party band, J. Geils personified the new "boogie" aesthetic: apolitical and hellbent on good times.

Other American late-'60s Blues purveyors included Canned Heat, from L.A., which was the opposite of the J. Geils Band, with their endless jams and fatal attraction to narcotics (singer Bob "the Bear" Hite died of a heroin overdose in 1970). There was also ZZ Top, who, like Johnny Winter, had roots in the first wave of Texas Rock. A three-piece, they shared with J. Geils and the Stones a direct instrumental approach that didn't leave room for long-winded jams. And, like those two bands, they were able to carry it successfully into the next two decades.

One shouldn't underestimate the enormous impact of either Cream or the Jimi Hendrix Experience on this generation of American bands, notably in the emergence of the classic "power trios": ZZ Top, Mountain, Wizard, Sir Lord Baltimore, Dust, Grand Funk Railroad, Beck, Bogart & Appice, West, Bruce & Lang, etc. Both the Experience and Cream were influential in another way—namely, the birth of Heavy. As a musical experience, so-called Heavy Rock was a natural by-product of technology: louder amplification, fuzzboxes, wah-wah pedals, and the like. Naturally the supergroups like Cream were the first to get hold of this technology. But due to the egalitarian nature of Rock 'n' Roll, this would soon trickle down to the sandlot leagues—i.e., the weeniest groups had the biggest amps. This made any idiots playing "Louie Louie" and "You Really Got Me" sound like Gods of Thunder.

These more aggressive tendencies first manifested themselves in the form of the garage bands for a couple of reasons: one was because their postadolescent suburban condition made them predisposed to angst; and second, their technical limitations as musicians made the new technology appealing to them. Bands like the Lollipop Shoppe, Other Half, Amboy Dukes, the Litter, and Black Pearl, although postpsych in origin, weren't real Heavy Metal. But their posture was a great deal more aggressive than previous bands, and their music was grounded in a whole new aesthetic that had to do with sheer power (usually through increased amplification).

The champions in this category were Steppenwolf, Canadians who moved to California in the mid-'60s after a somewhat fruitful career up North as Sparrow. They epitomized the greasy sound and tough-guy stance of the new Rock with songs like "Born to Be Wild," "The Pusher," "Rock Me," and "Jupiter's Child" which, if not actual Heavy Metal, definitely put the numbers in place (for others to paint by). Singer John Kay's gruff vocal style was a big influence on the macho direction of Hard Rock in the '70s, and his politics, although somewhat self-righteous, fit the hippie polemic: up on dope, but down on hard drugs ("Snowblind Friend," "The Pusher") and pervasively anti-establishment ("Monster"). With vague psychedelic traces still in the mix (Goldy McJohn ran his organ through the whirling sound of a leslie speaker cabinet) and wild flailing guitars, Steppenwolf aimed its music at hippies who'd rather ride hogs than farm them.

Another influential proto-Metal band was Blue Cheer. Looking like three hairy behemoths, they were the essential "power trio," generating more volume than even they could handle. Although they deserve credit for taking a stab into the abyss at the height of hippie-mania, most of their musical experiments were overwrought (like the gut-wrenching eight-minute climax of "Doctor Please"). Named after a particularly strong brand of acid, Blue Cheer mostly produced a headache. When original guitarist Leigh Stephens left to form

Silver Metre and was replaced by Randy Holden, they produced some "mellower" material ("Peace of Mind") that betrayed their Bay Area psychedelic roots.

Another Heavy band from this period was Iron Butterfly, the members of which literally came out of the back-alley teen clubs of Los Angeles to unleash their magnum opus, "In-A-Gadda-Da-Vida." Even they must have been flabbergasted when this nonsense song turned into a worldwide sensation. No one could forget the hammering chords, even if the words were phony hippie dreck. Obviously a by-product of Cream's grandiose ambition, the song ran seventeen minutes complete with drum solo, bass solo, and numerous variations on the same plodding three chords.

In-A-Gadda-Da-Vida was the biggest-selling album in the history of Atlantic Records. The label, which had become famous for its pioneering work in R&B, was finding out that the lucrative Rock market was the one paving the road ahead with gold. The label had already scored big with not only the Butterfly, but also Cream, Vanilla Fudge, and Buffalo Springfield. Oddly enough, all of these groups had been relegated to the Atco subsidiary, almost as if the parent stamp was too sacred a denomination. It took one group to break the barrier and Rock would never be the same again.

We must backtrack one minute, though, and once again emphasize the enormous significance of Cream. They were the first group, along with the Hendrix Experience, to overamplify their guitars to the high-pressure point, which helped birth the whole "guitar hero" concept, those swaggering Gods of the big stick....*the better to beat you with, my dear*! As this was an almost phallic fixation, it's not surprising that the audience was mostly male and a lot of the lyrics were Blues-derived misogyny aimed at "the bitch who dun me wrong." Then they'd hammer down on that whammy bar even harder, and the sound would reverberate in midair (symbolic of either pushing that bitch down— actually or metaphorically—or beating the meat until it fuckin' *cracked*). The sound became known as Hard Rock, briefly, and then Heavy Metal. The audience became known as Third Generation. This denoted that a whole new segment of the record-buying public had been born.

Into the foyer stepped Led Zeppelin, the group who—along with the MC5, the Stooges, and Black Sabbath—turned Rock 'n' Roll into Rock once and for all. Like Cream, Zeppelin qualified as a "supergroup," thanks to guitarist Jimmy

Page's stature as one of the top Brit session men of the '60s (he played on records by the Kinks, Them, and others) and his recent stint as the Yardbirds' lead guitarist (replacing Jeff Beck). Page's role in that institution could be likened to trying to save a sinking ship. When the band disintegrated for good in a drunken frenzy sometime during their final tour in 1968, Page merely recruited an all-new membership and rechristened them "the New Yardbirds." The new incarnation included a flamboyant lead singer named Robert Plant, former frontman of a California-influenced Brit aggregation called Band of Joy, and drummer John Bonham, a boozaholic lug whose Heavy sound fit Page's sonic concept perfectly. John Paul Jones, a bassist/keyboard player that Page knew from his session days, rounded out the line-up (Jones had recently worked with Page on Donovon's *Hurdy Gurdy Man* album).

At the urging of the Who's John Entwistle and Keith Moon, they became "Led Zeppelin," the allusion being that they'd sink like a "lead balloon." However, Page knew otherwise, as did his swift manager, Peter Grant, who, with his three-hundred-pound frame, was like a combination stormtrooper and linebacker, bullying promoters and record execs alike. This strong-arm technique was only matched by Zeppelin's Heavy, *Heavy* music. Grant was the consummate Rock mogul/hustler, and he coerced Atlantic's Jerry Wexler into giving the group a $200,000 advance. There was one other provision: they would be the first Rock group to appear on the Atlantic label proper, as opposed to Atco.

When Zeppelin hit the road with entourage in tow, it was like a Viking invasion. Their backstage debauchery was truly legendary. As *Life* reporter Ellen Sander found out, these were not the bucolic English dandies like Donovon, Ian Whitcomb, Graham Nash, and Stevie Winwood; these guys were *louts*, a fact confirmed when she went backstage at the Fillmore to "congratulate" them on their first New York appearance and they practically raped her. She was saved only when the massive Grant pulled the burly Bonham off her. Needless to say, the *Life* article never appeared, but Zeppelin band members were the first to act as if they didn't need it.

The first Zeppelin album signified a whole new *sound* in Rock, just as Elvis's Sun Sessions, the Beatles' early singles, and Hendrix's first album had. The sound was expansive—as a song like "Good Times, Bad Times" progressed, it got bigger! This not only had to do with Page's production techniques, but also with the dynamics of the band and the "ensemble" setup, whereby Bonham's drums were recorded in equal sonic density with the other members of the band. This contributed to the band's thunder-horse overdrive. Many of the songs were based on blues ("How Many More Times") or folk ("Babe I'm Gonna Leave You") but the approach was far from "traditional." Zeppelin was, by and large, about redefinition: they approached Rock in a wholly new manner, music-wise, lifestyle-wise, and in their overbearing manner (Page's publishing company was called "Superhype," after all).

The idea of a Rock group producing itself was novel, but Page made it clear from the start that Zeppelin was *his* monster, and every album had thousands of guitar overdubs in which Page wanked endlessly. Fortunately, Page blew a good load most of the time, but unfortunately in lesser hands it amounted to a generation of impotent jack-offs pulling their pegs endlessly to no one's satisfaction. Page, after all, was capable of producing climax, if nothing else. Along with the squealing guitars and big bottom (pun intended), there was Robert Plant's screeching falsetto, which was designed to show how much of a "heavy" he was on his respective "instrument" as well.

The first round of critics in this country missed the irony, however. John Mendelsohn, writing for *Rolling Stone*, dismissed the band as a Yardbirds-derived hoax. In all probability, the critics resented a young new band like that having such instant corporate clout. But they were missing the point—the subsequent history of Rock would have little to do with the "communal" spirit of the '60s and everything to do with greed and hype.

Although the next Rock group signed to the Atlantic label, Crosby, Stills, & Nash, were starkly different from Led Zeppelin in both sound and stance, they were every bit as prescient. Emerging from the splinters of three famous groups—Buffalo Springfield, the Byrds, and the Hollies—they were a supergroup also. Buffalo Springfield had been the first white group signed to Atco/Atlantic, and Ahmet Ertegun had apparently been impressed enough with them to keep the door open for ex-member Steven Stills when the whole thing came crashing down. At about the same time, David Crosby had been thrown out of the Byrds, and Englishman Graham Nash was becoming bored with the teenybopper direction being purveyed by the Hollies. It was inevitable that they'd hook up, and when they did, it was in a flurry of hype equal to Zeppelin's.

Crosby, Stills, & Nash had many distinguished people pulling for them from the start—not only Ertegun but David Geffen, the hip young mogul who was just fresh from a stint managing Laura Nyro. Geffen didn't even smoke dope. He was the first Rock 'n' Roll yuppie. He made it pay off, too—in 1971, he founded Asylum Records, which would soon become the domain of "adult Rock": Jackson Browne, the Eagles, Linda Ronstadt, Joni Mitchell, and other million-selling artists.

Considering that their name sounded like a corporate firm, I guess it's not too surprising that Crosby, Stills, & Nash manifested the first flowering of adult Rock. Their arrival heralded a whole new demographic: people getting near thirty, who'd grown up with Rock but put away their boogie shoes. These were the proto-yuppies, perhaps fresh out of college and buying their first homes while many of their peers—or perhaps, at this point, younger siblings— were running wild in the streets. What they were really looking for was music that soothed, and CSN was happy to oblige. Sure, their subject matter got heavy on occasion, especially after Neil Young joined ("Ohio"), but they were also the first rockers to voice domestic concern: "Teach Your Children," "Our House," etc. Everything from their attitude to their impeccable harmonies reeked of maturity, which was, of course, the great bane of '70s Rock ('til the Ramones, anyway).

Atlantic profited so totally from Led Zeppelin, Crosby, Stills, & Nash, and other subsequent signings like Yes and Bad Company that, by the mid-'70s, the former indie-label-founded-in-a-shoebox became one of the three major record labels (a merger with Jac Holzman's Elektra and David Geffen's Asylum also helped). But along the way, as they were making the transition from R&B to business as usual, they got burned a few times. A perfect example was their experience with the MC5. From Detroit, the group had been attracting an enormous amount of publicity due to their members' affiliations with radical John Sinclair's White Panther party. Sinclair acted as a de facto manager for the group, at least until he got sent to jail. The center of the auto industry and America's murder capitol, Detroit in the '60s was a bastion of fear. Despite the fact that it was, at that time, America's fourth-largest city, it was surrounded by an outback so rural that, by 1967, only thirty percent of the state's population was hooked up for television. Due to Detroit's immense Black population, when the cities began to implode with racial strife, Detroit was among the first to go up in flames (an event the MC5 memorialized with "Motor City Is Burning").

In many ways the Punk aesthetic, away from the fuzzy-headed disorienta-
tion of people like Roky Erickson and Sky Saxon, originated in the Midwest.
Such Punk classics as Them's "Gloria" and "I Can Only Give You Everything"
probably entered the vernacular as a result of Midwestern cover versions (the
Shadows of Knight in the case of the former; the MC5 and Little Boy Blues in
the latter). In Michigan, whether the bands played in a modernized R&B vein
(Mitch Ryder & the Detroit Wheels, Rationals, Reflections, Bob Seger, the
Woolies) or the new Brit-influenced style (Amboy Dukes, Iguanas, MC5,
Unrelated Segments, Terry Knight & the Pack), their musical approach only
made sense within the landlocked confines of the region. For this reason,
Detroit was full of "local legends" like Ryder and Seger—raw talents who
couldn't seem to break out on the national level. It was this experience that the
MC5 came out of.

Because of the hype, Atlantic misunderstood and thought the band were
basic hippie types. But they should have conferred with their future business
partners, Elektra Records, who'd dropped them from the label over such
offenses as using the word "motherfucker" on an LP and taking full-page ads,
affixed with the Elektra logo, that said "Fuck Hudson's" after the popular
department store chain refused to stock the offending album. The album was
called *Kick Out the Jams* and was recorded at the Grande Ballroom, their home
stomping ground, and it played up their associations with the radical underground. But as bassist Michael Davis remembers, it was mostly a hoax: "We
admired the Panthers for their stance. Like them we set up a 10-point program,
but it was conceived with a sense of humor. They were out marching in pla-
toons, they were practicing for something. We were just sitting around the din-
ing room table getting high and cracking up." [2]

Musically, the MC5 was based in the most rudimentary structures with a
lot of emphasis on feedback and distortion ("Looking at You," an earlier
recording, broke the sound barrier). They covered Chuck Berry and Little
Richard but jammed with Sun Ra, so who knows what they were really up to?
Drugs obviously played a big part—when a musician can't feel his hand on the
strings, he may be tempted to whack down a little harder on that power chord,
and that's what the MC5 did. Far different from Led Zeppelin's expansive
Heavy Metal, the MC5 were raw and sometimes sloppy, but never less than sincere about their revo-rhetoric. This was brutal, honest Rock 'n' Roll, which is

why they so shamelessly divulged their uninhibited teenage lust at every turn. Unfortunately, most of the turns were bumpy, which is why they're so often looked upon as the first real Punk band. Because in 1969, at the very height of the peace and love era, they went so directly against the grain of everything that was going on that they had to suffer the fate of outcasts.

Atlantic slicked them up with a "hip" producer, Jon Landau, and the subsequent album, *Back in the USA*, became the quintessential American Hard-Rock riot-in-the-streets manifesto with its unique blend of Chairman Mao and Chuck Berry. A lot of skeptics questioned the band's absurd hippie politics, but the important thing was, *as a band* they were taking the form to a whole new level. The album was as chock-full of grit as a dozen Rolling Stones albums, but they took a beating from critics and the record-buying public alike. The critics expected White Panther polemics and got "High School"; the public expected Led Zeppelin and got "The Human Being Lawn Mower." As a result, no one was happy—least of all Atlantic.

There was at least one group even more reviled by the record industry than the MC5—the Stooges, their "baby brother" band that also hailed from the environs of Ann Arbor. The Stooges were so prole that they apparently considered even the MC5 to be elitist to some extent. For example, the communal vibe apparently bugged original Stooges guitarist Ron Asheton: "At the MC5 house if you brought any beer or pot over everyone was like, 'Alright, give it up man!' We hated that." [3]

Undaunted, Asheton formed the declassé Stooges with his brother Scott on drums and a few friends including James Osterberg (a.k.a. Iggy Stooge, a.k.a. Iggy Pop). The young debating-team-captain-turned-delinquent (the classic '60s story) had studied drums with bluesman Sam Lay in Chicago and had previously belonged to such primal garage outfits as the Iguanas. He'd known the Ashetons and Stooges bassist Dave Alexander since elementary school.

Taking a cue from the MC5, the Stooges were also demonstrably primitivesque but, like the Five, they stabbed into the void enough to legitimately claim homage to Free-Jazz as well. Although the MC5 baited their lyrics with sister/brother rhetoric, the Stooges' lyrics, in a clear premonition of the Ramones, were disarmingly simple. The feeling was always the main thing. Iggy voiced these sentiments with a vengeance, and the Asheton boys and Alexander were never less than compelling.

Borrowing a little of the "evil" mystique of the Doors, Rolling Stones, and Velvet Underground, the Stooges were among the first groups to be truly *feared*. This was not only because they hit their instruments so hard (they used to hold football-style rallies of "kill kill *kill*" before every gig) and voiced contempt—it was also because, at the core, guys like the Ashetons and Iggy really didn't give a shit. This was not only an affront to the Lefty politics that had invaded the '60s Rock consciousness—which even the MC5 paid lip service to—it was also virtual suicide as far as career goals went. It was also the birth of the true Punk aesthetic, and virtually every musician of *that* generation would pay homage to the Stooges.

The Stooges understood the oncoming apathy of the next generation before almost anybody. As Iggy explained: "Sinclair would say, 'We are going to politicize the Youth!' But the kids were like, 'WHAT? Just gimme some dope.' They didn't care. That's how it really was." [4]

According to drummer Scott Asheton: "Peace and love wasn't a big part of it. We really didn't care that much about making people feel good. We were more into what was really going on, and how boring crap was, and how you're really treated." [5]

Creem magazine in Detroit became the bastion of the new fuck-all mentality as well as the Motor City aesthetic. Those were the days when people actually read Rock magazines. Those were also the days when people had attention spans longer than ten minutes. It was easy for an upstart magazine to come along and propagate its own unique philosophy. In the beginning they mouthed the same left-wing platitudes as the other hippie mags, but when Lester Bangs became the editor in 1971, *Creem* became the literary equivalent of the Punk ethos being fostered by groups like the Stooges and MC5 (whom they championed). *Creem*'s staff were the first to directly acknowledge the lowbrow implications of the impending culture. That's why their niche became Heavy Metal, but not before spawning a whole aesthetic based on love of rudiments that would inevitably lead to Punk.

The proletariat factor had something to do with it. To this new generation of Rock critics (which included Nick Tosches, Mike Saunders, Robot A. Hull, Andy Shernoff, Rick Johnson, and Peter Laughner, as well as the spiritual forefathers Bangs and Richard Meltzer), ineptitude in Rock was always preferable to studied virtuosity (which they saw as "anti-Rock"). The problem began when groups started purposely trying to be inept (Pussy Galore) as opposed to simply *being* inept (the Seeds, Blue Cheer, the Stooges). Bangs was perhaps the most pervasive champion of this anti-aesthetic, and even though his interest in music was primarily allegorical, he would have as much impact on the future of Rock as almost any musician of his era. Meltzer also deserves credit for his unique literary style that was one part wrestling manager to two parts carney barker. Clowns like Bangs, Meltzer, Tosches, and even John Mendelsohn were so intent upon *not* taking Rock seriously that they more often than not didn't even write about their subject matter. There was the famous incident in 1971 when Meltzer, who was supposed to be reviewing a Cactus album, reviewed the *cover*! Rock criticism soon became a forum for a whole school of would-be Kerouacs and purveyors of the confessional first-person narrative.

The contrast between the two schools of Rock criticism—Marcus/Landau/ Christgau vs. Bangs/Meltzer/Tosches, Punk vs. hippie, rudiment vs. refinement, "serious" vs. stupid—was largely symptomatic of the ever-divisive nature of Rock itself. With increasingly more people listening to Rock, there was no way they were all going to agree on what was "cool" or "hip" or even acceptable. No group pointed towards this impasse more emphatically than Grand Funk Railroad, who held the dual distinction of being not only one of the most hated groups of the era, but one of the most successful as well.

Originally from Flint, Michigan, Grand Funk fit the profile of Motor City Madness: a power trio, they arrived at just the right time to cash in on all the money a-flying in those days of industry overload. The thing was, in the post-*Sgt. Pepper* era, Rock had ascertained its large market share mainly through album sales, which is why all the Heavy groups of the next era—Led Zeppelin, Black Sabbath, Uriah Heep, Yes—didn't care about having hit singles. The idea was, you had to ingest this stuff *whole*. So much so that the Heavy bands fashioned a great number of their songs at eight- or nine-minute lengths, leaving room for a lot of supposedly Jazz-like soloing—which in the case of a band like Grand Funk, was a big mistake!

The industry was faced with an interesting proposition. On the one hand, the artists who were garnering favorable reviews from the critics—Laura Nyro, Randy Newman, Van Morrison, the Band—weren't really selling; at least not selling in the way that the bands they hated—Led Zeppelin, Grand Funk, Steppenwolf—were. The labels were faced with a dilemma: should they hold onto their hippie idealism and support those artists whose "cause" they supported, or should they just go for the gold? It's not hard to figure out what their decision was.

As for the critics, even Punk thud-lovers like Lester Bangs and Dave Marsh were left with an aesthetic conundrum as far as bands like Grand Funk went—mainly, how far were they willing to accommodate music that was basic sludge in order to fulfill their populist notions? In the end, the masses didn't care anyway, as they'd prove time and again throughout the '70s by embracing those artists the critics loathed the most: Kiss, Aerosmith, Ted Nugent. What it proved was how superfluous Rock criticism had already become by 1970.

This was the day and age of "freaks," when people took as many drugs as humanly possible just to stay awake. The great mortal exodus of Jim, Jimi, and Janis hadn't occurred yet. In England, the ultimate freak band were the Deviants, who were kind of the isle's version of the Fugs, with their tie-ins to various radical organizations and their penchant for performance-style spectacle. Fronted by noted Brit music scribe Mick Farren, the Deviants provided an exemplary transition between the hazy heyday of classic British psych and the Punk/Heavy Metal aesthetic of the new age. (Farren made it a point to visit the MC5 commune whenever he was in Detroit, which was a *lot*, if you know what I mean, heh-heh.) In the Deviants' sound, one could hear everything from classic Doors rabble-rousing ("Somewhere to Go") to trippy psych ("Jamie's Song," "First Line") to harmonica-wheezing Thirteenth-Floor-Elevators-style garage grunge ("You've Got to Hold On"). The more musically inclined members eventually went on to form the archetypal space/heavy/glam Pink Fairies, and Farren wrote sci-fi novels and a book about Elvis (the epitome of Third Generation consciousness, in other words).

Although the freak scene captured most of the hype in the late '60s–early '70s, there was another, quieter revolution going on that would have perhaps even more lasting implications. The whole outbreak of "do your own thing" and the overriding desire to be "free" had led to extensive inner exploration on the part of the Baby Boomers. After the massive rethinking of sex and social mores that had accompanied the Boomers' coming-of-age period, there was a turn toward a more inward-leaning direction. The '70s would become known as the "Me Decade," and this kind of solipsistic soul searching was the reason why.

As opposed to the previous generation with its heavily decorated World

War II Daddies, the Baby Boomers sought antiheroes: effeminate boys like the Beatles, Rolling Stones, and Bob Dylan. By the late '60s, the image of the anti-hero had invaded Hollywood. Actors like Robert DeNiro, Dustin Hoffman, Woody Allen, Elliot Gould, and others were more apt to shrug their shoulders than bust up a barroom à la John Wayne. Then they'd look into the camera with their puppy-dog eyes and go into a soliloquy about their "feelings." The "sensitive" guy was suddenly everywhere. In a way, it was just an extension of James Dean's whole confused style of method acting, but it also had to do with the antiwar movement and new issues like feminism. In general, the world was softening, and the old Hawkishness of the WWII Daddies was seen as barbaric. To believe in *anything* was becoming passé—in the modern world, everything was "relative." The consciousness raising brought about by LSD and the Movement had produced a sound conclusion on the part of the new disaffected generation that it was a multifaceted world and there was no one way of looking at anything. People were suddenly being encouraged to display their differences and doubts.

As far as music went, it was much easier to pull off this kind of self-conscious act as a soloist than in the group setting, where collective ID is everything. It all goes back to Dylan and his conversion to a kind of more "personal" statement (as opposed to "protest"), although he actually longed for the yin/yang interaction of the band setting and pursued it with the Band. The singer–songwriters of the late '60s–early '70s were doing just the opposite: abandoning the collaborative format to perform solo and shed their psychic demons. It was a deeply personal form of art, which is why it was sometimes self-indulgent and its legacy was more worthy of Tin Pan Alley than Rock 'n' Roll. But it *was* different than folk music because it was the first time young singers weren't expected to adhere to any particular "folk" formula. In fact, it was more of a straight-out Pop formula absorbed from the Beatles as well as Dylan. The Tin Pan Alley comparisons come back to haunt us again—a great many of the first wave of the singer–songwriters had commercial songwriting backgrounds (Randy Newman, Carole King, Harry Nilsson, Laura Nyro, Jackson Browne). A few others (Neil Young, James Taylor, Todd Rundgren, Rod Stewart) had broken free of the band format. In the case of the Brill Builders, they were probably sick of hearing their material mishandled and sought to clear their own emotional decks ("make their own statement," as it were). The band breakaways, on the other hand, no doubt felt that the collaborative vibe was crimping their style. They were sick of being emotionally sabo-taged by the restraints of interactive musicianship.

In light of all the techno-spasmodic twists that Rock was undergoing in the late '60s, the new wave of solo troubadours proved that the human voice was still a powerful tool of self-expression. But it wasn't necessarily for the same reason that people had listened to Joan Baez's glass-breaking voice for its puri-ty of notes. In terms of the singer–songwriters, it was important that all the flaws were left in—and that meant emotional ones in the lyrics. It was the anti-hero stuff again, and it contrasted greatly with the mythic warrior stuff of Led Zeppelin et al. Such was the chasm of early '70s Rock. Collective consumer mass would never reach the same level of cohesion that it did in the '60s with the Beatles/Stones/Dylan. The impasse would continue to grow—the hippies who dug the singer–songwriters would drift quickly into genteel old-fartdom and wind up with Bruce Hornsby; the Hard Rock hordes would continue to cheapen themselves until they'd digressed to cartoon-show irrelevance (Kiss, Ted Nugent). The '60s were over, in other words.

There's no denying that the singer–songwriter trend had a lot to do with the whole "mellowing out" phase of '70s Rock and the growing-old mentality of the graying '60s dino-farts. An even more insidious factor was that so many '60s holdovers quickly switched to the more placid waters once the decade was over. Paul McCartney, Van Morrison, Carole King, and Carly Simon all paint-ed a picture of the domesticated hippie, still liberal in outlook but ultimately self-involved with a papoose or two tying 'em down. In an indirect way, this whole mentality led to John Lennon copping out of the scene altogether to raise children and bake bread in 1975. It's also what led to pabulum-slingers James Taylor and Carly Simon tying the knot in public in a highly publicized "Rock star" marriage in 1973.

There were two schools of singer–songwriters: the more Tin Pan Alley/Pop-derived composers, who usually accompanied themselves on piano (Laura Nyro, Randy Newman, Carole King, Carly Simon, and, to some extent, even Elton John) and the folk-derived acoustic troubadours (Jackson Browne, James Taylor, Neil Young, Cat Stevens, Jim Croce). The lyrical content was essentially the same (love and self-reflection). Once and a while there was an idiosyncratic artist like Newman, who, not without good reason, ended up in the Warner/Reprise loony bin of the early '70s (alongside Captain Beefheart, Frank Zappa, Wildman Fischer, Essra Mohawk, Tim Buckley, the Fugs, and Alice Cooper—need I say more?). Singing in a plain and dry voice, Newman often took the role of first-person protagonist, like on "God's Song" in 1972, in which he literally played God looking down on the whole human race as mere boot-stomp material. By the time of *Good ol' Boys* in 1974, in a song like "Rednecks," he takes the imaginary defense of Lester Maddox against "niggers" and "Jews" everywhere (Newman, like King, Nyro, and Paul Simon, was Jewish). It was artists like Newman who helped introduce irony to the forum, but it's debatable whether, other than that, he had any influence on Rock at all. But he did serve as a consciousness-raising example of what could be done in the name of Rock. What it proved was, Rock was becoming merely the medium, as opposed to the raison d'être.

Like Newman, Carole King, and Jim Webb, Laura Nyro was a successful songwriter outside of her solo pursuits, but her own albums were a more idiosyncratic blend of Tin Pan Alley and Broadway sensibilities mixed with Jazz and Rock 'n' Roll elements. Being from Brooklyn, she seemed to absorb the influences of the pre-Beatles girl group/street-corner harmony era. She billed herself as "Laura Nyro Accompanying Herself on Piano," which apparently wasn't good enough for the hippies—they booed her offstage at Monterey. When she auditioned for Columbia, she demanded that it be in a candlelit setting. This was a whole new age of sensitive artists to whom such nuances were essential to the whole "aura" of the proceedings. It wouldn't be long before Rock stars were demanding ice buckets filled to the brim with heroin and, miraculously enough, being obliged.

Joni Mitchell was a perfect example. She'd waif'd down from Canada during the Folk phase in the early '60s and made a groin-galvanizing impression on almost every flutter-brained hippie songman in Los Angeles, from David Geffen to the various members of Crosby, Stills, Nash, & Young. Her quivering voice was a thorn in the side to the Hard Rock audience all throughout the first half of the '70s, as she scored million-selling albums like *Blue*, *For the Roses*, and *Court n' Spark*. Expressing a jaded sense of sorrow that sometimes bordered on contempt or self-pity, Mitchell was among the most exponentially personal of the singer–songwriters. Her incline was so inward, in fact, that, in 1975, she gave up live performing altogether.

Because she was female, Mitchell's blunt lyrics about love were taken as feminist statements. As their sardonic name implies, the California five-piece band, Joy of Cooking, were also proto-feminists, thanks to leadership in the form of two female singer–songwriters, Toni Brown and Terry Garthwaite. The Women's Movement really came to the fore in the early '70s. The new sensitized male à la Jackson Browne or James Taylor was the other side of the coin: mainly, the hippies knew they'd better be sympathetic to their sisters—or risk not ever getting laid again.

Despite these few improvements, the male singer–songwriters were inherently sexist. A perfect example is Neil Young, whose childlike demeanor led him to relegate the opposite sex to the role of "maids" or "cowgirls." Despite the sexist implications of "A Man Needs a Maid," in Neil's case there might have been a simpler explanation—as a hippie, he may not have liked having to pick up after himself. That didn't appease feminists, but it did differentiate him from his peers, so much so that he's endured to this day as a hero to not only his original audience but a whole new generation of underground and indie-Rock fans who like the way he plays guitar. Like Joni Mitchell, Young had originally hailed from north of the border, but many of his songs contained acute political commentary about the state of things on the American cultural frontier: "Ohio," "Soldier," "Campaigner," etc. A romantic as well, his more forlorn tendencies made him the captain of some of the most poignant melodies of his era ("Don't Let it Bring You Down," "Pardon My Heart"). Young was also one of the first to grow increasingly cynical in his view of the counterculture. In "Ambulance Blues," from the underrated *On the Beach* (1974), he warbles in a druggy voice: "All along the Navaho Trail/Burnouts stub their toes on garbage pails." It wasn't exactly Pete Seeger, in other words.

Jackson Browne, Leonard Cohen, James Taylor, Paul Simon, John Denver, and Todd Rundgren were the archetypal "sensitive" guys. Browne's woeful tunes like "Fountain of Sorrow," about Life After Break-Up, and "Here Come Those Tears Again," about the suicide of his ex-wife, were as important to the development of true '70s consciousness (i.e., self-absorbed) as Led Zeppelin's swaggering cocksmanship. Although technically not really a singer–songwriter, Todd Rundgren rode the wave of solo voices after departing from the Philly-based psych band Nazz in 1970. One of the most promising songwriters of the era, Rundgren was capable of suite-like grandeur on an almost Brian Wilson level, with just the right degree of shy, antihero distance. Songs like "Hello It's Me" and "I Saw the Light" presented the sensitive male stereotype but were believable, and "Couldn't I Just Tell You," with its hook-laden formula, was as vital in the development of "power Pop" as Big Star. Despite a few hits, Rundgren proved too complex and eventually too drug-riddled to ever achieve mainstream acceptance, and in many ways his shy-guy balladeer style was usurped by an even more saccharine tunesmith, from England this time—Elton John.

The less Pop-oriented and more Folk-oriented singer–songwriters—Cohen, John Prine, Loudon Wainright III, David Blue, Jerry Jeff Walker, Don McLean, Gordon Lightfoot, Tim Buckley, Tim Hardin, Jesse Colin Young, Eric Anderson—although aesthetically more challenging, had little chance of affecting the tastes of the mainstream. Dylan-style troubadouring had been dead ever since Dylan himself turned his back on it for the more genteel pursuits of Pop—there was little chance it was going to make a comeback in the '70s. Surprisingly, the straight Folk preoccupation would actually blossom again in the late '70s in the form of Ricky Lee Jones, and then in the '80s in the form of Tracy Chapman. In both cases, these were examples of the feminist strain of liberal-think invading the subtext—in either case, the implications were far more sociological than musical/aesthetic. It should also be mentioned that ex-'60s superstar group voices like Rod Stewart, Van Morrison, Stephen Stills, and the various ex-Beatles—although, like Rundgren, not outright singer–songwriters—made extensive use of the solo voice in plumbing their own confessional narrative depths.

In the quest for soul searching, there remained one relationship that had yet to be delved into—that between the hippie iconoclast and his maker (i.e., God). Maybe it was all the acid, but suddenly there was a desire on the part of the countercultural hordes to be *cleansed* from the free-for-all that was the '60s. This is where the whole notion of having one's own "guru" came from. Many of the dinosaurs thought redemption was possible via the teachings of a readymade spiritual leader. This included Pete Townshend's allegiance to Meher Baba as well as Carlos Santana's devotion to Sri Chimnoy. These dilettantes hadn't had to answer to anyone for so long that apparently the notion of that one divine figure whose feet they could kneel at appealed to them greatly, once again as a humanizing factor that would atone for their guilt in being such capitalists. It was only a matter of time before cut-rate hustlers like Charles Manson and Mel Lyman were exploiting the salvation seekers for all they were worth.

The whole notion that Jesus may have been just another wandering hippie bard seemed very plausible to the dope dupes. Within a short time, God-Rock was upon us. This took the form of such bombastic stage productions as *Jesus Christ Superstar* and *Godspell.* It was also apparent in the religious imagery evoked by artists like George Harrison, Van Morrison, the Band, Cat Stevens, Brewer & Shipley, James Taylor, Seals & Crofts, Coven, Aum, Norman Greenbaum, Neil Diamond, Black Oak Arkansas, and Black Sabbath.

Such sanctimonious gestures weren't about to invade the mainstream. This heavy-handedness helped widen the divide that had been growing between the Pop audience and the Rock underground since the days of psychedelia. Into the void stepped the new popsmiths, hip to hippie ideals but expressing the lachrymose sentiment that had always characterized popular songwriting. In many ways, they were just the same old pros (David Gates, Neil Diamond, Paul McCartney, Paul Simon) but with long hair. This was the new Tin Pan Alley: Bread, the Carpenters, Three Dog Night, Seals & Crofts, Chicago, America, Helen Reddy, Gilbert O'Sullivan, etc. Only vaguely "Rock"—if at all—these manufactured entities dominated the radio in the early '70s. Already the trend was being established—there was an easier way to do it other than having to deal with all those vulgarians.

But the vulgarians would have one last hurrah, and it was to be an orgy of mythic—if not damning—proportions.

CHAPTER 10

THE STRUGGLE

BY THE LATE '60S THE FACE OF WHITE ROCK 'N' ROLL HAD BECOME FULLY RAD-ICALIZED. Some of these sociopolitical forces were also creeping into the area of Black music, but this created a much more complex scenario because the purveyors of "soul" music were decidedly down-home in their origins. For them, musical expression had been an outgrowth of a healing process—from slavery—that went back to the church. Most of them hit the road when they were very young and, despite their soulfulness, considered themselves "entertainers" first and foremost. This was still the day and age when white Rock 'n' Roll and Black music weren't entirely separate. Race as a definition of their music was something that would be imposed upon them by whites. Black performers, because they were coming at it from such organic origins, weren't devoid of white Pop influences like Dean Martin and Frank Sinatra—or Hank Williams for that matter. It was just music they heard on the radio. That can probably be said of some white artists as well, as far as their take on Black resources—at least the more down-home ones like Hank Williams or Elvis Presley.

In the '60s, nothing had stirred the radical movement more than the Civil Rights struggle. Although Vietnam would prove to eventually have an even larger impact on the long-term ideology of America's Left, the course of nonviolent resistance practiced by Martin Luther King and his fellow Freedom Fighters in many ways set the tone for the social upheaval of the whole decade. For Blacks in America to defy one hundred years of racist policy so defiantly at a time when the media was coming into its own was an event that was bound to have everlasting implications. To be Black in the '60s (and ever since) meant asserting racial pride. That was the whole point of the Civil Rights Movement—to take it to the people so that King's dream would someday be realized.

To Black musicians, this created an interesting and sometimes problematic scenario. First there was the matter of the record industry itself, which was 95 percent run by whites. Then there was radio. There was also the press. In short, living in a country that practiced virtual apartheid, it wasn't likely that Black radicalism was going to be given equal voice. Soul performers like James Brown, Wilson Pickett, Otis Redding, Joe Tex, Ray Charles, Solomon Burke, and others, many of whom originated literally down on the farm, may have sensed injustice, but they didn't intend for their music to be a mouthpiece for radical ideas. What they were preaching was a more universal ideal. Considering the times, however, they couldn't avoid being mixed up in politics by the end of the decade, even if it took the form of nappier threads and afros. Black *identity* had become radicalized, and this couldn't help but affect the music.

In the late '60s the most pivotal figure in Black American popular music was James Brown. Born in rural South Carolina in 1933, but raised in Augusta, Georgia, Brown's musical experience had come from equal parts church and whorehouse—which was the classic breeding ground for so much of the important music of the twentieth century, white and Black alike. As Brown recalled: "I'd have to say that I was poorer than most of the other kids, and a different kind of poor, too. I was poor because nobody was really taking care of me. I came from a roadhouse, not an organized home." [1]

When Brown speaks of a certain kind of poverty, he is speaking in spiritual terms as well. The impact of racism was inherent in the whole experience, naturally, but what Brown is declaring is that there were even more pressing needs that informed his day-to-day existence. Music was one way Brown could transcend his own dire circumstances. Like a lot of Black Southerners, his first exposure to music came through the church, where the theatrical exaltations of the preachers undoubtedly influenced his own performing technique many years down the road.

Louis Jordan was another early influence. As the leader of the first intentionally scaled down Rhythm & Blues band, the Tympani Five, Jordan was a

likely prototype for all future Black bandleaders, especially one like James
Brown, who from the very start was very much in command of his whole stage
act. Recording independence would come later, but even as early as "Please
Please Please" (1956) he was attempting the same kind of sanctified/secular
crossover as Ray Charles and Little Richard. By doing so, he was putting himself at odds with the very source of his inspiration—namely, the church. When
they threatened to throw Brown and his Famous Flames out of the congrega-
tion, he must have felt genuine anguish. The church was the one area that a
poor Southern Black man felt he could always turn to, in light of society's indifference, and they were turning their backs on him. Because religion was the
way in which a person's identity was defined in the Black Southern community, the earliest Soul performers felt as if they were struggling for their very
humanity while they struggled with such conflicts.

Ray Charles, who was born in Albany, Georgia, in 1930, was perhaps the
most controversial agent of the Gospel influx in popular music. The fact that
he was blind helped intensify his mystique, because it meant that he carried an
even greater burden than the average Black, and that, of course, made him a
symbol of strength and self-determination within the community. The effects
of Charles's blindness on his vocal technique were profound; blindness being a
kind of isolation in itself, Charles sounded literally *possessed*. One of his last
memories before he lost his eyesight completely was the sight of his brother
drowning in a washtub. For Ray Charles, like James Brown, poverty was an
even more damning reality than racism at that time. As soon as he could break
free of the South, he did, hitting the road and eventually ending up in Seattle
and then L.A., where he cut his first sides (1949). But no matter how far from
the Deep South he journeyed, the intense fervor of the Baptist revival meetings
never left him. This was apparent on recordings like "I Got a Woman," which
caught fire from both sides—white radio programmers thought it was "too
Black" and were offended by its raw sexuality; Blacks thought it was making
light of the Gospel.

A skilled pianist who'd taught himself to read and compose in Braille,
Charles utilized both Jazz and Gospel rhythms, while using the "oral" tradition
of the Blues to tell his story. Again, the fact that he was blind made this tradition even more valuable, because the sense of sound itself carried much more
profundity to him than it did to the average person. In that case, he used his

voice to reach deep into his most primal source of emotional depth. This really is the definition of Soul music—a kind of naturalness that could only come from total emotional involvement with the world, but also the sense that the world itself is indifferent to one's concerns as a sentient being.

Ray Charles was lucky that he eventually ended up recording for Atlantic, a label with a strong relationship to the Black community. Perhaps because it was run by two Turks, they trusted Blacks more than they did whites, but Atlantic's early sides weren't all Black by a long shot. It was only after Ray Charles's success that Atlantic became America's leading resource for both Jazz and Rhythm & Blues. Atlantic was one of the first of the independent labels to get into the album market, and Ray Charles tended to be more adventurous on his LPs than his singles. What it proved was that there was a long-playing market for Black music as well, and Atlantic generally treated their artists better and presented them with more class and sophistication than their competitors. Being foreigners, the heads of Atlantic better understood the strange plight that confronted Blacks in America, making them foreigners in their own native land.

Blacks, meanwhile, could relate instantly to someone like Ray Charles, because many of them came from similar backgrounds—dirt-poor towns where *everybody* in the community went to church. Even when Ray Charles went Country, he never lost the Black audience. His effect on Rock 'n' Roll was equal to that of Little Richard—a liberating force that was steeped in Blues and Gospel tradition. One must remember, most Northerners didn't even see Ray Charles or Little Richard until their popular success brought them to television. To most Americans, there was a mystique to these artists that verged on *fear*. For all the impassioned phrasing and raw abandon of something like Ray Charles' "What'd I Say," to most whites it was the equivalent of speaking in tongues.

The natural reaction of the record industry was to bleach the music of its "color" and resell it to the masses in a watered-down rendition. Initially this was accomplished by having white artists cover Black material, like the McGuire Sisters doing the Moonglows' "Sincerely" or Pat Boone covering Little Richard's "Tutti Frutti." By the mid-'50s, however, a number of authentic Black Rhythm & Blues records were crossing over to the mainstream charts. Producers and arrangers found that it was just as easy to take an authentic Black act and mold it as to get a white man to mimic a Black man. The artists were actually encouraged to emphasize their blackness, but white Tin Pan Alley–style musical ideals were imposed upon them. This resulted in much of the commercial Black music of the '50s, from the Clovers to Frankie Lyman & the Teenagers.

Perhaps the classic example was the Coasters, a West Coast group who had several Top Ten hits that combined street slang with sophisticated arrangements. But this was Atlantic again—pairing the group with the composing team of Jerry Leiber and Mike Stoller resulted in a prosperous swap of talent for all parties involved. It also gave Atlantic a permanent inroad into the Brill Building, an endless resource of potential chart-topping hits. All Atlantic had to do was come up with the talent, and they got that right off the streets. For instance, the Drifters, another Gospel-influenced vocal group who'd been recording for Atlantic for several years, finally struck gold when they entered into a relationship with Doc Pomus and Mort Shuman, another pair of white composers from the Brill Building. Atlantic was also the first label to add strings to a Black record: the Drifters' "There Goes My Baby" (1959). Such bids towards "sophistication" were bound to have a drastic impact on the way Black music was recorded and produced outside of the Atlantic studios as well.

Sam Cooke was initially a controversial figure in commercial Black music because he was the first artist to come directly from the field of Gospel into the new Pop realm. As a member of the Soul Stirrers, he'd been recording since 1951. It wasn't really that big of a stretch for Cooke to cross over to the Pop market, especially since his sleek crooner style was having the same effect on the female portion of his audience that Elvis's hip-wiggling was having on his. Once he did so, his subsequent recordings were surprisingly tame. The same goes for Jackie Wilson, another crooner, whose recordings were saddled with strings that could've been intended for any number of white singers.

A lot of the more tough-minded R&B simply didn't cross over, particularly the gritty electric blues of people like Howlin' Wolf, Muddy Waters, Magic Sam, Ike Turner, John Lee Hooker, Elmore James, Pee Wee Crayton, Smokey Smothers, and Sonny Boy Williamson. These artists combined more hip urban sensibilities with distinctly down-home flavor and sold fairly well in the Black community. The arrival of Rock 'n' Roll no doubt didn't hurt them, but it also had little influence on their musical approach or recording policies. They remained solidly outside of the mainstream, as did most Black Jazz musicians at that time.

The pop/crossover model was perfected by a label called Motown, which was founded in Detroit in 1959 by Berry Gordy, Jr., an ex-boxer who became one of the most successful Black entrepreneurs in the country. He did so simply by cultivating that which was in his own backyard, culling these urchins out of the ghetto and polishing them until they shined. Gordy sent his charges to an actual "finishing school" so they would appear more sophisticated than their peers and thus more radio-and-TV-ready. At the same time, groups like the Miracles and the Temptations were doing dance moves no white acts would touch, and each band was Black, and generally excellent, for the most part just a bunch of guys right off the streets of Detroit (Gordy always worked cheap). The assembly line approach extended to songwriters as well: at Motown, one was only as good as one's last hit, and Gordy had a virtual pecking order among composers like Holland/Dozier/Holland, Whitfield/Strong, Smokey Robinson, and Ashford/Simpson. Gordy was no fool—he knew that creating such fierce competition would result in an abundance of quality product, and no label placed more songs in the hit parade during the '60s than Motown. For a Black-owned independent that wasn't too bad, and naturally it was bound to have sweeping ramifications.

It's interesting to note that many of the grittier, more soulful Black acts that recorded for Motown—Martha & the Vandellas, the Contours, Barrett Strong—didn't cross over as well. Whereas the Supremes, who weren't really that hip to Blacks due to their supper-club style, were the most successful act on the label. This was undoubtedly setting a precedent for the Black popular music of the future. Marvin Gaye, a soulful and evocative singer, straddled the line between R&B and Pop with his tuneful crooning, but his duets with female singers like Kim Weston were more naturally funky.

The other major Soul-provider in the '60s, the Stax label in Memphis, was gritty by contrast. The irony was, where Motown employed chiefly Black musicians, the Stax house band employed whites. These were Southerners who'd grown up listening to Country & Western and Gospel—Ray Charles in reverse, in other words. An integrated band like Booker T & the MGs provided for a uniquely cross-pollinating musical experience with an abundance of far-reaching social implications as well. What the Memphis sound added to the realm of Soul music was the stomp-beat. This in turn made the exaltations of Southern performers like Otis Redding sound like the most frenzied kind of sanctified testimonial despite the fact that, by this time, Black popular music was becoming an increasingly secular art form.

Chicago Soul, in contrast to Motown, had a much more down-home feel due to the fact that, because of its largely transplanted population, the city enjoyed a direct mainline into the South. Even the full-scale productions of Curtis Mayfield and his group, the Impressions, were musically grittier and more church-inflected than Motown's. Chicago's Black musical community was not attempting as broad a crossover as Motown, who actively strove to reach out beyond the Black community and into the white one. Maybe that's because there was no centralized powerhouse equivalent to Motown. The only potential hit-making factory was Chess/Checker, but as a label specializing in gritty Blues, they couldn't really compete with Motown's calculated charm. Nevertheless, by the mid-'60s, artists like Gene Chandler, Fontella Bass, Little Milton, and the Dells were taking a more deliberately "soulful" approach, partly because Motown had established that Soul music now worked as "pop" music as well.

Despite this inevitable incline toward more upwardly mobile pretenses, Chicago was still primarily a breeding ground for Blues. This brings up an interesting point, because it proves that even at the height of Black music's whole evolution into Pop, there were still these isolated pockets of neotraditionalism that went on devoid of the mainstream. Blues, which really hadn't changed since the postwar years, was its own reward. Although in certain quarters, it was perceived as being somewhat Uncle Tom-ish—partly because it had been effectively pillaged by white musicians, but also because it denoted the day and age of the Black man before he was enlightened to racial issues. Nevertheless, in Chicago, inner-city Blues continued to flourish in the form of Magic Sam, Buddy Guy, Junior Wells, J. B. Hutto, Hound Dog Taylor, and others. New Orleans, another city credited with introducing the ethnic element into American music, produced a whole new line of neotraditionalists who turned the city's rich musical heritage in on itself to produce a compelling legacy of their own. This included the Meters, Wild Tchoupitoulas, Allen Toussaint, Shirley & Lee, and the Neville Brothers, as well as the rise of Cajun and Zydeco as viable subcategories of semipopular music.

The whole time this evolution was going on, James Brown, perhaps Black music's pivotal figure, had never left the road (earning him the epithet "the hardest-working man in show biz"). As far as creating popular and still artistically valid Black music, James's vision was at least parallel to that of Stax or Motown. Initially he was a smoothie who liked to do ballads, but by the time of "Please Please Please" (1956) he was already striving for something more primal in his vocal style. This came directly from the church, and although these records sold incredibly well regionally, James Brown still hadn't crossed over by the dawn of the '60s.

As a performer, James Brown reached his peak during the whole transition between the roadhouses and the new auditoriums. The larger traveling Black road shows like the Motown Review or Brown's own entourage (which included musicians, dancers, and comedians) were reaching a new, hipper, more affluent—and most importantly, *integrated*—audience. But despite the success of the groundbreaking *Live at the Apollo* album, which was the first time most people had ever heard a Black concert in its entirety, James Brown's style was still too raw for most whites. Assembling a tight band of mostly down-home pros who'd all been playing for over a decade, Brown ran his organization like a drill sergeant, imposing fines on band members for missing notes or dance steps and firing them outright if they challenged his authority. The result was a musical revolution that would inject Black rhythms into the structure of American popular song once and for all.

The essence of Brown's rhythmic technique was making his band play on the beat of one instead of three. The effect was a stabbing staccato beat whereby every instrument, from the horns to the guitars, acted as a form of rhythm. Perhaps the first record on which Brown really found this groove was "Out of Sight" (1964), and once he found it, he never let go. But James Brown's influence as a Black consciousness-raiser was multifold. In the '60s, not only was he changing the *sound* of Black music, but the business as well. He did this first by wresting control from his record company as an independent producer as well as entrepreneur. Brown set up his own label with its own production company and publishing firm, enabling him not only to get independent royalties but also do his own A&R. As far as his relationship with King, the parent label, Brown had originally had to finance *Live at the Apollo* on his own because label owner Syd Nathan doubted the viability of such a raw document; however, when the album took off, James Brown was vindicated and took charge. By asserting his independence in this way, James Brown became a symbol of Black pride to African-Americans.

In the '60s there was "Black pride" and there was "Black power." All through the decade Martin Luther King's credo of passive resistance had been challenged—first by Malcolm X and then by the other radical factions within the movement itself, like the Black Panthers. What this meant for someone like James Brown, who through his immense talent and success had become a "symbol" for his people, was that there were going to be a whole lot of expectations thrown onto him by the guardians of the Movement. After Martin Luther King was shot, in April 1968, these expectations rose: in the eyes of the Movement, for a Black artist to *not* make a statement about his identity was seen as a capitulation to whitey.

This caught Black entertainers off guard, because the whole nature of their business had always been to be "accepted" at any cost. No matter how much of their ethnicity artists like Otis Redding, James Brown, Aretha Franklin, Marvin Gaye, and others had maintained during their popular ascent, they still considered themselves "entertainers" first and foremost. Politics never entered into it. Traveling the U.S.A. during the '60s and being Black, they couldn't have helped being affected by the racist conditions and racial unrest. But the whole notion of "soul" was that a kind of inner strength would conquer all. Once again, this whole attitude is very derivative of the church experience. In a sense, "soul" music was the musical equivalent of King's credo "We shall overcome." But the new, heavier music, known as Funk, was a more turbulent mix that represented the more hipped, radicalized Black. Through strength comes power, the new music seemed to be saying, and the strength was contained in the massive rhythm, which perhaps reached a primal part of the nervous system that a white person couldn't fully appreciate.

This wasn't the first time this had happened. In the '40s, the pioneers of Be Bop—Charlie Parker, Dizzy Gillespie, Thelonious Monk, Kenny Clarke, etc.—had purposely made their music so "weird" and harmonically complex that it seemed impenetrable to anyone who wasn't "hip" (read: Black). As Ben Sidran wrote: "Parker's generation, having intuitively recognized that the ground rules were stacked against them, was the first to declare the 'game' not worth playing and so became the first to articulate isolationism in a socially aggressive manner." [2]

In the case of Parker at least, the overriding need to express this separatism from mainstream culture unfortunately caused him to become a junkie. In a way this was desirable, because the junkie is the ultimate "outsider" in regard to cultural acceptance. So not only were the Bebop musicians isolating themselves via their musical approach, but also via their lifestyle choices. There's no doubt that the proliferation of heroin among musicians in the post-Bop years was not only a blatant attempt to emulate Parker but also another device to assert spiritual independence. Of course, the irony was, addiction was the ultimate slavery, but at least it was a choice made independently.

The rites of the junkie weren't exclusive to Black musicians either. White America has a strange way of responding to Black cultural activity—usually it mimics it, in an attempt to make it plausible to whites. And although whites could never really do this with Be Bop, they created their own alternative in the form of "cool" jazz, which originated on the West Coast and whose practitioners were chiefly white. The one legacy of Bop that extended into Cool was the junk and white musicians like Gerry Mulligan, Art Pepper, and Chet Baker followed Black musicians like Parker, Jackie McLean, Fats Navarro, Miles Davis, John Coltrane, Sonny Rollins, and others down the path of addiction.

While the West Coast subversion was going on, some of the original purveyors of Be Bop like Dizzy Gillespie were trying to find a way to further their search for Black identity through music, first with the Afro-Cuban movement, which Gillespie led, and then by making actual pilgrimages to Africa. In the '50s, musicians like Gillespie, Art Blakey, and Randy Weston traveled to the continent courtesy of the State Department-sponsored USO tours. Some of them, like Gillespie, embraced the garb; some of them, like Weston, the rhythms. Some, like Art Blakey, added actual African musicians to their bands, which opened the door for Afrocentric players like Sabu and Olatunji to introduce their polyrhythmic proto-"world" music. Many Black American musicians converted to Islam, which they no doubt saw as a way to purify themselves after the drugs. This resulted in musicians like Yusef Lateef and Kalaparusha taking Muslim names, as well as the preoccupation with spiritual matters by artists like John Coltrane.

By the late '50s, a lot of Jazz musicians were getting sick of the policies of the white record label and club owners. A giant stride for freedom came in 1960, when a group of Black musicians staged what amounted to an "alternative" version of the Newport Jazz Festival at the Cliff Walk Manor, an off-site venue. The dissidents, led by Charles Mingus and Max Roach, performed on their own terms, without the normal compromises that one had to make when participating in a corporate spectacle like Newport. As it said on the back of the resulting album, *Newport Rebels*: "It was exhilarating for the musicians involved to realize that for once in their careers, they were capable of formulating and sustaining their own ground rules without booking agents, impresarios and other middle men."

One of the things to come out of it was the foundation of the first independent Jazz guild, which led the way for Wildflowers, Charlie Haden's Liberation Music Ensemble, the Association for Advancement of Creative Musicians (AACM), etc. There was a whole new generation of musicians who were looking for a way out of the conventional power structure of Jazz. This also tied in with their desire to "leave" the United States. Embracing more Afrocentric tendencies allowed them to do this, at least spiritually. Musically, this translated into less of a reliance on song structure and more of an emphasis on such intangible, but liberating, factors as rhythm, energy, and sheer force of will. As Sidran wrote: "What distinguished the new music from what had come before it was its incredible dynamism: the new musicians *would* be heard. There was no way to be exposed to it and remain indifferent." [3]

In other words, like the Movement itself, Jazz was becoming confrontational. A perfect example of this was Ornette Coleman, the alto sax player from Texas who was almost universally panned by the critics but was respected, and copied, by other musicians. Eventually, musicians like Ornette and Cecil Taylor won out, commanding large sums of money for performances, but this victory came with a price, and the price was for Jazz in general, which had simply become too complicated, with too many intellectual implications, to ever satisfy a mass audience again. The Free-Jazz men had "blackened" the waters, so to speak. But this perfectly suited their own artistic needs, because they were approaching their music at this point from a Black nationalist perspective. What that implied was that there was a separate Black nation within the United States, a concept articulated by writers like LeRoi Jones and athletes like Muhammad Ali as well as the purveyors of the new Jazz.

The central figure in this New Thing was John Coltrane, an incredibly gifted tenor sax player from North Carolina who'd come up through Miles Davis's group and made a name for himself with his harmonically dense style. By the '60s, however, Coltrane was using his music as a vehicle to explore his spirituality, which was reflected in his use of exotic Eastern ("India") and African ("Kulu Se Mama") textures. It also led him to explore the farthest parameters of sound itself. His style became more intense and atonal, almost as if what he was ultimately striving for was silence, which could only be achieved by playing literally every possible variation of the Blues idiom. As tributes like Albert Ayler's "For John Coltrane" and Frank Lowe's "In Trane's Name" attest, when he died in 1967, it was to a martyr's requiem.

Although Coltrane had originally gained recognition in Miles Davis's band, Miles was one of the few Black musicians of his generation who remained resolutely anti-"New Thing." With *Kind of Blue* in 1959, which featured Coltrane, Davis had introduced the modal approach to Jazz improvising, which meant that the soloists were free to play without regard for the actual modulation of the chords (thus freeing up harmonic "space"). Free-Jazz offended Davis: he thought players like Ornette Coleman and Don Cherry were making a mockery out of the music, and he even denounced Coltrane's own farther-reaching experiments. One thing that did interest him was the new electric Rock, which led him to pursue his fusion experiments like *Bitches Brew* in the late '60s. This would have an enormous effect on the further homogenization of the Industry, because it would help erode the distinctions between Rock, Rhythm & Blues, and Jazz—Miles was combining Rock and Jazz instruments to produce what amounted to Funk (and Pop). The rolling polyrhythms were coming from the same place as the ones being employed by James Brown and Sly & the Family Stone—and the musicians, afros and all, seemed to be saying that place was *Africa*. (Never mind that several members of Miles' band, as well as Sly & the Family Stone, were white).

Miles's prompting of Fusion only completed the cycle that had begun with Be Bop, the intellectualization process that eventually drove Black people away from Jazz altogether. With the arrival of the "New Thing," there was a whole generation of musicians willing to follow the most experimental wing of Jazz as far as they could. As a result, a good portion of the audience felt left out. In a way it was the end of Jazz progression for a mass audience. At the same time, there was a whole new generation of college kids who just wanted crazy shit. At this time, post-"New Thing" bands like the Art Ensemble of Chicago emerged with a more theatrical brand of Jazz that bordered on performance art (they often employed dancers dressed in traditional African garb). Sun Ra became a big hit on college campuses in the psychedelic age, probably due to his album covers and his strange style of dress more than his music (which could be brilliant, or disjointed to the brink of utter chaos).

There was no question that by the late '60s the Black audience for Jazz had all but diminished. Free-Jazz had disenfranchised them. The more intellectual Jazz became, the less Blacks were interested. The Black musical experience in America came from the church, the dance halls, and the juke joints. Black music is a *social* music. Having to sit around and think about why an artist is doing something just takes away from that. That's a white concept (i.e., "chamber music").

In Chicago, the AACM—or Association for Advancement of Creative Musicians—synthesized some of the more interesting elements of the New Thing with a community overview. From this collective came the Art Ensemble of Chicago, Muhal Abrams, Maurice McIntyre (a.k.a. Kalaparusha), etc. The theatrical approach of these artists brought out Blacks, but the minute they left Chicago they were playing for white folks, and that's certainly who their albums were selling to. Still, the self-determination of the AACM inspired other similar independent collectives like the Black Artists Group (BAG) in St. Louis, from which came the sax players Oliver Lake and Julius Hemphill. Meanwhile, the Last Poets, true to their name, extended the oral tradition of Africa into the realm of angry rhetoric and, by doing so, premeditated Rap music.

Influenced by events like Muhammad Ali's refusing the draft on Islamic grounds and the assassination of Martin Luther King, Black popular music was beginning to reflect the racial turbulence of the times. Although James Brown had begun doing "message" songs as early as 1966 ("Don't Be a Drop-Out"), there were rumors that he was coaxed by the "community" to pursue a more "active" path. After all, even as late as 1968, J. B. was still processing his hair. There were also issues over his embrace of white politicians like Hubert Humphrey, whom he endorsed in '68, and Richard Nixon, whose inauguration he played in January of the following year and whom he would also endorse during Nixon's '72 campaign. Given the contradictions inherent in those two choices, it's evident that J. B.'s political motives could best be summed up by the phrase "Just gimme me the man with the power, I want to shake his hand."

Raised in a whorehouse, tied in a gunnysack and beaten by his father as a youth, and sent to adult prison when he was sixteen, there's no doubt James

Brown's relationship to his own cultural roots carried with it a certain degree of denial. As the first truly independent Black popular artist, Brown could not have helped but be aware of the irony of his situation. Feeling a need to make a statement about racial issues, in 1968 he cut "Say It Loud—I'm Black and I'm Proud," which became the anthem of the Movement. Based on a skittering guitar riff played by Jimmy Nolen, "Say It Loud" pointed the way to Funk. From that point on, James Brown's music became increasingly Black-oriented. When trombone player Fred Wesley took over as Brown's bandleader, they began forging the rhythms that would help invent Hip Hop many years later—in other words, the rhythms that would permanently change the face of Black popular music forever.

Despite their rhythmic, as well as cultural, differences, Black music and white Rock 'n' Roll were nonetheless reaching artistic parity in the late '60s. Just like in the '50s, the electric guitar would prove to be the leavening influence. Although the electric guitar was unquestionably the predominant instrument in white Rock, in Black music it was more often used as a subtle embellishment. A notable exception was Steve Cropper's work with Stax, but then Cropper was a white man playing Black music, and even then he never overplayed. As far as actual Black guitarists go, at least until the mid-'60s, the majority of them—Chuck Berry excepted—plied the Blues. As far as the audience went, that was the one form of Black music that Blacks didn't want to be associated with, because to many of them it conjured images of plantation days. But in the late '60s, one man would come along to change all that—Jimi Hendrix. The ironic thing was, perhaps because of his white bandmates, or maybe because of his musical approach (heavy), Hendrix's primary audience was white. But his impact on other Black *musicians*, from Miles Davis to Sly Stone, was profound. And he proved that a Black man could wank off on his instrument with as much wild abandon as any honky. Hendrix may have jammed with a couple of white cats, but he was nobody's Uncle Tom. He was, in fact, a Super Niggah.

Just as the Movement had coerced James Brown into digging deeper into his dark roots, Hendrix was also urged to get closer to his "spiritual" center. In Hendrix's case, this took the form of the psychedelic space-Blues of *Band of Gypsies*, recorded with Buddy Miles and Billy Cox on New Year's 1970. No one knew it at the time, but Hendrix actually wouldn't see much of the new decade, fatally succumbing to his excesses in September 1970. Posthumous evidence like *Nine to the Universe* suggests that he perhaps would've continued to pursue this more ethnically "pure" direction.

Other pioneers of Black Rock (or "psychedelic Soul") included the Chambers Brothers, four Mississippi brothers who were originally a straight Gospel act before adding a white drummer in the mid-'60s and pursuing a more amped-up direction. The classic was "Time Has Come Today," one of the pinnacles of '60s psychedelic excess. Like Hendrix, they liked to experiment with a multitude of special effects, including wah-wah pedal and the leslie, among other things.

Dallas-born Sylvester Stewart, a.k.a. Sly Stone, another performer whose musical roots stemmed from the church, took a more direct route into the world of white Rock 'n' Roll, producing albums for the Bay Area record label Autumn in the mid-'60s. Among the acts who recorded for the label, owned by Tom Donahue, were some of the proto-"San Francisco sound" groups like the Beau Brummels and Great Society, so Stewart experienced the psychedelic hippie explosion firsthand. His career as a disc jockey opened him up to perhaps a wider scope of influences than other musicians/bandleaders had the privilege of. When Sly finally formed his own group, called Sly & the Family Stone, he found himself incorporating many of the newer psychedelic/heavy Rock effects, but the group also featured horns. This was a unique fusion of Soul and Rock that turned out to be immensely popular with both Blacks and whites.

In songs like "Everybody is a Star," "Don't Call Me Nigger, Whitey," and "Stand," Sly was also addressing social issues in a more profound way than most Black performers of the time. This had a great impact on the direction of Soul in the late '60s. Even Motown became more politicized with such "protest" numbers as the Supremes' "Love Child," the Temptations' "Cloud Nine," and Edwin Starr's "War." By the time Sly was cutting J. B.-influenced dance grooves like "Thank You (Falettinme Be Mice Elf Agin)" as well as the murky, suite-like *There's a Riot Goin' On* album, the turbulent new "downer Soul" had become the norm. Curtis Mayfield testified to the disillusioning state of affairs with the ominously titled "If There's A Hell Below (We're All Gonna Go)," which took Nixon to task and painted a grim vision for Black America. The Temptations warned of "Smiling Faces," while the Watts 103rd Street Band urged Blacks to adopt a more uplifting, but still empowered, mantra: "Respect Yourself." War, a Sly-influenced band from L.A., presented a bleak smog-filled vision with "Slippin' Into Darkness."

Sly & the Family Stone were revolutionary in many other ways. In the area of diversity, Sly was an equal opportunity employer: white and Black, male and female. They were also the first Black-oriented act able to break the more lucrative album market, and this was a crucial turning point for Black music in general. After Sly, even Motown artists like Marvin Gaye and Stevie Wonder struggled for their artistic independence and produced albums of enduring worth (as opposed to collections of "hits" surrounded by filler). Marvin Gaye's 1971 album, *What's Goin' On*, was a bluesy evocation of the urban landscape. Wonder's early '70s albums like *Talking Book* and *Innervisions* were among the most sophisticated albums of the day, combining social concerns with Pop arrangements and selling in numbers to rival popular white hacksmiths like Elton John.

The tumultuous urban Blues being pumped by James Brown, Sly Stone, Curtis Mayfield, Marvin Gaye, and Stevie Wonder was a reflection of what was going on in the ghettos of America's largest cities, where Black folks were becoming increasingly disenfranchised. The heroin that was first introduced to the Black community on the wings of Be Bop had trickled down to the masses, and its use had reached epidemic proportions. Not that Be Bop had anything to do with it, because Black folks in the ghetto seldom listened to Jazz anymore, preferring popular music like Motown. More than likely, it was the force of organized crime flooding the ghettos with the most addictive drug possible, thus ensuring a long-term market. This equation led to the massive increase in criminal activity that occurred in America in the late '60s when the ghettos became war zones. This led to a radical demographic shift in the larger urban areas, where the minority population grew and the white one decreased. The result was neglect by city governments for certain low-income areas. In New York City in the late '70s, certain parts of the Bronx had all but been abandoned by the city. As these communities were becoming more self-contained, they felt even less inclined to assimilate white culture. And as they came to consider the white culture the oppressor who'd kept them in the ghettos, they made it a point to pledge separatism through means of their own ethnicity. It's not surprising that Rap music, perhaps the most self-consciously ethnocentric music ever, emerged out of the Bronx at the time when the borough was in its most desperate state of decline.

Black identity in America increasingly became about "street culture." Whereas performers in the '60s like James Brown, the Supremes, the Temptations, Marvin Gaye, and others had attempted to appeal to a crossover audience by at least behaving graciously, the new breed increasingly played up their essential "blackness" in a way that would confuse whitey. As urban Blacks turned more inward, the trappings of ghetto life began to infiltrate the music. This also corresponded with the rise of recreational drug use and the hedonism of the new decade.

Funkadelic, from Detroit, were essential in this urbanization process. Formerly a vocal group in the Temptations vein called the Parliaments, their leader, George Clinton, took a note from Sly and Hendrix and turned the group into a freak-out-inspiring ensemble. Detroit in the late '60s was the high-energy Rock epicenter, and Clinton later claimed that it was seeing the massive amplification systems used by white Rock bands like the MC5 and Stooges that influenced him to seek a more amplified sound. The other thing was the acid, and as their name implies, Funkadelic was psychedelic music for Black folks. They were lucky to be signed to a fairly offbeat local label called Westbound, who indulged them their creative preferences—at that time, still not a given for Black recording acts who sought to explore new tangents with their music other than the formulated R&B groove. That was about to change, and Funkadelic were harbingers of the great unveiling.

One thing that made Funkadelic unique from the start was that, like Hendrix and the Chambers Brothers, they eschewed the horns altogether. This break with tradition represented the final freeing-up process for the band. Heavily influenced by Sly & the Family Stone, particularly in the guitar playing of Eddie Hazel, Funkadelic offered a swirling maelstrom of driving rhythms, Black street slang, and general weirdness. Under Clinton, the whole notion of "the funk" became a kind of epistemology that bordered on cultlike dedication (the band were devotees of a weirdo religious organization of the time known as the Process Church). Later on, the extended Funk family would come to encompass two bands when Clinton revived the Parliaments in the '70s, under the more updated singular moniker, Parliament. That band would incorporate horns as well as a more dance-oriented groove, but even when

Clinton was making a bid for the dance floor audience, he was subtly making fun of them at the same time. Nevertheless, the P-Funk empire was unbelievably prolific, particularly in the late '70s, when all the various spinoffs—from Bootsy's Rubber Band to Eddie Hazel to the Brides of Funkenstein—produced albums of their own, all pledging devotion to the overriding funkentelechy. Along with Sly, Clinton was the first to approach Black popular music with the same kind of conceptual approach as Jazz musicians like Charles Mingus or Miles Davis. It was a giant step for Black artistic freedom and it paid off—in the annals of Hip Hop, only James Brown has been sampled more than P-Funk.

Another Midwest band, the Ohio Players, who'd backed Wilson Pickett on several recordings in the early '60s, were right behind Sly and P-Funk in embracing the new progressive tendencies of Rock-influenced Black music. Their early demos show a heavy James Brown influence, but by the '70s they were experimenting with jazzier rhythms. Utilizing horns, keyboards, and an emotive vocal style that had its origins in Gospel, songs like "Pain" were among the most sophisticated Black music of the day, going through several musical movements in its six-minute-plus span and never running out of steam. Recording for Westbound as well, the Players were decidedly more polished than P-Funk, but they shared the pimp ethos: their album covers were notorious for their depictions of S&M scenarios, all featuring the same bald Black model. Later on, after they'd sign with Mercury and make some more commercial-sounding records, they'd drown a bitch in honey ("Sweet Sticky Thing" indeed).

Black, or racially mixed, bands sporting horn charts and Funk rhythms became a regular commodity in the early '70s. Groups like Bagatelle, Mother's Finest, New Birth, Bloodstone, Mandrill, and Osibisa attempted to inject Jazz and Soul influences into what was basically a Rock format. The Crusaders did just the opposite: a straight Jazz band, they applied an electrified, and thus more commercial, approach to what was still a rhythm-based music. Never mind that most of their fans were white—from this point on, the majority of Blacks would almost unanimously prefer vocal-based music. This helped further screw up the progress of not only jazzmen like Pharaoh Sanders and the Art Ensemble of Chicago—who now had *no* chance of getting their music heard by Black audiences (even though it was heavily Afrocentric)—but also of funkmeisters like Sly Stone, James Brown, and Funkadelic. By attempting to elevate the whole art of Black music to the album-oriented state of "maturity" already forged by the Beatles and others in the sphere of white Rock, they were unwittingly alienating the dance/vocal-oriented masses of their own constituency. And although their records continued to sell in the Black community, at least through the mid-'70s, the intellectual implications were totally lost on the intended audience.

The harbinger of '70s Soul was Isaac Hayes' landmark *Hot Buttered Soul* album. Released in 1969, the album aspired to progressive heights by featuring a seventeen-minute suitelike version of Jimmy Webb's schlock hit "By the Time I Get to Phoenix," which Hayes transformed into an impassioned testimonial on the "power of love." The lofty string sections anticipated the swank "make out" Muzak of Barry White as well as Disco. There was still a down-home flavor, because Hayes was still recording for Stax in Memphis with homegrown talent like the Bar-Kays backing him up, but the wave of the future was upon us. Soon Black popular music would have two primary imperatives: to serve as rump-shaking fodder or to further the art of seduction.

The Gospel imperative wasn't totally lost in the '70s—performers like Al Green and Gladys Knight still pursued the emotional content of Soul music, but they couldn't fight the corporate tide in the form of an industry seeking to make all music more of a commodity. Black music lent itself more easily to it than white music, perhaps, because most Black artists had never sought "independence" to begin with. Music factories like Stax and Motown had established in the '60s that Black Pop music could be totally manufactured and still preserve its essential ethnic flavor. In the '70s, Willie Mitchell's productions at Hi Records in Memphis—including Al Green, Ann Peebles, Otis Clay, and others—were the bridge between Stax and Motown: smooth but still earthy/funky. They were successful, too—that is, until their biggest moneymaker, Al Green, proved the authenticity of his Gospel roots by denouncing the secular lifestyle to become a born-again preacher. He still holds service every Sunday at the Full Gospel Tabernacle Church in Memphis, and tourists from all over—white and Black—flock to the attraction as if Green were still a matinee crooner (a fact that the good Reverend, who's desperately trying to live down his secular past, probably abhors).

Black music went back to being a producer's art, much to the detriment of the music. Disco fit efficaciously into the equation. But Disco didn't only represent the subversion of Black music, but *all* music, and, as a *method*, Disco would unfortunately set the pace in the industry from here on out. Eventually, record companies would figure out they didn't even need *musicians*, per se. Unlike white performers such as, say, Paul McCartney, it wasn't a choice among Black artists to self-consciously make bad records. It was the fact that the whole industry was changing—if a white artist didn't stand a chance any longer of making a significant musical statement, where did that leave Blacks? The days of albums like *There's a Riot Goin' On* and *What's Goin' On* were over, at least for a while—Rap would avenge this transgression fittingly in the decade to come, but even by then, Rap's musical notions would have ultimately been corrupted by Disco. Disco changed everything—for the worse. But Black music went Disco at the same time Country went Kenny Rogers. It was purely a symptom of commerce.

But if Blacks didn't self-consciously create Disco, they lent themselves to it easily with the increased softening of Soul music in the early '70s. Groups like the Chi-Lites, Spinners, and Stylistics, while soulful enough, were actually a throwback to the vocals groups of the '50s, style-wise. Like Clinton's crew, they actually dated from that period anyway, but where Clinton psychedelicized his sound, these groups changed little about the vocal-group format other than their dance steps and stage wear (the ever-present bell-bottoms). Most importantly, they were strictly song-and-dance men, a mere tool for a producer to use. The production team of Kenny Gamble and Leon Huff in Philadelphia revolutionized the Black record industry with their chugging productions for acts like the O'Jays and Harold Melvin & the Blue Notes. Elsewhere, fat man Barry White was ruling his own empire, and milky-smooth productions like "Love's Theme" by the Love Unlimited Orchestra can in a way be seen as the first real Disco records. There was no "soul" left, just a lot of repetition. Motown naturally jumped on the bandwagon with the Jackson Five's "Dancing Machine," the Commodores' "Machine Gun," and Eddie Kendricks' "Keep on Truckin'," all of which signal the birth of Disco as much as anything. The whole notion of "down-home"—which was the essential resource for all Black music—was becoming more and more of an anachronism as Blacks became increasingly ashamed of their relationship with America itself. Increasingly, Blacks were viewing the grits-and-Sunday-morning-prayer-meeting truth of musical forms like Blues, Jazz, Gospel, and Soul with circumspection. The music became almost irreversibly urban.

At approximately the same time, another Black musical phenomenon, Reggae, represented a more organic solution, but Blacks wanted nothing to do with it. There are several reasons for this. One is the fact that Reggae, as a Jamaican hybrid, made use of a lot of cross-cultural influences (i.e., white), like Country & Western, for instance, that stateside Blacks were alienated by. It's been a fact for several decades that Black youth shies away from guitar-based music, which apparently they view in the same category as the sharecropper's sickle. But more than likely, it's simple racism—Blacks in America have never accepted the dark-skinned people from the island regions as being their equals. Ironically, when Reggae was at its creative peak in the '60s, the studio system set up by producers like Lee Perry and others borrowed wholesale from the whole Motown principle.

The Soul music performers of the '60s—Ray Charles, Aretha Franklin, Ike & Tina Turner, Otis Redding, James Brown, Wilson Pickett, Sam & Dave, the Temptations, Marvin Gaye, Martha & the Vandellas, Sly, Isaac Hayes—established an *identity* to go along with the music. This helped raise the profile of Blacks in general and created a new ethnic pride. But it didn't impose racial terms on the music itself—which is why some of the most soulful manifestations of the era were the results of Black and white musical interaction—such as Sly & the Family Stone or the products of the Stax studios. Never again would the Gospel be evoked with such nondogmatic fervor. Such color blind purity could not survive the coming age, and separatism once again became the norm.

CHAPTER 11

EXCESS

AS THE '60S TURNED INTO THE '70S, WHAT HAD ONCE SEEMED SHOCKING NOW SEEMED TAME. A good example was long hair on men, which had become readily acceptable—as reflected by Hollywood as well as the TV news, where the manes of most newsmen had grown by several inches. Although the World War II daddies were beginning to figure out that long hair didn't necessarily mean gay, actual homosexuality was still extremely feared within the culture at large. Given the liberation of the '60s, it was inevitable that gays were the next ones to throw off the shackles of imperialist repression—after Blacks, women, and freethinkers of all kinds.

The roots of gay liberation went back to the '30s, but the only area of mainstream culture where it was even remotely accepted was the art and theater world. Not surprisingly, the first outward expression of homosexuality in America was the '50s productions of Tennessee Williams, who touched on the subject in *Cat on a Hot Tin Roof*. But the crowd who twirled around this scene was still basically closeted. By the mid-'60s, however, a new, campier element had emerged. The new queens were inextricably tied to the flashier aspects of Rock n' Roll and other modernist preoccupations. The new scene centered on the downtown art contingent, led by Andy Warhol and his various acolytes.

In the fall of 1965 a club owner named Mickey Ruskin opened a bar/restaurant in New York called Max's Kansas City. For the next ten years it would serve as the headquarters—a virtual den of iniquity—for the whole downtown scene, including the emergent glam rockers as well as the whole hard-drug culture. The Warhol crowd had a table in the back room. To be welcomed into their lair—to be asked to sit with them at the round table under the glare of the ten-watt florescent red bulb that gave the place its decadent aura—was considered the pinnacle of having "arrived." While freaks made vain attempts to gain the Master's attention, Warhol would whine and feign indifference. This brought out the worst exhibitionist traits of some of the more desperate followers, like Andrea Feldman, an "actress" who'd starred in a couple of Warhol's movies and who eventually committed suicide by jumping out of a window clutching a crucifix, declaring, "I'm heading for the big time."

At Max's, Rock stars mixed with debutantes mixed with aged society hags mixed with gay painters mixed with ballet stars mixed with film students mixed with beatnik has-beens mixed with whores and junkies and media freaks and name droppers. The whole scene was so "open" that any kind of "freak" felt at home. As Paul Rothchild, producer of the Doors, remembered: "The first broad expression of homosexuality in New York City I saw there at Max's—embracing, kissing, great jealousies displayed for the world to see. Before it had been a confused, almost proper, European kind of homosexuality, but with the Warhol wave it became very theatrical, direct and out front."[1]

In 1969 the Stonewall Riots became the first incident to propel gay rights into public focus. The Stonewall was a gay bar in the West Village. On this particular night, tired of the usual police harassment, a queen had decided to fight back by smashing an empty bottle over a policeman's head. When other officers arrived to quash the uprising, the denizens of the tavern chased them out. This was an incredibly symbolic victory for the queens (and an embarrassment for the cops). No matter how sensationalized the event became, it proved one thing: homosexuals weren't going to remain in the closet much longer. Like everyone else in the '60s, they had been liberated.

Despite this fact, in the eyes of the mainstream media, homosexuality was still being treated as a form of deviant behavior. *Time*'s cover story dated October 31, 1969, was the usual sensationalism—mainly, they were still acting as if homosexuality was a "disease" that could be "cured." In Hollywood, meanwhile, homosexuals were still being portrayed as mincing queens (*Midnight*

Cowboy) or transsexual freaks (*Myra Breckinridge*). In other words, Hollywood's new embrace of "fags" was no one's idea of liberation.

In the early '70s there was little affinity between the sexual underground and the counterculture. In what amounted to his theory of what was wrong with the New Left, Paul Morrisey, Warhol's director, sniffed: "They had an opportunity to find an alternative to Nixon in, let's say, Ted Kennedy or someone who was responsible. But their alternative was just as dreary and vomit-making....Jimi Hendrix and Janis Joplin and Timothy Leary and Abbie Hoffman and those *ninnies*!" [2]

And who were the ninnies? These are people who died: Brian Jones, Jimi Hendrix, Janis Joplin, Jim Morrison, Duane Allman, Pigpen. Within a couple years' time span, all of these reckless adventurers had kicked the bucket. The mortality rate of the so-called revolutionaries was proving itself to be particularly low. This kind of dimmed the credibility of the "revolution" as well—it seemed incredibly facile to believe in a popular revolt in which the movement's prime foot soldiers couldn't even get out of the way of their own indulgences. The tide was changing—the subsequent history of Rock was going to be less inclined toward political posturing and more inclined toward the politics of pleasure. The trappings of the counterculture seemed too doctrinaire to the denizens of the new wave. As David Bowie would later say: "Too many *snags...*"

And snags were something that people got caught up in, and that was one thing that the increasingly disaffected youth audience wanted no part of. The new youth brigade realized that the '70s were less about "realism" and more about self-invention. The tension that had marked the '60s had been anesthetized. Perhaps it was the drugs. Far from "I can't get no satisfaction," the new credo was "I can't get *enough*."

A perfect example was the Rolling Stones. As the '70s dawned, they were getting off on their myth as "survivors"—they'd outlasted the Beatles while doing twice as many drugs and being on the wrong side of the law. The Stones were Rock's first living examples of successful excess. They would not be the last.

As decadence became a popular motif, the Stones found new ways to exploit their darker obsessions. For one thing, there was the tragedy of Brian Jones's death, which occurred shortly after he'd been forced out of the group he'd founded. "Mick and Keith killed Brian" rumors have circulated ever since. Then there was Altamont—the Stones play, people *die*, man. The fact they'd exploited the event by making a *film* out of it only made matters worse. But there they were in *Gimme Shelter*, sitting around demurely watching the playback of Meredith Hunter's stabbing while saying things like "far out."

The year 1970 was a year of many cinematic ventures for the Stones, and Mick Jagger in particular: early in the year he'd starred in *Ned Kelly*, about a displaced Australian gangster on the run in the outback (think of it as a milquetoast version of *The Outlaw Josie Wales*). It was the lingering legacy of the '60s preoccupation with "outlaws"—that gunslingers were cool people too.

Jagger's next movie project, *Performance*, attracted more attention, because in the film Jagger basically played *himself*: mainly, a decadent Rock star holed up in a country estate with two women. The best thing about the film was its theme song, "Memo From Turner," in which all the decadent underpinnings the Stones had been flirting with since *Aftermath* came crashing through the velvet curtain. Jagger and his cohorts were defining what the term *Rock star* would come to mean to future generations. This was a whole new type of celebrity: young, arrogant, and *very* rich.

Apparently, in the case of the Stones, the decadence was real, not imagined. For example, during the filming of *Performance*, the Stones' drug runner at the time, "Spanish" Tony Sanchez, caught Jagger fucking his costar Anita Pallenberg, who only happened to be the common-law wife of his best friend and songwriting partner, Keith Richards. It hardly mattered to Richards—by this time, he was a notorious junkie and didn't really care about getting laid.

Jagger, however, never seemed to tire of it. Considering how much flirting with androgyny he'd done since the video for "Jumpin' Jack Flash" in 1968, people began to question whether his carnal appetites extended to members of the same sex as well. Those looking for an answer didn't have to wait long: "Cocksucker Blues," delivered at the end of 1970 as a contract breaker with Decca, was a startling ode to sadism and homosexuality. Around the same time, when asked about his sexuality, Jagger told a reporter, probably for shock value: "If God wants me to become a woman, then a woman I will become."

Once freed of Decca's shackles, the Stones rolled out their own record label—backed by Atlantic—featuring its famous trademark red tongue logo. This was symbolic of the sybaritic excess that was now part of their lifestyle. *Sticky Fingers*, the first album on the new label, was knee-deep in decadence. As British critic Roy Carr noted: "This album abounds with so many overt drug references that it seems likely should you lick the label or sniff the sleeve, you'd probably get off for the rest of the week." [3]

A lot had changed since the veiled drug references of "She's a Rainbow." The Stones and other groups were *flaunting* their excesses now. This was to be the way of the '70s. To alleviate the heavy tax burden imposed by England on its more affluent denizens, the Stones became Rock's first millionaire tax exiles, relocating to a chateau in the south of France. This befitted their image as jet-set royalty. The group seemed to thrive in the environment, creating *Exile on Main Street*, which is often considered their best.

Groupies were another quintessential fact of the aristocratic Rock lifestyle. Girls devoted to pleasing you sexually—how much better could it get? It was part of life on the road, and all the forlorn Rock star wives waiting back in England knew it and accepted it. Even Rock critic John Mendelsohn of the instant-failure group Christopher Milk could brag about his groupie conquests in a five-page spread in *Rolling Stone*. For musicians that were always on the road, the whole system worked perfectly. Some groupies, meanwhile, became so notorious that they became virtual stars in their own right, like the Plaster Casters, a Florida enclave who sculpted Rock stars' penises. Or the GTOs, consisting of the famous groupies Miss Christine, Miss Pamela, et al., who got picked up and produced by Frank Zappa. In a certain way, their one and only album, released in 1969, foreshadowed some of the ironic "chick-Rock" of the '90s (the Breeders and Veruca Salt among them). In February 1969 *Rolling Stone*, by that time the premiere counterculture journal, took out a full-page ad in the *New York Times* to herald the groupie phenomenon. In typically elitist fashion, they asked: "When we tell you what a Groupie is, will you really understand?"

Every band of the late '60s/early '70s had its own groupie-grope road stories. Take Black Sabbath for instance, whose singer, Ozzy Osbourne, recalled: "She went up to Geezer's room and...took all her clothes off, and lay down on the bed with her legs apart. 'Well, isn't somebody going to fuck me?' she says to us. We just stood there looking at her kind of horrified. She looked pitiful and disgusting. The next time I'm not going to stand there. I'll fucking piss all over them." [4]

Or how about the Stooges? According to Ron Asheton, "It's always this way. The chicks are hung up. They're just making the scene. One good fucking and they begin to see what it's all about." [5]

Added Iggy: "I kicked her out of bed. Her whole story was a lie, really a bogus chick." [6]

Clearly, this form of sexual liberation had done little to promote "equality," as the male Rock stars obviously viewed the groupies with swaggering contempt. Obviously, this was a form of worship few mortals would ever be accustomed to.

In England the same kind of fanaticism shown by groupies toward Rock bands accompanied the football scene, but it wasn't necessarily sexual (although there were surely homosexual overtones). In the early '70s, the English football crowd was legendary—every Sunday they'd queue the trains to Derby, where they'd cheer on their teams and get into violent confrontations with fans of the opposing side. There were more youthful riots in England than at any time since the mid-'60s, when the Rockers hunted down Mods on the beaches of Brighton, Dover, and Clacton. And the football louts were just as staunch about their musical preferences. Like the Mods, they favored danceable forms like Reggae and Soul, but unlike the Mods, they weren't clotheshorses, instead dressing in butch-boy fashions like jeans, jackets with football patches all over them, and heavy leather boots designed for kicking your opponent's face in. But the most startling contrast between the football boys and the rest of Britain's youth at the time was that the football boys had short hair. For this reason, they were nicknamed "skinheads." In a sense, their mania preceded the Brit Punk scene a few years later.

Part of it had to do with the backlash that many kids were feeling at the time against the Left. The conceits of the peace-and-love generation didn't really concern the denizens of London's East End, a typically middle class suburb not particularly sympathetic to the plight of the oppressed—especially if they were colored. The Skins applied these base sensibilities to their musical tastes as well—they hated the inflated pomp-Rock of groups like Led Zeppelin and Yes, favoring instead the new bubblegum sensibilities of groups like Slade, Sweet, Mud, Wizzard, and T. Rex. This also had to do with the Back to the Roots Revival: the Skinheads were rejecting the slick, rarefied tendencies that had overtaken Rock since the days of *Sgt. Pepper*, an era many Brit Rock fans still blamed for the death of the first Mod era.

Many of the British groups of this era naturally catered to this element of hooliganism with a Stones-derived style jokingly referred to as "lad Rock." Once again, this was an important step toward Punk, best reflected by Slade ("Cum on Feel the Noize," "Mama Weer All Crazee Now"), the Faces ("Borstal Boys"), and Mott the Hoople ("One of the Boys"). All of these groups shared a preference for a sound that was, in light of their Prog Rock cousins, decidedly unembellished.

Into the midst of this came the film premiere of Stanley Kubrick's *A Clockwork Orange*, a futuristic psychodrama that painted a grim premonition of the future with its portrayal of hoodlums roaming the streets inflicting senseless "ultraviolence" on their unwitting victims. At a time when football rioters were tearing up the subways every other weekend, it was a pretty frightening vision. But some of the more primary aspects of the movie, like the fashion statement (derby hats and long johns with mascara and other androgynous touches) or the language (a kind of cockney bip-bop), would not be lost on a youth culture anxious to distance itself from the previous generation's mores. They would soon discover that shock value was perhaps the best way to accomplish this.

As for *A Clockwork Orange*, the ultraviolent pursuits of the Droogs were only slightly more sinister than the actual activities of most Rock stars at the time. Like Led Zeppelin, for example, who were riding the world with one big erection, dressing up in their Clockwork-ian gear and bullying men and women alike; or the Stones, as reflected by the lavishness of the '72 tour: typical of their immense narcissism, they wanted to capture the whole thing on film. The fact that filmmaker Robert Frank caught the group engaged in activities of questionable legality meant that the resulting film, *Cocksucker Blues*, would never officially see the light of day. Hadn't they learned their lesson at Altamont? Jagger had to settle for marrying his own spitting image in Nicaraguan wife Bianca.

Speaking of narcissism, on album cover after album cover in the early '70s, Rock stars would pose nude, shedding their hippie threads: Man, Three Dog Night, Steam, Dr. Hook, the Doobie Brothers, Orleans, even Herbie Mann. This directly presaged the phenomenon of streaking (running naked through a public area). Nudity was faddish in the early '70s, but this was before most people bothered to get toned, so it was usually a case of "Put 'em back on!"

Recreational drugs in the '70s were getting harder. Grass and acid were still popular, but the new drugs of choice among the younger kids were downers: Quaaludes, Seconal, Phenobarbitol. This was the '70s idea of a kick: a drug with no uplifting qualities, but rather a numbing form of intoxication that bordered on unconsciousness. *Creem* summed it up best with their cover story, "The Sopor Generation," in October 1972: "The new drug for the young who think down."

Elsewhere in the article they came up with perhaps an even better description: "Chickenshit heroin."[7]

The soundtrack of the Downer-Rock hordes became Heavy Metal, that ponderous form of overamplified Rock that dealt exclusively with sagging tempos and even more sagging spirits. By far the most worthy exemplars of the genre were members of Black Sabbath, the Clown Princes of Downer-Rock. They were the big Heavy band out of England after Led Zeppelin. Their popularity astounded everyone, just as Grand Funk's had—in their day they were continually referred to as "Punk Rock." Taking their name from an obscure Boris Karloff movie after a run with the more hippie-sounding Earth moniker, Sabbath did more to advance the presence of His Satanic Majesty in Rock than anyone else. There was a twisted hippie moral to their whole witches-and-goblins persona, although writers like Robert Christgau failed to see it ("an amoral exploration," he gasped).[8] There was nothing hippie about the sound, though—except for the Stooges, *no one* pounded their instruments harder. Pound for pound, the modern age of Rock was beginning and, after Black Sabbath, it was never going away. The kind of *force* Sabbath employed on their instruments suggested something even more ominous than the presence of Satan—namely, the presence of an overbearing male hormone. Not coincidentally, the subsequent Heavy Metal hordes would be predominantly male.

A lot of Sabbath's first album was influenced by Cream, but the first cut, "Black Sabbath," with its "spooky" graveyard sounds and lumbering power chords should have tipped off listeners to what was coming. Unlike Zeppelin, and unlike almost anyone else in Rock, for that matter, their songs weren't about girls. They were more like grim foreboding premonitions of the future. Stuff like "War Pigs" proved that "protest" music didn't have to be wimpy or Folky in order to be taken seriously. The fact that Sabbath, in their own time, *wasn't* taken seriously other than by a handful of critics was no fault of their own.

By the time of their legendary third album, *Master of Reality*, the sound had grown so thick it literally vibrated. *Master* became kind of the *Sgt. Pepper's* of the Quaalude kids, despite the fact that radio totally ignored it, as they did all Black Sabbath albums. But Sabbath represented a whole new niche in the marketplace—namely the "Heavy" groups who didn't need to have hits to be "popular." The result was a whole new breed of Heavy Metal and Prog bands that concentrated on one full-length work per year and eschewed singles altogether. As for Sabbath, there was something wildly comical and theatrical about the whole pose, particularly after singer Ozzy Osbourne became addicted to cocaine: he evolved into a sort of self-parody as the paunch-king of Rock, a kind of Benny Hill for the Sopor Generation. The 1972 "Snowblind" was like an advertisement for coke, and the accompanying LP, *Black Sabbath Vol. 4*, even contained the slogan "enjoy coke." Such decadence!

Another post-Psychedelic British band that evolved into one of the premiere proto-Heavy Metal outfits was Deep Purple. Their original forte was pseudomystical jive like "The Shield" combined with souped-up semi-orgasmic versions of pop hits like Neil Diamond's "Kentucky Woman," Joe South's "Hush," and the Beatles' "We Can Work it Out." They seemed like a bunch of poseurs without hope, but heaviness lent itself nicely to their cause, and soon their narcissism began to manifest itself in almost mythological terms. Their album covers were a perfect example: one of them showed the group embossed onto Mount Rushmore; the next one showed them shooting through the stratosphere like a collective comet, their leonine manes flying behind them like those of mythic warrior-Gods.

As with Sabbath, all the critics hated them, at least until *Machine Head* in 1972, a Heavy Metal masterpiece that came to define the genre as textbook accurately as *Master of Reality* or *Led Zeppelin IV*. The songs were tight time bombs of chugging riff motion, featuring wildly heavy drumming, fog-thick organ, flailing guitar, and castrated-gnome vocals (the last courtesy of lead singer Ian Gillan). Not only was "Smoke on the Water" a Top Forty hit, a rarity in these stakes, but it also became the preeminent guitar finger exercise for a whole generation of dunderheads, at least until Aerosmith's "Walk This Way" came along. It propelled the band to stardom and, judging by the title of their next album, *Who Do We Think We Are*, it was a position that suited them nicely. The liner notes contained all the recent press clippings, including a quip from guitarist Ritchie Blackmore that exemplified the band's arrogance: "It's not that I think I'm the greatest guitarist in the world—I *am* but that's got nothing to do with it." Purple were also among the first to cash in on the dreaded double live album syndrome, first pioneered by Grand Funk, in which a group could stretch a song that was normally four minutes long to a whole side of an LP. But Purple was plagued by nonstop personnel realignments, perhaps as a result of their massive egos, and by the mid-'70s their popularity waned and their beacon was summoned back to Earth.

If Led Zeppelin had made use of the Blues idiom, albeit in a hyperbolic version, to prove their "authenticity," groups like Black Sabbath and Deep Purple had shorn whatever "authenticity" they had in exchange for sheer bombast. This was the essence of '70s Rock.

No one personified the new decadent ethos more emphatically than Alice Cooper, whose very existence provided a constant source of anguish to those who wished to hang onto '60s values. As one hippie fumed upon his initial encounter with the artist: "*Mmmmmmm!* I've never seen anything like it! The very thought of it is enough to make me sick. *Alice Cooper!* I thought it was gonna be like Judy Collins or something! It was the most revolting thing I've ever seen."[9]

Alice and his whole band originally came from Arizona (and were called, at one time or another, the Earwigs, Nazz, etc.). Even before they'd left their home base, they had an interest in the macabre (an early single was entitled "Lay Down and Die Goodbye"). But it wasn't until they moved to L.A. in 1969 and hooked up with Frank Zappa that the group began attracting attention for their bizarre stage manner and style of dress. Alice more or less invented the stage show: sure you'd had Screamin' Jay Hawkins coming out of a coffin in the '50s, more recently Arthur Brown occasionally dropping his pants, and Hendrix and the Who smashing their instruments. But that was nothing compared to Alice, who chopped his own head off with a guillotine and then played dead while the fake blood oozed over his topless ninety-pound frame. The name Alice Cooper originally meant the whole group, but it eventually came to mean Alice himself, who was the poster boy for the malnourished (unless you count an endless flow of Budweiser).

The turning point for the group occurred when they moved to Detroit in 1970. This led not only to them hooking up with a Canadian-born producer,

Bob Ezrin, who gave them a heavier sound, but it also made them aware of such high-energy bands as the MC5 and Stooges and of such outlandish bizarros as Funkadelic. Their music transformed overnight, from a vague, almost Folky Post-Psychedelic vein into this bratty Heavy Metal snarl. "The Ballad of Dwight Frye" on *Love it to Death* (1971), Ezrin's first production with the group, was one of the most scarifying testaments of Rock's new decadent ethos, a song so chilling and macabre that Sonic Youth found it fit to cover more than a decade later. Like Black Sabbath, Alice Cooper had grasped the theatrical mechanisms of the new heavy Rock, and there was no going back.

Cooper was the first Rock performer who said *outright* "I play golf" and who shilled for breakfast cereal. The really great thing was that his music didn't suffer one iota for it. His influence on Punk is profound—when Johnny Lydon auditioned for the Sex Pistols a few years later he did so mouthing the words to the Coop's "I'm Eighteen." The kind of orchestrated chaos that made up classic albums like *Killer* and *School's Out* was a prototypical '70s sound, one that would be copied by Kiss, AC/DC, Aerosmith, and a lot of the other punched-up Heavy Metal that would grace the turntables of the subsequent burnout generation. The sensibilities were decidedly Third Generation: "I came into this life/Looked all around/I saw just what I liked/And took what I found." It was a long way from "Blowin' in the Wind," in other words (although no one less than Bob Dylan himself has claimed that Cooper is "underrated as a songwriter").

The message was: the new kids didn't care (and Cooper was the king of the Not-Carers).

Alice Cooper also helped birth the whole occult-Rock craze, as he'd originally taken his name from the Ouija board. Cooper may have hanged himself on a cross, or staged his own mock suicide, but he did it while wearing a *dress*, so how could anyone take him seriously? He was about as "satanic" as Mickey Mouse, in other words, but his flirtations with "evil" heralded a whole new era of occult-Rock and devil-schlock (culminating with the Misfits, death metal, and "goth"). In the hands of practitioners like Alice Cooper and Black Sabbath, the whole devil-worship syndrome was a dumb tag line, a form of *theater* that was essentially secondary to their music (which was excellent). They didn't go home and worship totems of the devil, nor did they perform blood rituals in private. But there was a more bogus side to Satan-Rock, and in the early '70s, more people than ever before were embracing the occult fix.

Not the least among them was Led Zeppelin's guitarist, Jimmy Page, who became so enamored with turn-of-the-century Black-magic meister Aleister Crowley, that he purchased Crowley's mansion, presumably to get the right vibes. One night while tripping on acid, Page thought the ocean was coming to get him, perhaps in retribution, and wrote a song about it ("The Ocean," 1973). Other artists also made bids toward occult trappings: Funkadelic, the heavy Black psych-Funk band from Detroit, devoted their third album to the Process Church, a.k.a. the Church of the Final Judgment, which propagated such uplifting philosophy as, "The tide will not ebb until all is destroyed." But like Alice Cooper, Funkadelic was basically a good-time crew who looked at such deviance as just another form of freakiness. Ditto for clowns like Black Oak Arkansas, Southern boogie boobs who played up the biblical analogies on their second album, *Keep the Faith*. There was also Louise Huebner, supposedly an actual witch, whose *Seduction Through Witchcraft* album was a fairly popular item among hippie couples trying to foment the love-buzz in the early '70s.

Blue Oyster Cult may not have been outright "evil," but they were at least *sinister*. Their first album, released on Columbia in 1972, sounded like it was recorded in a dungeon, and the cover featured a satanic symbol hovering above an endless abyss of identical trap doors, all presumably leading nowhere. As with Alice Cooper, their lyrics were among the first to explore the previously unexplored area of Rock star contempt ("Stairway to the Stars"). Insiders with connections in both the record industry (Murray Krugman) and Rock press (Richard Meltzer, who wrote lyrics for them, including the aforementioned ditty), the Cult was wise beyond their years. They were "underground" without eschewing Rock star aspirations (or chops). Their first three albums, released from '72–'74, were the salvation of the hipper Rock critics during the dry years when Hippie hadn't been totally killed off yet, but everyone knew it was on the way out. Just a sample of their song titles tells the tale: "Hotrails to Hell," "Dominance and Submission," "Career of Evil," "Flaming Telepaths." They broke down barriers, but got sick of waiting around for superstardom to befall them. As a result, their music grew a lot more "professional" but ultimately suffered in the long run (they're playing redneck bars in upstate New York now at age fifty). The first three albums are still the high-octane experience.

With their weird sado-fascist connotations, the Cult were an exception to the intellectual simplicity of most early '70s Heavy Metal bands, who played to the basest working class instincts of their audiences. These were the kids who were *not* going to college but were the future grease monkeys of America. This was the beginning of the bland '70s syndrome of nondescript burnout Rock— and also of the class split among the Rock audience. Working class Rock fans smoked pot and wore t-shirts and jeans and spent their money on albums by groups like ZZ Top, Foghat, the J. Geils Band, Grand Funk ("We're an American Band" being perhaps the classic in this genre), the Edgar Winter Group, Montrose, Lynyrd Skynyrd, Aerosmith, Bachman-Turner Overdrive, UFO, and April Wine. Although musically, these bands varied, the thing they had in common, besides the fact they all had long hair and mustaches, was their dedication to the eternal Party—they were mindless exponents of Rock-as-escapism, and the audience responded in kind.

Not everyone was satisfied with the drab neoconformity that was quickly coming to characterize the Rock of the new decade, however. There were still plenty of posh glory boys and girls who'd become attracted to Rock because of its flashier impulses and didn't fancy the pregrunge farmer fashions of the denim-clad early '70s. Most of them came from England, where the fashion industry had always had a farther-reaching impact on Rock (hence the whole relationship between fashion photog David Bailey and the Rolling Stones). Also, without a real hippie/antiwar movement of its own, England was quicker to get over the '60s. England experienced a mind-expanding psychedelic heyday, but it was less overtly political than the one in the United States, and, once again, more entwined with flashier notions (e.g., the Beatles' psychedelic suits for *Sgt. Pepper*). It seems that England has never been able to shake their whole preoccupation with the Shakespearean theatrical tradition. Combined with the gender-bending implications of the new polymorphous sexuality, this made for a whole movement based on somewhat frivolous (read: campy) notions.

To the rockers, the glam-boys were "faggots"; to the glam-boys, the burnouts were "hippies." And so it's been ever since…whether it's punks staring down poof-haired synth-poppers circa 1983, or the hordes of retro-punks facing off against Black lipstick-wearing goth kids nowadays. Never shall the twain meet, I guess.

In the early '70s, when the whole bisexual phase was just beginning, half of the artists weren't even remotely gay but knew that queening it up with a dash of makeup would be a guaranteed attention getter. After all, even John Lennon was appearing in army-surplus types of clothes, and the public image of the hippie was a decidedly drab one.

So here comes T. Rex (a.k.a. Marc Bolan), as flamboyant as a female film star, without a hint of musical knowledge, claming to be the biggest thing in the world. What did it mean for Rock? Not much—T. Rex's shuffling midtempo boogie wasn't quite the bridge to Punk that many pundits hoped it would be. What did it mean for fashion? Everything! He was the first to get by on his looks and image alone, at least as far as Britain goes, and it's been an endless parade of preening pretenders ever since.

Bolan got his start in Tyrannosaurus Rex, a duo consisting of him and partner Steve Peregrine-Took. They were a Folky oddity on the British psych scene whose albums bore titles like *My People Were Fair and Had Sky in Their Hair But Now They're Content to Wear Stars on Their Brows*. Admittedly unique—Took played bongos—they were ultimately too bizarre to ever transcend their cult status. Consider 'em a Brit equivalent of the Silver Apples, only with bongos instead of the Simeon. However, this kind of marginal notoriety was not what the starstruck Bolan aspired to.

Enter Tony Visconti, a producer who'd already worked with that other ingenue on the British scene, David Bowie. As Visconti would later recall: "Marc gave off an air of being very precious, very special and very charismatic. I fell in love with him."[10] It wasn't long before he was whispering sweet nothings into the would-be superstar's ears: mainly, that *he* was the real star of Tyrannosaurus Rex, and if he were to drop the bongo player he could really ascend the heights of fame. It wasn't long before Bolan re-emerged under the slightly modified T. Rex moniker. Only this time, there was no question about who the real star was and, like Alice Cooper, the name soon came to signify the group's flamboyant leader more than it did the band.

The gatefold of *Electric Warrior*, released in 1971, told the story: an androgynous-looking Mickey Finn, the band's percussionist, stands demurely in the background as Bolan stares intently into the camera with a glass of something—scotch? champagne?—on a table in front of him. The whole thing is a picturesque reminder of British Rock star decadence in the '70s.

But despite his "superstar" pretensions, T. Rex never really caught on in America, save one big hit, "Get it On," a decent enough rocker in the Stones/Who tradition. In England, however, T. Rex was *the* teenybop sensation of '71–'72. Dick Clark, the impresario who, more than anyone, represented mainstream America, offered an interesting observation about why T. Rex didn't level 'em over here: "He thought he was Mick Jagger. He was Donny Osmond…The poor fellow believed his own publicity, when you had Ringo Starr running around taking pictures of him with an 8-millimeter camera…he has been so ill-advised—a man of obviously great talents, but no business acumen. And so therefore…he went into the sewer."[11]

David Bowie also had a difficult time breaking the American market initially. When he first came to America in 1971, wearing a dress, he was considered an oddity. But Bowie used his campier sensibilities to inflate his own myth. When asked if he was really "bi," Bowie replied: "You'll know when I end up in bed with Raquel Welch's husband." Although Bowie flirted with androgyny, he was no more of an actual homosexual than Mick Jagger—marrying a woman in 1970, Bowie would continually alter his persona to suit his career needs.

A perfect example was the stylistic mutation between his first album, *Space Oddity*, which was actually hippie Folk-Rock in the Tyrannosaurus Rex/Syd Barrett vein, and his second album, *The Man Who Sold the World*, which was almost Heavy Metal. Even on that album, he was sprawled out in a dress on the cover, holding a fan. Everyone thought he was gay at this point, so he decided to play it up even further with his third album, *Hunky Dory*. Although it was vaguely Folk-Rock and hardly a huge seller, it was at this point that he first began to get noticed in the States.

Bowie's transformation from hippie–mime–minstrel to bisexual pagan god was a gradual evolution. If there was any direct catalyst besides wife Angela, an ingenue from the theater scene who helped liberate Bowie to the concept of wearing dresses, it was Bowie's infatuation with Andy Warhol and the whole New York Factory scene. Bowie was particularly enamored with Lou Reed, the former singer/guitarist of the Velvet Underground, whose influence on the whole subsequent glam camp shouldn't be underestimated. By 1971, however, the Velvets had splintered somewhat acrimoniously. Literally *exhausted* by his halcyon days in the New York underground, Lou Reed retreated to Long Island to work as a typist at his father's accounting firm. It wasn't long before he became restless to once again explore his more savage inclinations. He headed for England, inspired by the kind of success his glitter progeny like Bowie and T. Rex were experiencing. He made an album with some slick Brit session men, mostly consisting of the material he was working on with the Velvets when they unexpectedly fizzled. By then he'd started to make a name for himself, because his whole seamy history had begun seeping into the public view and the Velvets were soon to become the apostles of the new wave. This was good news for all the carpet crawlers that wanted to follow in his footsteps—like David Bowie.

Bowie had already established a somewhat testy relationship with the whole New York scene via "Andy Warhol," his "tribute" to the artist/filmmaker (which Warhol apparently hated). It was inevitable that when Bowie finally hit New York, he'd stop by the Factory. Apparently the two imagemongers, Warhol and Bowie, found common ground re: the latter's alligator shoes. When Bowie returned to England, stiff on this symbolic victory, it was inevitable that he would hook up with Reed. In the perfect role reversal, Bowie became Reed's producer/liaison. The result was *Transformer*, which was bubblegum Frankenstein-in-a-dress but wielded the biggest hit of Reed's career in "Walk on the Wild Side," a kiss-and-tell memoir of the Warhol regulars that became historic for getting the phrase "giving head" onto the airwaves. Lou ultimately chickened out, though, letting his friend Ernie Thormahlen appear in drag on the album cover instead of doing it himself.

Which is symptomatic of Lou's entire solo career—a series of basically unfulfilled promises, however not without some merit. Like *Berlin*, for instance, the ultradecadent dragged-down drama on wax produced by Alice Cooper's boy, Bob Ezrin; or *Metal Machine Music*, which Lou actually tried to pawn off as being "an electronic experimental composition" when actually it's just four sides of totally random shrieking noise. This isn't surprising, considering that when he made the album he was living on a diet of amphetamine, cigarettes, and Johnny Walker Black and weighed ninety pounds in his t-shirt and leather jacket, complete with an iron cross emblazoned into his forehead.

Bowie was no fool—once he'd usurped Reed in Phil Spector fashion, he aspired to do the same with a variety of other semi-washed-up sleaze-rockers. This meant Iggy & the Stooges and Mott the Hoople, two of the most notoriously misbehaving Rock and rumble units of the era, both of which had been unceremoniously dumped by their respective labels recently: Elektra in the case of the Stooges, Atlantic on Mott's behalf.

In 1972 Bowie launched MainMan, his own management company, which was run by Tony DeFries, a shuckster with a never-ending flair for publicity-generating antics. As Cherry Vanilla—a leftover ingenue from the Warhol scene who acted as Bowie's "publicist" during the '72 tour—recalled: "If there was some disc jockey in, oh, Cincinnati, who was halfway cute—and I knew by fucking him he would put David's record on the air, I fucked him. Then I'd hype my image and pretend I'd fucked every *one* of them. Really, we made the whole thing up as we went along."[12]

She must've got to the hippies at *Rolling Stone*, because Bowie ended up on the cover, under the clever heading: "Are You Man Enough for David Bowie?" Despite the hype, *The Rise & Fall of Ziggy Stardust & the Spiders from Mars*, supposedly Bowie's magnum opus, only made number 54 on the charts, but you'd be hard pressed to find a pundit nowadays who didn't claim it was the musical event of the year. Same thing would happen with Patti Smith, the Ramones, the Clash, and others a few years later—groups or artists with marginal sales but mega significance. We were entering the age when the pop and Rock audiences were splitting almost totally in half. Rock 'n' Roll was busy building and rebuilding its own legacy, but the marketplace wanted none of it.

No group signified this impasse more emphatically than the Stooges, the nihilistic combo from Michigan who'd helped invent Punk, Heavy Metal, and Motor City Madness in general. By 1972, after only a couple of years in the "business," they'd completely wiped out, victims of their own insatiable excesses. Turned onto smack by the P-Funk roadies in the back of their equipment van, the Stooges flung themselves into heavy drug addiction like they had everything else (full-throttle). They shot up so much that the walls of their hippie crash pad were covered with bloodstains. Not surprisingly, Elektra dumped them shortly thereafter. The famous truck driving accident didn't help—that's when drummer Scott Asheton, in a direct foreshadowing of *Beavis and Butt-Head*, tried to drive a twelve-foot truck through a ten-foot bridge. The Stooges: the name fit.

A lot of people blamed the reappearance of James Williamson as the catalyst for the Stooges' decline. Another high school buddy, Williamson was an ex-army colonel's son who just showed up one day at the Funhouse, the group's communal crash-pad. He also happened to be a hell of a guitar play-er, and with original guitarist Ron Asheton now bumped to bass duties, the realigned group entered a truly manic phase of nihilistic overkill. The song titles alone tell the story: "I'm Sick of You," "Beyond the Law," "Your Pretty Face is Going to Hell," "Gimme Some Skin." Needless to say, no record company was going to touch this stuff at that time.

That is, until David Bowie came along. Just as he'd sought out the Warhol crowd when he first came to America, upon his return in '72, he dutifully inquired: "Where's Iggy?" Being fairly desperate at the time, Iggy was looking for a lift, and Bowie's star was rising. The two became friendly, and Bowie promised Iggy a trip to England, management with MainMan and, eventually, a new record contract with Columbia. The only provision was that Iggy drop those ruffians the Stooges and bring only James to England with him. As he'd done with Lou Reed, Bowie would equip Iggy with a top-flight battalion of stu-dio pros.

But there was a difference—Iggy wasn't Lou Reed. He didn't stand at the mike and deadpan sordid lyrics about decadence and then simulate shooting up. Iggy jumped and screamed and rolled around and dived into the audience. And he showed up to recording sessions naked. It took a certain breed of musician to hold his concentration when Iggy was in the room. In the end, the only musicians up to the task were the Stooges themselves, so after literally *hundreds* of auditions, the Asheton brothers were flown to England as well.

The resulting album, *Raw Power*, was one of the few Hard Rock albums to ever live up to its name. Under Williamson's sonic guidance, the sound had become totally overpowering, a sledgehammer attack of brutal ill will. When it was first released in 1973, it seemed incongruous to just about everything else that was going on in music. But a few years later, it would start to make sense. As the guitar armies of the '70s, '80s, and '90s took formation, the influence of the album would be unmistakable. From the Dictators and the Cleveland groups (Dead Boys, Pagans), to the Sex Pistols and Motorhead in England, to the Saints in Australia and, of course, endless bands all over the globe, *Raw Power* would become the Punk prototype.

Meanwhile, Bowie seemed to be shocked into remission by his experience with the Detroit bad boys. After that, he concentrated almost solely on show-biz shtick and stopped flirting so heavily with decadence, excepting *Diamond*

Dogs, his last real stab into the void, which featured songs about other boys and featured him naked on the cover sporting dog genitals. After Alice Cooper became a "regular guy" who admitted that he liked to play golf and Elton John admitted that he really *was* gay, David Bowie came to dominate the Glitter camp in the eyes of the press. However, in England, during the years '72–'74, there was one group who gave him a run for his money: Roxy Music.

Roxy were the first group to epitomize a purely '70s aesthetic. They laughed at tradition, unlike Bowie, who paid constant homage to it: Beatles, Anthony Newley, Warhol, Dylan, Lou Reed etc. Roxy's only "tradition" was for patrician estates and haute couture. Their interest in electronics, particularly keyboardist Brian Eno's wild synthesizer frolics, made them weirdly "progressive" even though the Prog Rock audience always scorned them for being too "pop." This probably had something to do with their tastes in feathered boas and the like—oddly enough, the real Progressives like Yes, despite their upper-crust pretensions, seemed to pull the strictly prole t-shirt-and-jeans crowd.

A good example of Roxy's decadent persona was the cover of their first album, which featured what looked like a bounteous babe in a nightie sprawled out on a satin pillow with a gold record. Until one looked closer and realized that "she" was a "he"! It was just this unsettling air of sexual ambiguity that Roxy Music exploited. That's why on the cover of their next album, *For Your Pleasure* (1973), they put Amanda Lear holding a dentured ocelot on a leash while the limo driver looked on with a shit-eating grin.

Album packaging in the '70s was rife with decadence. First the Rolling Stones got their pal Andy Warhol to design an album cover, *Sticky Fingers*, with a built-in moveable zipper. Not to be outdone, Alice Cooper's next album, *School's Out*, included an actual pair of pink panties, which one was presumably supposed to wear.

There was also Sparks, who wore dresses on the cover of their *Kimono My House* album. From California, they were another group who tried the going-to-England-as-a-shortcut-to-stardom route. When it didn't work, they returned home with a chip on their shoulder, as epitomized by tunes like "This Town Ain't Big Enough for the Two of Us." The group was led by Ron and Russ Mael, a pair of former boy underwear models who never lost their affinity for playing dress-up, only eventually it came to encompass Nazi drag as well (brother Ron had a Hitler mustache). Such trappings only helped their U.S.

stock fall even lower, despite the fact that *Indiscreet*, the next album, was a unique fusion of grotesque orchestrations and the pseudo-operatic vocals of Russ Mael, who sang fiercely bitter ditties about revenge. Robert Christgau, ever a defender of family values, fumed: *"Mmmnnn!* They're *hateful!"*[13] They influenced Queen, among others.

In the annals of sleaze, however, no group lives in infamy more than the New York Dolls. Their story can certainly be seen as eponymous with the times they lived in, the Dark Ages prior to Punk, when the parameters of what was considered shocking were being expanded upon. The Dolls helped push these boundaries into the realm of drooling maniacs, stumbling junkies, and hopelessly narcissistic poseurs. By doing so they helped secure the fate of the next generation of Rock bands—mainly, that the hallowed doors of corporate America would be forever closed to all such violence-prone nonready-mades. The Dolls, perhaps more than anyone, hailed the birth of the true underground.

It wasn't meant to be that way. The Dolls, in their original form, were merely another early '70s Rock band sick of the arty pretensions and musically aloof concepts of the Art-Rock set. As their songs demonstrated, they had legitimate R&B and oldies roots, as well as a style and stance similar to that of the more aggressive '60s Brit bands (Yardbirds, Rolling Stones, Pretty Things). David Johansen, the singer, even played harmonica, and onstage he and guitarist Johnny Thunders parroted Mick n' Keef, a routine that would also be appropriated, to much cheekier effect, by Aerosmith approximately a year later. There was one distinct difference between the New York Dolls and other Rock 'n' Roll revivalists of the day, however: the Dolls were in *drag*! Not *actual* drag, like being particularly meticulous about removing the stubble or anything, but in the sense that they looked like they'd rifled through granny's attic and picked out the most garishly outdated threads and donned 'em just for showmanship's sake! It didn't take long before, at least in New York, their picture was in all the hip journals like *Rock Scene*.

The downtown scene of the early '70s was in transition. The Warhol era was ending, but there were still runaway offshoots like Charles Ludlam's Theater of the Ridiculous, a theatrical troupe consisting of a lot of the Warhol castoffs, particularly the drag queens. It was the Theater that was credited with introducing glitter to the general populace, via a stash of sequins that they affixed to virtually everything they touched during their off-*off* Broadway productions. Reputedly, when David Bowie first came to America in 1971, he was in the front row every night.

As the story goes, Johansen had originally viewed success in the Theater of the Ridiculous as his ticket off Staten Island. He'd already starred in a couple of sub-Warhol back-room skin flicks, so his credentials were in order, but apparently he couldn't get to first base with Ludlam, who gave him one non-speaking role in one of his productions. At that point, Johansen apparently decided to forsake his thespian inclinations to pursue Rock n' Roll and founded the New York Dolls, who took their name from the New York Doll Hospital, a curio shop across the street from where drummer Billy Murcia's mom worked.

The group took residence at the Mercer Arts Center, a dive located on the Lower East Side that was a typical downtown mixed-media venue: in one room they showed films; in another was a cabaret bar. The Dolls played in what was known as the Oscar Wilde Room, a makeshift concert hall originally launched as an experiment. Those were the days before Max's Kansas City allowed live bands, and before CBGB's got off the ground, so venues for Punk acts were limited. As David Johansen described the scene at the time: "It was real easy to take over because there was nothing happening...we were the only band around, really, so we didn't have to be that good."[14]

The thing about "not being that good" is important—this was the day and age of Yes, Led Zeppelin, and other so-called dignitaries. The Dolls by contrast were direct, honest, youthful, vigorous, spontaneous, and all the other things always associated with Rock 'n' Roll, including crass and sloppy—and that went for their sound as well as their makeup techniques. Like the Stones, they were a five-piece, but unlike the Stones, they weren't rehearsing in a chateau in the south of France. Rather they rehearsed in a bicycle shop in Manhattan where the owner would literally lock them in at eight every night and wouldn't come back with the key until the next morning. It was under these conditions that they produced the demos that were later released under the name *Lipstick Killers* on the ROIR label.

As their (bad) reputation grew, record companies began bidding for their contract, and the group somehow lined up a backing slot on a British tour with Rod Stewart & the Faces. Then tragedy struck: while in London, drummer Murcia died of a drug overdose in somebody's bathtub. All of a sudden, the bidding war ceased. Luckily, Rock critic Paul Nelson, one of the group's biggest proponents, was at that time the A&R director of Mercury Records, and at his behest the label signed the group. With the Dolls' longtime friend Jerry Nolan replacing Murcia, thus adding an even more tripped-up level of attack, the '70s were suddenly on again.

Next began the task of finding a producer who could hone their sound into a somewhat saleable product. It was decided that Todd Rundgren would do the honors, as he had somewhat underground credentials. He may have had a pair of recent Top Forty hits, but he still hung at Max's and wore a dress.

As Rundgren recalled: "The Dolls were the first of a whole set of New York groups who were springing up at the time, and I felt that as their album was the first, and therefore, most important…it better be at least half decent…and I succeeded. The Dolls themselves were barely capable of a half-decent effort anyway. I always had to keep the first take that wasn't literally offensive to the ears."[15]

The thing about the Dolls was, they were just too outrageous to ever extend their influence outside of their own immediate urban surroundings. The Dolls didn't catch on in the heartland, not to mention the South. They had a following in music centers like L.A. and New York, but that wasn't enough to keep them afloat in the increasingly homogenous music industry. We were soon to enter the era of Disco, when hit records could be manufactured without ever needing actual musicians. Producers and record execs were coming to the conclusion, "Who needs arrogant junkies?" That's precisely what happened to the Dolls: like the Stooges, they were victims of their own overkill.

Because of the Dolls, the underground got pushed even further underground. But that underground would continue to grow all through the '70s, first in the form of the glitter bands who sprung up in the Dolls' wake: Ruby & the Rednecks, Teenage Lust, Suicide, Wayne County & the Electric Chairs, the Neon Boys, the Magic Tramps; and then, in the form of the *actual* Punk bands that began playing CBGB's in '74–'75: the Ramones, Television, Patti Smith, Blondie. What all these bands took from the Dolls was the demon sense that "anyone can do it."

The Dolls' influence extended beyond the underground as well. There were many bands willing to subvert the danger factor but maintain the outrageous glamour pose. In the case of Kiss, perhaps the most successful of these postglam bands, the influence of the Dolls was obvious: all Kiss did was make it a little less drag and a little more Marvel Comics. Kiss roomed with the Dolls, gigged with them a lot in the early days, and appropriated a lot of their tricks. But Kiss took it to the level of actual dominance. Whereas the Dolls got off on the punk/glitter pose, Kiss turned both the music and the image into an artifice of control, power, and media manipulation. They were pros, unlike the Dolls, but at least they had the foresight to challenge the pseudo-Art Rock pomp of dinosaurs-in-their-own-time like Led Zeppelin and Deep Purple with a more razor-cut dynamic. What Kiss did for Heavy Metal was to extricate the Blues influence altogether.

Aerosmith, whose members hailed from Boston, performed a similar cleanup routine, although they were actually more derived from the Rolling Stones tradition than the New York Dolls in the first place. The fact that they were a five-piece made this even more obvious, especially in publicity photos where, initially, they struck the same androgynous poses as the Stones. They didn't really become popular anywhere outside of New England until the release of their third album, *Toys in the Attic*, which unleashed the Heavy Metal classics "Walk This Way" and "Sweet Emotion." The latter was classic '70s bad boy myth-making: "I pulled into town in the police car/Your daddy said I drove you just a little too far." The formula worked, and they became poster boys for the burnout generation without doing anything more offensive than bragging about their sexual conquests (and drug excesses). The main thing about post-Glitter bands like Kiss and Aerosmith was that they dropped the blatant gender bending. This made them seem like "regular guys" and thus accessible to the t-shirt-and-jeans-wearing hordes who were scared of the "drag" implications of the Dolls, Lou Reed, and David Bowie.

In an even more innocuous way, the Dolls can probably bear some responsibility for phenomena like *The Rocky Horror Picture Show*, a popular British stage production that ran all through the '70s and eventually, when it got turned into celluloid, became the most popular "cult" film of the era. Part of the whole '70s spirit of abandon was that every Friday night, hordes of nimbos would go to midnight screenings of *Rocky Horror*, dressed in drag like the various members of the cast, and pelt the screen with rolled-up toilet paper. Even as late as '76–'77, ridiculous readymade groups like Kim Fowley's all-girl sleaze-bait Runaways and Venus & the Razorblades were modeling themselves after the Dolls' whole glamour-puss image.

Besides transvestism, the big thing in the '70s was the advent of the synthesizer and the prevailing theory among technocrats that it was going to replace the guitar as the preeminent instrument in Rock. As Rock had accomplished somewhat of an artistic breakthrough in the '60s, it would only figure that any kind of eclecticism would be welcomed, and the keyboard wasn't originally intended to have a softening effect, but to forge a whole new sonic frontier of its own. Its inventor, Robert Moog, had based his early model on the mysterious theremin, a strange instrument invented by Leon Theremin that is played by waving one's hands in front of it. At the very least, this technique assured that no two theremin solos would ever be exactly alike. In the '60s, Brian Wilson used the instrument on "Good Vibrations," and a psychedelic band from New York called Lothar & the Hand People recorded two albums for Capitol employing a full-time theremin player.

The first "mini moogs" as they were called were actually souped-up keyboards. The sound was still analog, based on modular equipment that produced a strange whooshing noise. What Moog didn't know at the time was that these noises would soon give way to full-blown "space Rock." This also coincided with the moon walk and the futuristic appeal of music made *entirely* by machines.

When synthesizers first arrived on the scene, their primary exponents weren't Rock groups, but the purveyors of "electronic" music, which more often than not meant Classical musicians on a binge. Walter "Wendy" Carlos worked in direct cahoots with Moog to create the first popular Electronic-Classical LP, *Switched-On Bach*, a surprise bestseller in 1969 that took the synth off the pages of *Electronics World* and into the popular arena. By the early '70s, groups like Traffic, the Who, and the Band were using the instrument for subtle embellishments, and Black artists like Sly Stone and Stevie Wonder were already creating the kind of dense keyboard-laden Funk that would eventually lead to Disco.

This all corresponded with the rise of "head" music in the mystical '60s. The synthesizer was another way to add trippy special effects to Rock—thus making it more engaging to someone who was tripping. Although proto-Space Rock pioneers like the Grateful Dead and Pink Floyd didn't use synthesizers outright, they made extensive use of keyboards to create their embryonic pastiches. From there, it was only a short step to groups who used *all* synthesizers to weave opuses of incredible complexity (as well as clinical sterility). In any case, a machine that supposedly could never play the same note twice and could reverberate unto infinity if left unattended—i.e., *a machine that could play itself*—lent itself well to the rarefied atmosphere that was overtaking Rock at the time. Called "art-Rock," "space-Rock," "head music," and, ultimately, "progressive Rock"—or "prog" for short—the new Highbrow Rock was perhaps the most misunderstood and vilified category in Rock's history.

Blamed by the critics for almost singlehandedly gutting Rock of its primal instincts in the '70s, the purveyors of Prog were looked upon as humorless stiffs with an inflated sense of self-importance. Nevertheless, during the years 1970–1975, the Progressives ranked among the most lucrative recording acts in the world. Groups like Yes, ELP, Pink Floyd, and Jethro Tull routinely sold out huge concert halls and wracked up successive gold albums. These artists didn't even bother with singles, because the whole format was anathema to their grandiose concepts. What good was the three-minute single to groups who generally filled whole album sides with one twenty-minute song? More than anyone, it was the Prog rockers who turned Rock into an album-oriented medium.

In the '60s, groups like the Dead and Pink Floyd were pivotal, but so were lesser-known synth practitioners like the Silver Apples, 50 Foot Hose, and United States of America. These groups applied high art concepts to basically simple songs. But their spirited synthetic embellishments predated the Germanic onslaught of heavy Space Rock pioneers like Amon Düül (I and II), Can, and Faust. Influenced by the San Francisco groups, these German bands' whole modus operandi was to live communally, do *tons* of drugs, and wait for the jams to come. For the most part, all these groups were sincere hippies (albeit a Euro version): they truly believed that sitting around tripping and playing music was going to save the world. Boy, were they in for a big surprise.

Despite the toolings of these nascent Prog tripsters, there was an even more synthetic alternative brewing. Given their Teutonic nature, the Germans have always had a disposition towards technology—in the late '70s, they would become leaders in Disco, a form of music created almost entirely by machines. Earlier in the decade, groups like Tangerine Dream and Kraftwerk created pastoral suites of endless dribbling space. When the whole wave of "ambient" sounds—Eno, Laurie Anderson, Philip Glass—took hold a few years later, it sounded very much like the aural landscapes of Tangerine Dream. Kraftwerk was one of the only German groups to actually make a dent in the United States, charting in 1975 with a shortened version of the twenty-two-minute travelogue "Autobahn," a song created entirely by synthesizers, a fact Kraftwerk's two android-like members were proud of.

Android rockers weren't only searching for an antidote to the human condition, but to any earthly structure whatsoever. On the wilder side of Space Rock, there was the British band Hawkwind: they wowed 'em at all the festivals, so I guess they were good hippies after all, but persona-wise they were strictly badass, which was a twist on the whole celibate image of most immaculately buttressed progsters. One of the more futuristic—as well as horrific—bands, Hawkwind basically grew out of psychedelia, which meant they had a built-in propensity for taking drugs. In a way they were kind of a Brit version of the Dead, who also wowed 'em at the festivals, only Hawkwind was less organic and more krypton-fed. Despite the insanity of some of their farther-reaching space probes, they never let their prog ambitions overshadow their distinct Rock drive—which was among the most violent of the time. Then again, what would you expect from a band that once incorporated Lemmy?

The post–Syd Barrett Pink Floyd was also capable of trance-inducing stabs into the void. Britain's primary acid rockers, the Floyd became chiefly the domain of bassist/singer Roger Waters after Barrett downed one too many thimbles-full of acid. From that point on, Floyd took a turn toward creating aural wallpaper. Not surprisingly, they ended up doing a lot of film soundtracks. Like the Dead, they could jam for twenty-three minutes straight, as the side-long "Echoes" from 1972's *Meddle* amply demonstrated. They eventually found the right marriage of murk and cynicism and were able to achieve superstardom on their own terms, in the form of *Dark Side of the Moon* and other over-inflated monstrosities like *Wish You Were Here, Animals,* and *The Wall.* Harbingers of Punk by dint of their delicate stance, they provoked the provocateurs to no end with their noble indifference.

Soft Machine, part of the same Canterbury scene as Pink Floyd and Caravan, was never able to capture the American market in quite the same way, despite the fact that it was among the most legitimately progressive acts of the era. After two LPs of clever, cinema verité-style Art-Rock, Soft Machine released the two-record *Third* featuring four side-long excursions that combined everything from Grateful Dead-like noodling to jazzy runs to *Sgt. Pepper*-ish psychedelic textures. While other bands pursued suitelike conceits to stultifying limits, Soft Machine was tight and effluent in its jamming. "Facelift" borrowed from John Coltrane, with some Herbie Mann flute thrown in. These were indeed heady concepts for so-called rockers, but Soft Machine proved that the Jazz and Rock camps didn't have to be mutually exclusive. (Frank Zappa's fusion efforts like *Hot Rats* and *The Grand Wazoo* count here as well.)

King Crimson, another British band, also employed saxophone, but they weren't Jazz by any means. Starting as a quintet in 1969, their work was some of the most high-minded of its era, right down to the album packaging. The opening track on the first album, *In the Court of the Crimson King*, told the tale perfectly: "Twenty-First Century Schizoid Man," based on an ultraheavy ominous riff, was the kind of grim, futuristic vision they'd come to epitomize. With flailing saxes, maddening changes in tempo, doomsday lyrics, and Robert Fripp's searing guitar, it bespoke "seriousness" all the way around. Fripp, who once claimed to be influenced by Hendrix and *Sgt. Pepper*, seemed like one of the most pretentious assholes to ever pick up an axe. However, as Crimson evolved, Fripp's increasingly complex musical ideology exposed him as a genuine crank, as eccentric in his own way as the more punkified Art-Rockers like John Cale and Brian Eno, both of whom he eventually collaborated with.

Fripp tossed members in and out of King Crimson as if they were well-tooled components of a much bigger machine. The turning point occurred with the addition of drummer Bill Bruford, who quit Yes to join, and bass wizard John Wetton, a refugee from Uriah Heep. Revolving around this three-person nucleus, the group took on a more polyrhythmic approach culminating in the swan song tour de force *Red*, a masterpiece of embryonic Rock improv that wove through many scintillating twists and turns. That album, as well as the earlier *Starless and Bible Black*, would prove a huge influence on a whole school of complex latter-day bands like Primus and Soundgarden.

Another British band to arrive in the late '60s with rather high-minded concepts was Genesis. Like many of their peers, they were trapped somewhere between psychedelia and heavy pretension, at least at first. The central talents in the band seemed to be keyboardist Tony Banks and vocalist/lyricist Peter Gabriel, who combined to create expanding realms of sonic poofery. Like all Brit Prog bands, Genesis was seemingly always evolving, and the turning point came in 1972 when they added drummer Phil Collins and guitarist Steve Hackett. It was then that they embarked on a series of suite-like concept albums such as *Foxtrot*, *Selling England By the Pound*, and *The Lamb Lies Down on Broadway*, which merged pseudo-literary flourishes with densely enveloping keyboards and Collins's polyrhythmic drumming. Verging dangerously close to Muzak at times, Genesis ultimately exposed their true colors when they became a full-blown Pop band during the Age of Reagan. As with the Beatles, it wasn't that long of a fall from their high horse to end up producing what basically amounted to nursery rhymes. Other Brit Prog Rock bands like Yes also incorporated these twee traits.

Why Britons seemed so ready to embrace the pomp of Prog Rock probably has a lot to do with cultural factors. Classical music was conceived in Europe; therefore a fundamental appreciation of the form is probably more inbred in their culture than ours. It is a conceptually more "dignified" approach than the earthy sensibilities of America's indigenous musical forms (i.e., Blues, Jazz, Country & Western, and Rock 'n' Roll). Americans tend to consume things faster and reduce them to fodder; most Americans who have any interest in Classical turn it into a stylized kind of Pop art verging on self-parody (Frank Zappa being a perfect example). Whereas the English Prog bands who emerged at the end of the '60s, like the Nice, Yes, Emerson, Lake, & Palmer, and King Crimson would have you believe that their Classical embellishments were not affectations at all but a neoclassicist form unto itself. They were, in essence, claiming they were the "modern Beethovens."

Yes was a perfect example. Their backgrounds were certainly earnest enough, having covered the usual Brit bluespan. Throw some *Sgt. Pepper* eclecticism in and you've got the basic workings of any English supergroup of the era. Guitarist Steve Howe came from the influential "underground"/art band

Tomorrow, and Yes's early work was characterized by a kind of precocious psychedelic quality and an earnest Folk–flower child root: they covered Paul
Simon's "America," and their vocal harmonies often aped their Atlantic label-
mates Crosby, Stills, & Nash. The group hit the height of '70s arena-Rock pretentiousness when keyboardist Rick Wakeman joined in 1971. Although he'd
previously tinkled the keys as a session hack behind the likes of David Bowie,
Lou Reed, and Cat Stevens, none of that could have prepared audiences for the
kind of confrontational theater Wakeman evoked during his tenure in Yes, not
to mention his subsequent solo career. Wakeman brought the Classical influence into the group full force with endlessly Rotarian efforts like "Cans and
Brahms."

Emerson, Lake, & Palmer—or ELP for short—were even more important
in the annals of Prog Rock because they were the first group to eschew the guitars. For this reason, when the whole guitar vs. synth debate arose at the dawn
of the '70s, ELP was at the center of the controversy. On the one hand, their
Classical-influenced bombast—consisting of ex-Nice keyboardist Keith
Emerson, ex-Atomic Rooster drummer Carl Palmer, and vocalist/bassist Greg
Lake, who was recruited from King Crimson—was "heavy" enough; but a good
deal of their output was filled with pseudo-orchestral pretensions and tedious—
and interminable—musical interludes. Their attempts to synthesize the classics, at the very least, showed a great deal of chutzpah—like the 1972 *Pictures
at an Exhibition*, which painted Mussorgsky into a corner. Perhaps their ultimate descent was the three-record *Works*, a self-indulgent monstrosity containing one disc devoted to each member. Such things made them the whipping
boys of the critics. As *Creem* said at the time of the album's release: "*Works*...but
only as a frisbee!"[16]

The Electric Light Orchestra—or ELO—also harbored Classical pretensions but took it a step further by incorporating actual strings. What started off
as an experimental offshoot of the Move concocted by Roy Wood and recent
Idle Race abortee Jeff Lynne turned into a full-fledged band after Wood left to
form Wizzard. In their earliest incarnation, ELO were a novelty at best among
the FM-Rock hordes of the early '70s. Their symphonic version of "Roll Over
Beethoven" was a concert standout, and they gained a reputation as a flamboyant live act—due mostly to the freak appeal of having cello and violin players
in the context of a Rock band. On their records, however, the strings were just

an embellishment—the songs were almost entirely steeped in the Pop tradition (e.g., the Beatles). This tilt toward the center eventually paid off in a big way. By the late '70s they had become one of the top touring attractions, at one point even bringing an actual spaceship onstage. Such theatrical embellishments were another big part of the pomp and circumstance of early '70s Rock.

No one epitomized this more than Jethro Tull, who started out as Blues bohunks but evolved into archetypal art-Rockers with an endless stream of overblown "concept" albums, starting with *Aqualung* in 1971. The sacrilegious tone of that album was carried on by its successor, *Thick as a Brick*, which was also the first Jethro Tull album to feature one song over both its sides. Obviously Tull leader Ian Anderson considered himself a thematic genius on the scale of a Miles Davis or a John Coltrane. Some of the jams on albums like *Brick* and *A Passion Play* jelled in places, but in the same way as similar excursions by Yes: in the end, the whole effect sounded forced, as if they were leaping from stanza to stanza with automatic precision just to prove a point. The point was valid—Rock musicians were now entitled to the same "freedom" that Classical and Jazz artists had always maintained, which gave them the impetus to explore their music to the fullest. But the great thing about Rock 'n' Roll had always been that, by its very nature, it overcompensated for people who weren't that talented to begin with. It was the spirit that counted, and that's what a band like Jethro Tull was missing.

Anderson as a frontman certainly made a case for Rock 'n' Roll extravagance as well as anybody from the era. A raving bearded satyr who looked like he hadn't taken a bath in two months, his stage antics included leaping around the stage wearing a codpiece and honking on his massive flute. The most well known flautist in Rock, Anderson was also an outspoken detractor of other bands and a tireless promoter of himself. His air could be summed up in one word: pompous. If any Rock artist of the era considered himself a modern composer, it was Anderson, and on occasion he showed hints of brilliance in his ability to combine Folk, Jazz, and Rock textures with biting social commentary. But too often, it was grandiose posturing, and it fell considerably short of genius, to say the least. When Tull tried playing shorter songs, perhaps because they hadn't had a hit in two years, all they could come up with was "Bungle in the Jungle." Nevertheless, it paid off, and the song was a number one hit in 1974. But their days as members of the Rock aristocracy were numbered, just as for others of their ilk. Punk and Disco were right around the corner, with their celebrations of decadence and irony, respectively. The grandiose notions of the progressive rockers were soon to give way to a new, frivolous kind of postmodernism. Tull were merely "modernists."

They weren't the only ones to fall prey to their pretensions. Another victim of overkill was Todd Rundgren, who started out as one of the most promising songwriters of the early '70s with a pair of excellent LPs. By the time of the third, *Something/Anything?* he'd become narcissistic enough to believe he warranted a double album, but in this case, he was able to pull it off. It was on the next album that he began to veer closer to sheer self-indulgence. Entitled *A Wizard, A True Star*—which he apparently considered as much a self-fulfilling prophecy as David Bowie on the similarly egotistical *Ziggy Stardust*—the album was an incoherent hodgepodge of half-baked tunes strung together through sonic fission. He followed that with another double, the eponymously titled *Todd*, which showcased Rundgren's increasing reliance on the synthesizer. Within months of that album's release, he formed his own Prog Rock nightmare, Utopia. This was the band in which he pretended to be "one of the guys," only it wasn't just any bunch of guys, as Utopia featured no less than three synthesizer players. The classic track was "The Ikon," which ran thirty minutes on their first album. Such self-indulgence was short-lived, however, perhaps once again because of marketplace considerations. Before long, Todd was issuing *Faithful*, his note-for-note rethinking of the '60s artists who'd influenced him, and Utopia were resorting to the Beatles parody *Deface the Music*.

It took Brian Eno to make the synthesizer an effective Rock instrument, and even then that was only for two albums. When Eno first exited Roxy Music in 1973, he really wasn't that different from fellow Englishman/keyboard whiz Rick Wakeman, who'd recently left Yes under the same terms (i.e., bad). But where Wakeman posed a grim façade, Eno was as "colorful" as the most prancing dandy-Warhol (including Bowie, with whom he'd soon spark a collaboration). The mascara could not disguise a genuine talent at work, and *Here Come the Warm Jets* (1973) and *Taking Tiger Mountain By Strategy* (1974) retooled the landscape of British Rock for the next generation. Combining Velvet

Underground-type drone, Roxy Music Hall pomp, and King Crimsonoid noise (Fripp even played a scorching guitar solo on "Baby's on Fire" from *Warm Jets*), these records made Art-Rock palatable to the postmodern kids who were soon to explore the realm of Punk and "New Wave." Particularly in England, these records were the harbinger of a whole new style of clever songwriting, which could be heard in the twisted pop vocabulary of bands like XTC, the Soft Boys, Tubeway Army and others.

On those first two solo albums, Eno was still utilizing basically a band format. On subsequent efforts, he was to explore what others like Wakeman and Mike Oldfield had already done—mainly, the keyboard as its own universe. Albums like *Discreet Music* and *Music for Airports* were OK as aural wallpaper but almost negligible in Rock terms. By the end of the decade, Eno had shored up his credibility with the Rock/underground audience once more via his production of American New Wave groups like Devo and the Talking Heads, who bore his influence from their beginnings. There was also the "Berlin trilogy," the series of influential albums he made with Bowie: *Low*, *Heroes*, and *Lodger*.

Magma, who hailed from France, were so far out that they actually invented their own *language* and recorded all their albums in this absurd dialect. Capable of Hawkwind-scale outbursts, the group was masterminded by Christian Wander, who apparently ruled with an iron fist, disposing of members with Frank Zappa-like alacrity. Wander led his charges through various drills that were all part of the group's ever-expanding science fiction plot. Flirting with both Jazz-Rock fusion and intense Prog space-stab, Magma was genuinely weird, but hardly ever dull (unlike most proponents of this genre).

Prog groups were abundant in those extravagant times, right before Disco and Punk happened and the record industry tightened up for good. Groups were indulged a little more in those days and were encouraged to experiment. A lot of it was self-indulgent, but some interesting music could still be heard through the din. The Dutch band Focus created a seminal slab of Heavy Metal in the form of the immortal "Hocus Pocus"—which combined yodeling with a pounding riff— but couldn't remain focused long enough to up the ante. The Brit-Germanic hybrid Nektar was capable of lengthy excursions that combined electronic wizardry and space-Rock jamming. The British Van Der Graaf Generator were no strangers to lengthy extrapolations, combining elements of Jazz, Rock, Classical, and even Folk, all in the same song (albeit a twenty-minute one). Be Bop Deluxe, led by guitarist Bill Nelson, combined keyboards and monumental guitar pyrotechnics to occasionally brilliant effect. Ex-Procol Harum guitarist Robin Trower utilized the power-trio format to underscore a rockingly lyrical approach that nevertheless reeked of high-mindedness.

One of the best Psych-Prog bands came from Canada, although they were basically unknowns in their time: Simply Saucer. Influenced equally by the heavy space jams of Brits like Hawkwind and the Pink Fairies and by the seminal drug-roar of primal American geniuses like the Velvet Underground and Stooges, Saucer actually served as a worthy premonition of some of the more challenging—and intelligent—aspects of Punk (Ohio's similarly adventurous Vertical Slit falls under the same category).

Along with the Prog groups, the other exponents of "Head" music (called this because it supposedly stimulated the frontal lobes) in the early to mid-'70s were the Jazz-Rock fusionnaires. The purveyors of Fusion were no less pretentious about their chopsmanship than their classically trained contemporaries. Most of Fusion's front line consisted of alumni from Miles Davis's groundbreaking experiments in the late '60s. The double album *Bitches Brew* (1969) was particularly influential, with its massive polyrhythmic structure and extended jams featuring Rock instruments like keyboards and electric guitars. In both cases, it was white men who were helping Miles make the transition: the keyboards were provided by Joe Zawinul, an Austrian; and the guitars, by John McLaughlin, an Englishman. Zawinul went on to form Weather Report with the venerable sax player Wayne Shorter. McLaughlin formed the Mahavishnu Orchestra. Between them, these two groups represented the two major schools of Jazz-Rock Fusion.

Weather Report was more immediately Jazz-like, centering on Shorter's punctuated soloing and the rolling multiple rhythms underneath. Although the group was three-fifths Caucasian, there was an African sensibility—as well as an Eastern lilt—that put Weather Report closer to experiments done around the same time by actual jazzers like Pharoah Sanders. Mahavishnu, on the other hand, were almost uniformly Rock in intent—the only thing that made them "jazz" was the presence of polyrhythmic percussionist Billy Cobham and the fact that the music was almost entirely improv-based. At times they sounded like King Crimson and basically appealed to the same audience.

Herbie Hancock, another Davis spinoff, did some successful things in the Jazz-Rock vein. *Head Hunters* in 1974 was a roly-poly mixture of Funk charts, synthesizer vamps, and Jazz soloing, courtesy of reedman Bennie Maupin. *Return to Forever*, led by another Davis alum, pianist Chick Corea, was similarly stylized, only with Latin traces this time. Eventually Corea betrayed his roots altogether for full-blown electric Rock à la Mahavishnu: the aptly named *Hymn of the Seventh Galaxy* was closer in spirit to a psychedelic form of Heavy Metal than it was actual Jazz. Corea has to bear the responsibility also for introducing Al DiMeola, a sub-sub McLaughlin guitarist who came to epitomize the worst pretensions of the "guitar hero" genre.

For all the Jazz musicians who "went Rock," there were an equal number of rockers willing to jump the fence in the other direction in an effort to gain "respectability." Jeff Beck, the superstar British guitarist, is a perfect example: after leading a boogie trio—Beck, Bogart, and Appice—for the first half of the '70s, he began churning out a stream of Fusion albums like *Blow by Blow* and *Wired* featuring very tasteful, fluid licks. Carlos Santana, the Latino guitarist and leader of Santana, was equally guilty of wank: what started out as a fairly tight hybrid of Latin, Rock, and Jazz resources back in the Psychedelic Era soon became a forum for semi-mystical self-indulgence. Frank Zappa, meanwhile, had been doing what amounted to Jazz-Rock ever since he waxed *Hot Rats* in 1969.

Zappa was an anomaly, however: a genuine Rock superstar who eschewed the use of drugs. In the '70s he was severely in the minority. One of the probable causes for Art-Rock's and Fusion's popularity was probably the huge amount of marijuana being smoked by the general populace at the time. Recreational drug use was at an all-time high, at least according to polls that claimed that one out of every three high school seniors smoked dope. This was the day and age that Cheech & Chong romped through albums—and eventually movies—acting like the Two Stooges of the dope generation. In 1974 Tom Forcade founded *High Times*, a magazine devoted to almost fanatical recreational drug use. No underground rag, the magazine—at least then—employed top-flight writing talents and eventually achieved newsstand hegemony despite its editorial policy of total, unrelenting advocacy and its presentation of profiles of drug-culture heroes.

In this age of pot permissiveness, the next big trend on the horizon was

Reggae. It caught hold with the critics first, who were looking for a new Black music to martyr in light of all this Euro-derived Prog. Before Punk, Reggae was the great savior—an outsiders' domain that seemed like the final holdout against corporate Rock. The thing was, by the time Reggae caught hold in America—mostly through the popularity of one man, Bob Marley—the music was already more than a decade old in its native Jamaica. With the success of Marley and the subsequent whitewashing of the form (e.g., Eric Clapton doing "I Shot the Sheriff"), Reggae became as mainstream as anything else.

Marley summed up the mystical quotient of the form this way: "Rum mosh up your insides. Just kill ya, like the system. System don't agree with herb because herb make ya too solid. When ya smoke herb ya conscience come right in front of ya. Yes, Rasta! Herb is the healing of the nation."[17]

In the mid-'70s, the "nation"—real or imagined—had a lot of healing to do.

CHAPTER 12

DAYS OF MALAISE

THE PALLOR OF THE '70S WASN'T ALTOGETHER UNKIND: the war was over, Nixon had been given the boot, pot was de facto decriminalized and there were loose morals but no AIDS yet. One thing was for sure: the "struggle" of the '60s was behind America and it seemed, at least for a time, as if the libertines of the New Left had won. In the '70s, folks were *relaxed*. "Mellow" became the new mode (with "lame" being the other side of the coin).

As far as music went, in the '70s there'd be a general slowdown of the '60s life-and-death imperative into a kind of blasé I'll-take-my-time approach. The music of the '60s had equaled a complete remake/remodel of Rock's basic framework. The '70s represented a refinement of the body and engine of Rock 'n' Roll and, later, a complete smash-up and reassembly (Punk). Artists like Alice Cooper, Elton John, and David Bowie used the Rock medium for self-serving purposes, and the music industry hasn't been the same since. In the '70s, people's preoccupation with the personal (Tom Wolfe's 1976 use of the label "the Me Decade" in *New York* magazine stuck) brought on an accompanying lust for celebrity: magazines like *People* and *Interview* prospered, creating a whole new subgenre in itself (*Lifestyles of the Rich & Famous*). It was a whole new ideal, fostered by the leftover hippie aesthetic of self-help and spiritual awareness, that the only true reality was subjective anyway—it was a godless world. Therefore go for the visceral, the *now*, no matter how superficial. Whatever excites. Apparently, the sight of Elton in a dress did—and has ever since (i.e., Boy George, Marilyn Manson, et al.)

A lot of this was brought about by the not-so-simple advancement of the media itself; that is, with more bulbs a-flashin' and cameras cocked there was more of a need for shameless self-aggrandizement. By the '70s, the whole notion of becoming famous had become an aesthetic in itself, not to mention the somewhat cynical realization that anyone could do it—that is, it didn't intrinsically have to do with talent but more with an individual's particular thirst for the object of fame itself. This was the root of the Madonna syndrome. All it required was an understanding of media technique and the ability to manipulate it. This was definitely a more contrived approach than the guerilla tactics of the '60s.

The whole notion of cool arose in the '70s. The '60s thing had been a feel-good let-down-your-guard uninhibitedness. In the '70s another popular expression was "Looking Out for Number One." Hence the rise of self-help and weirdo religions, not to mention the Sexual Revolution—the prime concern seemed to be self-fulfillment. What that meant was that the supposed "community" of the '60s had finally fragmented into a million pieces. And the laidback "hey man, I'm just doing my thing" mentality of the '70s would soon give way to the mean-spiritedness of the '80s—or "get out of my face!" With so much of a consciousness overload coming at once, something had to get cut from the collective psyche: mainly, caring for one's fellow man.

Ever since the '70s, people (particularly liberals) who want to show that they actually care about other people have embraced causes. As for how they actually treat anyone outside of their social caste, well, you know the score: be clipped, don't let one's guard down, and be suspicious. This is all a result of the mass cynicism of the '70s, and this came about, at least partially, because of Vietnam and Watergate: if you couldn't trust your own *government*, how could you trust your fellow man?

A lot of Rock groups and artists had already exploited this cynicism: Alice Cooper, the New York Dolls, Kiss, Blue Oyster Cult, and David Bowie, among others. This post-everything mentality had infiltrated the actual music *business* in a less obvious manner: mainly, the way popular music was produced and marketed. A band like Kiss wasn't expected to *believe* the infantile swill it rendered; it was all hype! What David Bowie had once referred to mockingly as "the hard denim truth" was beginning to evaporate—the preoccupation with "realism" that had characterized the '60s was giving way to hype and fantasy. These were the great new factors of Rock 'n' Roll, a fact that would soon carry over to MTV and its progeny. In the '70s, the money was flowing at labels like Casablanca, and they were laughing all the way to the bank. There were legendary anecdotes of execs snorting heaps of cocaine off of glass-topped tables…clearly this was not your daddy's vision of corporate America—or of show biz, for that matter.

What the public didn't realize was that beloved stars like Kiss and Freddie Mercury were actually kicking sand in their faces. It had become a culture of total narcissism: celebrity, in any of its forms, was superior to mere mortality at *any* cost. This was the final triumph of Andy Warhol's immortal comment: "In the future everyone will be famous for fifteen minutes." Warhol meant it somewhat contemptuously, as if to say, "In the future maybe you measly little nobodies will know what it's like to be *me* for at least fifteen minutes of your miserable little lives." Sad fact was, there seemed to be a whole element of the culture that were perfectly willing to accept their footnote—or human-interest story—status just to satisfy their desperate urge for "celebrity." Hence the rise of shows like *Oprah* in the '80s on which people would essentially air their dirty laundry in public and, in the cynical climate of the time, get *praised* for it!

Journalism had also changed in the '70s; this was partly because of Vietnam and then Watergate, and partly because of television news journalism (i.e., *60 Minutes*). The mavericks of the "new journalism" like Norman Mailer, Tom Wolfe, Joan Didion, and Hunter S. Thompson put themselves right in the center of their dispatches, but what made these writers and others like them different from the Beats, who used a similar narrative style, was that they weren't the product of the underground but of the mainstream press: Wolfe of The *NY Herald Tribune*; Thompson, *The Nation*; etc. Whereas the Beats had been apolitical, the "new journalists" were directly a result of the post-JFK/Berkeley/Vietnam era—they were the New Left. This movement also encompassed Bob Woodward and Carl Bernstein of the *Washington Post*, who broke the biggest story of the era, Watergate. Surely the new journalism was a factor in getting Carter elected—and Nixon ousted.

As personified by a writer like Thompson, this was a new kind of liberalism: there was a cynical snicker to it all, as opposed to the blind optimism of the Left in the '60s. Another area in which this new cynicism was being tested was in the field of comedy. In this case, the Beats can be seen as a direct influence. After all, their coffeehouse readings often took on the fervor of performance art. Lenny Bruce was the most obvious by-product. His whole ad-libbed narrative style proved to be *the* major influence on almost all of the subsequent new-school comedians like George Carlin, Martin Mull, Steve Martin, Richard Pryor, Albert Brooks, Robert Klein and the members of Chicago's influential Second City troupe. Second City was particularly important considering that its alumni would ultimately go on to make up the cast of the most popular show of the late '70s, *Saturday Night Live*. Along with England's *Monty Python's Flying Circus* and the TV version of *Second City Television*, *Saturday Night* was an absurdist form of almost-guerilla theater that took satiric aim at such previously forbidden—on television anyway—targets as police, the government, the clergy, and the family unit. It was still kind of an underground cult thing (read: drug culture) because it was on late at night. The whole triumph of *Saturday Night Live* was that so many people would stay home on a Saturday night to watch it. This was definitely a turning point in the counterculture. *Saturday Night* was so popular that, a few short months after the show's debut, its cast members would become the first TV stars to take on the same mythic Godlike status of the Rock stars—whom they partially usurped and soon shared drugs with.

The "new journalism" and the new comedy commingled in the form of *National Lampoon*, the successful monthly "adult" humor mag that started as an offshoot of the original Harvard Crimson *Lampoon*. For a few brief months in the early '70s, it was the most cutting-edge satirical magazine in the country. It was also the spawning ground of *Saturday Night Live* writers like Michael O'Donoghue and Anne Beatts. Performers like John Belushi and Dan Ackroyd actually lent their voices to the syndicated *National Lampoon Radio Hour* and, eventually, a string of best-selling albums with tasteless titles and album covers and parodies of music icons like John Lennon and Neil Young. In the hands of *National Lampoon*—the magazine *or* the radio program—nothing was sacred. Nixon was, of course, the most brutally flogged sacrificial lamb. It was *National Lampoon*, the magazine, that coined the phrase that perhaps summed up the whole era: "It was the worst of times, period."

One of the first Rock groups to epitomize the transition to true '70s consciousness was Steely Dan, a group pioneered on Zappa/Traffic-esque pyrotechnics, Dylanesque cynicism, and Beatles/Spector studio reclusiveness. They also took their name from William Burroughs, which shows the stronghold the Beatniks still had on the whole posthip crowd. In perhaps the most cynical move of all, Steely Dan weren't really even a *band*—they were, or it was, the brainchild of a songwriting duo from New York named Walter Becker and Donald Fagen. They'd previously gone the Brill Building and backup musician routes, so they weren't the typically unskilled hippie dirtbags. We were entering the era when that kind of unprofessionalism would no longer be accepted. Southern Boogie would be the last stand for this kind of earthy, feel-good mud wallowing, a symptom left over from Woodstock. In Steely Dan's eyes, Woodstock was *definitely* over. Calculating in their cynicism, they personified the new elitism even as they castigated it: "Show business kids making movies of themselves/You know they don't give a fuck about anybody else."

Hiring studio musicians, expert ones—Phil Woods, Denny Diaz, Jeff "Skunk" Baxter, Tom Scott—to play on their albums, Becker and Fagan had perfected the ultimate vacuum. There was only one tour during the '70s, decidedly a mistake/failure. Although still hippies at heart with their "bad sneakers," they were unabashedly materialistic—a '60s no-no—with "a whole lot of money to spend" ...show biz kids! The music was impeccable, with jazzy fifths and weird time signatures, an eclectic mesh woven of such non-Rock elements as blazing saxophone and Bebop piano played by Fagan. None of it, save perhaps Diaz's immortal classic-Rock guitar solo in "Reeling in the Years," was particularly *hard rockin'*, but the new mood was mellow, and Steely Dan personified that more than anyone, being entirely a high-gloss product of the modern recording vestibule. On the back of their fourth album, *Katy Lied*, they provided precise details about the kind of microphones used. This was the peak of audiophile mania, of *Stereo Review* and quadraphonic sound. Steely Dan was "art" or "progressive" Rock as much as King Crimson or Yes, but they sought to create "Pop" as well. Much smarter than the average white band, Steely Dan borrowed freely from Jazz, Classical, and good old show biz technique. The attitude was an ultracool detachment, personified by Fagan's vocal sneers as well as his lyrics, mostly narratives in the first person. This was finger-pointing music at its best, influenced by Dylan's mid-'60s period and Zappa's scornful indictments of the in-crowd. Musically, the Jazz trickery was also zapped from Zap, but Steely Dan was more tasteful in its usage. In "Midnight Cruiser," for instance, the intricate music wove an evocative tale of an aging cruiser still looking for kicks even as he raced the clock towards thirty. It was a preoccupation much of Steely Dan's audience could identify with.

If Alice Cooper, Kiss, and the rest were the glam-rock messiahs to a new generation of teenyboppers, Steely Dan appealed to a much older, nonflashy audience—they were among the first to de-emphasize the glamour potential. Partially, this was the casual, laid-back exterior of the Me Decade coming into play: mainly, Why shouldn't I be able to go onstage looking like I do when I walk down the street? This dusty, rusty plainness first emerged during the singer/songwriter heyday of the early '70s: McCartney grew a beard and cuddled his papoose openly; James Taylor wore non-fop floparounds, and his wife, Carly Simon, banished her bra and let her nips poke through. The undressing of the Great Glamour God was at work. This is something many of the aging Baby Boomers could relate to. Robert Christgau, the *ultimate* aging Boomer, wasn't wrong when he labeled Steely Dan "the first post-boogie band."[1] The sound was softer, the look *lighter*. Another term that emerged during the time, supposedly coined by Rock scribe Mike Saunders, was "lightweight."

The "boogie" culture, from Hippie to Heavy, was kind of a commingling of the lumpen masses, a get-down-and-rub-against-yer-brother (and perhaps even a wild oak tree) aesthetic. Post-boogie, as well as lightweight Rock, was, by contrast, almost exclusive. Most of its purveyors lived in Hollywood, which is probably farther out of the mainstream than any city in America. In the '60s, L.A. had been the center for many important musical innovations: the Beach Boys', and particularly Brian Wilson's, studio perfection; the Byrds and their Folk-Rock progeny; and the chaos politics of the Doors and other radical hippie acts. Although vast, the L.A. Rock community has remained fairly incestuous over the years. Club owners there have always maintained an L.A.-first mentality, which has led to many out-of-town bands being given the shaft. Drink prices at the Whiskey A Go Go were outrageously high, and the drinks were served in paper cups by mascara'd waitresses who'd rather you just *died*. To someone coming from outside, L.A. seemed like the capital of all that was phony and illegitimate about the '70s. Clubs like the Troubadour, once a drinking hangout for the likes of Jim Morrison, were among the first to upscale the clientele by allowing comedians to open for "rock" acts, raising the prices, and generally ridding themselves of the downer-gulping teen pestilence. This left an audience consisting primarily of somewhat affluent white liberals with droopy mustaches and Earth shoes to fill the tables and help maintain the profit margin.

At the same time, yet another drug was coming into prominence: cocaine. Although it was instantly branded "nonaddictive," the ego-enhancing self-assuredness the drug provided, not to mention the short-term effectiveness, led many on the scene to develop an insatiable appetite for the drug. Because it was expensive, coke also provided the necessary elitist trappings: unlike speed or smack or marijuana, one had to be *rich* to afford a habit. This fit right in with the egotistical mentality of the L.A. Rock scene.

Along with the bullying club scene and the proliferation of coke, the other trademark of the L.A. music scene in the '70s was the sterile production values of most of its major recording stars. This can once again be traced to the close-knit environment of the L.A. entertainment industry. Many of the musicians who played on the most popular recordings of the era had come up through the ranks as studio hacks. As in Nashville and New York, there is a proliferation of this kind of work in L.A. Most of the musicians in this scene have backed one another or have collaborated in some way. The Eagles backed Linda Ronstadt on her albums, and Jackson Browne has composed songs for both of them. Artists shared the same musicians, producers, managers, and, in many cases, record labels. The whole WEA family—particularly David Geffen's Asylum records, launched in 1972—came to typify the "mellow" trend, with the Eagles, Joni Mitchell, Ronstadt, and Jackson Browne. This is what, to a great degree, accounted for the vacuity of the "L.A. sound" in the '70s. The whole notion of studio refinement has always been a vital part of the L.A. music scene. In this regard, Lou Adler's recordings with the Mamas and the Papas seem like the direct antecedents for the sound of Hollywood in the '70s—lush, well-orchestrated pop creations performed mostly by studio musicians. Likewise, Buffalo Springfield, another L.A. band, was probably the earliest progenitor of the laid back Country-Rock groove that equally came to typify the West Coast sound.

This was a very macho scene in the Burt Reynolds sense of the word—most of the musicians were men and, in contrast to the contemporaneous glam camp, they were decidedly he-male in looks and demeanor. Sexism was rampant in '70s "adult Rock": the man as a she-bedazzlin' cowboy with a heart of gold but a ramblin' jones that kept him skirting commitment as he lasso'd lass after lass. Don't laugh—this seems to be the mentality that Bill Clinton adopted. Since he named his kid after a Joni Mitchell song, it all makes sense. The women involved in the L.A. scene—Joni Mitchell, Linda Ronstadt, Stevie Nicks, and Christine McVie (the last two of Fleetwood Mac)—waxed vulnerable as they waited around for the perfect cosmic cowboy to sweep them off their feet, preferably on a cloud of white powder, and braced themselves for the inevitable put-down. Fueled by the coke, it was the Great Western Myth of the Rock-Star-as-Outlaw, epitomized by the Eagles' lame "concept" album, *Desperado*, which showed 'em on the cover lined up with gun belts slung ashoulder like the most macho lady-killers imaginable. Or so they thought…because of their lightweight sound, the Heavy Metal kids branded 'em "wimps" almost immediately. Such was the schism of '70s Rock.

The female counterpart was Linda Ronstadt, the prototypical El Lay chanteuse. Although the possessor of a rich soprano, the singer—who originally came from New Mexico—had a limited range, which made her the queen of bland. But what she lacked in delivery she made up for in kittenish sex appeal. Ronstadt personified the vulnerable waif: "All these boys won't let me be," "People try to *rape* me," etc. Even if she didn't write her own songs, she made the songs famous for their respective writers like Karla Bonoff, J. D. Souther, and Warren Zevon. Her theme song seemed to be Bonoff's "Someone to Lay Down Beside Me." She went in and out of affairs as if they were limousines, with Steve Martin, Glenn Frey, and her most famous catch, California governor Jerry Brown. So prevalent was the counterculture at the time that there was even talk of a "Rock 'n' Roll presidency" with Linda Ronstadt as the swingin' first lady. Linda's dehydrating nature made her one of the major sex objects of the era, at a time when there were sex symbols galore (Farrah, Cheryl, Cheryl, Suzanne). Larry Flynt over at *Hustler* apparently offered her a cool million to shed all but her cowboy boots, but she politely declined.

The L.A. rockers like Linda Ronstadt and the Eagles represented the first breach of faith between the Rock critics and the Rock musical establishment. An interesting contrast to today's slick stuff is that, in the mid-'70s, the musicians still, to some extent, took what the critics wrote about them seriously. They looked upon liberal mouthpieces like *Rolling Stone* as allies: there was still a Pop-politik at work, unlike today's pseudo-agenda, which is why, at that time, *Rolling Stone* looked more like a tabloid à la the *Village Voice* and now looks more like *People*. Artists like the Eagles felt betrayed when the critics attacked their work for its blandness and lack of depth. The critics, in turn, felt equally hurt that the Eagles hadn't tried to assume the gauntlet laid down by the Beatles, Dylan, and the '60s dream. The only artists to earn that distinction from the critics in the '70s were Bruce Springsteen and Neil Young. This highly personal—some said "solipsistic"—music simply wasn't as exciting to the Rock literati as the more universalist stuff of the '60s like "Street Fightin' Man." Using these terms, the critics vilified bands like the Eagles.

The pull of the critics was weakening anyway—it was becoming evident that the standard of "good music" was no longer a reliable barometer for social acceptance. While the critics moaned, the groups they hated the most—the Doobie Brothers, the Eagles, Wings—were well on their way to becoming the biggest-selling Rock acts of the '70s. The chasm between the popular and the aesthetically satisfying became so divisive in the mid-'70s that a number of artists like Joni Mitchell and the Eagles stopped talking to the press altogether. Mags like *Rolling Stone* found themselves devoting more and more space to politicians, the new comedians, even Hollywood movie stars—who, at that point, weren't all that different from Rock stars anyway. All the while, the critics never stopped slogging their albums. To supposedly "settle the score," the Eagles' manager, Irving Azoff, arranged a softball game between *Rolling Stone* staff and his charges. The Eagles won, proving their manly mettle once again.

The Eagles found the perfect formula when they adopted producer Bill Szymczyk in 1974. Sensing that, as the Dictators prophesied, "Country-Rock is on the wane," he upped the guitars a notch. The result was a hybrid of Country-Rock weepiness and Rolling Stones–type boogie, a sound that became known as MOR, or "middle of the road." Or as Donny and Marie Osmond put it: "A little bit country/a little bit rock 'n' roll." It was the adultrified hard-sobbing of modern Nashville combined with L.A. good-livin'/good-lovin' hippie sentimentality and just enough guitars to still be considered "Rock." This "Rock" was certainly not for rebel-rousing purposes like once upon a time. It's amazing how fast so many folks succumbed to the armchair.

Ohioan Joe Walsh, for instance, was supposed to be a typical Hard Rock badass with his band of gringos, the James Gang, back in the early '70s. However, he found the good life in sunny L.A. irresistible and soon forsook his Hard Rock background, at least enough to pass from semistardom to superstardom. Szymczyk slicked him up with the typical El Lay production, and he produced best-sellers with sardonic titles like *The Smoker You Drink*, *The Player You Get* and *You Can't Argue with a Sick Mind*. He may have still come off like a wild and crazy guy, but when an opportunity to join the Eagles—anything but a wild and crazy aggregation—knocked, he didn't flinch. With the band, he helped create what was perhaps their signature statement, *Hotel California*, which was Classic Rock heaven with the single "Life in the Fast Lane," which condemned the whole L.A. M.O. (i.e., lame-o) while at the same time celebrating it. It took the group another three years to come up with the less-than-satisfactory follow-up *The Long Run*, and when they did, it was loaded with cynical crap like "King of L.A.," a not-so-clever retelling of the old Hollywood casting-couch fable. Walsh kept busy in the meantime with the self-serving anthem "Life's Been Good," which told how groovy it was to be a stoned L.A. cowboy.

Along with Joe Walsh, another '70s L.A. act whose roots dated back to the pre-prefab era was Fleetwood Mac, which was actually three-fifths English. Although they'd logged much time in the London Blues scene during the late '60s, after the departure of guitarist Peter Green in 1970, they struck out on a mellower course. Their early '70s phase with American Bob Welch is probably their least known period, although they did score one hit with Welch's gently rocking "Sentimental Lady," a sign of things to come. This led Welch to quit Fleetwood Mac, first to front his own group, Paris, and then to strike out on a solo career. In a typical Beatles coattail-riding maneuver, it was only after Fleetwood Mac had become huge *without* him that he scored his own Top Forty hit, "Ebony Eyes."

The idea of working with Americans stuck with Fleetwood Mac, however. Recruiting a dopey male/female pair of Californians named Lindsay Buckingham and Stevie Nicks, the group seemed intent on once and for all burying their Blues roots. They called the new LP *Fleetwood Mac*, as if to prove that they were being reincarnated, and when they were, it was as a Pop band. "Rhiannon," the first hit from the album, introduced Nicks's witchy ways. Meanwhile, Englishwoman Christine McVie's "Say You Love Me" exposed the other side of the coin, mainly the fragile vulnerability. "If you use me again it will be the *end of me*," she sang. There was also Lindsay Buckingham's male sensitivity on "Monday Morning." In many ways, Buckingham was the one most responsible for the group's revival. His whole style of songwriting was yet another offshoot of the Brian Wilson School of Pop-craft, but it was cynical enough to still epitomize the '70s languor.

Between the recording of *Fleetwood Mac* and its follow-up, *Rumours*, in 1977, there was a lot of personal turbulence within the group. At the time, the group was comprised of two couples and one odd man out, John McVie, whose ex-wife had become lovers with fellow Englishman and original group member, Mick Fleetwood. Confusing enough? Well, consider this: Buckingham/Nicks came into the group as a swingin' '70s *couple*; however, by the time Fleetwood Mac became a household name, their relationship had deteriorated as well. By the time of *Rumours*, most of the songs chronicled all the interband fucking that was going on. The kiss-and-tell lyricism would prove to be a major influence on the next generation of songwriters—particularly the female ones, like Courtney Love, who covered Nicks's "Gold Dust Woman," or Liz Phair, whose "Six Foot One" was a musical as well as spiritual descendant of Nicks's "I Don't Want to Know."

Despite a few exceptions like the Mac women and Ronstadt, the L.A. scene was mostly male-oriented. Warren Zevon came on like an offscreen vampire, but the Muzak on the LPs, save for some token Rolling Stones guitar, was the usual studio swill. Neil Young managed the unique feat of being very in *and* out of the L.A. circle at the same time through his quirky style shifts, playing the El Lay hayseed on idiosyncratic albums like *On the Beach* and *Tonight's the Night*. When he needed a hit, however, he reverted to dizzy-headed Country mawkers, from "Heart of Gold" to "Lotta Love," actually a hit for his girlfriend at the time, Nicolette Larson (apparently, Neil couldn't do anything with it due to his wheezy voice).

Lameness in the mid-'70s wasn't restricted to Los Angeles by any means. Middle of the Road, or "MOR," represented a successful genre in itself. By the late '70s, MOR became, along with Disco, the preeminent sound of Top Forty radio, which was a fading category anyway. With the rise of things like Lee Abrams' "Superstars" format, the difference between AM and FM, formatwise, was becoming slim. FM had de facto turned into Top Forty, even as it made a pretense of "seriousness" via support of so-called album-oriented artists like Led Zeppelin and Pink Floyd. This classification also included soft-rockers like the Eagles, Fleetwood Mac, and Jackson Browne, if only because they subscribed to the same long-winded formula. Unlike the hard rockers, these artists also had "crossover" hits on AM. When AM evaporated, more or less, by 1979, these crossovers crossed *back* over, and FM radio found itself with a surplus of tunes known equally among nonrockers. This also led to white rockers giving up on singles altogether, because a "hit" was ultimately defined more by airplay than by actual sales of 45s. For example, the biggest FM radio "hit" of the era, Led Zeppelin's "Stairway to Heaven," was never even released on a single.

This left actual hit making in the hands of such schlockmeisters as Pablo Cruise, the Little River Band, Orleans, Firefall, and other mediocrities. What they all shared was a basic nonflex, non-Rock sound: all highs, no lows. This was the essence of MOR: tingling saxes, weeping guitars, soulless vocals, and greeting card-style lyrics. Looking back, it seems amazing to think of how many performers there were who, at that time, fit almost exclusively under the MOR banner: Olivia Newton-John, Billy Joel, Andrew Gold, Stephen Bishop, Rupert Holmes, Gerry Rafferty, Benny Mardones, Nick Gilder, Leo Sayer, Dan Hartman, Dan Fogelberg, Dan Hill, Al Stewart, Jay Ferguson, Melissa Manchester, and countless others. It's amazing because MOR isn't a category at all—it's a denial of all styles. Most of these performers were aging hacks so cynical by this time that even they hated the swill they were producing. But it was easily adaptable to Top Forty standards because, with less and less freedom occurring in the field of broadcasting, programmers were looking for a safe alternative. Soon the public had no choice but to accept this swill as the "standard" by which all Pop music would be measured. And that's what led to such future monstrosities as Mariah Carey.

Middle of the Road, as its name implies, was an aging Boomer fantasy. Because Nixon had fallen and Carter had been elected, the liberals truly believed they'd won the "revolution." So now that the wall had been torn down, there was plenty of time for fun and the pursuit of hedonism. But it was very uncertain and cynical, because, even a couple years into the Carter presidency, the optimism had dimmed as even the most sun-dazed hippies had to deal with the very real problems of the gas shortage, inflation, and unemployment. This made it easy for the Republicans to come in and quash the Dems again after only four short years.

As the cultural imperative of Rock in the '60s had demanded that the music take on sociopolitical trappings, the rockers of the '70s who were still tied to this myth found that there were few things their audiences were willing to get fired up about during this apathetic decade. No Nukes was one issue that rockers found solidarity on. But, for the most part, the Carter years—those years after Vietnam and Watergate, before Punk, when the '60s were finally hissing to an end—were starkly apolitical. There were issues at stake, but, true to form in the '70s, they were more personal issues as opposed to the kind of divisive ones that polarized the nation and the world in the previous decade. After all, it was hard for anyone to come out in favor of unemployment. As a result, what we saw in the '70s was the birth of normal-guy Rock: rockers who staked their identities on appealing to the long-neglected working class. This made sense, because they represented a previously untapped segment of the market. And this crossover would have a huge impact on two of the most successful musical trends of the era: Disco and Heavy Metal, both categories that appealed directly to the working class. Although no one realized it at the time, it would also help break down the barrier between Black culture and white culture that had been erected during the hippie takeover. Whereas the intelligentsia and radical Left were chiefly white, the working class was a melting pot made up of different social and ethnic composites.

In the '70s, working class Pop could encompass Steve Miller, who sang "I've been working real hard and I'm a-trying to find a job"; Tavares, who made reference to "standing in the unemployment line"; Bob Seger, a working class hero who revealed genuine angst in "Feel Like a Number"; and the Cate Brothers, who paid tribute to "Mr. Union Man." As the decade wore on, Bruce Springsteen became the leading spokesman for working class normal-guy Rock. There were many others: Southside Johnny & the Asbury Jukes, Tom Petty & the Heartbreakers, and Eddie Money, an actual ex-cop from New York. All of these acts were in stark contrast to the Rock superstars like Bowie and Led Zeppelin in their non-freaky normalcy. These were typical blue-jeans-wearing "normal guys" whom the average working slob could relate to. The "outlaws of Country music" trend that occurred midway through the decade can also be partly attributed to this working class ideal. Besides Waylon Jennings and Willie Nelson, there were Emmylou Harris, Tanya Tucker, Dolly Parton, Linda Ronstadt, Jerry Jeff Walker, and other cowboy and cowgirl types, as well as the endless and almost interchangeable string of Southern Boogie bands: Allman Brothers, Lynyrd Skynyrd, the Outlaws, the Marshall Tucker

Band, Wet Willie. Politically, they were Democrats all, especially with region-al fave Jimmy Carter in the White House, but they embraced the same work-ing class values of a Springsteen or a Bob Seger. You wouldn't see any member of, say, the Outlaws wearing any prissy makeup, in other words. Which meant that mainstream Rock was no longer very glamorous.

The Pop had gone out of politics as well. Times were unutterably grim under Carter and, for the first time since the Depression, people were actually whispering that perhaps America was no longer the Greatest Power on Earth. At home, the country's collective self-esteem had been greatly damaged by Watergate and Vietnam. In the case of the latter, resentment continued to grow long after the war had finally ended, as Vietnam vets came home to unemploy-ment telling horrifying tales of merciless torture at the hands of their captors, as well as poisoning, via Agent Orange, by their own government. After wit-nessing America's failed policy in Southeast Asia, many Americans felt that redemption was only possible through a denigration of Old Glory.

In terms of national public image, the Lefties were definitely in control: even Carter sported longish hair and attended Rock festivals. The suit-and-tie Pat Buchanan Republican was definitely on the run—which is why they sooo vigorously led the counterattack in the '80s. The liberal posture then was social-ly near Libertarian and, foreign policy–wise, isolationist. This led to the Iran cri-sis, which was probably the prime catalyst for Reagan's election in 1980. For Carter, the honeymoon was over. The United States soon returned to its tradi-tional Get Tough posture all over the world. Domestically, the economy became the prime focus again. The social agenda was relegated to the back burner, lead-ing to even greater crises like AIDS and the rise of the American ghettos. With Reagan, the Republicans successfully purged the Democrats just as the Dems had done to them four years earlier. Together the two sides have continued to play this ideological chess game of one-upmanship ever since, at the heighten-ing expense of the "people." Revolution never looked better, in other words.

There was no talk of revolution in 1976, however, other than the faux rev-olution of America's Bicentennial celebration, epitomized by the Freedom Train, a traveling exhibition that turned out to be a big financial bust like every-thing else in the late '70s. Along with *lightweight*, *laid back*, and *middle of the road*, apathy was another important watchword of the '70s. This malady gave rise to a whole series of utterly passive pastimes: '50s nostalgia, the Bicentennial, CB radios, disaster movies, Skylab, and, ultimately, video games, which took over in the early '80s.

The American character was being eroded in ways other than becoming passive or apathetic. Americans, who'd always walked tall and carried a big stick, were now falling prey to the victim's syndrome—instead of owning up to their problems, they were learning how to shift the blame, just like Nixon had. Whereas in the days of the World War II daddies, people were taught to keep a stiff upper lip and not air their dirty laundry in public, in the '70s, with the rise of self-help and weirdo religions, the whole notion of personal responsibility became a thing of the past. Now there was always something or someone else to blame. For the Black criminal, it was growing up in the ghetto; for the rapist, it was the fact that he was neglected, abused, and abandoned as a child; and for the white-collar thief, it was the pressure of "keeping up" that got to him.

In the modern-day United States, this preoccupation with the "victim's syndrome" has evolved into a culture in which a person's weaknesses or misfortunes become his or her *whole identity*. What that's done is to diminish one's ability to see oneself as a microcosm of a much larger world. In the '70s, this was just beginning: if you feel you've been wronged, make an *issue* out of it, and live off the fumes of your failure for the rest of your life. Somehow by bringing it out in the open it's supposed to remedy the pain—but it's added up to a hundred million "causes" and a guileless society who've made a form of sociology out of what might have been a mere peccadillo. The search for a reasonable definition of every deviation from so-called "normal" behavior has led to a nation of dullards who are always looking over their shoulders. Let's face it, the best way to deal with one's problems is to get over it, move on.

Starting in the '70s, however, the majority of people didn't want to move on. They became stymied by the nonutopian surroundings of their own existence and turned to nostalgia, dreaming of a past that never really existed (e.g., *Happy Days*). In the dim light of the Carter years, the past had never looked better. And this "jump back" mentality definitely had something to do with Reagan being elected in 1980. Socially, we have become a reticent nation: the true harbingers of revolution, when presented in their nonbuffed element, are greatly feared. This malaise has also led to the majority of Americans becoming disinterested in the arts, science, and even politics—and anything else that doesn't turn the profit margin.

Disco was by definition the blandest of musical forms, because it represented the systematic mechanization of rhythm itself. Despite current attempts to make Disco "cool," there's no denying that Disco was completely sterile and devoid of emotion. The preponderance of Techno in the '90s, however, forced a reevaluation of some of the more technocratic aspects of Disco.

Since Rock began, rhythm has always been its basic excitability agent. Rock 'n' Roll from the start was dance music, particularly the Black forms of Rock/Pop. Dancing-as-metaphor-for-lovin' is as old as roll-out-the-barrel. What Disco did was turn the rhythm into the mere *messenger*—the producer and, ultimately, the DJ and the way he programmed the music became the whole show. Disco in its earliest manifestation was "disco" only because it was played in discos. Otherwise, the music constituted straight R&B.

One of the reasons DJs in New York, as well as in Europe, were playing these records—long grooves like Manu Dibango's "Soul Makossa"—was because radio wasn't. FM was the domain of the hippies, and AM still constituted the usual Top Forty mash. No one was playing all that post-*Hot Buttered Soul* murk or the chugging rhythmic frenzies of Polydor-era James Brown. However, club DJs found that this was the music that people wanted to dance to. It was hard to dance to Led Zeppelin, after all.

The impact of the Sexual Revolution on the rise of Disco cannot be underestimated. For all their talk of free love and sexual freedom, the hippies were actually a rather asexual lot, with all their drab dungarees, lack of underwear, and long, unwashed hair. As the World War II daddies always said: "*Waaah!* You can't tell the girls from the boys!*" Disco, on the other hand, coincided with the rise of Glam-Rock. It was an uptown phenomenon, accepting of "alternative" lifestyles and based strictly in hedonism.

A lot of this had to do with the fondue-cocaine culture. In the '60s, on grass or acid, people wanted to feel those bonging chords up close—hence amplification and psychedelic light shows. But the coke made people twitchy. They didn't want *that* much out of music. Disco was perfect: it was all a mechanical pulse, like breathing (which under excessive coke wasn't always that easy). There was no experience behind it, no tradition. You didn't—nor were you expected to—"get" anything out of it. It was just there. Considering the times, this was more or less apropos.

With the rise of DJ culture, the separation between live music and dancing grew larger. Live music came to be associated with arenas (Kiss, Aerosmith). Before the rise of the underground in the mid-'70s, there simply weren't many bands existing on the grass roots level. There was the gay factor as well: when Disco started, it had a lot to do with the fact that a lot of bar bands in 1971 simply wouldn't *play* a gay bar. This left the field wide open, so to speak, for the DJs, who became mainstays at the gay clubs in the Village as well as out on Fire Island. DJs weren't the only ones who were pivotal in the emergent disco culture, though: there were also the producers, particularly those in Europe, who looped endless rhythm tracks together until the "song" was not a song at all, but merely a *groove*. Producers had always made mere mouthpieces out of artists and turned them into "product"—that's why they were called "producers." But this was different than the manufactured singing groups of the '60s (i.e., the Monkees), who at least still had personality. Most disco artists were just faceless voids.

Given their tradition of silly club laws and curfews, Europe was particularly accepting of Disco. The continent became a perfect bastion for Disco to grow. There was a whole new wave of Euro-producers churning out rote-a-tote rhythm tracks, often with some kind of autoerotic embellishment, such as Donna Summer's "Love to Love You Baby" (1975), one of the first international Disco hits. International because, even though Summer was a Black diva from the town of Boston, it was German producer Giorgio Moroder who laid the mark of distinction on that particular ditty. Once again, the artist became merely another tool in the ultimate product. The twenty-minute track became famous for its length as well as Summer's increasingly heightening yowls. Couples were supposed to *use this*, as either a dance track or an accompaniment to sex. This was a whole new twist, because, after that, Disco became a heterosexual phenomenon as well. Then it became popular.

The Disco sound, as noted earlier, was merely an extension of R&B, from James Brown to Memphis soul. The basic rhythmic feel of these sources was being married to the technological innovations of the Progressive rockers. Synthesizers were important, not only because they could readily produce the endlessly chugging mechanical repetition of Disco, but also because they could take the place of actual musicians. You didn't need a band, or even "musicians," to produce Disco, but you did need a rhythm track. The endless thumpa-thumpa of the programmed synth-drum took care of that.

Disco producers like Moroder came to define the role of the synthesizer in modern Pop much more than their Prog-Rock counterparts, many of whom were still using it for Phantom of the Opera-style hijinks. In pure Rock terms, synthesizers never really did become an innovative part of the musical landscape, but instead a tool of formalization, making contemporary Muzak indistinguishable from TV commercials.

The homogenous mixture that came to be identified as Disco, as well as MOR, was the final nail in the coffin for the traditional Rock form, which had always been rough-hewn and raw. From then on, anyone who left the rough edges in was "Punk" because, once the industry proved how easy it was to mass-produce such gloss, real bands were expected to shine up their rough spots or hit the boot trail. It only figured.

One of the prime factors of the Disco culture was a kind of upwardly mobile assimilation urged on by the promise that if one had the right clothes and the right moves, he or she would get laid, thus achieving forward thrust, real or metaphorical (in other words, goodbye to the hippie shitballs and *Rocky Horror* clowns). Disco was the first "rock 'n' roll" with a dress code. Blue collars were allowed to intermingle with highbrows at the communal haven, providing that they had the right threads as well as the right moves.

Wasn't this the whole point of *Saturday Night Fever*, in which Revolta-as-Tony-Danza danced his way into everyone's hearts? Based on a fictional story by the writer Nik Cohn that first appeared in *New York* magazine, the film version of *Saturday Night Fever* was the single event that blew Disco out of proportion. It was also the beginning of the soundtrack album syndrome that became so big in the '80s, when the record industry figured out that they could milk the success of popular movies by giving them all-star soundtracks and vice-versa.

Disco culture was about communal escapism, but the "community" only included the rich, famous, and beautiful or, at least, those who *aspired* to these things above all. The "values" taught by *Saturday Night Fever* presented a side of society that people had previously been ashamed of: tackiness, glitz, superficiality, vanity, greed, gaudiness, and immorality. But in their ever-fattening and supine position, most Americans embraced these flaws as an excuse to let their guards down even further—that is, to fail to exercise any self-discipline over their more wanton tendencies. We were proceeding into what Hunter S. Thompson would later term "a generation of swine."

In music, the demand for product was increasingly coming from the dance floor. A record like Gwen McCrae's "Rockin' Chair" could be an enormous hit in the discos before it spread to the charts. As discos became more widespread, so did prefabricated dance crazes like "The Hustle," which an R&B hack named Van McCoy rode to national prominence. That kind of fleeting appeal created a multitude of one-hit wonders. It was like the '50s again: you're only as good as your last record. Disco was soon overrun with silly novelty records like "Disco Duck." It was a genre ripe for exploitation.

No one understood this more than Neil Bogart. In the '60s, he'd been the key puncher behind the Disco of its day, "bubblegum Rock." Like Disco, bubblegum was primarily created by studio musicians, and its "artists" were more or less interchangeable. Founding Casablanca with his wife in 1973, Bogart had lucked upon a knockout act with Kiss, the most popular and instantly recognizable group of its day. This helped build the empire. The basic thrust from the start was a fantasia-like play world where anything was possible, a multipurpose Magic Kingdom of hits and hype. *All* of Casablanca's acts were outrageous, from Kiss to Parliament-Funkadelic. Given to nepotism, Bogart operated the label like an extended family, throwing lavish parties and paying exorbitant wages in an effort to match the grandeur of the film from which the label took its name. This was Hollywood, '70s-style, with employees snorting coke off of glass-topped tables and executive decisions made by dart board. It couldn't last, of course.

In their heyday, Casablanca launched two of the ultimate manufactured Disco acts: Donna Summer and the Village People. Summer was important because she was the first artist to be specifically pegged as Disco and to supposedly do "creative" things within the format. Her "Love to Love You Baby" had taken up a whole side of an LP. Subsequent albums like *Once Upon a Time* were suitelike "concept" albums with *Sgt. Pepper* pretensions. She was also the first Disco artist to be accepted by the critics, who were desperate to prove to themselves that this was the '60s again with their whole Disco-equals-Motown rationale. "Aw gee, it's not really *that* bad," went the refrain from the aging Boomers. Summer's "I Feel Love," from late '77, with Moroder's whirl-o-matic production, was a likely prototype for Blondie's heavily acclaimed Rock/Disco fusion "Heart of Glass" a year later. But at that time, the two camps couldn't have been farther apart.

No one proved this more than Casablanca's other major act, the Village People, who were the very antithesis of "serious." Or were they? More than anyone, the VP brought Disco's underlying gay subculture into the mainstream. They were an interracial act as well, and their smash hits like "YMCA" were bubblegum in the truest sense: even if the eight-year-olds didn't understand the blatantly gay connotations, they could sing along. Bogart understood this. He also understood the cultural need for gay kitsch.

Like Malcolm McLaren with the Sex Pistols, the purveyors of Disco culture realized the vivid appeal of the fetish. Not only did Disco bolster the rise of gay chic, but S&M chic as well. In the West Village, there were already S&M clubs where bizarre tastes could be satisfied. Barry White's moaning and groaning had been a harbinger of Disco in that it was an attempt to not only adultrify Pop music, but to porno-ize it as well: those little moaning epics were soft-core sleaze. With the rise of Disco culture, Pop turned more pornographic in general, from Donna Summer to Madonna. For some reason, a lot of this took the form of bondage-type afflictions.

One thing about S&M is that it's a powerful *image*—the psychological yin/yang of dominance/submission lurks somewhere in everybody's subconscious. The print media had been exploiting this since Robert Harrison's *Confidential* in the '50s. The first Pop hit to exploit the power of the fetish was Nancy Sinatra's "These Boots are Made for Walkin'," a kinky song if ever there was one, hence its being rerecorded by hundreds of Punk groups.

The group who really advanced fetishism as an art form was a gritty R&B unit from the Midwest, the Ohio Players. Recording for the local Westbound label à la P-Funk, they became famous for a string of album covers on which the images were much closer to Mapplethorpe than Hipgnosis. One of them, entitled *Climax*, featured a woman plunging a long dagger into the back of her lover, producing little droplets of blood that actually looked like raspberries (a not-so-subtle parody of the snuff-film genre that was flourishing). Other covers featured group sex and tricks with fruit.

All this kinky stuff wasn't really raising anyone's ire when it was Black-on-Black. But when the *Stones* did it, that was a different story! The Stones had been taking a nod from Black tastes and trends for years, but their essential kinkiness came from within. The promo for their 1976 album *Black & Blue* showed a girl savagely bound with rope and covered with bruises under the heading: "I'm Black and blue...and I love it!" The billboard ran on Hollywood

Boulevard before groups of angry feminists demanded its removal. The Stones once again reaped the benefits of the negative publicity.

Outlandish publicity-mongering was rampant in the mid-'70s: just witness Grace Jones, a Black ingenue who was the diva of the downtown Disco set for a season with her futuristic space-dominatrix persona. There were also brazen Black women like Millie Jackson, who said "fuck" on her records; or Betty Davis, who sang, "He was a big freak/I used to beat him with a chain." The most notorious kinky queen of Disco was Amanda Lear, who for years perpetuated the myth that she was actually a *man* until she put out an album in 1978 called *Sweet Revenge*, featuring a nude picture of her. Her ruse fully exposed, she lamented to *Creem*'s Jeffrey Morgan: "Take all my clothes off in magazines— that's *wrong*. Because...people don't *want* that from me. They do not want to be confronted with a close-up of my pussy. They want to *dream*. Amanda Lear is a fantasy for these people..."[2]

There was an aura of fantasy to the whole Disco experience that matched the futuristic escapism of *Star Wars*, which was a big hit at precisely the same time. Both the disco and the spaceship promised the same thing: a flight from reality to a place where time ceased and *motion* was everything. At the Disco— particularly in New York—the dancing never stopped. The Magic Kingdom of the Disco universe was Studio 54, the trendy downtown disco owned by Steve Rubell. Here the cognoscenti snorted its collective nose. The club was so trendy that, at its peak, there wasn't only a line around the block, but a two-month *waiting list*! Of course, celebrities like Andy Warhol never waited, but that was all part of the Disco mentality: elitism and snub-you. The doormen at Studio 54 took great pride in the number of people they turned away nightly.

This sort of elitism infuriated the populist-Rock types, particularly the typical blue-collar Hard-Rock muttonheads. Oafish hippie types had been getting a break for years, but now the Disco boys were coming on slick, sleek, and strong—and getting the girls! As the Sweet, a glam-band from England, lamented ca. '79: "The only way to get in the girls' pants/Is to dance." The Who, using one of Pete Townshend's typically "brilliant" metaphors, sang "goodbye sister Disco" as if their grand dismissal would shake it off for good— boy, were they wrong! Bob Seger belched "don't try n' take me to a *disco*" as if his indignation was a great political act. To the pot-smoking masses of the mid-'70s, that's about as "active" as it got. It *was* political for a while—Disco put

SONIC COOL: THE LIFE & DEATH OF ROCK 'N' ROLL

musicians out of work. Therefore the populist Rock hordes were dead set against it, a fact epitomized by the infamous "Disco bonfire" in Chicago's Comiskey Park during a White Sox–Tigers game in the summer of 1979. Rock fans were up in arms, but what they didn't realize was, by then, what constituted Rock was equally constipated. Frank Zappa, always an arch social commentator, rendered a couple of appropriately scathing anti-Disco putdowns, but most anti-Disco sentiment came off like sour grapes.

At that time, the realm of popular Hard Rock consisted of bogus corporate-Rock bands with innocuous one-name monikers like Boston, Foreigner, Toto, Styx, Queen, Kansas, Triumph, and Heart. As their names imply, their music was sterile, to say the least. The first Boston album had been a phenomenon, if only because it proved that a group could become a serious commercial entity without actually having cut any chops at all. In this case, the mastermind behind the group, Tom Scholz, quietly earned his degree at MIT while recording his elaborate demo in the basement with his cohorts. After Scholz sold the tape to CBS, the subsequent album went on to become the biggest-selling debut in Rock history. Tight as a drum, Boston's sonic assemblage of ten thousand overdubbed guitars and whooshing synthesizers was the perfect formulaic backdrop to all those "good times" in the late '70s. It also established a precedent in which a "Heavy Metal" band didn't have to have any grit, balls, or stage presence—or identity. The only requirement was that the sound was dense and clean. Ironically, two years later, another group from Massachusetts, the Cars, would establish the same precedent for "New Wave."

Heavy Metal in the late '70s was in sorry shape, its thunder having been stolen by the upstart nature of Punk. At least two groups, though, were adding something new to the same tired old formula. One was ,Van Halen, a group of L.A. rich brats who upped the energy level considerably while adding a lot of show biz clichés and half-assed novelty to the mix. This helped found the basic precepts of MTV on which, through no coincidence, they became matinee idols, setting the precedent for the whole L.A. school of "hair" metal in the '80s. The other one was AC/DC, who hailed from Australia and dealt ferocious staccato blows based on the most simplistic rhythms, albeit accelerated to absurd levels of testosterone overdrive. Meanwhile, English dinosaurs like Bad Company, Led Zeppelin, and even Foghat were able to remain credible to the metal minions, even as their pulse grew weaker as the years went by.

A lot of the glory had disappeared from the Hard Rock ethic. In the '60s, rent was cheap—ten hippies could live in one "crash pad" and basically do nothing but devote their time to the lifestyle of spiritual fulfillment (sex) and self-expression (drugs, or vice-versa). In the '70s, with inflation (not to mention drug prices) on the rise, the burnouts—who were the younger, more disaffected siblings of the hippies—were forced to take some dead-end job to support their indulgences, which included expensive concert tickets to see groups like ELO and Boston. This put them on the same timetable as the "squares"—only with less education. The lines weren't quite so clearly drawn anymore. The music became more conservative. For the first time in Rock's brief history, the mainstream American teen wasn't necessarily rebelling against anything. To the contrary, teens were actually quite content with a basically apathetic existence that included smoking lots of pot and watching *Saturday Night Live* every weekend. From *Saturday Night Live* to *Saturday Night Fever*, everything centered on the weekend. In the realm of Heavy Metal, it took on an almost mythic significance, as epitomized by Boston ("Smokin'," "Party"), Ted Nugent ("Weekend Warrior"), and Loverboy ("Workin' for the Weekend").

Another interesting phenomenon was occurring in the record industry: the market was expanding in droves due to the audience's growing both younger *and* older at the same time. On the one hand, the teenybopper demographic was multiplying at an alarming rate due to all the teens and preteens discovering Rock 'n' Roll for the first time, even if it was in the form of such artifices as the Bay City Rollers, Shaun Cassidy, and Kiss. At the same time, Rock 'n' Roll had been around more than twenty years, and a whole generation had grown up with it. Although this generation was supposed to be a fleeting nova who were born to be wild and hoped they'd die before they got old, they ended up being as sentimental about their past as the World War II daddies, thus inventing Boomer culture in the '80s. The whole process of aging became an obsession with many '70s rockers: the Who, the Rolling Stones, and Bob Seger all exploited this preoccupation. These dinosaurs became fossilized by the industry because they represented long-term sales potential. As FM radio had become merely an appendage of corporate Rock itself, it readily enshrined the old farts—and ignored new and unproven music unless it was something formulaic like Boston or Foreigner. The kids, meanwhile, didn't know the difference—they believed the hype and went on the attack against Punk and Disco, not seeing the real enemy within—corporate dinosaur Rock.

By the late '70s, the industry was forced to pay for this stagnation. Their failure to nurture new talent, relying on proven winners like the Stones, Bob Seger, and Fleetwood Mac to pad their sales figures, backfired. A perfect example was Peter Frampton, who'd exceeded all previous market expectations with the success of *Frampton Comes Alive*, his 1976 double live album (another syndrome-in-the-making in the increasingly parrot-like record biz). Despite the hype, when it came time for the follow-up, he wasn't able to capitalize on his cutie-pie teenybopper success. The follow-up album, *I'm In You*—to which *Creem* responded: "Call the Exorcist"—was a disappointment, not only sales-wise, but also to the fans who'd inhaled bong hit after bong hit to the flexing wah-wah pedal of *Comes Alive*, an anthem-packed jamfest to rival *Boston*.

Boston was another group that was unable to follow up its initial success. Believing his own hype, Scholz sat on the follow-up, *Don't Look Back*, for almost two years, perfecting every twizzle and turn of the knob. There was actually speculation in the press about "when's *Boston II* coming?" Such was the lack of imagination within the industry at the time that it was automatically assumed that the album was going to be called *Boston II*, following the inane syndrome set forth by Chicago. When it finally came out, it was a big letdown, mainly because it sounded almost *exactly* like its predecessor. This was the dreaded "second album syndrome": a band has their whole lives to come up with a first album, but only a few months to come up with the follow-up. This is the challenge of Rock 'n' Roll. All throughout Rock history bands had been taking this challenge and succeeding. But, in the '70s, the labels were no longer willing to nurture bands to the point at which they could progress into their inevitable "next phase" like, say, the Byrds, the Beatles, or the Rolling Stones had in the '60s. What they wanted was a repeat of a proven winner.

Another thing the record companies were doing in the late '70s was overshipping albums to retail outlets in an attempt to shore up chart positions in *Billboard*, whose charts were based on how many items were shipped as opposed to actually sold. A perfect example was the infamous *Sgt. Pepper* soundtrack album in 1978. Because of the success of *Frampton Comes Alive*, not to mention the Bee Gees' success with the *Saturday Night Fever* soundtrack, the masterminds behind each of those monstrosities—Dee Anthony in the case of

Frampers, Robert Stigwood on behalf of the Bee Gees—came up with the ulti-mate corporate co-op. They would combine the two in a movie based on the Beatles' most famous album, get bad boys Aerosmith to play the villains, and even toss in Earth, Wind, & Fire in a token attempt to sucker the R&B/Disco crowd. It was just the type of cookie-cutter focus-group mentality the record companies were beginning to incorporate. But it backfired, because the movie was a terrible bore, and *Rolling Stone* instantaneously labeled the accompanying soundtrack "worst album of the decade." The label, RSO—which had former-ly belonged to Atlantic but had recently merged with the much-less-visionary MCA—hyped the album to stores, accounting for the rapid sales figures dur-ing the first four weeks of its release. Once people read the reviews or, worse yet, saw the movie, the album just sat there. A platinum album can't be revoked once it's been awarded, but this crib death for *Sgt. Pepper* hurt the parent com-pany, because they had to refund all the advances they'd accepted from their distributors. In the trickle-down syndrome that exists in the record business, this only resulted in the further paring down of A&R, which meant that labels were now willing to spend even *less* time—and, more importantly, less money—nurturing new acts. In the long run, this would have hurt them, but then MTV came along to solve all their problems. The companies didn't need long-term "artists" anymore—just a handful of trained acrobats like Van Halen and Foreigner. This also represented the death of Hard Rock Neanderthals like Ted Nugent and Foghat when they weren't able to assimilate. *"Too animalistic,"* said the Powers That Be.

For a couple of years, the industry would smart from the recession. The soundtrack-album syndrome had proven to be an almost guaranteed formula, but the failure of *Sgt. Pepper* showed that even this supposedly failsafe method was vulnerable. The Disco glut that came on the heels of *Saturday Night Fever*, in which companies loaded the market with anonymous Disco garbage, back-fired also: other than a few name acts like the Bee Gees and Donna Summer, most Disco artists proved to have *very* little staying power. But that didn't stop the whole squishy sound of Disco from becoming part of the overall Pop fab-ric, not only on radio, but also in such insidious places as TV commercials, tel-evision, and movie themes. The whole record industry had actually become more like the ad industry than any "art form," because its sole objective had become to make money. Therefore, a record had become little more than an advertisement for the artist in question (not to mention the record company). This would become painfully obvious in the age of video. What other purpose did the medium serve than to advertise available product?

Another failure during the dying Disco season was the Bee Gees' long-awaited follow-up to the *Saturday Night Fever* soundtrack, *Spirits Having Flown*, which came out in February '79 and promptly received the Frampton treatment. Clearly this kind of indifference would hurt the industry if it continued. One solution was to consolidate. Subsequently, most of the remaining indies were bought up by the larger corporations: Motown by MCA, A&M by RCA, and Sire by Warner Brothers. This further limited whatever artistic freedom remained at these labels.

In a very telling statement, Gil Freisen, president of A&M, told Marc Eliot in *Rockonomics*:

"We went to branch distribution with RCA on February 15, 1979, and I'd have to say that it was a genius move. The timing was perfect because the record industry…went into the toilet. All the records we had out with independent distributors began to come back. We really didn't know how many we had out there; we had no specific control, no computers the way we have them today. We would ship records to Detroit, or we'd ship them to New Jersey, and they'd ship them to Florida or St. Louis, all over the place, with no exclusive territories and everything on consignment. I'd have to credit Jerry Moss with saying, enough, we don't know where our records are, and deciding to make the move to RCA, just as the industry was starting to crash…In some ways, it might have been the best thing to happen to the business…It was no longer a free-for-all expanding market. It was, going into the eighties, an industry where there was going to be tough competition for market share, with business principles that governed."[3]

What that meant was that the excesses of people like Neil Bogart were coming to an end. Even the overly pampered Rock stars were feeling the pressure of the economic squeeze—touring was cut back, and with it went the perks that had become associated with the traveling Rock 'n' Roll road show. No more jelly donuts, in other words. Regardless of how proven an act was, all tour expenses were paid off against royalties. This didn't hurt the real Rock dinosaurs like the Stones or Led Zeppelin, but it put marginal acts like Cheap Trick and Tom Petty temporarily out of business.

Many Rock dinosaurs who felt the brunt of the corporate squeeze attempted to cash in on Disco to revive their sagging careers, even as they risked their credibility within the Rock camp by doing so. To aged faghags like the Stones, this was hardly a very risky proposition—they'd already been trashed by the Punks in their homeland of Britain, and had of course laughed all the way to the bank. For the Stones, it wasn't that drastic of a move anyway—they'd always been chiefly derivative of Black/R&B stylings, and they'd always shown a propensity for cashing in on any trend that came along, from Baroque-Rock to psychedelia to Country. Flirting with Disco as early as 1976, with "Hot Stuff," it wasn't until 1978 that they finally found the right groove with "Miss You," a record that played through that whole summer and not only put the Stones back on the map, but helped resurrect old-guy Rock in general.

Despite his hall-of-mirrors sensibilities, David Bowie was another British artist who wasn't a total impostor as far as Disco went, exploring the form as early as 1975 with *Young Americans*. By the time Disco reached its heyday, he was embroiled in his arty period with Brian Eno, producing some of the most influential work of the '70s. Other English poseurs weren't quite as calculating about their conversion to Disco—Rod Stewart, ELO, Elton John, and the Kinks all tried their hand at the big beat-off. Roxy Music's attempt at Disco, *Manifesto*, was also passable, if only because the elite trappings of the form fit leader Bryan Ferry's aristocratic sensibilities perfectly. It got a little ridiculous, though, when even *Kiss* had a Disco hit!

The New York Punk group Blondie pulled off the most significant Rock-Disco fusion of the era. Their first album was a brilliant pastiche of '60s girl group foxiness and Punk cynicism, but from the very beginning the band had their eyes on mass acceptance. This success was basically assured through the playful sexploitation of their lead singer, Deborah Harry, whose platinum pout, laced with irony, carried with it as many mixed messages as the band's oddly-retro-yet-still-hip music. Already featured on the cover of every underground journal in America, from *The New York Rocker* and *Punk to High Times* and *Interview*, Deborah Harry just needed a hit to cross over into the mainstream. In 1978 a song from Blondie's *Parallel Lines* album called "Heart of Glass" achieved this crossover, and for good reason: the song was pure Disco.

When accused of being a sellout, Chris Stein, Harry's partner and the de facto leader of Blondie, had an interesting take on the situation: "I think the anti-Disco movement is a bunch of bullshit with very heavy racist overtones. And if you remember correctly, back in the late '60s, all the great Black music people now accept as the best...was considered sort of the same way...People saying it's just background, but Procul Harum is...*really* happening."[4]

Stein had a point—by understanding that Disco was now a thoroughly ingrained phenomenon that wasn't going to go away, he shored up his band's street credibility at a time when almost all of their New York peers were being ignored anywhere outside the underground. For better or worse, Blondie's notions were correct: a great deal of the post-Punk that emerged in the years to follow was Disco-influenced, from Killing Joke to Big Black.

In the late '70s, enthusiasm for typical Hard Rock had run dry. The last stab for guitar-driven Rock in the '70s was the endless parade of redneck rockers who constituted "southern boogie": Lynyrd Skynyrd, the Outlaws, Blackfoot, the Rossington Collins Band, the Marshall Tucker Band, the Charlie Daniels Band, and Molly Hatchet. Keyboard-embellished schlock-Rock of the type practiced by Boston, Foreigner, Journey, Styx, Kansas, Loverboy, REO Speedwagon, and Toto reigned supreme.

Despite this complacency, there were a few bright signs on the horizon. Considering the cultural state of affairs, it's actually no surprise that an alternative was brewing. To discover what that was, we must once again turn our attention to New York.

CHAPTER 13

ƎPUNK

PUNK WAS A REACTION AGAINST THREE THINGS:

- The pompous airs of the Rock Messiahs

- The corporate sterility and predictability that was making the music stale and turning its idols into brittle old farts

- The liberal agenda of the Rock Aristocracy

Punk as a musical form evolved almost unequivocally out of the embers of two original and, for the most part, unheralded '60s bands: the Velvet Underground and the Stooges. The two, in fact, were semirelated: Danny Fields was an intimate of the Velvets who managed the Stooges; John Cale, a member of the Velvets on the first two albums, produced the first Stooges album; and Nico, another VU alum, was Iggy's first superstar girlfriend. What these two groups constituted wasn't so much a conscious epistemology like the hippies— it was more a cultists' fixation, an almost intellectual fascination with primitivism. At the time, the *popular* Rock music (*Abbey Road*, CSN&Y, Led Zeppelin) was becoming more ornate. The urgent primal need for scraping noise was not being satisfied except by a handful of groups. But these groups would spawn the future, because in their rejection of the gloss they were letting their basic musical instincts run wild. This is the only way a legitimate Rock movement can grow—by accident.

Punks were buttheads—they butted their heads against the cultural elite: the big-name critics and record companies. They weren't commercial.

When the Stooges were launched, they were probably expected to *sell*. That's what Elektra had in mind when they marketed them as a riot-inducing teen nightmare. But that's not what the group saw themselves as. They considered themselves creative geniuses—they definitely had musical progress in mind, hence the startling difference between albums one and two. Unfortunately, this equaled failure in the increasingly conservative eyes of the industry, so, like most bands of their ilk (including the earlier prototype Velvets), they got the shaft.

Rock had reached the crossroads where popularity and creativity would separate as they had in Jazz during the previous decade. But it was more complex than that—Jazz had never really been absorbed into the mainstream, at least not since the Big Bands. It was *Black* and thus feared by the power brokers who controlled what constituted popular music. Rock consciousness, on the other hand—even if it was the '50s surfboard/hamburger stand/drive-in variety—was absorbed. Rock became synonymous with the major cultural movement of the times. The first generation of Rock—the Baby Boomers—had evolved together by sharing many of the same social trappings (dope and long hair being the longest-lasting). Subsequently, these things took a long time to overturn.

The early '70s Punk or underground bands were a lot closer in spirit to Jerry Lee Lewis or the Hamburg-era Beatles than they were to Led Zeppelin. This all had to do with the Back to the Roots Revival (see chapter nine). In the late '60s, a lot of folks felt that Rock had grown too grandiose (*Sgt. Pepper*). But it only seemed that way if you'd been following all along. To the kids growing up with Led Zeppelin who'd never known anything before that, it was a moot point. Rock was reaching into its Third Generation and had become part of a much larger industry—there was no longer much conscious consideration of "roots" by its practitioners and consumers. The heavy arena-Rock band had forever obliterated the kind of intimate audience/performer interaction that once existed. Nevertheless, many musicians sought to return Rock to this grassroots level.

The audience they attracted consisted of cultists—reverential nerds who spent their whole lives trying to validate their obscure tastes. But their reverence wasn't based on a move-backwards philosophy—they applauded the latest high-tech fad gadgets, and their attitude was decidedly Third Generation (the generation who'd stopped caring about the bomb). What they wanted to preserve was the more subterranean aspects of Rock 'n' Roll, which, like avant-garde cinema, had developed a cult following, particularly in Europe, where a mystique had formed around failed American bands like the Stooges and Flamin' Groovies.

The term *Punk* was originally coined by collector types and critics to describe any loud, greasy band with attitude: from garage-Rock pioneers like the Standells and Chocolate Watch Band to protometalloids like Dust and Black Sabbath. They were making it up as they went along, like the catalysts of any historical movement. In the glut of the Rock revolution, hundreds of obscure records were languishing in the department store forty-nine-cent bin. And because these records epitomized a moment in time that obviously wasn't coming back—in this case, the mid-'60s—they became collector's items, much like Rockabilly records had a few years earlier.

Until that time all of this crassness had been left out of Rock history because the few scholars who'd bothered to chronicle it subscribed to the hippie doctrine, which pooh-poohed such animalistic proceedings. Their big man was Pete Seeger, not Ersel Hickey. As with any countermovement, an alternative press arose: journals like Greg Shaw's *Who Put the Bomp* went to great lengths to refute the heretofore chosen "truths" about Rock music, even if that meant publishing something like Lester Bangs's raving ten-thousand-word appreciation of the Troggs. These were the first "fanzines," and they can now be seen as a logical extension of the underground press in the '60s (which *Rolling Stone* was never really part of).

Rock culture had become a culture of its own, eclipsing mainstream culture in the minds of its faithful. The real dope fiends and record collectors simply didn't care about politics. The '70s were all about apathy. Bored middle class kids with nothing better to do became record collectors and read Rock magazines like *Creem*. They also, consequently, picked up guitars and formed bands.

The term *Punk* first found its application in *Creem* and *Who Put the Bomp*. The critics who helped popularize the term—Bangs, Dave Marsh, Mike Saunders—applied it not out of any perversion but because they really believed the artists they were applying it to, from Paul Revere & the Raiders to Black

Sabbath, were just that: punks, or more aptly, hoodlums (e.g., the Stooges). The rebellious nature of Rock had never left, but adultrified rockers like Crosby, Stills, & Nash were making it more refined. It was the lack of glorious teenage angst that the critics were lamenting. Therefore, *any* scrunge-Rock at that time—be it the Raspberries or Alice Cooper—seemed a testament to this missing primal element.

The real seedlings of Punk as a movement stem back to Glam-Rock. Not so much musically, but image-wise, David Bowie represented a new dawn of both pretense and media manipulation. His flirtations with shock-theater were camp to the farthest extreme—something the punks duly took note of. His whole persona was gloriously amoral, as was Lou Reed's (Bob Dylan in a dress). Meanwhile, glam bands like Mott the Hoople, Slade, and the Sweet were a high-energy antidote to the slow snooze of either Pink Floyd or the Grateful Dead. They would definitely influence the first-generation punk bands.

Decadence came naturally to the bands who were born in New York City in the early- to mid-'70s: Blue Oyster Cult, the New York Dolls, Kiss, Ruby & the Rednecks, the Magic Tramps, Suicide, the Ramones, Television, the Stilettos, Blondie, the Patti Smith Group, the Dictators, the Marbles, Teenage Lust, Tuff Darts, the Shirts, and the Heartbreakers among them. Stylistically these bands varied, but the one thing linking them together was attitude—they all shared a post-post-everything demeanor. They had spiritually—and in almost every other sense—*decayed*. At the time, Max's was still the nexus for this kind of posture, but soon new venues would emerge, including the Mercer Arts Center and CBGB's.

The last has somewhat rightfully been acknowledged as the birthplace of Punk and has taken its place alongside the Cavern Club in the annals of Rock landmarks. Located right smack in the Bowery, the club was originally a non-Rock joint (CBGB's stood for "Country, Blue Grass, and Blues"). However, in 1974, a young guitarist from New Jersey named Tom Verlaine convinced owner Hilly Kristal to let his—Verlaine's—band play there on Sunday nights. Named Television, the group specialized in long, torturous guitar duels between Verlaine and guitarist Richard Lloyd. Learning to play in public wasn't always easy, but it was the only way a band earned their chops, and Television were just one of many groups who'd find the stage at CB's to be their nurturing ground. It was a tough audience made up of drunks, flops, junkies, and slumming art-literary dropouts. In other words, jaded hipsters who were mad at the world. But Kristel must have been impressed—if not wholly satisfied—because he soon switched to live Rock altogether.

At the time this scene was so far removed from the mainstream Rock industry that it was free from the corruptive influence of record company money that had soured so many scenes in the past. It was a collaborative, self-supportive outpost that revolved around, basically, the same thirty people. Taking place in New York, however, it was bound to catch the attention of a lot of influential media sources.

After the bath Mercury took signing the New York Dolls, the major labels were wary of New York underground bands. That didn't stop Terry Ork's little private, eponymous label from releasing the first recorded works of Television and Patti Smith. The early indie labels were founded on the same do-it-yourself spirit as the fanzines. It was kind of like when R&B emerged in the '40s and '50s; it was all released on independent labels to compete with the dreck the majors were serving up. The difference was, the denizens of the new underground (read: Punk) realized that, at this point, there was *no* chance that anything they did was ever gonna be popular. That gave the whole thing an ironic edge: Pop as an unpopular form.

The first of the CBGB's artists to record was Patti Smith, a twentysomething songstress from Jersey who'd written for *Rolling Stone*, published reams of poetry, and generally been active on the "scene" a long time. Smith was a chronicler of a whole new kind of postelectric tradition: dope, Rock 'n' Roll, comics, beat poetry (one of her pieces was entitled "High on Rebellion"; another, "Rape"). She was just as apt to drop a reference to Rimbaud or Baudelaire as she was to drop one to Jim Morrison or Bob Dylan: the neobeatnik scene tied the auteurs of the past with the electric troubadours of Rock. This movement also included downtown denizens Richard Hell and Tom Verlaine. They certainly weren't just plain old rockers. They saw themselves as intellectuals, but not in a smarmy collegiate way (most of 'em were dropouts). Call them new urban realists: they'd absorbed the streetwise ethos personified by everyone from Charles Bukowski to Lou Reed (not to mention the Jazz hipsters). They were building a new legacy, one that would ultimately make Rock more intellectual than ever. Which would only further alienate the mainstream audience.

Patti Smith's first release, on the microdot Mer label, told the story. The title alone, "Piss Factory," guaranteed that it would never penetrate the mainstream. Like ESP-Disk in the mid-'60s, this was urban music with little hope of branching out into the general marketplace. The song was a maddening mosaic featuring jazzy guitar (courtesy of Rock critic Lenny Kaye) and a somber piano riff (played by Richard Sohl). The lyrics told the tale of an urban nightmare comparable to *Last Exit to Brooklyn*. Smith's delivery was a kind of foul-mouthed street-smart staccato, all phrased on the downbeat. It was effective stuff, and it garnered great reviews in magazines like *Creem* and *Rock Scene*—magazines that Smith, not coincidentally, sometimes wrote for.

At that time, Clive Davis had left Columbia to start his own label, Arista, which had successfully cashed in with the likes of Barry Manilow and the Bay City Rollers. Davis apparently thought the New York underground was going to be the Next Big Thing and signed Lou Reed and Patti Smith to the label in 1975. For Smith, the result was *Horses*, which actually made number fifty-five on the charts, which was an estimable position for an album that was a volatile mix of beat poetry, the Ronettes, Reggae, and the Velvet Underground. The fact that John Cale produced really drove the Velvets thing home, tying the album in with a proto-Punk family tree that included Nico, the Stooges, and the Modern Lovers.

That year, Patti Smith was overshadowed by another product of New Jersey who preached the urban ethos: Bruce Springsteen. She'd have to wait three more years to achieve her commercial breakthrough and, when she did, it was not coincidentally in tandem with Springsteen, who cowrote her big Top Forty hit "Because the Night," which took her out of the CBGB's milieu once and for all.

Back on the Bowery, the club was just beginning to receive its first burst of media attention, and soon other bands would make their first stabs at recording. Tom Verlaine had played on *Horses*, and Television had released their first single, "Little Johnny Jewel," on the Ork label in 1975. Reviews in the underground press and eventually the *New York Times* landed the group a deal with Elektra. But the album took two years to complete, and by then other bands had beaten them to the punch (like the Ramones, for instance). When *Marquee Moon* was released in 1977, it revealed Television as by far the most accomplished musicians in the scene, but by then the definition of Punk had been subject to so much wrangling debate that no one knew anymore whether that was a plus or minus.

Another vital participant in the scene's evolution was Verlaine's boarding school buddy from Tennessee, Richie Myers—soon to be rechristened Richard Hell. Often credited with inventing the *visual* style of Punk—short, spiky hair; leather jacket; cheap sunglasses; ripped t-shirts (all of which was appropriated by the Brits)—Hell was the original bass player/singer in Television, but apparently two such massive egos as his and Verlaine's couldn't be contained within one group for long. Verlaine told *Creem* in 1977: "I haven't spoken to him (Hell) in a year. Every time I read something he's so mad at me. And I'm so tired of him." [1]

From there, Hell joined up with Johnny Thunders and Jerry Nolan, newly departed from the New York Dolls, to form the original Heartbreakers. Once again, Hell's unique persona seemed to create friction with his bandmates. According to Nolan: "Richard Hell is the most boring person I ever met. He never laughs…never smiles…talks about himself all the time. I mean, that's all I heard—about him! How fuckin' boring can you get?" [2]

The only solution was for Hell to form his own unit, which he did in 1976 with the VoidOids. During this time he wrote the Punk anthem, "Blank Generation." By declaring "I was sayin' let me out of here before I was even *born*," he was expressing a kind of nihilism that helped distance the new urban realists from the hippie utopians. The punks' enthrallment with '50s cultural chic like funny shades and leather jackets further emphasized their rejection of hippie trappings. But this wasn't nostalgia of the Sha Na Na variety—it was shock treatment. For instance, in the case of the leather, the punks understood the sado-masochistic imagery as well (which most of the '50s "greasers" probably didn't).

Punk was shock-Rock, but its inventors realized that Rock itself had become so insular that the whole mom & pop culture it had set out to dispel was now insignificant. Rock's self-fulfilling prophecy was a fait accompli, in other words. Now it was the Rock culture that needed puncturing. Punk was a rebellion against Rock culture more than it was against mainstream culture.

Like disco, Punk was a very '70s thing: they'd seen the fall of Nixon, the failure of war, and now a souring economy. New York City itself was bankrupt. Clearly there was a mandate to live for the moment, whether that was dancing the night away or indulging in the most self-destructive behavior possible.

Love was another concept that was expelled from the shaggy carcass of Rock n' Roll during Punk's implosion. Love songs had been part of the whole process ever since Rock n' Roll became pop in the '50s. But in the cynical '70s, the concept of belief in *anything*, or of sincerity of any kind, was instantly circumspect. It wasn't just the Punks—everyone from Kiss to Steely Dan was declaring the Death of Love. But Punk was even more savage in its decimation of the romantic urge—artists like Richard Hell and, later, the Sex Pistols made any offering of physical or emotional love seem like an exercise in humiliation. To believe, *really believe*, in anything, with no irony behind the façade, was looked upon as the new squaredom. This is the aspect of Punk that would have the longest-lasting cultural implications.

The alternative to Love was, of course, Hate, and Punk was hate-Rock pure and simple. Of course that meant, to a certain segment of the Rock audience, that it was music they'd been waiting to hear their whole lives. That's why it seemed so exciting in 1976: the culture seemed flaccid, the audience gullible and utterly passive. Punks reacted by embracing all those things that were alien to the mainstream culture—from S&M to mass murderers. It had nothing to do with morals—they were considered outdated. The whole concept of "sincerity" had become an anachronism. This was a TV culture that grew up on spoon-fed reality—impact was far more important than "content."

This is what led so many less-than-perfect musicians to go onstage falling all over each other and emitting pure squall. The idea of formal musicianship was as outmoded as "formal" anything—street ethos was what counted. When they threw bottles at you, you wouldn't run and hide. Bands like the Stooges, MC5, and the New York Dolls had taken a real beating from the record industry. By the time Punk happened, bands said fuck the industry altogether. In the beginning, it really was a street phenomenon.

That would change, of course, but at the time, as long as a self-supportive scene existed, its denizens didn't really care about outside involvement. This was evident in the creation of the scene's first "fanzine," *Punk*, founded by two Connecticut transplants, John Holmstrom and Legs McNeil in 1975. Here was a magazine about the "culture" that centered at CBGB's, where Holmstrom and McNeil hung out every night, becoming scene luminaries in their own right. They got Lester Bangs to write for their 'zine, and the name *Punk* helped give the scene identity. Meanwhile, the content personified the new indifference—like *Mad* and *Creem* before them, they made fun of everything. *Punk* was also the first mag to highlight the new visual-art style of Punk in the hideously deformed cartoon images drawn by Holmstrom, who eventually went on to do a couple of Ramones album covers. It was *Punk*'s singlemindedness in fostering the myth that a "scene" actually existed that may have first led the majors to the back door of CBGB's.

Punks never claimed to have "purity"—they simply refused to play by the rules. Greed and money were OK, but not *success*, per se: there had to always be that disclaimer, that self-imposed double negative, that irony—the name *punk* in a sense meant *failure*, after all.

In the mid to late '70s, the major labels consolidated, creating, basically, three empires: CBS, Warner/Atlantic, and Polygram. These three majors were made up of a half dozen subsidiary labels apiece, smaller labels that had been bought out by these conglomerates and now operated as a wing of the parent organization. In many cases, these subsidiaries were allowed to operate as if they were de facto independent labels. One such label was Sire, which was owned by Warner Bros. In the early '70s, the label was a wayward wing of London Records, reserved for eccentric British psych-folk and Prog acts. London itself was devoured in the Big Takeover—what was left of Sire's roster was salvaged, but that wasn't much. At that time, their two most popular acts were Renaissance, an obscure British Folk group, and Focus, a pretentious Dutch band. The label wasn't exactly prospering, in other words.

In 1976, Warner's hired a young executive from New York named Seymour Stein to head the label. Initially Stein aimed at the burgeoning oldies market with innovative and well-done repackages emphasizing the rawer side of '60s Rock: Troggs, Pretty Things, *History of British Rock*, *History of British Blues*, as well as a reissue of Lenny Kaye's original *Nuggets* album. He was no fool, in other words—he had an eye and ear for the obscure and primeval. Living in New York, he couldn't have helped but catch a whiff of what was going on in the Bowery. Anyone with an intellectual link to Rock's past would have been interested.

In that case, the Ramones arrived at the perfect time. Like Larry Bird with the Celtics, they basically saved the franchise—in this case, Sire. Friends from high school and the same neighborhood, they'd originally formed a band together in 1974, writing their own simplistic songs because, supposedly, they couldn't play anything else. But it was a double-edged sword, because no one could play what the Ramones played either. It was always tongue-in-cheek—

they were never as "dumb" as they seemed. Where the "Ramone" identity came about is anybody's guess. It must have occurred sometime prior to their first gig at CBGB's in November '74, because that's what they were calling themselves then.

Crowds at first were shocked by the simplistic brutality of their sound and appearance: accentuated by counts of "1-2-3-4" from guitarist Johnny, the Ramones hammered out twenty tunes in ten minutes, each one at a faster tempo than the last, each one revolving around sometimes only a simple phrase. What they lacked in musical proficiency they made up for with speed. Wearing ripped jeans, t-shirts, and leather jackets, the group's appearance was basic to the point of startling. It was a look everyone in New York had seen before on thousands of white middle class mid-'70s burnouts—but turned into a stage uniform, it was almost frightening, like something out of *Night of the Living Dead*. The subject matter of the songs, although equally basic, was just as unnerving, from Nazis to woman-beating to murder. But the songs sure were catchy!

How much the Ramones realized the polarizing effect they would have on the Rock audience has been subject to debate for years. They always claimed to be four kids from Forest Hills inspired by the primary Heavy Metal groups of the day. Black Sabbath was an obvious influence in the arched chord structure as well as the distortion level and the way guitarist Johnny made those chords resonate in the air. But where the metal brigade was getting further and further into ten-minute opuses and the like, the Ramones were closer structurally to the previous generation of bands (Beatles, etc.): short, concise, tuneful with proper choruses and breaks and no excessive soloing. That the subject matter happened to be about sniffing glue or just plain boredom was the ironic factor that other less-lethal Rock revivalists, from the Rubinoos to the Bay City Rollers, had missed.

There is a kind of Jewish humor that has run through show business and the media ever since the '50s, from *Mad* magazine to Lenny Bruce to Mel Brooks: it's a kind of sick poke at the freaks and invalids and a celebration of the truly weird. The Jews felt they'd suffered enough in World War II to earn the right to laugh at everything. So "sick" humor dared dwell in areas that traditional comedy wouldn't: mainly in all the grotesquerie and deformity and all the sick, perverse, but plainly obvious, parts of everyday life. The Ramones were the Rock n' Roll equivalent of this comedic tradition.

But here we must backtrack—there was a group over in the Bronx emerging at approximately the same time that received far less credit in the long run: the Dictators. Also Jews, their name alone shows how determined the new super-bright mensch was to disavow the sad-eyed legacy of the Holocaust: fascists, Nazis, murder…it was *funny* now (much to the horror of their parents). The kids understood the irony of these images and exploited them. In the media culture they'd been born into, Hitler was as much of a caricature as Marilyn Monroe or Elvis Presley. An *image*, that's all. Suddenly, existence itself—feeling, caring, all that—seemed supplemental to the Big Buzz. Life had—how does one say it?—lost its *meaning*.

The Dictators were an ad absurdum cartoon equal to the Ramones, and they carried out their assault with aplomb aplenty—a few of their tricks were even copped by the Rama Boys, such as the "let's gos" of "Master Race Rock" and the idea of covering "California Sun." If anything, the Ramones were the more stripped-down version—the Dictators, who got to vinyl first, in 1975, were caught somewhere between Heavy Metal and Punk. But even then, their "metal" was more of the Stooges *Raw Power* variety than it was Deep Purple. In any event, the great billowing pyrotechnics of axeman Ross "the Boss" Funicello would've sounded absurd on a Ramones album. Dictators leader Andy Shernoff, another Rock critic, was perhaps the most astute profiler–chronicler of the mid-'70s cultural malaise *ever*: TV equaled success, drugs and sex equaled recreation, and nothing was sacred, right down to taking a shit. "Don't forget to wipe your ass!" Shernoff bellowed at the end of "Master Race Rock," the band's magnum opus. In a mad stab at lowbrow culture, partially inspired by the band's buddy Richard Meltzer, the 'Tators effectively brought the aesthetic of *Championship Wrestling* to the Rock forum.

Despite the fact that their visionary antics were a great influence on a lot of important bands—the Angry Samoans, Meatmen, Minor Threat, AntiSeen, Band 19—the Dictators were not well-received, least of all by the mainstream critics. A perfect example was Dave Marsh, who shuddered in fear over what he perceived as the 'Tators' assault on all human decency. Despite having once been a hippie, he sounded like his aging hag-grandbag now: "A new low—Rock songs about wrestling and contempt, not just for the music and the audience, but even for themselves." [3]

When the Dictators and Ramones arrived, there was very little legitimate *Rock*, let alone Punk Rock, on the horizon. This was perhaps the driest period in Rock history, with *nothing* happening on the grassroots level. It wasn't like it is now, when there are a thousand bands and a couple dozen clubs in every major city so that even the most inept bands can get a *taste* of the Rock n' Roll experience. In the mid-'70s, Rock had become the domain of the record companies and FM radio stations—and they fought hard to uphold their dominance against the threat that the Punk groups represented. That's why Punk encountered such tremendous resistance at first. Only after the labels sensed that there might be some marketable "gimmick" did they began sniffing around CBGB's with anything resembling enthusiasm.

Seymour Stein, on the other hand, had actually gone down and hung out at CBGB's, so he had a more realistic idea what was really going on. His first signing was the Ramones; in the ensuing months, he'd go on to sign Richard Hell & the VoidOids, the Dead Boys, and the Talking Heads. When *Ramones* was released in May 1976, the band was perceived by most outside of the city as ultimately another '50s nostalgia act like Sha Na Na (as epitomized by the haircuts, leather jackets, and other retro tendencies). It took a few months for the momentum to grow. Meanwhile, the number of bands playing at CBGB's had swelled to such proportions that, before long, there were new ones playing every night, and even some out-of-town ones. The club had initiated the Punk gigs in 1974 as a Sunday night exception to the house rule. Two years later, the club offered nothing *but* original Rock—no Blues or Bluegrass.

The Ramones' first album split the history of Rock in half, serving as the blueprint for almost all subsequent New Model bands—the emphasis was on *songs* as opposed to jams. In many ways the group's methodology was startlingly similar to the Beatles: four-men-with-funny-haircuts-in-matching-suits-playing-seven-songs-per-side-in-two-minute-bursts-of-energy. They were a conceptual package, masterminded by their manager Danny Fields and their photographer/road manager Arturo Vega. They were *not* just another Rock band. Their arrival was immediately hailed as a major breakthrough.

Unlike the Beatles, their appeal wasn't universal, however. Many people recoiled at the sight of these four ragamuffins from Queens. Radio, for one, was in total fear, and airplay equaled zero. Without radio, there was no way to make the big money. Bands like the Ramones barely survived without having to hold day jobs; a few years later, a reasonable percentage of "important" bands—Yo La Tengo and others of their ilk—had to cop the copy shop jobs just to remain above the poverty line. We were entering the age when anyone doing *anything* creative in the name of Rock 'n' Roll existed within the membrane of the underground, because mainstream Rock had become just another wing of the entertainment industry.

Those who heard the Ramones' first album knew instantly that it was a historic turning point. How often does one hear a truly *original* sound? It usually happens once per generation: Charlie Parker, Elvis Presley, the Beatles, NWA. The Ramones laid that same vital stake in the heart of the '70s. Dead in the middle of the doldrums, they arrived with their mercurial brand of inspired idiocy. A whole generation jumped up and down in place.

In the ensuing years, speed would become such a vital factor that "Blitzkrieg Bop" almost sounds slow nowadays. But when one first heard the Ramones, the most immediate factor was the tempo—the guitars were so muted by distortion that it sounded as if whole lines were being played with a mere strum. It was ceaseless rhythm, and it was extremely powerful. Then there were the lyrics, mere slogans really: "Beat on the Brat," "I Don't Wanna Walk around with You," "I Don't Want to Go Down to the Basement." All negative, which is precisely what a lot of people were feeling at the time. Unlike the Dictators, who asserted "gasoline shortage won't stop me now," the Ramones were totally resigned to losing, to the point of stupefied indifference. But they rendered it so powerfully that they made it sound attractive.

The Ramones might have absorbed the distorto-guitar mainframe of the Who/Black Sabbath/Alice Cooper, but what they didn't absorb—and aimed to obliterate—was the ponderous heavy-handedness. Utilizing such long-discarded pop stylings as "yeah yeah yeah," their music was a rejection of all the pretensions that had come in the wake of the British bands and the hippies. Mick Jagger had once sung "I can't get no satisfaction," and when he finally got satisfaction, the kids kind of resented it. It was almost as if the whole point of Rock was that you're not *supposed* to be satisfied. The Ramones fulfilled this negative prophecy. Although they were from a middle class section of Queens, in those early years, they paraded around as if they'd actually come off the Bowery, like Rock's own version of the Dead End Kids.

The whole routine was strangely exhilarating. There was genuine glee and exuberance in the execution. The songs built to exciting crescendos, and the pace never lessened for one second. Emotionally, they were tough as well, which was a welcome antidote to the usual liberal posture (i.e., always complaining). The Ramones weren't exactly happy, but they weren't sad either, and their ability to turn the most meager of resources into a positive force resonated loudly. In the hands of the Ramones, Rock n' Roll became a fierce urban roar—despite the fact that they aimed it at "the kids," it was conceptually far too sophisticated for all but the most twisted gym-class dropouts.

The Ramones might have played it dumb, D-U-M-B, but they were actually very smart—their second album, *Leave Home*, featured a cover photo by Moshe Brakha, who'd done the Rolling Stones' *Black & Blue*. All over, they were being courted as media darlings even as they failed to sell records. One thing that put them ahead of the run-of-the-mill garage band was the brilliant production of Tony Bongiovi and Tom Erdelyi. a.k.a. Tommy Ramone, who was soon to drop drum duties altogether to concentrate solely on production. On *Leave Home*, the sound had grown into an immense, densely laden wallop: Super Rock!

As the Ramones' notoriety grew, they continued to persist in the charade that they were "just another Rock band," but it was evident that they were something much more sophisticated. Their simplicity was only simplistic if one thought of Rock in the conventional manner that had become the norm. To be able to actually play as fast—and as tight—as the Ramones was another thing entirely (Johnny's hands bled after every gig). In an atypically candid comment to *Rolling Stone* in 1979, Erdelyi summed up the Ramones' whole modus operandi this way: "If every untrained musician doing the best he can decides to make a record, he's *not* going to get a Ramones LP out of it." [4]

Ramones and *Leave Home* served as the Punk Rock Primer, Books I and II, for bands all over the globe, but the commercial failure of the Ramones was a sobering reality to Sire, as well as other record labels who might have taken a chance on Punk. Because of the previous two decades with their respective "pop explosions" of Presley and the Beatles, everyone expected it to be their birthright that, every ten years or so, someone would come along and shake up the industry and save Rock 'n' Roll. Everyone with even the slightest Rock aptitude knew in the '70s that Punk was it, but trying to convince record executives, not to mention radio programmers, proved not so easy. With the hippies it had started slowly, moving from "yeah yeah yeah" to "fuck you." Punks were claiming to be anti-industry right up front, and the industry, comfy as it was, was not going to concede easily. Time and again, the record companies, in cahoots with FM radio, now under the reign of the ever-tightening Lee Abrams format, would try to fabricate a "Next Big Thing" with Fleetwood Mac, Boston, Peter Frampton, the Bee Gees, Donna Summer, and other hypes. These acts would prosper for a while, but when it came to any kind of staying power, they fizzled. It wasn't the next Beatles, in other words.

Sire didn't get discouraged. To their credit, they continued to pursue Punk Rock fervently with a handful of truly inspired signings. The Talking Heads, a bunch of art school dropouts from Rhode Island, were instrumental in inaugurating New Wave, a term invented by the media to cope with the only "Punk" they could find even remotely palatable. Originally a term applied to cinema, it was a way of glossing over the undoubtedly antisocial characteristics of Punk by making it merely another form of entertainment. But that wasn't the Heads' fault. Although they were collegiate, preppy even, they never came out and said, "Hi, we're a New Wave band." All of these bands in their early days assumed they were playing good old *Rock 'n' Roll* (albeit with a definite irony).

People outside of New York, who'd read about the Talking Heads within the context of the "punk" movement, were surprised when they heard the band's debut album and discovered an above-average Pop band that, by all accounts, sounded fairly radio-friendly. It would take a couple of albums before radio dared to venture that far—*Talking Heads '77*, their first, fared little better than either of the first two Ramones albums. The "punk" tag hurt them, in other words, especially because the only thing that made them "punk" to begin with was singer David Byrne's unabashed nature when it came to things cutesy-pie. In the post-Watergate/Bicentennial era, one just wasn't supposed to take lyrics like "I feel nice inside now that it's summer again" and "I'm a lucky guy to live in my building" seriously. The suspicion was that Byrne didn't either. This built-in "ironic" disclaimer would become an important part of all post-punk stylings (i.e., R.E.M.). Meanwhile the Talking Heads laughed all the way to the bank later on when radio programmers weren't able to gauge their cynicism and took them at face value.

The Heads were the first American underground band to prominently feature keyboards (unless you count Richard Sohl's Freudian piano playing in the

Patti Smith Group). Roxy Music was a prominent influence: Byrne's vocal enunciation at times emulated the foghorn wail of Bryan Ferry, and the group's abstract use of keyboards was clearly Eno-derived (Eno repaid the compliment by becoming the Talking Heads' producer for the next several albums).

In many ways, the Talking Heads represented the revival of preppy/collegiate sensibilities before the Reagan era made that fashionable. This was reinforced not only by Byrne's upwardly mobile lyrics ("mommy daddy come and look at me now") but also by the fact that two members of the group, Tina Weymouth and Chris Frantz, were actually married to one another, reaffirming the vision of semi-domestic bliss the lyrics painted. The fact that Weymouth seemed to exist in a state of semi-equality with her band counterparts was a groundbreaking factor also: the "chick" bass player has become a mainstay of "college Rock" bands (Sonic Youth, the Pixies, Smashing Pumpkins) ever since.

Blondie featured a female lead in the person of Deborah Harry, one of the most visually arresting frontpersons any band could ever hope to "get behind" (which Debbie's boyfriend/svengali, Chris Stein, who was the group's de facto musical leader, realized). Calling the group Blondie was the ultimate post-everything irony, but Harry was no dumb blonde. A veteran of the whole Warhol scene, she'd even waitressed at Max's. Blondie's first album, released in 1976, was perhaps the all-time masterpiece of ironic Pop: the songs plunder Rock's past, from girl groups to the Beach Boys, but the sensibilities are post-Warhol hip and the presentation is *tough*. That was the reason it failed to make it on the radio.

When Blondie finally did make it two years later, it was with a Disco crossover hit called "Heart of Glass," which got 'em hailed as the vanguard of New Wave—and Deborah joined the ranks of Farrah as a pinup princess. Only with a twist—on a popular poster of the time, photographer Francesco Scavullo portrayed her as a dominatrix, clutching a whip, her eyes icy blue, cheekbones flaring. Ironically, it was Harry who was in bondage, to her bombshell image and the fickle expectations of fame. When Blondie tried to make purely commercial records later in the decade, they lost a lot of their downtown charm and succumbed to a more formulaic approach.

Like Blondie, the Modern Lovers, who hailed from Massachusetts, were also heavily Velvet Underground-influenced. Their leader, Jonathan Richman, was such an obsessive Velvets fan that he'd followed them around backstage whenever they came to Boston. For this reason, the Modern Lovers got John Cale to produce their early demos. Richman's first, independently made, single, "Road Runner," was the ultimate Velvets homage, stealing its riff from "Sister Ray." Through the Cale connection, Richman got signed to Warner's in 1972, but when they heard the resultant album, they politely declined: skeletal songs with jangling guitars and lyrics about sexual insecurity delivered in a plaintive monotone that made Bob Dylan sound like Pavarotti. To many it seemed as if Richman was the ultimate Pop ironist, but, as the years passed, bringing about all his trilling little tunes about leprechauns and the like, it became painfully obvious that he was *serious!* As for the group, one could easily make the argument that they were the prototype for New Wave, having spawned members of the penultimate New Wave aggregations, the Cars and the Talking Heads, in drummer David Robinson and keyboardist Jerry Harrison, respectively.

Alex Chilton was another oddball on the early '70s landscape whose influence wouldn't become fully recognized until Punk happened. Originally a teenage star with the Memphis band the Box Tops, Chilton had also tried his hand at drug-immersed psych-folk à la Syd Barrett, but his heart and soul were still in Pop heaven. The reason this qualifies him as Punk is because, in light of Led Zeppelin and all the rest, the anti-macho sentiments of Pop were a kind of freak-outsider stance in itself. In that case, Chilton's next experiment was a primary building block of New Wave consciousness. Called Big Star, even the name was ironic, because at that point—roughly '72—no one had any hope of being big stars performing that kind of chrome-plated Pop (marketed teen idols like the Raspberries ultimately don't count).

Due to the fact that they were from Memphis, Big Star were signed to the Stax subsidiary, Ardent, and made two brilliant albums in the early '70s: *Number One Record* (more irony) and *Radio City*. The latter contained one of the most heartbreakingly beautiful songs in the annals of Rock in the form of "September Gurls." For Chilton, having once been a teen idol and now faced with the prospect of becoming a *cult* idol, the irony rang true. So much so that he pretty much became a head case thereafter. Meanwhile, Robert Christgau, writing in the *Village Voice*, found the perfect term to describe Big Star's music: "semipopular." In that case, Big Star has impacted "semipopular" music ever since with an interloper's accuracy, and its influence on such acts as Game

Theory, R.E.M., the Replacements, Matthew Sweet, Velvet Crush, and Teenage Fanclub is unmistakable.

The renewal of "pop" sensibilities was a direct reaction against the heavy-handedness of '70s pomp deities like Yes, ELP, Pink Floyd, and Led Zeppelin, who refused to even bother with singles. Punk, on the other hand, was entirely devoted to the concept of the three-minute burst of energy that had always made up the foundation of Rock n' Roll. This would be even more evident in England, where the provincial nature of the record industry allowed many indie-Punk singles to become actual hits. With the rise of Jake Rivera's Stiff empire (Nick Lowe, et al.), "power Pop" would constitute a whole new genre in its own right. By the late '70s, the renewal of pop tastes represented not only an ironic statement, but a somewhat elitist one as well, the implication being that it took a certain kind of "cleverness" to produce or even comprehend this music. This empowerment of the nerd would blossom more fully in the next two decades, first with the "indie-Rock" revolution, and then with the computer revolution. The other influence on the rise of New Wave sensibilities was the whole "record collector" mentality—the more obscure singles there were, the more obscure singles there were to collect.

In New York, this took the form of such brilliantly self-conscious retro-Pop as the Speedies' "Let Me Take Your Photo," which poked fun at the whole Pop process while it slowly raised the stakes of just that with one of the most dynamically charged readymade "pop" opuses of all time. And the ages burned...

Although many artists were devoted to reconstructing Pop, many others were devoted to deconstructing Rock itself. This included the whole "skronk"/ "no wave" brigade: Richard Hell & the VoidOids, Teenage Jesus & the Jerks, Mars, DNA, Bloodless Pharaohs, Red Transistor, Theoretical Girls, and any aggregation fronted by James Chance. Several of the aforementioned used such traditionally non-Rock instruments as saxophone in an attempt to bridge the gap between Rock and Jazz in a manner distinctly different from the soppy fusion of Return to Forever, Herbie Hancock, etc. A lot of these artists identified with the jazzer persona, especially the allure of the junkie. Before long, actual Jazz artists like Ornette Coleman and James "Blood" Ulmer were coming down to jam with them, which led to the reality that, nowadays, the Free Jazz scene is much closer aligned with the white indie-underground than it is the mainstream Jazz industry. The involvement of these musicians also heightened the interracial quotient (although not as much as one might assume). This milieu represented the height of "no commercial potential" in modern-day ESP-Disk fashion, and as such constituted a new kind of boho-elitism (which would result in Sonic Youth) as well as a liberating new reality. Once a musician or artist is no longer aiming at the "pop" target, the possibilities become endless.

One thing's for sure—there's no way a Teenage Jesus or a DNA could've come from anywhere but New York, with its endless urban landscape and vast array of lofty late-night resources. But New York in the late '70s wasn't limited to skronk. The city was active with underground energy in a variety of mutated forms: the Stimulators, for example, offered a kind of prehardcore thrash; the Fleshtones were working in an updated neo-garage Rock vein, complete with '60s haircuts and Rickenbacker guitars; Student Teachers were a worthy premonition of later synth-pop stylings (all primarily Roxy-derived anyway). There were also the various incarnations of the Heartbreakers, Johnny Thunders' post-Dolls unit, who were Punk-ready and Rock-readymade.

All over America, in every major city, pockets of resistance were forming. If you'd grown up in the '60s, you'd come to believe good radio was a birthright, with AM's innovative mix of various cultural and class implications and FM's early progressiveness. However, by the mid-'70s, real Rock fans knew they could no longer turn to either side of the dial for musical enlightenment. Left with no alternative, many of them formed their own bands just to hear the kind of music they were craving, whether freeform or Hard Rock. They had no hunch that they were inventing the next wave. They were just doing what came naturally.

One of the most potent underground scenes emerged in Cleveland. According to historian Mike Welden, there'd always been an underground faction in the city, and residing as it does on Lake Erie, Cleveland's always been a major Midwestern media outlet. More importantly, it was a decidedly *ugly* place, skies gray from the smog of the factories that usurped the city like an iron veil. No surprise, a lot of the bands that emerged from the region echoed the clanging industrial hum of their immediate surroundings. People had said the same thing about the Stooges and MC5, who were from the industrial wasteland of the Midwest as well.

Along with their "industrial" preoccupation, the Cleveland groups drew their inspiration from the same sources as the New York no-wavers: Free Jazz, Captain Beefheart, and the Velvet Underground. Many of them also shared the poetic sensibilities of a Patti Smith or Richard Hell, and the nihilistic traits of Hawkwind, the New York Dolls, and Iggy & the Stooges. Most particularly, there was an avoidance of anything remotely "hippie"—the new aesthetic was individualistic, not group-harmonious; pro-industrial, not pro-nature; disturbing, not soothing; hate, not love.

David Thomas of the Cleveland band Pere Ubu, once told *Creem* that the band used to keep their roadies awake at night by telling them Cleveland horror stories—indeed, the industrial Midwest was like the climate out of a horror movie. It being a mill town, a redneck mentality prevailed. Whereas on the Lower East Side of New York, these kind of things were expected, people in Cleveland had no precedent for the behavior of bands like the Electric Eels, whose members would purposely go to working-class bars and dance with one another just to provoke a reaction.

Many of the bands in Cleveland were directly confrontational not only in their musical attack—which was Velvets raw—but also in their utilization of any disturbing symbolism they could drum up, most notably the swastika. The Stooges had already displayed the Nazi emblem, and the Ramones, who were Jewish, were soon to sing: "I'm a Nazi schatz you know I fight for the Fatherland." These groups were trying to be offensive in any way possible to eradicate any identification with the previous generation of Rock fans (not to mention their parents' generation). There was a self-conscious attempt being made by these musicians to bury the past. What it would be replaced with was the same old Rock 'n' Roll clichés as ever: dope, leather, ego, self-parody, and self-destruction.

A perfect example was Peter Laughner, who fronted the pivotal Cleveland proto-Punk outfit Rocket from the Tombs. Befriended by Lester Bangs after a late-night phone call confirmed their mutual adherence to speed and the Velvet Underground, Laughner became a Rock critic, and his byline began appearing in *Creem* regularly. The nihilism that lay at the root of their friendship would take its toll on both of them—by 1982, both of them had already checked out (Laughner answering the call in '77).

Laughner's self-destructive tendencies were apparent in Rocket's music. The Velvet Underground were the primary catalyst, but tracks like "Cinderella

Backstreet," an early demo, reveal a Dylan influence as well. It has to be remembered that, at this time, Dylan was still a major influence on a lot of proto-Punk stylists: Ian Hunter, Elliott Murphy, Tom Verlaine, Richard Hell, Patti Smith.

No song summed up Rocket from the Tomb's message more aptly than "Final Solution," the foreboding title of which was only the beginning. Mapping out its destiny with seismographic precision, the song grew more unruly with each verse. As the frustration grew, the industrial noise accents became more pronounced. This only helped underscore the negativity of the lyrics: "Girls won't touch me coz I got a misdirection/And livin' at night ain't helpin' my complexion." This was loser Rock pure and simple, fed by the sentiment of Iggy & the Stooges' immortal line: "There's nothing left of life/But a pair of glassy eyes."

Songs like "Final Solution" represented the politics of boredom. We'd reached the stage at which young people who could afford the luxury of playing Rock 'n' Roll strictly for the amusement of it had grown so blasé that they literally wanted to see the world disintegrate for their own amusement. Far from being antiwar like the hippies, the new kids welcomed carnage of any kind as a kind of liberation from their dull shopping mall surroundings. This was the inevitable message behind "Final Solution" as well as the Nazi stuff and later celebrations of destruction like the Weirdos' "Neutron Bomb": push the button!

Pere Ubu was the first of the Cleveland groups to gain national prominence by being the first to play CBGB's. Their early singles were in a noisy, post-Beefheart vein, but *The Modern Dance*, their first album, proved they were equally comfortable with more straight Rock sounds, albeit Rock punctuated by random spurts of feedback and other ugly noise. In the mode of Beefheart, former Rocket from the Tombs vocalist David Thomas croaked like a bull-frog—and looked like one too—and the music underneath was dark and moody with quirky time signatures and lots of industrial hum. The group even decorated their album jackets with pictures of deserted factories in hometown Cleveland. This was the beginning of the era when groups would have their friends design their album covers for that homemade look: the whole idea was to be anti-industry, outsider, and, ultimately, loser. Perhaps despite themselves, Ubu was signed to Mercury Records in the mad dash to catch the (new) wave. There they were relegated to the label's Punk subsidiary, Blank, which attempted to rival Sire but soon faded into oblivion despite a handful of excellent sign-ings, including Ubu as well as Texas weirdos the Bizarros and Minneapolis's underrated Suicide Commandos.

The other notable spinoff from Rocket from The Tombs was the Dead Boys, formed by guitarist Cheetah Chrome after leaving Laughner's unit. The Dead Boys weren't entirely a Cleveland group, as they moved to New York shortly after being signed to Sire and their sound was less "industrial" and more Dolls/Stooges speed and fury. Singer Stiv Bators' stage jackoffs were directly "pulled" from Iggy, but he advanced it a step further towards the G. G. Allin level of intentional lewdness. They weren't winning any sympathy from femi-nists, either, with lyrics like "Don't look at me that way, bitch, your face is gonna get a *punch*!" New limits were being tested constantly. It was almost as if the punks were saying: "How much can you tolerate, how long can you ignore us without breaking down?" In other words, they were pushing the supposed-ly open-minded hippie liberals to the philosophical breaking point. It was pure outrage. To further emphasize this polarization process, the Dead Boys wore ridiculously short hair, almost in a '50s vein, which once again reaffirmed their intentional estrangement from the hippies.

The Dead Boys' nihilistic ethos spread to other important Cleveland bands like the Pagans, who asked the metaphysical question: "What's this Shit Called Love?" The band's sound was typical Ramones spawn with some '60s refer-ences thrown in, but the attitude was *all* bad, as epitomized by their eternal credo: "Not now, no way/It's the wrong time and it's the wrong day." They were "difficult" to deal with, in other words.

In nearby Akron, an even uglier city than Cleveland, bands played a clank-ing brand of post-Velvets Rock mixed with the kind of irony that could only come from living in the rubber capitol of America. Once again, it was an indus-trial wasteland, and the bands there realized the bleak symbolism of their immediate surroundings. They seemed more sympathetic to Prog resources than their New York counterparts, perhaps because the mechanized texture of keyboards seemed more compatible with the industrialized way of life. Devo, whose name stood for "de-evolution," mocked the mechanized uniformity of modern culture by wearing plastic radiation suits and having assembly line names like "Bob 1" and "Bob 2." It was a very dadaist concept, influenced by Frank Zappa, but Devo took it much further. The first group to broadly explore the video medium, they made horror–futuristic shorts to accompany songs like "Mongoloid" as well as their de-evolutionized version of "Satisfaction," which angered old hippies. This mangling of the hits was soon to become a big part of New Wave consciousness, especially for less imaginative bands like the Flying Lizards, who desecrated "Money" and "Summertime Blues."

Devo's arrival was greeted with disdain by almost everybody, including high school hippies and jocks to whom "Rock" always represented something "cool." Devo represented something different: the triumph of the nerds. If irony ever meant anything, it was in the hands of the group who sang, "It's a God-given fact that you're gonna get dumb." In a song like "Sloppy," Devo even took on the sacred target of sex, pointing out that our inherently lustful inclinations had become a kind of mechanization itself. This kind of knowingly antimacho posturing was new to Rock, and it was bound to have an effect. Which is really all Devo wanted: ultimately, they became as much of a novelty act as Kiss.

Other groups from the region also toyed with the mechanized/industrial aesthetic. Tin Huey, whose name was symbolic of this technological preoccupation, did a song called "I Could Rule the World if I Could Only Get the Parts." Kids all over realized that, in the '70s, it was a snap-on world. A band like Huey toyed with the nouveau symbolism enough to prove that a band no longer had to fit the same old stereotype to make a "Rock" record—and remember, at that time, the stereotype was still Bad Company! Bands like Devo and Huey were a stark contrast, as were other freedom-seekers like nearby Bloomington, Indiana's MX-80 Sound, whose deformed rhythms echoed the twisted algebra of mystical outfits like Captain Beefheart & His Magic Band and the Hampton Grease Band.

By the time *The Akron Compilation* was released, with its scratch & sniff emblem that smelled like burnt rubber, the Midwest underground had made its impact worldwide. That was the beauty of the new groundswell—the local scenes that were formative in shaping the sound of Rock in the '50s and '60s had all but disappeared in the corporate-Rock takeover of the '70s; with the rise of Punk, things began happening on the grassroots level again. Most of the participants on *The Akron Compilation* were far too quirky for mass consumption (although Tin Huey did get signed to Warner's on the coattails of Devo). Their messy music barely masked the contempt these artists felt for even the most basic of human emotions. Love—the concept of emotional love—was once again a big target of their disdain. A group called Sniper took a dip in the Velvets' tank with a tension-building tug-of-war called "Love is Making Me Bleed." Chanteuse Jane Aire out-iced Deborah Harry in the cockteasing opus "When I Was Young," reversing twenty years of Rock 'n' Roll tradition by victimizing the male as the rhythm pole-vaulted around in Ubu fashion and the band added some much-needed Thirteenth Floor Elevator jug-noise. It was a perfect example of Punk's ability to turn the tables on its audience's expectations. In the ultimate postmodern twist, Aire blames the *past*—her parents' generation—for her callousness: "That's how *they* always told me how to do it," she sang offhandedly, proving that not only was this the brightest generation ever, but the most irresponsible one as well.

In England, social conditions also played a large role in the shape of the independent music scene. The record industry in England during the mid-'70s was split between teenybopper hit makers like Sweet and the Bay City Rollers and the Arena-Rock dinosaurs: Rod, Elton, Bowie, the Who, the Stones, ELP, Led Zeppelin. The Pop process was a lot more localized than it was in the United States: radio was run under a rigid format, as was television. There was little room for expansion. The only plus was that an artist didn't have to actually *sell* that much to get into the Top Forty. England was a relatively small territory overall. This meant that once and a while, an independently produced record could still make the charts, which just didn't happen in America anymore. This would help Punk gain a stronghold in England that it never could in the U.S., where industry support was negligible.

As for the dinosaurs, they had ceased having "hits" altogether to concentrate on mythic album-making procedures, a process that went back to the '60s and *Sgt. Pepper* pretentiousness but now took the form of pomp-Rock like Led Zeppelin's year-in-the-making *Presence* and Pink Floyd's painstakingly crafted *Wish You Were Here*. Despite the fact these dinosaurs were national heroes at home, most of them lived outside of the country to avoid England's burdensome tax penance. The young fans that would soon make up the Punk audience viewed these expatriates as effete snobs and hated them accordingly.

The pub scene in England provided the spawning ground for many distinguished musical units. The prototype Pub-Rock acts—Ducks Deluxe, Brinsley

Schwarz, Dr. Feelgood, the Kursaal Flyers, the Count Bishops, Rockpile, Kilburn & the High Roads—played rootsy music that was well-suited to drinking. But the self-consciously "retro" style of these bands did not hold up well in the post-Ramones era. Yet this is what was happening in pre-Pistols Britain, and some of it would play a role in the origins of Brit-Punk.

Economically, England was in even worse shape than America in the mid-'70s. The Nazi decimation of England during World War II—and the subsequent Allied bailout—had placed the country in debt ever since. Their role as an industrial center had more or less diminished entirely: in July 1975 the country saw its worst unemployment figures since before the war. The country was plagued by "school leavers" and "squatters," which were groups of youths who moved into abandoned buildings and collected their money from the "dole."

This hopeless predicament fueled the rise of ultra-Tory organizations that played on people's fear and paranoia. Ironically, these were the same devices Hitler used to gain power in Germany during the '30s: xenophobia, hysteria, racism, and censorship. The IRA (Irish Republican Army) was a militant organization that specialized in terrorist-style bombings against civilian targets. The National Association for Freedom (NAF) emerged with similar hard-line tactics. Later, the outright fascist National Front came along. This only followed the increasing popularity of fanatical terrorist organizations all over the world (this was, after all, also the age of Patty Hearst and the Symbionese Liberation Army).

In England, this right-wing fervor was a reaction against the effects of "Swingin' London" in the '60s, when the so-called new permissiveness ruled. This sort of conservative backlash would also happen in America a few years later with the election of Ronald Reagan. Playing on people's gut fears—bombs in the streets, unemployment, miscegenation—the new conservatives placed the blame for England's decline on the shoulders of the liberals.

Into the fray stepped Margaret Thatcher, who was soon to emerge as a figurehead for conservative leadership worldwide. In 1975, as the Secretary of State for Education, she defeated twice-run Edward Heath for leadership of the Conservative Party. Her stern, matriarchal manner gave people the impression that she was somehow in control, even as things crumbled around her more noticeably every day.

The whole "permissive" culture that Thatcher was a reaction against had begun on the King's Road, where the hip, young fashion designers had suited the stars in the '60s. From there the psychedelic revolution swept Carnaby Street and Portobello Road, legendary clotheshorse hangouts. But by the mid-'70s the whole scene had washed out like so much tie-dye ink. In its stead, a thousand fringe elements had emerged, from anarchist to retro-rocko.

Standing among them was one Malcolm McLaren, who'd taken over proprietorship of one such clothing stand in 1971 with his female counterpart, Vivienne Westwood. Calling the shop Let it Rock, to cash in on the back-to-the-roots trend, the pair specialized in tacky threads from the '50s—sequined suits and the like. This was in *direct* reaction against the blue-jeans-wearing hippies. McLaren had been exploring such contrary politics since the mid-'60s in a variety of different incarnations. The French student uprisings had left a deep impression on him. Even back then he was espousing the tenets of "anarchy." It was a sentiment popular in England at the time, with crude, spray-painted symbols of "revolution" popping up all over the W.9.

McLaren was different than other politicos, however, because he'd also adapted to the dandified flair of the pop culture. With a twist—it wasn't Warhol he championed, but Warhol's would-be assassin, Valerie Solanis. Even back in '71 McLaren was practicing adverse shock therapy on the masses. By the time the hippies were a permanent fixture on King's Road, his tastes were running more toward zoot suits than "flares" (British for bell-bottoms).

Malcolm had adopted some of his fashion sense from his protégé, Vivienne Westwood, daughter of a cotton weaver, which must have implanted some fabric-working handicraft in her somehow. During the '60s she went through her share of artful frolics before settling on a career as a schoolteacher. Soon after she met McLaren, the two had a child out of wedlock. Although they never officially married, they would remain "partners" for the next fifteen years. The store was kind of a fluke that McLaren just inherited from an acquaintance, Trevor Miles. But once engaged in this endeavor, the young couple never looked back.

Westwood made the clothes, while Malcolm played the congenial host, offering crumpets to patrons and playing records. Westwood's short, spike-haired appearance might have evolved from some weird hybrid of Edie Sedgwick and David Bowie, but it predated the garish self-mutilation of Punk by several years. McLaren dressed mostly in hideous '50s garb with a big gob of grease in his hair. The '50s style was very much in vogue in England during the early '70s. In fact, one of Let It Rock's first big accounts was to provide costumes for Ray Connolly's retro-flick, *That'll Be the Day*, which starred David Essex and ex-Beatle Ringo Starr.

In order to accomplish this, Westwood and McLaren began applying silver studs to old leather jackets. As they progressed, and as the costumes grew more bizarre and fetishistic, McLaren began to realize the shock appeal of one of his future obsessions: S&M/bondage. Another innovation was to superimpose glitter onto cloth, a procedure that enabled them to imprint t-shirts with ambiguous slogans. Naturally, many of these images possessed sexual or political connotations. In what was perhaps his most telling statement, McLaren summed up his aesthetic this way: "You never wanted to be part of that Rock 'n' Roll liberal tradition, looking like you were doing good things." [5]

With this in mind, McLaren and Westwood continued to manufacture clothing that would shock and polarize. By 1973, they'd changed the name of the store from Let It Rock to Too Fast to Live, Too Young to Die in an attempt to rid themselves of the teddy boy types who were hanging around. The shop's clientele now included bondage mistresses as well as a flamboyant clique of teenagers. Because so much of their clientele at this point consisted of "professionals" in the underground sex trade, they changed the name of the store to Sex in 1975.

Like so many hustlers of his day, McLaren had become enamored with Rock 'n' Roll as a mouthpiece for his radical notions. His involvement in the Rock process was gradual—he was still very skeptical of the whole hippie thing and its lingering effects. Nevertheless, Sex soon began selling records as well. It was during this period that McLaren found a strange correlation between prepsychedelic "mod" outfits like the Small Faces and the more-aggressive-but-still-basic Rock acts of the day: the Modern Lovers, the Stooges, the Flamin' Groovies, and the New York Dolls.

McLaren was particularly enamored with the Dolls, partly due to the fact that they frequented his store whenever they were in England, but also because of their fuck-all attitude. When he heard that the band was in danger of being dropped by its American record label, Mercury, he flew to New York, supposedly to bail them out. Although the Dolls' reputation by then was mud, McLaren somehow convinced the owner of New York's Little Hippodrome to allow them to play a Saturday afternoon concert to "preview" their next album.

The fact that, at that time, there was no plan for any such album didn't really matter, because McLaren was making it up as he went along.

For the occasion, McLaren decked the group out in Westwood-designed red patent leather with a huge hammer-and-sickle backdrop. The Dolls had already paraded as transvestites, and now they were playing "commies." Shortly thereafter, McLaren became their ersatz manager. But the streetwise group—particularly guitarist Johnny Thunders and drummer Jerry Nolan—soon tired of Malcolm's grooming and left to form the Heartbreakers. That left Malcolm little to show for his trip to the States except, reportedly, a bad case of the clap.

When McLaren returned to London, his experience managing the renegade New Yorkers had left him hungering for a mouthpiece that could be more easily manipulated. He didn't have to look too far—a pair of his regular clients, Steve Jones and Paul Cook, had formed a group specializing in the typical "lad rock" à la the Who and Small Faces. At this point, they were just average guys looking to have a few pints and pull some birds. They certainly weren't thinking along the same revolutionary lines as Malcolm, but ideologically they were malleable. What was more important at that time was that they were both adequate players. As a drummer, Cook could keep a steady Rock 'n' Roll beat, and guitarist Jones came up with a simple-but-effective style utilizing such influences as the Who, the Stooges, the Dolls, and Chuck Berry.

The proletariat qualities of Cook and Jones made them infinitely appealing to Malcolm. Jones became one of the earliest exemplars of the Punk fashion code. McLaren also encouraged Jones's criminal activities, especially his habit of procuring expensive musical equipment from big-name acts like David Bowie by sneaking into their rehearsal spaces at night. By McLaren's standards, this was the ultimate "revolutionary" act.

The group would've never evolved beyond the level of an above-average Punk band had it not been for the addition of John Lydon. At the time, they needed a singer, and if the bug-eyed Lydon couldn't sing, he made up for it with sheer *attitude*. He was *nasty* and he knew it, so much so that, after his first audition—which consisted of mouthing the words to Alice Cooper's "I'm Eighteen" on the jukebox—Steve Jones renamed him "Johnny Rotten." The name stuck, and the Punk movement had its first visible front man.

The bass player in the group was a fresh-faced lad named Glen Matlock, whose tastes ran more towards conventional Rock 'n' Roll and even Pop. He did *not* hit it off with Rotten, but, for the time being, this was the band's nucleus. Sometime in 1975, McLaren changed their name to the Sex Pistols. Ironically, at that time, he actually envisioned the group competing with the Bay City Rollers. This more or less matched the Ramones' admission that they saw themselves on the same level as Kiss and Ted Nugent.

Rotten added a lot to the group. As he told Jon Savage: " 'Sod them,' I thought, 'they're gonna do Who rip-offs, I don't care. I'll write the songs I want to write.'" [6]

Rotten's Roman Catholic brand of alienation fit McLaren's blueprint perfectly. Like the Ramones in the United States, Rotten was exploring the politics of boredom: "We're pretty vacant...and we don't care!" Boredom had been a successful motivating factor in Rock 'n' Roll since Eddie Cochran sang "Summertime Blues" in 1958. Cochran, who'd died in a car crash in England in 1960, was an early role model for McLaren (which he later projected onto Sid Vicious). In the mid-'70s, there was a consensus that, after the tumult of the '60s, not much was really happening. Rotten attacked the boredom head-on, proclaiming: "I don't pretend coz I don't care!" As the ominous date of Orwell's *1984* loomed, it was still a very pertinent cultural reference point. The other work of futuristic fiction that appeared to be coming true was *A Clockwork Orange*, which seemed more believable everyday with men like Rotten running around.

In the '60s, Jim Morrison had epitomized the nonconformist mentality with his eternal credo: "There Are No Rules!" To the Sex Pistols, this included smashing the corporate stronghold of contemporary Rock where everything was so pristine and choreographed. This meant getting onstage without even knowing how to play one's instruments. As groups in New York and Ohio had already found out, this could have an extremely polarizing effect on stunned audiences, who sometimes reacted violently. This was the "chaos" factor that McLaren so loved.

It can be argued that all throughout Rock history, bands and musicians have failed to master the simple mechanics of their chosen instruments (the Seeds). But the difference was that, in the past, musicians who were technically deficient were, in a sense, bluffing and hoping nobody would notice. The Sex Pistols and their ilk were saying, in essence...*so what*! They seemed to derive glee out of seeing their audience squirm. It wouldn't be long before the band's hoodlum friends all began turning out, which transformed the gigs into volatile "events." The music was almost secondary, but somewhere in the din a genuine style was emerging. As Al McDowell told Jon Savage: "It was immediately attractive to anyone who was feeling hostile."

McLaren squired the boys through a series of live appearances at offbeat locales, including universities in the darkest corners of England. Although the group was still chiefly unknown at that time, their entourage behaved threateningly enough to gain attention. This was the reality of *A Clockwork Orange* come to life—no one had ever appeared so unyieldingly *nasty* (rotten) before.

During the summer of 1976, the Ramones toured England, and young Brits finally witnessed Punk Rock in the flesh. At the same time, the home-grown Sex Pistols were also making the local club circuit and gaining attention. For one thing, their appearance was immediately photo-worthy (and much imitated): in contrast to the American Ramones, the Pistols sported *short hair*, an immediately polarizing effect, considering that long hair had been such an essential part of the counterculture. The Ramones were no hippies, however—they were apolitical mostly, as were the Heartbreakers and most of the other American Punk groups. Which is why they ultimately couldn't capture the international media the way the Pistols did.

As the Pistols evolved, they eventually mutated their influences—the Dolls, Stooges, and Ramones—into a more thrashing attack. As a vocalist, Rotten spawned a whole new school of painful post-Iggy expression. Where Iggy screamed in whoops of unadulterated agony, Rotten carefully mangled his words until they were razor-sharp with toxic rolls of the tongue. No one had ever appeared as *unashamed*—not Iggy or Jim Morrison. Rotten was twenty years old, thin, with rotting teeth; a freak with orange hair, dressed literally in rags, and he was singing "I don't care, I don't care." For the time being, the public said "no thanks."

Those whom the Pistols did attract appeared in similarly mutilated form and attracted quite a bit of attention themselves. Most of them were hangers-on from Malcolm's shop like Sue Catwoman and Siouxsie Sioux. These girls preferred heavy makeup, short hair, and fetish clothing. At this point, McLaren and Westwood were still making more money off the clothing store than they were the Pistols. In many ways, these kids were the progenitors of Goth fashion, and when their pictures began appearing in the paper accompanying the shock wave that greeted the Pistols, it became a big fashion statement as well.

In about a year, punk boutiques like Manic Panic would open in New York, and Punk "fashion" would take hold throughout the world.

Back in America, where the scene was based on a more complex avant-garde ideal mixed with some dark humor, no such fashion renaissance occurred. But the sight of these miscreants in their war paint and pantaloons at least gave the scene a visual identity to go along with the musical one.

Punk had such a polarizing effect that, in the actual '70s, to be committed to liking it was to socially ostracize oneself from one's peers. As the first antipopulist Pop form, Punk effectively disintegrated the whole notion of Rock itself. But it couldn't have done this if the Pistols hadn't played Rock to begin with and, for all their bluster, Steve Jones was still basically playing Chuck Berry riffs. The Sex Pistols gave more to Rock 'n' Roll than they wanted from Rock 'n' Roll in the first place—their music demanded a commitment, even if it was a commitment to being immoral. You were supposed to understand the contradiction.

During the summer of '76, the band played—and got banned from—every major venue in England: the 100 Club, the Roxy, the Marquee. Despite the industry's trepidation in approaching these rabble-rousers, the kind of publicity—albeit negative—that they were attracting almost guaranteed that, at some point, one of the major labels would come dangling their carrot. It turned out to be EMI, who took a chance with the group in November 1976. From the label's vantage, they clearly expected the group to make money. So confident were they in their investment that they gave the Pistols a forty-thousand-pound advance. This was the group's first coup on the road to the Great Rock 'n' Roll Swindle.

The advance was nonrepayable, which meant the group got to keep it regardless, meaning the deal was slanted in the Pistols' favor from the beginning because the label felt they had to get the best out of their investment and thus humor the group through all their shenanigans. Almost from the start, there were fireworks. EMI began to realize that they might not have long to milk their investment. They urged the group to release their most "pop"-oriented song to date, "Pretty Vacant," but the group stood firm and went for the Big Statement. Lucky for them: "Anarchy in the U.K." proved to be a major turning point in Rock history.

The Pistols by now had garnered an inordinate amount of publicity, so it was vital that their first recording delivered. The title alone said everything about what that they were trying to accomplish—this was the most overtly political single in England since Paul McCartney's "Give Ireland Back to the Irish," and it was banned immediately, even as import copies began being distributed all over the world.

"Anarchy in the U.K." instantly equated the Pistols with their New York counterparts on a musical level. From the opening roar of the guitars to Rotten's vicious snarl, "Anarchy" was a thoroughly compelling Rock record with almost melodic soloing from guitarist Steve Jones, as well as a thousand overdubbed guitars creating a wall of sound and a pulsing rhythm section. This can be partly attributed to producer Chris Thomas, who'd previously worked with Roxy Music. But it mostly had to do with the band—not content to be merely another group of rude lads, they aimed straight for the jugular. What else could you say about a group whose first utterance in their musical lifetime was "I am an anti-Christ"?

Politically, such statements were perceived as way more of a threat in England than they were in the USA. In a country the size of America, things tended to get filtered out. Most Americans didn't concern themselves with, say, the political implications of a Rock record because they felt it didn't directly affect them. But England, which was essentially a small island, was constantly worried about its national stability. In the mid-'70s, the neo-Conservative factions had taken hold amidst the paranoia and they did *not* welcome the arrival of youngsters like the Pistols—*especially* after the William Grundy episode.

Grundy was an aging talk show host on Thames, the most liberal of the three major British television networks. His *Today* program aired during the supper hour and was widely viewed by the whole country. From time to time, the acerbic Grundy would host "pop" groups, often making fun of them. With the Pistols, he bit off more than he could chew.

It all came about when the British superstar group, Queen, cancelled, supposedly because singer Freddie Mercury was offended by Grundy's fashion sense—or lack thereof (*toupees*...yuck!). The Pistols had been getting a lot of publicity, and Grundy apparently figured their appearance would boost ratings. He also figured they'd be young and naïve enough to rake over the coals. So he sent a line to McLaren inviting the Pistols to appear live that afternoon (December 2, 1976). After a few hours in the pub, the Pistols showed up, with their entourage—Siouxsie, etc.—in tow.

The show progressed through some rather typical goading by Grundy, but there were a few good exchanges, like the one in which Steve Jones and Glen Matlock informed him that the money from EMI was already spent and he exclaimed "good Lord!" in a voice reserved for British broadcast announcers. The chitchat eventually broke down into a back-and-forth exchange of tease-and-taunt, but it was slightly revived by Grundy's apparently lecherous advances on Siouxsie after she remarked: "I've always wanted to meet you!" (Which proves what a dumbo she always was.) This prompted Jones to remark: "You dirty sod." Testing the limits of his guests once again, Grundy then goaded Jones to "say something outrageous" to which Jones replied, in succession: "you dirty bastard...you dirty fucker...you *fucking rotter*!"

Overnight, the Sex Pistols became a household word in England. The papers the next morning rang with headlines like: "The Punks—Rotten and Proud of It" as well as the immortal "Foul Mouthed Yobs." McLaren couldn't have been more delighted. This kind of publicity was, of course, any manager–exploiter's dream. In a classic example of postmodernism, the group later used all the negative headlines as song lyrics, like the classic blurb from the *Daily Mail*: "Never mind moral standards—the only notes that really count are the ones that come in wads!" Apparently, a forty-seven-year-old truck driver named James Holmes had been so outraged by the Grundy broadcast that he had kicked in the TV screen. As reports of this furor spread back to America, record collector types began speculating on the possibilities of British Invasion II.

Up until this point EMI had been fairly supportive of the group despite their nonconformist agenda. "Anarchy in the U.K." had been selling briskly, and the group was ready to embark on a national tour with the Clash and New York's Heartbreakers. However, after Grundy, many stores refused to stock the record, and radio play was out of the question. Thus the great irony that would govern Punk's future: one could be "famous" but have no actual hits. And record companies didn't necessarily care about fame or notoriety unless it resulted in record sales.

Being the media-savvy generation they were, the Punks understood this complex dilemma—they realized that if they backed down, they'd lose everything and their moment would pass, as it had for the mods, as it had for the hippies. So they rebelled even further—and continued to solidify this everlasting impasse with the Powers That Be. The example set by this kind of blatant defiance helped attract legions of fans the world over. Punk's power lay in its nihilism—the essential belief that "nothing mattered"—not even fame and money. Of course, if it was all laid out for the taking, punks took it. Or, as Rotten sang on "Anarchy": "I use the best/I use the rest/I use the enemy…"

After Grundy, the Pistols were released from EMI, which they promptly wrote a song about—once again, the new aesthetic: *use* everything. By this time, they were in the unique position of having any negative publicity actually work in their favor. At the same time, their nihilistic ethos meant they were free to do anything they wanted (as they "didn't care" anyway). Anarchists broke down all sense of moral reason: the end justified the means every time. Punk was more meaningful and lasting than any similar movement in modern times because it went beyond the realm of mere *ideas* and moved into the terrain of actual violence and self-sacrifice.

Nobody embodied this more than Sid Vicious, who was a lifetime friend of Lydon's and was one of McLaren's inner circle at the clothing boutique. According to Lydon, Sid was always a clotheshorse, and he was to become the ultimate vehicle for McLaren to project his nihilistic fantasies upon. Lydon was too strong-willed. Jones and Cook too basic. But Sid (born John Ritchie) was the perfect symbol of fallen youth: barely eighteen, he'd been brought up illegitimately by his hippie-vagabond mother. He was wont to do himself physical harm and to do virtually anything else for attention—including the inevitable clotheshorse stuff, which made him an early Punk fashion plate. Sid would later brag that it was beating up British Rock critic Nick Kent that got him the bass player job with the Pistols, but it was actually Lydon's intense dislike for Glen Matlock. "Either he goes or I go," Lydon told McLaren, who promptly fired Matlock, leaving the bass player with—literally—tears in his eyes. As a bluff, the band told the press they fired Matlock for "liking the Beatles." There was a constant attempt to bury the past. On the other hand, when faced with the future, the band declared: "No future!"

Ultimately, any movement based entirely on negative energy wasn't likely to flourish. Eventually some "optimism" arose in the Punk arena. When it did, it was mostly provided by the Clash, who emerged as the Pistols' biggest competitors in 1977 and were, in fact, managed by a former member of McLaren's inner circle, Bernie Rhodes. If guys like Jones, Cook, and Sid Vicious embodied the "rocker" elements of the new movement, the Clash were the closest thing Punk had to "mods." They wore much of the same union-jack garb as the Who a decade earlier, as did such shameless mod wannabes as the Jam. Mod itself would have a full-blown revival before the days of Punk had come and gone. Even the Clash's sound was influenced by the Who—they "borrowed" the "Can't Explain" riff on several occasions. The Clash was poppy and amphetamine-driven. And they helped bring Reggae into the whole spectrum. The Black   mpathetic cousin to the punks in a country where raci   nbers of the Clash were good   nstant loggerheads with the

The   sm had more to do with an   prescribed doctrine. They tr   ped in an inkwell of frustrat   ng these elements is what g   he Pistols, they were unaba   od old-fashioned dose of Ma   nto a political agenda later   ancisco Bay Area scene in th   vement worldwide, the influence of the Clash   's look—scowls, combat boots, the shortest hair ever—was to become the blueprint for many bands to come. The Clash was *admired* for their stance—by fans, musicians, and critics. When the Rock Against Racism resistance movement emerged, the Clash played all the benefits and rallies. They also got their first album out before the Sex Pistols.

Although the Pistols were desperate to make a full-length LP, the ongoing controversies, internal friction, and lack of industry support kept them from doing so for almost a year. They signed with A&M in a big media blitz outside of Buckingham Palace. The grannies were outraged, but they hadn't seen anything yet—the Pistols' next single was entitled "God Save the Queen," and it arrived just in time to toast the monarch's Silver Jubilee. "She ain't no human being," Rotten sang in his gutterwurst cockney accent. The single was historic for another reason: despite the fact that, after it was finally released by Virgin Records in late May 1977, it topped the charts, it couldn't be listed in the Hit Parade under its name because it had been "banned." Consequently, that week, there was a big blank spot at the top of the charts. This was the epitome of the "Blank Generation."

The Pistols were so shrouded in controversy at this point that they could hardly make a move without having to go underground for six months. It really had reached fever pitch on the strength of a few songs: "Anarchy in the U.K.," "I Wanna Be Me," "God Save the Queen," "Did You No Wrong," "Pretty Vacant." In the summer of 1977, *Rolling Stone* sent their wild-and-crazy-guy Charles M. Young to London to do a cover story. When Young arrived, McLaren looked at him straight-faced and said: "They hate you, you know." He meant the whole *Rolling Stone* hippie tradition. Ironically enough, the story—which was entitled "Rock is Sick and Living in London"—ran in the issue immediately following the one memorializing Elvis Presley. Rotten's immortal comment on the passing of the King was a classic case of Slay Thy Father: "Fucking good riddance to bad rubbish."

Meanwhile, the Clash was releasing powerful singles like "White Riot" and "Remote Control." Their deal with CBS had reportedly been a lucrative one, but they had their rows with their record company as well—especially when, in the summer of '77, the label released the *wrong song* as a single. Wasting no time, the group responded by making the next single *about* the incident in question. The Pistols had already roasted EMI, after all. The Punks were learning how to use the record industry to make powerful, ironic statements against the industry itself. As the first effective form of "protest" music since the hippies, this was yet another way that Punk fulfilled its promise.

CBS also fucked up by not releasing the Clash's first album in the U.S. Claiming "no interest," both American branches of the label, Columbia and Epic, declined (Epic would eventually handle the group). The album quickly became one of the most sought-after "import" records, a burgeoning territory previously reserved for oldies but now being rejuvenated by Punk. This would help spawn the whole record collecting syndrome that has become so much a part of "punk"—artists were putting out interesting singles/albums, but only in limited quantities. The reasons for this were: 1) that's all they could afford; 2) that's all the record company would allow them; and 3) they got banned so fast that they were virtually impossible to find and thus became sacred objects. The hush-hush tendencies of early Punk—that feeling that the listener was in on a truly underground explosion—was what made it so alluring.

As for the Clash album, here was the true test, what many had been waiting to see: could the British Punks deliver a full-length musical document that rivaled the work of their '60s Fathers (whom they wished to kill) or their Reggae Brethren (whom they sought to emulate)? In the case of *The Clash*, the answer was yes. The Clash succeeded on their own terms in much the same way as the Ramones (i.e., they succeeded on the Ramones' terms): their album was a full-speed whirlwind designed to knock you out.

If there was ever an album that epitomized "Oi!" this was it. Singers Mick Jones and Joe Strummer sang in cockney accents so strong that they convinced American journalists like Lester Bangs that they really were the working class louts they pretended to be, even though they were actually middle class kids slumming. This didn't mean their music wasn't legitimately working class, because in an effort to authenticate the "punk" quotient, they slummed to maximum effect, living in abandoned flats, taking amphetamines, and "busking." If times got too hard, they still ran home to mommy, but that didn't make them any different than 97 percent of everyone else in Punk Rock, American and English alike. Punk was a genre ripe for poseurdom from the start, but more importantly, it was a way for angry white intellectuals and smart-asses to cop "street" sensibilities. Punk was often referred to as "street Rock," and *The Clash* evoked the sound of a thousand young feet running, probably from the cops, as pictured on the back of the LP in a mad equivocation of the Clash's own "White Riot."

The Ramones had upped the energy level, and the decibels too, earning the distinction of "buzzsaw guitars." The Clash embodied this completely. It may sound a bit dated now, but when "Janie Jones" came out, it was completely exhilarating, like a volt of instant energy at your disposal—aural lightning. The lyrics were pseudo-working class liberal bile: "The factory's killing all of us," a predicament they ultimately confronted with the conclusion: "but what can I do?" That was the "loser" ethic of Punk once again, but it was rendered with raw power. The song ends, and, as the Ramones had taught, 1-2-3-4, they launch another missile: "White riot/I WANT A RIOT!"

The lyrics on *The Clash* revealed the antimaterialist instincts of the ultra-proletariat Punks. As Johnny Rotten would tell an interviewer in his best schoolboy-with-a-hand-grenade-in-his-pocket voice: "I don't *want* a Mercedes." But that was because every Rock star of the previous generation had owned one, or some equivalent. Once again...*Elvis*: "Fucking good rid-dance to bad rubbish!" By disowning the more opulent trappings of Rock star-dom, the punks earned the respect of younger fans that couldn't conceive of such self-indulgence. After all, the Eagles would never cop to such a thing.

Although the Pistols and Clash signed to major labels, most of the early British Punk bands that emerged during the first wave were on independent labels. This provided a forum for totally untrained acts like the Damned, who recorded for Stiff, a label that was to become an important outlet for British independent music in general. Stiff's output included geeky guys like Nick Lowe, Elvis Costello, and Wreckless Eric, who were as important to the birth of New Wave as the Talking Heads or Blondie. These bands were Pop crafts-men, but they still favored the raw sound of Punk. This went for the Damned as well. The opulence of some of their work bespoke latent hippie or pub roots but, then again, every band had to start somewhere. What defined "punk" more than the cover of the Damned's first album, with four shorthairs shoving pies in each other's faces?

That was a joke the Jam never got. They got their album out before the Pistols, too, but their whole corny mod-revival bit, not to mention their liber-al politics, proved that, in some quarters, Punk had already been subverted to the nostalgia level. Although successful in England, the Jam were basically snubbed by the hip record-buying circles in America, a fact that so enraged mouthy leader Paul Weller that he later wrote a three-hundred-page anti-American diatribe based solely on what he perceived as the nation's inability to comprehend his "art."

The Vibrators could never have done that, because they were never "arty" to begin with. By the sounds of it, they were a jaded pub band overcome by the sensibilities of Punk with some gnawing Velvets traces. They got signed to CBS along with the Clash, but for all we know they might have been plucked out of the mailroom at corporate headquarters and told to play some of that "punk" music. The great thing about the Punk explosion was that it didn't matter—it was all about *just doing it*. The Vibrators were plucky enough in their adherence to the chainsaw technique to earn kudos from Robert Christgau of all people, who blushed: "*Mnnnn*! They're *narsty*!" Despite their defiant pose, the Vibrators had a hint of "virtue" hiding underneath that would dim their credibility with the "real" punks. This was best epitomized by the lyrics to "Keep it Clean," which admonished hooligans of every stripe: "You'll never get to heaven," they warned, as if they were Dionne Warwick. Even when they tried to get tough, as in "No Heart," in which they threatened to "send her up to heaven with my .38," they didn't get it: baby wasn't going to heaven. Baby had been a bad girl.

The Buzzcocks, from Manchester, had played some early gigs with the Sex Pistols. Their first single, "Orgasm Addict," was an utterly frank description of obsessive male masturbation—it was Devo's "Uncontrollable Urge" without the sly, rubber-suited innuendo. The author of that song, Howard Devoto, split the group shortly after to form his own band, Magazine, leaving the Buzzcocks with Pete Shelley at the helm. The string of brilliant singles like "What Do I Get" and "Ever Fallen in Love?" written by Shelley were the next step in male vulnerability and sexual insecurity after Jonathan Richman. While the other Punks were busy castigating Love into the garbage pile—none of the Clash's songs were about girls—Shelley was obsessed with the subject and felt victimized by its all-powerful allure. This kind of irony would not escape the young teenagers who would soon make up groups like R.E.M., the Smiths, Game Theory, and other pioneers of the next wave. To admit to being so willy-nilly and weak-kneed was like a betrayal of the whole macho Rock tradition. Shelley's essential *ginchiness* was akin to saying "oh go ahead, walk on me, it's better than *nothing*." It was sex as *validation* and, as the Pagans sang, "anything could be better than nothing." Although they were a dark horse in this country, in the years since, the Buzzcocks have taken rank alongside the Ramones and Sex Pistols in the annals of Punk by critics who apparently had their heart broken to the sounds of "Why Can't I Touch It?"

The Buzzcocks represented the more self-conscious strain of British Punk. These are groups who took the basic buzzsaw anarchy of early Punk and added their own embellishments. In the case of the Buzzcocks, that was a poppier sensibility; in the case of Wire, it was an artier one. Wire codified the Ramones into an even more tightly woven formula that seismographed its message in staccato bursts. When the first album, *Pink Flag*, came out in early '78, the big deal was the brevity of the songs. The Ramones had already shortened the playing time of the basic Rock song, and Wire, true to their name, were making an even slimmer statement. Little did anyone realize that when Hardcore came along, the songs would get even shorter…thirty-nine seconds, *twenty-four* seconds. Meanwhile, as Wire progressed into more abstract territory, their songs got longer but no less conceptual; only by now the Ramones' influence had given way to a plethora of artier touchstones.

The Fall, who came from Manchester, soon to be the locale of a major Brit youth subculture, rocked consistently but with an artier jagged edge. Singer Mark E. Smith established the band's acerbic direction with the most distinct British male vocal applications since Johnny Rotten, a kind of biting staccato bark dripping with sarcasm. The angularity of the guitars, and the twisted sense of rhythm, made the Fall not just the regular old Punk Rock, but at the same time there was little self-effacing or pretentious about it. One of the more pro- lific British bands, they were also indie-pioneers with their own Step Forward label, proving once again that effective—and lasting—musical progress could occur outside the realm of the majors. Needless to say, this would have enor- mous impact on the post-Punk hordes of the next two decades.

If Wire, Magazine, and the Fall represented the artier realm of Brit-Punk's first wave, there were still plenty of straight-ahead buzzsaw-rockers emerging every week: the Adverts, Radiators from Space, Skrewdriver, Satan's Rats, Slaughter & the Dogs, the Users, Sham 69, Rezillos, Sniveling Shits, the Cortinas, Eater, Chelsea. Most of these bands, although enjoyable enough, added little to the overall Punk-Rock palette, but their very existence proved that the bracing fury of the music—the speed/aggressiveness factor once again—was here to stay. In this case, in these bands' uniformity lay their essen- tial "charm."

A notable exception was Motorhead, who also emerged from England around this time ('77) and overcame the odds through sheer grit, self-determi- nation, and brute force. Although they've often been classified as "heavy metal," their basic remake/remodel of the whole Rock idiom itself was as com- plete as that of the Stooges, Ramones, or Sex Pistols. Clearly they were not another puffed-up Heavy Metal act à la Led Zeppelin. One of the reasons they got classified as "heavy metal" probably had to do with the fact they had long hair. Actually, it was groups like Motorhead who began pointing out in the late '70s the latent similarities between Punk and Heavy Metal, a fact that became clearer to the musicians of the '80s as the curse of MTV-sponsored dross set in. At that point, any music that was organically conceived—as opposed to clever- ly choreographed—was in short supply, and the definitions between different types of Rock began to shrink under the weight of the more important question of whether it was Rock at all. Motorhead clearly were, and when they got the classic line-up in place of Lemmy (bass/vocals), "Fast" Eddie Clark (guitar), and Philthy Animal Taylor (drums), they steamrolled through more consecutively good albums than anyone this side of the Ramones.

Also slightly older and less stereotypically "punk" was the Stranglers, who sported leftist dogma underneath the safety pins, despite reintroducing some mildly hypnotic Doors organ to the spectrum. The Stranglers were older and uglier, so they were able to push the kids around. Their image was ultra-narsty, like sending dead rats in the press kits that accompanied their *Rattus Norvegicus* LP. They were signed to A&M, the company who dropped the Sex Pistols over "God Save the Queen." In an ironic twist, they later had some "pop" sellout success.

The Stranglers may have represented the same old sexism in new garb, but Punk actually acted as a sexually liberating factor in many ways, particularly in that it finally gave women equal footing in the male-dominated field of Rock. Punk had so expanded the limits of "style" that it helped rectify some backward notions about gender. All-female bands like the Slits, who played every bit as Velvets/Stooges/Ramones-intense as their male counterparts, were like an injection of estrogen into the bloated, sagging contour of Rock's slovenly white underbelly. This was especially true in England, where, discounting the Folk scene (Maddy Prior, Annie Haslam, Sandy Denny), women had played a minimal role in the music's definition. In the wake of Punk, all-female bands like the Raincoats would approach the music from an entirely feminist perspective (thus influencing later "riot grrls").

Other important Brit-bands of the era had female frontpieces. Like Blondie's Deborah Harry in New York, these women were busy twisting people's notions about traditional sex roles. Siouxsie Sioux, of Siouxsie & the Banshees, came right out of the Sex Pistols' inner circle, being the girl Grundy tried to "meet" after the infamous broadcast. She became one of the most photogenic emblems of early Punk "style," mostly by evoking the image of the dominatrix. The influence of bondage and domination as a visual motif should not be underestimated in the Punk pantheon. At war with the concept of "love," it was no wonder the Punks embraced the one form of human sexuality that had to do with pain and humiliation. And when it came to violence, Punk rockers rebelled against the liberal tradition of always identifying with the victim by identifying with the perpetrator—hence the Ramones' (or AntiSeen's) embrace of Charlie Manson or Siouxsie's (or Chrissie Hynde's or Deborah Harry's) personification of the Bitch Goddess. No surprise, Siouxsie has often been hailed as the godmother of "goth," although the best work on the Banshees' debut album was more rooted in typical New York Dolls/garage sensibilities.

X-Ray Spex offered an even more hilarious sendup of traditional sex roles with their Black, braces-wearing, five-foot-tall teenage female singer, Poly Styrene. With a voice somewhere between a siren wail and an alley cat yelp, Styrene turned the tables on victimization itself, alternating between singing "I want to be a slave to you all" and "oh bondage up yours!" When she sang "The Day the World Turned Day Glo," it was only half-mockingly: at this point the whoops took on the tone of fear, and ultimately of pure insanity. The first Brit-Punk band to prominently feature a saxophone player, X-Ray Spex's first and only album, *Germ Free Adolescents* (1978), was an incredibly perceptive commingling of Punk stylings and postmodern observations.

Well into its second year, U.K. Punk became increasingly political. In Ireland, the sense of fear that ruled the streets in light of the IRA bombings spawned Stiff Little Fingers, who named themselves after a Vibrators song. Their first two singles, "Suspect Device" and "Alternative Ulster," were among the most politically charged statements ever. Like the Sex Pistols and the Clash, Stiff Little Fingers proved that it was possible to make a record as defining as all those "classic Rock" singles of yore: "My Generation," "Satisfaction," etc. For years, the crumbling relics of the '60s had maintained that their legacy was untouchable. Now here were these upstarts literally coming out of nowhere and making tribunal-Rock statements that put to shame anything the dinosaurs had done in years. It was hard to deny the power of a record like "Alternative Ulster" on sheer Rock terms, which meant that it was indeed the musical and cultural equivalent of "Satisfaction": a complete explosion born out of the fury of the moment. Except that, in Rock terms, it was even more powerful, and in popular terms, far less successful.

Which, once again, was the irony of Punk in the first place. Politicos like Stiff Little Fingers may have been even more naïve and idealistic than their '60s counterparts, but as far as sheer Rock went, they were several calibrations higher than anything that had come before. Punk's commercial failure was attributable to a mass wimping-out on the part of everyone. But that didn't mean that the small fragment of the population that it appealed to didn't warrant some kind of "culture" of their own. With the arrival of groups like Stiff Little Fingers—youngsters whose whole histories didn't include much prior to Punk—it finally happened.

In other words, Punk was the self-conscious rebirth of Rock itself on a smaller scale.

Most of the other Irish Punk bands weren't as politically conscious as Stiff Little Fingers. The Undertones, for example, were like Ireland's version of the Ramones: goofy and poppy, expressing frustration certainly, but basically apolitical. The Boomtown Rats created a well-textured swirl that borrowed its street ethos from Bruce Springsteen more than the Sex Pistols. Not surprisingly, they were one of the few groups from this whole discussion that later hit gold. The Pogues mixed traditional Irish drinking music with the post-everything irony of Punk. And of course, later on, U2 would appropriate all these aspects to create their world-winning formula.

Australia experienced a Punk boom of its own, much like it had experienced a Rhythm-and-Blues boom in the '60s. The musical, as well as spiritual, foundation for much Aussie punk seemed to come straight from the United States: the Saints certainly learned from both the Ramones and Stooges: from the Ramones, they borrowed the downstroked repetition of the rhythm guitars; from the Stooges, particularly the *Raw Power* era, the menacing shrapnel-inducing squeal; from both bands, a general kind of anomie/"no future" ethic. Their second album effectively mixed these elements with more politicized sentiments and, believe it or not, *horns*. The Saints' counterparts were Radio Birdman, who played the MC5 to their Stooges (or vice versa). Birdman was capable of the same bracing speed as the Saints, but with some rootsy elements thrown in. Their embrace of an authentic garage-based aesthetic seems to have been passed on almost immediately to primalists like the Lyres and, later, the Hellacopters.

The other Australian band of significance from this era was, of course, AC/DC. Not a "punk" band by any means, they nevertheless seemed more open to many of the attributes of Punk—shorter songs, faster tempos—than most of their metallic brethren. Maybe it was their provincial proximity that rendered them just savage enough to appreciate the fury and angst of the form, or maybe it was the fact that they were sponsored by Australia's premiere hit-making factory, Vanda/Young, which went all the way back to the Easybeats in the '60s. In other words, they were based more on structured songwriting than they were on "jams." Like the Ramones, AC/DC were never as dumb as they seemed. What they were was a harmonically compressed engine that reached peak performance around the time of *Highway to Hell* (1979), which, in this country, accomplished what the Ramones and Sex Pistols never could: mainly, it became the soundtrack for social dropouts—i.e., literally, *punks*—everywhere. Along with Motorhead and Van Halen, AC/DC were instrumental in gearing Heavy Metal back toward a more streamlined attack, which would result in the Punk/metal fusion of Metallica et al. in the '80s.

In England, Punk was becoming more political. Take, for instance, Sham 69, led by the irrepressible Jimmy Pursey. Not a great singer by any means, Pursey nevertheless embodied the "oi" aesthetic. Decidedly prole ("Hey Little Rich Boy"), Pursey and the Shams spoke the voice of the rabble. In a premonition of Hardcore, their heavily politicized gigs were often violent. In a way, they were like a marriage of Ramones chug-a-lug and Clash working-lout sensibilities. But unlike the Clash, they really were "street." And when they settled down to rock, they were capable of epic statements like "Tell Us the Truth" and "The Kids Are United."

The "oi" spirit led to a whole second wave of Brit-Punk bands: U.K. Subs, the Exploited, the Crass, Discharge, Anti-Nowhere League, Skrewdriver. But despite this preoccupation of politicos, the scene still had the smarty Pop of the whole Stiff Records brigade to contend with. One of the first important indie labels in England, Stiff was quick to apply the Punk aesthetic to marketing terms: an early advertising slogan was "if it ain't stiff it ain't worth a fuck."

Even before Punk, Nick Lowe had been kicking around, first as a member of the perennial pubbers Brinsley Schwarz, then as a producer (he produced the Damned, the most important band signed to Stiff). When he came out in a gold lamé suit in 1977 with an album called *Pure Pop for Now People*, he offered up a whole new side to the "punk" aesthetic. Two songs were about the Bay City Rollers, and Lowe arrogantly took pride is his appreciation of "pop" (as opposed to Rock). He told the American comedian Robert Klein: "There's been this snobbery against the Osmonds too long!" The new target of contempt was no longer "Pop" but what, at that time, passed itself off as Rock: the

Rolling Stones, the Who, Pink Floyd, Led Zeppelin, Rod Stewart, and the other dinosaurs. Stuff like the Osmonds had become perversely hip. This was an important turning point in the development of the post-Punk aesthetic in which irony would rule all. Soon you had college kids listening to Slim Whitman to make some ironic statement about the pop culture itself (but mostly just proving they were idiots).

This kind of knowing irony would have a pervasive influence on New Wave, which was Pop with Punk sensibilities. Nick Lowe's "Marie Provost" was a perfect example: although it was a Beatlesque popper, the lyrics were about cannibalism. In the same vein, Lowe's one and only American hit, "Cruel to be Kind," had such a pretty melody and lush texture that it disguised the song's more subversive content (mainly, the fact it was a paean to S&M).

Stiff heralded the coming age more than anyone, with the proliferation of all those cute promo buttons that would become as popular as skinny ties by '79–'80, as well as with their endless assembly line of smarmy creations: Rachel Sweet, Wreckless Eric, Mickey Jupp, Lene Lovich. Their most famous discovery was a young man named Declan McManus, who, the minute Elvis died, took the sacred name for his own and rechristened himself Elvis Costello.

Working as a computer operator eight hours per day, Costello was this mad, obsessive songwriter in his spare time. When he finally took to the stage, he brought the nerdy, pigeon-toed, suit-wearing demeanor of the office clerk with him. This was another part of Punk undoing hippie: there's nothing the hippies loathed more than the short-haired junior executive, but that's what Costello was and what a whole generation would become with pride (i.e., the yuppies)—much to the chagrin of the leftover '60s "revolution" types.

Like Jonathan Richman before him, Costello was brutally frank about his sexual inadequacies, but once again, this fit the Punk polemic. In the '60s, "sex" had ceased to be "love," but this was much more—in the '70s, "love" had become war, and no one epitomized this more than Elvis. As Travolta was ripping up the dance floor, here was this bug-eyed troubadour spouting venom. It caught on, and Costello was hailed as an "angry young man" and "poet." The New Wave had its Bob Dylan and, like grandpa, he was signed to Columbia. His first album, *My Aim is True*, was Brinsley Schwarz-level pub Rock with more vitriol, musically not that different from another would-be Dylan signed to Columbia at that time, Bruce Springsteen. But Elvis was a nasty little bugger, and the mystique grew. Despite this fact, he still never got played on American radio.

Starting with *This Year's Model* in 1978, Costello formed the Attractions, a semipermanent backing band that gave him a more intense, organ-laden sound and a sturdier rhythm section to base his vitriol on. Never was it more intense than on classics like "I Don't Want to Go to Chelsea," "You Belong to Me," and "Lipstick Vogue," which completely desecrated the notion of romance with lyrics like "love is like a tumor/Sometimes you have to cut it out." By the time of *Armed Forces*, they were even beginning to play him on regular American FM-radio rotation, sandwiched between Journey and Lynyrd Skynyrd. Then came the ill-fated Tour of Hate.

Touring the U.S. to support the album in the winter of '79, he ended up in a barroom brawl with aging hippie singer Bonnie Bramlett. Apparently Costello referred to Ray Charles as a "blind half-assed old nigger" and Bramlett responded with a right hook. This was part of New challenging Old once again: hippies were sanctimonious about their relationship with Blacks. Punks, on the other hand, while not inherently racist, refused to pay lip service to such politically correct protocol. In the end, it was nothing more than what traveling musicians and other barroom types experience every night of their lives. But because the bastions of the liberal press like *Rolling Stone* got a hold of it, Costello's name in America temporarily became mud. His next three or four albums stiffed before he finally pulled a Clash and sold out completely with *Punch the Clock*, the title of which harked back to his junior-executive roots. Welcome to the working week, indeed.

About the same time *My Aim is True* was released, the Sex Pistols' album finally came out. This was Punk's crowing achievement—far from some grungy basement LP, *Never Mind the Bollocks* was as full-bodied as any Kiss album, thanks to Chris Thomas's brilliant production. Overdubbing what sounded like one thousand of Steve Jones's guitars to create an absolutely pulsating attack, the album thrilled Punk fans, but the majority of Americans were swept up in Disco and played dead. And they have ever since.

This did not bode well for the Pistols as they got ready to embark on their first American tour, which, ironically enough, was centered in the South and Southwest. This was part of McLaren's weltanschauung: snub New York and the major media outlets and take it directly to the people. But it backfired, because the press in the region didn't know what to make of the group and the "people" didn't either. A few New York journalists like *Punk*'s Legs McNeil and John Holmstrom flew in and accompanied the band, and there were predictable flare-ups at every roadhouse along the way. For instance, Sid outtoughing a Texan who'd burned himself with a cigarette by cutting himself open and bleeding all over his scrambled eggs and then eating them. Suffice to say, British Invasion II—which was supposed to be spearheaded by the Pistols—never happened.

The Pistols had other things to worry about. There was internal tension in the band, which eventually equaled separate travel arrangements for the warring factions: in typical rocker fashion, Jones and Cook supposedly couldn't abide by all the Reggae being played on the tour bus and eventually opted to fly with McLaren by plane. Sid had become particularly unruly, cutting himself, getting into fights, and, worst of all, becoming hooked on heroin. Johnny Rotten was openly critical of his old friend, but McLaren seemed to delight in the controversy, molding Vicious into a Frankenstein like he had done with the Dolls. But the Dolls had basically told McLaren to fuck off; Sid was young and impressionable and kept indulging in increasingly self-destructive behavior in order to live up to the "punk" ethos. It had been ex-Doll Johnny Thunders and his band the Heartbreakers who'd introduced Vicious to junk during the famous "Anarchy in the U.K." tour in 1977 (which also included the Clash and Damned). They also introduced him to Nancy Spungen, which was really his downfall.

There were other factors that contributed to the Pistols' imminent demise. McLaren had inked a deal for a movie entitled *The Great Rock 'n' Roll Swindle*, in which he outlined his ten-step program to Rock 'n' Roll suckerdom. It was originally supposed to be directed by tit-king Russ Meyer and contain such poignant scenes as Sid making it with his own mother (played by Marianne Faithfull). But the Pistols hated Meyer, branding him a "dirty old man." Eventually, Rotten had a bitter falling-out with McLaren, not only over the direction of the film but the band as well, and over the distribution of moneys from each. Reportedly, the final blow came when Rotten did a radio interview in San Francisco prior to the band's final gig, in which he claimed he was not McLaren's "puppet." During the same interview he also said: "Rock 'n' Roll is finished. We killed it."

Despite their worst intentions, the Pistols didn't kill Rock 'n' Roll—they rejuvenated it. To a whole new generation bred on an "underground" networking aesthetic—based on corporate indifference to "real" Rock—the Pistols were the founding fathers: they financed their own tour, played in out-of-the-way villas, invented their own visual style, and didn't compromise. All of a sudden, there was great freedom in forming a band. The Sex Pistols may have been a Rock band in that they played Chuck Berry riffs, but the bands that followed didn't know or care about such rootsy definitions—as it was in the '60s, that would come later. The kids of the '70s were the first generation to grow up with Rock 'n' Roll as their birthright—that is, inbred into the fabric of the culture at large. As such, they'd grown up absorbing a thousand different variations of the basic Rock structure as their daily bread. What Punk did was decontextualize all of this: the basic four-person bass/drums/guitar/vocal format stayed intact, but the Do It Yourself aesthetic gave bands the freedom to alter the form through whatever means necessary. It was no longer unusual to see a skronk-blaring saxophone within the context of a Rock band—or four women sweating onstage until their nipples poked through their ripped t-shirts.

In the wake of their demise, the Sex Pistols' legacy seemed to take its greatest stronghold in California (not ironic, as the scene of their last performance ever was San Francisco on January 14, 1978). L.A. in particular was an early spawning ground for Punk. The climate suited the bored/no-future ethos of Punk perfectly: America's second-largest city, and one of its most dangerous, Los Angeles was the home of Hollywood and the television industry, and miles and miles of endless suburbs. The center of vacuous hipness and decadent pop culture, it was renowned for its smog and endless traffic jams. But at the same time it was in many ways a virtual Promised Land of sunny beaches, beautiful girls, and eternal sunshine. It was this paradox that provided the philosophical basis for L.A. Punk.

The Rock scene in L.A. was very distant from the average kid in the suburbs—clubs like the Whiskey were elitists who made bands work like dogs to back up itinerant major-label acts. L.A.'s own denizens saw the city as a cultural dead end. Frank Zappa had been parodying L.A.culture since the '60s. In the '70s it seemed as if Zappa's "Plastic People" prophecy had come true.

Although a large portion of the music industry was based in L.A., there was no real Rock scene, at least not on the local level. Glam bands had ruled since the '70s, but by '76–'77 the clubs had given themselves over to half-assed kozmic cowboys and mediocre comedians. There was a metal scene, but surprisingly, few noteworthy bands emerged from L.A. in the mid-'70s. The city had experienced its heyday, as far as Rock goes, in the '60s with the Byrds, Love, Buffalo Springfield, the Doors, the Beach Boys, the Mothers, Captain Beefheart, and others. In the '70s, L.A. became the idyllic capital of the singer/songwriters. These troubadours saw the lit-up city as their cruel but understanding mistress. This laid back attitude was epitomized by one of the most popular albums of the mid-'70s, the Eagles' *Hotel California*: "You can check out any time you like/But you can never leave." Time and again, Rock artists have portrayed Los Angeles as an inescapable Gomorrah.

However, by the late '70s, L.A. was about to experience a reawakening, as was San Francisco—one akin to what happened in the '60s, only this time instead of thousands of bands with long hair forming in the foothills, thousands of bands with *short hair* began forming in the foothills.

In March 1977, a dive called the Hollywood Punk Palace opened; a few months later, the Whiskey inaugurated "New Wave weekends." At that time, virtually all live music was in jeopardy because of Disco, and the club owners hoped that New Wave would help revive the flagging club scene. It was in L.A. that the *look* of New Wave really came into being (sound-wise, it was still Ramones cloning). Punk musicians in L.A. seemed to absorb a lot of the Damned's visual panache: short hair, kooky shades, etc. The Damned were one of the first British Punk bands to play Los Angeles, and during the occasion, bass player Captain Sensible shed the emerald dress he was wearing, a gesture that caused a riot. It was a sign of things to come.

The symbolic birth of L.A. Punk can be traced back to about the time legendary Rock critic Richard Meltzer first arrived from New York in 1976 and quickly became an integral part of the burgeoning Punk scene, thanks to his membership in the ultimate amateurish aggregation, Vom. Meltzer was one of the inventors of the "punk" aesthetic: his 1972 book, *Gulcher*, celebrated the lowbrow anti-intellectualism that would soon characterize bands like the Dictators and Ramones. His rewritten lyrics to early Blue Oyster Cult songs were laced with bitter contempt, like the great line from "Stairway to the Stars": "Should I sign it/Just for you?" Although he was well over thirty by the time he came to L.A., he had not tempered his abrasive punkitude one whit. Meltzer was the thinking man's Peter Laughner, and he'd been one of the first to turn his back on the corpse of corporate Rock. Naturally he was in his element amongst the decadent descendents of his barbed aesthetic.

So much so that when the Pistols invaded San Francisco for what would be their last-ever gig, Meltzer was the emcee. However, not before having to out-fox the show's promoter, Bill Graham, who disliked Meltzer from an earlier N.Y./California rivalry that went back to the hippie days and barred him from the club. Reportedly Meltzer turned his leather jacket inside out, sneaked past Graham, and proceeded to unleash a torrent of drunken profanities onstage, which later caused Greil Marcus to fume: "*Mmmmnn!* This from the man who co-wrote 'Stairway to the Stars'?" Of course, this was just the sort of genera-tional treason that made Meltzer a hero to the coming Punk hordes.

Another pioneering L.A. Punk outfit were the Weirdos, who relied on the by-now-patented Punk fashion statements (*kookie glasses!*) combined with the usual Ramones buzzsaw attack. The Weirdos reached their pinnacle on the L.A. Punk apotheosis, "Neutron Bomb" b/w "Solitary Confinement." Released on the indie label Dangerhouse, it was another sign, along with the stuff com-ing out of England at the time, that the 45 was back as a viable Rock 'n' Roll medium. It had taken a dip during the bloated Album-Rock era of Yes, Led Zeppelin, and Pink Floyd, but Punk bands who otherwise would've never had a chance to record were finding the format to be ideal for their momentary bursts of brilliance. It didn't take that much imagination to conceive two songs, nor that much money to produce the record either.

Equally important, and also on Dangerhouse, were X, led by the charis-matic duo of John Doe and Exene Cervenka. They were definitely the fore-runner of all the other indie-Rock husband/wife teams, from Sonic Youth to Yo La Tengo. Thus, along with the Talking Heads, they were among the first true college Rock bands. When they shifted gears to a more Rockabilly/roots-influ-enced sound a few years later, they actually experienced some college-radio suc-cess. Bright, young, and suburban, their relationship with their city was one of genuine fear and loathing. Their anthem "Los Angeles," with its racing tempo, was the equivalent of eight million people racing to get out of Gomorrah before the walls came tumbling down. As Exene told *Boston Rock* magazine years later on the subject of growing up in public: "I was 18 years old. How do you think I felt? I was *terrified.*"

Other bands proliferated: the Dickies did a wild take on cool kitsch—the next step in "nerd" after Devo—with a surging tempo three times the normal Ramonespeed and cartoony falsetto vocals that mouthed platitudes to Twinkies and bondage, equivocating both of them as mere symptoms of modern disposable living. The Dickies, with their black-taped glasses and songs about getting beat up, were defying every macho principle of Rock from Elvis to Sid (so were the Ramones with their limp-dumb persona).

Bands like Vom, X, the Dickies, and the Weirdos shared a common camp sensibility—like movie stars, they all sported made-up monikers: Billy Zoom, Darby Crash, Chuck Wagon, etc. Far from being a "street" rebellion based on class values, L.A. Punk was a bunch of suburban kids reacting against the media culture that they'd grown up in the shadows of.

Other important L.A. bands included the Screamers, whose contributions to the field of video were years ahead of their time; and the Flesheaters, who burned a hole through typical Stooges-style riffings with a more Blues-based crunch that helped pave the way for the whole Green River school of ballistic guitar abandon.

The group that best epitomized the sound and fury of early L.A. Punk was the Germs. This was bored adolescent fantasy driven to EXTREME proportions: a group in which all the members were between the ages of fifteen and eighteen, led by the Michael Jackson of Iggy imitators, Darby Crash. This was Punk at its most nihilistic: a kid cutting himself, bleeding, screaming and retching, driven to exposition not by some grandiose ideal about the proletariat, but by raw desire—growing up and acting out his basest adolescent fantasies entirely in public. More than Iggy, this was the root of someone like G. G. Allin (who was already older than Darby when Darby debuted). What it proved was that a whole generation was awakening to the reality that the void was inescapable.

There was one escape, though, and it was the same one as ever: Darby "crashed" from a heroin OD shortly after the Germs' first (Joan Jett-produced) album came out.

The scene typified by bands like the Germs soon became known as Hardcore because of the self-mutilation as well as the degree of audience participation. Punks were finding out, like stand-up comics before them, that by being so accessible to their audiences, they had become targets for their fans' wildest aggressions. At the time, heckling was one of the lost arts of Rock 'n' Roll, with arena artists being too aloof and godlike and physically distant to entertain audience response of any kind (other than lumpen worship). But Punks played in sweaty basement clubs and venues where Rock artists had never played before, like VFW halls, biker hangouts, and drag bars.

Hardcore was where toughness finally came into full display—playing until one's hands bled and all. Melody, harmony...it all degenerated into a massive metallic KO. Crowds who'd already learned to "pogo"—which meant to jump up and down in place—were now starting to push each other around. Spitting, or gobbing as it was called in England, had already become the standard form of "tribute" to Punk bands by their adoring fans. The next step was throwing actual bottles as well as trash. Punk gigs began to draw audience members who were primarily interested in violence, not music. Of course this played to the Punk ethos even more, because it meant that one was risking his or her own life just to be involved in Punk.

This was a lot different than the peaceful campaign of the hippie, which seemed to say that, as long as one took drugs, he or she was "cool." But Punk demanded a more physical commitment. Almost as if to bury any trace of hippiedom, Punks for the most part eschewed drug use—especially marijuana, the sacrament of the hippies (as well as the Rastas). By that time, marijuana use was at an all-time high, and to *not* use it was a kind of self-imposed ostracism. This also went along with the Punk desire to make oneself as ugly as possible (short hair, ripped clothes, garish makeup). A scene that had initially been open to women now became more male-dominated than ever, particularly after the blossoming of Straightedge, which was the ultimate extremist manifestation of the whole No Sex/No Drugs/No Booze doctrine. In the form of Washington, D.C.'s Minor Threat, it was also perhaps the most intense, streamlined distillation of Rock in theory/practice *ever*.

The Punks used warfare tactics but, ultimately, Hardcore was a musical war, not a social revolution. A few thousand faces got stomped—like the poor John Denver look-alike who tried to stage-dive into a teeming pit of shaveheads—but, in the end, Art was the enemy: Hardcore was a stripping down process meant to unload all the excess baggage Rock had taken on over the previous two decades. As for the so-called violence factor, none of the original scenes revolving around such genres as Honky Tonk, Rhythm & Blues, or even Mersey beat were that genteel either. In each case, it was foreign sounds being presented to an unsure audience, and sometimes their reactions were not con-

THE RUNAWAYS
The Donnas' favorite babysitters.

John Fahnley

X_X
It sure ain't the Allman Brothers.

Tom Warren

DNA
Making a case for urban decay.

Tom Warren

THE FEELIES
They go through chicken and fish phases, but no meat.

Tom Warren

THE LOUNGE LIZARDS
Trans-topology.

Tom Warren

JOHN LYDON
Piss off, mate!

John Fahnley

JOE STRUMMER OF THE CLASH
Raising collars so that you don't have to.

John Fahnley

THE FLESHTONES
Just say "Eeeeh…"

Anne Streng

D. BOON OF THE MINUTEMEN
Get the pizza delivered next time.

John Fahnley

UPSIDE DOWN CROSS
No, no NO, buddy!

Taaang! Records

SONIC YOUTH
The return of dating.

Michael Galinsky

KING BUZZO OF THE MELVINS
Ten seconds after this was taken, someone pulled his pants down!

LIZ PHAIR
In 20 years she'll be Hillary Clinton.

Mellow Lomba

Allison Tanenhaus

LOVE CHILD
4.0 GPA, 3.2 Beer.

Michael Galinsky

MUDHONEY
Anarchy in staggered animation.

Michael Galinsky

SHELL
Our parents voted for Reagan.

Bortz/Dagley

TRIS McCALL
Uncovering New Jersey brick by brick.

Tris McCall

BILLY OF THE BLACK HALOS
Hey Billy, who dresses you? King Buzzo?

Lisa LeeKing

GLUECIFER
Huns give frosty reception for the MTV "rockumentary" crew.

Electralux

structive. Hardcore represented the Rock audience turning violent on itself: much more than an Us against Them mentality, it was the perpetrator-as-victim, which translated into a kind of paranoia that had everyone looking over their shoulder while still trying to maintain "cool."

Into the fray came Black Flag, a group from Redondo Beach that, perhaps more than anyone, defined Hardcore. From the beginning, their gigs were the scene of some of the most widely publicized cops vs. kids bloodshed, which resulted in their name becoming mud to the local authorities. Banned from every venue in town, the group was one of the first to network with friends in other cities and arrange out-of-town gigs. Soon this would become common practice within the underground.

Dedicated to the indie spirit, Black Flag owned their own record label, SST, eliminating the middleman once again. Soon they would discover just how difficult it was to get a record distributed once you'd made it, given the politics of the record industry. But for the time being, they were banking on Art—they correctly assumed that the break with the corporate record business was the only way anything "authentic" was ever going to happen in the name of Rock 'n' Roll again. That was the great thing about Punk and Hardcore all along—the freedom that came with saying "fuck them" and just blasting away and actually rendering all these great songs with no frills and nothing going for them other than the fact that they *were* great songs. And that's what Black Flag's early works were—some of the most amazing Rock 'n' Roll ever put onto wax, in many ways the last true Rock 'n' Roll as far as the ultimate paring down of the whole Chuck Berry technique. One could make the same argument for any of a dozen groups of the same era, but none of them were as *ultimate* about their intentions. Black Flag were on a mission.

Few debuts were as quintessential—or dramatic—as "Nervous Breakdown" (1978): Stooges/Ramones riffing at twice the normal speed with the guitars all racing each other to get to the final apocalypse. It was maddening stuff, one minute and twenty-two seconds of sheer physical/emotional release. The vocals, especially the ones by original singer Keith Morris (who later joined the Circle Jerks), were a post-Iggy post-Rotten type of manic insanity. Whereas, the later vocals of Henry Rollins were just pure rage! This would be a big influence on the future direction of Rock, from the howling feminists of Riot Grrl to the crunching oppression of Industrial music. This was the music of the *Clockwork Orange* generation—the malt shop had been detonated for good. Fun was dead—to deny the pain and agony was to shirk your savage duty. This was the angriest Rock *ever*: "I've Had It," for example, was a brilliant deconstruction of Led Zep's "Communication Breakdown" riff in which the sheer physical force of the music anchors the most hate-ridden angst of all time with amazing clarity. In this case, Zep's ornate embellishments would be superfluous (which was the whole point of Punk).

Flag continued to maintain their position as the figureheads of the movement right up until the time their first album, *Damaged* (1981), was released—and subsequently banned. Although the band had released the album on SST, their own label, they'd agreed to a distribution deal with MCA, a deal that ended when an MCA exec, Al Bergamo, "found it to be an anti-parent record." This was an important turning point: whereas Punk's first wave—the Ramones, the Sex Pistols, the Clash, Patti Smith—had more or less been signed to major labels, the second wave—Black Flag, Dead Kennedys, Minor Threat—had to face the daunting prospect of the majors, for the most part, staying home.

Which is where labels like SST came in. Like the purveyors of Rhythm & Blues in the late '40s/early '50s, the early Punk labels saw an untapped market and jumped on it. Perhaps an even clearer antecedent was ESP-Disk, the New York avant-garde label that, in the age of the Beatles, released records by proto-Punk bands like the Fugs, Godz, and Pearls Before Swine (not to mention their impressive roster of Jazz greats like Ornette Coleman, Sun Ra, and Albert Ayler). Bearing that in mind, consider how incongruous the Minutemen's jazzy skitter or the Meat Puppets' warped Country-Punk wail sounded in the midst of Hardcore circa 1981. Even the "speed-metal" sound that became so popular later on (Metallica) was influenced by SST's early "crossover" acts (St. Vitus, the Stains, Overkill). And where would the future practitioners of "alternative Rock"—Nirvana, etc.—be without Husker Du? SST found itself in the unique position of predicating national trends from their little four- or five-man operation in Lawndale, California. So it would go throughout the '80s (and, yawn, the '90s): dedicated starving artists would weld the latest innovations only to be ripped off by joyriders and Johnny-come-latelies.

As the majors grew increasingly oblivious to what was going on at the grassroots level, the indie market expanded. At the majors, money that once went into "artist development" was now going into promotion. They banked on the biggies, in other words, but no longer bothered to build a solid base of long-term talent underneath. The major labels had put all their hopes in Disco, cashing in with all kinds of insta-product, which they bullied their distributors into buying, thus guaranteeing the cherished "gold record." At that time, "gold" meant "one million copies shipped" but not necessarily *sold*. So while *Billboard* awarded its token gold star, the worthless "product" languished on the shelves, eventually having to be returned. It's easy to see why the majors were losing money.

The industry itself was getting older and thus less inclined to kick out the jams. Most of the young mavericks had become wine-sipping snobs—it's no wonder they were indifferent to Punk. After all, many of the major Rock artists of the day—the Rolling Stones, the Who, Bob Seger—were getting older and *singing* about it. This made them a perfect target for the reactionary Punks. From the beginning, one of Punk's biggest deviations was its lack of respect for its musical elders, all of whom were put down even as their riffs ran through the songs of the New. This caused a schism that could never be mended between the Punks and the Boomer-controlled industry.

To the old hippies, it was absolute anathema that these kids weren't traditional liberals—that their scene was based entirely on irony and that they didn't care about issues like civil rights, Watergate, and Vietnam. Soon Punks would purposely take an adversarial role on these issues, just to piss the liberals off. After being considered "rebels" for so long, the '60s hippies had quickly become the old fogeys, which is why they despised Punk with such vehemence. Punks were laughing at them, and kicking their canes, so to speak.

This all had to do with the further constriction of FM radio, which had become as formulaic as AM once was. Worse actually, because at least in the Rock-daze of yore a runaway hit that came out of nowhere could top the charts (e.g., "96 Tears"). By the '70s, everything adhered to strictly controlled playlists—which the majors pumped up with advertising money to get their music on the charts. Many listeners lamented that Rock was dead and turned elsewhere: Folk, Reggae and, if the companies were lucky, Disco. But in reality Rock hadn't gone anywhere—it was being twisted through more creative mutations than at any time in its history. But the kids were being sold a bill of goods in the form of processed pseudo-Rock pabulum: Boston, Styx, Foreigner, Triumph, and the rest of the single-moniker brigade. The problem was, the average kid no longer knew what constituted Rock. Once a secret language amongst the young, Rock was now merely another suburban birthright, like owning a car or getting laid. FM provided an endless soundtrack of nearly identical bands that personified the kind of "laid back" cool personified by equally obnoxious films like *FM*, where the hippies stood up to the greedy programmers in what was perhaps the final confrontation of '60s free-spiritedness vs. modern-day mean-spiritedness. It was a communist plot.

The few bands playing anything remotely "Punk" that were allowed on the airwaves were usually of the readymade "new wave" variety, which the industry helped invent as a safe alternative to Punk: the Knack, the Cars, Sniff & the Tears, M, Flash & the Pan (from Australia), the Vapors. None of these, save possibly the Cars, were a "real" band in that they'd ever been an active part of any local scene. It was if they'd popped out of nowhere. By 1979–1980, New Wave had hit the high school cafeteria as the betokened new trend after Disco.

When the majors did handle Punk acts, they did so from a distance. Sire's whole relationship with Warner's set the pattern for other in-house subsidiaries like IRS (which was owned by A&M) and Slash (which belonged to Warner's). The former was the vanity project of millionaire Miles Copeland, but initially their roster included several important and great bands: the Buzzcocks, the Fleshtones, and the Fall among them. They finally made amends to the parent label by launching the Go-Gos, the most manufactured Pop act since the Monkees, and almost as successful with New Wave hits like "Our Lips Are Sealed" and "Vacation." Slash, which was originally a spinoff from the fanzine of the same name (another first that would be repeated by Touch & Go, Sub Pop, Kill Rock Stars, et al.), was even braver in the beginning, scooping up the cream of L.A. Punk acts: the Germs, X, and Fear. But in the end, as they grew bigger, they vomited forth Mitchell Froom.

The major labels seemed intent upon colonizing the more radio-friendly English New Wave imports. A&M proper profited from both the Police and Joe Jackson. The Police played it cool, but they were actually a bunch of old session hands who'd gotten haircuts and jumped on board, practicing nouveau-cynique and playing a little faster. Jackson was a basic non-Rock person: his "Punk" hatred was based on a more traditional form of romantic cynicism. The music was never "music" at first: the lyrics were always the heart of the song, and they usually described the pitfalls of love. Both acts were significant, however, for helping to introduce the Reggae downstroke to the common vernacular, which led to the Ska revival. The Clash bears a lot of the responsibility here as well. Speaking of everyone's favorite socialists, CBS were about to cash in on them in a big way when *London Calling* became the soup du jour of the brat-o-phile set.

Meanwhile, the do it yourself scene was flourishing with fairly successful indies like Bomp, Beserkley, and Ralph, labels who'd actually achieved some degree of financial stability (enough to advertise regularly in the back of *Creem*, anyway). Fanzines were popping up everywhere, and even above-board mags like *Trouser Press* at least tried to keep people informed about independent music. From this point on, the indie records never stopped coming—great and gloriously obscure stuff that bore absolutely *no* relationship to the general marketplace. This was music of limited quantity and sometimes quality, but it broke the mold of soundalike complacency. Something was indeed happening. Because once a band divorced itself from the realm of commercial music making, they were free to pursue their art to the farthest extent of their imaginations. Basement bands could bravely step forward—and they did, in alarming numbers. The whole phenomenon of Rock was becoming more localized again. Far from trying to be Rock stars, the early indie pioneers simply wanted to live the dream of having a piece of vinyl with their name on it. The quaintness of it all truly reeked.

In and of itself, a band like Detroit's Half Japanese, who released their first independent single in 1977, would never have made sense. They were brash, crude, atonal, and, at times, infantile. However, within the greater context of Punk, their music was like a great rallying cry for personal freedom—even if at that time its only audience was a bunch of hopelessly well-read Rock scholars (i.e., nerds who never got laid, even in the most promiscuous time ever, the late '70s).

The college market was an ever-widening sphere for the new Punk/underground rockers. Just as in the '60s, the college audience had proven a fertile breeding ground for Folk, the college kids of the '70s and '80s were both intelligent and jaded enough to figure out that there had to be something more challenging than Journey. At the same time, college radio didn't pay royalties and the DJs didn't get paid, so the egalitarian principles of Punk were appealing to college radio's perpetrators and adherents. Commercial radio had tightened up so drastically with its timid mix of Boston/Foreigner/Seger/Styx that the hope of any independent record getting played on the radio was gone. So why not fuck the industry?

Ironically, when FM began in the late '60s, it served much the same function as college radio today, exposing obscure and unusual talent without the stricture of format specifications. However, in the '60s a lot of truly underground music was still being licensed by the majors: Reprise's roster alone included Captain Beefheart, Tim Buckley, the Fugs, Essra Mohawk, Nico, and John Cale, for instance. At that time, FM was unsyndicated, which meant that each station's program director set the format, much like college radio today. This meant a lot of the programming was influenced by regional factors—that is, a programmer in Berkeley was probably going to play the Sons of Champlin more than a station in New York. By the late '70s, however, it was a mass web of schlock—stations all over the country sounded exactly alike.

Therefore, anything even remotely adventurous on the airwaves became the province of college radio. Along with fanzines and independent records, college radio was the third point in the three-prong crown heralding the arrival of the new American underground. College radio programming regularly jumped from genre to genre—Punk, New Wave, Reggae, Garage, Ska—and allowed songs that contained profanity or unpopular sentiment. In general, it helped foster the "fuck the mainstream" mentality.

The isolationist / "fuck off" stance was in place within the American underground, but as far as actual activism of the type that was already happening in England, it was limited. That is, until the Dead Kennedys and their flamboyant leader, Jello Biafra, came along. Hailing from San Francisco, the band was instrumental in introducing politics to the American Punk scene. However, by doing so they helped it splinter in two thousand different directions. Spreading his message through the band as well as its two multimedia offshoots—the *Maximum Rock' n' Roll* fanzine (actually the province of aging Yippie Tim Yohannon) and the Alternative Tentacles record label—Biafra's interest in politics was real: he later ran for mayor of San Francisco, but his campaign was cut off when some opposition thugs broke his knees. Nevertheless, he remained active on all fronts, collecting tapes of various bands from all over the world and releasing them in a series of compilation LPs that set the state for the whole indie onslaught, and later the barrage of genre-specific indie comps (Punk, Oy!, Metal, Folk, Garage). The whole point was, if a band wasn't good enough to make a whole LP, at least their one contribution to the overall body of independent music could be heard. And it worked, because the bands performed as well, and Punk gigs became multi-band extravaganzas, all-afternoon, "all-ages" slamfests.

In California, these were kids who'd witnessed the conservative revolution being born through the ascendance of two-time governor Ronald Reagan. Consequently, the music echoed chaos—abrupt time changes foreshadowed by bubbling bass lines and rapid right-turn rhythmic explosions. Whereas the hippies had been fogged out, as if in a blissful daze, the Punks were erect and rigid. They hated the elitism inherent in the counterculture and sought to stabilize it by embracing such pre-Rock values as family dedication, short hair, masculinity, anti-drug sentiment, paramilitary garb and, above all, *organization*. Punks were *united*. But although Punks were much more likely to embrace '50s culture over '60s, if only because they liked the hairstyles better, politically they were to the far, *far* left. This made Reagan the ultimate symbolic bogeyman—and the most hated president, as far as Rock 'n' Roll went, since Nixon.

Now with a target for their rage, the Hardcore hordes could become even more focused. But despite the committed social agenda of a few people like Jello Biafra, the whole essence of American Hardcore became toughness-for-toughness's-sake: slam-dancing and playing until yer hands bled. It became very formalized. In England, the communal aspects of Hardcore gave way to tribes like the Crass who were important in establishing an international Punk overthrow. The English Hardcore scene seems to have blossomed almost after the fact, but, with the appearance of the Exploited, can probably be credited with reintroducing the mohawk to the vernacular, which was to have a big fashion impact via the New York group the Plasmatics, led by the post-porn queen Wendy O. Williams.

Along with the Dead Kennedys, there were a number of other interesting bands in San Francisco in the late '70s/early '80s. The Residents, who began recording for the indie label Ralph in 1973, were actually the city's pioneering indie trailblazers, but their weird dadaist music didn't really fit in with the scene at large, and their impact seemed to be restricted to the area of video. The Avengers, with a female singer, were perhaps the first Frisco band to sense the direction that was coming from New York, London, and, by that time, L.A., with their Ramonesean attack. The Nuns meanwhile possessed a "cabaret" quality enhanced by their Nico-esque blonde lead singer, Jennifer Miro. Flipper was the first Hardcore band to slow the tempo (Boston's Kilslug deserves credit also). And bands like Chrome and the Urinals added the damaged clang of the Velvets and other '70s noise to the rudimentary aesthetic of Punk. One of the more interesting Art-Punk bands to emerge from Frisco were the Toiling Midgets, whose singer, Mark Eitzel, croaked in a post-Beefheartian vein and whose somewhat askew rhythms predated much of the deconstruction of the '80s.

All over America, in the name of Hardcore, several distinct factions were forming, each one more microscopic than the last. By far the most celebrated offshoot was Straightedge, which represented the fiercest denouncement of the hippies yet thanks to the anti-drug crusades of its leaders—most notably D.C. Punk god Ian MacKaye of the formative Straightedge bands Teen Idles and Minor Threat. The Idles' first single, "I Drink Milk," was actually a pre–Hardy Har Hardcore anthem that made fun of beer drinkers. At that time, a good deal of the Punk audience consisted of under–twenty-ones who couldn't drink anyway—hence "all ages" shows. A lot of this was just youthfulness—the young kids entranced by the energy fix of Punk/Hardcore saw the slow-moving, paunchbellied sloths of the "burnout" generation as lame and ineffectual: as long as they had their beer/dope they were oblivious to the world around them, which the Punks saw as the ultimate cop out. Or as the credo, penned by MacKaye, went: "Don't smoke! Don't drink! Don't *fuck*! At least I can fuckin' think!"

A lot of this was sour grapes: young Punks like Minor Threat were, in actuality, too young to drink, too lame to score drugs, and too fucking ugly—with shaved heads and jackboots—to get laid. One thing's for sure: all that deprivation led to a welter-whip of fury: Minor Threat's debut LP was the most aggressive Rock album of all time. And it was Rock: the rebounding chords bespoke the entire power-Rock tradition, from the Who to the Dictators to the Sex Pistols, but the songs were played at such a furious pace, with such a high level of distortion, and the overall message was so extreme, that it came on like something totally original.

There was a macho polemic at play here also—the scene was almost entirely male-oriented, and the sheer physical force of Punk bespoke an almost bodybuilder level of dedication: one had to be in shape in order to keep pace— or to survive the slam-dance rituals. Bands like the Misfits actually began lifting weights. There was a genuine determination to rescue Rock from the slovenly slag heap of '70s self-degradation (Cheech & Chong, et al.). There was definitely a macho thing to it, in the way the bands were drawn into actual confrontation with the audience. The confrontational aspects of Punk began with gobbing, and now it had reached such ridiculous proportions that even non-macho bands like the Angry Samoans and the Minutemen were forced into mindless standoffs with their audience—these led the Samoans, at least, to say "fuck the scene" entirely.

Straightedge attained its most solid footing in Boston, where bands like SSD Control, DYS, and the F.U.'s dominated the local scene. But the temperance of the original movement was soon to fade. Almost as if to defy the unshakable dictum that had been laid down at that time, some bands even began sporting actual *long hair*—notably, Husker Du (from Minneapolis) and Black Flag's latest (and last) lead singer, Henry Rollins, who, with his poetry readings and flowing locks, became the closest thing the scene had to a Jim Morrison. With a twist, however—he pumped iron, had tattoos, and *didn't* imbibe.

In a musical sense, many bands were beginning to find the relentless crank tempo of Hardcore—eighty-eight beats per minute—to be constricting. Since these were kids who grew up in the '70s, the turn they took was naturally one toward metal, even though, during Punk's inception, that was the chosen enemy. Part of the reason for this was the metal hordes' shortsightedness when it came to Punk—although they should have recognized the Ramones and Sex Pistols as their natural brethren, they turned their backs on them, brainwashed as they were by the forces of commercial FM radio. Meanwhile, the Punks' dismissal of the metal hordes as dope-smoking burnouts didn't help matters either. The fact remained, though, that growing up when they did, most Punk fans had albums by the following artists in their record collections: Black Sabbath, Led Zeppelin, Kiss, Aerosmith, and Ted Nugent. So when the dust settled, there was common ground there. With first Disco and then MTV threatening to decimate all Rock, the two camps—Punk and Metal—found they had more in common than they'd ever dreamed possible.

A nod in this direction came in the form of the "New Wave" of Heavy Metal that barnstormed out of England in the late '70s: Judas Priest, Iron Maiden, Saxon, Def Leppard, Motorhead, and the newly revamped Ozzy Osbourne. These bands had their asses kicked into high gear by the energy of Punk. Gone were the twenty-minute solos of Led Zeppelin/Deep Purple. This, in turn, influenced legitimate Punk bands to pick up the Metal chalice. Among Brits who jumped the gun on the Punk-Metal merger was Discharge, whose brutal and chaotic thrash set the pattern for the violent splatter of speed-Metal acts like Slayer. Venom was another important Hardcore-cum-Metal act: whereas Ozzy Osbourne and Black Sabbath had foretold the hand of doom falling on the devil worshipping hordes, Venom celebrated the lurid presence of His Satanic Majesty. Speaking of Ozzy, the Clown Prince of Heavy Metal experienced a major rebirth in the early '80s: after bottoming out with Sabbath in 1978, he reappeared with a revamped lineup, including neo-guitar god Randy Rhoads, to become an icon to a whole new generation of death-wishers. Van Halen is another outfit that also can't be discounted in the reformation of Metal that occurred during the post-Punk era, if only because they upped the tempo somewhat and also changed the subject matter from Zep-derived mystical jive to pure hedonism. Which ultimately signaled the birth of the '80s MTV glam-Metal poseurs more than anything (and that kind of collective cutesy-pie was something Halen readily succumbed to any chance they got).

In America, the scene was evolving at a rapid pace. It was inevitable that the Punks would experiment with guitar leads and different tempos, and that metalloids would speed it up and make it more streamlined—the whole nature of playing an instrument is to explore new musical territory, and there are only so many things one can do with the basic Rock formula. By combining influences, purveyors of both genres—Punk and Metal—found a way to not let either get boring. The genuine metalheads realized how enthralling the fury-pace of Punk was—if they believed there was ever "danger" in Heavy Metal, then they must have realized that the genuine carnage of Hardcore had its place. The kids who grew up to form bands like Metallica and Slayer may have actually been more Zep/Sabbath-derived than Stooges/Ramones-oriented, but, as a result of Punk, they speeded it up and made it nastier. The Punks, meanwhile, were influenced to explore different rhythmic avenues other than the same old 1-2-3-4 slamfest.

After '83 many Hardcore bands made the move metalward, some more subtly than others. Groups like Husker Du, SSD Control, and Bad Brains increased the use of leads, but this was probably due to their own organic musical progress than any blatant attempt to go Metal—even though that's what they got accused of by many Punks at the time.

The Misfits were an interesting transitional band. Many of the demonic trappings later copped by bands like Slayer seem derived from the Misfits' per-verse—and ironic—celebration of guts n' gore and all forms of horror-kitsch. It all goes back to Alice Cooper. By the time of *Earth AD* in '83, the Misfits' chug-ging juggernaut was beginning to sound more metallic every day. When they eventually disbanded, leader Glenn Danzig formed an actual Metal band named Danzig. Other Punk bands who showed evidence of the Metal influx included DRI (Dirty Rotten Imbeciles), Corrosion of Conformity, Poison Idea, Battalion of Saints, Powertrip, Suicidal Tendencies, Die Kreuzen, and the Cro-Mags. In a sense, the hyperdramatic Super Rock of groups like the Angry Samoans, Bad Religion, the latter-day Minor Threat, the Meatmen, Gang Green, Band 19, the Bags, Redd Kross, and Urge Overkill owed something to metal in its whole use of guitar-as-punctuation. Actually, it all goes back to the Dictators...

The most startling Punk-Metal merger in many ways was pulled off by Black Flag, who merely reversed the trend started by bands like Metallica and Slayer by *slowing down* the tempo to quivering proportions on the classic *My War* (1983). The kids cried "treason," especially when they saw singer Henry Rollins' newly shorn locks, but Flag were busy working on a synthesis that would prove incredibly influential once "grunge" took hold later in the decade. With their new, strange kind of Punk-Jazz-Metal, Black Flag were consciously testing the boundaries of all they'd helped create, without succumbing to mere "crossover" technique. By the mid-'80s, on albums like *Slip it In*, *Loose Nut* and *In My Head*, they'd reached a kind of crazed, metallic ultra-core sound—and in the process speeded up the tempo once more.

The whole SST roster was influenced by Flag's intense variations on the basic Punk formula. Husker Du, from Minneapolis, carved out an even more ornate landscape with just a three-piece. They also proved to be one of the most influential bands of the era. Overkill L.A. took their name from a song by Motorhead, which tells you something right there—due to the growling vocals of singer Merrill Ward and the bombastic approach of the whole band, they felt right at home among the spandexed hordes that were starting to populate California with increasing rapidity. St. Vitus at their best approximated a neat fusion of Black Flag/Black Sabbath with a little Blue Oyster Cult thrown in. The BOC influence wasn't limited to them either—Swa, another SST group, also echoed the sinister sound of Long Island's favorite miscreants. It wasn't unusual for bands to whip into an impromptu "Cities on Flame with Rock 'n' Roll" as a set closer. This ironic embrace of the metal ethos was best typified by head Meatman Tesco Vee, whose '84 EP *Dutch Hercules* parodied the neo-Metal scene with songs like "Wine, Wenches, and Wheels."

Bad Brains, one of the only visible Black bands on the Punk horizon, combined elements of Metal, Punk, and Reggae with the kind of ferocious velocity that made their attack instantly convincing to all those who witnessed it. Although Brains constituted the most original Black approach to Rock since Hendrix, *Rolling Stone* and others of their ilk criminally ignored them. Ironically, these institutions had been clamoring for such an ethno-fusion for years, but when confronted by the real thing, they retreated because the group's politics didn't fit the liberals' idealized stereotype of the appropriate Black activist posture. They liked their Black musicians to be more Uncle Tom, in other words. As such, Prince and Michael Jackson would get the nod as the acknowledged Black musical geniuses of their day. If *Rolling Stone* had really been doing its job, it would've given Bad Brains the lead review—possibly the cover—in 1982.

In truth, Blacks had been turning away from guitar-oriented Hard Rock since the late '60s, so it's no surprise that most of Punk's practitioners were white. Because Punks had placed themselves in the position of being social outcasts just because of their chosen music, they understood racism a lot better than their white peers. As such, they were responsible for some of the staunchest antiracist sentiment since Bob Dylan's "Only a Pawn in Their Game." Take, for example, the Dead Kennedys' "Nazi Punks Fuck Off" or Seven Seconds' "Racism Sucks." But because Punks weren't afraid of being ostracized by the liberal media establishment, they were free to explore such forbidden topics as reverse racism, which was run down by Minor Threat ("Guilty of Being White") and Johnny Thunders ("Just Because I'm White"), among others. This wasn't about racial differences—there were no antiblack sentiments to these songs. These artists were simply sick of being vilified for a posture they would never consider in the first place—mainly, white supremacy. Whereas at first, punks merely wanted to go against the grain of everything, in time the smarter ones realized that their contradictoriness-for-the-sake-of-it might have certain ramifications.

There was racism in Punk of course, notably in the proliferation of the swastika and later in the embrace of the music by actual Nazis. But these people were Nazis to begin with, and Punk gigs, because of their violent nature, provided them with an opportunity to twist heads. But ultimately, Nazis had no bearing on the *sound*—or "official" stance—of Punk.

In England, where the social and economic structure had crumbled drastically, racism provided an easy way out for disgruntled proles looking for a scapegoat. The U.K. had seen a proliferation of racist hate groups since the mid-'70s, culminating with the dreaded National Front. Punks had been at the forefront of opposing these forces, thanks to such efforts as the Rock Against Racism rallies, where artists like the Clash and Elvis Costello readily offered their services. Because of the social order, racial issues had a much larger influence on the Brit Punk scene than they did in the United States. Still, it was hard for Punk to resolve its anarchistic impulses in light of this fact. In many ways, race-baiting was just another guaranteed offense: in other words, if you were *really* desensitized—the essence of being "cool," after all—then *nothing* would offend you, right? So what was the big deal about a few swastikas? It was all a test.

Nobody embodied this more than Sid Vicious, but he was dead by 1978. He left behind a brutal legacy, however: heroin addict stabs girlfriend and, while awaiting trial, ODs in front of his own mother. As for Punk, this was the turning point in terms of the record industry. They took a dip after that and conveniently invented New Wave and later, synth-pop. They were abated by MTV in both areas. Turncoats like the Clash were free to make their bids, but anyone continuing in the rabid flesh-wound style of Sid was instantly excommunicated. Either that or they followed him to the grave: Darby Crash (Germs), Will Shatter (Flipper), etc. Punk was dead, *literally*, but by divorcing itself from the Pop marketplace once and for all, Punk was able to flourish from the ground up, almost as if Rock 'n' Roll was being reinvented again.

The Rock being played on the radio was Rock in name only. Those who really wanted to be challenged by the band concept had to look elsewhere. But the music being produced on the local, independent level could no longer be called Punk, because it no longer necessarily meant bands with short hair playing music at breakneck speed. It now meant *any* music that challenged the restrictions of the mainstream record industry—which was growing more restricted every day.

The term *post-Punk* was used for the first time by columnist Penny Valentine in her "Letter From Britain" column in the February 1980 issue of

Creem. At that time, England had been swamped by what amounted to a second, artier wave of independent-music making bands: Gang of Four, Joy Division, Throbbing Gristle, the Comsat Angels, Public Image Ltd., the Raincoats and the Psychedelic Furs. These groups represented the turning point of Punk Rock in England as much as bands like Black Flag, the Minutemen, and Toiling Midgets did in the United States. The slowing-down process had begun, but in England it was less in the form of Sabbathian grind as it was a kind of post-industrial clank. Bands like Joy Division and Ultravox used synthesizers, but Rock rhythms still mulled around in the mix. The attitude was still cynical, but instead of Punk's basic "fuck everything" premise, which in a way was kind of celebratory, the new gray "doom and gloom" brigade waxed almost fatalistic. At least in the case of Joy Division, it was a predilection that proved to be all too true when lead singer Ian Curtis hanged himself.

No matter how sincere Joy Division's alienation was, their transmusical atmospherics were easily translatable to Synth-Pop standards (as the spinoff band New Order proved). This didn't really help the cause of Rock at all, but in a way that was the whole point—a band like JD never claimed they were Rock in the first place.

John Lydon's own post-Pistols project, Public Image Ltd., was central to Britain's post-Punk musical development. After the Pistols' breakup, Lydon was quick to denounce his former group. This meant he had to, in essence, put up or shut up, and it's to his credit that, for at least the first two PiL albums, he was able to successfully accomplish this. This was the essence of post-Punk: namely, that someone who was considered the very essence of Punk Rock could come back as something totally different and succeed. He could *evolve*, in other words. PiL sounded nothing like the Sex Pistols—no Chuck Berry licks this time—and Rotten was no longer rotten, but Lydon.

In many ways, PiL may have been even more influential than the Sex Pistols. The enormous bass-line, borrowed from Jamaican "dub" music, provided an easy transition to Disco, which is the route Lydon and many other Brits—like the surviving members of Joy Division—eventually took. Keith Levene's snake-like guitar lines were not Rock-forceful, but they helped construct jarring soundscapes nevertheless. Rotten finally got to utilize his lifelong love of the German Prog band, Can, and in the next few years, as all the veins were plucked from the rotting corpse of Rock 'n' Roll, such obscure references would come out of the woodwork. We were entering the era of extreme cultism, when the more obscure a band was the first time around, the more heartily it was championed in post-Punk terms. So while something like the Velvet Underground, which had been done to death in the hands of neophytes, was now considered almost "mainstream," the truly obscure bands like Can and Big Star, who had almost no impact the first time around, were seen as the true titans. Which means that Rotten achieved his initial goal with the Sex Pistols—mainly to deconstruct the legacy of Rock 'n' Roll itself.

Another important band on the Brit post-Punk frontier was Throbbing Gristle. Although they arrived concurrently with the Sex Pistols, their music could never have started a revolution. In its odd, amoebalike way, it was background Muzak à la Eno's *Music for Airports*. There's no doubt it was one of the roots of Industrial music with its non-instrumentally derived mélange of "sounds," including what amounted to some of the first "samples." The group's image was that of the effete noncommunicators—it wasn't Handsome Dick Manitoba, in other words. In terms of calculated detachment, they were only outdone by Laibach: a Yugoslavian enclave, they borrowed TG's clinical approach to further their own neocommie propaganda.

There was also a neopsychedelic scene in Britain, particularly in Liverpool, where such bands as the Soft Boys, Echo & the Bunnymen, and Teardrop Explodes reiterated '60s influences that had long been discarded in the aftermath of Punk. The Psychedelic Furs also pumped out a kind of careening post-Joy Division/Velvets-derived wail complete with saxophone, but the problem with all these bands was that their more melodic inclinations tended to meld easily with the less-aggressive Pop-oriented New Wave bands that were also pouring out of the U.K. at the same time: New Order, Soft Cell, Ph.D., Spandau Ballet, Human League, the Cure, A Flock of Seagulls, Cabaret Voltaire, the Smiths. This helped effectively neuter them in their prime, in other words.

In America, all those college-bred twentysomethings reading *Rolling Stone* produced a neoclassicist thread of Rock that boiled down to "name that influence." The Byrds (Bangles, Rain Parade) and Velvet Underground (Dream Syndicate, Human Switchboard) seemed to be among the most-imitated prototypes. R.E.M., from Athens, Georgia, managed to effectively usurp the influence of both bands. By this time, we were into a whole new era:

this music wasn't even vaguely Punk, but it sprang out of the same Do It Yourself aesthetic.

Minneapolis provided a breeding ground for at least two notable post-Punk aggregations: the Replacements and Husker Du. Both paraded as Hardcore until it was deemed permissible to do otherwise—which, in the case of the Replacements, was a more roots-derived sound, and, in the case of Husker Du, a more embellished heavy Rock attack. Both groups were full-blown substance abusers as well: the 'Mats (as they affectionately became known) with cocaine and alcohol, and the Huskers (as they affectionately became known) with speed and heroin. This was the crux of both bands' inability to achieve the same kind of mainstream crossover as R.E.M. Needless to say, Minneapolis never became the epicenter of the post-Punk universe that it was touted as.

With its heavy working class element and its reputation as an old, cold Colonial town, Boston was a natural spawning ground for Hardcore and Straightedge. But the proliferation of colleges made it conducive to other, arti-er forms of post-Punk experimentation as well. Mission of Burma used abrupt rhythmic shifts learned from Hardcore, but their approach was brainy and cerebral. Despite being one of the more forward-leaning units of the day, they hardly received any notice outside of New England. The same could be said of the Girls, who embraced many of the same musically deconstructionist traits as Burma while being products of an art-loft scene that encompassed a multitude of mixed-media trappings. Because of its provincial nature, this problem has plagued Boston again and again: inescapably cliquey, its bands have had to make do with being "local legends" at home—and "well-kept secrets" every-where else.

The one area in which Boston excelled was the retro scene, starting with the Real Kids in 1976 and progressing through the whole DMZ/Lyres axis as well as the various aggregations fronted by Kenne Highland. Other bands like the Outlets, La Peste, the Slickee Boys and the Neats treaded on this kind of raw energy factor also. Although these bands may have been unembellished, they were thankfully not undernourished, especially when it came to their basic Rock instincts.

The neoretro scene came alive in the early '80s with New York's Fleshtones, Rochester's Chesterfield Kings, Rhode Island's Plan 9, and England's Barracudas, among others. Nowhere was the garage-Rock revival more prevalent than Down Under, where Aussie's favorite Stooges/MC5-worshipping sons, the Saints and Radio Birdman, had set the precedent—whether directly or indirectly—for such other energy-related outfits as the Hitmen, the Visitors, the New Christs, Lime Spiders, and New Race (the last a supergroup of sorts featuring ex-members of Birdman with expatriated Detroit legends Ron Asheton, ex- of the Stooges, and Michael Davis, ex- of the MC5). New Zealand's Punk scene, meanwhile, gave way to the whole Flying Nun empire in which bands like the Tall Dwarves, the Clean, the Chills, the Bats, the Verlaines, and the Spines did a jangle-Rock redefinition of the Velvets and other '60s influences that would bear enormous import on the indie aesthetic worldwide.

In the post-Punk era, bands attempting a self-consciously retro "psychedelic" sound tended to concentrate less on the more cerebral acid-Rock pioneers and more on the rawer garage-psych practitioners like the Standells, Love, Blue Cheer, Captain Beefheart, the Thirteenth Floor Elevators, the Seeds, and the Stooges. Many Rock fans that had been drawn to the energy of Punk had not disowned their record collections either. Now they were discovering a direct lineage between these '60s thrashers and the new Punk aesthetic. More often that not, this bridge was provided by the Velvet Underground, the quintessential missing link between primal '60s (nonironic) "authenticity" and post-Punk consciousness.

With the re-emergence of the psych-garage element, the question of drugs once again entered the picture. Groups like the Dream Syndicate, who sounded a lot like the Velvets, were directly following in a path that was almost entirely drug-influenced. Beyond that, more and more bands were discovering what musicians from other generations, from Be Bop to psychedelic, had known before them: taking drugs abetted the whole creative process. Bands like Black Flag and Husker Du "evolved" in the classic '60s sense—longer songs, more ornate structures, and a focus on improvisation. Husker Du even covered the Byrds' "Eight Miles High" in a version totally true to the "spirit"—if not the sound—of the original.

The Butthole Surfers, from Austin, Texas, were the perfect example of what drugs could do to mutate the fleshy membrane—if not the psychic ID—of Punk Rock. Like Sonic Youth in New York, they were primarily involved in a deconstruction process, jamming in a nonprescribed way à la Beefheart. They were purposely offensive, from their name to their shock-theater technique, such as showing crash-test dummy films behind them as they played. Such assaults on the senses were a kind of "happening"-related psychedelic performance art. And, like most of the important post-Punk bands, they evolved musically from album to album. The first EP, complete with naked men on the cover, was like a more abrasive update of the Fugs' whole tribal-lunacy shtick. By the time of workouts like "100 Million People Dead" and "PSY," they'd actually perfected an almost Grateful Dead-like psychedelic skill, particularly in concert (Sonic Youth, not coincidentally, also evolved along these lines but was more ether- than acid-based).

Although they weren't overtly drug-influenced, the Minutemen perfected a similarly disarming right-hand turn on the Rock 'n' Roll highway when they appeared before stunned "punk" audiences in the early '80s. Here was a seemingly confrontational challenge to preconceived notions about what constituted lo-fi credibility. A little fatter than most, with beards, and acting as if they remembered King Crimson, the three members of the Minutemen were kind of a comic-snickery frontal-lobe assault. How much influence their music had is debatable—to this day no one has ever matched the kind of Funk/Polka/Punk mesh they achieved on their magnum opus, *Double Nickels on the Dime*, and their other albums are filled with challenging material, most of it resting solely on the uniqueness of its architects. Mike Watt's bass was always the foundation, the factor that made them so distinct, but nothing about the Minutemen was routine—least of all their adherence to any preconceived notions about what "punk" constituted. With the Minutemen, one gets the feeling that if the "revolution" had never happened, they would've evolved in some muted form anyway. And because of their natural outsider inclinations, when it *did* happen, they were content to stay home, sit around on the couch, and goof. They weren't lining up for haircuts, in other words.

Within the American indie milieu, there were flirtations with such retrostyles as Surf and Rockabilly as well. In the best-case scenario, this took the form of subtle embellishments, such as the Southern California band Agent Orange's mild usage of surf textures to underpin their basic Punk rhythms. On the other hand, the groups that outright aped these styles—be it surf (Jon & the Nightriders) or Rockabilly (Robert Gordon, the Stray Cats)—were novelty acts at best. But a group like the Cramps, originally from Ohio but destined for the N.Y. scum heap, were a more aesthetically challenging merger of old styles and new sensibilities. The Cramps incorporated a high level of camp, but unlike other such experiments, they didn't compromise their raw instincts in the name of nostalgia. Treading on trash elements from pulp to horror to psychedelic to smut, they were instrumental in rendering kitsch a new nasty kind of post-everything irony. In lead singer Lux Interior, they had (another) one of the great post-Iggy belchers.

Speaking of the Stooges, they continued to be a formidable influence on post-Punk development right into the '80s. Particularly in their maiden region of the Midwest, their impact was estimable. Ohio bands like the Dead Boys and Pagans seemingly knelt at the shrine of Detroit's gnarliest darlings. In Detroit, bands like Cynecide, the Mutants, and Destroy All Monsters (featuring ex-Stooges guitarist/bassist Ron Asheton) preserved the legacy. In the New York "no wave" scene, the Stooges' second album, *Funhouse*, with its atonal honking sax, was particularly influential.

L.A.'s Angry Samoans had absorbed all the elemental grist of the Stooges, but they also borrowed heavily from the Dictators' comic crusade. This was all part of the process of not-taking-Punk-so-seriously, which was a turn away from the whole Straightedge crusade, not to mention the volatile politics of activist fronts like the *Maximum Rock N' Roll*/Alternative Tentacles empire. As far back as '78, the Samoans were masterminding a post-everything aesthetic that would influence such later institutions as *Forced Exposure* and the Sub Pop record label (Mudhoney covered the Sams' "You Stupid Asshole"). This was total suburban sprawl—but the Samoans came with a resumé: Rock critics Mike Saunders and Gregg Turner had been pivotal in introducing the Punk aesthetic to the world via their writing in such '70s journals as *Creem* and *Rolling Stone*. Saunders had been one of the first critics to heap praise on the likes of Black Sabbath, Grand Funk, and Uriah Heep while everyone else was mired in hippie muck; Turner's debut in *Creem* was a slam-job of Iggy, which was perfect—slay thy father and take it from there. As one of the preeminent post-Meltzer scribes, Turner left his imprint on future generations as well (Byron Coley in particular). He routinely called people "fags," and the Samoans were the epitome of political incorrectness—which made them outcasts in the increasingly doctrinaire climate of Hardcore.

The Samoans became notorious in L.A. during 1980 when their vengeful debasement of local legend Rodney Bingenheimer resulted in a lawsuit. The whole situation was only exacerbated further when Richard Meltzer read the lyrics to "Get Off the Air" *on* the air, during his "Hepcats from Hell" radio show on KPFK. Displaying a mastery of the new ironic, detached post-everything mean-spiritedness, the band used Rodney's cease-and-desist summons as a *handbill* for one of their shows. Their take on Rock itself was equally comedic and dark-humored, but unlike so many later joke-rockers, the Sams didn't treat the music itself as a joke. In fact, with their massive overstated Super Rock dynamics—three rhythm guitars at once all going "rk-dk-dk"—they self-consciously advanced the whole Stooges/Ramones/Dictators formula to its next logical stage.

The power chord had always held manly denotations, but in the '80s, in the hands of groups like the Meatmen, it took the form of an overexaggerated machismo that said: "No wimps allowed." It was all starting to break off into various camps: tough guys (Meatmen, Misfits) vs. "wimps" (R.E.M., New Order) vs. weirdos (Minutemen, Butthole Surfers). The whole absurdist context of the Dictators and Angry Samoans gave way to "hardy har Hardcore," which meant groups who were "funny" ha-ha (Dickies, Adolescents, Murphy's Law, Angry Samoans) as well as "funny" ironic (Dead Milkmen, Happy Flowers, Camper Van Beethoven). Although these groups varied musically, what they shared theoretically was a usage of the "punk" ethos to express their own satirical impulses.

Despite the best jibes of these would-be bozos, the Reagan Era meant that their message would no doubt be lost on the increasingly homogeneous youth populace. Majority would soon come to rule, and these guys and others of their ilk were decidedly in the minority. Mainstream culture was moving away from the idea of rebellion in general—although the ironic twist that these paupers proffered wouldn't be lost on latter-day "ironic" claim-jumpers like the Pixies. But for the most part, as far as the popular picture went, the Top Forty was almost entirely Rock-free from 1980–1985. In the late '80s, manufactured glam-Metal bands like Motley Crue and Poison (not to mention Bon Jovi and the revivified Aerosmith) reintroduced guitar-based rhythms into the popular vernacular, but only of the most choreographed variety. Guns n' Roses, a by-product of this, actually proved to be somewhat more legitimate and helped introduce Hard Rock back into the mainstream, but that wasn't until 1988. By that time, a legitimate American "underground" had been thriving for at least a decade.

So where was the Rock press during that time? Well, except for the fanzines, nowhere to be found. Confused by what they perceived as Punk's betrayal of their '60s-bred populist ideals, most of them sought to repeat the past and ignore the future—hence their embrace of such neodinosaurs as Bob Seger, Bruce Springsteen, and John Cougar Mellencamp. The other alternative was to plunge headlong into what amounted to Disco—Prince, Michael Jackson, Madonna, and even, to some extent, U2—and eschew the Rock quotient altogether. Anyone listening to guitar-oriented music in the '80s knew better than to consult *Rolling Stone*. Consequently, with no true Rock fans still reading the magazine, *Rolling Stone* was free to pursue what was its ultimate agenda all along—namely, to turn the '60s into a permanent time capsule and forge ahead with the materialistic manifest destiny of the yuppies.

Punks, meanwhile, were left with the challenge of whether or not to pursue it for one more day and confronted by the grim reality of almost universal indifference. But in a way, this freed many bands to pursue a more progressive agenda—with nothing to lose, why not? From this generation of musical experimenters would come the groups who represented the future of Rock 'n' Roll: Sonic Youth, the Butthole Surfers, Husker Du, the Replacements, Black Flag, the Minutemen, the Angry Samoans, the Dream Syndicate, Minor Threat, the Meat Puppets, Flipper, Bad Brains, Mission of Burma, Big Black, Dead Kennedys, Half Japanese, the Descendents, Green River, Dinosaur Jr., and, ultimately, Nirvana.

Industry-wise, the majors had miscalculated first Disco and then Punk. MTV solved this impasse, because it borrowed much of its cynical veneer from Punk ideology while utilizing the glossy mechanized process of Disco. The end results were the post-everything icons of the '80s: Madonna, Prince, Billy Idol, R.E.M., and U2, who at least learned some of their notions about irony—if not hairstyles—from Punk.

The real "Punk" ethic has been part of Rock *music* since its inception—purveyors of either one know that the two are inseparable. What the Punk revolution symbolized was a self-conscious rebirth of this aesthetic from the ground up. It was also the first generation of total media cool.

Those who care continue; those who don't never did.

CHAPTER 14

THE EIGHTIES

THE '80S BEGAN THE GREAT CULTURAL SOBERING-UP PROCESS AFTER THE '60S AND '70S. The Reagan era revoked the "revolution"—and the new conquerors took no prisoners. Despite its many obvious flaws, the '80s were probably the real turning point of the twentieth century.

Looking back, it's technology that most often affects any modern-day revolution. The Pill, for instance, obviously abetted the Sexual Revolution. Rock 'n' Roll, meanwhile, would never have happened without the invention of the electric guitar. In the '80s, computer technology took over and forever tied the world together into an interactive web of information processing and distribution.

This all happened by accident: in the early days of computers, they were the cumbersome monstrosities that are now seen as the Edsels of the industry, and one had to be a certified genius to run them. As time progressed, there would be bright young engineers who would refine not only the intricate programming features of the computer, but the whole method in which it was used. Thus, the whole unapproachable aura of computers—that one had to be an egghead/genius to program them—would change. This whole evolution would take years, but if any event can be seen as the major technological turning point of the modern age, it was the invention of the PC. This not only revolutionized the economic factors of life in the capitalist system—banking and the stock market—but human interaction as well. In the '80s, people *became* the machines the way futurists had always predicted. Some people got so tied up in their computers that they took a trip into cyberspace and never came back—and while they were at it, they came up with the next major technological breakthrough.

It didn't happen overnight—it took a long time for the personal computer to become entrenched in American society. Sometime between 1971–1979, the microchip was invented, which changed the whole nature of computer engineering. After Bill Gates at Microsoft shrewdly discovered a way to market the software that went with the new machinery, it became an endless quest for information, information, and more information, until no bit of data would remain unturned in the modern world and we would eventually come to *know everything*. In *Accidental Empires*, his excellent summation of how the cyberculture was created, Robert Cringely posits an interesting theory about the modern-day deification of mortals like Gates:

> "What we're often looking for when we add…a computer into our businesses and our lives is certainty. We want something to believe in, something that will take from our shoulders the burden of knowing…In the twelfth century…such certainty came in the form of a belief in God, made tangible through the building of cathedrals—places where God could be accessed. For lots of us today, the belief is more in the sanctity of those digital zeros and ones, and our cathedral is the personal computer. In a way, we're replacing God with Bill Gates."[1]

By perfecting the software it took to run the machines, Gates and his partner at Microsoft, Paul Allen, made home computer use possible. That made them gods. Because Gates chose to eventually ally himself with IBM, he was in the twilight of the gods—and he made IBM buy back something that was theirs to begin with. But there was one major setback when IBM commanded microtechnology: nobody could *use* it except IBM. Once other companies like Apple made computing accessible to everyone, including non-computer programmers, IBM realized they would have to follow in suit to maintain control of the industry they'd always been in command of. And they knew that in order to do this, they'd need Bill Gates, which is basically the story of the Harvard dropout who eventually became the most unlikely Great American Hero.

As the story of Rock had already proven, heroes can come from unlikely places. But the heroes of the future were no longer Rock stars like Mick Jagger—they were geeky but brilliant young men like Gates. The tides of the culture were turning toward a more high-minded ideal. The party was over. Now it was time to get down to business and, aided by Gates and his cohorts, that's just what the United States did in the '80s.

Soon the big mergers that would consolidate the world into the domain of several large corporations would spawn the global economy. From corporate boardrooms everywhere came cries of "I'll buy that," and buy it they did, in ever-larger chunks. Corporate America was the biggest beneficiary in all this greed, and what really happened in the '80s was something even Marshall McLuhan hadn't pictured.

In the U.S., the changing of the guard from Democrat to Republican aided the corporate takeover. Under Carter, the economy had been a disaster. His foreign policy had been a fiasco. So in 1980 it was easy for virtually anyone in the opposing party to sweep in there. But Ronald Reagan wasn't just anybody: a four-time successful governor and former Hollywood actor, Reagan had been in the conservative mainstream for years. In the '60s he'd helped outlaw LSD and supported the war in Vietnam. In the '70s he led the cry for a return of "family values" to oppose what he perceived as the moral pallor that had befallen the nation in the wake of the '60s revolution.

Watergate helped erode people's trust in the Republicans, which helped Carter get elected in 1976. But the Democratic Party had changed since the days of Camelot and LBJ: both Kennedy and Johnson were old-time hard-line Dems who supported a strong military along with all the social programs. As the '60s wore on, the radical bent that was influencing the whole country eventually seeped into politics as well. This was unavoidable: ever since the Berkeley Free Speech uprising in 1964, the radicals had increasingly become involved with a kind of high-profile political theater that culminated in the Chicago riots during the '68 Democratic convention.

In the '60s, radical factions were making themselves visible all over. The rush of technology, the firmament of what the '80s would ultimately be all about, had produced such massive change in such a short span of time that people were simply reeling with newfound freedom of thought. This made it more difficult for the various governments around the world to suppress the masses—once anything seemed at least possible, there were bound to be certain people who were going to attempt to break down the remaining barriers. In America, the momentum of this resistance made it seem, at least for a time, as if a true "revolution" were taking place. It was only in '72, when Nixon defeated McGovern in the election, that people realized how small the movement really was.

To the average Americans who made up the general consensus, America was a country to be grateful to because of its immense prosperity. These people believed in the old adage "love it or leave it." Most of them had every reason to love it, of course: they weren't intellectuals or politicos; they were people who came of age before World War II who'd either served in the war in some way or felt grateful for its aftermath. They didn't question it when their government lied to them, or plotted to kill foreign leaders, or effectively degraded its own citizenry. They didn't care—they felt they'd "paid their dues" (which, having survived the Depression, many of them had) and were now enjoying the "American Dream" in progress. These believers had nothing but contempt for those who deviated from the norm. But the world was becoming a more "open" place through forces beyond their control, and with this came a requestioning of the values that had stood unyieldingly in place for so long.

The Civil Rights, Anti-War, and Free Speech movements had helped consolidate a genuine opposition. These were issues most Americans felt strongly about, one way or another, and they were bound to explode across lines of class, age, gender, and geography. In the '60s, as they exploded, more people found themselves drawn to the opposition. More often that not, these were the younger, more educated, idealistic ones. But as the "revolution" raged on, there were still millions and millions of poor or middle class families whose lives still revolved around the ideals of the American Dream. That is, one serves his country when he is called upon, etc. (even Kennedy had said "ask not what your country can do for you"). The *real* revolution had been that kids learned to smoke dope, play with newfangled machines on a daily basis, and expect partners to fuck on the first date. As for their politics, most of them remained as oblivious—or mutton-headed—as ever. The attention the media had paid to the Civil Rights struggle—not to mention the hippies—only bred resentment from the white working class. All through the "revolution," Americans continued to get up at 7 a.m., go to work in warehouses and on loading docks, come home and eat steak and drink beer, and fall asleep in front of the television. The

kids played Little League and had hoops erected in newly blacktopped drive-
ways. On weekends, Dad mowed the lawn and took the family on a picnic in a
beautifully groomed state park. Life was good. In fact, a lot of Americans felt
that the only thing "wrong" with the country were the "freaks" and "niggers"
themselves.

The liberals had overestimated the extent of the "cause." True, many
Americans were disgusted by the war. True, a lot had changed in the '60s, and
millions of people had become more open-minded about issues like sex, religion, and race. But the liberals were duped into believing that the "cultural revolution" was more widespread than it actually was. If you look at any high
school yearbook from Anytown U.S.A. from, say, 1972, 90 percent of the boys
still had crew cuts. But any Hollywood movie from the same era will depict a
cultural landscape in which everyone had been hipped—because, of course, in
Hollywood, everyone had. But Hollywood isn't "America," not by a long shot,
and neither is Berkeley or Greenwich Village, which is a fact a lot of academics and radicals misunderstood in the aftermath of the '60s.

In 1968, in order to win a close election against Hubert Humphrey, Nixon
called on the "silent majority"—those Americans who'd worked hard and still
believed in the American Dream. Suddenly songs with traditional, working
class themes like "Okie from Muskogee" and "One's on the Way" became popular. Country music had a legitimate revival. And construction workers lined
the streets to beat hell on the hippies. Because Nixon had called upon them,
and because they represented the America that was slipping away, the
Republicans became the "conservative" party and the Democrats, by default,
became the liberals. This was the Democrats' unraveling, as most Americans
didn't feel that liberal about most of the issues.

One look at Hunter Thompson's *Fear and Loathing on the Campaign Trail
'72* tells the story: disregarding the usual babbling of the good doctor for a
minute, all one really has to do to understand why the Democrats lost the election is look at the picture in which Senator Gary Hart, sporting long hair and
wearing a casual western shirt, is chatting with Warren Beatty. This was the
image the Democrats were trying to propagate to oppose the gray vision of
Nixon: hippified, *loose.* There was no precedent for this, no reason to believe it
would work, other than the media's success at fostering the countercultural
veneer all through the '60s. In other words, the Beatles had ultimately influ-

enced politicians like Hart in their decisions to wear long hair. As far as presidential politics went, this apparently cut little muster with voters, excepting the newly eligible eighteen-year-olds, who proved to be far less of a significant factor than initially suspected. Even then, there were plenty of Young Republicans who were happy to vote for Nixon. To most Americans, politicians like Hart and, ultimately, McGovern, came off as *irresponsible*—would you entrust America's national security with someone who'd hang around with Warren Beatty (not to mention Hunter Thompson)? True to form, when the liberals failed to capture the popular vote in '72, they turned to more inward pursuits like Disco, self-help, rollerblading, kinky sex, drugs, spiritual concerns, and private enterprise. Nixon began to pull out of 'Nam, and many former radicals, who were pushing thirty after all, began convincing themselves that the "revolution" had been won.

Watergate only seemed like a further vindication of the liberals' assumed moral fortitude. As an aftereffect of Nixon's disgrace, Carter beat Ford in 1976, and the Democrats held the White House for the first time in eight years. But it was a Pyrrhic victory: Carter's 22 percent inflation made him an even more unpopular president than Nixon. When Ronald Reagan offered a restructured economy, it seemed like a viable alternative to Carter's morass, which, besides inflation, also encompassed the Iran Crisis and the gas shortage.

What this all proved was that, except in the minds of a few radicals, scholars, Rock stars, journalists, actors, and intellectuals, the "revolution" was a bust. In any true revolution, the system being opposed must totally crumble in order for the new one to be erected. But capitalism wasn't likely to crumble, and when Americans started being hit in their pocketbooks, their political affiliations fluctuated.

So in 1980 Ronald Reagan came in shooting his guns. The former Hollywood actor had made a career out of shoot-'em-ups and the order of virtue, and his image was white teeth and gloss; plus, he was a geezer to boot—at sixty-nine, the oldest president ever. But the age factor actually helped him, coming on the heels of the naïve "youth culture" that many Americans felt had "ruined" the country. Behind the doddering old man persona, however, Reagan had brought with him the most ruthless political minds of the far Right. When the libs tried to counter with the kind of elitist devices that had carried them through the '60s and '70s, they found they were dealing with a more ruthless enemy than they were accustomed to on the opposing side. Reagan and his merry men came on like a super-jet of high sheen after the more casual stance of the Carter administration. The '80s quickly took on a shiny veneer: tall, "straight," and decidedly not fogged out.

There was "fun" in the '80s, but it was of the manufactured variety and fell in with the Reagan doctrine. There was no way the radical element could've just disappeared. There was undoubtedly an organized attempt to silence the dissenters—i.e., Punk Rock was *not* going to be played on the radio. There was witch-hunting left and right in the '80s, but as with the commie scare in the '50s, it came under the jurisdiction of ridding the country of unwanted louses. Part of Reagan's conquest was his whole bring-back-the-'50s mentality. Anybody who "got theirs" in the '50s was surely aghast at the subsequent generation's excesses. With Reagan, old farts were in vogue again, and the talk of "new values" was actually a retro-program aimed at returning the country to the values of a previous generation—values that were hideously anachronistic at that point. In cahoots with Reagan, the militialike Moral Majority took hold and put heavy pressure on the media to become, if not outwardly retrogressive, at least more "conservative." The '80s were the first time the term "conservative" had desirable social connotations. As Huey Lewis noted, in the '80s, it was "hip to be square."

Religion also made a comeback in the '80s. It had never really gone out among the working class, not to mention minority factions. American culture was founded on Christian principles, and a big part of the Cold War hype was that the Russians were the godless atheists. The Republicans believed that religion should be part of the nation's agenda in order to salvage the country's "moral fiber."

This reversion couldn't happen overnight. The revolution had wrought many internal changes in the country's psychological manifold. In the high schools at the time, the parking lots were an endless whirl of grass, speed, acid, booze, downs, dope, and a general I-don't-give-a-fuck malaise. Under Reagan, stricter drug enforcement laws were inevitable, and the next generation would be less apt to experiment. The new drugs were mind-numbing leisure activities like video games. The muttonheads of AC/DC Land had so blatantly *misused* the drugs—by devaluing the Ramones, for instance—that they made it easy for anyone reasonably intelligent to believe the hype (i.e., drugs equals loser). In

1982, a *very* popular actor/comedian, John Belushi, died of a drug overdose, which helped exacerbate the antidrug furor. It seemed that a certain lifestyle, a certain belief in the abyss as a spiritual pool, was coming to an end.

Reagan tried to convince people that he'd get the economy rolling again. But as the cliché went, the trickle-down economics where the rich just kept getting richer created a nation of burger flippers. The real new jobs were in the field of business and technology, which meant that the working class was going to be left out of the prosperity. Despite Reagan's immense popularity—there was even talk about repealing the twenty-second Amendment so that he could be re-elected for a *third* term—it was obvious that there was an ever-widening gap within the society itself. Most often, it was minorities who felt the most left out of the "Reagan revolution." Reagan was basing his whole neoconservative model on the kind of cultural hegemony that existed in the '50s. He didn't understand that, by the '80s, there was such immense diversity within the culture that there was no way his conservative agenda could speak for everybody.

Under Reagan, Blacks saw virtually *no* representation of their interests in government. All they saw was the old man smiling and talking about how great things were. Not only did this cause bitterness; it made Black politicians like Jesse Jackson, Al Sharpton, and Louis Farrakhan start speaking in a separatist tone. During the '80s, among the Black community, the ideology of Malcolm X—which pledged the concept of a nation-within-a-nation—seemed more viable than the assimilation preached by Martin Luther King. Deep in the boroughs of America's largest city, young Blacks were beginning to formulate a whole new kind of culture to counteract the indifference of the nation at large.

The Bronx in the late '70s was not a pretty place—it actually looked more like a bombed-out Third World country after a costly war than a borough of what was supposedly the world's greatest city. According to John Goodwin's book, *Murder City USA*, published in 1978, 40 percent of Bronx residents were on welfare, 30 percent were unemployed, and 25 percent were illiterate. For twenty years, there had been an exodus from the Bronx by the original Jewish, Italian, and Polish immigrants who'd settled there. Because of the deteriorating conditions, property values decreased substantially, making way for thousands of low-income families. With this shifting demographic came many of the problems that had plagued minority housing elsewhere in the nation: drugs, vandalism, arson, and rampant lawlessness.

In the early '80s, the Disco phenomenon was waning. Perhaps its most enduring legacy was the whole concept of music as endless groove. Rap music, a mechanical rhythm with someone literally *talking* over it, came from Disco in this sense, but there was rebellion inherent in it, just as there had been with Punk. Since it came from the ghetto, it was the domain of the street, and it sounded the roar of the underprivileged. Like Punk, it evolved almost totally outside of the mainstream music industry.

For years, Black DJs who were hired to play block parties in the Bronx had been utilizing a technique whereby they talked through the extended funk-jams on records by people like the Ohio Players, Isaac Hayes, Sly & the Family Stone, the JB's, and Funkadelic. This may have stemmed from the Jamaican technique of "toasting," a game of verbal one-upsmanship that had been going on since the '60s (in 1970, a group called the Pipkins had a small hit with a song called "Gimme Dat Ding," which is often cited as an early example of Rap/toasting). As one of the original Bronx rappers, Kool Herc, was originally from Jamaica, it's likely that toasting was an influence on at least some of the people involved with the scene.

Picture this: it's midsummer 1979 and, in Manhattan, Studio 54 is raving with lines around the block. However, if you're a Black teenager in the Bronx, Brooklyn, or Long Island and not one of the privileged set, you have to make do with a phonograph and a microphone, and that's what the earliest rappers did, siphoning the power from a city light pole. With new technology introduced in the '80s, home recording became more feasible. It also made it possible to literally plagiarize other people's recordings, even if it meant mom's old Aretha albums. This was how Rap began.

Disco as a musical form (if it could be called that) had derived from Black R&B, but as culture it was racially mixed with a lot of antecedents in the New York—and Euro—gay sub-culture. Rap, on the other hand, was principally Black-oriented, and decidedly heterosexual. There was a new urban-based ideology brought on by the perception that the government had abandoned the ghettos. Despite basic novelty attempts like Blondie's "Rapture," this didn't translate quickly to commercial terms.

For Rap to really catch the attention of the media, it had to move out of the Bronx. In 1978, DJ Kurtis Blow and a friend, Russell Simmons, opened the first Rap club in Queens, which, in a sign of the times, was called the Night

Fever Disco. It should be noted here that Blow and Simmons were not ghetto youths, but more privileged Blacks who came from the suburbs and went to college. Simmons' sociology degree would come in handy when it came time to sum up the demographic he knew existed for Rap.

Around the same time, a promoter in Harlem named Randy Sanders had transformed his Harlem World disco on 116th Street into a Rap emporium. By then virtually every star of Rap's first wave had arrived: Grandmaster Flash & the Furious Five (including DJs Kid Creole and Melle Mel), the Treacherous Three (featuring Kool Moe D), the Cold Crush Brothers, the Disco Three (who later became the Fat Boys) and Spectrum City (featuring future Public Enemy producer Hank Shocklee and his brother Keith).

Considering Hip Hop's origins from the mean streets of the Bronx, there was already an air of danger and an "outlaw" mentality accompanying the phenomenon. For this reason, many uptown clubs were hesitant about opening their doors to Rap. But a whole new ghetto culture, based on the same kind of urban sensibilities as Rap, was manifesting itself in other ways. By the late '70s—the era of inflation and inhalation—New York was covered in graffiti, which was considered by some to be a new kind of urban folk art. Break-dancing was another aspect of Hip Hop culture: the acrobatic movements were like a rebellion against the lock-step of Disco, and they signified the same kind of in-yours directive as Rap music itself. The militant face of Rap was apparent from the beginning: in 1979, the pro-Africa organization Zulu Nation, became involved in the burgeoning Hip Hop community.

In the early '80s, the increasingly portable nature of recorded music also played a part in Rap's evolution. The portable "boom box" (a.k.a. ghetto blaster) became as much a part of Hip Hop's cultural identity as breaking or graffiti. The other major portable fixture was the Walkman, developed by Sony in 1979. Consisting of a small headset and a tape deck that could be attached to the listener's belt, it made cassettes so accessible that, briefly, they became the preferred method of music dissemination. One reason for this was the increasingly shoddy quality of the vinyl product the major record labels had been putting out; meanwhile, to suit the new technology, they'd actually been improving the quality of cassettes. This helped make music itself just another form of instant gratification. Whereas before, for a person to buy a record, it required some kind of active pursuit, some kind of *commitment*, now it merely constituted one more stimulus to plug into. Ultimately this resulted in a further dumbing down of standards, whereby any old thing was all right because it was all "background" music anyway (for jogging, or whatever).

Around this time, the song that would define Rap to the general public came along in the form of "Rapper's Delight" by the Sugarhill Gang. There was some resentment from the original Rap community, because these upstarts hailed from New Jersey instead of the Bronx. The group had been discovered in a pizza parlor by Sylvia Vanderpool, who, as one-half of Mickey & Sylvia, sang on the '50s Rock 'n' Roll classic "Love is Strange" and, more recently, had a horrible hit with "Pillow Talk." She was a music industry insider, in other words, and she helped launch the first important Rap label, Sugarhill. When it came time to get to get the whole thing off the launching pad, Sugarhill found itself going through the same sleazy channels that record labels had since the '50s—namely, Morris Levy, the legendary ex-owner of Roulette Records who'd been embroiled in controversy since Rock was in its infancy. He no doubt viewed the Sugarhill Gang in much the same way as he had Frankie Lyman & the Teenagers: an easy mark.

There were other problems brewing for Sugarhill, however: Vanderpool's husband, Joe Robinson, who was the producer, snatched the bass line from Chic's recent hit "Good Times" for "Rapper's Delight." By doing so, he had inadvertently created the first "sample." This fact was not lost on Chic's Bernard Edwards and Nile Rodgers, who sued Sugarhill and eventually secured a copyright credit on the song—which must have pleased them considerably, given that at one time Sugarhill was shipping 75 thousand copies of the record per day. This was only the tip of the iceberg as far as lawsuits would go, and as Rap continued to gain momentum and the practice of sampling became more commonplace, there would be much controversy over rights of ownership.

Rap got a big boost in 1980 when the number one American New Wave group Blondie released "Rapture," with Deborah Harry's mock-"toasting" and its gratuitous mention of Fab Five Freddy, a Brooklyn rapper who'd been featured in the first Rap movie, Charlie Ahearn's *Wild Style*, that fall. But Blondie wasn't the only white band to embrace the coming Hip Hop culture: during a 1981 tour of the U.S., the Clash hand-picked Grandmaster Flash & the Furious Five to accompany them, which met with predictable scorn in the Bible Belt. Mick Jones would later fume: "*Mmnnn! We went*

down South and you know what they called us? *Nigger lovers!*" Apparently
shocked by America's racial divide, which they saw coming alive before their
eyes (possibly in the form of angry rednecks bearing the proverbial pitch-
forks) they politely asked Grandmaster Flash to exit the tour ("no offense,
guys") and replaced them with the more pedestrian lite-Reggae act Jo Jo Zep
& the Falcons.

Grandmaster Flash, meanwhile, went back home to create the masterpiece
that would finally get Rap noticed by the mostly white, liberal Rock press. "The
Message," released on Sugarhill in 1982, was voted "record of the year" by
Rolling Stone and the *Village Voice* as all the critics made apologies for its incendiary lyrics, which in many ways foreshadowed gangsta Rap. With its hypnotic refrain—"It's like a jungle sometimes/It makes me wonder/How I keep from
going under"—"The Message" would serve as the pivotal record of Hip Hop,
much like *The Harder They Come* had for Reggae ten years earlier.

Despite the success of "Rapper's Delight" and "The Message," Sugarhill
never became a viable commercial entity. Many people who were around at the
time attribute this failure to the fact that the label wasn't willing to nurture new
talent. As DJ Silk remembered: "Sugarhill just got lost. They didn't put out
LPs, they didn't put out videos. They made a lot of money, and then they felt
'We got the cream of the crop.' They didn't stay with new groups, they stuck
with the originators." [2]

Rap wasn't a form of music about "originators," however—it was all about
reinvention. If Disco had been the first truly mass-produced form of popular
music, Rap was the first music based entirely on technology, which meant its
practitioners had only to wait for the next technological innovation before
they could spring into the future. This gave them incredible freedom, when
you think about it. By far the most controversial practice among the nascent
rappers was sampling. In 1982/1983, Afrika Bambaataa began releasing a
string of recordings for the Tommy Boy label that relied heavily on programmed samples. Although this may have caused controversy among purists,
it did have a few positive side effects. As Kurtis Blow recalled: "Sampling
brought a lot of these groups back in the forefront: P-Funk wasn't doin' nothin'…the Meters, the JBs. Sampling…resurrected their careers. Back then, the
stuff was going for ninety-nine cents, but people didn't want that, they wanted what was happenin' then." [3]

Most likely, when artists like James Brown and Kool & the Gang first heard their work being "sampled"—i.e., plagiarized—they weren't too happy. But, slowly, it helped bring them back into the public consciousness, where they'd been absent since the rise of Disco. Rap reawakened Black consciousness. This meant the work of musical pioneers like James Brown, Sly Stone, Marvin Gaye, and George Clinton was justifiably enshrined alongside the crusading efforts of Martin Luther King and Malcolm X. All of a sudden, young Blacks were listening to P-Funk and James Brown, if only to pull samples from their albums. And in the end, this helped no one less than Mr. J. B. himself—which is the real reason that he and other members of the old school were so slow to take legal action against the samplers.

Along with sampling, another audio attribute that Rap was making more plentiful was the use of the drum machine. The heavyweights in this category were Run-DMC, a duo from Queens featuring Russell Simmons's brother, Joe, and Darryl McDaniels (a.k.a. DMC—rappers were all starting to have funny monikers). The fact that they rapped simultaneously, often completing one another's stanzas with perfectly timed—and oft-sarcastic—rhymes was definitely a turning point, along with the fact that they created a whole new persona for Rap. As Def Jam publicist Bill Adler recalls: "They were self-consciously 'new school,' which was how the old school felt: 'Who the fuck are these interlopers from Queens! Fuck them!'" [4]

But if the old guard couldn't appreciate these new stylists, the kids could relate. Adler again: "Run came out with sneakers and dungarees: 'I'm like you, I'm from a neighborhood like yours.'" [5]

Run-DMC helped foster the rise of B-Boy culture as a social trend that could be appreciated by young whites as well as Blacks. The key word here is "young"—to anyone "old," meaning the aging Baby Boomers, Rap was completely unfathomable. This irritant factor was appealing to young whites also. Meanwhile, because of their suburban background, rappers like the Simmons brothers were perhaps more familiar with white Rock n' Roll stylings than their ghetto counterparts. As a result, Run-DMC was the first Rap act to sample white resources, like the AC/DC lift on "Rockbox," which more or less made the Profile label.

Rap in the beginning was almost exclusively an indie phenomenon—but then, where have we heard that before? Rock 'n' Roll in its infancy was also mostly the domain of independent labels. And while in the late '70s and early '80s everyone was looking around wondering what the Next Big Thing was going to be—Disco, New Wave, ambient, synth-Pop—Rap was happening right underneath the record industry's collective nose.

Russell Simmons, meanwhile, was responsible for one of the preeminent early Rap labels, along with his white partner, Rick Rubin. In 1984, the two founded Def Jam, which eventually became the most successful Rap label of all time. Simmons had built an impressive network of contacts from his days in college radio. Rubin, meanwhile, showed an astute knack for taming raw talent into studio-wrought perfection. Over the next few years, he would discover the Beastie Boys, EPMD, Slick Rick, DJ Jazzy Jeff & the Fresh Prince, and the Geto Boys, to name a few. Simmons, on the other hand, was responsible for LL Cool J and Public Enemy. When the money started coming in, the records got better: now artists like Public Enemy were free to pursue limitless soundscapes wrought by endless studio overdubs. Albums like *It Takes a Nation of Millions to Hold Us Back* (1988) were multilayered affairs that revolutionized the realm of recorded sound overnight. For better or worse, it was also acts like Run-DMC, Public Enemy, and the Beastie Boys who brought dirty words to Rap.

The Beastie Boys were the ultimate paradox: a trio of foul-mouthed upper-middle-class Jewish kids who'd originally been a Hardcore band before they put the instruments down and began imitating the Black rappers they heard in their native New York. The irony was not lost on Rick Rubin, nor was it lost on Madonna, who invited the Beasties to tour with her in 1985. The outrage voiced by the group's detractors, many of them Black, was akin to those purists who claimed in 1956 that Elvis was subverting Black Rhythm & Blues. But the Beasties' bastardization of Rap was inevitable, and their five-million-selling debut, *License to Ill*, released in 1986, was the album that turned Rap into a profitable commodity once and for all.

A whole new epidemic was sweeping the ghettos in the '80s—mainly, the rise of crack, a synthetic, smokable form of cocaine that sold in bit-sized configurations that made it easy for dealers to pack. Highly addictive, but relatively cheap—especially compared to the raw coke that had dominated the Disco scene in the '70s—crack was a phenomenon lawmakers weren't ready for. In L.A., the crack epidemic produced a "gangsta" subculture, which in turn led to the West Coast's answer to the N.Y. axis in the form of Ice-T, NWA, and other "gangsta" rappers. Perhaps the criminal backgrounds of most of the L.A. rappers taught them valuable lessons about entrepreneurship as well because, after NWA got off the ground, they certainly made more money than their East Coast counterparts ever had.

But that would come later: in the early '80s, such an insurrection was inconceivable. The record industry at the time was undergoing massive tightening-up measures. The cutbacks of the late '70s had yielded no sympathy for ne'er-do-wells or starving artist types. With fewer albums being made, and even fewer groups being signed, the record companies were now putting all their money behind a few well-chosen acts. That's why in the '80s, again and again, we'd see a group or performer getting an all-out media blitz that produced a million-plus selling album, only to fumble on the follow-up and never be heard from again (Men at Work, the Hooters, Tears for Fears, Midnight Oil). But the record companies didn't care—as they'd invested very little in nurturing these acts, the windfall created by their one big hit more than compensated for their lack of long-term potential. And there were no temperamental prima donnas to baby-sit, seeing as these performers were utterly malleable and succumbed easily to the major labels' marketing whims.

In the '80s, the major labels had no practical use for any artists who didn't make fame-seeking their top priority. If a group or artist wasn't braced to "make it," he or she had no inherent worth as far as the company was concerned. This was just another sad economy-driven fact of the '80s. But it created a vortex for Rap and underground Rock to thrive. As has been noted again and again in this book, in a way the industry's indifference created the greatest freedom of all. The perpetrators of the new music figured that as they had no chance whatsoever of "making it," they might as well follow their artistic inclinations to the fullest. But it would take a long time before they'd be appreciated for their efforts.

The record industry was suffering a recession in the late '70s/early '80s due to shoddy workmanship and the subsequent disinterest of the public. Other forms of disposable entertainment were now encroaching upon the turf that had been established by Rock in the '60s and '70s. Video games like Pac-Man provided the same kind of leisurely pursuit as recorded music had, with even less aesthetic engagement. Once VCRs as well as home video games took flight, Americans became more affixed to their televisions than ever. It was inevitable around this time that Rock and television would merge.

Ever since the '50s, music-oriented shows had been popular television fixtures. Most of these consisted of variety-show type programs with performers lip-synching their current hits. In the '60s, there had been a whole stream of sitcoms based on musicians, from *The Monkees* to *The Partridge Family* to the cartoons: *Archies*, *Jackson Five*, *Josie & the Pussycats*. The advent of MTV—or "music television"—was different because there wasn't any emphasis on music-as-*performance*, per se. Whereas the theme of *The Monkees* or *The Partridge Family* had always been "the show must go on," music video was different: it was predominantly fantasy-oriented; there was no pretense that it was "real." It was also consumer-driven: the whole concept from the start was to show the targeted audience what they could buy. In this sense, many of the most popular "hits" of the '80s constituted nothing more than jingles designed to sell the wares of their creators.

MTV was not the first network to venture into the area of video TV: that distinction belongs to the USA Network, which, in 1980, began broadcasting *Night Flight*, a program consisting of videos by the few artists who were making videos at that time: Devo, Blondie, the Residents, David Bowie. There was also HBO's "Video Jukebox" segment, which aired video clips between movies when there was some filler time. But none of this could have prepared the music industry for MTV and its complete devouring of the whole hit-making *process*. "Music" as we once knew it would never be the same again.

MTV was originally conceived by corporate giant Warner-Amex, as an outgrowth of their 1980 two-way interactive cable experiment, QUBE. These were the early days of cable, and the field was wide open. There was actually a lot of creativity flourishing at the time, as evidenced by such daring non-network shows as *Fernwood Tonight*, *Mary Hartman Mary Hartman* and *The Uncle Floyd Show*, all of which were a result of cable broadcasting. However, far from being experimental, MTV from the start was based on the blandest, most commercial idea possible: namely, FM radio's AOR format (Adult-Oriented Rock), which was responsible for the insipid nature of mainstream radio in the early '80s. For this reason it's not surprising that the major labels, which were responsible for keeping the AOR format afloat, seized the opportunity to further expand the market, this time into the kiddie cartel. By far, the largest TV viewing audience was the twelve- to twenty-year-old range, and the whole idea of creating Rock that appealed to an adolescent audience only meant the whole mentality was going to be lowered a notch. What's really amazing is how fast so many so-called Rock musicians willingly succumbed to this subversion and aimed for the lowest common denominator.

With the advent of MTV, Rock 'n' Roll finally became absolute *product*. However, it took a bit more fine-tuning: the initial format, featuring the white dinosaur acts, didn't work. This caused the network to adopt an even lower standard—mainly, CHR, which in radio jargon meant "Contemporary Hits Radio." This meant swill like Men at Work and Hall & Oates more than it did Rock. No small wonder that, as the years went by, it became increasingly difficult to distinguish between the videos on MTV and the ads for Pepsi. In a strictly creative sense, the advent of Rock video did much more to revolutionize the advertising industry than it did Rock 'n' Roll. Not only did the manufacturers of items like ski togs, soda pop, automobiles, and other consumer items have a whole new field of innovative video technique to work with, but one that tied in with the billion-dollar recording industry as well. From there it was only a short step until recording artists were making actual ads themselves and putting all the muster they'd once put into their music towards Pepsi—who just happened to be sponsoring their latest tour.

In the early days of MTV, one of the major gripes among its critics was that it was inherently racist due to the dearth of Black artists being represented. The network's adherence first to AOR standards, and then to CHR ones promised that the public would not see a proliferation of Black musical acts on MTV, as those formats were basically devoid of color. But MTV's inability to secure more than a 1 percent Nielsen rating in the early days saw the network widen its umbrella slightly to include such soft-Pop/"adult contemporary" Black performers as Michael Jackson and Lionel Ritchie. They wouldn't mess with Rap until it was a proven commodity. Thus one sees the whole crux of the MTV mentality: eventually everything becomes compressed into a homogenized mix catering to show biz notions learned from TV and movies, as opposed to Rock 'n' Roll.

Video killed the radio star; however, by that time, radio was already dead. In fact, it was probably the blandness of FM radio that created the void for MTV to step into. But it would have happened anyway, because the world was shrinking and everything was becoming interconnected, and it was inevitable that the forces of TV, Rock 'n' Roll, movies, and advertising would all merge.

MTV was the final turning point away from the era when the words of fuddy-duddy Rock critics would even matter anymore. In the early '70s, a good or bad review in a magazine like *Rolling Stone* actually could make a difference. However, with the advent of MTV, serious analysis of Rock 'n' Roll became irrelevant—interesting to someone with an arcane interest in the form perhaps, but extraneous to the consumer. While certain pundits were decrying MTV as the death knell of Rock, a whole new nation of kids were learning how to exercise their freedom of choice by simply turning on their televisions. This was a lot different than the "underground" buzz that Rock represented in the '60s and '70s, where the whole sense of discovery was part of the process. Now Rock had become just another commodity.

Although the majority of old-school critics found MTV inherently offensive, the war against the new medium basically yielded losers. A perfect example was Dave Marsh, the Springsteen-touting liberal Rock critic who'd begun publishing his own anti-industry broadside in the early '80s, *Rock n' Roll Confidential*. Month after month, good old Dave bemoaned the deteriorating standard of Rock, the lack of "community" within, and the inherent racism of MTV. Although once an influential critic whose opinions influenced the public's tastes (e.g., about the Who, Springsteen), Marsh found himself on his own when it came to trying to buck the trend of Music Television, especially among his old comrades at *Rolling Stone*. Jann Wenner has never been a detractor of anything that made money—on the contrary, when it came to MTV, he wanted a piece of the pie (which he eventually got). The end result was that, around the time Marsh began issuing his stinging indictments—mostly in the form of his own aptly named "American Grandstand" column—he was relieved of his duties at Rolling Stone.

Someone like *Rolling Stone* contributor Kurt Loder fared much better, eventually becoming a kind of ersatz elder statesman who headed up MTV's "news division." This allowed him to still retain some distance from the kids while at the same time remaining neutral on such MTV-approved—and anti-Rock—sensations like Sting and Madonna. Considering that, in the *Billboard* Twenty-Fifth Anniversary of Rock special, Loder had selected albums by the Velvet Underground, the Ramones, and Stooges among his all-time favorites, he must have had to swallow pretty hard to now endorse such MTV swill. Indeed, his smirk often betrayed genuine contempt for the subject matter at hand. Then again, with the yuppification of New York that had occurred in the '80s, rents were rising. Bohemia was no longer an option.

In the early '80s, synth-Pop, which represented a fusion of Disco and New Wave, was all the rage: from New Wave came the whole waxed-down "futuristic" approach; from Disco, the mechanized hum of the synthetic rhythm track (although in the case of synth-Pop, it was often trance-inducing as opposed to dance-inspiring). The antecedent to the *look*—a kind of manqué skeleton—was David Bowie, who'd already shamelessly dabbled in Disco and would again with *Let's Dance* in 1984—when he also did the whole '80s Michael Jackson/Madonna thing of the album-of-the-movie-of-the-book-of-the-tour. Brian Eno, Bowie's collaborator on albums like *Low* and *Heroes* in the late '70s, was also extremely influential, particularly in England. His synth experiments like *Another Green World* and *Before & After Science* were just the kind of spongy aural wallpaper that groups like Human League were incorporating into their sound. Kraftwerk, from Germany, can't be discounted either: in 1975, their *Autobahn* album, made up entirely of synthesizers, was a worldwide smash. Later, they'd claim in interviews to actually be machines! Devo took this a step further with their mechanical goose-step, but ultimately their sense of humor revealed them for the "punk" band they actually were. Not ironically, the various ex-members would all go on to be MTV insiders in the late '80s.

Devo's whole man/machine persona was a natural extension of the age itself—in the race toward the year 2000, the group mentality had taken precedence over individual identity. This was surely the essence of '80s culture—a kind of mass homogeneity. This was also the era when people were talking about clones, and the test tube baby was also in the news. It seemed as if we were reaching an amoeba-like state as a species. Subsequently, there was a whole crop of Anglo-New Wave robot men adhering to this inhuman facade: Thomas Dolby, Gary Numan, Peter Schilling, Steve Strange.

As far as the synth-Pop groups went, most of them looked/sounded the same, especially after they discovered that, in order to make music this instinctively inhuman, one didn't need to be in a *band*, per se. Hence came the synth duos: first Kraftwerk, and then Ph.D., Soft Cell, Tears for Fears, and others. The more popular synth groups modeled themselves after the Beatles (Duran Duran, for instance). This was all enhanced by MTV: naturally this type of easy-to-assemble Muzak was an easy commodity for the fledgling video industry to foist on the public, as all the acts were more or less interchangeable. Even groups who may have started with good intentions quickly got sucked up into the MTV vacuum. For example, the Bangles, a female band from L.A., were originally part of the so-called paisley underground, a loose collective of bands who adhered to '60s styles in the era of post-Punk revisionism (this included the Dream Syndicate, the Rain Parade and the Three o'Clock as well). It didn't take long in the age of video for some slick CBS producer to figure out the appeal of four females, particularly lead singer Susanna Hoffs, whose curly Black hair and dark eyes marked her as a potential sex symbol for the '80s. It wasn't long before the Bangles were doing cute pajama-party videos on MTV and having Prince write their hit singles for them.

In other words, Rock music, which had reached its creative peak in the '60s with things like *Sgt. Pepper* and *The Velvet Underground and Nico* and all the adjacent trappings (Folk-Rock, Symphonic Rock, Art-Rock), had been completely turned back to the level of Frankie and Annette in less than twenty years' time.

I remember when Cyndi Lauper's first album, *She's So Unusual*, came out: I was working in a record store in a suburban shopping mall. By that time, music chains had become as constricted as format radio. It used to be that the record store was the sanctum of musically hip people who would lounge behind the counter spinning whatever discs they chose and bullshitting with the customers all day, with a few covert excursions into the back room to perhaps smoke some grass. By the '80s, chain outlets like Sam Goody and Musicland had actually resorted to *playlists* telling employees what records could be played in the store during operating hours.

Because of these playlists, I had to endure *She's So Unusual* ad infinitum. I remember telling a drummer friend of mine at the time: "If this ever makes it big, it's all over..."

It made it big. And, as far as the ideal of Rock that had existed for two decades went, it *was* all over.

As for the white, college-educated Baby Boomers, it wasn't really that surprising that they sold out their radical ideals for a house in the suburbs and 2.4 kids. Especially since those ideals were never really theirs to begin with. The majority of them were only attending the peace rally in hopes of getting laid. What kind of "struggle" did most college-deferred pseudo-radicals endure in the '60s, other than risking a little tear gas on a Saturday afternoon? Certainly their sacrifices were nothing compared to the Blacks in this country at the same time, not to mention the working class kids who actually went to Vietnam. Once college was over, the more affluent Boomers dove right into corporate America as readily as their parents once did.

In the '60s there was a belief running through the counterculture that if you're young, you *understand*. However, in the '80s, the reverse turned out to be true—in many ways it was the new kids who were the most closed-minded of all. They'd grown up in a filtered society, with all inputs duly sanctioned and approved. As the ages progressed, it would only get worse.

Much of the activism of the counterculture stemmed from massive opposition to the Vietnam War. Naturally, when the Boomers felt threatened that they might be taken away from their suburban Shangri-la, they protested. However, with the elimination of the draft and the end of the war, a lot of that fear subsided. Carter's resumption of draft registration in 1980 spurred a hint of fury amongst the decaying factions of the radical Left, but Reagan's subsequent ironhanded foreign policy and tough military stance pretty much eliminated the threat of war in the minds of most Americans. Reagan had fought the lewdness of Hollywood and won; he'd fought the LSD freaks and won; and now he was going to finally stare down communism. When the Iron Curtain finally came crumbling down in 1989, Reagan's pundits liked to say it was his get-tough stance that helped bring the commies to their knees. Nationalism made a big comeback in the '80s—especially in light of the fact that the Japanese were busy making "investments" in America by buying up such media outlets as CBS and Radio City Music Hall.

Consumerism as a way of life was also reflected by the first generation of MTV idols: Prince, Madonna, and Michael Jackson among them. These artists corresponded with the Reagan doctrine, because they were all basically working class and from mid-America but upwardly mobile and unashamed to reveal their greater ambitions (e.g., "Material Girl"). The invention of the compact disc was only a further incline toward blatant consumerism. By literally compacting recorded music to the size of a small commodity, the industry found that they could move even more units at cheaper cost. Meanwhile, as the CD was supposedly a "superior" format, the industry raised the price on the consumer. At first, CDs were sold in tandem with records, but slowly they came to replace records entirely. Retro clowns lamented the passing of the LP for aesthetic reasons, but they should have known—in the '80s, it was always going to be aesthetics that would suffer.

Companies weren't signing that many artists anymore: since the recession in the '70s, most of them had trimmed their rosters considerably. Because fewer artists were recording for major labels, fewer albums were actually being released. Each one had to be a major "event." Whereas in the '60s, artists like the Rolling Stones, the Beatles, and Bob Dylan were good for at least one album a year, in the '80s and '90s it wasn't unusual for an artist to wait *four years* between LPs. This was due in part to the coaxing of the record companies, who wanted to milk a single release for as long as possible. Also, it took longer to make an album in the '80s because of all the accompanying horseshit like videos. Michael Jackson, for instance, accompanied his *Thriller* album not only with several grandiose video productions, but also a video about the making of the video. Madonna, Prince, and Bruce Springsteen all followed Michael into the realm of megalomania: Madonna not only made albums, hit singles, and videos, but also posed for glamour photo shoots and made movies; Prince made movies and staged grand-scale tours with all the accompanying baggage; and Springsteen, already an established marketplace entity, rode his *Born in the USA* album for two years straight with books, tours, and TV specials. All the "creativity" in Rock n' Roll was going into marketing. Apparently, *Saturday Night Fever* in the now-already-quaint Disco era was only the beginning of how much a product could be milked. In any case, it was definitely the forebear to all this mass-produced swill.

However, unlike in previous musical eras, this "swill" wasn't just swill—these were considered major works by major artists, and the critics capitulated accordingly. In the '60s there were the Beatles, Dylan, and the Rolling Stones. In the '70s: Led Zep, Pink Floyd, whatever. Madonna was a little different: although she had many "bones" in her body, not one of them was musical. Can you imagine the type of society a world inundated by "Maneater" and "Like a Virgin" was breeding? Performers like Madonna were getting greater and greater media exposure than any previous musical acts ever. Michael Jackson's *Thriller* sold twenty two million copies. A lot of selfish, spoiled, greedy little "maneaters" were being born.

At the same time, the Baby Boomers who supposedly made up the "love generation" were showing their true colors by following in the same path as their parents: buying homes, raising families, and spending their hard-earned dollars on an ever-widening array of consumer items. The "revolution" had been a hoax. This was the generation who supposedly caused the "Generation Gap," but it was amazing how quickly they were willing to be put out to pasture. Ultimately they'd grown up to be a generation of consumers, not revolutionaries. In the '60s the unprecedented number of Boomers inadvertently aided the cause of "revolution" by lumping everyone within a certain age into a specific social demographic (even if it never proved very potent at election time). This distortion by the media—partly propagated by the hippies themselves—made the ranks of dissent appear much larger than they actually were. By the time the '80s rolled around, the party was over but the demographic was still there. This meant that the largest generation in American history was achieving its greatest buying power as consumers. This gave them a lot more clout in America than they'd ever had politically.

Suddenly the '60s were everywhere, even if it was an amalgamated version being used to sell Honda scooters and Coca-Cola to the tune of "Born to Be Wild." Despite the fact that the whole '60s youth movement had been based on the ethos of "hope I die before I get old," by the mid-'80s the Boomers were simply too pooped to pop. That rendered the rebellion of the '60s into nostalgia, which in turn sapped it of whatever strength it once had. This rested all future hopes of Rock 'n' Roll on the shoulders of Punk, a self-negating movement based on "no future." This dashed all hopes for real Rock to ever become a popular phenomenon again. It also opened up the door for the readymade nostalgia of classic Rock.

The whole notion of classic Rock was an anachronism, of course. Rock n' Roll has always been about seizing the moment and electrifying it, not about venerating the past. But the companies who owned the back catalogs of '60s superstars like the Beatles, Rolling Stones, the Doors, the Who, Jimi Hendrix, Eric Clapton, and Led Zeppelin realized what a valuable commodity they had on their hands—especially given the huge demographic represented by the Boomers and the new consumer format of the compact disc. In essence, the Boomers could have their past sold back to them—at a price. Meanwhile, radio stations that were resistant to the new schlock like Madonna and Duran Duran and still touted themselves as Rock stations, if only by brand name, adapted to the classic Rock format and became, in essence, the oldies stations of tomorrow.

The Boomers were typically self-righteous about all this nostalgia. Suddenly everyone in that age demographic was a supposed expert on '60s Rock even though, in actuality, the bloated pontificator in question had probably never inhaled. There was even an ad on the Nickelodeon channel in which a paunchy Boomer told his son, "Sorry son, no more fun. We used it all up in the '60s." What was really insidious, though, is that a lot of kids believed it. This was the kind of job the Boomers were doing on their own kids' self-esteem, eventually adding up the X Generation's whole sense of loss. It was as if the Boomers, having suffered arrested development as a result of their own privileged upbringing, couldn't bear to pass the torch of youth to the subsequent generation.

Meanwhile, the kids growing up listening to FM radio were left with few options. Faced with either "adult contemporary" crap or regurgitated oldies, it was easy to see why many of them believed all the good Rock had happened in the past. Unlike the original '60s generation, the '80s kids had no hope of ever hearing what the most creative musical minds of their generation were up to (save for the outlet of college radio). Given the choice of listening to what few bogus "new" groups made it across enemy lines and onto the airwaves—the Police, U2, the Cars, Tom Petty—or the music of the previous generation, many of them chose classic Rock. Which pleased the record companies to no end, because no artist was easier to A&R than a dead one (e.g., Jim Morrison). It also pleased the Boomers because it validated their assumption that, because their cultural artifices proved so enduring, their legacy would stand (i.e., the "revolution" was real after all).

As for the kids growing up listening to classic Rock in the '80s, consider it this way: it was the cultural equivalent of the hippies listening to Benny Goodman in the '60s. But of course they weren't—they were listening to artists who could acutely sum up their own feelings of frustration. The other side of this was, they *never grew out of it* either, which was unprecedented. Weaned on Dr. Spock and child psychology, they were taught to believe their every whim was important. They were also taught to believe that their legacy was infallible. This enabled them to chime on forever with "Light My Fire" and somehow think it was still radical—or stop listening to music altogether.

In the '80s, actual youth were the "silent minority." Suddenly, the Rock market was glutted by elder statesmen: Bruce Springsteen, the Rolling Stones,

Steve Winwood, Neil Young, Pete Townshend, Tina Turner, Paul McCartney, Eric Clapton, Peter Gabriel, Phil Collins, Paul Simon, John Fogerty, David Bowie, Jefferson Starship—all had "hits" and staged comebacks in the post-MTV era. Meanwhile, hack acts like ZZ Top, J. Geils, and John Cougar Mellencamp proved that if an artist just hung in there long enough he'd eventually make it. The word "survivor" was bandied around a lot, and the whole notion of longevity in Rock became a symbol of pride. Thus you had Pete Townshend, who'd once written "hope I die before I get old," singing: "I've *got* to stop drinking/I've *got* to stop smoking." Bands like the Who and the Stones became unsolicited overseers for a generation who didn't have a clue in the first place. Now people who'd, for all intents and purposes, missed the '60s the first time around, could claim: "I was *there*, man."

MTV had initially been launched as an entity that was supposed to vanquish the pre-existing Rock hegemony with something new and vital ("Video Killed the Radio Star"). When they found they could also exploit the new trend toward aging, they hopped on that, too. All of a sudden, prancing fortyish twits in leisure suits replaced synth-Pop groups as the synthetic of choice (drugs were out in the '80s, of course). A new feature of MTV was the insipid interview session, when they allowed some aging '60s hack to mouth platitudes between videos about how lucky they were to have "survived" the revolution, unlike poor old Jim or Jimi.

In light of this, it was amazing how fast supposed New Wave bands like U2 and the Police became "respectable" overnight. Semi-old farts like Tom Petty and the Dire Straits were quick to team up with graying edifices like Bob Dylan in order to reap mainstream respectability. The common ground seemed to be such causes-of-the-moment as USA for Africa and Amnesty International, which resulted in the inevitable video and video-of-the-making-of-the-video, which made such feel-good liberalism a hot MTV commodity as well.

Performers like Sting, who'd had their origins in "punk," suddenly found they had much more in common with elder statesmen like Springsteen (although, in Sting's case, he was almost as old). Would-be dinosaurs like John Cougar Mellencamp, Tom Petty, Elvis Costello, Huey Lewis, and Dire Straits played along as if they were a full decade older than they actually were. Perhaps the most symbolic popular record of the era was Dire Straits' "Money For Nothing," which arrived square in the middle of the '80s and summed up in plain terms what many people knew all along: "That ain't working!" An ironic ditty about how Mark Knopfler had overhead some knuckleheads in an appliance store musing about what it constituted to become a Rock star, one couldn't help upon hearing it but sense that Knopfler realized that, if it weren't for a few lucky breaks, he could be in the same position. Almost as if to underscore the irony, there was Sting singing backup vocals. And what was he singing? "I want my MTV..."

In 1978, the Rolling Stones, the ultimate pseudo-dilettante group, sang: "We're so respectable." The sad fact was, by the '80s, Rock really *was* respectable. Whereas in the days before MTV, Rock had merely been a livable commodity, still somewhat outside the fray of the mainstream "entertainment" industry, by the '80s it was big business. Suddenly, so-called Rock riffs were popping up in commercials, like Pontiac's "we build excitement" campaign. Meanwhile, MTV icons like Michael Jackson sold Pepsi, and beer companies such as Schlitz and Budweiser sponsored tours for artists like the Who and Rolling Stones, respectively. Rock stars even sold their *own music* to companies like Coke and Pepsi. Although Jazz musicians in the '50s had supplemented their income by performing jingles or television themes, they did so anonymously. This was a lot different than Paula Abdul shilling for Coke (although the Cola Wars *were* a major issue of the '80s, along with Madonna's belly button, ad nauseum).

The final proof that Rock had become "respectable" was when Lee Atwater "rocked and rolled" at George Bush's inauguration in 1989: here was the establishment itself exploiting the very devil it had once so vehemently sought to exorcize. By then, even the government knew the demographic they were aiming for—mainly, the yuppies who had grown up with Rock n' Roll and were now the nation's number one consumers. Rock, meanwhile, was ultimately doomed to become just another generation's version of "popular music." Almost as if to underscore this fact, the Rock Hall of Fame opened in 1989—in *Cleveland*, no less! But you can't enshrine the intangible spirit of Rock n' Roll: ultimately the Hall of Fame was just another consumer warehouse filled with high-priced memorabilia, a study in cheap nostalgia only a few notches higher than the ultra-commercial Hard Rock Café.

So while Rock's past—or an extremely muted version thereof—was being filed away in a museum, the only new groups making it big in those days playing guitar-based music were poodle-haired bands like Bon Jovi, Poison, and Def Leppard. Even then, their Muzak wasn't actually Rock, but a video director's rendition of what Rock constituted—which, of course, fit evenly into the MTV Magic Kingdom. The poodle bites.

Women in the '80s had achieved marketplace equality for the first time, and with this came a new independence about everything, from careers to sexuality. For the first time ever, a woman could have her cake and eat it too: the new thing was for a woman to have both a career and a family, even if that meant the male stayed home changing the diapers. A lot of this was the upwardly mobile pattern established by the yuppies: with a host of challenging employment options opening up under the new revivified economy, it was unlikely that any educated woman would want to be a simple housewife anymore. In fact, in the dual income households of the '80s, very often the woman was the breadwinner. This naturally resulted in a whole new sexual dynamic as well.

While people like Ronald Reagan, Pat Robertson, and Jerry Falwell were trying to turn back the hands of time, and people were continually looking to the past for inspiration, there were changes being wrought in the culture that would permanently alter the concept of the American family once and for all. In the '80s, the whole notion of the single mother was born, not just in the unwitting example of the millions of unwed Black mothers in the ghettos, but also the kind of dilettante maternity (epitomized by the famous *Murphy Brown* episode) in which a woman pushing forty chooses to have a child out of wedlock before her biological clock runs out.

The new independent woman was totally unprecedented, and American manhood was going to have to learn to deal with her, even as all the old familiar sexist stereotypes were still promoted in everything from *Playboy* to Budweiser ads. Many women felt that, because the balance of power had been tipped against them for so long, they had to go to absurd lengths of self-empowerment to achieve equality. This resulted in a genuine Battle of the Sexes.

Some of the purveyors of this new form of women's liberation were fiercely aggressive, almost to the point of wanting to tame—or maim—their male counterparts (whom they saw as repressors). Divas like Sheena Easton, Annie Lennox, and Janet Jackson readily emasculated their would-be suitors in massive video campaigns broadcast all over MTV. Madonna was, of course, the most successful practitioner of this kind of female self-empowerment, but it wasn't a Gloria Steinem type of liberation urging women to be less catty and to stop using their sexuality to get what they want and to adapt more manly attributes. On the contrary, the thing about Madonna was, she was urging women to actually be ultrafeminine to get what they want—by wearing bustiers in public or whatever. After the rise of Madonna, the whole notion of a butch kind of women's liberation became antiquated. The new feminine role model was someone who could be fully aware of her sexual prowess, while at the same time being selective and also in control.

The '80s were also the beginning of the era when people began going to exercise clubs and working out on a massive scale. Everyone got into health in the '80s, as a way to turn back the tide of all the recklessness and drug consumption of the previous two decades. Early-to-bed/early-to-rise fit in a lot better with the yuppie lifestyle than three-day acid trips. "Control" was a big issue in the '80s, so much so that Janet Jackson named her album just that, and she wasn't only talking about her workout regime or vegetarian diet (which Madonna also adhered to), but control over her male oppressors as well.

There were many ways men in the '80s responded to the new female empowerment. Some of the liberal types tried to appear sympathetic, but many women viewed this genteel response as a form of pandering and treated its purveyors with even more scorn and derision than they did the most offensive type of male macho slime. They cut their balls off, in other words. In the age of feminine conquest, the passivity of the male was inevitable, and some of the new TV ads with dad burping baby while mom buzzed around getting ready for work helped reinforce the new stereotype of the totally emasculated male. The implication was that the male, by dint of merely being male, was inherently guilty of the kind of sexism that had rendered women "second class citizens." Therefore he must be hung out to dry.

Madonna, meanwhile, straddled the fence (and everything else) by proclaiming herself a "boy toy" but then having it her way—a perfect paradox, in other words. Just the fact that she made the most money made her a symbol of winning womanhood in the ultramaterialistic '80s, even though her image was merely an amalgamation of the whole American pinup tradition and other ironic symbols of mass consumption. It really had little to do with female empowerment, other than the fact that she could choose her own sex partners—and subsequently discard them at will. Many female artists went to even further lengths to assert their unmistakable "control." The male response oftentimes was a kind of baffled resignation, which resulted in many of them receding even further into the depths of porno and pinups, a trend that would only accelerate with the birth of the Internet.

In the '80s, the previously clandestine terrain of sadomasochism came out of the closet: to the newly emasculated male, the image of the dominatrix—or untouchable Bitch Goddess—seemed eminently comforting because, with her, the male could finally be relieved of his "control" once and for all. Many men figured that, as women were taking their jobs away, the next step was to relinquish control in the bedroom. In the field of popular music, this resulted in a vast array of readymade divas slipping into the dominatrix persona: Deborah Harry, Jennifer Miro, Chrissie Hynde, Janet Jackson, Sheena Easton, Madonna, Wendy O. Williams, Grace Jones, Amanda Lear, Annie Lennox. Tina Turner did them one better by hanging her deadbeat—and physically abusive—husband, Ike, out to dry in public, while she glided to the top of the album charts with *Private Dancer* as well as the best-seller lists with her tell-all bio, *I, Tina*.

Reaction to this was varied on the part of male rockers: sure there were symps like the Violent Femmes, who tried to placate the feminists by being the perfect submissive counterparts. But in the male-oriented sexist domain of Rock 'n' Roll, there were bound to be those who reacted violently in the opposite direction. When such reaction was limited to the Punk Rock gutter—like G. G. Allin or the Meatmen, for instance—it went largely unnoticed. But when albums like NWA's *Straight Outta Compton* began to sell three million copies, a few watchdog groups like the PMRC began to make some noise. After all, in the newly emergent world of Rap music, the words "bitch" and "hoe" had become synonymous with "woman."

When the Parents' Music Resource Center (PMRC), a watchdog group consisting of congressional wives, first took aim against sexist content in popular music, their primary target was Heavy Metal. The music, so named because it conjured the stomp of industrial mayhem, had been reduced to a shadow of its former self in the '80s. Whereas acts like Led Zeppelin, Black Sabbath, the MC5, and the Stooges had been called "heavy metal" precisely because that's what they sounded like, by the '80s, with a few exceptions (Motorhead being the most obvious one), that essential heaviness had been usurped by Punk groups like the Misfits, Bad Religion, Husker Du, Minor Threat, Swans, Big

Black, Die Kreuzen, Black Flag, and others. The glam posturing of bands like Kiss and Aerosmith had spawned a whole new generation of harmless haircut bands who affected the pose without the pulse, so to speak. As far as having any sense of history, these kids had none—they didn't know that Jimmy Page stole a good portion of his act from the Blues, and didn't care. The new generation of metal bands worshipped Rock heroes like Led Zeppelin or Kiss solely for the fact they got laid a lot and made lots of money. In other words, Beavis and Butt-Head were being born unto the culture for real.

In the '80s, the whole concept of being a Rock star became just another career choice. A lot of musical aspirants enrolled in the Berklee School of Music in Boston or Juilliard in New York where they learned to play scales ad infinitum. The whole sense of doing anything musically constructive was lost. It now became a contest between who could outplay whom. A lot of critics blamed Page or Sabbath's Tony Iommi for this syndrome, but it wasn't really their fault—they'd come to their self-indulgences by accident. It was simply a matter of following where the technology led them. Consequently, they grandstanded a little.

By the time Metal became institutionalized, it was an accepted fact that one could play scales in rapid succession at ninety miles per hour. Now it was just a matter of who had the best haircut. After the rise of Eddie Van Halen, there was a whole series of fast-fingered hacks with names like Yngwie Malmsteen, Andreas Vollenweider, and Joe Satriani who appeared in succession to try and unseat Edward as the supreme fretboard monger. Although popular with the *Guitar Player* crowd, they didn't really catch on with the MTV Metal audience, which, by that time, was the domain of big-haired bubblegum groups like Quiet Riot, Motley Crue, Ratt, Poison, Dokken, Enuff Z'Enuff, Kix, and Axe.

In the '70s, Heavy Metal had somewhat of a bad reputation, and its adherents were generally perceived to be drug takers and devil worshippers. With the input of MTV, the whole persona of Heavy Metal became more mainstream: most of the musicians still took drugs and toyed with death/Satanic imagery, but (following Van Halen's cheeky lead) with a wink of an eye. The Metal pose was still based on Zeppelin's original premise—the preening leonine singer and the show-off Guitar God—but like everything else in the '80s, that merely became a syndrome, with all the fear—and thus the "reality"—extricated. It became an *act* because it was no longer being aimed at a musical audience, but a television one.

Perhaps Kiss was the first band to approach Rock as total show business. With them there was never any of the pseudomystical mumbo-jumbo of a Zeppelin or even a Sabbath. Kiss had roomed with the New York Dolls and played gigs with the Stooges—believe me, they knew the scene inside out. It was a self-conscious decision on their part to become cartoon characters, thus foreshadowing the whole MTV Magic Kingdom where every band or artist from Madonna on down signified some kind of persona, just like any matinee idol. Another thing to carry over from Kiss to the "new Metal" was the sexism—songs like "See You in Your Dreams," "Ladies in Waiting," "Room Service," "Ladies Room," and "Calling Dr. Love" signaled the birth of a whole new category in the late '70s: "cock Rock."

By the mid-'80s, the PMRC was recommending that albums carry warning stickers like cigarettes did, because of the sexism and violence being reflected by Heavy Metal and other forms of popular music. "Popular" is the key word because truly offensive underground rockers like G. G. Allin were being overlooked in favor of the readily available MTV mock-Metal. The main targets seemed to be clowns like Twisted Sister, whose leader, Dee Snider, rose to prominence as one of the key speakers during the proceedings (the other being Frank Zappa). The PMRC's complaint centered on the fact that the video for the group's hit, "We're Not Gonna Take It," glorified domestic violence by showing the old man getting blown out of a window by his seemingly "possessed" son. In other words, it was more *Animal House* than something actually dangerous like the Stooges or G. G. Which is where Kiss comes in once again—when it comes to faux rebellion, it's harder to find a clearer precedent for all this stuff, especially considering such mass-marketing attempts as *Kiss Meets the Phantom of the Park*, a network TV special they made in 1978.

Ultimately, the PMRC was a paper tiger—by that time, the real enemy came from within, not without. As the PMRC didn't know anything about *real* Rock and were basing all their opinions on what they saw on MTV, the targets they sought to eradicate were bogus non-Rock artifices anyway. Nevertheless, even supposedly hip underground acts like Sonic Youth apparently considered them enough of a threat as late as 1990 to issue a promo photo for the album *Goo* containing the legend "Smash the PMRC."

Sonic Youth could have only *hoped* to get that much attention in 1985, because, at that time, the world of the "underground" and the world of mainstream Rock couldn't have been farther apart. The self-appointed guardians of morality concentrated their attack almost solely on Heavy Metal (this was before Rap had really caught on in the mainstream). The irony was that groups like Twisted Sister, far from representing any actual threat, were merely *acting* like they thought Rock stars should act. Among the biggest targets of the PMRC was the whole wave of "satanic" metal bands like Slayer, Venom, and Witchfinder General, who adorned their albums with satanic symbolism and sped up the whole process with superaccelerated riffs (influenced by Punk and Hardcore). Most of the bands in this genre that had any serious musical claim to fame (the British band, Sacrilege, comes to mind) went unnoticed by the PMRC and the public alike. Instead, the hearings focused on silly son-of-Satan bands like WASP and Dio, whose album covers featured kitschy illustrations of little red devils and the like. As the always-caustic Zappa, holding one of the offending album covers, told the committee, "As a parent my first reaction to this record is to laugh."

The defamation of women at the hands of Heavy Metal bands was a big media issue in the '80s, with album covers featuring women dismembered, or tied to a cross, or worshipping slavishly at the feet of Rock deities (a trend started by Kiss). Videos were even worse, routinely showing a bevy of bikini'd bimbos bouncing around, which was demeaning not just to women but also to anyone with an IQ over fifty. There were also the lyrics, which, in the case of Metal, had been misogynist since the days of Zeppelin. But at least Zeppelin, or even Van Halen in their early days, had some musical merit—a group like WASP relied on shock value alone. Which was easy to do in the age of MTV.

In the underground, the sexism came across in a more subtle way, because the mostly collegiate audience was supposed to be "hip" and intelligent enough to understand the irony. Nevertheless, a lot of genuine sleaze seeped into the scene. There were bound to be those who wished to push the buttons of these jaded hipsters in more extreme ways—nine times out of ten, they came not from the college scene, but from the white-trash redneck frontier. The most potent example was G. G. Allin, an outcast from New Hampshire who was always on the front line when it came to being offensive. Not only did he advocate rape ("I'm Gonna Rape You") but child rape as well ("Ten Year Old," "Expose Yourself to Kids"). These were the days before Rap really hit—in a few years you'd have someone like Slick Rick proclaiming "Treat Her Like a Prostitute" and actually having a hit with it.

In the '80s such raunch was still the exclusive terrain of sub-subterranean acts like the Mentors, a bunch of fat thirtysomethings from Seattle who'd been on the fringe of the underground for years and who cashed in on the West Coast Metal trend with albums like *You Axed for It*. Only their whole approach was much more self-parody, in the league of Tesco Vee, than it was legitimate Heavy Metal. Nevertheless, they got signed to the prestigious Enigma label and were able to expose such unrelenting slabs of sexism as "My Erection's Over" and the immortal "Sandwich of Love" to a fairly sizeable audience. These songs epitomized the new mentality that had actually begun with Kiss— mainly, that "scoring" wasn't just about self-fulfillment anymore; it was about total mental and physical dominance.

The other side of the coin was the Madonna syndrome: mainly, that the "slut" stigma no longer carried the same negative connotations it once had. If it was true that, as Van Halen preached, "everybody wants some," then sluts, as they got a *lot*, were actually cultural icons in the '80s. For a while, there was even such a thing as Slut-Rock. Its perpetrators—Pat Benatar, Bonnie Tyler, Berlin, Heart, Samantha Fox—fucked freely, but never learned. As a result, were always receiving "the short end of the stick" so to speak. These were the sub-Madonna types who were sexually liberated but not emotionally mature enough to handle the consequences. Therefore, the girl fans who grew up listening to them were already resigning themselves to a life of unrequited nonliberated love. The end result would be the whole *Springer* syndrome a few years later in which a whole generation of white-trash losers would get off watching their counterparts air their dirty laundry in public.

That was the equalizing factor of MTV and '80s culture in general. It was the beginning of the era when lowbrow culture would invade the mainstream, as epitomized by such phenomena as professional wrestling and Rap music. Needless to say, the culture would never be the same again. One by-product of this decline was a whole new school of ultraprofane comedians like Andrew Dice Clay, who routinely ran down women with alarming alacrity. As the rappers did, comedians like Clay routinely referred to women as "bitches."

Naturally, any man who slaps bitches around would hate "fags" also, so there was plenty of antigay sentiment in the '80s to go along with the misogyny. Being gay in the '80s wasn't the best of times—the rise of AIDS had in many ways reversed the kind of acceptance gays experienced during the freewheeling Disco era. Homosexuality wasn't in line with Reagan's vision of America, and just as the administration had waged a war on drugs, they were ready to go to war over "alternative lifestyles" as well. There was a lot of speculation about how perhaps the government itself had manufactured the AIDS virus to whip up antigay hysteria and in essence revoke the permissiveness of the previous era—which Reagan was trying to do in other ways as well, from attempting to overturn Roe vs. Wade to recommending that prayer in public schools be resumed.

The antigay climate produced some stunning examples of intolerance, such as Guns n' Roses' put-down of "fags" (along with "niggers"—besides being sexist, the group were apparently racist as well). Meanwhile, NWA speculated about the cops who routinely searched them: "I don't know if they're *fags* or what." Later, NWA member Eazy E, on his first solo album, would conjure a fag-assault fantasy culminating in the verse "that was one faggot I had to hurt." Heavy D & the Boys, another Rap group, mused about a rival rapper who was "happy as a fag in prison." Tone-Lóc perhaps summed up the climate best with his proclamation in 1989: "Ain't no plan with a man!"

Fag baiting was popular in the "underground" as well, but it's harder to gauge the intent, considering the pervasive irony that ruled all such postmodern exploits. Tesco Vee was chief among the gay-bashers with not only the antilesbian "Death Dyke Dirge" but also the anti-male fag "Tooling for Anus." The Dead Milkmen rhetorically asked their collegiate audience: "You know what you are, don't you?" Before answering: "A bunch of art fags." Byron Coley and Jimmy Johnson over at *Forced Exposure* magazine routinely called other fanzine editors—as well as bands—"sissies." And the Angry Samoans, in their inimitably venomous style, offered "Homosexual." At least they had the good sense to give Jerry Falwell the songwriting credit.

Increasingly, the culture was being driven by senseless provocation. The proliferation of "culture" that had resulted from the media age had cheapened its value—with the invention of television, culture suddenly belonged to everyone, including the lower classes. By the '80s, this cheapening of the cultural landscape took the form of such crass icons as Madonna, Andrew Dice Clay, and Mike Tyson. Bad behavior became the norm, and when that happened, those who were consciously seeking to "shock"—like the members of the underground, for instance—had to dig even deeper into the gutter of depravity to remain outside the mainstream. This included the worlds of crime/gore, pornography, drugs, and death-exploit. Through these and other "sleazo inputs," the underground in the '80s got a lot grimier.

The definition of "culture" had expanded. Now network news shows had segments on "entertainment" and a host of "human interest" stories. Because of this, history itself was being mutated—more people now remembered the Beatles than the Tonkin Gulf Resolution. Modern history was increasingly becoming a kind of glorified folklore. Consciousness was being affected by *symbols*, not so much actual feats. Television had a lot to do with this—momentous events became insignificant trivia (what Norman Mailer disparagingly termed "factoids") while insignificant celebrity types like Madonna took on mythic importance.

This slavish worship of fame spawned the insta-celebrity syndrome. It also resulted in a kind of warped appreciation of infamy as celebrity, resulting in the celebrity status of famous criminals like Charles Manson and Richard Ramirez. Manson's story was too perfect to ignore in the overdramatized swirl of the modern media culture: a "hippie" whose followers murdered a famous actress, supposedly under telepathic direction from the Beatles. The whole saga tied in so many disparate elements that it became a kind of parable of the counterculture, with Manson emerging as a "cult" hero in his own right. Perhaps the first criminal to understand the media, Manson was actually somewhat of a charismatic speaker, even if what he was saying amounted to hippie mumbo-jumbo and sociopathic raving. By the '80s, Manson's name was as synonymous with evil as Beelzebub's himself.

Not surprisingly, those who embraced the more antisocial side of Rock turned Manson into a kind of hip mascot (after all, he couldn't hurt them from behind bars). Among the Rap and Rock groups who evoked his image were the Ramones, NWA, the Geto Boys, Sonic Youth, Lydia Lunch, Gangsta NIP, and the Pixies. Many post-everything combos even slipped his ugly mug—usually in the form of the famous *Life* cover photo—onto their LP sleeves: Poison Idea, the Lemonheads, Negative FX, etc. Guns N' Roses and G. G. Allin covered Manson material, and AntiSeen's Joe Young perfected the ultimate Manson "tribute" with "Charlie's Blues," which sampled a crazed Manson speech to the dirge of a Black Sabbathian riff.

In the case of AntiSeen, no group was better suited to comprehend the white-trash ethos lying at the root of Manson's mania than the boys from New

London, North Carolina. Their subject matter ranged from spousal abuse ("Wifebeater," "White Trash Bitch") to incest ("Little Sister") to fistfights ("Face Full of Teeth"), all conditions they were infinitely familiar with, given their humble redneck origins. All of this was delivered with a sort of Southern pride and the most turbo-charged update of the grinding Stooges/Ramones/Motorhead formula to emerge during the '80s. This was a whole new element in Rock: the belligerent hick or white-trash degenerate who, at the same time, wasn't necessarily anti-intellectual. AntiSeen were the kind of punk kids who wrote letters to Manson in prison simply because they knew they could and wouldn't have to face retribution from the devil. It was another gag, another cultural land mine waiting to explode in the face of the politically correct intelligentsia, who were quickly becoming the neo-"old ladies" of the new age.

New Hampshire's G. G. Allin came from the same hick origins as AntiSeen and even made an album with them. But whereas AntiSeen's angst was somewhat righteous, G. G.'s was merely pointless. Referring to what he did as "the mission," Allin's path of celebrated mayhem—fighting, shitting onstage, massive intoxication—took him to the cultural podium for a brief spell. It also took him to jail and, eventually, the grave. During his peak, he had bragged that he was going to commit suicide onstage during Halloween 1989, but kept conveniently pushing the date forward. When he finally died, it was in the most predictable Rock burnout manner—a heroin OD.

In his time, G. G. was often referred to as a "porn rocker," not only because of the subject matter of some of his songs, but also because he often performed in the nude. Actual pornography was another one of the sleazy elements making inroads into the Rock scene in the '80s, from Madonna's various nudie exploits in *Playboy* and *Penthouse* to lesser-known chanteuses like Lydia Lunch, Wendy O. Williams, and Bebe Buell baring it all in skin mags like *Oui*, *Club*, and *Swank*. The truth is, for the women of the New Wave, posing nude or working in strip bars was often more lucrative than their chosen art—particularly in New York. As Tommy Dean, the second owner of Max's Kansas City, recalled: "Almost every musician had a girlfriend out in New Jersey doing table dances all day to pay the rent. I always used to say that if the topless industry broke down, it would have killed the Punk scene in New York instantly."[6]

As Cosey Fanni Tutti of Throbbing Gristle, perhaps the first New Wave waif to dabble in porn, found out, it was also a way to make an ironic statement about the exploitation of women. Because if an intelligent woman chose to engage in the sex profession willingly, then who was really being exploited, the woman or the men who pay for the fantasy? This was an important part of the post-Punk aesthetic as practiced by aggregations like the Swans, Sonic Youth, and Pussy Galore (all of whom employed female members).

It was almost as if it was becoming a contest among the hip downtown groups like the Swans and Sonic Youth over who could stomach the most sleaze. This meant that the audience was also having its resistance to sleaze worn down. That's why you had audiences of superhip white college intellectuals standing around in smoky clubs trying to look bored while the Butthole Surfers performed with an actual stripper and showed car-crash films behind them. It was also why a group like Pussy Galore stormed to fame on the strength of songs like "Cunt" and "You Look Like a Jew" and why leader Jon Spencer told *Spin*: "I know my girlfriend is a cunt." (His girlfriend, Christina Martinez, was, of course, also in the group.)

The contradictions apparent in this kind of ultrahipsterism were brought to the fore when the indie-Rock factions were confronted with such non-ironic practitioners as G.G. Allin or AntiSeen. That's when their "cool" was tested, because it was supposedly not hip anymore to *mean* what you said, but a performer like G. G. *definitely* meant it. But at the same time, to pooh-pooh someone like G. G. would betray some sort of moral objection, which was perceived as square. So it got complicated for the young hipster-on-the-make.

Others, meanwhile, wanted to delve as deep in the sleaze as possible, in a vain attempt to reach the philosophical threshold of seen it all/done it all. Here's Swans leader Mike Gira describing a typical scene in Venice Beach, California circa the late '70s:

"The Nitsch event was more of a ritual than a performance and it lasted about four to six hours and right there all around—not on a stage—in a storefront...Strung up in this white room were the skinned carcasses of two lambs...so the dead meat was suspended in mid-air. Something like a hundred gallons of lambs' blood and entrails had been supplied in vats as well, and a series of young boys, naked and blindfolded, were brought out on the stretcher, the blood, etc. was poured through the carcass and over the tender youths' bodies, into

their mouths, etc. This obscure series of ritualized actions was directed by...this little fat guy dressed in black like a priest without a collar...and he was wearing this one oversized black rubber glove on his
white hand, and with it he'd direct people. Everyone was drinking lots
of wine from jugs that were passed around; the idea was to get as drunk
as possible and revel in the blood and sound, and eventually it just built
to a point where the boy-volunteer sacrifices started shaking in uncontrollable convulsions. By this time...the room had filled a couple of
inches deep in the blood and offal and everyone was just wallowing in
it. Half the audience was naked by this point and in a drunken dream
state. Eventually the blood was pouring out the door onto the street
outside and the police came...the main thing I took away from the
event—besides a stink I couldn't wash off for weeks—was the sense of
being overwhelmed by the blood and sound, the way it slowed down
time, and I wanted it to go on forever. In a way it was a really pure religious experience."[7]

Granted, not everyone's idea of a night out, and it's hard to tell how much
of Gira's description is meant to be tongue-in-cheek, but it just proves how far
out some people were willing to go to experience what the Cramps called
"Some New Kinda Kick." This also accounted for the rise of sadomasochism
in the '80s and of voyeurism in general. The spread of AIDS had attached grave
risks to frequent casual sex, and a lot of people found a safe alternative by
voyeuristically experiencing as many shocking deviations as possible. Human
sexuality had become an artifice to be manipulated like everything else. This
contributed to the rise of "performance art."

Performance art was the ultimate postmodern manifestation, because it
acknowledged so many latter-day art forms. From conventional art, it absorbed
the whole notion of trying to do something visionary and intellectual. From
Rock n' Roll, it borrowed its brashness and confrontational style. As far as the-
atrics went, it was a combination of actual theater and stand-up comedy. The
moral content, meanwhile, was derived from the world of hardcore pornography, whereby exploitation of the human form was its own kind of ironic statement. In the '80s, it wasn't unusual in the art community for a performer like
Annie Sprinkle to stick a speculum in her vagina and ask audience members to

come up and take a peek, or one like Karen Finley to confront male viewers by reaching out and grabbing their wee-wees. In the press, even G. G. was erroneously labeled a "performance artist" but, as he proved, in his case it was no "performance"; it was real.

G. G. doesn't really concern us here, but his biggest disciple, Lisa Suckdog, does. The thing that made Suckdog important was that she did all the things G. G. did—shit onstage etc.—but she was a *woman*, which made it even more shocking because there was simply no precedent for this in the indie-Rock world, which she casually got lumped into/under by dint of her musical exploits, which couldn't be called "Rock" unless one considered the works of Yoko Ono to be musical masterpieces (don't laugh—in the ultra-ironic post-everything era, people did). The fact that she was also from New Hampshire, and her father was a legendary ex-con dope smuggler, only contributed to her white-trash allure. There was also the matter of her insatiable sexual appetite—she would later go to work as a prostitute and then describe her exploits in the pages of her 'zine, *Rollerderby*. That was another important part of the underground in the '80s—the revolution brought about by the PC had made desktop publishing a reality. Now anyone could publish his or her own fanzine for a small price. People like Lisa Suckdog, who reveled in self-publicity, could spread their message far and wide providing they were just a little more organized than, say, G. G.

In the end, many of the concepts rampant in the field of performance art eventually made inroads into more conventional art forms. The controversial photographer, Robert Mapplethorpe, raised the hackles of Reaganites when it was discovered that the National Endowment for the Arts funded one of his exhibits featuring bondage photos of male homosexuals. Similar furor erupted over Andres Serrano's sculpture of a crucifix submerged in water (entitled "Piss Christ"). Even though such blatant sacrilege was already commonplace in the field of "underground" Rock—for example, the Feederz's "Entering Jesus from the Rear"—its entrance into the field of high art was unprecedented. Meanwhile, long after Mapplethorpe died of AIDS, his work would influence artists like Madonna, who put out her own artsy-smartsy book of black-and-white bondage photos entitled *Sex*, which became one of the biggest turnbacks in publishing history when it was discovered that the pages fell out.

People were becoming desensitized on a mass scale, not only to strange sexual practices but to forms of violence as well. It was clear that violence was becoming a routine factor of American life, judging by the TV shows (*Miami Vice*) and movies (*Rambo*, *Friday the 13th*) that were popular at the time. To the underground, the exploration of human pain and suffering was just one more hipster kick. We've already discussed the cult status of Charles Manson and other mass murderers. A popular book in the hip record stores during the post-Punk era was *Tortures of the Medieval Era*. There was also *Faces of Death*, a popular video rental during the age of irony that supposedly featured the *real thing* (even though it was exposed years ago as being partially fake).

Hardcore had done a lot to introduce *real* violence to Rock. It was music of extremely jacked-up emotions and, as such, was bound to inspire some degree of aggression in its participants. The Hardcore slam pit routinely became a bloodbath: suburban jocks would come into town during the weekend to bash with the locals. This scene was perhaps best epitomized by the Slammies on "Gonna Slam": "I'm gonna sneak up from behind/I'm gonna hit him in the head/Gonna rip his 'Rock Lobster' shirt…"

So while you had one faction of post-Punk development going into the hypnotic sex-ritual direction of the Butthole Surfers or Sonic Youth, there was also this whole militaristic army of male suburbanites who were being influenced by the violent philosophy of hate groups and gorehounds. And never the twain shall meet (thank God).

As far as blending the misanthropic carnage of gore-schlock like *Faces of Death* with the primary musical impulses of Hardcore, the Misfits were champs. Leader Glenn Danzig was admittedly a big comic book buff, and the Misfits' whole death-mask Halloween get-ups were in a way just a cruder version of Kiss (the band also hailed from the New York area). However, Danzig's descriptive lyrics weren't for the kiddies—he could describe violence with a passion and bluster that would have been truly frightening if he hadn't been five foot four! No matter—along with his pal Henry Rollins, Danzig was one of the biggest muscle-builders in Punk Rock. It was cathartic the way he sang: "I'll put a knife right in you" in "Horror Business." The guitars naturally reinforced the sentiment.

In a way, the Ramones were responsible for this casual, offhand manner of dealing with violence. That's because they were TV kids—violent events like the war in Vietnam, the terrorist bombings in Beirut, and the space shuttle disaster were just that: events. That is, they were "objects" and thus not real. Once again: *folklore*! That's what it was all becoming. More and more, what little "real" Rock there was left was becoming a form of literature: it described things, represented opinions and philosophy. It aligned itself with various causes, or it told stories (or, in the case of the Misfits, ghost stories). It was journalism. More than that, it had become a folk form. Rock was actually the last true folk art left.

What else would you call it when some of its most noble practitioners had to sustain themselves with day jobs right up through the '80s? But that's how it went for bands like Boston's Kilslug, who were the next step after the Misfits in the gore-Rock department, only where the Misfits played extremely fast, Kilslug played extremely slow, because their musical birthright was not the Ramones but Black Sabbath. A little older than the average "punks," Kilslug found themselves ten years too late for the gladiatorial stuff, so they had to find their niche among the indie hordes. Having never been afforded the grandeur of their heroes—Cooper, Sabbath, Kiss—they had to work the blue-collar jobs, which not only intensified their angst, but also built their muscles. Consider them a Northeast version of AntiSeen—and grasp the irony of such lone desperados—and others of their ilk like Poison Idea, the Mentors, and even G. G.—trying to survive in the increasingly ginchy climate of the '80s.

Despite the Reagan administration's attempts to formulate a war on drugs, on the music scene, drugs were prevalent as always. Drugs and musicians have always gone together, and the self-destructiveness of Punk guaranteed that the whole tragicomic notion of the suffering-artist–junkie would continue into a whole new generation. Most often, heroin was the drug of choice. Each generation has its mavericks who think they'll dabble and not get addicted—and each time, the same thing happens: they get addicted. It's amazing how many tortured souls dive readily into its grasp. The fact that the narcotic problem in the Rock scene grew worse in the '90s is only further evidence of the incredibly seductive powers of the opium plant and all its synthetic variants.

The proliferation of heroin in the late '80s–early '90s can be traced directly back to the Hardcore scene. This was a scene given to violence and self-negation. Although the punks originally sputtered self-righteous venom against "drug-addled hippies," they seemed all too ready to succumb to the same vices once they'd grown old enough to appreciate their "healing" powers. The only difference between the punks and hippies was that the hippies grew complacent on the drugs and "mellowed out," and the punks grew more violent and self-destructive. Which is why in the '80s, no "Punk" bands ever made it—because those who were courted by major labels, like Husker Du, were, by that time, suffering from drug addiction. This meant that they were of no use to a record company that was accustomed to Madonna's regimented gymnastics. Once again, it was the artist's misconception that the drugs were "freeing him" that ultimately led to his enslavement to a seedy lifestyle in which pulling into each town meant another risky attempt to cop.

Drugs sidelined the career of many a potential Rock star during the Blunder Years of the '80s. Steve Jones, the original guitarist of the Sex Pistols, found himself in Hollywood doing session work here and there and going to cop—when he finally woke up, ten years had gone by. There were also the exploits of the Guns n' Roses crew who, in typical *Oprah* style, went public with songs like "Mr. Brownstone." We've already discussed Husker Du. Perhaps even more ridiculous in their cart-before-the-horse readymade-Rock-star antics were the Replacements, who, like the Huskers, hailed from Minneapolis. Their guitarist, Bob Stinson, lived out the whole junkie-flunkie-punky ethos before he was even remotely "famous." In a few years, he'd be dead. Don't forget Johnny Thunders, who was kind of the Dean Martin of the junkie generation: the fans expected him to shoot up, just like they expected Dino to have a full cocktail glass, and Johnny never let them down, even if he was falling off the stage. Like Dino, he slapped "broads" around as well.

In the field of Punk, drugs were a particularly unfortunate plague, because the artists weren't making much money to begin with. Therefore, virtually all their money went toward drugs, and all their creativity went into finding ways to cop. It wasn't like with Keith Richards, who could merely wait at the estate for the heroin to be delivered by limo. The street realities of junkiedom beat the shit out of many notable performers. One of them was Dee Dee Ramone, who finally quit the Ramones in 1987, after serving as the group's chief musical director for more than a decade. Apparently he'd become too fierce of a junkie to function any longer in a working band. Handsome Dick Manitoba of the Dictators was another perfect example of someone with good intentions who got sidelined by the dope. When he finally made it out of the sewer, it was in the form of the somewhat redemptive Metal-mockup Wild Kingdom, who rendered cautionary tales like "Had It Coming."

The laugh of it all was, through this whole era, Reagan and his cohorts were patting themselves on the back for the job they were doing in the "drug war." In the abandoned ghettos, however, no amount of law enforcement was effective. Statistics proved that one out of every three Black males ended up in prison. In other words, to young Blacks, there wasn't really much of a deterrent against using drugs and resorting to crime—they figured they had nothing to lose. There was also the allure of money and the macho image of the mack daddy. Surprisingly, some of the strongest antidrug statements came from within the Rap community itself, such as Ice-T's "You Played Yourself" or NWA's "Dopeman."

It's hard to envision a world now where gangsta Rap doesn't exist, but in the early years of Rap, there was little talk of guns or criminal acts, at least in the first person. Groups like Run-DMC were streetwise, but almost in a Big Brother way: they were *warning* young brothers about the dangers of the street, not personifying the perpetrators of the violence. However, by the end of the '80s, with actual ex-cons staking out careers as rappers, the narratives were bound to become more "realistic." L.A.'s Ice-T, for instance, spoke from experience, having been a major coke dealer before picking up the microphone. Urban melodramas like "Six in the Morning" offered an almost cinematic portrayal of life on the mean streets. The difference between performers like Ice-T or Chuck D (of Public Enemy) and old-school R&B stars was that the rappers weren't trying to distance themselves from the acts they described. They also weren't necessarily trying to sap the aggression they saw in the nation's Black youths—they were merely saying to harness the power.

Perhaps because of economic realities in the United States, the natural inclinations of Black performers have always been to seek power through ascendance. That is, their popularity among whites would give them more "power" than they could ever attain otherwise. Rap changed all that by making *Black identity* a reality that every Black person in America had to deal with on a daily basis. Black musical performers and athletes in the '80s felt committed to providing what was essentially a separatist/Black-nationalist role model to young Black Americans. Blacks saw the Republicans roaring and realized there was nothing in it for them. Far from trying to assimilate, they sought to divide, while not adequately facing down the real problems that plagued the "community"—like unwanted teen pregnancy and drug addiction, for instance. It became the blame game—but what was sad was that this kind of finger pointing became institutionalized through Rap. Given the proliferation of Black-on-Black violence in the ghettos, it seemed that Blacks were taking out their hostilities on each other and not affecting the balance of power at all. The whites simply moved further out to the suburbs, and the cities fell to the minorities, who continued to destroy their own neighborhoods.

The grim realities of life in the ghetto, and Black awareness in general, became the central theme in Rap once Public Enemy arrived. Although they weren't ghetto youths by any stretch, the Long Island group changed Rap from a get-down dance party in the Bronx to the incendiary sound of a thousand feet marching in lock-step. Public Enemy made Rap *militant*: "Yo Chuck, we gotta dust these guys off," sang Flavor Flav as sirens went off around him. PE was the first serious Rap *group* as opposed to a lead singer with a bunch of backup rappers (Grandmaster Flash & the Furious Five) or a duo (Run-DMC). Chuck D was the undisputed spokesman, but not necessarily the leader; for publicity direction, Harry Allen—the "minister of offense"—was equally important. Public Enemy functioned like an organization, somewhat similar to the MC5 in the early days.

It wasn't just their political zeal that made them distinct. Their sound was as revolutionary as the Beatles or Led Zeppelin as far as changing the way everything in the genre sounded after them. Once Public Enemy came out with their maddening cacophony of multitracked samples—courtesy of DJ Terminator X (the name says it all)—all other Rap sounded outdated. PE brought the NOIZE—the multiple overdubs created massive sheets of rhythm, all manufactured by machines. This not only influenced other Rap artists, but the whole field of "techno" and other synthetic forms of music as well, which were becoming more commonplace as the '80s came to a close—further sealing Rock's coffin.

Public Enemy was a totally postmodern phenomenon: Chuck regularly made reference to movies and current sports stars. This was one of the things about Rap—it was modern folklore. Black kids—or, for that matter, white kids—in the '80s didn't read their history books; they watched TV and listened to CDs and the radio. It was a culture juiced with electricity, short on patience, needing immediate gratification because TV had conditioned them to expect something happening every minute. In this case, Rap ideally suited the needs of the attention-deficit generation because in the maddening embryo of sound there were a thousand things going on at once. Which is also why it sounded so foreign to Baby Boomers or those older.

To young Black teenagers, Public Enemy represented sheer strength, not only due to their association with such radical Black-consciousness raisers as filmmaker Spike Lee and Islam leader Louis Farrakhan, but also because of their own attack battalion of politicos who carried actual guns and wore paramilitary garb. Chuck D spouted mean-spirited invective, and he outright bragged, which had been a mainstay of Rock n' Roll since Jerry Lee Lewis but was a little different when the bragging was about killing people. Or as Chuck sang on the first album, *Yo! Bum Rush the Show*: "Kill a cop a day."

The whole cop killer/street violence thing was what really put Rap over the edge. When PE's first album came out, some of its biggest boosters were punks who'd become disillusioned with the increasingly politically correct environment of Hardcore and were looking for a new kind of kick. The Beastie Boys had already proven that there was a white audience for Rap, but Public Enemy was even hipper—the fact they were actual Negroes added to their street-cred with the skinhead hordes. The first time I'd ever seen white rockers taking an active interest in Black music of any form was at those shave-head soirees where skins 'n Blacks grooved equally to the raucous rhythms of Public Enemy. This was a generation of white kids who'd grown up in the '70s, and as such they tended to associate Black stylings of any kind with Disco. In PE they heard something that was clearly more streetworthy. Ironically, Chuck D, who'd grown up in a white section of Long Island, was singing lyrics like "can't deny it coz I'll never be white." It was the beginning of the hand-gesture generation.

Public Enemy's first album became a huge seller. It was obvious that, despite its incendiary nature, this kind of angry Rap was going to catch on in a big way. The Beasties had already broken new ground via their use of sampled Rock licks and rampant profanity, but they were white, and thus apolitical (which was ironic in itself, considering that they'd originally stemmed from the field of Hardcore, which was political to a fault). At the same time PE were launched at Def Jam, so was LL Cool J, who was the New Jack version of the same old swank-jive R&B—he was Teddy Pendergrass in tennis sneakers without the five-octave range. It was all coming down to sheer *attitude*: between the time of the first two Public Enemy albums, "gangsta" Rap as a genre had emerged with the first albums by Ice-T, Eazy E, and KRS-One/Boogie Down Productions. But Public Enemy had caught the momentum and, having done so, were the primary catalysts for this phase of Rap's development.

When Public Enemy released their second album, *It Takes a Nation of Millions to Hold Us Back*, it was treated as an event by the critics, and rightly so: here was the most tightly structured sample-woven sound ever, an endless barrage of mechanical rhythm with song after song testifying to pure Black rage. Public Enemy spared its listeners the usual boasting about sex, which gave them an air of dignity that even Black cultural leaders like Farrakhan could appreciate. They were "serious" from the word *go*, which made their rage all the more believable. What *Nation of Millions* really accomplished, in its suitelike grandeur, was to turn Rap, and thus all Black music, into an album-oriented genre. Groups like the Sugarhill Gang and Grandmaster Flash & the Furious Five were known for their singles and extended twelve-inch dance mixes of those same songs, but Public Enemy raised the standards by such a degree that any rappers worth their salt now had to compete on the album market as well. Most of all, Public Enemy wanted to change the white public's perception of Black artists as song-and-dance men and entertainers into something more serious. That's why there was such an affinity between Rap and the new, arrogant sports heroes like Mike Tyson, Dennis Rodman, Deion Sanders, and Charles Barkley: these were the first "attitude Blacks" since the heyday of Muhammad Ali, and soon *all* Blacks—indeed, all *people*, for that matter—were going to follow en suite or risk being perceived as milquetoasts.

Even more than the lyrics, perhaps the most controversial aspect of Rap was the issue of sampling. Although at this time there had only been isolated incidents of legal action taken over sampling—like the Sugarhill Gang getting sued by Bernard Edwards for "Good Times"— Rap's detractors claimed that sampling was outright musical thievery. While in some cases this was true, with a Public Enemy, the samples were so hyperkinetically rearranged that they elevated the practice to an art form. Like the Pop artists of the '60s who made high art out of items one could find in the supermarket, the purveyors of Rap realized that, in the modern vernacular, everything had been reduced to fodder. That meant that one's influences were only important in the way they could be used. Sampling was the ultimate realization of this, because the artist didn't seek to merely replicate his source, but to manipulate it to suit his needs and then discard it. It was almost as if the program mixers were saying that by placing a previously recorded sound into a whole new context, they had rendered it another "object" entirely. The sample, be it borrowed from an old R&B album or a movie score, was merely a source of "raw material" to throw onto the canvas, like the proverbial pine cone or paper cup picked up in the school playground to use in a collage. The rappers had no remorse about this method of audio pilfering either. As Flavor Flav said on *Nation of Millions*: "Hey Chuck, you can't license a beat. What, are they crazy?"

Rap was the Rock 'n' Roll of the modern age. It offended as many people, and sounded as foreign to its detractors, as Rock had in the '50s. Once again, it was the prompter of new styles of dress and language. No one epitomized this more than NWA, who helped introduce the West Coast school of Rap to the general populace. The name stood for "niggas with attitude," and the group hailed from Compton, California, a violent section of South Central Los Angeles. They brought the ghetto mentality into mainstream culture, where it has remained until the present day.

NWA was the first Rap group whose members sported separate identities. They were *all* MCs, which meant that, as with the Beatles or Kiss, there were three or four strong personalities in the group. Although they didn't realize it at the time, this would cause much ego-fueled friction in the future. It was also a play on the old gangland mentality of organized crime, in which every don or wiseacre had his own identity: Joe "Fingers" Carr, Sammy the Snooper, Bernie "Jowls" Jacoby, Stan "The Hit Man" Giancuomo, et al. It was this adherence to criminal posturing that made West Coast Rap different from the East Coast version—its ethos was based on the tenets of hoodlums and hustlers instead of activists and philosophers. It was the essence of the life-is-cheap philosophy that had begun to infest the culture at large ever since the '70s. In the vision presented on the group's first album, *Straight Outta Compton*, absolutely nothing was sacred or profound. As the group themselves put it, "Life ain't nothin' but bitches and money."

Public Enemy was fairly righteous; NWA wasn't—the crucial difference. Which one do you think became more popular?

NWA were the beginning of the melismatic style of Rap, in which all the words ran mellifluously together. The barking oratorio of Chuck D had become orthodox. Chuck & Flav had taken Rap vocalizing to a whole new level when they kind of weaved in and out of each other's verses, but the members of NWA all took turns and spit out their vitriol in staccato bursts. The lyrics voiced their anger and outlined their intentions—all of which were bad.

The institutionalization of the words "nigger" and "bitch" also originated from NWA. "Nigger" was even in the group's name, a fact that may seem commonplace now but was still shocking when they first emerged in 1987. For years, good liberals had been taught to never utter the word in public, and now here were these defiant young Black men claiming the vile epithet as their own! It was all part of the '80s irony, ultimately no more profound than Morrissey singing "I'm a girl and you're a boy," but much more threatening (and thus effective). Race relations in the '80s were on shaky ground anyway (thanks partially to Reagan), and the reintroduction of the word "nigger" didn't help matters. It became a kind of I-dare-you-to-try-it taunt from the Blacks to the whites. Or to put it more bluntly: in the postmodern era, only a "nigger" could call a spade a spade.

It was this lack of remorse on the part of the latter-day rappers when it came to issues like violence, sexism, and racism that really ruffled the feathers of the Robert Christgaus of the world. Actually it wasn't that different from the Ramones, who sang "one bullet in the cylinder" a decade before. It was just that, coming from white semi-intellectuals, or at least culturally attuned hipsters like the Ramones, it was "ironic": the critics assumed they actually "knew better" and thus didn't take the violent or misogynist content of their lyrics seriously. But Black music as a popular phenomenon has never been about irony, and the liberals just weren't ready for a new race of young Black men who were unapologetic about their politically incorrect stance.

As for women, when NWA routinely labeled them "bitches," it was coming from an experience that a Robert Christgau could never hope to understand, because the modern girls weren't all sugar and spice either. The point was, *everything* and *everybody* had gone to hell—the only thing left to be determined was who was king of the slag heap. It all came down to bragger's rights. In the '80s, mean-spiritedness was the new social activism, and Rap music was one of the principal driving forces in this campaign. We'd reached the breaking point in the culture, at which nobody felt the need to be nice anymore, from commercials that literally insulted us (Joe Isuzu), to the smarmy attitude of President George Bush, to women in the workplace who were sick of dumb pickup lines. Everything was ready to explode into a fit of anger. It's no wonder why, for millions, Rap artists like NWA, Public Enemy, and Ice-T summed up the moment perfectly.

Ice-T was another Rap artist who couldn't get his stuff played on the radio. To underground rappers, this became kind of a badge of honor, whereas rappers who compromised the language and attitude, like LL Cool J, were instantly branded sellouts. In 1988, nobody had more street-cred than Ice-T, who boasted: "Even if I'm banned/I sell a million tapes." He even appeared on an episode of ABC's *Nightline* with Richard Goldstein of the *Village Voice*, which was a chance to witness the cultural paradox in living, breathing action. Goldstein tried to maintain his freedom-of-speech posture while pooh-poohing Ice-T over his supposed "sexism." Ice wasn't buying it: "Yo, man, he's contradicting himself," he said as he smirked and made fun of Goldstein's pompous tone. Ice-T was raising an important question to a whole new generation. Mainly, who *was* this guy? And why did people keep asking his opinion about things like Rap? To Ice and his ilk, being the features editor of the *Village Voice*—an esteemed position in the literary world—meant nothing. Having millions of dollars like Michael Jordan—or having spent six years in San Quentin—*that* meant something. Once again…street cred! It was a cultural showdown. Rap was the final triumph of lowbrow.

Up until the late '80s, there wasn't really that much camaraderie between the Old School and the New School. It was only after rappers like Ice-T, Eazy E, and the DOC began paying homage to people like George Clinton that these older funkmeisters gave their blessing to the New Jacks. Probably they were just grateful for all the royalties the samples were bringing in, which enabled them to finally pay off their enormous coke debts from the '70s and early '80s. Black music had gone through some pretty lean years in the '80s when Disco-fied pabulum like Michael Jackson, Prince, and Whitney Houston was being passed off as state-of-the-art. In light of this bland preoccupation, old-schoolers like Clinton and, to some extent, James Brown, recognized Rap's vitality. The rappers, meanwhile, were consciously trying to live up to the legacy of their funk heroes. This was just one more way for Rap to achieve staying power. On *No One Can Do It Better*, his first album, the DOC declared Rap "rhythmic African poetry," and indeed, the Hip Hop nation was the biggest consolidation of Black identity since Be Bop.

Rap also utilized the "buddy system" to great extent—that is, the more visible rappers brought their less fortunate—and, in many cases, less talented—brothers from the ghetto along with them. This was total empowerment, and it made Rap seem like a conspiracy. For instance, NWA launched Above the Law. Part of their hype was that three-fifths of them had not only been to jail, but to college. This was the new hardass Rap role model: hip enough to have hung in the 'hood but smart and talented enough to have gotten out. Which was the gangsta thing, which they learned not from the streets, but from movies. The new Rap was very cinematic, like Above the Law's "Another Execution," in which the protagonist shoots somebody over a casual diss. A sane person couldn't imagine taking another life over such an insignificant thing. But come the late '80s, it was happening every day in every big city in the United States.

A Clockwork Orange really *did* happen, but not in the romanticized way that many pseudo-anarchists imagined it. Instead of white English boys in their underwear running around perpetrating "ultra-violence," it was young *Black* kids in baggy pants and baseball caps. The musical accompaniment was not Beethoven, or even the Beatles—it was NWA. And this wasn't "science fiction"—it was really happening. The beat went on, more propulsive than ever.

At the point when Rap was at its height, its most controversial group, NWA, became enmeshed in a controversy of its own—specifically, the departure of group leader Ice Cube over "creative differences." It didn't take Ice Cube long to come up with his first solo LP, which was just an example of the kind of velocity Rap was moving at. Like the dispatches from reporters in the trenches in Vietnam, Rap lyrics had the same kind of immediacy. Given the circumstances surrounding Ice Cube's departure from NWA, it's no surprise that *Amerikkka's Most Wanted*, his first solo LP, was received as a broadside.

Somewhere in the album's maddening swirl, it became apparent that Ice Cube had become militant. Perhaps it was his disillusionment about the whole NWA/Jerry Heller fiasco. The fact that Heller, the group's manager, was white seemed contradictory in light of Ice Cube's increasingly militant posture. Perhaps it was his friendship with Chuck D that helped clue him in to more radical Black consciousness raising endeavors. In any case, he knew that his first post-NWA effort was a potentially powerful statement within the Rap community, and *Amerikkka's Most Wanted* was as convincing an argument for Rap's musical merits as any.

After Ice Cube departed, NWA remained popular but lost a lot of their firepower. They also lost credibility within the movement. Although, like the Beatles, every member would eventually have a successful solo career, only Ice Cube and Dr. Dre proved to have any longevity. In Ice Cube's case, it was a conscious process of redefinition—he donned the wool cap, shed the curls, and converted to Islam. He also got married and dropped the trash-talk about women.

Afrocentric concerns were a major part of the new Rap consciousness, and many rappers adapted traditional garb like the fez or dashiki to further display their devotion. But even Allah couldn't save Rap from degenerating into self-parody. Particularly after NWA, the poseur quotient increased to epidemic proportions. Once it became implanted in a thousand young turks' heads that attitude was all it took, suddenly everybody had attitude. In the case of most rappers who glutted the market in the post-NWA era, attitude was *all* they had. Some of them were funny (Tone-Lóc), and others were merely foul-mouthed (2 Live Crew, Slick Rick), but very few advanced the musical language of Rap, not to mention the Nation of Islam. What Rap did was break down the whole notion of graciousness that had surrounded Black music since its earliest inception as an American show biz entity. Now instead of Marvin Gaye trying to coax a bitch into bed with songs of sweet seduction, it was Slick Rick treating her like a prostitute.

This was the era of rude records by johnny-come-latelies like Special Ed, whose "I Got it Made" in 1989 pretty much took bragger's rights with its assertion: "I got in bed/I just got laid." As predicted by Marshall McLuhan and other '50s sages, sex had become the ultimate acquisition of power. That's why rappers like Tone-Lóc and MC Hammer surrounded themselves in their videos with beautiful women—oftentimes beautiful *white* women. As Hammer bragged, as his bevy of beauties wiggled their behinds temptingly in your face: "You can't touch this."

Rap had quickly reached a critical mass whereby its own audience didn't know or care about "street" ethos. After all, white groups like New Kids on the Block could effectively pillage the style for their own formulated brand of bubblegum, and even TV commercials were using Hip Hop to hock their wares.

Fools were dancing all over the land, and within the Hip Hop community "credibility" became a big issue. With sellouts everywhere, those rappers who maintained their street cred were utilizing an even more hardcore method of verbal and rhythmic warfare.

The stab wound caused by NWA on the heart of American Pop music was so severe that virtually every Rap act *after* NWA had to be judged on those terms. And those terms were *fuck you, bitch,* etc. Rap groups became "posses," a term that came straight from gangland. Now within the context of Rap, there were a lot of metaphors between gang-style violence and the art of rapping. No one epitomized this more than the Geto Boys, a foursome from Houston with the added freak appeal of having a little person, four-foot tall Bushwick Bill, in the group.

After a couple of local releases on their own Rap-a-Lot label, they caught the attention of Rick Rubin, whose flourishing Rap label, Def Jam, was looking for a "gangsta" group to compete with NWA. The first album, *The Geto Boys*, was actually comprised of more solidly produced versions of material that had already been issued on Rap-a-Lot, but just as the album was taking off, Rubin pulled out. All subsequent releases would be distributed by Priority, the company NWA had founded several years before. There was also an attempt at a distribution and management deal with Geffen, but they proved apprehensive about the group's lyrics. Bushwick: "Shee-it. I think David Geffen's got sugar in his veins."

Brian DePalma's *Scarface* had become the favorite movie among young Black rappers. The Geto Boys sampled not only every James Brown album they could find, but also the soundtrack to *Scarface*, with Al Pacino yelling "fuck you, manck!" With its portrayal of a Cuban immigrant who, through the drug trade, obtains everything that had previously been off-limits to him—money, power, white pussy—the film became an inspiration to ghetto youth everywhere. Influenced by the movie, the Geto Boys also wrote their own seething phantasmagorias like "Mind of a Lunatic," which were universally decried for their violent content. They also weren't making friends with feminists for lyrics like the one in "Gangsta of Love," which said: "Whatever you got, you deserve it, *bitch.*" All they were really saying, to the most propulsive James Brown rhythm ever, was what James Brown had been saying all along: "It's a man's world." Only they were saying it in language that would make even J. B.'s old Methodist ass cheeks blush.

For a short time, the Geto Boys were able to justify their reprehensible message because the musical backing was so intense it sounded like nothing less than the apocalypse. They were so intensely *on time* that the whole thing literally exploded in their faces, and they eventually had to taste the malice that it bore. To be specific, Bushwick had one of his eyes shot out during a doped-up struggle with a female companion. If you think you've heard hard-luck stories before, just imagine what it's like to be a four-foot one-eyed little person. Then again, in typical postmodern fashion, they exploited the event by putting a picture of Bushwick, sans eye, on an album cover. The whole realm of the Geto Boys seemed inhabited by science fiction, witchcraft, and horror-movie scenarios. In many ways, they were the true heirs to the Last Poets, and their vision of America as a violent wasteland was as realistic as it was repugnant.

For Black Americans, at no time was this more apparent than on March 3, 1991, when a speeding motorist was pulled over and severely beaten by the LAPD. The driver was a Black man named Rodney King, who'd been in and out of jail several times—not a model citizen by any means. But the fact that he was Black and the cops were white, not to mention the severity of the beating they gave him for a mere traffic offense, escalated the incident into a racial issue. Coming three years into the Bush administration, at a time when it seemed like racial issues had been swept under the rug, the event polarized the nation. It didn't help that a passing motorist had captured the whole thing on videotape and that the vivid spectacle of a half dozen cops beating one man was replayed endlessly for the whole country to see. When the cops got off scot-free, Blacks in L.A. rioted in the first widespread act of race-related civil disobedience since the '60s.

To old liberals who'd once championed the cause of civil rights, it might have seemed like a rebirth of their ideals if it hadn't been for one thing—this time around, Blacks didn't want any "sympathetic cousins" from within the white community. Whites were unequivocally seen as the enemy, and the L.A. riots began an era of tension between the races that has yet to be fully resolved. Despite the calls of Affirmative Action, the races were farther apart than ever.

To young rappers who sympathized with his plight at the hands of the LAPD, Rodney King became a martyr figure. One thing the race riots in L.A. proved was that this country's racial problems were no longer restricted to

Black/white confrontation: some of the real estate hardest hit in the looting belonged to Asians who had moved into previously all-Black areas and started their own businesses. Even Ice Cube issued an extremely foreboding invective against these so-called intruders with a song called "Black Korea" (as in "don't try to turn my neighborhood into…").

The country's complexion was changing rapidly. The influx of Latinos in particular affected American popular culture in profound ways, as it produced a whole new sector of consumers. Although these immigrants on the one hand were eager to suck up as much American as they could, they still wished to maintain their own cultural identities. This created a perplexing problem for the record industry, as they hadn't yet mastered the art of promoting Latino music and culture like they later would with Ricky Martin. The most popular Latin crossover act of the '80s was Gloria Estefan and the Miami Sound Machine, which was light Disco with a samba twist. Later on, Paula Abdul, who was partly Hispanic, became a popular recording star. Both Estefan, who sang: "all I want to do is keep lovin' you," and Abdul, who sang: "I'm forever your girl," were throwbacks to the pre-Rock flights of Tin Pan Alley in style and execution. But being primarily Catholic, the recent Hispanic immigrants were staunchly working class and family-oriented. Unlike with the Blacks, the concept of monogamy suited them fine.

AIDS had put a damper into the Bacchanalian spirit of the previous decade. Suddenly such concepts as monogamy and, indeed, dating, were acceptable again. There was a proliferation of dating shows, like *Love Connection* and *The Matchmaker*. A show called *Studs* went even further by taking the formality of the whole dating concept—a throwback to the '50s actually—and marrying it to the loose morals that were now generally accepted. As the name implies, the female contestant who won the "date" with the stud in question was supposed to sleep with him in order to assess his studlike qualities—and then tell everyone about it. This was the ultimate form of public spectacle (and sometimes public humiliation). What were once the most intimate details of our personal lives had now become a spectator sport. The knife was driven in even further by the acidic commentary of host Mark DeCarlo, whose contemptuous attitude was akin to that of Joe Isuzu. It was bad enough when television merely insulted our intelligence—now not only was it insulting our intelligence, it was *telling us* that it was insulting our intelligence. Check out this choice bit of cheeky commentary from Mr. D as he auctioned off a pair of studs to some eager ladies in waiting: "One is a courier, the other is a political science major, but who's the bigger stud? If you knew American history, you'd know the answer. But *since you don't*, let's ask the ladies…"

In other words, it was automatically assumed that the audience was made up of total idiots.

Perhaps it wasn't idiocy as much as it was sheer indifference. As *Beavis and Butt-Head* would later exemplify, to a youth population totally raised on TV, all of life had been reduced to fodder.

As the writer Paul Simon Zmieski remarked: "It's the Reagan and post-Reagan kids who are really hip in the truest sense of the word: uninvolved, cynical, unwilling or incapable of having any strong beliefs about anything. All they have left is making a buck and buying more stuff. I feel sorry for them."[8]

What Zmieski didn't grasp was, there was no reason to feel sorry for them: ignorance is bliss, and the kids didn't know what they were missing. As the Geto Boys would say, "I don't love me/How the fuck am I gonna love you?" Ice Cube had said the same thing, and later '90s singer/songwriters like Kurt Cobain and Billy Corgan would evoke similar self-loathing. Even on television, the Fox Network had set the precedent for the new cynical TV with shows like *The Simpsons* and *Married . . . with Children*, which never missed an opportunity to drive the spike in further. In both cases, the classic "family unit" was being boiled down into a kind of theater of pain (where usually the father came off looking like the imbecile, kind of like in the Twisted Sister video, only worse).

At least the Bundys and the Simpsons were traditional family units—in the culture at large, however, the role of the traditional family unit was disintegrating. This was particularly true in the Black community, where single motherhood was becoming the norm. Is it any wonder that the ghettos exploded with the kind of music that hailed forth in a thunder of bullets?

Ultra-ultra-hardcore Rap was best epitomized by Gangsta NIP's *South Park Psycho* album. NIP was the Geto Boys' bodyguard until one day, drunk on Skunky Monkey, he got up before the microphone and started singing: "I gut some *co-caine!*" NIP did what real Rock was supposed to do: he tested friendships. I knew people who'd lived through the whole Punk thing and had been junkies, and I almost came to blows with them about the lyrical content of the album. One close friend in particular had a nine-year-old son who went to school in a heavily Black area, and to him NIP's loose talk about shooting and killing was anything but entertaining. In fact, he was morally outraged by it, and this is someone who'd *hung out with Kilslug*! NIP was crossing the line into territory where even ultralibertarians had to rethink their opinions on free speech. It wasn't "ironic" like so much Punk rock, which is what scared most white college audiences away from Rap altogether.

The Geto Boys themselves weren't sleeping either. By the time of their first post-Rodney King album, *Til Death Do Us Part*, the posse had expanded to such swelling ranks that it was difficult to keep track of who was actually in the group anymore. Big Mike? Who the fuck was that? Even NIP was in there. "Bring It On" was perhaps the final apotheosis of all Gangsta Rap, a six-minute blast of hardcore Funk with all the momentum of a subway train, in which every member of the posse got to mouth off. The fact that the riff was as funkified as anything J. B. ever created and the vocals were almost a kind of gospel call-and-response made this classic Black music. But there was an even more insidious side to it: as the Geto Boys turned such classic blues phrases as "shake your money maker" into nihilistic postmodern statements, one realized that, for all the white critics had romanticized them, the original bluesmen like Elmore James, who'd coined such phrases, were probably a lot closer in spirit to Rap than they were to the emancipating principles that white liberals (like Greil Marcus) had attributed to them. The only difference was, the Geto Boys had found a way to make money at it, and Elmore hadn't. The tide had turned for Black badasses everywhere—which ultimately scared the white critics.

Another factor that influenced the increasingly depraved nature of the popular culture was the fact the audience was getting younger. With less adult guidance and more exposure to media input, kids were reaching consumer age before they'd even reached adolescence. This meant their whole sense of history was completely compressed into momentary intervals. It was the reality of McLuhan's world come true—whole decades were being shrunk.

In the early '90s I heard a seventeen-year-old girl remark about Grandmaster Flash's "The Message" (basically the prototype for all modern Rap): "My grandmother has it." As the record was only about ten years old at that time, "granny" must have been only about forty. But this was another changing facet of the culture: because of the whole "babies makin' babies" syndrome that was happening in the ghetto, the span between generations was shrinking. The whole notion of "granny" as a little old white-haired lady holding a pan of freshly baked cookies was becoming a thing of the past. Now granny was a former coke whore who chain-smoked and spat venom.

As the Geto Boys, who understood the whole syndrome, said it best, perhaps summing up the whole culture: "Now granny's on her way to meet the devil."

CHAPTER 15

POST-EVERYTHING

AS THE '90S BEGAN, WHITE-BOY FUNK, IN REACTION TO RAP, WAS THE BIG THING: the Beastie Boys' *Paul's Boutique* (Punk/Funk/Hip Hop); Living Colour (Black Rock); Urban Death Squad (euro-Funk/Rock/Rap); and the West Coast wave (Faith No More, Primus, Limbomaniacs, Jane's Addiction, the Silly Peppers).

The other big trend was readymade "classic Rock." To wit:

Spin Doctors=Steve Miller

Jayhawks=Nils Lofgren

Black Crowes=Faces/Stones

Lenny Kravitz=Beatles/Hendrix

A rather inauspicious start to the decade as far as Rock was concerned.

Although sappy critics looking for a story jumped all over the white-Funk thing as a harbinger of long-awaited pararacial osmosis, most of the bands exhibited little actual "soul" or earthy Funk-derived passion, opting instead for a minstrel version that ripped off the most obvious (and thus stereotypical) tendencies of Black music while missing the essential quality of the acts they were aping (James Brown and Parliament-Funkadelic being the most ripped-off funkmeisters by that time). The Funk revival—although hyped to death by fly-by-night Rock mags at the beginning of the decade—was not the big breakthrough. It was dumbass '70s Rock with slap-bass.

In the early '90s, anything deviating from the mainstream in the slightest was lumped under the banner "alternative Rock," probably more because of the way the bands *looked* rather than any discernible musical variants. This was the MTV age, after all, when bands were judged first and foremost by their image. The mainstream at that time, particularly in the area of music video (i.e., MTV), was still dominated by cabaret sluts like Madonna, George Michael, Paula Abdul, MC Hammer, Taylor Dayne, Janet Jackson, and Vanilla Ice. On MTV, so-called alternative music was relegated to the Sunday midnight grave-yard. The radio, meanwhile, wouldn't touch it. In turn, college radio kept its own charts, documented in mags like *CMJ* and *Alternative Press*. This small phenomenon had been going on since the "college Rock" days of R.E.M., who were hailed as "alternative Rock" pioneers when the meaningless phrase—which was probably borrowed from "alternative lifestyles" (i.e., gay)—first became a music-biz cliché.

The term "alternative Rock" was meaningless because anybody who made it in the Entertainment Industrial Complex in the '90s was not an "alternative" to anything—they were foisted upon us by the same record companies who'd always force-fed us swill. There *was* a legitimate underground thriving at the onset of the '90s, in Rock as well as Rap, but as far as the stuff that was being played by MTV and on commercial radio, it was the usual corporate cop out. Even the labels that were responsible for the purest distillations of "Rock 'n' Roll" in the very beginning—King, Savoy, Aladdin—were never bastions of integrity. A record label is out to make money, and if they think something will sell, they'll promote it by whatever means necessary. As the '80s turned into the '90s, it was inevitable that someone would make the move back toward guitar-dominated Rock after almost a decade of synth crap. When it happened, the Industry was there as always, ready to exploit it. This time it just happened to work in the Rock aesthetes' favor—or so it seemed.

Although he probably didn't realize it at the time, David Geffen was initially responsible for the move back toward Hard Rock in the popular market. He'd already proven his business acumen by launching Asylum, the label that came to typify the "mellow"/laid back atmosphere of L.A. in the '70s with its roster of artists including Linda Ronstadt, Jackson Browne, Joni Mitchell, and the Eagles. In the '80s, after scoring major successes in the area of film with bogus entities like *Risky Business*, Geffen sold Asylum and launched a new label, this time bearing his own name à la Donald Trump (another '80s icon). Eventually, he would sell Geffen Records to MCA for big bucks, but for a while in the late '80s, Geffen himself maintained stewardship of the label. Not surprisingly, in the early days he loaded the roster with MTV mavens like Don Henley (big surprise, he was in the Eagles) and Aerosmith (they came from the right era anyway and had cleaned up their act by then). But Geffen was not afraid to take risks—by signing "underground" bands like Sonic Youth, Teenage Fanclub, and, eventually, Nirvana, he was probably more responsible than anyone for bridging the gap between the "college Rock" audience and MTV/commercial radio.

Actually, the trend started in the mid-'80s when Warner Brothers had tried to nurture Husker Du, one of the few "underground" acts at the time seen as having "crossover" potential, into the world of limousines and sushi luncheons. The public proved unready, but the industry was already starting to crank its collective eye begrudgingly towards the underground. Although, at the time, the major labels were scoring hits with artificial acts like Def Leppard, Bon Jovi, Poison, Great White, et al., *someone* must've realized how silly these eunuchs looked and, more importantly, sensed that the public would soon lose interest.

The transition was slow. In the mid- to late '80s, haircut metal was the *only* guitar-driven Rock allowed on either MTV or the radio. No one deviating from the teenybopper mode was going to burst through the void right away. Rock 'n' Roll really hadn't changed that much since the days of Fabian. Which is why Guns n' Roses were the perfect paradox in the summer of 1988—in many ways, they were just another one of the L.A. spandex bands. But some of their songs actually showed signs of a legitimate Rock 'n' Roll sensibility ("Night Train" pointed towards the crossroads where Van Halen and AC/DC met). They weren't total crap, and they seemed more than willing to assert their Punk roots at a time when most MTV idols were giving kissy-poo kudos to their hairdressers and set directors. When ex-Sex Pistol/junkie Steve Jones made his ill-fated "comeback" album in 1988, several members of G n' R made cameos. Not that Guns n' Roses weren't susceptible to the whole MTV charade—Axl Rose was the most obnoxious Rock frontman since Steven Tyler, and it was clear early on that he was a vacuous asshole. It all had to do with the whole MTV/*People* magazine syndrome—the members of Black Sabbath and AC/DC were none too eloquent either, but no one thought to ask them their opinions about racism and other social issues. Now the camera was always on, and the clock was always ticking. Axl, Slash, and all their cronies cracked under the pressure, but not before helping reintroduce Hard Rock to the mainstream. They weren't real Rock, but they cracked the windshield a bit.

The real insurrection at that time was Rap. Whatever rebellious edge Rock tried to assert in the '80s was quickly usurped by the very real call-to-arms of stuff like Public Enemy and NWA. Rap was perhaps the final emasculation of the hairspray Metal—whatever luster so-called "heavy metal" once held with working class knuckleheads was soon to be jettisoned forever by the revolution that was Hip Hop. All subsequent Rock that would succeed on this working class level would in turn borrow something from Hip Hop (Rage against the Machine, Korn, Limp Bizkit). Guns n' Roses were essentially the last group to model themselves on the Stones/Zeppelin/Aerosmith Rock star prototype and succeed on those terms (the Black Crowes were too "formal" about their affectations to even matter, except as neo-old fart Rock of the type begun by retroists like John Cougar Mellencamp in the '80s).

The Death of Rock didn't *have* to happen, providing that the record companies in the late '80s were willing to do what record labels have always done during any prolonged slump—namely, reinvent Rock 'n' Roll and sell it back as something new. But in the post–Hip Hop era, Guns n' Roses wasn't it. At the same time, the record companies grappled with the question of whether the idiosyncratic "college Rock" bands like Fugazi and Sonic Youth were "the next big thing." Geffen signed Sonic Youth hoping that by doing so they could tap into what appeared to be a small but very loyal audience. The resulting album, *Goo*, proved entirely inaccessible—it still sold to the core "alternative" audience, but failed to win converts among the MTV kids (which, of course, was what Geffen was hoping for). This was the dilemma the record companies faced at that time. On the one hand, the underground/college Rock groups had carved out their own self-governing niche: since they'd more or less resigned themselves to the Punk/Hard-Core notion of artistic freedom at all costs, they weren't really interested in becoming "stars." It was difficult for the major labels to persuade them into compromising their "art" in order to morph into passable commercial entities. At the same time, the labels had to at least try to come to terms with the underground. What they misunderstood, however, was that, when it came to the underground groups, once they were removed from the self-nurturing indie-Rock environment and placed within the confines of corporate Rock, the same kind of chemistry wouldn't exist. There was no way a label like Geffen's could take a Sonic Youth and simply snap it into the mainstream alongside Paula Abdul—at least not yet.

In the Pacific Northwest, a scene was coalescing that would have great consequence on the national music scene in the '90s. All through the '80s various towns that were exploding with indie-Rock fever were hailed as the next Liverpool: Athens, Georgia was the first, because of R.E.M. Minneapolis, home of critically acclaimed indie-gods Husker Du and the Replacements, was another prime candidate for the indie Mecca. There was even a thriving college/indie scene in Madison, Wisconsin. The Chicago scene that played host to noisy anti-social acts like Naked Raygun and Big Black and the whole Touch & Go and Amphetamine Reptile empires was another indie-Rock epicenter. But it didn't happen because, as vital as all those scenes were, they still lacked that central unity that is so essential to spearhead a major movement. The Beatles and their cronies had this when they were parading up and down the banks of the Mersey in 1963; so too did the hippies in San Francisco in 1967. The Ramones, Patti Smith, and the other harbingers of Punk represented this same kind of united front in New York in 1974. The Sex Pistols and their ilk would only elongate this unified spirit in London a few years later. In the late '80s it was Seattle, Washington where the ruckus was about to begin. Not only would it put the Northwest region on the map as a cultural hotbed, it would also completely revolutionize the face of Rock 'n' Roll—perhaps for the last time.

Like Liverpool, another seacoast town, Seattle's principle strength as a spawning ground for youthful insurrection was its isolation. Unlike, say, Los Angeles—where the two most commercially successful "Hard Rock" acts of the late '80s, Guns n' Roses and the Red Hot Chili Peppers, hailed from—the city was not the home of a million starry-eyed aspirants who came there for the sole purpose of striking it rich in the entertainment industry. Right through the '80s, the city got very little attention in the national media. This would change gradually as the city became one of the fountainheads of the burgeoning high-tech industry. Until that time, because of its enormous wealth of natural resources, Seattle was chiefly a logging and fishing town. World War II brought the city into the modern age as far as industry went, and by the '50s, Seattle began to acquire an image as one of America's most "livable" cities. The first mall was built there, as well as the protruding Space Needle, which was the city's most visible feature on the national landscape. For the most part, however, Seattle was merely a distant second to Portland, Oregon as the most notable American city north of San Francisco (plus, it rained all the time).

In the '60s, the region was bursting with raw Rock 'n' Roll talent. The Wailers and the Sonics toughened up what was then the standard garage band formula and could arguably be considered the first "Punk" bands. Undoubtedly, the purveyors of "grunge" considered them a valuable influence. Jimi Hendrix originally hailed from the city, but uprooted quickly via a stint in the Air Force and an endless string of traveling R&B road shows as a hired gun on the chitlin circuit. Like almost every large city in America, Seattle experienced a bohemian takeover in the '60s, but compared to other West Coast cities like San Francisco and Los Angeles, it was relatively subdued. In the '70s, the Punk movement helped revive the club scene, which had lain dormant in the hippie era. By the dawn of the '80s, the city had at least a half dozen clubs sponsoring regular Punk shows. There was also a broadcast forum for Punk, thanks to the radio station at the University of Washington in Olympia, the aptly named KAOS.

One of the DJs at KAOS was named Bruce Pavitt, a Chicago transplant whose interest in Punk Rock was so immense that he started the city's first fanzine, *Subterranean Pop*. Pavitt was a serious promoter of not only Punk but of the whole do-it-yourself mentality as well. Early editions of the 'zine came with a giveaway cassette compilation of local bands (a much-emulated ploy among mainstream and underground publishers in the years to follow). By establishing this kind of philanthropic niche amongst local musicians, Pavitt essentially had a permanent "in" with everyone in the community. This would prove immensely beneficial in a few months, when he launched what would become the most important American record label since SST: Sub Pop.

The Seattle sound was unique because, until that time, the city was a nonentity as far as trendiness was concerned. MTV wasn't out there doing specials every ten minutes yet. The scene was really isolated, split up among a few dozen factions. As we look back at the history of Rock, isn't that the way it always happens? It's always a small group of miscreants who follow their instincts. Then the rest of the world comes running.

In the early- to mid-'80s, they weren't running yet. Seattle was just one of many cities that had begun sporting a grassroots outgrowth in the years following Punk, a small coterie of bands, club owners, and record collectors who were in on a private joke that no one else got. Half of Punk's conceit was that Rock 'n' Roll was dead and the public's indifference didn't matter. The "no future" ethos worked in the bands' favor, as it guaranteed artistic freedom—it was a foregone conclusion that their work wasn't going to sell anyway. When the hopheads that would eventually fuse the loner aspects of Punk with the stoner traits of '70s Hard Rock began to formulate "grunge," it was mostly to amuse themselves and their friends. Like the denizens of every other city in Indie Rock USA, they didn't expect fame to come knocking on their door.

These were ugly bands that really had little hope of ever being noticed by anyone: Malfunkshun, Skin Yard, and the Melvins. Their lumbering tempos showed the influence of Flipper as well as the later incarnation of Black Flag, when the band began slowing the tempo and singer Henry Rollins grew his hair to Messiah-like lengths. The Melvins—named after a fifty-year-old who'd been caught stealing Christmas trees from a local Safeway—were the most influential of the early Seattle bands. Hailing from the small logging town of Aberdeen, they inspired a young Kurt Cobain to hump their gear around for a while so he could sniff their aura. As head Melvin Buzz Osborne explained of the Aberdeen scene: "It's so backward, it's forward. There are only cover bands here, so we don't have no real competition." [1]

This meant making up their own rules as they went along. The primary outsource for the Seattle Punk/indie sound was the small C/Z Records, which released an influential compilation in 1985 called *Deep Six* featuring the crème de la crème of the local scene, including the by-now legendary Melvins as well as upstarts Green River and Soundgarden. The record made evident the Seattle bands' embrace of a lot of the '70s influences that had been duly rejected by Punk—everything from Neil Young to Led Zeppelin. Unlike arty punks like X in Los Angeles or Sonic Youth in New York, or even the Butthole Surfers in Austin, Texas, the participants in this scene weren't that hip. Away from the highly politicized Punk scenes of Washington, D.C. or San Francisco, youths were free to pursue their musical interests unencumbered by any particular social doctrines. As Chris Cornell of Soundgarden explained: "We talked about music, and drank a lot." [2]

Reconfirming this roll-up-your-sleeves-and-roll-your-own mentality, Ron Nine of the Seattle band Love Battery told me during an interview for the 'zine *New Route* in 1991: "I've been friends with Mark Arm (of Mudhoney) for a long time, and he'd come over to my house and always put on my Neil Young records."

They were hippies, or, if not hippies, just good old stoners. As common as that sounds now, in the mid-'80s it was sacrilege because the one thing the Punk brigades hated was the "classic Rock" of the '60s and '70s (not to mention marijuana). However, to a bunch of Northwest hicks growing up with only one of two options available to them—fishing or logging—the sounds of something like Creedence Clearwater Revival's "Fortunate Son" made a lot more sense to them than the Velvet Underground. This is how Grunge as a style evolved: the antihipster's sense of "hip."

The first band from Seattle to have any impact beyond the local scene was Green River. Named after a song by Creedence, they epitomized the spirit of Northwest Grunge with their plodding chords and strangulated vocals. The whole thing sounded like Led Zeppelin fed into a meat grinder, but in singer Mark Arm they had one of the great post-Iggy screamers. The influential New York indie label Homestead released the band's sludge-o-phonic first EP, *Come on Down*. As far as indie credentials went, it was overshadowed by another Homestead release: the first one by Dinosaur Jr., whose proximity in the landlocked region of western Massachusetts made them almost as much of an anomaly at that time as Green River. Despite the lack of national recognition, the Green River EP had considerable influence on the scene back home. Bruce Pavitt, in particular, was listening. He'd already been writing his influential "Sub Pop" column—shortened from *Subterranean Pop*—for Seattle's premiere music paper, *The Rocket*, and his coverage was some of the first local musicians like the Melvins and Malfunkshun received. When Homestead swooped down and snatched up Green River right from his own backyard, Pavitt decided to launch a label of his own.

Fortune smiled on Pavitt one day when guitarist Kim Thayil of the band Soundgarden introduced him to Jonathan Poneman. An Ohio transplant, Poneman had also done his own radio show as well as a stint as a guitarist in the band the Treeclimbers. He'd also promoted shows at the Rainbow, one of the first clubs in Seattle to feature Punk/Hard-Core acts. Between the two, they were able to amass forty thousand dollars, which they used to launch Sub Pop in 1986.

Keeping with the indie tradition that had already been established by labels like SST, the first two releases on the label were EPs. The "extended play" record was a mainstay of the indie era. For a new band that might not have warranted a whole LP but were still eager to get something on vinyl, EPs were more efficient. Given the volatile nature of the scene at the time, in which the mortality rate of most bands was short-lived, EPs were an assurance that a band would at least get to wax their own little slice of indie-Rock history. EPs were also cheaper, which worked for the target audience, who were notoriously short of funds due to their indie-Rock/thrift store existence (the whole motif that would later become known as "slacker"). This same sensibility also led to the revival of 45s as a worthy medium, first with Punk and then indie. Sub Pop became the chief exponents of the revival with the Sub Pop Singles Club, issuing a different single each month by a different band in a limited edition. Over the years, Sub Pop were able to entice just about every major band/figure in the American underground to record a single for the club at one time or another, which enhanced their hip credibility considerably.

The first two EPs issued by Sub Pop—*Dry as a Bone* by Green River and *Hunted Down* by Soundgarden—sold only modestly, especially outside of the Northwest. However, both were important for helping to introduce some of the trademarks of the "Seattle sound": in the case of the former, it was the production of Jack Endino, who'd later work with Mudhoney and Nirvana; in the case of the latter, it was the Heavy Metal sensibilities, which had lain dormant for so long per the command of the hippie/stoner-hating Punks. The Seattle kids were among the first to start sprouting actual long hair again, and that was significant in 1986–'87. Like the hippies, their drug policy was basically anything-all-the-time, and this was a scene wracked by drugs from the onset. Like so many suburban communities, its youthful denizens simply felt that there was nothing better to do. Right from the start, the stoner/I'm-fucked philosophy was a key characteristic of the Seattle sound/scene. No one did more to promulgate this "wasted" ambiance than Pavitt and Poneman. They were well aware that they were bucking the clean-cut mood of optimism that had swept the country in the Reagan/yuppie years. In a prescient move that predated Beck, Sub Pop issued a t-shirt in 1988 that proudly proclaimed "loser." Things like this, and the singles club, which was inaugurated with the release of Nirvana's first single, "Love Buzz," helped raise the label's profile in the "underground," which at that time included not only college radio but a plethora of fanzines like *Forced Exposure* as well as more mainstream magazines like *Option*.

Across the nation, 1987 had been a pivotal year for the underground scene in the United States. As Byron Coley, who wrote the "Underground" column for *Spin*, said: "There's a lot of stuff that has been gestating a while, but people just started to recognize it in 1987. Bands that you used to be able to go and see, and no one would be there, their shows are completely filled with college students capering around. Bands that people are recognizing now, have really extensive and elaborate discographies by this time, which is different to what happened in the past. There's a large number of records coming out of America, too, wherever you go. When you go out to buy a record and see 200 new releases by bands you never heard of, I think that's a little daunting."[3]

By 1988, page after page of all the hip music journals were full of adds for Sub Pop, whose unique logo, not to mention marketing strategy, made them instantly name-droppable. Like other mystical labels in the past such as ESP or International Artists or SST, the label focused on a certain sound/stance and didn't let go, not wanting to extend its boundaries too far into other areas and cloud the already muddy waters. When one thought of Seattle, one thought of Sub Pop. The city's status as a somewhat remote locale to most young Americans gave it an edgy allure. The fact that it was also the suicide capital of the US is a distinction that, as our story evolves, will perhaps become more significant. Just like in the '60s when San Francisco briefly dictated the nation's musical trends, the most innovative sounds in Rock were once again coming from the West, but as the sounds moved eastward their attributes began to infect the scenes in other regions. These included the slower rhythms, the abrupt stop-start time changes, the heaving vocals, the metallic veneer, the long hair, the "loser" posture, and, of course, the drugs.

In Chicago, demons like Naked Raygun, the Effigies, and Big Black actually predated the Grunge groups with some of the rudest sounds imaginable. In 1988, Touch & Go released Slint's *Tweez*, perhaps the quintessential American indie album until Pavement's *Slanted and Enchanted*. With guitars that hummed like insects and bass that sounded like a police car alarm underwater, the album was a downer all the way through. This was epitomized not only by the say-nothing lyrics but also the fact that there were no credits on the LP. Slint, who hailed from Louisville, Kentucky, were as important as the Seattle bands in establishing a directive for American independent Rock in the late '80s. The other important Touch & Go band that heralded the coming age was Urge Overkill, with perhaps the first indie-rockers to affect a glam-Rock pose. What made them significant was their embrace of the kind of riff-Rock that most hip folks (including Coley) thought had gone out of style. "Candidate" on their first record had a tight, compressed riff sound, not unlike Kiss. Along with their Heavy Metal harmonics, Urge Overkill band members also prided themselves on their whole glam/ladies' man image. A couple of years later, when the thudding staccato Hard Rock band Helmet hit the big time, Blackie Onassis, the spokesman for Urge Overkill, told an interviewer: "Helmet's whole attitude is very stand-offish to women."

Other Chicago bands like Tar shared with their Seattle counterparts the same penchant for sluggish tempos and traffic-jam clashes of guitar/bass/drum in a style that could only be called "grunge." Miscreants like the Jesus Lizard soon joined the ranks of the most prominent noise merchants on the indie scene. Not surprisingly, Lizard vocalist David Yow was an old friend of Sub Pop founder Bruce Pavitt and was in the seminal Texas band Scratch Acid, which Kurt Cobain, among others, acknowledged as an influence.

As far as Chicago went, Touch & Go wasn't the only label trumpeting the indie sound. Equally important was Amphetamine Reptile, founded by ex-Marine Tom Hazelmeyer in 1986. The imprint became famous for their *Dope, Guns, and Fucking in the Streets* compilations, which oftentimes included contributions from Seattle bands like Mudhoney. This kind of charitable interchange was at the heart of the whole indie-Rock movement. Given the grim state of the record industry at that time, these bands really felt a call to arms. There was legitimate solidarity whereby label owners allowed their charges to freelance for other labels simultaneously because they believed it was all working towards the same end. Ultimately, though, once Nirvana got signed to a major label and became superstars, the feeding frenzy didn't exactly make room for everybody, and that caused resentment.

There was no resentment in those golden days of '88. Bands toured together, sold each other's gear at shows, and recorded for each other's record labels. Sonic Youth, perhaps the theoretical figureheads of the whole "movement," cut a split single with Mudhoney for Sub Pop's singles club in 1988 on which they

covered a Mudhoney song, and vice versa. For Pavitt and company, the solidarity was paying off.

1988 also saw the first Sub Pop release by Mudhoney, who were, along with
Nirvana, the quintessential Seattle "grunge" band. The term "grunge" suited
them well—this was Rock n' Roll barely to the point of competence. But when
had that ever stopped anyone in Rock, from the Stooges to the Germs? Those
influences could be heard in the chaotic guitars and droning rhythms of
Mudhoney, but the attitude was an even more hopeless brand of "who cares"
intensified by singer Mark Arm's manic vocals—no one had yelped as uninhibitedly since vintage Iggy. Arm hung off the mike stand with his shag haircut like
one of those droogy mid-sixties garage-Punks like Sky Saxon or the guy in the
Electric Prunes. Dressed in t-shirts and jeans, swilling cans of beer and acting like
they didn't give a fuck, Mudhoney were early heroes of a juvenile delinquent
ethos that wasn't new but seemed like it in the heyday of Reagan, Madonna,
Prince, and *Oprah*. Arm and guitarist Steve Turner had already logged time in the
proto-Grunge band Green River, so they already had a leg up as far as credentials went. In those dim years, Mudhoney were not only fairly big sensations on
the admittedly limited indie circuit; they were something even more important—
cultural heroes. Their whole "wasted" demeanor ("fuck you/keep it out of my
face" went the lyrics to an early single) couldn't help but attract the attention of
not only journalists, but fellow musicians as well—like Kurt Cobain, for instance.

Bands like Mudhoney helped remind Punk Rock fans of their eternal legacy:
the unwound mania of the Sonics, the Stooges, '60s Garage Punk, B-movies (the
band took their name from a tit-happy Russ Meyer flick), comic books, dope, booze,
and the strange warp of American Hard Rock, from Mountain to Aerosmith. The
mania was decidedly heterosexual, which is worth noting in an era that made superstars of Morrissey, George Michael, Boy George, and Michael Jackson.

Mudhoney toured extensively during its first year and a half of existence,
bringing the sound of Seattle to the U.K. during their successful engagement
abroad in cahoots with eternal indie patrons Sonic Youth in 1989. That appearance sparked a cover story in *Melody Maker* in March of that year, which was as
symbolic as *Rolling Stone's* cover story on the Sex Pistols in the middle of
1977—mainly as an acknowledgement of the "next big thing" coming from
across the pond. Sub Pop suddenly found itself inundated by orders from overseas, particularly for the first Mudhoney EP, *Superfuzz Big Muff*. During the

summer of '89, representatives from Island records met with Poneman and Pavitt to discuss a distribution deal with Sub Pop. It didn't happen, but it was becoming apparent to Poneman and Pavitt that the label's eventual compromise with the Powers That Be was inevitable.

That summer brought the debut album by the band destined to finally put the "Seattle sound" on the map once and for all: Nirvana. No one could have guessed this at the time, however. When *Bleach* was released, it seemed like just another noisy Seattle record, not that different from ones that were then circulating by Tad, Soundgarden, and Mudhoney. Like a lot of the swamp Rock that was seething forth from the Northwest, the sound was ugly, the attitude grim. The release of *Bleach* corresponded with the hiring of Sub Pop's house photographer, Charles Peterson, whose pics would give the "Seattle sound" a visual image to go along with the music: sweaty Neanderthals with leonine hair bashing into each other and their instruments with wild abandon. Together with the crunching guitars and surging bass lines of the songs on *Bleach*, these images helped portray a stoned ambiance that, in the day and age of Reagan/Bush, was like a big "fuck you" to everything and everybody—especially the record industry. For this reason, the industry stayed away.

In 1989, Nirvana was the ultimate cult band. Plus the whole name, "Nirvana," implied drug use. There were also lyrics like "I'm a negative creep/And I'm stoned." Aptly enough, a few months earlier, Mudhoney had waxed: "I'm a creep/and I'm a *jerk*." There was definitely something going on here: a direct rebellion against the conformity of the Reagan/yuppie age. These stoners, locked in the Pacific Northwest, were directly thumbing their nose at any kind of "acceptance."

The reality was, many young Americans felt left out of the optimism of the '80s. Reagan had, essentially, not only declared war on the less privileged factions of the country by cutting back on welfare payments and services, but he'd also turned his back on the homeless, had refused to effectively address the AIDS dilemma, and had allowed crippling new censorship measures to invade the arts and media. There was also the war-hawking mentality of Reagan and his successor, George Bush, to effectively wage vain battles overseas for strictly diplomatic purposes. As Poneman postulated at the time: "The past eight years have created an environment in this country where what we are doing is actually a viable form of rebellion. It's a liberating factor. It's amazing that this stuff can still rile people. We like the idea that we can get a reaction."[4]

The key sentence there is *it's amazing that this stuff can still rile people*. By 1989, it seemed unlikely the notion of Rock as revolution, or at least as mass rebellion, would ever raise its muskets again. There was the dreary deadlock of prefab Hip Hop lite in the form of MC Hammer, Paula Abdul, Vanilla Ice, and New Kids on the Block, and, on the other hand, made-for-MTV crotch-stuffers like Def Leppard, Motley Crue, Warrant, and Winger. The thing that made the "underground" thrive in those days was the fact that it had become so insulated from what was going on in the mainstream. To the members of the underground, it seemed as though Rock was dead as a populist form. Like art or underground movies, Rock as we once knew it had come down to a balka-nized cult whose members relished their own obscurity. On the other hand, it seems evident that Nirvana was doing it for the same reason kids always have: because they were pissed off and felt lonely and disenfranchised. This convic-tion was apparent on the best songs from *Bleach*.

There was no great indication that Nirvana was the group that was going to push "the movement" to its next frontier. Their free-form jamming was admirable in a sense—it certainly wasn't "commercial"—but they did tend to get lost sometimes. They were a four-piece at that time, and the band's rhythm section—consisting of drummer Chad Channing and bassist Krist Novoselic—was definitely its heart. Singer Kurt Cobain was not any more polished than Mark Arm and employed a similar guttural delivery. Although Mudhoney tended to take their influence from a long legacy of American Punk, Nirvana tended to be more metallic. The riffs were ugly, the album cover was ugly, and the attitude was even uglier. There was no indication that singer/songwriter Cobain was any kind of budding musical genius—even the "ballad" "About a Girl," was a very basic drone. No true melodic gifts were apparent yet.

What was apparent was that Kurt Cobain was a fucked-up angry kid who wrote angry songs with titles like "Blew," "Scoff," and "Downer," that, rather than screaming for vengeance like previous hard-rock licks, actually called out for sympathy. It was rock from the point of view of arrested development and psychological despair and it would be very influential on the music of the nineties. Within the swirling haze of Cobain's misanthropy was a dim kind of ambivalence that said: "I give up." Although the band functioned as a democ-racy at this point, it was evident that, within the grinding-and-halting tumult of the music, it was all about Cobain's angst.

Kurt Cobain had reason to be angry, like any other sensitive kid growing up in a town full of lumberjacks—in this case, Aberdeen, Washington. In the early '80s, the logging industry was flagging, which lent the town the same grim air of desperation that surrounded many of the Detroit suburbs at the same time, when a lot of the auto plants began closing. Not only did mental illness run extremely high in Aberdeen; so did alcoholism. There's little doubt that Cobain, a victim of a broken home since age nine, who spent his formative years being shuttled between two parents and various relatives, witnessed his share of both syndromes. The other thing he was subjected to constantly was the scorn of the redneck jocks at his junior high school, who treated the delicate young man as a target for their hostilities. As with a lot of Rock n' Rollers, from Elvis to Jonathan Richman, this kind of abuse left deep scars on his psyche.

There's no real indication of when Cobain's musical inclinations became apparent. Supposedly a period of residence with an aunt provided some of the inspiration, as she was young enough to appreciate "classic Rock" like the Beatles, and she encouraged Kurt's own latent talents. A tenure in the Columbia Record Club while living with his dad in a trailer park led to Cobain's appreciation for the more decorated elements of '70s Hard Rock such as Ted Nugent, Aerosmith, and Blue Oyster Cult. Like just about everybody else growing up at that time, Cobain's musical environment was surrounded by Heavy Metal. His world was basically untouched by Punk until he discovered the Melvins sometime around 1983, just before he graduated from high school. But, as Kurt Cobain would prove time and again, he was a quick learner.

It was through the Melvins connection that Cobain met his future musical co-conspirator, Krist Novoselic. Two years older than Cobain and about six inches taller, the L.A. transplant had moved to the town of Grays Harbor when he was fifteen due to his father's job in the logging industry. The sheltered working class environment didn't settle well with Novoselic—like Cobain, he was a rebel, and, like Cobain, he gravitated toward Punk in general and the Melvins in particular. When he met Cobain, their mutual insolence led them to form their first band, Ed, Ted, and Fred, with Cobain playing drums and Novoselic, guitar. The third member—"Fred," as it were—was a kid named Steve who cut his finger off during a logging accident, leaving Cobain and Novoselic a duo. It was during this period that the displaced youth Kurt Cobain, fresh out of high school, was busted for spray painting "Quiet Riot" on a bank in downtown Aberdeen. The fact that he chose to immortalize such a lame Pop-Metal outfit tells you something about Kurt Cobain's musical sensibilities circa 1984. Actually, Cobain was ahead of his time, because when Grunge finally happened a few years later, it was obvious that there was as much Heavy Metal influence as there was Punk.

The turning point came in 1986, when a demo on which the increasingly versatile Cobain played guitar and bass and sang, and Dale Crover played drums, convinced Novoselic that the "project"—known at various times as Skid Row, Fecal Matter, and Nirvana—was for real. After refining the line-up to Cobain on guitar and vocals and Novoselic on bass, the twosome moved to Seattle. It was a logical move for a band-in-training to move to the nearest big city. Sub Pop was still an unknown entity, and the world hadn't discovered Seattle as a new musical nexus. The move was more of an escape from Aberdeen than a conscious career decision.

Once they'd arrived, they didn't waste any time, cutting a demo with guitarist Jack Endino, who was quickly becoming the major recorder of "the Seattle sound." A member of Skin Yard, his production credits included Mudhoney, Tad, Soundgarden, and just about every other notable band on the Seattle scene. In their rebellious infancy, Nirvana seemed a natural for not only Endino, but for Sub Pop, which is why shortly after the tape was made Endino midwifed it to Jonathan Poneman. Meanwhile, the band found a "permanent" drummer in Aaron Burkhart (the Melvins' Crover had played drums on the Endino-produced demo). They gigged frequently, at the kinds of venues bands play when they're just starting out—that is, gigs where the whole band ends up splitting twenty dollars among them. The members of the band were strict adherents of the whole thrift shop mentality—a mentality that would soon sweep the world. Eventually there'd be whole books about "thrifting" as a major cultural preoccupation.

By the time Nirvana got signed to Sub Pop, Chad Channing had replaced Burkhart on drums, and the band had added a second guitarist, Jason Everman, even though Everman barely played a note on the first album. He *did* agree to put up the $600 to record it, because that's the way indie-Rock worked in those days. When the pressures of the road turned out to be too much for him, the band bounced him but put his picture on the cover. Kurt: "Eeeh, it was the least we could do—we never returned the $600."

Whether or not Nirvana ever intended to be part of the Grunge movement, getting signed to a label that, at that time, was becoming more prestigious by the minute was a fortuitous move. Within a few short months, Sub Pop and, with it, Grunge, would become an international phenomenon. Nirvana would go along for the ride, but it wasn't entirely unjustified. Although *Bleach* consisted of some pretty ugly noise, there were signs of a legitimate musical foundation underneath. At that time, it didn't matter—as long as the band had long hair and a sludge heap of guitar/bass/drum noise, they could be included in the panoply of Grunge. The major label feeding frenzy would soon begin: A&M grabbed Soundgarden; Columbia went after Screaming Trees and Alice in Chains. That left the Seattle supergroup Mother Love Bone—the half of Green River that didn't become Mudhoney, plus Malfunkshun's lead singer—for Polygram. But the heroin overdose of singer Andy Wood in 1990 nipped their career in the bud just as they were poised to become the first Seattle band to break out nationally.

Back in the underground, Sub Pop was having a hard time maintaining its indie cool while being constantly feted by the industry reps who were now flooding to Seattle on an almost daily basis. A distribution deal with Sony fell through, but Poneman and Pavitt were being constantly wined and dined. All over fanzine America, the label was still garnering accolades, and their roster of "hip" bands continued to grow in size and diversity. Some of the label's newer, nonindigenous acts included Pittsburgh's the Dwarves, a garage-Punk-speed-core aggregation that took Mudhoney's whole fucked-up/scumdog image a step further with anthems like "Skin Poppin' Slut" and "I Don't Give a Fuck (About Anybody but Me)." In an interview with the magazine *Seconds*, the Dwarves' singer, Blag Jesus, explained the band's gestalt this way: "Aggression is the only emotion that's real. I mean, we don't make any money doing this. We're a broke band, we lose money, and we're certainly not clockin' the pussy like all those faggot ass other Sub Pop bands who do boring college Rock." [5]

One of those "faggot ass" bands was Nirvana, whose ascendance on the whole college Rock circuit was directly tied to their Sub Pop seal of approval. With the ambitious Kurt Cobain at the helm, there were already some rifts between band and label. Cobain claimed that *Bleach* hadn't been promoted properly or with much enthusiasm. He also complained that the sales figures were shrouded in mystery. What really influenced Cobain to start looking beyond the limited realm of "indie Rock" was Sonic Youth's "success" with Geffen, a major label which had allowed the New Yorkers to maintain artistic integrity while still benefiting from the kind of exposure that Geffen's status ensured. This was a big influence on the whole underground. In summer 1990, Kurt Cobain remarked: "It's not hard to keep your dignity and sign to a major label. Sonic Youth have been really smart about what they're doing. I feel we're experienced enough to deal with it now. We're changing a little bit, we've been into more accessible Pop styles of music for the last two years, and finally we're able to relieve ourselves of some of that. So we figured we may as well get on the radio and try to make a little bit of money at it." [6]

The Sonic Youth connection can't be understated. These archangels of the underground had already bestowed their blessing on dozens of promising young bands, from Mudhoney to Dinosaur Jr. to the Japanese noisemongers, the Boredoms. In the case of Nirvana, it was singer Kurt Cobain's songwriting plurality that first impressed Sonic Youth, and bassist Kim Gordon in particular. SY also couldn't help being bowdlerized by Nirvana's immense stage presence, which by now involved epic instrument smash-ups à la the Who. To the members of SY, Nirvana spelled excitement. They liked Nirvana so much that they dragged them along on a series of tours and had someone wear a "Nirvana" t-shirt in the video for "Dirty Boots." The fact that Sonic Youth were on a major label was no mean feat. For Nirvana, it offered a bridge to something that Sub Pop was simply incapable of—the option of "making a little money at it."

At Sonic Youth's recommendation, Geffen became interested. The whole Grunge phenomenon occurred at a unique juncture in the history of the record industry. As with a lot of events in the history of Rock n' Roll, fate dealt a certain group of outcasts a fortuitous twist. In the case of Nirvana, it was the fact that a whole new generation of music listeners were finally moving into the ranks of A&R and promotion within the industry itself. As the '90s dawned, young adults who'd been weaned on R.E.M., Husker Du, and the first inklings of indie-Rock were making decisions in an A&R capacity at the major labels. They obviously were disillusioned with the whole Glam-Metal charade. The field of Hard Rock, once dominant, had now been reduced to a handful of puppet bands, most of whom were incapable of producing a legacy beyond one megaplatinum LP. The industry needed an overhaul, and Grunge arrived just in time. But unlike either hippie or Punk, it didn't take long for the perpetrators of Grunge to engage in the eternal meat grab. Grunge was the most rapidly subverted form of Rock ever.

Nirvana's deal with Geffen was the enabling factor in this subversion. The major labels had already experienced success with vaguely "alternative" bands like Living Colour, Jane's Addiction, and the Red Hot Chili Peppers, all of whom can be given credit for softening the blow. But these bands weren't Nirvana, whose credibility within the "underground" was secure. Consciously, they carried this hipness factor into the mainstream. With their management in the hands of Danny Goldberg, who'd done a stint with Led Zep's Swan Song in the '70s and had more recently taken control of Sonic Youth's fortunes, Nirvana were ripe for mainstream pickings. Cobain's insistence that "we're changing a little bit" was a dead giveaway: the band was ambitious, and they stylistically progressed to a level of aesthetic improvement. This included tightening the sound with the addition of a new drummer, Dave Grohl, a mainstay of various D.C. Punk and Hard-Core outfits whose pounding style fit the harmonics of Cobain's new, more melodic songs perfectly. It also included a new producer, Butch Vig, who was able to capture the band's vitality while still constructing the multi-overdubbed wall of Grunge that made the subsequent record, *Nevermind*, slide right onto FM radio alongside more mainstream Rock. The songs, the *attitude*, were "punk"—but the sound was like a slightly more chaotic version of the first Living Colour record.

Before Cobain and Company could slip calmly into major-label stability, there was still one loose end to be tied up—what to do about Sub Pop. Technically, the label still owned the band's contract, and while the band's relationship with them hadn't always been harmonious, they were still largely indebted to Poneman and Pavitt. In a classic move rivaling Sam Phillips selling Elvis's contract to Colonel Tom Parker/RCA for 35 thousand dollars, Sub Pop accepted a buy-out price of 70 thousand dollars with a 3 percent royalty rate and a guarantee that the Sub Pop logo would appear on every release Nirvana put out for Geffen.

It's symbolic that the week Nirvana began recording *Nevermind*, the United States, under President George Bush, began bombing Iraq. Symbolic because the kind of staunch patriotism that had flourished in the 1980s under Reagan and Bush had directly contributed to the disillusionment of kids like

Kurt Cobain, Chris Novoselic, and Dave Grohl—which was the basic theme of
Nevermind. Within a few months, it would become apparent that they were not
alone—whatever "American Dream" the Republicans' militarism supposedly
represented, it apparently excluded a lot of Americans. Soon the chickens
would come home to roost, but not before a few more asinine months of Bush's
92-percent approval rating and other trappings of the ersatz-patriotic shell
game.

The coming of Grunge signified that the '90s were going to be a lot different from the '80s. To those who'd been listening to underground radio for
the previous three or four years, it seemed anticlimactic. If you weren't watching MTV or listening to commercial radio, you might've missed it.
Nevertheless, Nirvana was the group that finally broke the history of Rock in
half. The Sex Pistols and Ramones had laid the groundwork, but their impact
had been kept a secret. To the average music listener, Punk had never mattered.
The difference was, Nirvana—a "punk" group by definition—made the trappings of Punk unavoidable. Suddenly, everything that had been festering in the
"underground" for fifteen years came floating to the surface. The culture
would never be the same again.

What people had been decrying about Rock for years was that it had ceased
to be significant, that its ability to act as a seismograph of cultural change had
evaporated. Surely this was true in the cabaret charades of U2 or R.E.M., two
bands who were at least declared by sociologists/critics looking for the missing
link as the great populist-Rock messiahs of the '80s. What critics failed to realize was that the unanimity encompassed by the Beatles and Elvis had not been
based solely on record sales. It had also rested on their influence on their immediate musical peers as well as their cultural impact. Like those artists, Nirvana
struck a chord that resonated with millions. Hype was part of it, just as it had
always been in Rock n' Roll, but by actually *being popular*, Nirvana had an
impact even greater than the bands who'd influenced them—like the Ramones,
for instance, who retired in defiance shortly after Nirvana's ascendance.
Whether *Nevermind* was even "punk" anymore after Butch Vig threw it in the
musical washing machine was a moot point—the fact that it inspired what
became the youth culture of the '90s was enough.

"Smells Like Teen Spirit," the first song most people heard by any Seattle
band, was the defining musical moment of its generation. Pulling in influ-

ences like a boat trolling Puget Sound looking for suicide victims, it managed to sound raw, alive, and redolent of change. Apropos for the time, the video helped sell the song to the masses. Its vision of a high school hop from hell, complete with the image of Kurt Cobain's greasy, unwashed hair falling in his face and the kids getting down with the band, was a much more populist message than the imperialistic preening of most Heavy Metal videos. Suddenly the garage band down the street that everyone loathed—the honest underdogs—were outselling the manufactured Pop darlings. Nirvana may have been no less manufactured, but what they were manufacturing was a bit more toxic. No one ever got the idea from Kurt and Co. that they were ever anything more than a bunch of kids down the street trying to kick up a little revolution. This appealed to a lot of kids at the time—otherwise, it wouldn't have sold. It was clear that Nirvana was reaching a whole new audience, and that was bound to have an effect on the commercial music environment, which had been saturated by the likes of Poison, Bon Jovi, and even the new, drug-free Aerosmith.

Most of my friends were all pushing thirty "the year Punk broke." The sight of a bunch of grungy boys jumping around with their hair falling in their faces wasn't enough to impress us, especially as we'd lived through the Stooges, the Ramones, Sex Pistols, Black Flag, Motorhead, and other "punks." Half the songs on *Nevermind* were filler—rants designed for the sensitive Kurt Cobain to throw a tantrum atop Krist Novoselic's ultraheavy bass lines. But as the months of the '90s wore on—as Bush's "no new taxes" pledge helped scuttle his insane popularity in the aftermath of the Gulf War; as personal computers began to line every desk and people all over learned to say "Microsoft;" as Clinton and his clan from down in Arkansas began to construct a new yuppie American Gothic; as the skirts began to get shorter and the hair longer; as bored youths in baggy pants with skateboards and funny little beards began to invade the city squares; and as the culture in the larger cities began to permanently change its complexion from white to every color in the rainbow—the vague angry songs began to make sense.

The youths of America were in turmoil, as the subsequent decade would prove. As always, Rock was the voice of the disenfranchised. Rock n' Roll, in the ensuing decade, was rarely, if ever, going to express a positive thought again. There would be good-time music again, but it would be rendered with stabbing irony. This was the final triumph of postmodernism: no one gets out alive—least of all Kurt Cobain.

Listening to *Nevermind* at this point, it seems like Cobain's persistent self-doubt was actually a prophecy. The throwaway lyric that he used to end the last verse of the anthem of the decade—namely, "Teen Spirit"—was perhaps the fitting summary of his generation: "I found it hard/it's hard to find/the will/whatever, nevermind." Nirvana added an almost Lennonesque melodic flair to basic Punk rhythms, but lyrically their songs were endless odes to doubt and self-loathing. Kurt Cobain was not a happy soul, even then, and the flush of fame, coming as it did, was a major disruption to his bleak but ultimately safe little world. Here was this small-town reject from a broken home who, like millions before him, found solace in the strings of an electric guitar. When that actually made him famous, he didn't know how to handle it. This is ultimately what killed him. His Rock star matrimony to human viper Courtney Love didn't help either. The most egregious hanger-on since Nancy Spungen, Love brought an equally damning fate to her own Rock star boyfriend. Long before that, though, Cobain had already demonstrated an unusual ambiguity about fame and success that was more or less a first in the world of Rock. This was just the opposite of the whole '70s superstar mentality. There's an interesting moment in the British exploitation film, *Kurt and Courtney*, when Cobain describes fame as being less cathartic than going to thrift stores and trying to discover that one elusive treasure. As Cobain explained, it was the thrill of the chase and the uncertainty of it all, not even knowing whether or not you could afford the item in question, that made it so exhilarating. Fame, he seemed to be saying, was mundane and spiritually degenerative.

This is why all post-Punk Rock music had to be ironic—the modern-day practitioners were trying to put distance between themselves and the corpse of Rock 'n' Roll. That's why there were so many parodies of Rock star pomp and preen in the world of post-everything Rock, from the Upper Crust to Urge Overkill—by the '90s, the grandiose excess of a Kiss or a Led Zeppelin seemed ridiculous. The difference was, when those groups came into their own, no one had ever been *that* famous before; they had no time to think about it, and their reaction was to embrace it and go overboard. But Nirvana's generation had been witnessing this obsessive degree of fame from the sidelines for their entire adult lives, all the contradictions intact. They'd witnessed the casualties, and of course the deadly, calculating cynicism of big-league Rock. Thus, they approached fame itself with trepidation. For this reason, Kurt Cobain was probably the first Rock star who wasn't a total asshole. And this hurt him in a way, because in the Rock n' Roll business, everyone around you is a total asshole. Cobain, being generally passive, became an easy target for the sleazier elements of the industry. When he couldn't take it anymore, he jumped.

Fame is a void that opens up and devours even the unwitting. Nirvana had been a phenomenon partly built by MTV and its trappings. It would have been impossible for them to avoid the baggage of fame, no matter how much it bugged them. Although their disaffected behavior endeared them to millions of like-minded youths, it also ensured that they'd turn into the "role models" they desperately wanted to avoid becoming. In their honor, the world would soon be filled with saps with low self-esteem writing anthems of failure, a damning fate for a youth culture already on the ropes. Cobain's own Rock star suicide, the most martyred Rock death since Lennon, was the ultimate affirmation of this.

Because the whole flannel-shirt/loser posture was so easy to copy, it wasn't long before there was an abundance of groups willing to step into the void that Cobain and company had, de facto, abdicated. Sony Records, who'd already had some success with Alice in Chains, got lucky when they signed Pearl Jam to the label, shortly after Geffen had taken the plunge with Nirvana. Cobain dismissed them almost instantly as "the curse of corporate Rock," but their roots in the Seattle scene were actually even deeper than Nirvana's. Guitarist Stone Gossard and bassist Jeff Ament were by-products of two formative Seattle bands, Green River and Mother Love Bone. The former was important because they played slowly; the latter, because they featured extended jamming. These were both musical attributes that had long been abandoned in the wake of Punk/Hard-Core, but they were about to make a comeback.

When Love Bone vocalist Andy Wood OD'd just as the band was on the verge of making it, Gossard and Ament joined forces with Chris Connell and Matt Cameron of the stalwart Seattle band Soundgarden under the name Temple of the Dog for a one-album deal on A&M, Soundgarden's label. A supergroup of sorts, the Dog was basically a side project for the Soundgarden guys that left Gossard and Ament looking for a more permanent situation. A set of demos they recorded as a duo eventually found their way into the hands of drummer Jack Irons, who'd played with the Red Hot Chili Peppers and

Redd Kross, among others. At the time, Irons was living in San Diego, and it was through his acquaintance that Gossard and Ament finally found their singer, Eddie Vedder. A loner who worked at an all-night gas station in San Diego and hit the surf the minute he was off the clock, Vedder was actually enough of a visionary to not only give the band its messianic connotations but also their name: Pearl Jam.

The band struck a chord immediately with "Alive," an anthem to rival "Teen Spirit." Within its oceanic framework were a lot of dynamic highs and lows that suggested that Pearl Jam were throwbacks to '70s dinosaurs Bad Company. Gossard's fret-fingered guitar work didn't dispel this comparison, nor did Vedder's gruff vocalizings and flowing locks. A moment became frozen in time. The image of that moment was one from the Pearl Jam video for "Alive": bodies triumphantly being heaved into the air in a show of solidarity to the new Rock of Ages. By the time "Alive" had stamped its way up the charts to number one, where it stayed for five weeks in the waning days of 1991, the industry was being rocked by the most unified Rock explosion since the Beatles.

From that point on, there was no turning back. In spring of 1992, Cameron Crowe's screenplay for the movie *Singles* portrayed a bunch of twentysomething slackers against the backdrop of Seattle. Soon thereafter, Grunge "fashion" began to take hold. This was one of the first signs that the '90s generation was going to have an identity of their own. Along with the baggy pants and backwards baseball caps brought about by Rap, there were now thousands of young men running around with little beards, or "goatees." Long hair was back, as well as earrings, body piercings, and, most of all, tattoos. Shorts were also in, which was part of the almost jock-Rock nature of Grunge. In the '90s you'd also have professional athletes who were de facto Rock stars, like White Sox pitcher Jack McDowell, who fronted his own "alternative Rock" band, or Alexi Lalas, a soccer player who looked as though he did. For women, it wasn't quite as unanimous: let's just say any ironic manifestation of noir/girlie/retro stylings—from thrift store faux leopard-skin coats to garish hornrims—was definitely *in*. This kind of ironic style manipulation was considered a form of feminism in itself. In reality, Grunge fashion had been around a long time. As a friend of mine remarked: "There is no such thing. Grunge was some yuppie term for those of us who grew our hair and never wore suits."

Another friend, a small-town lawyer in upstate New York, said: "The Grunge kids dress like *farmers*. Where I'm from, everyone dresses like that."

In the '90s, after all those years of yuppies with short hair just saying no, a new generation was ready to get dirty again. As subsequent fests like Woodstock II and III would demonstrate, the Manson family had nothing on these kids—when they got dirty, as in rolling-naked-in-the-mud dirty, they got *dirty*. The workplace was changing too, so now if you were a grimeball you could still go to work as a computer analyst making fifty dollars per hour and wear shorts, a t-shirt, and sneakers, and the CEO wouldn't even question it. In a few years, he—or she—would be wearing jeans into the office, too.

There was also the whole coffee-shop phenomenon, which was mass marketed by Starbucks Inc., a Seattle enterprise, natch. That was when a bunch of goateed slackers sat around sipping latté and discussing their apprehensions about the future and their philosophies on life. It was neobohemianism of the worst kind, but it did help define the '90s as something other than the yuppies.

The enormous popularity of Nirvana, Pearl Jam, and coffee—the caffeine also went along with that whole Silicon Valley/*Wired* nerd mentality—put the focus of the music industry on Seattle. For a while, the town played victim to the same migrant plague as San Francisco in the '60s. Endless streams of aimless travelers descended romantically upon the city, hoping to find an enlightened wonderland. This also included musicians hoping to cash in on the trendiness of the town. Of course, the industry hacks were perfectly willing to sniff their butts and probably, for a short time, shove rolls of fifty dollar bills up there. Can you blame them? By spring of '92, Nirvana, Pearl Jam, and Alice in Chains had gone platinum, and Soundgarden and Temple of the Dog had gone gold. All of these groups dominated MTV and FM radio. The next step was inevitably readymade knockoff groups like Stone Temple Pilots, who didn't even hail from Seattle but from Edward Vedder's home of San Diego. The only thing any of these groups had in common was the drugs they used. That is, except Soundgarden, who were the sensible Zappa-esque pyrotechnicians of the whole scene, thus eschewing drug use altogether.

By the time Grunge was sweeping the Top Ten, the real underground had moved from Seattle to the nearby burgh of Olympia, a town on the southern tip of Puget Sound with a population of four and a half million, where the top industries were fishing, tourism, and the aerospace industry. In the late '80s and early '90s, Olympia would become the home of two of the most promising upstart record labels of the indie-Rock era: K Records and Kill Rock Stars. Both labels operated on the same liberating principles and low budgets. K was instrumental in fostering the whole spirit of dual-gender equality and do-it-yourself accessibility. Kill Rock Stars was the harbinger of the next major movement in Rock music after Grunge—namely, Riot Grrl.

What were "riot grrls"? Well, Suzi Quatro had been one. So had Joan Jett and the Runaways. Now it was the '90s, and girl-Rock was laced with not only a heavy quotient of feminism, but irony as well (the crucial difference, as always, when considering any of this postmodern stuff). Why the Puget Sound happened to be the ideal location for an eruption of grrl power is anybody's guess. One explanation is this one offered by Gilly, a member of the band Calamity Jane: "I felt very discouraged about the whole grunge thing, because it was so male-dominated, all that Sub Pop stuff. The attitude that was coming out of Seattle was a Seventies male rocker attitude."[7]

In Seattle, all-female bands like 7 Year Bitch began to compete with Grunge-oids for local stages. By far, the most important band in the Northwest Riot Grrl scene was Bikini Kill. Although they had a male guitarist, their idealism came from an almost exclusively girl-centric point of view. Their unofficial "leader," Kathleen Hanna, was one of the most controversial figures in the whole '90s fem-lib debate. She was also one of the most prominent and outspoken role models for the posthip crowd. In short, she helped define '90s culture, for better or worse, as much as Kurt Cobain did. What Kathleen Hanna did was something that, at this late date, sounds incredibly unremarkable—no less than the first totally all-female-controlled Rock n' Roll: chicks played the music, ran the record label, and defined the scene.

There'd been self-defined female Rock personalities before, such as Patti Smith or even Grace Slick. Kathleen Hanna was aware of these influences, but her "feminism" was rooted in something more visceral than most of the previous female role models. Think Lydia Lunch, who was quickly rising on Patti Smith as the high priestess of Punk amongst the post-everything factions. Lunch helped turn the tables on how "sexuality" was defined by turning victimization into power, pain into liberation, victory into salvation, and sin into pleasure. Lunch made ugly music and, at first glance, appeared ugly—but she wasn't "ugly," just shocking…and ultimately she used this realization like the proverbial Black Widow, using her sexuality, twisted as it was, to ensnare the bait (which, in her case, turned out to be underage boys). This bitter twist was not lost on a host of female musicians who hated the dumb stereotype of American femininity as much as creeps like Cobain hated the male equivalent. Women hadn't actually been encouraged to explore all the confused repositories of their sexual ids like men had, at least not in public, so when they finally did, it was with all the drama of a dam breaking.

All through the age of Punk, brave female pioneers persevered: the Raincoats, the Slits, Poly Styrene, Joan Jett, Poison Ivy of the Cramps, and others. In the '80s, the visibility of females became even more pronounced. It wasn't just the presence of the Bangles or other MTV kissy-face posers…it was in the democratic interaction of male/female bands like the Dream Syndicate, Black Flag, Sonic Youth, Yo La Tengo, the Pixies, Beat Happening, et al. Something like Kim Gordon's "Halloween" from Sonic Youth's *Evol* LP was an enormous influence on Kathleen Hanna, not just for its Lydia Lunch-inspired noirish depravity but for the sense of Punk Rock empowerment that came from hearing a feminine voice say "fuck" so uninhibitedly. In the '80s, as the media extolled the virtues of Madonna as a feminine role model, a huge percentage of America's female population knew that this was a paper tiger. That exposing one's belly button and learning to say "I want product" louder wasn't exactly a form of liberation. Just as Rock n' Roll had provided the perfect outlet for male miscreants for the last half century, it proved the ideal spawning ground for a whole major radical feminist insurrection. This was perhaps was the final cock-cutting irony of Rock n' Roll.

From the start, the movement was conceived as a political entity. Hanna did the fanzine thing, but it wasn't just any fanzine—it was one sprinkled with the politics of the new grrl power polemic. Because it was in homemade fanzine form, it didn't come off doctrinaire, like many feminist tracts, but instead as an honest source of dialogue between the differing factions of "the movement." Unlike Grunge, which actually had no self-identity, the purveyors of Riot Grrl were glad to assert themselves. Like many Rock crusaders in the past, Kathleen Hanna wanted to change the world. In Bikini Kill's best music, this imperative comes across.

Bikini Kill were consciously following in the Punk tradition, which is why when they recorded their first single, they recruited Ms. Joan Jett to come in and play den mother. The similarities between "Rebel Girl" and Ms. Jett's own recorded output—with or without the Runaways—end there. "New Radio," and particularly "Rebel Girl," had that same sense of surprise, that same sense of starting over, as "Anarchy in the U.K." or "Smells Like Teen Spirit." These are the songs that launched the movement.

There were female-empowered bands before Bikini Kill, like L7 or Babes in Toyland, who were spouting some of the same rhetoric. As far as breaking down the barriers that had previously existed between women and the music industry, L7 were particularly important. Signed to a major label, Reprise, in the post-Nirvana feeding frenzy, the band helped forward the image of the empowered female rocker. There was even a popular t-shirt at the time that said "L7" with a drawing of a victorious female forcing a man's head into her crotch.

In the case of Bikini Kill, however, it was the sense of raw discovery that made it so convincing. It wasn't just finding out that the world was gonna be a place where a whole heap of shit was stacked in front of you; it was the passionate sense that, in light of such adversity, one could still find something liberating. REBEL GIRL! Just like Nirvana wasn't your dad's Punk Rock, this wasn't mommy's feminism either. As Hanna screamed in "New Radio": "Let's wipe our cum on my parents' bed."

There was also the dyke thing to consider. The radical feminist wing of American liberalism, whose profile had increased sharply in the '80s even as Reagan had them on the run, had long embraced what was essentially an anti-male stance. As the '80s became the '90s, the bastions of the politically correct—particularly those in institutes of higher learning—had imposed a doctrinaire pall on the female gay movement. This was unfortunate, because there were thousands of young women who may have been confused about their sexuality, or maybe realized they were gay, but didn't necessarily hate men. There were also those who swung both ways. Although the whole idea of "liberation" should mean "anything goes," that wasn't the case. The bloated whales in flannel shirts who helped define the more extreme radical reaches of the feminist movement weren't too amused by the riot grrls. That's because the riot grrls, like all Rock girls, embraced a lot of cutesy-girly stuff as well, mostly as a form of satire, but also as an honest acknowledgement of their own sexuality. In the early '90s, the face of feminism had a few moustache hairs. That's what made the riot grrls different—dykes or no, they were still "girls." It was almost as if they realized that by not betraying their own femininity, they were actually empowering themselves more. They were almost saying let the pains of womanhood—menstruation, sexism, victimization—be turned back on those who'd inflicted the pain in the first place. It wasn't just men—it was the male-oriented society that perpetrated all the dumb stereotypes that had objectified and maligned women in society for so long. It was just this kind of stereotype that the Riot Grrls exploited—which is why they all wore lipstick, and put barrettes in their hair, and talked in this campy, dumb Valley Girl voice. They were, in essence, throwing American society back in America's face like a bloody tampon and thus freeing themselves of their shackles.

Whether they were actual lesbians or not didn't matter. Kathleen Hanna may have been hetero, but her love for her sisters was universal, which meant that it could be manifested in the form of actual physical love as well. In "New Radio," she sang, "Come here baby let me kiss you like a boy does." In "Rebel Girl" it was, "I wanna take you home/I wanna try on your clothes." There was the essence of the "movement" right there…turning the whole thing into camp. The "movement" actually came down to a bunch of ironic college girls named Jen and Amy, carrying Partridge Family lunch boxes and wearing thick-framed black glasses, saying "likelike" and "y'know" every other word and thinking they were making some grand commentary on sexuality in the '90s. When actually, they were the same clotheshorses that American girls had always been, only now the clothes came from the thrift stores as opposed to the mall, and they were wearing them for the appreciation of other girls as opposed to boys. In a way, this was the ultimate feminist statement, because it seemed to be saying to men, "You're just not needed anymore." Women like Lydia Lunch and Kim Gordon had, in a classic role reversal, already objectified males as sex objects. The fact that the guitarist in Bikini Kill was a guy suggests that men could still function as accessories in the realm of riot grrls. This also left the door open for experimenting with lesbianism. Even to nondykes it looked appealing, because it was the ultimate statement of sister-solidarity—and male exclusion. It was also a way to get back at daddy—and in a classic Oedipal twist, this was perhaps the ultimate goal of the new feminism, because "daddy" was to blame for everything.

The other song Bikini Kill cut during the Joan Jett sessions was "Demi Rep," which begins with Hanna and company doing a girlish clap-along to the

old nursery rhyme, "Miss Mary Mack," to show their solidarity with their sisters once again. This was no nursery rhyme, however. It was an angry manifesto which expressed how a lot of young women felt about having to fulfill typical sex roles: "I'm sorry that I'm getting chubby/And I cannot always be happy for you/And I am not some lame sorority queen/Taking you home to meet my daddy." By playing second guitar on these tracks, Jett helped shape the young band's attack into a classic Punk wall of sound. Jett had also produced the first Germs album, which should be noted as an important influence on this kind of youthquake Punk. It's interesting to contrast the sound of these early Bikini Kill sides with either the later singles recorded with John Goodmanson or the tracks on the band's first full-length LP, *Pussy Whipped*. It was musical chaos, to put it bluntly: two-note riffs, mellifluous usage of swearwords like "pussy," "cunt," and "fuck," gnawing guitars, trash can drums, and Hanna's voice doing all kinds of wild things, often in the same range—and with the same unreserved manner—as Yoko Ono. On *Pussy Whipped*, the Sonic Youth stigma still ran strong. By the time of *Reject All American* in '96, the band had honed their sound into a tight Punk package that smoked from start to finish. The end result was perhaps the most politically incendiary American Rock n' Roll LP since the MC5's *Back in the U.S.A.*

The name Bikini Kill itself was a commentary on the dumb sexual stereotypes the media hurled at us on a daily basis, via TV and advertising. Of course, nowhere was this more prevalent than in the record industry, where dumb-ass stereotypes were a way of life. For this reason, Bikini Kill named their record label Kill Rock Stars.

The group's politics directly influenced the way they ran their record label. They didn't allow journalists to have guest-list privileges, and the office was run like a kind of extended sisterhood, staffed mostly by the siblings of the bands. Kill Rock Star's famed publicist, Maggie Vail, was the sister of Bikini Kill drummer Tobi Vail. Eventually she'd form her own band, Bangs, who'd also record an album for Kill Rock Stars. It was not unusual to find the various members of bands like Unwound or Cold Cold Hearts answering the phones or running the copy machine in the office during their nontouring time. It was as close to "communal" as anything since the early days of the San Francisco hippies.

The hype spread—suddenly girl-rockers were everywhere. But too often, Riot Girl bands like 7 Year Bitch and Babes in Toyland were just annoying. Was it really "liberation" for females in Rock to finally act as obnoxious as men had been acting for years? It wasn't just the dumb reverse-macho attitude chick-rockers copped from metallic male assholes; it was the destructive lifestyle as well. This is what really scuttled the movement (along with boring riffs). Within a year, after the dual ODs of 7 Year Bitch guitarist Stefanie Sargent and Hole bassist Kristen Pfaff, and the shooting death of Gits singer Mia Zapata, the industry had backed off. Unfortunately, this hurt the more legitimate factions of the riot Grrl movement, although Bikini Kill, who were probably offered a ride on the major label gravy train, admirably refused 'til their dying day. The movement also opened the door for imposters like Courtney Love, whose aptly named band, Hole, despite some fine songs, turned out to be a mere artifice masking Love's megalomaniacal ambitions. Not the least of which was marrying Kurt Cobain, who just happened to be the most famous Rock star in the world at the time, which was a fitting conquest for a lifetime star fuck-er/name dropper.

While the media focused its attention on Seattle and the surrounding 'burbs, and flogged both Grunge and Riot Grrl into submission, California had not yet detonated nor fallen into the sea. There was still an active Punk Rock scene that had been going strong since the late '70s. This was the essence of indie Rock as much as the more visible Northwest music scene. In many ways, the entire West Coast D.I.Y. movement owed its existence to the L.A. Punk scene and the more eclectic Bay Area scene to the North. San Francisco, in particular, was home to a variety of difficult, complex, and anticommercial bands and labels in the late '70s/early '80s, such as Flipper with Subterranean and the Dead Kennedys with Alternative Tentacles. In L.A., the original breakneck, shorthair, three-minute ethos of Punk had never really died. Within its own milieu, it had only gotten bigger. Punk was not only part of the L.A. musical legacy; along with haircut Metal, it *was* L.A.'s musical legacy.

The Punk fervor spread up and down the state of California all through the '80s. It's difficult to say why California has been the utmost preserver of Punk Rock, other than to mention the obvious fact that the weather is more conducive to skateboard parks and buzz-cuts. L.A. had been the stronghold of Hard-Core in the '70s and '80s, and a lot of the bands were merely following in that path. The most prominent of these were Redd Kross, the Descendants, and the Angry Samoans. These bands specialized in a tongue-in-cheek brand of Rock, critic-reference Rock—that is, they were smart enough to know better, but played it d-u-m-b anyway. With their melodic songs and satirical lyrics, these bands proved that Hard-Core didn't have to be jingoistic. Green Day was one band that was no doubt listening.

Even as Grunge was rearing its ugly-*ugly* head, there were still plenty of bands playing Punk-is-as-Punk-does. In L.A., the Leaving Trains had long established a legacy of being a good old Heartbreakers/Ramones style Punk band. Recording for SST, the band found itself wedged firmly in the Punk tradition. Unlike other mid-'80s SST bands such as Husker Du, Dinosaur, Jr., Soundgarden, the Screaming Trees, and Sonic Youth, all of whom sensed a major post-Punk renaissance coming, the Trains were more or less oblivious to the posturing of "college Rock." This hurt them as far as the "hipness" factor went (although it should be noted that leader James Moreland was actually married to Courtney Love briefly before she married Kurt Cobain). "Rock n' Roll Murders" from '91 still stands as their magnum opus. By lumping all the dead Rock stars' deaths with such factors as the Kennedy assassination, they were actually treading on Oliver Stone territory but with a caustic twist. As always, the question remained: did he fall or was he pushed?

Following in the tradition of the Leaving Trains were a whole league of California bands like the Lazy Cowgirls (a transplant originally from Indiana), Creamers, and Chemical People, bands whose basic sound/stance was "punk" but who eschewed the political implications that had come to be the norm in Cal-Punk post-Hard-Core/Dead Kennedys. This was a revolution in itself, because Punk as a musical form would soon prove more viable than ever, whereas the doctrinaire, politically correct trappings of Straightedge/Hard-Core would more or less scream to a halt in the callous era of the Internet/*Seinfeld*/*Springer*/Bill Clinton. Punks had to learn to adapt to the new callousness—as if real Punks would've ever done anything else! Bands like the Lazy Cowgirls came off as a kind of brazen New York Dolls/Sex Pistols equivalent in light of Nirvana's Beatles, Hole's Fleetwood Mac, or Pearl Jam's Bad Company. There was nothing left to do but relive it AGAIN and AGAIN, and bands like the Lazy Cowgirls were wise in one way: they knew they'd never improve on the whole stance of someone like the Dolls, and they didn't try. In a way, these were the least pretentious bands since the early '60s because they set out to do nothing more than play some good Rock n' Roll. If any band made a convincing argument for Rock n' Roll "purity" during that whole '80s-'90s indie-Rock era, it was the Cowgirls.

Punk by then had become such a popular pose, and one so easy to assume, that it was hard to tell the pretenders from the actual practitioners. The Cowgirls had to be judged against masqueraders like the Dwarves, who just happened to have the more viable Sub Pop seal of approval. In light of commercial crap like Jane's Addiction and Living Colour, authentic Punk bands found themselves in the same position as Ventures-style instrumental bands did in the heyday of the Beatles: mainly, if you can't write the power ballad, dude, you're out.

So where did this leave a band like AntiSeen, possibly the greatest American Punk band of the era? Haling from New London, N.C. (population: approx. 4 thousand), they couldn't have been more oblivious to whatever posturing was sweeping the "underground" at the time. They built a recorded legacy far more impressive than most, and they did it the same way as many other bands in their shoes—through self-determination and the D.I.Y. spirit. Still, it was a little harder to get in the loop of that whole indie/D.I.Y. community when your philosophical message is kick-your-stinking-teeth-in and The South Will Rise Again. Nevertheless, on their own Destructo label, they unleashed a sterling legacy that was two parts MC5 to one part Hank Williams Jr.—with a little Charles Manson thrown in. It was as American as apple pie, but needless to say, it wasn't gonna win any kudos from indie champions who, at that time, weren't interested in anything that didn't come from the Pacific Northwest and wear flannel. Hell, AntiSeen wore flannel shirts too, but ones with "Don't Tread on Me" emblazoned on the back.

The hipster masses' indifference to AntiSeen was typical of the kind of buttress Punk was facing in the early '90s. About the only "punks" who were accepted into the sacred realm of hipster college/indie Rock were the Washington, D.C. segment led by Fugazi, and that was mostly due to the band's vegetarian/Straightedge philosophy. This fact annoyed their leader, ex-Minor Threat shavehead icon Ian MacKaye, who complained vigorously: "Mmmmnnnnnn fuck! No one wants to talk about the music! All they want to talk about is the fact we only charge five bucks!" What he was referring to was Fugazi's—and their record label, Dischord's—policy of imposing strict ceilings on the prices of both their shows and record albums, a fact that prevented distributors or promoters from gouging the consumer. This was the egalitarian legacy of Hard-Core, but few were as serious about it as Fugazi. After Nirvana broke, the sales figures generated by a Fugazi would appear modest, but for a while, in the late '80s/early '90s, when the band were at their greatest strength, the industry was appearing to take notice. Wave that carrot all you want though, boys—Fugazi wasn't biting. At one point Fugazi was selling about 40 thousand albums, and drawing fourteen hundred people to a single concert. For a band that released their own records, did their own promotion and advertising, refused to make videos, and shunned the mainstream press in favor of small fanzines, those were pretty impressive stats. The same D.I.Y. spirit would infuse the Riot Grrl movement, but unfortunately, there was no cohesion between the two movements because the politics were different. It was a scene we'd see repeated again and again during the age—and it was a guarantee that there'd be no massive "punk"/indie uprising until the bands put aside their politics for populism. Which is why the vague Nirvana and the poppy Green Day became the biggest "punk" groups of the era despite the fact that neither of them could hold a candle to, say, Fugazi as far as musicianship.

In California, three labels ruled the roost: Triple X, Lookout, and Epitaph. The latter are an interesting case, being the domain of Bad Religion, a Southern Cal Punk band whose antidogma message and rhythmic firepower earned them a sacred notch among the Punk ranks in the '80s. Amazing the number of Punk groups who actually started their own record labels during those years: AntiSeen with Destructo, the Dead Kennedys with Alternative Tentacles, Minor Threat with Dischord, the Angry Samoans with Bad Trip, and Black Flag with SST, among others. Bad Religion was no exception. They knew that what they were selling was good, and they were willing to take some risks. It paid off, at least in part, until their drug problems and pursuit of higher education sidelined them for a few years. However, by the end of the '80s, ennobled by the hiatus, they came back with a rejuvenated sense of purpose, epitomized by the classics *Suffer* and *No Control*. This was Punk Rock beyond the call of duty—a dense, layered mass of guitars all throbbing at once to a switchblade snarl. Few bands ever approached the level of sonic assertion that BR did on these discs. If Rock n' Roll had any purpose in the post-post-hip era, this was it—and that was to make everything that came in its path sound lame, wimpy. In their own way, Bad Religion was as heavily politicized as Fugazi, but their politics verged on a kind of anthropological/anarchist stance, partly due to lead singer Greg Graffin's pursuance of a zoology degree. They put humanity under the microscope only to conclude that the whole thing was a failed science experiment. There was a reason the band was called Bad Religion: they saved their most acute venom for organized religion, and their songs were nothing short of a complete denouncement of the whole Christian way of life embraced by Western Civilization. The music itself was such a firestorm of harmonic intensity that it deserved a classification of its own: "Super Rock." It would not go unnoticed: as the '90s dawned, Bad Religion found themselves in the unique position of being the big brother band to the whole West Coast wave of totem-Punk. Signed to a major label, CBS, in 1991, they continued to run Epitaph independently, helping to foster one of the most commercially successful California bands of the era, Rancid, whose success paid off for Epitaph in much the same way Nirvana's had for Sub Pop.

Triple X never got quite the same payoff, but their hearts were, and are, in the right place. Headed by Rock critic Bruce Duff, the label's whole modus operandi has always been somewhere between garage/glam and hardy-har-Hard-Core. Most of their entries, like the Creamers, have been worthy proponents of the kind of melodic Punk pioneered by the Ramones with the same fuck-everything stance. The label also played host to reconstituted glam-rockers like Jeff Dahl as well as having reclaimed a few of the old masters (Angry Samoans, Dickies). The label's purity has been the thing that's prevented them from ever crossing the line into Sub Pop/Epitaph style success. It might also be the fact that a lot of their records are simply boring—the same repetitious riffs that have ruled Punk for close to twenty-five years with the same dumb sub-Ramones posture. Nevertheless, given their self-appointed duty of being preservers of the Punk Rock faith, Triple X have done a better-than-adequate job of keeping the flame alive.

In Northern California, Lookout, based in Berkeley, proved to be the most venerable Punk indie. They were lucky initially to land one of the best, and most tireless, Punk bands in the country, the New Hampshire band the Queers. Not that the group would ever be a top money maker, but for credibility purposes, it helped to have a band of that prestige on the tiny label. The time-honored New Englanders were respected among the legions of Punk fans across the country for their endless touring as well as their melodic post-Ramones

Punk Rock. Queers leader Joe King was also a professed admirer of the Beach Boys, like Joey Ramone, so the two bands had a lot in common, a fact the Queers more or less acknowledged by covering the Ramones' magnum opus, *Rocket to Russia*, in its entirety. In Chicago, Screeching Weasel did a pretty fair facsimile of the Queers, even going so far as giving the Ramones' first album the same treatment the Queers gave *Rocket*. Likewise possessed of melodic abilities as they were, their songs were similar reflections on dead-end post-Punk consciousness. The group eventually spawned off into the Riverdales, who were one of the best son-of-Ramones bands of the age. The Queers and Screeching Weasel would in turn influence the most successful band on Lookout, and the group who'd turn out to be the label's Nirvana—Green Day.

An above-average Punk band from Berkeley, these upstarts had a lot of things going for them, not the least of which was youth. Taking up residence at a local dive called Gillman Street, which became their nexus in much the same way as the Cavern Club had for the Beatles or CBGB's had for the Ramones, Green Day soon found themselves spearheading a whole movement of youthful Punk-brat acts. Signed to Lookout in 1991, just as Nirvana was going national with Geffen, the band sold a remarkable number of units for an indie band at that time. Although most of the sales were in the Bay area, the band had estimable breakout appeal. Their second album, *Kerplunk*, was a masterpiece of melodic Punk riddled with tight arrangements; poppy hooks; and funny, self-deprecating lyrics. Their whole teenage appeal was bound to endear them not only to the generation who were getting into Grunge, but, perhaps more likely, that generation's younger siblings. Green Day weren't immune to what was going on in Seattle either: the churning tempo during the break in "Christie Road" was very reminiscent of "Smells Like Teen Spirit." Like Nirvana, Green Day offered a hope that hadn't been felt in Rock since its heyday—namely, that the most popular band in the world might also be the best.

Sometime in '93, watching the kids at Gillman explode on a weekly basis, and watching those impressive Lookout sales figures and watching Nirvana's ascendance, someone at Warner Brothers decided to take the plunge. It was risky: no "punk" band, homegrown or imported, had ever "made it" in the United States. For all their faults, that's one thing Green Day certifiably was: Punk. From the first note of the first song on *Dookie*, their Reprise debut, the LP bristled with a kinetic energy. The sound was based on guitars, guitars, and more guitars. Almost all the songs moved at breakneck pace. They were brats, and there was nothing innately threatening about them. The Stooges or Sex Pistols they weren't. They were, however, the best "popular" band in twenty years. Like Nirvana, they were aided by a good video: "Longview" showed Green Day leader Billy Joe Armstrong tearing up a sofa in a furious rage wrought by suburban boredom, which the song's lyrics paid tribute to as well with lines like "when masturbation's lost its fun/you're fuckin' breakin'."

One thing it liberated were the little bank accounts at Lookout. As with Sub Pop before them, when the payoff came from the major label buyout, they were able to expand their roster multifold with a variety of interesting bands, mostly in the same melodic Punk vein as the Queers or Green Day. Among these were the first openly gay Punk band, Pansy Division; the Ramones-clone Riverdales; and the all-female Donnas, the best band of their type since Green Day themselves. Playing on a straight Ramones formula and evoking the same cocktease image as their spiritual forebears, the Runaways, the Donnas person-ified the Californian ethos of kids who grew up with Punk *and* glam-Metal and refused to be apologists for either. The Donnas were hot with teenage lust, a factor made all the more enticing by the fact that, when they recorded their earliest records, they were still in high school. Rumors abounded that they did-n't play their own instruments, that they were merely the Go-Gos with a hard-er edge. Nevertheless, it was inevitable that they'd eventually become the next band on Lookout after Green Day to get signed to a major.

There was also an ardent "retro" scene in California in the early '90s, sup-ported by labels like Crypt, Estrus, and Dionysus (and to some extent, Triple X and Sympathy for the Record Industry). This scene existed harmoniously with the Punk scene, but its perpetrators were more consciously throwbacks to Rock's classic age, evoking the snarl of mid-'60s garage-Punk and any of its variants (Surf, Folk-Rock, Lounge-Rock). This also tied in with the emergence of thrift store culture and mondo video/horror schlock. The basic message was that the commercial Punk scene was no more radical than any other strain of the mainstream record industry; thus these groups eschewed all aspects of modern-day record making, including videos or heavy studio embellishment. A lot of these groups were so self-consciously "retro" that they even refused to make CDs, like the San Francisco area band, the Mummies, for instance. A lot of them concentrated on that dying medium, the 45 RPM record. Some labels like Crypt even offered reissues of genuine '60s Punk along with the offerings of the newer practitioners. And the phenomenon wasn't just restricted to California: in Massachusetts, Cheater Slicks did a gasohol-fueled take on scuzzy '60s Rock. In Pennsylvania, the Cynics offered a manic replication of Garage-Rock wildness. In England, the various aggregations conceived by Billy Childish—Headcoats, Delmonas, Milkshakes—evoked the unbridled spirit of everything from Rockabilly to Punk to girl groups. Even the state of Maine had its own all-girl Garage-Punk troubadours in the form of the Brood. Garage-Rock neoclassicism was not strictly a '90s phenomenon. Going back to the '70s and all through the '80s, there'd been a host of fine bands playing in a retro style: Boston's Lyres and Kenne Highland Klan, upstate New York's Chesterfield Kings, Rhode Island's Plan 9, and New York City's Fleshtones. However, the growing dissatisfaction many people felt with the increasingly commercialized world of MTV-sanctioned alt-Rock led many people to seek the only alternative they trusted—mainly, a return to the era before such falsification even existed.

In the U.K., any mention of the retro/indie scene begins with Billy Childish. Not only has he been recording for the longest duration of time; he's also been the most prolific. A writer and painter as well, he's also produced a wide variety of artists, as well as recording more than fifty albums, either under his own name or one of several all-purpose band monikers such as Thee Headcoats, the Milkshakes, or Mighty Caesars. Childish has been a one-man Rock 'n' Roll preservation society and has amassed a following in Europe, the United States, and Japan, where he helped influence Garage-Rock enthusiasts like Guitar Wolf. It was his notoriety among cultists that led to his being signed to Sub Pop in the late '80s. When Mudhoney toured England for the first time, they made it their mission not only to look up Childish, but also introduce him to Jonathan Poneman so that he could be suitably enshrined within the hipster elite.

Right behind Billy Childish in the Brit do-it-yourself scene was a similarly deranged miscreant named Nick Saloman, a.k.a. the Bevis Frond. Salamon's an interesting case: victim of an auto accident that had him laid up in a leg cast for more than a year, he received a lucrative insurance settlement and decided to fulfill his lifelong dream of being a '60s psych-god. Only problem was, he'd had the dream since the sixties. Saloman was no spring chicken, in other words—

by the time his first independently released album, *Miasma*, came out in 1987, he was already in his mid thirties. As was the case with Childish, in Saloman's age lay his authenticity—old enough to actually *remember* the glory days when they rocked the Roundhouse, he had no trouble recreating the kozmik '60s vibe. His first few albums were brilliant evocations of the period, alternating between melodic Beatles tunefulness and Hendrix/Deviants distortion-box freak-outs. Recording literally in his basement, perhaps the most amazing thing about the Bevis Frond was that he actually belatedly turned into the kind of cult artist he'd always wanted to be. So thick was the indie-underground membrane by then—through fanzines, college radio, and whatnot—that, by the late '80s, the Bevis Frond had actually established an intensely loyal following. The lesson being: it's never too late (and, as the Angry Samoans, another band with retro leanings, said: yesterday started tomorrow).

As far as longevity, the Mekons were England's reigning indie champs. They'd been around since the late '70s, when they emerged out of the same Leeds University scene that produced Gang of Four. Beginning as a clattering post-Punk aggregation and eventually going in a more roots-Rock direction, there was a lot of cockney in the mix. Later on, they adopted a fair portion of rustic twang, a trait garnered from listening to too many Hank Williams and Gram Parsons records—not surprising, as drinking was high on their list of priorities. By the late '80s, they'd gone the major label route, first with A&M and then Warner's, before finally being dumped right back into indie-ville where they made many of their most interesting records.

The Pastels were important for introducing a lot of the gender-interactive tendencies that would play such an important role in the indie scene in the '90s. Alternating between male and female vocals, and writing vague little love-Pop ditties that possessed some of the jangle tendencies of classic Pop/Folk, the Pastels were no strangers to the oceanic drifting quality of the Velvet Underground's third album either. Their childlike coyness and homespun amateurishness rivaled what Beat Happening was doing in America at the same time. One group they influenced was Teenage Fanclub. Another was the Vaselines, who, as their name implies, were more lascivious and harder-edged than the playtime Pastels. The Vaselines were downright sleazy-sounding, with songs about drugs, lust, and pleasure. They were "punk" by definition, but of a more enlightened variety in which women were equal to men and the macho pose of Rock that had carried all through Punk (Dead Boys, Dwarves, G. G. Allin) was being joyfully tossed overboard. So the attitude was still "fuck you," but the tunes were pretty with the girl's voice wafting waifishly above the fray, and the songs were basic and unadorned instead of heavy and ominous.

Taken together, the Pastels and Vaselines were the beginning of boy/girl indie-Rock in England, and their influence would not go unnoticed. Jad Fair of Half Japanese, for instance, claimed to be a huge Pastels fan; Kurt Cobain, meanwhile, readily acknowledged the Vaselines' influence by covering several of their songs.

An even more maverick and pioneering act were Spacemen 3, who exercised a similarly decadent spirit as the Vaselines, but with the emphasis more on drugs than sex. In fact, group leader Jason Pierce, apparently a trust-fund babe, organized the group around weekend getaways at his parents' estate, which would turn into marathon acid-eating parties and jam sessions. The group fancied themselves following in the same visionary path as the Doors or Velvet Underground, and, like those groups, their music seems inconceivable without the influence of mind-altering substances. They had a definite aesthetic, epitomized best by their eternal credo/statement of purpose: "Taking drugs to make music to take drugs to." Perhaps more than any other group to emerge in the '80s, Spacemen 3 were perfecters of the endless drone, and a lot of their songs amounted to nothing more than the same riff building and building for several minutes at a time, becoming more intense but not necessarily varying at all. They weren't really improvisers as much as repeaters, kind of like a Jimmy Reed for the space age. Although they weren't opposed to technology (particularly keyboards), the sound was basic, stripped down. The scenario evoked by their music was one of losing total control—as the songs slowly unwound in their repetitious but harmonically dense way, it was like watching something come unraveled, like your mind perhaps. For a three-piece, they had the most hypnotic sound this side of Galaxie 500, their American counterparts and the other vastly influential drone merchants of the era, although Galaxie's drones were of a more oceanic—and less alchemic—variety.

My Bloody Valentine, from Scotland, was another one of the most influential bands of the era. Certainly their layers of cascading guitars, all building up to a mesmerizing groove, mixed with electronics and ethereal vocals, seemed aimed at the tripping masses. Particularly in England, psychedelics were on the rise again, including newfangled designer drugs like Ecstasy and Ketamine that fueled the weekend-long dancing escapades in the new Rave capitol of Manchester. Belinda Butcher's blissful vocals in the droning rapture of My Bloody Valentine's "Only Shallow" suited the dreamlike drug experience perfectly, as did the fanciful dandy-boy antics of Manchester's own Rave bands: Happy Mondays, Stone Roses, Charlatans UK, and other flat-footers.

The ethereal phase of Anglo-Rock epitomized by My Bloody Valentine— nicknamed "shoegazers" because of the way the musicians detachedly refused to engage the audience, staring at their feet during performances—produced a stream of clever one-named bands utilizing swirling textures: Ride, Suede, Lush, Blur, Curve, Moose, Verve, Adorable, and Swervedriver. In most cases, their success in England failed to translate across the Atlantic, although they helped spawn many stateside imitators in the form of Smashing Orange, the Swirlies and the Brian Jonestown Massacre, among others. The Manchester bands, meanwhile, were the catalysts for the Brit-Pop explosion that reached its apotheosis with Oasis, the most successful band of its type since the Beatles.

In England, among the psychedelic faeries, were also some good rockers. The Hypnotics, for instance, did a fairly punched-up rendition of '60s garage-grunge-psych filtered through metallic Detroit and Aussie influences. The Wedding Present were wound as tight as a clothesline, and their skittering guitars effectively placated the indie-Rock masses for a few months in the early '90s. Scotland's Teenage Fanclub was one of the most successful bands of the era: copping Beatles and Big Star Pop textures, their claim to fame was being the band who was signed to Geffen *between* Sonic Youth and Nirvana. But they were still a little too ironic in their affectations to catch on with the mainstream audience. They left their spike in the ground nevertheless.

Most of the English indie-Rock bands were abetted by John Peel, the notorious host of BBC's "Radio One," who'd been championing what could loosely be called "underground music" since the late '60s. England only has one radio station, so no matter how they want to divide it up, it's still all under the same government-controlled umbrella. Due to some weird musicians' union rules, the BBC is only allowed a certain amount of air time for recorded music—this left gaps to be filled during the course of the average programming day. It was Peel's idea to bring live bands into the BBC studios to play during open air time. Initiated in 1968, these outings almost instantly become known as "the Peel Sessions." Peel had begun his career on one of Britain's legendary "pirate" radio stations, and his tastes had always been adventurous. The BBC apparently figured that the best way to destroy the illegal competition was to usurp it, so they lured him away from the pirates. The result was more eclectic programming than the BBC had ever known, as well as an open-door policy toward bands Peel wanted to have play on his show. In England, the whole division between corporate and indie Rock isn't quite as pronounced as it is in the U.S. Being a small island, England's tastes are much more provincial. There's much more of an emphasis on local sensations because, in a sense, in a country that small, every indigenous act is "local." Songs that could never become "hits" in America are actually able to climb the British charts. Peel was free to introduce mavericks like the Wedding Present and My Bloody Valentine to BBC audiences as well as host American indie acts like Love Child and Mudhoney when they were in the U.K. In America, these bands would stand no chance of getting anywhere near broadcast radio.

The indie scene down under also produced a wide range of exotic talent. New Zealand remained an untapped paradise of unbridled Rock n' Roll enthusiasm, a fact proven by the Tall Dwarves, a band fronted by ex-Toy Love members Alex Bathgate and Chris Knox. Toy Love deserves special mention for dating back to the birth of Punk and thus being partly responsible for the New Zealand underground itself. Like Half Japanese in the US, the Tall Dwarves were purposely lo-fi, recording in four-track and shunning the hype of the modern recording industry. That wasn't hard to do on an island known mostly for kiwi fruit. However, in the age of fanzines, it was inevitable that, with their homemade recordings, Tall Dwarves would soon become enshrined as hipster heroes in this incestuous little netherworld. Knox was even able to ride this pocket notoriety into a solo career, getting signed to the American indie Caroline in the early '90s and producing such brilliant work as "Belly Up and Grinning" with its hypnotic Lennon/Ray Davies-like transitions and tinkling piano minuets as well as the Velvets' third album homage, "Nothing Comes Clear." A gracious performer, Knox was a unique talent who deserved better than the indie graveyard.

Other important New Zealand bands included the Bats and the Clean, both of whom purveyed the jangling hypno-strum of the Velvets/Byrds but weren't necessarily "retro." The Clean went back the furthest—their single

"Tally Ho" was the first release on Flying Nun Records, which would become the flagship vessel for all subsequently significant NZ Rock. Eventually, bassist Robert Scott left to form the Bats, whose jangling guitars and droning melodies influenced the American singer/songwriter Barbara Manning immensely, so much so she even made the pilgrimage to Dunedin. On the fringe end of the NZ scene was Bailter Space, a more experimental group capable of surging power in their somewhat messy evocation of Sonic Youth/My Bloody Valentine drone and Toiling Midgets-style dourness. They got signed to the ultra-hip indie label Matador, but got dropped when label honcho Gerard Cosloy figured he was actually *losing* money on every album they released. The band didn't care—they moved to Brooklyn, lived communally, and started their own record label to combat the world's neglect. The result was a continuation, perhaps even a refinement, of their basic bulldozer methodology.

Perhaps New Zealand's premiere drone group was the legendary Dead C, perhaps NZ's ultimate "underground" act. Their double album, *Harsh 70's Reality*, was an ongoing drone that, over four sides, never got boring. Like a lot of the music of this era, it proved that noise could be spiritually uplifting. As far as the ultraunderground world of indie-Rock went, there was no limit to the microscopic density: Dadamah were one of the strangest and most wonderfully hypnotic space/drone/ethereal bands of the era, but their whole self-negating "obscurity," such as packaging their records in indecipherably blank sleeves and not listing personnel, ensured that their whole "revolution" would remain private.

In the '90s, this self-negating factor had to be considered time and time again. The indie rockers did what rockers in the past never had been willing to do—they gave themselves over to obscurity. The fact that Classical and Jazz musicians had previously done this tells you something about the state of Rock in the late '80s: mainly, that the only way to achieve any serious musical synthesis at that point was to ignore the temptation of sampling the major labels' sweet fruit. The musicians were noble to do what they did—it enabled them to actually accomplish something progressive in the name of music. But the *fans* were ultimately wrong—obscurity didn't necessarily equate to integrity, and a lot of indie-Rock was simply boring (like a great deal of New Zealand's indie heroes, for instance).

In America, a legitimate indie-underground was being assembled piece by piece. Any discussion of this has to include Dinosaur, Jr., if only because the group spawned two of the basic '90s prototypes: the mushmouthed stoner (J. Mascis) and the edgy nerd– dreamer–romantic (Lou Barlow). From their western Massachusetts environs, Dinosaur evoked a lot of '70s stoner-Rock clichés that the whole Black Flag/Minor Threat generation had rejected. Originally a drummer, Mascis claimed that John Bonham of Led Zeppelin was his biggest influence. In keeping with the times, he joined a typical thrash-and-burn style Hard-Core band called Deep Wound in 1983. When the band dissolved, Mascis and guitarist Lou Barlow decided to continue on, with a drummer named Patrick Murphy (a.k.a. Murph). With Mascis switching to guitar and Barlow to bass, they became Dinosaur, which was almost too honest a betrayal of their FM Rock roots. Over sprawling beds of distorted guitars, and Mascis's almost wistful-sounding vocal delivery, Dinosaur made a unique impression during that whole transitional era between Hard-Core and "alternative," when so many bands were stylistically pushing the envelope, from the Butthole Surfers to the Meat Puppets to Sonic Youth.

In 1985, another Western Massachusetts native named Gerard Cosloy, who'd recently relocated to New York to start a record label, Homestead, made Dinosaur one of his first signings. Cosloy was one of the pivotal figures in the evolution of the American indie scene. He'd done a college radio show at U-Mass. in Amherst, and before he was even twenty, his fanzine, *Conflict*, competed with *Forced Exposure* (to which he also sometimes contributed). An avid Punk Rock fan and record collector, he'd amassed a sizable network of connections by the time he moved to New York. This would enable him, several years down the road, to found perhaps the most successful "indie" label of the '90s, Matador. Dinosaur's debut had good company on Homestead's roster alongside such underground luminaries as Sonic Youth, as well as the first recorded evidence of the Seattle sound in the form of Green River (Cosloy had wisely signed them earlier that year).

Shortly after the album was released, a group of actual dinosaurs, called *the* Dinosaurs and led by former Grateful Dead lyricist Robert Hunter, demanded that the group change their name. Since they'd already established somewhat of a reputation on the underground by that time, Mascis compromised and added a "junior" to their name. Just as Sonic Youth would extend a helping hand to Nirvana a few years later, the New York scenesters also played Big Brother to

Dinosaur, Jr. Recording for SST at the time, SY persuaded the label's leader, Greg Ginn, to listen to Mascis's mangled guitar structures and drawling ambivalence. Fortunately, this kind of almost "retro" sensibility fit in perfectly with the direction SST Records was heading at the time. The pioneering label, which was partly responsible for Hard-Core, was also the first one brave enough to start exploring the boundaries beyond that ultimately limited genre. With such bands as the Meat Puppets, Husker Du, Sonic Youth, and the second incarnation of Black Flag, they helped expand the whole musical language of American indie-Rock, thus enabling Nirvana and their ilk to become a reality.

J. Mascis's persona—a shrug-shouldered, un-intense mopiness—helped define the essence of "slacker." He wasn't "emotional;" he was detached, sitting in the room of his father's house, strumming his guitar, loading bong hit after bong hit as he practiced the Neil Young songbook. Lou Barlow wasn't much different, only Barlow hadn't even been to college. He was Rock n' Roll all the way, even if he looked like an owlish suburbanite. In many ways, it was Barlow, along with Jad Fair and Steve Albini, who was the prototype for the whole "nerd" preoccupation of the post-everything era. By the late '80s, it was no longer a stigma to be a "nerd." As the desktop/Internet revolution would prove, the nerds were winning. And when the girls began believing this, guys like Barlow would clean up. However, at that time, he was just another depressed, lonely postteen with a romantic streak.

SST was able to extend the group a better budget than Homestead to record their next album, and the result was *You're Living All Over Me*, inarguably Dinosaur's—and J. Mascis's—masterpiece. Producer Wharton Tiers defined the sound of the times, multitracking layers and layers of riffed-out distorted guitars with Mascis's drawl emanating out of the mist. When Nirvana recorded *Nevermind* a few years later, producer Butch Vig would pull a similar trick for them.

The new indie-Rock was girl-friendly. That was an element that Rock had been losing throughout much of the '80s. Punks were just so damn ugly with their shaved heads. Then again, the pretty boys who passed themselves off as "Rock stars" in the '80s looked, and sounded, like eunuchs. By contrast, Mascis and Barlow came off as regular guys. This is the way it's always been in Rock— the guys down the street playing in the garage are always the truest exponents of the form. Like the Seattle bands, a band like Dinosaur, Jr. had no ulterior motives for playing music, other than that it felt good. At the same time, they couldn't escape their fate as children of the '80s—they saw the world through a detached, cynical perspective, and their senses had been dulled. Now it was time to just explode into the moment.

By '88, Dinosaur had a hip buzz going, particularly in the world of college radio. But the next album (and last for SST), *Bug*, showed signs of communal rot. Mascis's trademark drawl had become almost formulaic, and while there were hooks aplenty buried in the songs somewhere, there was only one real classic on the album, the epochal "Freak Scene," containing the verse that perhaps best summed up the whole era: "So fucked I can't believe it." There seemed to be a lack of enthusiasm on the part of the band; underlying this was the fact that, at the time, there were tensions between Barlow and Mascis. Barlow was trying to spread his wings as a songwriter, and Mascis, in truly dictatorial fashion, was having none of it. Lou had been allowed one original on *You're Living*, and it was a loopy noise experiment of the type normally favored by art cut-up types. On *Bug*, he didn't contribute any original songs. Outside of the band, however, Barlow had been making his own "bedroom music." The results were the songs that would eventually make up Sebadoh's first album, *Weed Forestin'*, which was originally released as a cassette in true indie-Rock fashion (remember, that's how Sub Pop started).

But the final spike that drove an end to the partnership of Mascis and Barlow had to do with an age-old Rock n' Roll conundrum—women. Barlow had become involved in a relationship, and his sappy tendencies had gotten the better of him. Flush with true love, he became obnoxious, talking about sweetie-kins all the time. As Mascis recalls: "Lou was a silent guy. When he got a girlfriend, he suddenly started talking. He was talking all the time, and I couldn't stand him."

However, when Mascis finally flipped Barlow from the band, his own music suffered. *Green Mind*, the next Dinosaur album and the first for a major label, Reprise, had Mascis basically doing a Stevie Wonder/Prince and recording all the tracks by himself because he apparently felt that no one else was capable of getting the right feel (although the stalwart Murph did appear on three cuts). Producing music in such a vacuum ultimately leads to sterility, and that's exactly what happened to Dinosaur, Jr's music in the '90s. J. has seemed to rediscover his Rock n' Roll roots of late, however, performing in an active

touring band called the Fog with ex-Stooges guitarist Ron Asheton and garnering rave reviews.

In the meantime, Barlow formed Sebadoh with someone named Eric
Gaffney. Right from the start, Barlow aimed to keep the band a more democratic
operation than Dinosaur had been. Whereas Mascis had maintained absolute
dictatorial power, Barlow allowed his bandmate Gaffney equal time (even
though, conceptually, the band was entirely Barlow's vehicle). Although Barlow
eventually matured into a capable tunesmith—some would say a better one than
his former bandmate, Mascis—Gaffney was more or less a Punk and a crank, a
noisesmith whose songs ruined the flow of any Sebadoh LP. The first album on
which their sound actually began to resemble anything even vaguely coherent
was *Smash Your Head on the Punk Rock*, their maiden effort for Sub Pop. Even
then, there was a lot of down time on the album, mostly due to Gaffney, whose
contributions like "Cecelia Chime in Melee" were inexorable train wrecks of
inchoate white noise. The guitars, on the other hand, were sinewy,
gnawing…insect noise! The covers—Nick Drake, the Byrds—betrayed their
ultimate folkie influence. In a few years, Barlow would have a side project called
Folk Implosion. Barlow's reflective poeticism made him a kind of Hamlet figure
on the underground scene. The girls were all saying: "Why is he so lonely? He's
so *cute! I'd* go out with him!" And there stood Lou frozen in a stoned soliloquy
saying things like: "There are no excuses—bitterness must not take hold."

Barlow's romanticism permeated every inch of Sebadoh's existence. This
endeared Sebadoh not only to boy fanzine editors who felt fucked up about
their sexuality, but *girl* fanzine editors as well. A lot of people on that scene
thought of Sebadoh as the band. One group they definitely influenced was
Pavement. Others like New Radiant Storm King and Purple Ivy Shadows
copied not only their whole indie-geek posture—or lack of it—but also the
whole hard/soft dynamic. If Barlow accomplished anything, it was exorcising J.
Mascis completely—by '92, among hipsters, Dinosaur was out, and Sebadoh
was definitely *in*. This didn't help Lou, who was still in search of his mythic
babe: "I dream of a goddess I admire and trust/To deal with my neurosis and
satisfy my lust."

On the next album, *Bubble and Scrape*, the guitars had become more Neil
Young and less Slint, but the band as a whole still had a hard time getting a
coherent message across. Or getting out of a song, even a good one like

"Bouquet for a Siren," which was ruined by a *bad* ending, the ultimate anti-Rock statement, I suppose. Bands like this really *were* "indie," or maybe just naive: they didn't understand that they were only shooting themselves in the foot by putting all this unlistenable crap on their albums—especially if, like Sebadoh, they'd previously proven that they were actually capable of writing decent material. They didn't realize that, as the Rock of the day, their work was later going to be analyzed, be taken seriously. They were just fucking around. Far from getting credit for having any artistic vision, they should be considered chumps who got lucky. A perfect example is the way they ruined a perfectly good album by tacking on an absolutely worthless song—drummer Jason Lowenstein's "Flood"—after what should have been an obvious side-closer, Barlow's "Think (Let Tomorrow Bee)." This was another indie trick—just to be sure you didn't think they were wimps or, worse yet, *lightweights* (all that talk about "love" be damned).

What's love got to do with it? Nothing. In another year's time, Gaffney was flipped as unceremoniously as Barlow had been from Dinosaur. History repeated itself, but at least Barlow didn't seem to be predisposed to the same kind of narcissism as Mascis, and Sebadoh actually continued to improve. *Bakesale*, from '95, was pretty damn near a masterpiece. Even Lowenstein had learned to write, but the album, good as it was, proved to be the band's creative peak before they retreated into the calmer—and more lucrative—realm of corporate whoring.

A band like Yo La Tengo gave whole new meaning to the term *college Rock*. Because they were so old, it was more like professor Rock, and with all their obscure covers and arcane reference points, they were in a way admonishing the kids and rubbing their indie-geek credibility in their faces. Given frontman Ira Kaplan's Rock critic background, they qualify as "Rock critic Rock" as much as the Angry Samoans. A Lou Reed look-alike/sound-alike, Kaplan played a mean distorted guitar, and his wife, Georgia Hubley, played drums à la Moe Tucker. Although they began pressing their own little homemade records from their home in Hoboken, New Jersey, they finally reached a stage, like all successful indie-Rock bands, at which the records stopped being little fuck-off projects and became something more legitimate. For Yo La Tengo, that point occurred with the release of *May I Sing with Me?*, which was at least as good as *Loaded*—that is, if you take away the musical imagination it took to actually *be* the Velvet Underground in the first place. Like their fellow thirtysomethings Sonic Youth, Yo La Tengo were able to incorporate feedback in an original manner, as opposed to merely producing noise for noise's sake. As a guitarist, Kaplan was never content to just pound chords; he actually put his instrument through provocative mutations. When Yo La Tengo finally nailed down a semipermanent line-up of Hubley, Kaplan, and bassist James McNew, they became improvisers to be reckoned with, turning concerts into enrapturing dronefests that went on for hours.

Existing on the same plane of indie infamy as Yo La Tengo was Olympia, Washington's Beat Happening. Whereas Yo La Tengo was urbane and sophisticated, Beat Happening was purposely childlike and primal—if any band personified the whole D.I.Y. aesthetic in those days, it was Beat Happening. Leader Calvin Johnson had founded K Records to put out his own odd little records and also nurture other similar naifs. Another record label that was a spinoff of a fanzine, K became the bastion of something that loosely got termed "love Rock"—giddy, guileless songs about very primal romantic urges. There was a heavy sexual element, but also a nursery rhyme quality. Johnson's approach was the next step beyond Jonathan Richman in terms of pure ginchiness, but whereas Richman had abandoned his Rock n' Roll sensibilities, Beat Happening always maintained a great thrashing Velvets-like quality throughout almost all of their simplistic songs like "Look Around," "Knick Knack," and "Other Side." When Johnson put the tiddlywinks down for a moment and reached inside his dark heart, he was capable of truly stunning work. Songs like "Cast a Shadow" and "Redhead Walking" were right up there with Lou Barlow's stuff in the annals of modern love songs—they were the first ones in a long time to say something other than "love bites."

If Beat Happening was childlike, Half Japanese was *infantile*. Such was their charm as well as wisdom. Formed in Detroit in the mid-'70s by brothers Jad and David Fair, Half Japanese adhered to the whole dumb-ass *Creem* magazine mentality of junk culture, Punk Rock, professional wrestling, and do-it-yourself, be it homemade horror flicks made with hand-held cameras or songs based on one chord. There were hundreds of bands like this during that era, but very few of them released a three-record set as their first offering like Half Japanese did with *Half Gentleman, Not Beasts*. Even as an ultra-underground self-produced indie record, it was a pretty bold move—three albums of absolute *din*: no chords, no song structure, untuned instruments, Jad's adenoidal vocals, and parodies of current Rock songs…parodies that adhered not even ever-so-slightly to what the songs actually sounded like. Half Japanese were smart, however—their amateurishness was so unabashed that it actually got them noticed, primarily by the big-name Rock critics who'd become disillusioned with the more ornate structures—and power structures—of contemporary Rock. Both Lester Bangs and Richard Meltzer gave thumbs up to *Half Gentlemen*. But it wasn't as though Half Japanese could actually take the ball and run with it, so to speak. It took 'em about six more years to learn to play their instruments at all. During that time, the band became a free-floating assemblage of various scenester types including Don Fleming, whose own well-sparked imagination matched the Fair boys'. They made friends with Moe Tucker and, like a hundred other bands at around the same time, saw themselves as the self-appointed torchbearers of the Velvets. In the end, what Half Japanese offered was almost as rich and inspiring. It was also original in a way that couldn't be said about most of the other bands of this era. *Charmed Life*, their absolute magnum opus, while still primitive, was a heartfelt evocation of the American spirit that combined the best aspects of vaudeville, Hank Williams, Rockabilly, the Velvet Underground, Free-Jazz, the Stooges, the Modern Lovers, and the Shaggs (the whole century, in other words).

Superchunk was another interesting case—although their buzzing guitar sound and Mac McCaughan's hollering vocals tended to grate after a while, no one could deny their integrity. Coming out of Chapel Hill, N.C. at a time when the industry had zeroed in on the town as a potential replacement for Seattle as an alt-Rock Mecca, they stuck to their guns even as several major labels dangled that carrot before their somewhat bunnylike noses. They could've possibly signed for major bucks during the years '91–'93, but McCaughan and bassist Laura Ballance were determined to do it their way. Sporting more integrity than any band this side of Fugazi, Superchunk continued to record for their own imprint, Merge, long after it was necessary. It paid off when the label grew into one of the more formidable indies, a legacy that remains to this day. For a one-time slacker like McCaughan, who wrote his most famous song, "Slack Motherfucker," about some yo-yo at Kinko's who screwed him by walking off the job, this may have been the ultimate vindication.

Indie-rockers were allowed to thrive—although not necessarily make any money—because, at least for a while, no one paid attention to them anyway. In the early years of indie-Rock, distribution was hard to come by because most distributors considered it a risky venture, especially after the demise of Rough Trade in the early '90s. The original Rough Trade emerged out of England during the Punk era, first as a record store and then an independent label. Sometime in '83, the shop divested from the label altogether, which freed them from culpability and allowed them to eventually expand into a chain of record stores with outlets in Paris and Tokyo. A record label remained in name only, but it asserted its influence upon a large number of independent labels, judging by the huge number of indie albums in the '80s that bore its imprint. One of their tactics as a distributor was to usurp another label's copyright of an artist's work. Being in the situation a lot of indie groups and labels were at that time, the other label would basically have no choice but to comply. The Butthole Surfers were one example; Galaxie 500 was another. Eventually the whole network collapsed, but as Rough Trade had also ventured into music publishing, a lot of copyrights remained in limbo. Galaxie 500, for instance, had to literally buy back the rights for their own songs from the auction block. In the end, the name "Rough Trade" got redistributed amongst a variety of labels and companies, many of which are still in operation.

At that time there was still virtually no interest from the majors. The reason for Rough Trade's dominance was simply acquiescence on the part of the mainstream. Nevertheless, it was a genuine Renaissance period as far as creativity went, and while it was becoming increasingly clear that there was actually nothing new under the sun, there were infinite *variations* on old formulas. A perfect example was Mark Kramer, the proprietor of Noise New York, the studio he owned in tandem with his record label, Shimmy Disc. Kramer's an important figure as far as helping sway the sound of independent music back toward a more drug-oriented sound (as opposed to the rigid lock-step of Hard-Core). The bands that recorded for Shimmy Disc—Bongwater, King Missile, Galaxie 500— were decidedly cerebral. As a producer, Kramer—who supposedly smoked an epic quantity of marijuana—was fond of reverb. He was also a student of the '60s: in 1992 he recorded *Guilt Trip*, his own three-record homage to George Harrison's excessive *All Things Must Pass*. Kramer was an active member of Bongwater, along with the actress/performance artist Ann Magnuson. This was a real turning point of '80s consciousness, when Magnuson could be on a successful network TV show (*Anything But Love*) and simultaneously be in a group called Bongwater. Packed with social commentary and full of swirling embryonic textures, the group were the best of their breed since vintage Mothers of Invention, and Shimmy Disc automatically established itself as purveyors of a hip new brand of doper cool for the emergent slacker culture.

This kind of hipster elite also included King Missile, perhaps the quintessential arty-snotty Lower East Side band circa the mid-'80s. With tie-ins to the whole "poetry slam" phenomenon, as well as performance art (Magnuson again), Missile never seemed as much an actual Rock band as much as an art-literary "project"(despite the membership of at least one admittedly excellent musician, guitarist Dave Rick). Their singular pretentiousness could be more or less accredited to their pompous leader, Jon S. Hall, a pretentious twit whose sophomoric utterings were actually mistaken for "visionary" by many naïve college students at that time. Anyone familiar with Missile's output knows the real bright light of the group was co-conspirator and fellow literary aspirant Stephen Tunney, a.k.a. Dogbowl, who wrote the all-time best S&M opus, "In Margaret's Eyes." This kind of eminence no doubt threatened Hall, and there were tensions within the group immediately. Like Cale/Reed in the Velvets and Ferry/Eno in Roxy Music, it was inevitable that a band could only carry two such fragile egos for so long, so Dogbowl soon departed. That left Hall free to pursue even more sophomoric mock-songs about Jesus and a detachable penis, while Dogbowl shined with a delightful solo opus called *Tit* (*an opera*). Perhaps the prototypical Shimmy Disc venture, it was full of swirling textures and eclectic musical embellishments from harmonica and sleigh bells to Hawaiian guitar and French horn, not to mention lyrics like "I have a hole in my pocket/And when it's unfolded it's bigger than the state of Texas."

They came and went fast in the world of indie-Rock, mainly because it was hard to remain steadfast with so little support from the industry at large. As the Rough Trade fiasco had proven, all the indie labels were extremely vulnerable, which meant that bands were even worse off. A group may be lucky to finally find a label willing to put out their little homespun treasures, only to have the label go belly up just on the eve of pressing the first two thousand copies of their single. This meant a lot of indie-rockers merely grew tired of the Rock grind and went back to college.

If "alternative" Rock was going to supplant dumb-ass MTV Rock, there had to be a solution. That ultimately meant that "alternative" Rock had to *become* dumb-ass MTV Rock—which it did with Nirvana, Hole, Pearl Jam, Stone Temple Pilots, Jane's Addiction/Porno for Pyros, and Green Day, among others. Before that, the indies were able to maintain their distance quite effectively, through the efforts of the fanzines and college radio. Absurd underground bands like Don Fleming's Velvet Monkeys were able to achieve legendary status via coverage in mags like *Forced Exposure*. There was definitely a sardonic quality to this, borne out by things like Fleming's statement that the Velvet Underground and the Monkees were "the two greatest bands of all time" (hence Velvet Monkeys). Or the fact that a band named the Moles wrote the song they imagined the Beatles would have, "What's the New Mary Jane," based on the title of an oft-circulated but seldom heard *Let it Be* outtake. Or that a band called Happy Cat wrote a song called "We'll Fuck You Like Superman," a phrase based on a quote Paul McCartney once made in a British underground paper in the late '60s called *The Rat*. Who would know about such esoterica other than those who literally "studied" Rock n' Roll? In the '90s, Rock became a major field of anthropological research.

Whether it was something the average kid in Tuscaloosa could get a grip on, who knows? What if Cobain and company had never come along? Would the scene have continued to just keep fragmenting into these little pieces? That might've been good, because all the "grunge"/alternative revolution accomplished was prolonging the inevitable—that Rock n' Roll would eventually run out of steam. In the meantime, the indie bands were figuring out that the best way to make a name in the increasingly fragmenting world of the "underground" was to go against the grain of what had already been against the grain to begin with—an alternative to the "alternative," in other words.

This kind of au contraire stance gets difficult after a while. If there really *was* such a thing as an alternative to the alternative, it was in the hands of ultra-obscure labels like Majora, Twisted Village, and Forced Exposure. These vessels weren't trying to slowly ingratiate themselves into the mainstream à la Sub Pop or Matador; rather, they were hell-bent on seeing what they could get away with—which meant releasing albums that no one else would touch with a fifty-foot hose. In this sense, these labels were the true inheritors of the whole ESP/International Artists tradition. Majora, for instance, operated out of someone's back room in Seattle, Washington, and their star attraction, the Sun City Girls, had been releasing cassettes of their pure weirdness since 1982. Their magnum opus was '89's *Torch of the Mystics*, a completely twisted mélange of Arabic music and ultra-weird experimentation. They played up their whole reputation as misanthropic independents whose music was so far beyond the masses that it was pointless to even try to sell it in the conventional way. Spinning their records off at the rate of whenever it struck their fancy, they were—like tapehounds before them—documenting virtually every stage of their existence. They sure didn't waste the money on promo. As a result, the albums and CDs all came in ornate handmade sleeves designed by either the band or their artiste buddies. It was a very personal thing, and it was also somewhat elitist. Unlike "underground" music in the past, the message wasn't that this music required a higher level of commitment on the part of the listener— the message was, don't bother, because you probably wouldn't understand it anyway, asshole.

Despite such elitist pretenses, it was hard to doubt the integrity of musicians who basically turned their backs on anything to do with the broader spectrum to pursue art for art's sake. In the case of Crystallized Movements, another husband–wife team, this time from Connecticut, albums like *This Wideness Comes* and *Revelations from Pandemonium* were well-executed Punk-psych ramble (despite the penchant of guitarist Wayne "Duane" Rogers for playing the exact same solo on almost every song). The Corwood label in Texas existed solely to document the insane Folk-drone-psych ramblings of the mysterious Jandek, who satisfied the indie crowd's thirst for self-imposed obscurity by refusing to reveal his true identity while releasing album after album from the nexus of his living room. To the purists, this made him the ultimate "artist," because his "art" was his only identity. There were none of the trappings of "personality"—or, worse yet, celebrity—to go along with it.

Perhaps the most positive development to come from the indie netherworld was the gender equality that resulted from having male and female musicians interacting together on such a grand scale. In the '90s, Rock became a cauldron for the psychosexual meltdown of the age, a litmus test for male/female equality (intellectual, sexual, or otherwise). It was the college thing again—that's where most of the band members met: either on campus, or as part of the whole postcollege "searching" process. In many instances, the search involved pursuing some kind of artistic endeavor, without necessarily carrying the promise of it coming to anything significant. Indeed, probably a decent number of prominent indie bands were merely vanity projects for slumming postgrads. But lo and behold, many of them actually amounted to something.

Some of the more notable bands sporting coed membership during that era included Sonic Youth, Superchunk, Yo La Tengo, Galaxie 500, the Pixies, the Breeders, Smashing Pumpkins, Smashing Orange, Hole, Beat Happening, Love Child, Butterglory, Tsunami, Versus, Bikini Kill, SF Seals, 11th Dream Day, Twig, Helium, Fuzzy, Bettie Seveert, Unrest, the Spinanes, Loud Family, Nightblooms, Stereolab, Madder Rose, Tuscadero, Veruca Salt, Velocity Girl, and countless others.

The inter-gender bands were inevitable. The heightened presence of women in all walks of life guaranteed this musical osmosis. Women have always made up a sizable portion of the Rock-listening audience; it was only a matter of time before they'd begin shaping the sound, as well as the vision, of Rock itself. When the floodgates opened, it provided not only a healthier dialogue between the sexes, using music as the medium, but an injection of some healthy female hormones into the pudgy, flaccid body of male-oriented Rock.

The presence of so many women in Rock also injected the music scene with a certain kind of vitality. What really separated these inter-gender bands from other female-inclusive bands in the past was that the feminine identity was coming to the fore. It wasn't just the neuter female musician like Tina Weymouth in the Talking Heads or Moe Tucker in the Velvets (or Kira Roessler in Black Flag). Music, like everything else, had become totally politicized and thus sexualized. That's not to say that every band that included females within its framework was making a sexual power play. However, it meant that if they wanted to, they could. There were just as many bands whose female members were equal partners as far as the songwriting and playing goes, but who chose to not necessarily make an issue of their femininity. Nevertheless, a Georgia Hubley of Yo La Tengo was obviously a lot more of an "equal" partner in her respective band than, say, Moe Tucker was in hers. Bands like Yo La Tengo, Sonic Youth, and Crystallized Movements revolved around husband-wife teams, which proved that the family that played together stayed together. In the '90s, being in a band became a common pastime for young married neobohemians.

The assimilation of the female in Rock was gradual—those early bi-gender bands like Yo La Tengo, Sonic Youth, and the Pixies weren't just flogging a dead horse, so to speak. This was an equal partnership, which could only happen when women not only interacted musically with their male counterparts, but infused the music with some of their own feminine identity as well. In a great deal of the early male/female bands, the male and female voices switched leads, like a perfect point-counterpoint dialogue. In the case of bands like Love Child or the Vaselines, this resulted in some hypercharged sexual chaos. The chick in the Vaselines waxed "I'm a real bitch/a twisted witch" with icy conviction. A group like Boston's Twig posed an interesting scenario—here was a *complete* role reversal of the Talking Heads/Velvets model, whereby the male in the group, in this case the bass player, was the token odd man out (literally as well as figuratively in this case). Somehow you got the feeling that he and others of his ilk, like the male guitarist in Bikini Kill, didn't really mind. Their bemused expression seemed to say: "Hey, don't *blame* me—I came to play."

Once the girly stuff came to predominate, there was no turning back. A lot of it hinged on a kind of noveau feminism that bordered on lesbianism, real or feigned. There were a lot of women celebrating other women, like Huggy Bear's "Aqua Girl Star" or Velocity Girl's "In Audrey's Eyes" or Lazy Susan's "Faith Has Another Lover." Who knows if they were all dykes? It didn't matter: it was ambiguous—they liked it that way. It was sexy to males, though, because it involved a preponderance of females cooing seductively about sheer femininity. A perfect example was Helium's "The American Jean," an incredibly sexy song celebrating the joys of being female in the U.S.A. and wearing blue jeans, rendered by singer Mary Timony in the "flat" vocal style that was becoming popular around the time. There was no question about Timony's sexuality, however—she wasn't making some big statement about feminism; she was merely celebrating her blue jeans like any other suburban mall rat. It was the hard/soft dynamic of the music itself that bespoke the song's inner sexuality.

The whole dynamic of having men and women coexist in a musical unit on equal footing charged the air with sexual tension; this was healthy for Rock music, which had been tension-free for far too long. Just when it seemed there were no more barriers to break down in the name of Rock, it became evident that there was still one—the sex thing. Within the next few years, every corner of our sexual psyches would be delved into, as if Rock had become some kind of forum for Freudian psychoanalysis.

The question arose: was it even Rock anymore? Musically, the prevailing influence on most of this stuff was the Velvet Underground. There were many reasons for this. For one, they were among the first to employ female members (Moe Tucker, Nico). Second, their association with Andy Warhol endeared them to college students, particularly the artier ones. Third was the fact that they were easy to imitate—through no fault of their own. Their use of dissonance and feedback made it easy for pretenders to disguise their lack of musicianship by evoking the lowest common denominator of VU musical appreciation. Then there was their appearance, which personified a kind of city street-sleaze that has yet to go out of style and is easy for starving musicians to emulate—just look tired, dirty, and strung out. One of the VU's big gifts was "realism," which earned them the admiration of several generations of Rock musicians. At least in their time, they personified the outsider ideal that most indie rockers aspired to. If, as has been suggested, the Velvets were twenty years ahead of their time, then it made perfect sense that in the '90s their music would become state-of-the-art. In the hands of bands like Yo La Tengo, Love Child, Beat Happening, Mazzy Star, Butterglory, Stereolab, the Clean, Luna, Spacemen 3, Trash, Smashing Orange, the Mistaken, and others, their influence was reiterated again and again. This was also the same period when the Iron Curtain was falling down to the sound of the Velvets-influenced Plastic People of the Universe, who had a very vocal fan in the person of Vaclav Havel, the playwright who eventually became the president of the Czech Republic.

The indie-rockers were actually the folkies of the new age. Like the original folkies, their scene revolved around the college campus, and men and women existed on the same intellectual/artistic par. The Folk scene in the early '60s was one of the few places where women stood on equal footing to their male counterparts, unlike the world of Rock, where women played an utterly subordinate role. The revival of the whole coffeehouse scene that accompanied the indie revolution only reconfirmed how much this new generation of affluent white kids had in common with their liberal Boomer parents. The indie rockers liked to sit around and discuss "causes," too—however, because it was the '90s, the cause was often something utterly solipsistic, which meant the issues involved were more personal ones...which meant feminist and sexual stuff. This meant we had to endure Ani DiFranco along with Bikini Kill.

It was obvious that the Rock community wasn't going to be able to ignore women for much longer. By the mid-'90s, they were asserting themselves in a myriad of ways. Fuzzy, a band from Cambridge, Massachusetts, in many ways personified the new role model: two fairly attractive chicks in the usual thrift store garb playing clever Pop tunes with the two mute male backup members. The whole name of the band absolutely reeked of the typical cutesy-girly stuff, not to mention the genteel strokings of their no-doubt liberal parents. "Warm fuzzy," after all, was a Mr. Rogers-type expression that evoked the maternal glow that keeps one close to the womb through his or her entire adult life, a '70s ideal for sure. Given this type of genteel nurturing, Fuzzy weren't without charm—their first album was a sparkling collection of '90s indie-Pop with chirpy female vocals, but if listeners were seduced by the cooing come-on, there was some feminist angst hidden within. Like a lot of songs in this genre, the whole *irony* was that the gossamer pop tunes actually contained sarcastic lyrics, mostly about the shortcomings of the male gender. A perfect example was Fuzzy's "Sports," which used baseball/football analogies—the domain of men, remember—to emasculate a would-be male suitor: "It's around you like a little ball/But forget it, you can't throw that far." Suddenly the intent becomes clear—it isn't a come-on after all, it's a completely penile-reductive salvo.

By the mid-'90s, there was no shortage of smarmy groups with pretty—and not-so-pretty—girl singers/leaders. As far as Rock 'n' Roll went, some of them were actually pretty good—in fact, at that time, they were generally a *lot* more interesting than their solidly male alt-Rock counterparts. Tuscadero is a typical example. The name referred to a female character on *Happy Days*, which was ironic in itself—increasingly, group and album names referred to pop-cultural reference points, especially ones grounded in "childhood." One look at the cover of their first album tells the tale—depicting a loose-leaf notebook, it had childlike innocence written all over it. But it was just a mirage, despite the inclusion of songs literally about *candy*. There was also a song about a domina-trix. "Just My Size" objectified the male with lyrics like "my friends and I will get together and trade"—male sex partners, that is—and "I keep him around as a spare date." "Dime a Dozen," which contained lyrics like "you were the biggest mistake I ever made/But I made sure you paid and paid," turned the table on the traditional macho Warren Beatty/Hugh Hefner philosophy: "good looking girls are a dime a dozen." But for all their venomous barb and bite, there were still inner-child-exposing paeans to mommy/daddy/childhood ("Nancy Drew"). One must wonder how mommy and daddy felt when they heard their daughters singing lyrics like "better fuck him before he's out of reach"? They probably thought it was a perfectly valid expression of feminist retribution circa 1995, being good liberals and all. This was a fitting legacy for the group that was the musical descendant of the Waitresses.

Whereas Tuscadero took their name from a '70s sitcom, Veruca Salt took theirs from the brattiest female character in *Willy Wonka and the Chocolate Factory*. More than any other band, they epitomized the essence of "chick Rock." This time the two girls up front positively exuded chicklike sexuality, as personified by their big hit, "Seether," which was the first song after the Breeders' "Cannonball" to get the "little girl voice" onto FM radio. In the video for that song, Veruca chicks Nina Gordon and Louise Post kissed, which made many suspect that they were lesbians, not to mention lyrics like "I'd like to shove her into my mouth." The drooling male fans knew better—the girls in Veruca Salt were all woman…and how! Their combination of wispy vocals and meaty macho guitars was, in many ways, the ultimate ironic statement. There was a reason their first album was named *American Thighs* in homage to AC/DC: the guitars had the same kind of ultrametallic bite. They could shoot straight, something no one could ever accuse Sonic Youth or Dinosaur, Jr. or even Nirvana of. Veruca's teeth-grinding riffs ("Victrola") were the ultimate metal parody, mainly because it was being rendered by these ninety-eight-pound creampuffs—and that was just the *boys* in the band!

The English division of "chick Rock" was perhaps even more explicit in sexual content—and even less musically inclined. Take, for example, Elastica, who had a big hit during the golden age of "alternative" with "Connection," which stole the riff from Wire's "Three Girl Rhumba" with a bit of X-Ray Spex's "I'm a Cliché" thrown in. This caused many people to claim that Elastica represented a revival of "New Wave" when all it should have really done was alert listeners to the fact that the band had a severely limited imagination. Nevertheless, the song became a hit on both sides of the Atlantic, partially abetted by an MTV video that depicted the female members of the band—singer Justine Frischmann (who was merely a third-rate Chrissie Hynde) and guitarist Donna

Matthews—tiptoeing through a field of naked boys. On the debut album, the band, and particularly Frischmann, fanned the flames of this perverse role reversal with songs like "Stutter" (which made fun of a guy for impotence), "Car Song" (which was about having it off in an auto), "Line Up" (which discounted the worth of male groupies), and "Vaseline" (self-explanatory).

Sleeper, a similarly female-fronted British band, was even more explicit. Their one great moment, which failed to even chart in America, was "In Betweener," which was the most blatant statement yet about role reversals in the '90s. The whole phrase "In Betweener" denoted a brief interim-fuck before the next dreamboat came along. At least, in this case, singer Louise Wener denigrated both sexes as she sang to the song's hypnotic strains: "He's not a prince/He's not a king/She's not a work of art or anything…" This was the perfect impasse in the whole '90s male/female thing…the battle of the sexes was declared a draw, and both sides lost.

Be it angry riot grrls or precocious brainy types, the biggest thing to happen to Rock in the '90s was women. The impact of women was so strong, not only on music but all of popular culture, that "feminism" of one form or another established the tone for the whole decade. Women certainly proved their power as a voting block, which directly resulted in a president whose wife was seen as the embodiment of the equal partner and self-empowered woman. The whole culture of the '90s was imbued with a feminine identity that also tied directly into the whole philosophy of the politically correct, which was originally an offshoot of radical feminism anyway. As far as Rock went, it seems absurd and somewhat condescending to speak of this kind of equality as any sort of revelation, especially considering the great advancements made by women artists in the two previous decades. However, when considering the Rock of the '90s, it's difficult to argue that at least the *visibility* of female artists grew considerably.

The new '90s Rock woman provided a whole new twist on the feminine identity. Even Madonna contributed to this, but if one goes back to the '80s, there were many other important role models. Tracy Chapman, a Black singer/songwriter who actually began her career busking for pennies in Boston, was in many ways instrumental for spawning the renewed interest in female Folk singers, if only because her first album sold an astonishing 3 million copies in the Dukakis/Bush election-battle summer of '88. Politically, her paeans were the usual liberal grandstanding, but musically she was important because she represented a return to the skeletal structure of the classic folk singers à la Joni Mitchell—an anomaly in the opulent days of Reagan/MTV. Her songs weren't that interesting, but at least they did represent a young woman voicing social concerns ("Fast Car"), which was to have a big influence on the next wave of female songsmiths, who not only explored traditional party politics but also the personal politics of feminism.

A perfect example was Suzanne Vega, a folkie who obviously came from privilege, attending the High School of Performing Arts in New York before finishing her education at Barnard (these '80s–'90s Rock ragamuffins always needed something to fall back on). In this sense, she predated just about all the other female noteworthys save Barbara Manning, who's about the only one in this survey who didn't come from an Ivy League background—and it showed. As for Vega, here was a legitimate female solo artist unadorned by producer's gimmicks. For instance, her first album was produced sparsely by ex-Patti Smith guitarist/Rock critic Lenny Kaye, which gave her vital "street" credibility. Vega's own tunes were skeletal, her persona that of the Greenwich Village waif/ingénue/urchin. Her use of a wafting monotone was a highly effective device that predated the "little girl voice" that became the trademark of '90s girl-Rock. Whereas the first album had been bare and skeletal, by the time of *Solitude Standing* ('87), she was decorating her songs with splotches of synth. After "Luka" became a fluke hit, Vega became a fashion victim and then faded away, but by then the "revolution" was right around the corner.

A good argument could be made that Barbara Manning's *Lately I Keep Scissors* was *the* prototype for the subsequent wave of quirky, eccentric female Folk-Rockers. Truth is, probably not many people heard it when it was released on a small San Francisco indie label, Heyday, in 1988. That doesn't take away from the fact that Manning was somewhat of a visionary. Whereas Vega was more or less a folkie-cum-commodity, Manning was an eccentric rocker whose tastes for the obscure matched that of most fanzine editors (she worked in a record store). Even when playing solo, she used weird tunings, and the songs were aloof and informed by such psych-Folk influences as Fairport Convention and John Fahey, not to mention the Velvet Underground, the Fall, Wire, Sonic Youth, and other brainy Punk rockers. An active member of the San Francisco underground, Manning was a key player in such groups as 28th Day and World of Pooh, prototypical hard/soft male/female aggregations. The ultimate "cult" artist, she never really broke the way she should have despite a stint at Matador, which was, by that time, the indie label with the hippest cartel. Nevertheless, Manning's guitar and vocal style would resonate for years to come in the work of others.

Still, one didn't hear the phrase "Women in Rock" on a mass scale until about the time of P. J. Harvey's *Dry* album appeared (1992). No wonder— Harvey, a chanteuse from England, was the most explicit yet in defining female sexuality in the new decade. Skinny as a twig, with an offbeat sexuality that could only be viewed as not the typical textbook version of female "good looks," Harvey delighted in twisting around the stereotypes that had previously defined the relationship between males and females. In this way, she was a liberator. The critics drooled all over *Dry*, and Harvey did plenty of drooling as well. The opening verse of the very first song was "oh my lover it's all right/you can love her and me at the same time." Was this a form of women's liberation? On the one hand, Harvey expressed a candor about female sexuality that was perhaps unprecedented. On the other, her insatiability ("come on boys let's push it harder" she sang on "Victory") merely pandered to a lustful audience. Actually it was somewhere in the middle—like Madonna before her, Harvey's whole routine showed that the new women's libbers were adapting to the more male-centric tenants of Rock/porno. As commonplace as that sounds now, coming off of a dozen years of Reagan/Bush it was a pretty headstrong formula. Harvey was saying perceptive things about sexuality—"Dress," for example, was a brilliant evocation of the way women feel trapped by having to constantly fulfill sex roles. But Harvey didn't sound victimized by this exploitation; she used it to empower herself. Like, "Take that, you *sucker*," then she shimmied like yer sister Kate, shaking her little A-sized rose blossoms in yer face from behind a retro '60s muumuu.

Which meant she'd never be mistaken for one Elizabeth Phair, who definitely preferred the vulnerable waif persona, albeit with a post-alt Rock twist. This was the feminine side of "college Rock," because it personified the young woman away from home in the big city for the first time experimenting with sex, which was something many people could relate to in the '90s—particularly college students. But Liz Phair was a paper tiger as far as female empowerment went—the only "liberation" she was forging was a new kind of flighty, callous, and ultimately self-destructive female behavior. This included not just the right to fuck whomever you pleased, but to stick your finger down your throat in order to maintain perfect waiflike physical structure. The message of Liz Phair's music was: "I like to fuck—I just don't like to fuck *you*." In her own way, the white intellectual hipster babe had become the ultimate high school cheerleader cocktease. The critics fell for it: when *Exile in Guyville* was voted Album of the Year in the *Village Voice* in 1993, Phair was on the cover straddling a pair of beds in a miniskirt humping a guitar, under the headline "Girls! Girls! Girls!" Obviously, feminism had come a long way since the days when the *Voice* was championing the bra burners of NOW.

Despite Phair's bravado, when it came right down to it, she waxed as vulnerable as female folkies had for years: "Fuck and Run," despite its risqué title, was the same old formulaic lovelorn lament we'd been hearing from supposedly "liberated" women all along—mainly that, for all their newfound sexual freedom, they still felt "unfulfilled."

Even Phair acknowledged this seeming contradiction. In an interview in 1993, she said: "No one ever asks me about my guitar playing. No one's ever fuckin' asked me about how I write songs. I have all these things to say about that, but no one cares, 'cause it really doesn't matter what I play on guitar. Even if I play really interesting guitar songs, the only thing they care about is what it's like to be an upper middle class cute girl with smart parents singing dirty words." [8]

The Females in Rock preoccupation spawned a whole breed of would-be chanteuses wearing their hearts, as well as their sexual psyches, on their sleeves: Juliana Hatfield, Lida Husik, Alanis Morissette, Meredith Brooks, Mary Lou Lord, Tracy Bonham, Jules Verdone, Heather Nova, and, ultimately, Jewel and Fiona Apple all added their own tortured take on sex in the '90s to the general medium.

The most celebrated female rocker of the era was Courtney Love, for obvious reasons: she was the widow of the martyred Rock star Kurt Cobain. Love's roots as a Rock 'n' Roll bad girl actually went back even further than that. Her own trajectory was the stuff upon which legends were built: daughter of former Grateful Dead roadie/acid casualty, Hank Harrison, she'd never gotten along with dad. Almost from the start, her rebellion against the pretense of her hippie upbringing drove her to explore any form of deviation. Sent to a detention center at age eleven for stealing a Kiss t-shirt, Love's future as a Rock n' Roll diva seemed predestined. She was adept at inflating her own mythos, too. This is probably how she ended up with a string of famous, or semifamous, Rock star boyfriends: Julian Cope, James Moreland (Leaving Trains), and eventually Cobain. It's also how she secured parts in movies such as *Straight to Hell* and *Sid and Nancy*. Unfortunately, in the case of the latter, she didn't get to play the role she was ultimately meant for—mainly that of the hydra-like Nancy Spungen, whom Rock fans worldwide would soon liken her to.

At that time, in the Northwest, the whole riot grrl/"foxcore" movement was breaking out. The inevitable thing for a restless female postcollegiate with not too much stage fright to do in those days was to join a band, so Love joined her friend Kat Bjelland's new band, Babes in Toyland (which, in typically self-aggrandizing fashion, Love later claimed she founded). Apparently, she was too much of an egomaniac, not to mention too undisciplined, at least at that time, to exist within a collaborative framework—that is, one in which she wasn't the center of attention. The inevitable thing for her to do was form her own band, but since, at that time, she didn't really *play* anything, she had to find some musically inclined cohorts. Moving to Los Angeles, she put an ad in that city's music free weekly, *The Recycler*, seeking recruits interested in playing a weird mélange of "Sonic Youth and Fleetwood Mac." The respondents included bassist Jill Emery, drummer Caroline Rue, and guitarist (and token male) Eric Erlandson. Love christened the band Hole, claiming she drew the name from the Euripedes play *Medea* (pretentious once again). She couldn't have been unaware of the sexual connotations of the name, nor the irony: was it making a statement against sexism, or was it actually a form of sexual exploitation in itself?

Hole's first album, *Pretty on the Inside*, was an unholy caterwaul influenced by everything that was going on in the world of "indie" Rock at that time—Sonic Youth, Mudhoney, the riot grrls, and possibly even the group whose career Courtney Love was soon to intersect: Nirvana. Yelling a lot, swearing a lot, Love was establishing herself as one of the most abrasive of the new breed of expositional female vocalists, and the band was a tangled mess of deconstructed high energy. "I'll be the biggest scar you ever had," she sang on "Good Sister, Bad Sister." Soon this prophecy would come true for one Kurt Cobain.

The second Hole album, *Live Through This*, was such a radical improvement over the first it was astounding. The songs were more structured, the passion and anger drawn into a straight line instead of a sprawling mass. There was a reason for this: by that time Love had married Cobain and been drawn into the same realm of major-label nurture, being signed to hubby's label, Geffen. During the recording Cobain croaked. This infused the music with a special significance as a kind of widow's farewell for the generation who mourned Cobain as some kind of antihero. Typical of her nature, even when Love was mourning her departed husband, she still waxed vindictive: "Someday you will ache like I ache." In "Violet," she belched out an admonition to all the wannabes who wished to follow her into the realm of MTV infamy: "When they get what they want/they'll never want it again."

Which is something you'd never hear from Lisa Carver, who preached "no mercy for the ne'er do wells" and once caused Courtney Love to have a hissy fit over the topic of cheese as they discussed the caloric properties of the dairy product in the pages of Carver's fanzine, *Rollerderby*. Carver exhibited her exceptional narrative gifts by portraying her own eccentric way of life as an irrepressible form of wisdom, something she'd done since her days performing as Lisa Suckdog. This eventually landed her the job she'd always wanted as kind of the Dr. Ruth of the "X" generation. *Rollerderby* was very influential: suddenly grrl-zines popped up all over, each one like an expanded version of a diary. In the case of most of them, one could argue, "Who cares?" Then again, because these zines were so achingly personal, they were ultimately a lot more fun to read than the dry interviews/profiles with worthless bands that filled the pages of most small-print manifestos. What put Lisa Carver ahead of the pack was that she refused to toe the party line, even during the most politically correct of times. In a debate with Bikini Kill's Kathleen Hanna and Cold Cold Hearts' Allison Wolfe over an article she ran about Chinese opera, she pithily explained her solution to racism this way: "Friendship is what breaks down racial fears and misinformation."

That's really what the whole fanzine network was all about—forging friendships and breaking down misconceptions about fringe elements. Because the fanzine writers probed the deepest corners of their psyches, they inspired other like-minded individuals to not only do the same, but to also perhaps feel like they weren't quite as alone in the world because their own particular fetish happened to be purple chiffon scarves from the 1940s or retro lunch boxes or whatever (there were whole 'zines devoted to thrift store culture). Because the feminist movement lent itself to the whole ideal of self-publishing, 'zines turned out to be an invaluable source of expanding the network of female self-determination. Before long, there were fanzines with names like *Bitch* and *Chick Factor*, and, eventually, web pages with names like Gurl.com. This translated to the literary success of such postfeminist writers as Lisa Carver, Elizabeth Wurtzel, Amy Sohn, Robin Shamburg, Courtney Weaver, and others, as well as a whole new wave of more challenging female singer/songwriters: Rebecca Odes, Jenny Mae, Diamanda Galas, Azalia Snail, Jean Smith, Edith Frost, Cath Carroll, Sue Garner, and Allison Faith Levy.

In the '90s, the new feminine identity was being felt in other ways. On television, shows like *Ally McBeal* depicted the newly liberated woman as one who fucked freely, leading to the ironic *Time* cover that equated the fictional McBeal with Susan B. Anthony. An inevitable result of all this female empowerment was the subsequent emasculation of the male. Sadomasochism, once utterly a fringe manifestation, suddenly became very popular. In the '70s, bondage gear had become less subversive; in the '90s, it hit the streets and runways. The whole "goth" thing, and the preoccupation with body piercing and body art (i.e., tattoos), was a direct by-product of the S&M scene. In the hip weekly *New York Press*, a professional bondage mistress, Mistress Ruby (nee Robin Shamburg) wrote a weekly column called "Whipping Post" in which she explained, "[To] be a good Mistress…you've got to know a little bit about human nature and the psyche. That's why most Mistresses have been to college or are Mistressing to put themselves through college. So here's the standard Mistress profile: an intelligent young woman with a wild streak who needs to make some quick cash in a nondemeaning, preferably interesting way. As a Dominatrix, you get to have that kind of excitement without getting your hands dirty. Then there's the illusion of power. Yelling at people all day seems a lot more dignified somehow than stripping and kissing some guy's ass as you're doing a backbend over his table, now doesn't it?"⁹

In a very telling statement, pornographer Diane Hansen described the appeal of female dominance this way: "Now we've had twenty solid years of feminism, of men being told, 'You're not doing it right, you're not satisfying us, we're angry, if you would *only* do it right we'd be happy.' I've been working in this field for years. In the beginning, the letters were, 'I'd like to fuck you, I'd like you to give me a blow job.' Then it started to be, 'I want to eat your pussy.'

Men were taught they had to eat pussy. And men, with their eagerness and their sex drive, would get into whatever it is the woman says she wants. In fact, they'd get into it so much that they give it to her *more* than she wants! And then she says, 'I don't *want* that anymore!' With women getting harder and harder to please, a lot of men are just going, 'I give up. You *tell* me. You *use* me.' And that's the sort of letters I get from young men now: 'Just take me and do with me as you will. Use me as your sex toy and get yourself off.' And then that relieves all that anxiety about pleasing the woman. Men have come to eroticize, for survival's sake, the woman's dissatisfaction." [10]

What Ms. Hansen was implying was that the appeal of sadomasochism in the modern era was inherently related to the manner in which men had been manipulated, by the media or whatever, to feel inadequate. Although some hard-core masochists no doubt enjoy having needles stuck into their nuts, or having an "X" branded on their warm and waiting fannies, the primary attraction of S&M is psychological. Perhaps it has something to do with guilt: Mistresses like Ruby claim it's always the most powerful male executives who crave the most degrading forms of torture. A corporate exec who laid off two hundred people on a Friday afternoon runs to his Mistress for his usual dose of bondage and degradation before returning home to the suburbs for the weekend. Somehow this treatment affords him the psychological clearance to continue pursuing the art of the deal.

It was one thing for a bunch of decadent freaks to get their jollies being humiliated by high-priced female sadists. It was another for a whole generation to assert their low self-esteem by embracing such lowlife forms as Hip Hop, Grunge, neo-retro Boomer envy, body piercing—not to mention an underlying level of cynicism and self-doubt that would get them instantaneously branded with the cultural nonidentity "Generation X."

Whereas all previous generations had more or less surpassed the achievements of their predecessors, the generation coming of age in the '90s found themselves dwarfed by the legacy of their parents, the Baby Boomers. Because the Boomers were the most voluminous generation ever, by the '90s, they totally controlled the cultural forum: media, and soon, politics (e.g., Clinton/Gore). The generation of the '90s—the "X" generation, as it were—couldn't escape this legacy, especially as the Boomers, a despicably self-aggrandizing lot, were constantly patting themselves on the back. This led to a serious lack of self-

esteem on the part of their offspring. When the Boomers should've been trying to raise their own kids' esteem levels and providing suitable role models,
they were trying to come to terms with their own "inner child." Their kids
would have to wear the brand of the "X generation," which basically said: "Our
generation ain't shit." Coupled with the social factors of the times, it guaranteed a generation of self-loathing, doubt, and anxiety.

The '90s generation was the first to whom the idea of the traditional
"nuclear" family meant nothing. With divorce and one-parent households on
the rise, the traditional grounding of mommy/daddy that all previous
American generations, including the Boomers, had enjoyed was becoming a
thing of the past. This contributed to the generally "lost" demeanor of much
of '90s youth culture. This was reflected in the angst of Rap as well as
Alternative Rock. Pearl Jam, among the biggest crybabies, expressed these
regressive tendencies most succinctly in their big hit "Jeremy": "Daddy didn't
give attention/To the fact that mommy didn't care." Whereas Rock 'n' Rollers
in the '60s like John Lennon, Bob Dylan, and Lou Reed had *rejected* those family ties, alt-rockers of the '90s were reaching out for something they never had.
Eddie Vedder was the product of a broken home. Kurt Cobain was the product of a broken home. Courtney Love was the product of a broken home. All
of the aforementioned, as well as a plethora of other '90s "alternative" bands,
displayed an almost debilitating lack of self-esteem, manifested most vividly by
Radiohead ("I'm a creep/I'm a weirdo"), Beck ("I'm a loser baby/So why don't
you kill me?"), Green Day ("I'm a user and a loser"), Alice in Chains ("Down
in a Hole"), and Smashing Pumpkins (Billy Corgan wore a "Zero" t-shirt in a
video and bemoaned "I'm just a rat in a cage!"). In the *Time* magazine cover
story on Alternative Rock/Generation X, Bonnie O'Shea, a student disc jockey at the State University of New York, explained the appeal of all this grum-
bling loser-Rock this way: "It appealed to me and my friends because our generation is so dead to the world. There's nothing waiting for us when we get out
of school." [11]

To a generation who'd had everything handed to them on a silver platter—
whose own parents had nurtured them to basically expect to be coddled, with
the whole legacy of Dr. Spock/*Mr. Rogers*/*Sesame Street*—capitulation came
easy. These were the Children of McGovern Voters! The defeat of McGovern
in '72 left a big scar on the collective psyche of the Baby Boomers. In many

ways, it can be seen as the main reason they turned away from social causes and turned inward (which meant basically that they became the greedy capitalists they'd decried in the '60s). It's also why they strived toward a politically correct hegemony that ensured that no one got their *feelings hurt*. Who were the main recipients of this prevailing wussydom? Why, their children, of course.

When said youths had to step out into the big bad world, they simply weren't prepared for the cold, harsh realities and blunt indifference of society at large to their coddled-and-milk-fed plight. This was Youth in Denial! It's interesting to note the preponderance of songs in the indie-Rock canon that expressed themes of sleep, which is the ultimate back-to-the-cradle cop-out. Twig sang "Singing in My Sleep." Veruca Salt expressed a sigh of relief that they could "sleep until the phone rings." Versus sang "I won't get out of bed today/I'll sleep my whole life away." Madder Rose blurted: "I want to sleep for a million years." Add to that the fact that Love Child, Beat Happening, and Deconstruction all had songs entitled "Sleepyhead" and that there was also a *band* named Sleepyhead, and you get the idea. At least Bongwater had the cool detachment to decree: "There's too much sleep."

Lying in bed with the covers pulled over one's head wasn't the only method of escapism purveyed by the X Generation. There was also a reversion to childhood and, worse yet, childlike kitsch, as manifested by the riot grrls who carried lunch boxes, wore hornrims, and peppered their speech with "like, like" and "y'know y'know." Add to that groups with kiddie names like Dressy Bessy, Huggy Bear, Letters to Cleo, Heavens to Betsy, and Bratmobile as well as a plethora of other indie-Rock bands who trilled in childlike fashion about their insecurities, if not their favorite ice cream flavors, and one could see where the frontier of '90s Rock led: back to nursery school! Tuscadero, another band with infantile leanings, even designed their album covers to evoke such childhood preoccupations as loose-leaf notebooks and cutout paper dolls, respectively. Boston's Twig—actually an excellent gender-swapping band capable of some genuine Velvet Underground-style mantra excursions—told the Boston fanzine *The Noise* about a "pajama party" they'd had with another band. In the good old days of the '60s/'70s, a "pajama party" would've translated to "orgy," but in the '90s, it meant just that—sitting around literally wearing pajamas with each one's significant other safely at arm's length, playing regressive games like "spin the bottle" and drinking soda pop.

Almost as a reaction against this kind of escapist fancy, maverick fanzine publisher Lisa Carver pulled the unthinkable "grownup" act of giving birth to a son in 1994. In contrast to what was going on around her, this action was a deliberate political act. The difference between Carver and many of her peers was that she came from a strictly working class background, as opposed to the Ivy League/prep school environs that the majority of "alternative" '90s cultural figures hailed from. As Carver herself explained: "I believe life is used time— at least a good life is. But the goal of Generation X is to get things for free, including time. And with this time that is all theirs, they sit in their room depressed, or in coffee shops talking about philosophical stuff that I can't believe anyone *really* cares about, or watching bands whose singers are just depressed and confused and mumbly as they are." [12]

Considering that indie-Rock had originally been an outgrowth of *Punk*, this preoccupation with childlike "innocence"—the opposite of Punk, in other words—left a bad taste in the mouth of a lot of the older denizens of the "movement." I recall in 1992-93 or thereabouts showing a friend of mine the Boston 'zine *Popwatch*. I liked the mag because I thought it expressed a certain vitality via its analysis of artists like Barbara Manning and Crystalized Movements. But my friend couldn't grasp it: "Eeeeh, it's got pictures of little *fishies* and stuff in it. What am I supposed to think?"

This wasn't exactly what the editors of *Forced Exposure* had in mind when they lent their praise to all this homespun stuff back in the mid-'80s. So, in 1993, the ultimate indie-Rock Bible called it quits. Thing was, by that time, editors Jimmy Johnson and Byron Coley realized that the whole distinction of "indie Rock" had lost its meaning, especially since stuff like Nirvana had entered the mainstream. There were just too many records coming out, and too many factions existed to even bother trying to come to terms with it.

Soon the alternative-Rock world would be shattered by an even more tragic loss—mainly, the suicide death of its theoretical figurehead, Kurt Cobain. The Cobain "tragedy" was symbolic of the whole state of mind of Gen X. Here was perhaps the most prominent X'er offing himself at the height of fame because he couldn't handle the "pressure" of stardom—the ultimate Gen X move. Not everyone was sympathetic, however. Once again, Lisa Carver: "I'm sad Kurt's dead because now I have to hear about him even more than when he was alive...My generation is trying desperately to be unacknowledged. They needn't fret so—I believe that's the one thing Generation X will succeed in doing. If Kurt Cobain really is responsible for homogenous clothes, pride at being a confused loser, and messy music I can't figure out a word of, then I'm glad he's dead."

The worst part about Cobain's death was that, as with G. G. Allin before him, it was the most predictable kind of Rock star croak crusade. Although he didn't actually die of a heroin OD à la G. G., he was a well-known user, as was his wife, Courtney Love. Heroin made a comeback in the '90s, which only makes sense, as it's a drug that provokes, ultimately, the denial of all feeling. It suited a generation with low self-esteem that aspired to nothingness.

This didn't just begin and end with heroin or meaningless music with mumbling lead singers and miserable lyrics betraying a general lack of self-worth. There was also a dumbing down of the mainstream culture due to the fact that, by the '90s, those in the industrial media complex (advertisers and the like) simply didn't feel that the youth were intelligent enough nor had the attention span for anything that wasn't strictly d-u-m-b. This resulted in ad campaigns geared around slogans for simpletons, like "Drink Pepsi—Get Stuff." Although such devices were partly tongue-in-cheek on the advertisers' part, the kids didn't know that. It was the prophecy of Joe Isuzu/ Mark DeCarlo come true. It was a proven fact that the literacy rate was declining in schools all across America. What did the educators do? Make the tests harder and discipline the young whelps that weren't a-studying? Of course not—they merely passed them through the system like so much prechewed mush through a garbage disposal.

It was becoming clear that a whole generation of copy shop employees named Jason with funny little half-beards wasn't exactly going to set the world on fire. Perhaps *Beavis and Butthead* was actually the most accurate portrayal yet of the '90s youth culture, but there was one problem—it was a cartoon, but in a way, in the '90s, all of life had become a cartoon, right down to the president (who did indeed "guest" on an episode of *Beavis*). And *Beavis* represented the triumph of computer-generated art and also of Internet commerce, because its originator, Mike Judge, lived down in Texas and sat home and fucked around with his Medi-Arts program while his wife worked to pay the bills. It was a '90s success story. Judge was actually part of the '70s generation, but the new stay-at-home method of creativity well suited a new generation with low esteem and a sluggish energy level who didn't dig actually having to be anywhere at a certain time, or interacting with other people.

Beavis and Butthead may have been fictional characters, but millions of kids could relate to their latchkey existence, because they undoubtedly did the same thing that B&B did when they got home from school every day—namely, sit in front of the TV, eat junk food, and say, "This sucks!" Ultimately, *Beavis and Butthead* and *The Simpsons* were the most accurate portrayals of American life on television since *All in the Family*—and they'd have just as great an impact. In a few years, you'd have *South Park* with even *more obnoxious* kids and even viler subject matter (like the notorious "Mr. Hanky" episode featuring a talking piece of doo-doo). With *Beavis and Butthead*, as well as *Springer*—which showed white-trash losers literally beating each other up onstage—"mainstream" culture had totally succumbed to lowbrow tastes.

In many ways, the kind of rebellion that once could only be satisfied culturally by Rock n' Roll had become part of the accepted norm (i.e., television). In other words, what were once vices were now habits. Rock 'n' Roll, by definition, had become merely a memory. Not to say there wasn't a fresh new generation discovering Rock 'n' Roll for the first time, but it's questionable whether the new heroes—Trent Reznor, Marilyn Manson, Korn, Eminem—really qualified as Rock n' Roll or whether that was just a tag that got put upon them by the media operatives of the previous generation, for lack of a better word. Wasn't it only fair to let this new generation enjoy a culture of its own separate from the one that came before, just like the Boomers had? But that would never happen, because the Entertainment Industrial Complex had erected this *institution* in the name of Rock 'n' Roll—hence such monstrosities as the Rock Hall of Fame. Which meant that Rock 'n' Roll had been reduced to nostalgia, even though when Rock 'n' Roll originally came along, it was to supplant nostalgia—the Doris Day/"Que Sera Sera" brand o' nostalgia—with something that was totally, inexorably part of the here and now. Now Rock n' Roll, which was entering its fifth decade, was proving to be just as stubborn about letting the new generation get out from underneath its overbearing shadow.

MTV had already produced a protracted version of Rock and its past—by turning Rock n' Roll into mere television, it ascertained that the scum would rise to the surface. TV, after all, isn't a medium that lends itself to a bounty of philosophical insight or complex analysis, least of all a brand of TV aimed at the lowest common denominator (i.e., the youth faction). The whole advent of "music video" was the death knell of Rock as music, because it signified the juncture where its perpetrators became preoccupied with style over substance once and for all. The popular music makers of the '80s and '90s—be they R.E.M. or Puff Daddy—had to think now about what kind of "image" they would shroud their music in before they even wrote the music. Artists like these and other posers like Nine Inch Nails, Oasis, No Doubt, and Korn now purposely wrote what amounted to jingles—that is, in their heads they already had the videos planned before they wrote the "music." The music was secondary, and it showed. It was only a backdrop to the way they would act—or present themselves.

In this glossy but ultimately cynical wonderland, there was no way the Rock of the past—say, the "golden era" of, approximately, '56–'80—could help but appear not only brazen and heroic, but ultimately old-fashioned as well. Rock's past had become the stuff of legend: a mythic part of the cultural fabric that had been institutionalized with schoolmarmish precision by VH1 and the Rock Hall of Fame, as well as aging Boomer Rock critics who'd assumed tenured positions at all the daily newspapers by now. They all applied a curator's sense about Rock, mixing and matching the actual events and participants to fit a fairy-tale version of what actually went down. If one were to judge by the evidence presented by these institutions and others, all the "revolution" had amounted to was a bunch of yuppies in the suburbs taking their kids to soccer practice in their SUVs.

A program like VH1's "Behind the Music," a documentary series based on the confession interview style wrought by *Oprah Winfrey* and on production values learned from MTV, was a perfect example. Following the Iggy Pop story with Whitney Houston the next night, the producers refused to exercise any kind of judicious critical standard. To them, it was all Rock 'n' Roll.

On the other hand, all the neat little pockets of alternative culture now had the means to perpetuate the implications of their own private revolutions ad infinitum. As Rock 'n' Roll, traditionally, had always favored the underdog, this enabled the meek to inherit the Earth—for at least their allotted fifteen minutes of fame. It also allowed a few persistent little devils to rewrite history altogether—and thus, at least in their own minds, revoke what had become the established gospel. The quintessential example of this revisionist gestalt was the

complete vindication of what had heretofore been considered the worst element of the entire Rock age—mainly, easy listening—which was pulled off
almost singlehandedly by the independent publisher, Re/Search, in San
Francisco via their *Incredibly Strange Music* volumes. In the early '90s, cocktail
music was "cool" again. Or not "again"—for the first time: because in the original Rock n' Roll era, it had been anathema, all that was uncool, everything
Rock n' Roll was against. However, because the vanguard of Rock had emerged
as this totally dogmatic entity, thanks to the aforementioned neogranddads, the
fact that cocktail music was initially anti-Rock made it all the more embrace-
able by a new generation of ironic hipsters. This was the kind of groundless
rebellion postmodernism has ultimately spawned—embracing something that
was ultimately bad just because it was obscure. Are you getting the point? Rock
n' Roll, a phenomenon that should've lasted twenty years tops, had reached the
ultimate point of self-imposed obsolescence, whereby the only people who
cared about it felt the need to impeach its own manifest destiny.

The lounge revival gave rise to neolounge, the most notable example being
Combustible Edison, who shamelessly tried to ape the trappings of squaredom
past by donning Lawrence Welk-style dinner jackets, playing Hammond B3
organs, and taking on the identity of fictional lounge lizards like "the
Millionaire" and Ms. Lily Banquette (formerly Mike Cudahy and Liz Cox of
the band Christmas). As Cudahy explained: "I could see this vast underground…of people fed up with people being slobs and going home early. Rock
clubs are lousy places to hear music, you can't talk to your friends there, you
can't *drink* there for God's sake—the drinks are overpriced and badly made.
That's kind of what this Combustible Edison is all about, it's a lot more civi-
lized way of life." [13]

Among the bastions of "hip"—a realm in which Cudahy formerly
"belonged"—this postmodern redefinition was not cutting the mustard. Jimmy
Johnson of *Forced Exposure*, shortly before he gave up the ghost altogether, dismissed Combustible Edison as "Mike Cudahy's pathetic ode to cocktail
nation." This just proved that even among the denizens of the ultra-ultra-alter-
native, it was far from a unified rah-rah lovefest. *Forced Exposure* was different
from other so-called fanzines in that they didn't try to promote any kind of
"scene" unity—in fact, they actively discouraged it, testing friendships and,
when it came right down to it, making enemies, left and right. They saved their

ultimate derision for rival fanzine editors, like the ill-fated Mike McGonigal, who published the New York 'zine *Chemical Imbalance*. Even among the chosen few, no one was safe from the poison pen of Johnson, who admittedly maintained an ivory tower distance from the actual "scene"—you wouldn't see him in the mosh pit, in other words. Take Half Japanese, for example. *Forced Exposure* had been one of the most vocal champions of the archetypal American indie-Rock band. But when leader Jad Fair began rendering actual children's music, he became the magazine's latest whipping boy. This provoked letters to *Forced Exposure* from Fair's wife, among others. Making matters even worse, Jad Fair had actually worked for the 'zine before, as an illustrator. Fortunately, this didn't prevent jazz editor Byron Coley from appearing in the Half Japanese "documentary" *The Band Who Would Be King*, perhaps the *ultimate* ironic revisionist statement.

This kind of ultrahipsterism could occasionally backfire. A perfect example is the time Boston "underground" DJ—and Johnson cohort—Conrad Capistran attempted an on-air interview with the Boston devil-Rock band Upside Down Cross (formerly Kilslug). Capistran was a typical record collector type, but his smarmy—and somewhat elitist—pretenses were not welcomed by the almighty Cross, who humiliated him in front of his "exclusive" college radio audience. Months later, he was still fuming: "*Mmmmmmn*! I couldn't *believe* it!"

All it proved was, when confronted by the "real" thing (i.e., actual "punk"), the new indie generation ran in fear. But that needn't have been a concern for too much longer, because hipsters were finding out there were much more benign ways to assert their independence. If the Velvets and Stooges had been all but totally exhumed by this point among the nerd/record collector crowd, the next step was the Teutonic humdrum of Germanic "prog" groups like Can and Faust. This kind of cultural strip-mining also led to things like the *Theremin* documentary about Lev Theremin. Utilized by groups like the Beach Boys and Lothar & the Hand People in the '60s, the weird instrument had all but been forgotten when groups like Stereolab revived it in the '90s. In the hands of postmodern groups like Apples in Stereo, it was merely one more method of reliving Rock's glorious creative past, one more kitsch item, a step away from Combustible Edison's embrace of Ferrante and Teicher. It was all kitsch now. There wasn't going to be any "breakthrough" because, at this point, Rock had become a neoclassic form doomed to forever keep repeating its own history.

Nowhere was this syndrome more evident than in the endless stream of "tribute" albums that began materializing in the late '80s and into the '90s. Originally the tribute albums had at least some claim to cultish merit. When groups like Redd Kross and Sonic Youth decided to do an album entirely devoted to the obscure female Japanese pop-Punk band Shonen Knife, it was at least novel. But the sublime soon became merely the ridiculous—from obvious targets like the Beach Boys, Velvet Underground, and 13th Floor Elevators, it went to Donovon, the Sonics, Joy Division, the Rutles, and finally Lisa Suckdog. After there was finally a tribute album to Saturday morning cartoon shows (once again, the childlike stuff), Kevin Burke, writing in *Hub* magazine, perhaps put it best: "Maybe this should be the last tribute...of anything. It almost seems trivial, a tribute to songs that were never intended to be remembered, bringing what has sometimes been an ugly trend to a resounding crash.

We'd reached the point of post-post revisionism. With so much information constantly being fed to us, history was open to constant re-evaluation. This resulted in things like *Spin* magazine's laughable cover story debating which 1969 phenomenon had the greater, and longer-resounding, cultural impact— Charles Manson or Woodstock (considering what's gone down ever since, it seems obvious that Charlie won).

Another by-product of the regurgitated culture, besides overkill, was the fact that, as a result of all this fodder, nostalgia itself was accelerating. Even fairly recent trends were being hyped as "the good old days." Even worse, there was nostalgia for the nostalgia! An article in *People* magazine from 1999 celebrating the revival of the movie *Grease* proclaimed: "*Grease*: Twenty Years Later." But when *Grease* came out in the '70s it was in the form of nostalgia for the '50s! What we're talking about is nostalgia that's already twice removed. With this necro-culture in effect, it's easy to believe there's nothing that's new happening.

The effect of this on Rock 'n' Roll is deadening, especially as almost all of current rockdom has become basically a rewrite of the past, with the current practitioners slipping into their roles as if they were actors. This is once more merely a result of the proliferation of cultural fodder as a means of inspiration. It also has to do with MTV and the prevalence of TV culture, whereby slipping into roles becomes second nature and takes precedence over core creative instincts. The creativity of the contemporary artist now goes into trying to ape whatever effects from the past seem applicable. In any event, history seems doomed to repeat itself again and again. In this sense, the contemporary culture appears ghostly familiar, at least theoretically, to the previous era.

NWA is the Beatles. Prince is Bob Dylan. Michael Jackson is Elvis. Bowie is Sinatra. Lenny Kravitz is Sammy Davis, Jr. Henry Rollins is John Wayne. Gerard Cosloy is Ray Charles. Alanis Morissette is Melanie. Love Battery is Crabby Appleton. Fuzzy is Whyte Boots. Letters to Cleo is Chi Coltrane. The Donnas are the Runaways. No Doubt is Pat Benatar. Mercury Rev is Supertramp. Pearl Jam is Bad Company. Elliot Smith is James Taylor. Barbara Manning is Judy Collins. Sonic Youth—or Yo La Tengo or Belle and Sebastian (or Marianne Nowottny)—is the Velvet Underground. The Strokes are the Boomtown Rats. Alice in Chains is the Little River Band. Abunai is the Strawberry Alarm Clock. Nick Cave is Dennis Hopper. Liz Phair is Joni Mitchell. Steve Albini is Phil Spector. Fatboy Slim is Rootboy Slim. Weezer is Ray Stevens. Ryan Adams is Bryan Adams. Jerry Springer is Andy Warhol. Andy Warhol is God. Charles Manson is the devil. *The X-Files* is *Moonlighting*.

The only thing that was certifiably *new* in the popular culture of the '90s was the Internet. Bright kids with newly acquired technical knowledge but perhaps fundamentally limited resources elsewhere—particularly social skills—could command large sums of loot from fledgling corporations for the simple reason that no one else knew how to do their jobs yet. These were the kids to whom Bill Gates was a sage and to whom the mythology of the modern-day tycoon went something like: "He started in the garage with a box of semiconductors and a dream."

Voice mail, faxes, e-mail, chat rooms, desktop publishing, conference calls...the world was becoming an intertwined network of costly intrigue. A cultural war was building between the wired and unwired. Now more people than ever had an excuse to be antisocial. It was an easy position to assume when one worked seventy hours per week, which the average yuppie did in the '90s. Then there was the time sanctioned for the gym, and taking the kids to soccer practice. All of life was becoming preordained allotments of time.

It was coming down to *cubist culture*. The new workplace consisted of endless rows of boxlike cubicles—the arrival of the computer on every desk and its function as the universal mind negated the need for individual personal space. The American entrepreneurial spirit wasn't dead—if anything, the computer revolution helped revive the spirit of American independence and enterprise, not to mention helping to spawn the most robust economy *ever*. Now every kid with a computer who could afford his own server could set up his own business, thinking he was on the cusp of…the next phase? This was the essence of the "startup"—companies with low, or no, overhead run by unconventional boy-geniuses who stuffed their dirty socks in the top drawer because they hadn't been home to mom's in a week.

There's a good story dating back to the birth of Microsoft: programmer Gordon Letwin invaded sales manager Vern Raburn's office one day to meas-ure it, to make sure the rumors weren't true that it was actually *three inches* big-ger than his! With that in mind, one can see where the impersonal nature of all those cubes might come in handy to a company trying to avoid such interoffice carping.

By the late '90s there was no question that the advent of the Internet had helped further the means of commerce, of business, of free enterprise, which was of course the basis of the American spirit. As far as creativity went, there were different opinions as to the merits of the new medium. Ken Kesey, the former acid guru, may have been correct when he said, "So much of this Internet stuff is kids playing with paper cups and string."

In the '90s, the same kind of creative energy that a previous generation had applied to Rock 'n' Roll was now being applied to the Internet. Rock 'n' Roll, as it once upon a time existed, presented too much of a challenge, too much *conviction*, too much *energy* for the denizens of the Prozac Nation to muster the strength for. It involved pratfalls and pitfalls—it involved humping gear at some dingy club at two in the morning and playing thankless sets in front of eleven people. The core continued to do it, and still do—but it was no longer the only option as far as youthful methods of expression go. On the other hand, the Internet didn't demand any actual interaction with people—all it demanded was some basic high-tech skills, which would soon be the domain of every school kid.

The Internet affected Rock 'n' Roll through the new downloadable medi-um of MP3, whereby one could—for a price—gain virtual access to recorded music without having to physically "possess" it. Was this the future of record-ed music? Well, it was a nice egalitarian notion that now everyone who was capable of stringing two notes together could produce and promote their musical output basically for free. But did it really further the progress of the art itself? As critic Erin Franzman wrote: "The ease of CD self-promotion means that any band with 72 minutes of music and $1,000 can get their sound out there. Part of me loves the possibilities of this, but part of me wonders if it *should* be hard to get your music recorded: Then the people who make music would do so because they want it more than everybody else. When it's easy, like it is now—and like it will be even more with MP3s—we are flooded with art that is meaningless. The more we're inundated with emotionally bereft music, the more our society learns to devalue that art. It drags down our already slumping cultural standards, which, looking at pop culture, are depressingly lax. And eventually your precious music, that which you can have and hold, becomes that much more background noise, indistinguishable from street sounds or the vacuum sucking away what little creativity we have left." [14]

As we drifted into the twenty-first century, the raging debate in the music industry was over Napster, a downloadable music resource on the Internet that was virtually "giving away" recorded music through its website, which anyone could access providing he or she had the software. That is, until the industry figured out that this resulted in a massive loss of revenue. The whole matter is, as of this writing, unsettled, but one thing's clear: the downloadable music medium is not going to go away. The inevitable result is that the industry itself will harness the potential of the Internet—and make you pay for it. What this inevitably means is that the industry will soon make the whole process of record making intrinsically related to owning a computer, which will be another step toward the "central mind." We will bank on our computers, we will conduct commerce through them, and we will listen to music through them. Now that the labels have figured out that people can download music through sources like Napster without having to actually *buy* it, they'll surely devise a way to make that the *only* format available and charge people $88.50 for the "privilege"—in the form of software—to use it.

There used to be a standard to determine who could create art and who couldn't. At least one person, even if it was Morris Levy, had to decree that your "art" was worth putting forth to the world at large. But within the easily accessible domain of the Internet, whereby total democracy reigns, Rock n' Roll, self-expression, the *arts* in general, have become completely solipsistic—if a person thinks his "art" is worth demonstrating to the world at large, then what's stopping him? As long as he can afford a basic hook-up with an Internet service provider, he has free rein to express himself, despite the actual value of his chosen art form. Which, in a way, is the ultimate triumph of Rock 'n' Roll—bad taste wins in the end.

At this point, the culture at large has much bigger problems. What if all these computers—supposedly the solution for everything—fail us? There's also the theory that the Internet was created by the government so they could keep track of us. It's already common knowledge that, if a person is connected to the Internet, then he or she is already on the government's radar screen. Credit card info as well as other personal data flies around like death ashes tossed into an uncaring ocean. If the Feds *did* invent the sucker, what purpose would they have in doing so—save for reasons of commerce—other than to tighten the harness on society at large?

It's an intertwined network of costly intrigue: given the mergers that went on in the past few years—be it Time/Warner joining AOL or Disney's takeover of ABC—it's not hard to imagine an ever-shrinking world where Big Brother is not only watching you, but, as Richard Meltzer has written, he's charging you for the privilege. There's no question that with the global economy in place, there are increasingly fewer places to hide. There now exists a service—which is actually advertised on TV—in which, for a fee, a future employer can find out anything he or she wants about a job candidate just by obtaining a few basic personal details (like the ever-present Social Security Number, which really has become the Mark of the Beast). There's no such thing as privacy, because in the mind of Big Brother it's irrelevant. If you've got nothing to hide, you won't have to worry. As a friend of mine once suggested, pondering the Disney-fication and Micro-softening of everything: "Soon we'll all work for the same seven people."

If the government doesn't get us, the new age of pestilence might. There are some nasty new diseases out there: diseases without names, diseases that are resistant to the traditional course of medicine. Disease is alive and well in the new millennium—and the next Black Plague is right around the corner, be it in the form of anthrax, the Ebola virus, Mad Cow Disease, or even new, more virulent strains of age-old favorites like influenza and tuberculosis. Not to mention the rise of "adult" diseases like diabetes in children (mostly due to their shitty eating habits and sedentary lifestyles). The weather's out of whack also—

not only in the form of global warming, but also massive natural disasters. The world itself could tilt off its axis. As the world becomes a smaller place due to our endless web of mass communication, it certainly seems like a more threatening one.

There's always the potential that some nut is going to go fully off his rocker and take a few—or a few thousand—victims with him. In the '90s there was the Oklahoma City bombing, the Branch Davidian siege in Waco, the Unabomber, the World Trade Center bombings, numerous acts of airline terrorism, and of course the legendary Columbine High School killings when a fifteen- and sixteen-year-old, respectively, gunned down a random assortment of their school peers. Yes, they had a website. Increasingly, fear about such random outbursts—perpetrated by an overactive media—only served as a further excuse to sweep the Bill of Rights under the rug. We were living in a time of fear and hostility. It seemed that, more and more, people were turning to violence.

Then came September 11, 2001, and all of our worst fears were confirmed. All of a sudden, it became clear to millions and millions of Westerners that we were vulnerable (a fact that had apparently never crossed our collective mind before). America's global economic reach in the '80s and '90s had put the nation squarely in the middle of the affairs of other countries all over the world—but while the Third World was ready to devour our hamburgers, they weren't necessarily ready to submit to our complete cultural hegemony. In the Arab and Islamic world in particular, America's continued support of Israel marked us as a perceived evil that ultimately had to be confronted. For years, the United States had resided in its ivory tower, reasoning that our borders were safe because of an enormous military deterrent. But as the attacks on New York and Washington, D.C. proved, the desire on the part of the Islamic world to do harm to the United States transcended any logical considerations—which is what currently has Americans in the most fear of all. The subsequent anthrax scare that occurred on the heels of September 11 only reaffirmed the way that, without warning, an agent of terror could disrupt the flow of American society in a totally unprecedented manner. With so many threats lurking right around the corner, is it any wonder people are paranoid? So paranoid, in fact, that they're willing to grant their government enormous liberties in the name of personal freedom. But whatever mawkish displays of patriotism and of caring for one's fellow humans was invoked in the months following September 11 quickly became obvious for the kind of hypocrisy it was when one really looked at how Americans conducted their everyday business—which was with the same callous pursuit of me-first aggression that makes the Arabs—and other civilizations around the world—hate us so much. It was always interesting to note, as I walked the streets of the city where I live in the months following September 11, how the SUV that most aggressively tried to run me down as I was crossing legally at an intersection was the one flying the largest American flag.

But Americans had better take heed—no matter how many times we have to quash rebel camps, overthrow governments, and pay off Third World leaders in order to fight the amorphous War on Terrorism, it's important to note that, numbers-wise, the Third World population is multiplying at a rate of five to one over its Western counterparts. Which means that, even in the United States, as more and more immigrants flood its borders year after year, the concept of white hegemony will be a distant one. The whites will ultimately become the minority. In fact, in cultural terms, we're already seeing it happen as the prevalence of "ghetto" culture rapidly overtakes more mainstream Western values. Miscegenation, a concept that, forty years ago, put the nation at large in a state of fear, is now being flaunted on MTV. This new nation of multicolored kids is actually bad news for the increasingly Anglocentric field of Rock n' Roll. Rock's roots may have lain in everything from slave field songs to southwestern brothels, but the actual phenomenon of *Rock*—the one that caused the uproar, the one that made all the money—was primarily a white one. Which is why the multicolored kids don't care about it anymore. Go to any urban high school in the United States—the majority of kids listen to Rap, not Rock. Take into account also the increasing ranks of the Hispanic population and the fact that they too have their own music—a hybrid of Latino and Hip Hop sensibilities—and one can see that the cultural meltdown may be the thing to deal Rock its final death blow.

Then again, who the hell ever expected Rock n' Roll to last forever? As far as numbers of bands go, Rock n' Roll is still alive and well, but it just doesn't matter anymore. Rock n' Roll had its moment—probably during its first three decades. That doesn't mean that its current practitioners are going to curl up and die. It just means that the thing that made Rock n' Roll what it was—that effervescent flash that made it, at one time, this revolutionary force to be reckoned with—no longer exists. What its current practitioners are is neoclassicists.

So every band just mines a style that suits them ad infinitum—a style that's already been done to death by eight million other people. The necro-culture ensures that there's still a lot of shelf life in this kind of stillborn redundancy. Which is the whole essence of postmodernism: something's only significant in the way it *comments* on something that already happened before.

The '90s were the final triumph of consumer capitalism, which was perfectly tied together by the homogenization of all entertainment media. There is no more "music," "art," "politics," per se. They have all become interchangeable product selections at the entertainment superplex. As McLuhan noted in the sixties, the *medium* is the massage—everything else just comes down to preference. The solution? Same as ever: change the channel.

Lester Bangs wrote in 1970: "Personally, I believe that real Rock 'n' Roll may be on the way out, just like adolescence as a relatively innocent transitional period is on the way out. What we will have instead is a small island of new free music surrounded by some good reworkings of past idioms and a vast sargasso sea of absolute garbage." [15]

Thirty years later, that seems like prophecy, particularly the part about "reworkings of past idioms." Considering that Rock was less than twenty years old at that time and Bangs was already noting that it was getting repetitious, it's not difficult to figure out where it stands now. Rock n' Roll, a form of music that was supposed to erase all tradition and exist fully in the moment, actually became the most musty, stagnant, stilted cultural dead end ever.

Part of it is the Baby Boomers. Fully in control of the media, they must be held responsible for our continuing indoctrination. Popular culture became the religion of the postwar generation, and they've been just as dogmatic about it as their own forebears were about that old-time religion.

A poll taken in June of 1995 on the TV program *Politically Incorrect TV* asked a sampling of Americans what meant more to their everyday lives, the Bible or *TV Guide*. Only 33percent chose the Bible. Meanwhile, to believers it must appear as though the devil has already won, given the current cultural climate: terrorism, biowarfare, renewed nuclear proliferation, mass greed, moral malaise, political scandal, school shootings, miscegenation, rampant vagrancy, illiteracy, teen pregnancy, "art" that rivals pornography, pornography on demand (via the Internet), disease, natural disasters. Despite these social maladies, apathy is rampant, which begs the question: What if they gave an apocalypse and nobody came?

The Baby Boomer generation was the first to embrace instant gratification as the be-all and end-all. That's why Bill Clinton was the first Rock 'n' Roll president, and his whole "when in doubt, *lie*" modus operandi was the ultimate terminal-teenager proviso.

A generation grew up—and went to sleep in their rocking chairs. The legacy of the '60s continued to fade into the realm of myth and nostalgia. In the '60s there was a kind of amazement with the world, like "Wow, we're going to the *moon!*" Nowadays, with cynicism and fear pervading every corner of modern life, it would be, "We went to the moon and caught AIDS from a Prozac-addicted baby-rapist."

We are once more becoming a tribal culture. One need only look at the demographic makeup of any major city to see this. Whole sections of each town exist in isolated fragments consisting of one cultural distinction or another. It's not just differences of race; the population is being separated by socioeconomic factors as well. But the real divide is cultural: there isn't really that much difference anymore between popular culture and what manifests itself as high art. The pursuers of high art are the ultimate isolationists, because it takes a conscious decision to turn away from the trash culture that permeates (i.e., television). Elitism has its rewards, but in a culture where the lowest common denominator rules and rules, it is the equivalent of backing oneself into a corner. I guess this is what "Cue Ball" there in Smashing Pumpkins meant when he wailed, "I'm just a rat in a cage."

The culture that Rock was born out of came from a mindset that doesn't exist any longer. The basic urge to rebel is still there, but now the rebellion is aimless because the kids have nothing legitimate to rebel against. Their parents spoiled them, the school system coddled them, and the government didn't try to draft them. *These* are the things kids used to rebel against. Rap music at least was focused in its anger—for Blacks in the United States, there was still plenty to protest. But white adolescent rage—which is what Rock has always been based on—is an empty shell at this point. To a whole generation of self-doubters addicted to mood-altering pharmaceuticals, the enemy exists from within. The kids are their own worst enemy, and they're not even aware of the *real* enemy—which is the system feeding them all this crap in the first place.

A conversation I heard between two kids, one Black and one white, on the subway one summer afternoon in 1998 describes the fickleness of the current generation. It also illustrates their complete lack of any historical perspective. To wit:

"Who's better? Puffy or D-Mob?" the white kid asked.

"Puffy," said the Black kid.

"Puffy or Biggie?"

"Biggie," he answered carefully, pondering his decision.

"Biggie or 2Pac?"

"Biggie."

The white kid raised the stakes: "Biggie or Snoop?"

"Snoop."

"Snoop or Dre?"

"Snoop."

"Digital Underground or Run-DMC?"

"Digital Underground."

"What song did they do anyway?" the white kid asked.

"'The Humpty Dance,'" the Black kid said. (Surprising that he actually knew, as it had been a hit eight years previous, which is, of course, ancient history to these kids.)

The white kid resumed his grilling, switching to female performers: "Missy or En Vogue?"

"Missy."

"En Vogue or TLC?"

"TLC."

"TLC or Boyz II Men?"

"Boyz II Men."

"Oasis or the Beatles?"

"Oasis," the Black kid answered.

This is the *real* cultural war, and it's one that the Baby Boomers cannot win. Despite the attempts of the Rock Hall of Fame and VH1 to try to institutionalize Rock, once the Boomers die off, no one will give a damn. And the Boomers, approaching middle age, will soon begin dropping like flies, thanks to their self-indulgent lifestyles. In the meantime, the kids have spoken: Oasis...*better than the Beatles*!

As the artist Fred Tomaselli told David Grad: "The unreal has become far more powerful than the real. Virtual reality, computers, the Internet, movies, drugs, theme parks, malls, gene splicing and plastic surgery all play a part in the vast menu of artifice. I firmly believe that the present mutability of reality is one of the main issues separating our culture from that of our parents." [16]

Another way "the present mutability of reality" has affected Rock is that it has contributed to the vaudevillization of the form—that is, because of the mutability of reality itself, it becomes easy for a band to assume the posture of another age, and that's what most current attempts at "Rock" constitute. This is not a bad thing if one argues that Rock is a fundamentally limited genre and that, therefore, there are only so many variations on its basic form—which means that the only way to keep it interesting is not to expand too far beyond its limited musical and sociopolitical framework and, indeed, to evoke, if not another act from the past deliberately, than at least an *ethos*, a celebration of a kind of tradition. Most of the contemporary Rock acts worth their salt are in fact very deliberate, staunch traditionalists—they are aware of their influences and flaunt them almost like a badge of honor, be that Hank Williams or G. G. Allin. Rock 'n' Roll has become a subculture, the only visible form of hipsterism left in the world. So we begin again, anew, in the new millennium—with one hundred years of cultural surplus to pilfer. Rock 'n' Roll makes for an interesting canvas for hipster intellectuals and even a few legitimately disgruntled youths (like the Punk scene, which continues unabated even though it's been deprived of a purpose for the past two decades).

And once and a while, in the name of Rock, something spontaneous and exciting still happens...like what happened with the Strokes, a New York pretty-boy band who are the latest in a long line of contemporary New York groups to evoke the "golden age" of New York Punk. Bands like this have been playing in lower Manhattan for years—D Generation, the Toilet Boys, the Realistics, Electric Frankenstein, the Mooney Suzuki. All of these bands in one way or another pay homage to the glam-Punk tendencies introduced by the New York Dolls and all their subsequent progeny (except perhaps the Mooneys, who are more based in Detroit-style ethos but still count in terms of New York's Rock revival). But the Strokes are different because they also have a poppier tone, which has enabled them to become the darlings of this whole scene while their peers have sat back and sneered at how these Johnny-Come-Latelies could slum around for a while and then wash their hands of the whole scene when the bright lights of MTV beckoned. Which is about what happened—good band, good album on a major label (RCA, in this case)...influences: Television, Only Ones, Human Switchboard, Velvet Underground. A lot of hype, and with the help of MTV, the Strokes, who are tunefully benign enough, have a hit on their hands...

But everything's relative in the post-Hip Hop/corporate conglomerate environment...the Strokes may have sold a half million copies of their album at this point, but we're not talking Rolling Stones or Nirvana or Green Day level of success; what we're talking about is still basically a "cult" thing. And that's what Rock 'n' Roll of the rough-hewn variety (which is the only kind, after all) has come down to. So, as encouraging as it looks for guitar-oriented groups like the Strokes to be facing mainstream acceptance once again, it may be a false alarm. The culture of Hip Hop pervades, and it's hard to see a massive analog rebellion anytime soon no matter what the latest generation of hipsters hopes for. In the meantime, there are plenty of groups to feed the frenzy, and if the groundswell is real, that can't be a bad thing for the art form itself. But the Strokes are about as representative of the New York "Punk" underground as the Knack were representative of "New Wave" in 1979, and their success lately is about tantamount to the Knack's—only with one important twist: the Knack were *much* bigger. Their album went to number one, but that would be almost impossible now for the Strokes, because Rock 'n' Roll albums simply don't go to number one anymore, even those of the manufactured variety.

That said, the Strokes are a good band, and the backlash against them by the hipsters is a perfect example of the self-negating nature of Rock and the Rock audience in this day and age—I mean, people finally get what they've been asking for, which is a populist Rock band who have kept the music—and for that matter, the image—fairly simple and honest, and then, because they suddenly become *too* hip too fast, the hipsters turn on them. A lot of their detractors have claimed that the Strokes are just a gimmick band, mostly because singer Julian Casablancas is some kind of fashion industry prince...but that doesn't really make him that much different from a lot of other middle class Rock stars like Lou Reed or Jonathan Richman, whose parents weren't poor by any means. It's been a long time since Rock has retained the shit stains beneath the fingernails that it might've known when it first came in from the shacks of Hank Williams and Muddy Waters. The Strokes are as convincing an argument as any that rich kids can indeed rock, and the Velvet Underground-isms of *Is This It* are a perfect contemporary backdrop to post-September 11 New York.

But the Strokes were one thing—them being from New York, and on a major label, their success, while still surprising, was not completely unprece-dented. The White Stripes, who are enjoying similar mainstream success right now, including massive radio play on commercial networks, are more of a total left-field entry: a brother-sister act from Detroit, they had their third album released on the ironically named California indie Sympathy for the Record Industry during the summer of 2001, and it suddenly broke out almost a year later with the success of one of the album's tracks, "Fell In Love with a Girl." The track just happens to be as close to real Rock 'n' Roll as you're going to hear on the radio today: great bursts of fuzzed-out guitar, stuttering Elvis-like vocals, and the sound of complete sexual unraveling. It's a masterpiece, and if you'd told me six months ago that it was going to be a hit, I would've scoffed at the possibility. But in the new post-terror post-ironic post-Napster post-Boomer postmedia postapocalyptic culture, anything is possible.

As for the new Rock practitioners, as always, it didn't happen overnight. The White Stripes, for instance, represent the periphery of a renewed Motor City scene that has been going on for a while and that pledges alle-giance to that city's hard-rockin' legacy in the form of such high-energy bands as the Go, Demolition Doll Rods, and Detroit Cobras (none of whom sound anything like Madonna, who is also from Detroit). Regional scenes like this are occurring organically, perhaps due to the negligence of the major labels, who have seemed in recent years to concentrate more and more on prefabricated creations that recall, if anything, the horrible teen idols of the '50s. However, a full-blown Rock renaissance seems unlikely, because the form itself has been all but totally delved and explored. As noted earlier, there are only so many things groups can do with the basic format of Rock n' Roll, and it seems, at least, as if all variations have been thoroughly explored. So what we're living with now is a great expanse of raw talent with no meaningful place to go. If we stopped comparing it to the '60s and '70s, we'd be a lot better off. But that's impossible to do because, despite numer-ous variations, the form has changed so little in forty years. Which is why even the dandiest of current practitioners are in some way reminiscent of something that happened in the past.

So why can't we just let it stand like that? That Rock 'n' Roll is this institutionalized form of music/culture that suits the needs of a certain bunch of neoboho intellectuals, all of whom understand its ironic retro implications? The problem is, at the same time Rock as a creative force was being spawned, there was a parallel Pop universe that was Rock in name only—the industry *can't* let Rock die, because they've laid their whole foundation on it. The obvious solution would be to let the real rockers like the Black Halos and Hellacopters run wild, but they're not going to do that because the industry discovered long ago that manufactured talents were easier to control and exploit than real ones. And never the twain shall meet.

What the general public perceives as Rock is what's being force-fed to them by the likes of MTV, VH1, and the Rock Hall of Fame…and *Spin* and *Rolling Stone*, and of course Hollywood. Those willing to delve deeper are destined to find a lot more interesting manifestations going on. Rock nowadays requires commitment—and the commitment is to a certain ethos that has, in many ways, taken the place of religion for at least a certain segment of the population. These, then are the current keepers of the faith.

Bands like the Strokes, White Stripes, Black Halos, Richmond Sluts, Hellacopters, and the Secrets consciously see themselves in the Rock tradition—which, to them, puts a heavy emphasis on the more Punk elements of Rock's trajectory and less on the classic Rock ones (i.e., Pop). These are groups who've done their homework—they ain't as simplistic as they seem, in other words. Their Chuck Berry riffs are, in a certain sense, affected. What makes them not a self-parody like, say, the Black Crowes is that they embrace the basic Rock methodology as if they were the first ones to ever do it. Perhaps subliminally they are aware of their influences, but the way they put it across is totally refreshing and doesn't sound borrowed. To extend the religious analogies one more time, it's almost as if these groups are proselytizing: they believe so totally in Rock 'n' Roll as a way of life that their music rings with conviction and almost a kind of triumph because, unlike previous generations of Rock musicians, these artists have the example of history laid out before 'em and understand the sacrifices it takes to preserve one's art in an industry that runs solely on greed.

It could be argued that these artists merely represent a neoclassicist *version* of Rock, an "artist's rendering," if you will. However, chances are, the kids who are just getting into it for the first time don't know the difference—and if they do, it doesn't matter, because no one expects or wants anything particularly "new" to happen in the field of Rock n' Roll anyway. Rock 'n' Roll has become an institution, and the Rock lifestyle a kind of cult, whose members are identified by several distinguishable traits including body piercings, tattoos, leather, certain hairstyles, and the ever-present cigarette. Much of it still goes back to the '50s, with a kind of mondo Punk twist. It's still a refuge of bad boys and girls, but now it's a somewhat contrived one—the real bad boys listen to Hip Hop, which usurped Rock's basic populist rebellion stance in the '80s and shows no signs of quitting. And that's only natural, because, once again, whoever said it was our collective birthright that Rock 'n' Roll would remain the preeminent form of popular music forever? The current champions of Rock are making a self-conscious decision to listen to this style of music, because it's not readily accessible and they must seek it out. The Boomers didn't have to do this: they merely liked Rock because it happened to be popular when they were growing up. But when they settled down and put the toys away, Rock went with it, except as repackaged nostalgia. Unfortunately, nobody in the media ever understood that distinction—which is just another one of the reasons that Rock no longer is the most popular form of music in the world. The kids have been denied, but at the same time, you can't really feel sorry for them when so much actual Rock is thriving right under their noses.

Point being, it would seem to me that a healthy adolescent culture would be much more likely to embrace a Black Halos than a Backstreet Boys—that is, if they *knew* about the Halos. But, of course, the mainstream media do their best to deny the kids this knowledge. However, to the cultists who happen to discover this music, it makes no difference that these acts are not "popular," because they can still go out and see these bands if they want and experience the ethos of Rock up close and personal, just like previous generations have. It doesn't matter who learned it first—all that matters is the conviction with which one pursues it.

In recent years, one of the best arguments for the "retro" stance has been the Brian Jonestown Massacre, a collective from San Francisco who almost seem to be reinventing the wheel with each album—each one sounding more '60s than the actual '60s did. The way the Jonestown approached it, however, it seemed like they'd organically arrived at this sonic frontier on their own, in thoroughly postmodern terms, no less. The effect was something akin to what the Stones might have been like if Brian Jones had lived and wrested control back from Mick and Keith. Despite another fine LP in early 2002 entitled *Bravery, Repetition, and Noise*, of late the group seems to be suffering the strain of ego and drug problems. Anton, say it isn't so.

The Jonestown has produced spinoffs, most notably the Warlocks and Richmond Sluts, both of which include former Massacre members. The Warlocks are thoroughly psychedelic, with a lot of droning ambiance as well as more jam-oriented improv; the Sluts are straight Rock, more like the early Stones than the later psychedelic period that the Jonestown evokes. All of these groups are active on their respective scenes, which is another crucial difference between this kind of indie/underground Rock and the more corporate entities: these groups are all approachable, not some stadium-Rock museum piece. You can go right up to 'em and throw a beer in their faces.

In many ways, the San Francisco area seems to have the most vital Rock scene in the country right now. Besides the Richmond Sluts and Brian Jonestown Massacre, there's also Vue and the venerable Loud Family. Vue is one of the most promising young bands in the country—although reaction to their first album was varied, the group's weird marriage of churning Velvets/Stooges/Television/Birthday Party decadence and New Wave influences made them distinct among their more prodigal peers. Their second album evinced a more straight-Rock direction that once again betrayed the influence of the Rolling Stones, who seem to be a popular antecedent these days.

Whereas Vue come off as a band that's young and inexperienced but that makes up for it through sheer arrogance, the Loud Family, under the aegis of the venerable tunesmith Scott Miller, comes off as perhaps the most sophisticated "pop" band that ever lived. As the leader of Game Theory in the '80s, Miller proved that he was capable of the same delicate balance between extremely lovely melodies and slightly demented sentiments as Todd Rundgren, Brian Eno, Elvis Costello, Alex Chilton, or Robyn Hitchcock—all of whom obviously influenced his pastiche-style songwriting technique. Where Miller outdistances them all is in his grasp of irony—the songs are beautiful, but they inevitably lampoon some aspect of the culture with biting accuracy. It's the perfect juxtaposition between old/new Pop/Punk that makes the Loud

Family simply too good to be true in this day and age. In the same token, one should also mention fellow Bay Area popsters Imperial Teen, whose grasp of the ironic mixed with the melodic is almost as profound as Scott Miller's. If there was any doubt, the group's coed membership and their reliance on such slightly "New Wave" embellishments as cheesy organ, hand claps, and group harmonies underscores their essential cuteness factor.

Most of these bright hopes record for small indie labels. And although a good number of these labels are doing it simply for the love of it and might not even be around a year from now, some indie labels have established themselves as long-term forces to be reckoned with. In a way, they've carved out a nice little niche/demographic that enables them to guarantee their artists complete freedom while at the same time offering them some degree of recording and touring stability. This is the ideal position for a creative Rock n' Roll band to be in nowadays, as the majority of indie artists who've gone the major label route, however temporarily, have all come rushing back to indie-land with tales of woe.

Speaking of indies, after a few years of floundering, Sub Pop has re-emerged as one of the more vital independent music strongholds. After the initial buyout accompanying Nirvana, Sub Pop had to refocus their whole music-making objective. On a smaller scale, the same thing happened with SST after Husker Du and the Meat Puppets bailed out for major label waters in the late '80s, but SST were unable to recover from the tumult; Sub Pop seems to have done so with flying colors. Of late, they seem intent upon keeping the faith.

A good example is the Hellacopters, a band from Sweden that was signed to Sub Pop in the late '90s after rocking the glacial expanses for years (and that has since moved onto the major label plateau in Europe, an arrangement that ultimately soured their U.S. deal with Sub Pop). Their first album, *Super Shitty to the Max*, which bore a lot of ominous Germanic-looking symbols on its cover, was actually released on the San Francisco indie Man's Ruin, and it was one of the ultimate triumphs of the '90s, a sonic juggernaut firmly in the tradition of such pulverizing Rock kings as the Stooges, Motorhead, and AntiSeen. The group's embrace of the whole *ethos de rock* is so utterly convincing that it sounds as if they're front and center in the Grande Ballroom and that "revolution" is still a viable option. If this—as well as the band's unmistakably "greaser"/scumbag image—comes off as "retro," so be it. What it really amounts to is basic Rock n' Roll, which, if the 'Copters are any evidence, will apparently never go out of style. Their 1999 LP for Sub Pop, *Grande Rock*, was kind of a *Back in the USA* for the '90s. Their latest, *High Visibility*, although sporting a slightly more mainstream sound, is a riveting tour de force that just might be their Valhalla.

Sub Pop's also recently signed Gluecifer, another Scandinavian herd in the same league as the 'Copters, from Norway this time, who are intent on the same kind of Rock-as-revolution rhetoric and storm-the-barricades musical prowess. Actually, the whole Scandinavian Rock scene, where bands like Gluecifer, Backyard Babies, Hives, and the Hellacopters reign supreme, has been one of the true bright spots on the current horizon. These bands display a conviction that is hard to match, almost as if their twice-removed status— geographically as well as decade-wise—provides them with just enough distance to really do it without holding back. Like the Brian Jonestown Massacre with their mod-psych affectations, bands like the 'Copters never come off as if they're aping something from the past. They make you believe that the "past" never really ended—and, let's face it, in the minds of the faithful, wherever and whoever they may be, it probably never really did.

Other recent Sub Pop signings include the Go, the Murder City Devils, the Makers, the Yo Yos, the Black Halos, and other bands adhering to the basic Rock-as-salvation model. All of these bands are expressing a certain vitality that has been missing from Rock for a long time, and they seem to be making converts. Although Sub Pop's influence now extends far beyond the regional sphere that they've always maintained, the Northwest continues to be a constant source of important and influential bands—most prominently Sleater/Kinney.

It was early 1997 when Sleater/Kinney first emerged as a dark horse candidate in that year's annual *Village Voice* "Pazz & Jop" critics' poll. At that time, the *Voice*'s music coverage was heavily feminist-oriented, thanks to the respective stewardship of Ann Powers and Evelyn McDonnell. That probably informed the fact that *Call the Doctor* placed number three on the charts. Anyone who remembers the '90s and knows anything about the way the media work realizes that, around '96–'97, nothing *but* a feminist group made up of dumpy-looking broads with glasses could've pulled such honors. Fortunately, there was more to Sleater/Kinney than their viability as mouthpieces for feminist-speak. The most important Northwest artists since Bikini Kill, Sleater/Kinney were like a refinement of riot grrl: the tempos were slower, the guitars more angular and less Punk-simplistic. Being an all-girl band, they inevitably were drawn into the whole feminist-Rock thing, but their actual songs, while angry, were less political than those of a lot of other bands of that time—as with most great Rock, their politics were mostly of the "you broke my heart" variety. *Dig Me Out*, from '97,and '99's *The Hot Rock*, although conceptually almost identical, showed a maturing process that not only brought them greater success but also helped define their status as populist outsiders. "Jenny," "Dance Song '97," "The End of You," and "A Quarter to Three" were all first-rate, spotlighting the band's intricate guitar patterns as well as the shrieking vocals of singer Corin Tucker, whose five-octave range enables her to hit notes that even some chipmunks can't. The band's most recent album, *All Hands on the Bad One*, although brilliant in places, shows that the formula, although still effective, may be getting a little predictable.

Another contemporary all-female band who've been hailed as a potential Next Big Thing are the Donnas. If they have a precedent, it's the Runaways, the Kim Fowley-masterminded teen-jail bait-spandex band from the late '70s. However, the Donnas have already surpassed the Runaways in musical terms. Starting as another Ramonesian combo with sprightly melodies and highly accelerated tempos, the group has evolved into a formidable metallic aggregation, despite their novelty status—which admittedly comes from the fact that they are women who, to no small degree, exploit their sexuality. Because of this, it's easy to see why they're currently on the verge of getting morphed into the mainstream via the usual corporate channels.

As the Donnas and others of their ilk prove, there's no shortage of good Rock bands playing in the basic tradition. A good example is Nashville Pussy, who actually got signed to a major label in 1998 on the strength of songs like "Go Motherfucker Go" and "All Fucked Up." Considering that, on the bad taste-o-meter, these songs—not to mention their whole demeanor—are only a step above G. G. Allin, maybe there's still hope. A lot of bands seem to be plying the neoredneck vibe. If nothing else, this has helped spawn the revival of cowboy hats. A good example of the new redneck raunch is Honky, a group founded by ex-Butthole Surfers bassist Jeff Pinkus that combines the shit-kicking white-trash ethos with typical metal-Punk grind, all with the same self-deprecating sense of humor as Nashville Pussy. It's the Jerry Springer of Rock n' Roll, and somehow, in the current cultural climate, it seems achingly appropriate. It seems to be spreading too, as the redneck stance is one of the last refuges left for politically incorrect sentiment.

The redneck thing gained popularity in the '90s, partly due to Bill Clinton. This has translated into a cadre of burr-heads on the current scene, starting with Southern Culture on the Skids back in the pre-Clinton era. The Country revival even spawned its own fanzine, *No Depression*. Memphis, in particular, seems to be undergoing a renaissance of sorts, as epitomized by indie-rockers like the Satyrs, who sound more like the Velvet Underground than a bunch of cornpone hicks.

The twang has been a presence for a while now. If there's one band that has effectively incorporated countrified musical attributes with post-REM ironic statements, it's Buttercup from Boston. The twang became more pronounced on their second album, *Love*, which, true to its name, was one of the most candid explorations of human emotion heard in many a year. The album they followed it up with, entitled simply *Buttercup*, was equally brilliant, albeit much more subtle. Unfortunately, as with many bands in this valediction, genius has had to serve as its own reward, as they've pretty much been left to vanquish in obscurity. Another countryesque band, Beachwood Sparks, who are equally capable of shimmering Byrds-like textures, may have more of a chance at broader acceptance due to the fact that they bear the prestigious Sub Pop imprint.

Obscurity suits some artists, especially during an era when going for the brass ring amounts to being turned literally into a show monkey. That's why, to this day, there are still artists out there dedicated to the indie spirit the way it first manifested itself in the early '80s. Ray Mason is a perfect example: a rawboned man who looks like a truck driver, he began making homemade recordings on cassettes two decades ago and distributing them through the mail. His music's a combination of smoky down-home atmosphere and working class sentiment, which suits his western Massachusetts environs perfectly. At his best he recalls the stately grandeur of the Band, but there are a lot of countrified as well as pub-Rock influences implicit in Ray's music as well. As he put it in his opus, "Got it Right": "It took us years to get a sound/We don't need no big label comin' 'round." Mason's got a point—whereas it seemed at one time that the only point of making Rock 'n' Roll was to become famous and get groupies, there are now many people who play it merely for the excitement it brings—to themselves as well as to others. In this way, Ray Mason's a throwback to the roadhouse era that predated big league Rock n' Roll, and his audience, who are every bit as passionate as previous generations about the kind of escapism a Friday night hoedown provides, probably don't take too kindly to the Jason figures.

Which brings us back to the White Stripes, who are the hippest thing going right now, the next group after the Donnas to appear vulnerable to major-label persuasion—which is unfortunately the inevitable next step when a group has reached this level of notoriety, unless they want to remain martyrs like Fugazi or break up like Bikini Kill. Anyhow, Jack White and his sister Meg make the bashin'est sound for a twosome since Suicide, only with a much different modus operandi: Jack sings and plays a heavily distorted guitar, and Meg plays drums. Jack's unassuming manner and ordinary appearance contrast sharply with his swaggering vocal style and live presentation, which is the ultimate postmodern trick, of course: the dork who becomes a sex symbol. Their instantly recognizable red and white stage uniforms, as well as rumors that the "siblings" were once husband and wife, haven't hurt them in gaining notoriety, and the inclusion of almost down-home material in their oeuvre has helped authenticate their sound. There are times when Jack gets a little too ginchy, and wrongheaded critics have made a big mistake drawing continuous comparisons to Robert Plant and Elvis when it's actually Blue Cheer's Dicky Peterson that he sounds like—hey, tell a kid that too many times and he'll actually begin to believe you and try to sound like Plant after all.

Which is the eternal point about postmodernism—an artist can steal everything that's come before and turn it inside out. Rock may be dead, but the few artists who are still bothering to purvey it are probably the best at it ever, simply because, absorbing the work of earlier artists, they can't help but transcend them.

The only way Rock matters anymore is conceptually. In the case of groups purveying the most simplistic Rock 'n' Roll, the same thing goes—the riffs are even more wound up; the lyrics, even more clever/sarcastic. Rock has become the ultimate postmodernist art form. Smart kids from all over who have real jobs on the side have embraced Rock 'n' Roll as their hobby, for the sole purpose of expressing themselves. They're not planning to make it big, because they know they would have to compromise the art to do so. Therefore, they toil away at their forty-thousand-per-year computer slacker jobs and do the band thing on the side. This certainly takes off the pressure of having to "tour" or any of the other protocols that have always accompanied Rock stardom. In many ways, this approach to Rock has freed its purveyors: as they know it's only a hobby, they're not afraid to take it to the edge. The lesson being: we live in the most democratic time ever for creating art…just don't quit your day job.

One of the best conceptual-Rock bands is Boston's Upper Crust, whose members wear Louis XIV get-ups—lace cuffs and powdered wigs—and ply kinetic AC/DC riffs. They sound more like AC/DC than AC/DC, except they render it all in character, so their songs are all mad celebrations of class warfare, with the band, of course, falling on the side of "royalty" (hence the name). Even the between-song banter at their live shows is delivered in the strict parlance of royalty. Songs like "Rock n' Roll Butler," "Little Lord Fauntleroy," "Friend of a Friend of the Working Class," "(She Comes From) Old Money," and "Let Them Eat Rock" put them in the same class as the Dictators, Angry Samoans, Meatmen, and so few others in the realm of "funny" Rock. But critics seldom write about bands like the Upper Crust because, for the most part, critics have no sense of humor, and the Upper Crust are not politically correct in the post-Sleater/Kinney era.

The general aura of "cool" that permeates the Rock media and that doesn't allow the critics to let down their guard for one minute is the number one reason they've so totally botched the job of leading the consensus instead of following it. That could be the only explanation why, in the annals of singer/songwriters, they've chosen to enshrine wimps like Elliott Smith and Ryan Adams and have ignored the more jovial, and thus more philosophically insightful, Tris McCall. McCall's whole lanky, self-deprecating manner doesn't sit right with a bunch of losers who are too self-aware to ever truly get the universal joke. Like a young Bob Dylan, McCall upsets people's notions about what a "folk" singer constitutes. His first album, *If One of These Bottles Should Happen to Fall*, which consists of songs about McCall's native New Jersey, is the best Elvis Costello album since *Armed Forces*, and McCall proves himself a master of the same kind of intricate wordplay as Dylan and Costello. More importantly, he bears the melodic influence of Scott Miller of the Loud Family, who produced McCall's album and is by far the reigning maestro of sarcasto-Pop. What other "hipster"—other than Miller, of course, who's a little too old to qualify—could come up with sly couplets like: "Unless this inter-office envelope contains dope/Or dog-eared treats/I'll take my beating/Thank you for all of this rope"?

McCall has taken the indie route of self-financing his own CD and then selling it through the mail. Another younger and even more eccentric "singer/songwriter" who also hails from New Jersey, Marianne Nowottny, has been lucky enough to receive the modest backing of the Abaton Book Company, a company that seems as devoted to nurturing oddballs as ESP-Disk did in the '60s. That's been easy so far, considering that Nowottny's their only artist—unless one counts the Shell album Nowottny made last year with her teenage partner, Donna Bailey, which explored postfeminist angst from the twisted realm of ultrabright adolescence. Shell was like a musical version of the Power Puff Girls—or Suicide, if they were flying on pixie dust instead of methamphetamine. The ultraweird soundscapes wrought by Nowottny and Bailey on their little toy keyboards achieved the rare (in postmodern times) phenomenon of a sound without a suitable reference point. If anything, it called to mind Lisa Suckdog during the *Drugs are Nice* era: all that submerged audio-murk combined with the swirling confusion of young female hormones run amok.

Nowottny's latest album is an even more ambitious project. A two-CD set, *Manmade Girl* proves that Shell was no fluke and Nowottny has a very bright future indeed. A pixie of a girl with a taste for outlandish dress—much like Abaton proprietress Lauri Bortz—Marianne proves herself a genuine prodigy of both vocal and instrumental prowess. Although Shell wasn't "Pop" or even "Rock 'n' Roll" in any sense, *Manmade Girl* is even less so. Most of it is just Marianne and her piano, and it shifts from cabaret-type outings to semi-Classical excursions to flickering weirdness of the Nico/Diamanda Galas variety.

Truly original music like this can't be stumbled across by turning on the TV or radio. That's the crucial difference between the Rock 'n' Roll of nowa-days and the Rock 'n' Roll of forty years ago. Nowottny's not a Rock performer in any sense, but her music appeals to the same kind of hipster minority who listen to indie-Rock and attend club performances—the only group of people who actively pursue music with any sense of enthusiasm these days (not count-ing the immense and very rabid audience for Hip Hop and other DJ-related forms, which,, of course, is a different thing entirely). Because of the preponderance of prepackaged swill, even musical forms that were once upon a time totally populist and accessible to everyone—like "soul," for instance—have become the dominion of a small, and somewhat elite, minority.

A perfect example is the Soul Fire label in New York. They put out absolutely pulverizing Funk records that evoke the golden age of American Black music. But there's one problem—to the world at large, Hip Hop is the only contemporary representation of Black music. There's no way Black radio is going to play anything as authentically "down-home" as the albums Soul Fire puts out by artists like Lee Fields, Calypso King & the Soul Investigators, J.D. & the Evil's Dynamite Band, and others. As far as music goes, slickness has won out over feeling, and raw soul is the last thing Black (or white) folks want to hear nowadays.

Nevertheless, Soul Fire's albums are the most hard-boiled Funk opuses since the mid-'70s. Putting the emphasis on the grooves, the bands are often anonymous; the albums, similar-sounding. But the sound is a thundercloud of soulful self-expression that's both infectious and powerful. Is this simply retrogressive, or is it a continuation of a long-standing tradition? Does it make a difference? The thing we should all be thinking about right now is, there's never enough good music—and there's *far* too much "bad" music. That's where Soul Fire comes in, but there's not much likelihood that any of their music will be heard by anyone, because magazines don't pay for stories about musicians; they pay for stories about celebrities, and therefore no one's writing about Soul Fire. And those who do write about it will no doubt stress the "retro" angle and miss the organic quality of the music entirely.

Still, Soul Fire presses on with its great-sounding, non-glory-seeking heavy Funk, rendered in what sounds like analog for that "authentic" quality. But there's a catch—although this music might sound reminiscent of the past, it's actually happening right now. Which only proves how, ever since Chuck Berry first struck that golden chord, Rock n' Roll as a form has been infinitely redeemable. What the artists who record for Soul Fire, as well as neo-Rock monoliths like the Hellacopters, understand is that less is more, and they've actually taken influences from the past and refined them into what we'd always hoped they'd become anyway. They are bettering the art itself, and in a strange way, that's progress.

What's really sad is that, listening to the albums on Soul Fire, it stirs memories of a time when that kind of down-home goodness actually grew on trees. The only thing that renders it "novelty" at this late date is how rare such musical excellence is in this day and age. Lee Fields, if he isn't the greatest James Brown imitator of all time, may just be the greatest living "soul" singer in the world. He's got no competition from the real J. B. these days, that's for sure.

Soul isn't the only music making a "comeback" either—Jazz is more popular than ever, but unfortunately, much of that means Jazz of the slick supper club variety personified by mercenary performers like Wynton Marsalis, Joe Lovano, James Carter, Diana Krall, and Cassandra Wilson. This is the Jazz equivalent of "Pop" and is thus musically insignificant. The real preservers of the Jazz faith are centered on a handful of small labels in New York and its outskirts, as well as in Europe. The performers are a close-knit alliance whose creative energies flow together to create a sound all their own, which is slowly being acknowledged for what it is—the most fruitful and cross-pollinating scene in contemporary music.

Perhaps the central figure in the "new music" is saxophonist David S. Ware—only, in his case, "new" is a relative term, considering that he spent twenty years in the pro realm before finally getting signed to a major label, Columbia, only to be subsequently bounced. For Ware, it made little difference—coming to prominence as one of the great post-Coltrane horn blowers, he's weathered the storm long enough to know that making quality music is its own reward, and that's how he's always approached it: as a quest and vision that must be fulfilled at all costs. This kind of dedication comes across in his immensely powerful playing. Ware's back home again on the independent Aum Fidelity label, which is currently the most important Jazz label in the world due to its pioneering efforts in the always risky terrain of Art For Art's Sake. Not surprisingly, its owner, Steven Joerg, hails from an indie-Rock background. There's been a genuine affinity between the Free-Jazz and Punk Rock worlds since the late '70s, because the purveyors of each recognize their similarities stance-wise, if not musically. They recognize the plurality inherent in their mutual embrace and have pursued it to the advantage of both genres. It's much more likely that a David Ware would be found jamming with a Thurston Moore than he would a Wynton Marsalis.

The downtown underground is thriving. Along with Ware, among its other more visible practitioners are pianist Matthew Shipp and bassist William Parker. Both of these musicians are more or less permanent members of the groundbreaking David S. Ware Quartet as well as remarkable bandleaders and soloists in their own right. Recording together or alone, they're capable of making music that echoes resoundingly in its musical vicissitude. Although he's a loner who doesn't play with the others much, the saxophonist Charles Gayle has also proven himself capable of some mighty testimonial. Other current luminaries like Roy Campbell, Daniel Carter, Rashied Ali, Hamid Drake, Tim Berne, Michael Formanek, Joe Morris, Tom Bruno, Rob Brown, Chris Lightcap, Mat Maneri, Rashid Bakr, Billy Bang, Whit Dickey, and Susie Ibarra prove that Jazz may have more of a future than ever seemed possible a mere twenty years ago.

The Rock underground thrives also, but in fragments. Because the indie scene is so vast and moves so quickly, there's little time for any collective identity to form like it has with the Jazz artists, most of whom live in New York. The Rock avant-garde spreads its tendrils all over the world, and sometimes bands that are lumped together as being part of a certain "scene" actually share nothing more than regional similarities. A good example is the Japanese scene, which has been one of the more fertile independent and experimental music outposts of the past decade. Not just in the form of better-known Japanese bands like Shonen Knife and the Boredoms but also a whole revo-retro scene centered around American trash and kitsch culture, including such raw exponents as Guitar Wolf and Thee Michelle Elephant Gun. These groups subscribe to a primal philosophy and take a lot of their stylistic identity from the more mondo elements of Punk Rock but render it through a Japanese sensibility that enables them to approach it with more wild abandon than their more reserved Euro and American counterparts. By far the most interesting group in Japan right now is Acid Mothers Temple, who, as their name implies, specialize in wild acid freak-outs not heard since the heyday of the original psych commune bands like Red Krayola and Amon Düül. Their music varies from almost traditional-sounding Folk haze to blistering guitar onslaughts to almost tribal chanting, but it's never less than interesting. Their recent *New Geocentric World* is one of the most amazing documents of the new millennium.

Not everybody has to get as wigged out as the Acid Mothers to make a contribution to the ongoing art of Rock. A band like the Figgs, who hail from New York, are perfectly capable of making a joyous noise that might sound a little

familiar at this late date but is no less stimulating because of it. In fact, what the
Figgs remind us most of all is that the whole beauty of Rock 'n' Roll lies in its
simplicity. Whether it's the Replacements-style bash they exhibit on *For EP
Fans Only* or the revved-up Real Kids-like chug displayed on their masterpiece,
Sucking in Stereo, the Figgs prove the old adage that less is more.

Which no one would ever accuse Belle and Sebastian of. The effete
Scottish band is intent upon using fairly baroque embellishments to augment
some of the most intricate Pop melodies heard since the Beatles, or at least the
Smiths. It's not straight Pop, though—like the work of R.E.M. and the aforementioned Smiths, it's rendered with detachment and irony, and a certain sense
of sullenness and contempt that's borrowed directly from the brooding mid-
'60s "male vocalists" who also inform B&S's music: Scott Walker, Serge
Gainsbourg, even Tom Jones. But it's rendered through the eyes of a kind of
posh Warhol/Morrissey-type quality. It's also some of the most intricate and
enduring work of the era, and among its fans the group inspires the same cultlike devotion that has followed other such visionary mystics as the Velvet
Underground, Joy Division, and the Smiths. That means they release all kinds
of neat little EPs and other notions that come straight from the heart of indie-
Rock, which they are still technically part of, being signed to Matador and all.

"Indie Rock" doesn't really mean much anymore, as all such distinctions
have been disseminated into their own private little villages like McLuhan predicted so many years ago. We live in a world where Belle and Sebastian and
Britney Spears can coexist—that is, if Belle and Sebastian, as well as their fans,
accept their outsider status. Which they do, gleefully—far from being "popular" music anymore, Rock n' Roll has become the biggest cult—some would
even say a religious one—in the world.

So where does that leave the nonholy Rock that rocks the mainstream?
Ever since Nirvana, there've been a million prepackaged groups of bellowing
boys in shorts screaming and yelling to the crunching overload of loud guitars:
Sublime, Tool, Korn, Limp Bizkit, Bush, Rage Against the Machine, Everclear,
Blink 182. But is it really Rock? Contrary to the indie bands—and, for that
matter, Nirvana—these groups don't seem to adhere to any tradition. It's as if
they were just hatched as a marketing scam by the record company, as their
music doesn't seem to come from any organic source. Some of these groups
incorporate elements of Hip Hop, which at least would indicate they're "mod-

ern." This ultimately would also mean they're not Rock, because Rock, ultimately, is no longer modern music.

Which is perfectly OK—Rock will survive, because it's lurking around every corner. It's easy to play, and it has its rewards—people will always play it. The difference is, in the "old days," if you were good enough, you'd rise to the top. Nowadays, that's not necessarily true. We've gone back to a pre-Renaissance era in which a Beethoven could easily languish in obscurity. In the name of hype and of the victory of style over substance, artistic purity has become the least significant factor. For the most part, the attitude of the industry—as well as the rabble—is "who needs it?" Art without irony, without cynicism, without the acknowledgement of a kind of cheeky detachment, and most of all without the overall driving desire for commerce, is ultimately a useless commodity. In this ultradysfunctional age, alas, everything must be functional.

In this sense, Rock has become ultrafunctional. Belle and Sebastian are nothing if not functional. The Figgs are functional. Even the Hellacopters are functional. They all "function" perfectly for whatever niche they belong to. The corporate Rock functions as well, mostly to feed the masses. Which only means we've devolved to a state of musical communism in which mainstream commercial Rock n' Roll is the opiate of the masses.

For Rock, a music that was once the bastion of nonconformity, this presents a challenging predicament. In order to truly be Rock, it has to keep expanding that rebellious factor—but that gets increasingly harder to do in a society that is jaded beyond belief. Rap music kind of usurped the "danger" quotient of Rock 'n' Roll by presenting a scenario that was much more palpable. Because Rap came from the ghetto, it wasn't an idealized version of a violent society, like Punk was—it was an actual product of it. Some of the chief principles of Rap were actually killed for their art—like Biggie Smalls and Tupac Shakur, for instance—reputedly by principles within the Rap industry itself. Rock hadn't seen that kind of danger since Bobby Vinton threatened to have DJs' legs broken if they played the Beatles instead of him. Over the past thirty years, any "danger" in Rock has been mostly of the self-destructive variety. The rebellion that Rock once manifested has been turned into a kind of benign theater, of which "Goth" and "Industrial" are the current epitome.

At least for a while, there will probably always be a market for the ersatz

Rock—the Korns, the No Doubts, the Marilyn Mansons. The fact that Rock n' Roll as we once knew it has become a mere demographic in a vast wasteland of mass-marketed swill shouldn't surprise anyone, seeing as, at its root, Rock n' Roll was never anything *but* that. Still, for a moment—probably in the '60s—it achieved the unique feat of being both commercially successful and artistically satisfying. That dream was squashed by a variety of cruel realities brought about in the post-Woodstock era when the big record labels realized they could formulate rebellion into a very effective marketing tool. Since that time, Rock has had little hope of escaping its inevitable servitude to corporate demands. There wasn't much room left for spontaneous combustion, because the Industry was now the self-appointed fire marshal, and it made sure that even the most minimal brushfires were well contained. Punk and indie represented an all-out war against the industry; the end result was Nirvana, which was kind of the record industry's Vietnam. Even today, they whisper in horror: "Never again…"

Ultimately, it's only music. The original purveyors of Rock 'n' Roll— Chuck Berry, Elvis, or any of the rest—had no idea that their legacy would be so eternal and would have to endure so many permutations. They were just doing what came naturally. If some fast-talkin' slickster put the bug in their ear that they might be able to make a buck from all this, that wasn't the same thing as consciously "selling out." But when Rock became a cultural commodity, an accepted part of the norm, it lost its reason to live. When you give the kids readymade rebellion to step into as a rite of passage, is it really rebellion after all? And do we really want any more rebellion in these chaotic times?

The apocalypse is over. All that's left is eighty-eight billion mass-produced pieces of plastic encrypted with sounds that will be with us, in one form or another, until the end of time.

Which is why there comes a time when we must go beyond words.

NOTES FOR SONIC COOL

Chapter 2

1 Malone, Bill C. Country Music USA. Austin, Tx.: University of Texas Press, 1985, 138.
2 Ibid., 154.
3 Mullican, Moon. Music City News (February 1967) 4(8):27.

Chapter 3

1 *Nation's Business* (February 1953):51.
2 Malone, Bill C. *Country Music* USA. Austin, Tx.: University of Texas Press, 1985, 204.
3 Hull, Robot A. and Joe Sasfy. "B-I Bickey-Bi, Bo-Bo-Go: Rockabilly's Rabid Moment." *Creem* (February 1980) 11(9):36.
4 Guralnick, Peter. *Feel Like Going Home*. New York: Harper & Row, 1971, 227.
5 Robert Palmer. *Deep Blues*. New York: Viking, 1981, 222.
6 Guralnick, 235.
7 Ibid., 179.
8 Ibid., 189.

Chapter 4

1 Arnold Shaw. *Honkers and Shouters: The Golden Years of Rhythm & Blues*. New York: Macmillan, 1978, 74.
2 Bangs, Lester. *Psychotic Reactions and Carburetor Dung*. New York: Alfred E. Knopf, 1987, 139.
3 Wolfe, Tom. *The Kandy-Kolored Tangerine Flake Streamline Baby*. New York: Pocket, 1966, 53–54.

Chapter 5

1 Gambaccini, Paul. *Paul McCartney in His Own Words*. New York: Flash Books, 1976, 14.
2 McCabe, Peter and Robert D. Schonfeld. *Apple to the Core*. New York: Pocket, 1972, 13.
3 Ibid., 11.
4 Meltzer, Richard. "Got Incredible Screaming Live Beatles If You Want It!" *Creem* (August 1977) 9(3):60.
5 Carr, Roy. *The Rolling Stones: An Illustrated Record*. New York: Harmony Books, 1976, 98.
6 Epstein, Brian. *A Cellarful of Noise*. New York: Pyramid, 1964, 43.
7 Ibid., 27.
8 Wenner, Jann. *Lennon Remembers*. New York: Fawcett, 1971, 14.
9 Schaffner, Nicholas. *The Beatles Forever*. New York: Stackpole, 1977, 17.

Chapter 6

1 Scaduto, Anthony. *Mick Jagger: Everybody's Lucifer*. New York: David McKay Company, 1974, 37.
2 Ibid., 46.
3 Ibid., 4.
4 Ibid., 248.
5 Jagger, Mick. 1972. In Roy Carr, *The Rolling Stones: An Illustrated Record*. New York: Harmony Books, 1976, 72.

Chapter 7

1 Scaduto, Anthony. *Bob Dylan*. New York: Signet, 1973, 36.
2 Ibid., 110.
3 Ibid., 204.
4 Rinzler, Alan. *Bob Dylan: The Illustrated Record*. New York: Harmony Books, 1978, 34.

Chapter 8

1 Welch, Chris. *Winwood: Keep on Running*. London: Omnibus, 1989, 56.
2 Schaumburg, Ron. *Growing up with the Beatles*. New York: Pyramid, 1976, 56.
3 Bockris, Victor and Gerard Malanga. *Uptight: The Velvet Underground Story*. New York: William & Morrow, 1983, 18.
4 Clapton, Diana. *Lou Reed & the Velvet Underground*. New York: Proteus, 1982, 12.
5 McLuhan, Marshall. *The Medium is the Massage*. New York: Bantam, 108–109.
6 *Making Sense of the Sixties, Vol. 3*. New York: Journal Graphics, 1991, 4.
7 Welch, 106.

8 Hamilton, Dominy. *The Album Cover Album*. London: Dragon's World, 1977, 13.
9 *Goldmine* (26 April 1996):72.
10 Dannen, Fredric. *Hit Men*. Random House: New York, 1990, 75.
11 Sanders, Ed. *The Family*. New York: Avon, 1971, 40.

Chapter 9

1 Bovis, Hercules. "Rock Critics: Why They're Morons." *Creem* (December 1987) 19(4):26.
2 Rubin, Mike and Rob Michaels. "Heroes, Homeboys and Has-beens: A Secret History of Detroit Rock." *Motorbooty* (1990) no. 5.
3 Henssler, Barry, Matt O' Brien and Phil Durr with Rob Michaels. "Ron Asheton: I Need Moe." *Motorbooty* (1990) no. 5.
4 McNeil, Legs and Gillian McCain. *Please Kill Me*. New York: Grove Press, 1996, 48.
5 Ibid., 74.

Chapter 10

1 Brown, James with Bruce Tucker. *James Brown: The Godfather of Soul*. New York: Macmillan, 1986, 15.
2 Sidran, Ben. *Black Talk*. New York: Holt, 1971, 109.
3 Ibid., 142.

Chapter 11

1 Stein, Jean and George Plimpton. *Edie*. New York: Alfred A. Knopf, 1982, 224.
2 Lombardi, John. "A Conversation with Paul Morrisey." *Rolling Stone* (15 April 1971) no. 80:35.
3 Carr, Roy. *The Rolling Stones: An Illustrated Record*. New York: Harmony, 1976, 67.
4 Green, Robin. "How Black Was My Sabbath: 12 Homesick Hours with the Dark Princes of Downer Rock." *Rolling Stone* (28 October 1971) no. 94:41.
5 Ehrmann, Eric. *Rolling Stone* (2 April 1970) no. 55:32.
6 Ibid.
7 Robins, Wayne. "I'm Down, I'm Really Down: The Emerging Sopor Culture." *Creem* (October 1972) 4(5):44.
8 Christgau, Robert. *Christgau's Record Guide: Rock Albums of the '70s*. New Haven: Ticknor & Fields, 1981, 49.
9 The Editors of *Creem*. *Rock Revolution*. New York: Popular Library, 1976, 150.
10 Paytress, Mark. "Unmasking the Tyrannosaurus." Liner notes from *The Definitive Tyrannosaurus Rex*, 1993

11 Bangs, Lester. *Psychotic Reactions and Carburetor Dung*. New York: Alfred A. Knopf, 1987, 138.
12 Clapton, Diana. *Lou Reed*. New York: Proteus, 1982, 50.
13 Christgau, Robert. *Christgau's Record Guide: Rock Albums of the '70s*. New Haven: Tricknor & Fields, 1981, 362.
14 McNeil, Legs and Gillian McCain. *Please Kill Me*. New York: Grove Press, 1996, 119.
15 *New Musical Express* (14 September 1974).
16 Genheimer, Air-Wreck. "Emerson, Lake & Palmer Works: But Only As A Frisbee." *Creem* (July 1977), 9(2):76.
17 Davis, Stephen and Peter Simon. *Reggae Bloodlines*. New York: Da Capo, 1977, 44.

Chapter 12

1 Christgau, Robert. *Christgau's Record Guide: Rock Albums of the '70s* (New Haven: Tricknor & Fields, 1981), 370.
2 Morgan, Jeffrey. "The Secret Life of Amanda Lear: Things Your Mother Never Told You." *Creem* (February 1979), 10(9):64.
3 Eliot, Marc. *Rockonomics*. New York: Citadel Press, 1989, 191–92.
4 DiMartino, Dave. "Meat to the Beat: Doin' It in *Roadie* with Blondie and Meatloaf." *Creem* (February 1980), 11(9):45.

Chapter 13

1 Stephen Demorest, "Television: More Than Just a Boob Tube." *Creem* (May 1977), 8(12):79.
2 Nina Antonia, *Johnny Thunders: In Cold Blood*. London: Jungle Books, 1987, 24.
3 Swenson, John and Dave Marsh. *The Rolling Stone Record Guide*, 1st ed. New York: Random House, 1979, 103.
4 White, Timothy. "Bang the Heads Slowly: The Importance of Being a Ramone." *Rolling Stone* (8 February 1979), no. 284:12.
5 Savage, Jon. *England's Dreaming*. New York: St. Martin's Press, 1991, 501.
6 Ibid., 126.

Chapter 14

1 Cringely, Robert. *Accidental Empires*. New York: Addison-Wesley, 1992, 48–49.
2 *Goldmine* (24 May 1996):52.
3 Ibid., 56.
4 Ibid., 56.
5 Ibid., 56.
6 *Details* (11 November 1995):110.
7 *Seconds* (1995) no. 30:24.
8 Peck, Abe. *Uncovering the Sixties: The Life and Times of the Underground Press*. New York: Citadel Underground, 1991, 335.

Chapter 15

1 Morell, Brad. *Nirvana and the Sound of Seattle*. London: Omnibus, 1993, 30.
2 Ibid., 35.
3 Ibid., 45.
4 Ibid., 46.
5 *Seconds* (1991), no. 13:18.
6 Morrell, 66.
7 Ibid., 78.
8 Becker, Scott, ed. *We Rock So You Don't Have To: The Option Reader #1*. San Diego, Calif.: Incommunicado, 1998, 107.
9 Shamburg, Robin. "Whipping Post." *New York Press* (10 July 1996), 14.
10 Carver, Lisa. "Diane Hansen: Pornographer." *Rollerderby* no. 21, 1997.
11 Farley, Christopher John. "Rock's Anxious Rebels: A Young Vibrant Alternative Scene Has Turned Music on its Ear. But are the new stars too hot to be cool?" *Time* (25 October 1993), 65.
12 "The 100 Visionaries Who Could Change Your Life." *Utne Reader* (January–February 1995).
13 "Combustible Edison." *Popwatch* (1993), no. 4:15.
14 Franzman, Erin. "MP3s Basically Suck: A Manifesto of Cautious Modernism." *The Stranger* (3 February 2000).
15 Bangs, Lester. *Psychotic Reactions and Carburetor Dung*. New York: Knopf, 1987, 46.
16 Viveros-Faune, Christian. *New York Press* (3 November 1999).

INDEX

877 694 8012
suite^C 12A